PLASTICS IN BUILDING

Edited by

IRVING SKEIST, *Chemical Consultant*

Skeist Laboratories, Inc.
Newark, New Jersey

REINHOLD PUBLISHING CORPORATION, New York

CONTRIBUTORS

J. A. BAUMANN
Project Scientist
Union Carbide Corporation
Plastics Division
River Road
Bound Brook, N. J. 08805
Chapter 4: CONSTRUCTION AIDS
Chapter 8: OTHER PLASTICS FOR WALLS
  ROOFS, DOORS, Part B: HONEYCOMB
Chapter 14: UTILITIES, Part A: ELECTRICAL
  FIXTURES
Chapter 16: PERMANENT FIXTURES

SVEND W. BRUUN
Consulting Engineer
Joseph R. Loring Associates
270 Madison Avenue
New York, N. Y. 10016
Chapter 15: LIGHTING

RICHARD E. CHAMBERS
Staff Engineer
Simpson Gumpertz & Heger, Inc.
1696 Massachusetts Avenue
Cambridge, Mass. 02138
Chapter 5: STRUCTURAL FIBERGLASS REIN-
  FORCED PLASTICS FOR BUILDING APPLICA-
  TIONS

ROBERT P. CONGER
Manager of Research
Congoleum-Nairn, Inc.
Kearny, N. J. 07032
Chapter 12, Part A: RESILIENT FLOORING

ANTHONY ERRICO
Editor
Paint & Varnish Production
855 Avenue of the Americas
New York, N. Y. 10001
Chapter 17: PAINTS AND OTHER COATINGS

GORDON E. HANN
Executive Vice President
The Tremco Manufacturing Company
10701 Shaker Boulevard
Cleveland, Ohio 44104
Chapter 10: SEALANTS

PAUL HARSHA
Public Relations Department
The Dow Chemical Company
Plastics Division
Midland, Mich. 48641
Chapter 9: PLASTIC FOAMS IN THERMAL
  INSULATION

FRANK J. HEGER
Consulting Engineer
Simpson Gumpertz & Heger, Inc.
1969 Massachusetts Avenue
Cambridge, Mass. 02138
Chapter 6: DESIGN OF REINFORCED PLASTIC
  SHELL STRUCTURES

CHARLES B. HEMMING
Director, Research & Development
U. S. Plywood Corporation
P. O. Box 126
Brewster, N. Y.
Chapter 7: RESIN BONDED WOOD STRUC-
  TURES

RAY C. HESS
Project Scientist
Union Carbide Corporation
Plastics Division
River Road
Bound Brook, N. J. 08805
Chapter 8: OTHER PLASTICS FOR WALLS, ROOFS, DOORS, Part A: VINYLS
Chapter 14: UTILITIES, Part B: HEATING AND AIR CONDITIONING APPLICATIONS

MASANORI KANAI*
President, Central Research Laboratory
Sekisui Chemical Co., Ltd.
Mishimagun-Hirose
Osaka, JAPAN
Chapter 19: PLASTICS ABROAD, Part C: JAPAN

ROBERT C. KENNEDY
Plastics Development and Service
The Dow Chemical Company
Plastics Division
Midland, Mich. 48641
Chapter 9: PLASTIC FOAMS IN THERMAL INSULATION

JOHN M. KING
Director, Research Operations,
NAHB Research Foundation
1625 L Street, N. W.
Washington, D. C. 20036
Chapter 20: THE NAHB RESEARCH HOUSES

JOSEPH R. LORING
Consulting Engineer
Joseph R. Loring Associates
270 Madison Avenue
New York, N. Y. 10016
Chapter 15: LIGHTING

KAORU MAEDA
Chief Researchers, Central Research Laboratory
Sekisui Chemical Co., Ltd.
Mishimagun-Hirose
Osaka, JAPAN
Chapter 19: PLASTICS ABROAD, Part C: JAPAN

*Deceased.

Z. S. MAKOWSKI
Head, Department of Civil Engineering
Battersea College of Technology
London S. W. 11, ENGLAND
Chapter 19: PLASTICS ABROAD, Part D: INTERNATIONAL DEVELOPMENTS IN PLASTICS STRUCTURES

LEONARD MOSER
Public Relations
American Carpet Institute, Inc.
Empire State Building
New York, N. Y. 10001
Chapter 12: Part B: RESILIENT FLOORING

HAROLD PERRINE*
Civil Engineer
New York, N. Y.
Chapter 3: BUILDING CODES AND REGULATIONS

JOSEPH W. PRANE
Consultant
Skeist Laboratories, Inc.
89 Lincoln Park
Newark, N. J. 07102
Chapter 18: PLASTICS IN ROOFING

HAROLD A. SARVETNICK
Consultant
Skeist Laboratories, Inc.
89 Lincoln Park
Newark, N. J. 07102
Chapter 2: THE PLASTICS MATERIALS

JERRY S. SCHAUL
Senior Development Engineer
Celanese Plastics Company
Clark, N. J.
Chapter 13: PIPE AND PLUMBING

GEORGE J. SCHULTE
National Industrial Sales Manager
3M Company
Adhesives Coatings and Sealers Division
2501 Hudson Blvd.
St. Paul 19, Minn.
Chapter 11: ADHESIVES IN BUILDING

IRVING SKEIST
Consultant
Skeist Laboratories, Inc.
89 Lincoln Park
Newark, N. J. 07102
Chapter 1: THE ROLE OF PLASTICS IN CONSTRUCTION
Chapter 19: PLASTICS ABROAD, Part E: OTHER DEVELOPMENTS OUTSIDE U. S. A.

Chapter 21: EXTENDING THE HORIZON

ARMAND G. WINFIELD
Plastics Consultant
562 West End Avenue
New York 24, N. Y.
Chapter 19: PLASTICS ABROAD, Part A: WESTERN EUROPE, Part B: THE SOVIET UNION

PREFACE
AND ACKNOWLEDGMENTS

Both the plastics chemist and the architect are designers of structures. The architect builds with units that the eye can see and the hand can weigh. The chemist's building blocks are tiny molecules, far smaller than one-millionth of an inch, which he strings together to make aggregates called *polymers*. These little chains, barely discernible by electron microscope, are entwined and sometimes tied together to give us the plastics.

Many of the most useful plastics are copolymers, made by combining two or more different building blocks to give a product that has characteristics superior to those obtainable from either unit alone. This book is a copolymer of a different sort—a composite to which chemist, architect and engineer all have contributed. Each of these groups is represented in our roster of authors. I am grateful to them for taking the time to share their expertise in this complex and rapidly changing field.

The following is only a partial listing of the scores of other scientists, technologists and entrepreneurs to whom I am indebted for help in this interdisciplinary undertaking:

Allied Chemical Corp., New York, N.Y. and Morristown, N.J., Mr. Richard Cooper, Mr. Sheldon H. Cady

American Cyanamid Co., Cambridge, Mass. Wayne, N.J., Mr. N. A. Plamondon, Mr. Keith W. Harrison, Mr. Staff Thompson

American Carpet Institute, New York, N.Y., Mr. Gerard J. Riley

American Society for Testing and Materials, Philadelphia, Pa., Mr. Fred F. Van Atta

Archer-Daniels-Midland Co., Minneapolis, Minn., Mr. H. B. Finch

Architectural Plastics Corp., Eugene, Ore., Mr. David S. Mulford, Mr. James Dobson

Architectural Record, F. W. Dodge Corp., New York, N.Y. 10018, Mr. W. Dudley Hunt, Jr.

Armstrong Cork Company, Building Materials Research, Lancaster, Pa., Mr. Jack E. Gaston, Mr. Harry A. Jensen, Mr. Clyde O. Hess

Bath Academy of Art, Corshan, Wiltshire, England, Mrs. Charlotte Enis

Battelle Memorial Institute, Columbus, Ohio Dr. C. W. Cooper

Bayvo Products Co., West Collingswood Heights, N.J.

Beetle Plastics, Airport Road, Fall River, Mass.

Berton Plastics, South Hackensack, N.J., Mr. Robert Handler

Bird & Son, Inc., East Walpole, Mass., Mr. S. H. Sallie

Birdair Structures, Inc., Buffalo, N.Y., Mr. Alvin C. Smith

Bouwcentrum, Rotterdam, Netherlands, Mr. H. E. Wulkan

Brooks-Borg Architects and Engineers, Des Moines, Iowa, Mr. John Rice

Building Construction, Chicago, Ill., Mr. Robert G. Zilly

Building Research Division, National Bureau of Standards, Washington, D.C., Mr. William F. Roeser

Building Research Institute, Washington, D.C., Mr. Harold Horowitz

Burson-Marsteller Associates, New York, N.Y. 10017, Mr. William F. Koelling

Butler Manufacturing Co., Grandview, Mo. 64030, Mr. Lewis H. Acker

Cabot Piping Systems, Plastics Division, Cabot Corporation, Louisville, Ky. 40201

Canadian Plastics, Don Mills, Ontario, Canada

Cast Optics Corp., Hackensack, N.J., Mr. Norman Germanow

Celanese Polymer Co., Newark, N.J., Mr. John L. Patterson

Chem-Seal Corp., Los Angeles, Calif., Mr. Fred Redman

Ciba Products Company, Toms River, N.J., Mr. G. M. Scales

Cirvac Plastics, Erie, Pa., Mr. R. W. Flint

Clearfloat, Inc., Attleboro, Mass. 02703, Mr. Coleman Seely

Clopay Corp., Cincinnati, Ohio, Dr. D. S. Threlkeld

Columbus Coated Fabrics Co., Columbus, Ohio, Mr. Edward L. Mahoney

Coralume Engineering, Inc., Littleston, Pa.

Cornwall Corp., Boston, Mass.

Crane Plastics, Columbus 7, Ohio, Mr. A. Lovell Elliott

Crown Line Plastics, Inc., Hamburg, Iowa, Mr. H. J. Somermeyer

Douglas Fir Plywood Association, Tacoma, Wash., Mr. David Countryman, Mr. Darwin Boblet

The Dow Chemical Company, Midland, Mich., Mr. Earl Ziegler, Mr. Donald Gray

James R. Dresser & Associates, Minneapolis, Minn.

E. I. du Pont de Nemours & Co., Inc., Wilmington, Del. and Trenton, N.J., Mr. Andrew Melrose, Dr. Russell Akin, Mr. H. H. Abernathy, Mr. James Maneval, Mr. E. Tufts, Mr. Jack D. Hunter, Dr. C. H. Topping

Eastman Chemical Products, Inc., Kingsport, Tenn. 37662

Eggers & Higgins, 100 East 42nd Street, New York, N.Y., Mr. G. R. Keane

Enjay Chemical Co., New York, N.Y., Mr. G. L. McIntyre, Dr. N. F. Newman

FMC Corporation, Packing Equipment Division, Riverside, Calif. 92502, Mr. E. G. M. Dykeman

Fabbrica Prodotti Termoplastici, Carlo Pasquetti & Co., s.a.s., Varese (Masnago), Italy

Fiat Metal Mfg Co., Inc., Plainview, L.I., N.Y., Mr. P. Robert Young

Fiberglass Evercoat Co., Cincinnati, Ohio, Mr. Gordon Overby•

Fiber Glass Plastic, Inc., Miami, Fla., Mr. W. T. German

Ford Motor Co., Aeronautics Division, Newport Beach, Calif., Mr. George Epstein

Yale Forman Associates, New York, N. Y.

Foundation Ratiobouw, Rotterdam 3, Netherlands, Ing. E. K. H. Wulkan

Furane Plastics, Inc., Los Angeles, Calif., Mr. Andre B. Kerr

Furniture City Plating Co., Grand Rapids, Mich.

Fylon Corp., Hawthorne, Calif., Mr. R. Merlander

General Electric Co., Pittsfield, Mass. and Waterford, N.Y., Mr. R. J. Kunze, Mr. J. C. Schroeder, Mr. R. T. Daily

General Homes Division, General Industries, Ft. Wayne, Ind.

Georgia Pacific Corp., Portland, Ore, Mr. F. B. Langfitt, Jr.

The Glidden Company, Architectural Products Division, Atlanta, Ga., Mr. Walter J. Maker

B. F. Goodrich Co., Cleveland, Ohio, Mr. M. D. Sellers, Mr. Robert Holtz

Graham Products, Ltd., Englewood, Ontario, Canada, Mr. David S. Graham

Hercules Powder Co., Wilmington, Del., Mr. J. R. Lewis, Dr. Thomas L. Martinke

George R. Hermach Associates, Eugene, Ore., Mr. George R. Hermach

Hess Manufacturing Co., Quincy, Pa., Mr. R. V. Emerson

Home Manufacturers Association, Washington, D.C., Mr. J. A. Reidelbach, Jr.

Hooker Chemical Corp., Niagara Falls, N.Y., Mr. C. R. Simmons

Farbwerke Hoechst, A. G., Frankfurt Main, Germany

Hostachem Corp., Mountainside, N.J., Mr. G. H. Lang

Hotel-Motel Management Review, Hayden Publishing Co., Inc., New York, N.Y. 10022, Mr. A. Stuart Powell, Jr.

Imperial Chemical Industries, Inc., New York, N.Y. 10022, Mr. F. R. Kipping

Imperial Chemical Industries, Ltd., Plastics Division, Hertfordshire, England, Mr. J. A. deNormann

Institut Battelle, Centre de Recherche de Geneva, Carouge-Veneva, Switzerland, Dr. J. Csillaghy

Interchemical Corporation, Clifton, N.J. 97015, Mr. Paul Blackmore

Johns-Manville Research Center, Manville, N.J. and New York, N.Y., Mr. Robert Crouch, Mr. S. Lauren, Mr. Eldredge Miller, Mr. D. H. Anderson

Kalwall Corp., Manchester, N.H., Mr. Richard R. Keller

Kawneer Corp., Niles Mich.

Kaykor Products Corp., Yardville, N.J., Mr. J. L. Huscher

Keller Products, Inc., Manchester, N.H., Mr. Robert R. Keller

Kemlite Corp., Joliet, Ill., Mr. John H. Sergeant, Mr. Alfred B. Menzer

Koppers Co., Inc., Panel Dept., Pittsburgh, Pa., Mr. B. R. Sarchet, Mr. W. Edberg

Lightolier, Inc., Jersey City, N.J.

Lunn Laminates, Inc., Wyandanch, L.I., N.Y., Mr. Frank M. Stagl

Manufacturing Chemists Association, Washington, D.C., Mr. William Demarest

Marbon Chemical Co., Washington, W.Va., Mr. L. C. Oberholtzer, Dr. Kenneth A. Erwin

Massachusetts Institute of Technology, Cambridge, Mass., Prof. Marvin E. Goody, Prof. Frederick J. McGarry, Prof. Albert G. H. Dietz

Materiales Plasticos, S. de R. L., Col Roma, Mexico 7, D.F., Mr. E. Cortes S.

M-H Standard Corp., Hamilton, Ohio 45011, Mr. Andrew Kornylak

Miracle Adhesives Corp., Bellmore, L.I., N.Y., Mr. L. Cutler

Mobay Chemical Co., Pittsburgh, Pa., Mr. Samuel Steingiser, Mr. William F. Gauss, Jr.

Modern Plastics Magazine, New York, N.Y. 10021, Mr. Joel Frados

Molded Fiber Glass Co., Ashtabula, Ohio

Monsanto Company, St. Louis, Mo., Mr. David Plumb, Mr. Carl R. Martinson, Mr. W. D. Hill, Mr. R. D. Williamson, Mr. Lloyd D. Shand, Mr. R. M. Parks

Multiplastics, Inc., Addison, Ill., Mr. Robert McKirnan

National Association of Home Builders, Washington, D.C., Dr. M. H. Rogg

National Building Code, National Research Council, Ottawa, Canada, Mr. J. M. Robertson

National Homes Corp., Lafayette, Ind., Mr. James R. Price

National Lumber Manufacturers Association, Washington, D.C., Mr. Robert A. Holcombe

National Paint, Varnish & Lacquer Association, Washington, D.C., Mr. Neil B. Garlock

Naugatuck Chemical Co., Naugatuck, Conn., Mr. H. C. Bendel

Navaco Co., Dallas, Tex., Mr. George E. Watson, Mr. H. E. Adams

New York World's Fair, Flushing, N.Y., Mr. William J. Kelly, Gen. John L. Whipple, Mr. William Douglas, Mr. William Burns, Comm., Robert Moses

Owens-Corning Fiberglas Corp., Toledo, Ohio, Granville, Ohio and New York, N.Y., Mr. Joseph L. Pokorny, Mr. George Medinnus, Mr. R. L. Rosenfield, Dr. William E. Cass

Panel Structures, East Orange, N.J. 07017, Mr. J. W. Ratner

Pittsburgh Plate Glass Co., Pittsburgh, Pa. and Bloomfield, N.J., Mr. Robert W. McKinley, Mr. Bernard Gould

Plastics World, Boston, Mass., Mr. D. V. Rosato

Joseph Platzker, New York, N.Y. 10038

Plyco Corp., Elkhart Lake, Wis.

Polyfiber Ltd., Renfrew, Ontario, Canada, Mr. E. A. Brown

Polymer Corp., Ltd., Sarnia, Canada, Mr. T. L. Davies

Products Research Co., Burbank, Calif., Mr. H. J. Hoag

Raven Industries, Sioux Falls, S. Dak., Mr. Robert Ludlow

Raymond Development Industries, Inc., Huntington Park, Calif.

Reichhold Chemicals Co., White Plains, N.Y., Mr. J. S. Brown, Mr. Frank X. Ambrose

Dr. Frank W. Reinhart, Silver Spring, Md.

Rensselaer Polytechnic Institute, Dept. of Civil Engineering, Troy, N.Y., Prof. John P. Cook

Rohm & Haas, Philadelphia, Pa. 19105 and Bristol, Pa., Mr. O. L. Pierson, Mr. J. R. Hiltner, Mr. Ben Allen

The Ruberoid Co., Building Products Division, New York, N.Y. 10017, Mr. Harold Lundby

Russell Reinforced Plastics, Lindenhurst, L.I., N.Y., Mr. A. Russell

Sheraton Ritz Hotel, Minneapolis, Minn.

Society of Plastics Engineers, Stamford, Conn.

SPE Journal, Stamford, Conn., Mr. Louis I. Naturman

Society of the Plastics Industry, Inc., New York, N.Y. 10017, Mr. Bert Montell, Mr. Charles L. Condit, Mr. Robert Gutzeit, Mr. Joseph Broslaw

The Society of the Plastics Industry (Canada), Inc., Toronto 17, Ontario, Canada, Mr. E. G. Salmond

Structural Plastics Corp., Osseo, Minn., Mr. J. C. Stuebner

Thiokol Chemical Corp., Trenton, N.J.

Tile Council of America, Princeton, N.J., Dr. J. V. Fitzgerald

Underwriters ' Laboratories, North Brook, Ill. 60062, Mr. A. A. Briber

United Shoe Machinery Corp., Cambridge, Mass., Mr. Robert McA. Lloyd

U. S. Army Mobility Command, U.S. Army Engineers Research & Development Laboratories, Ft. Belvoir, Va., Mr. F. B. Swenson

U. S. Forest Products Laboratories, Madison, Wis., Dr. Richard Blomquist

U.S. Natick Laboratories, Technical Services Div., Natick, Mass.

U.S. Dept. of the Navy, Bureau of Yards and Docks, Washington, D.C., Mr. R. J. Schneider

U.S. Plywood Corp., Los Angeles, Calif., Mr. F. B. Smales

University of Michigan, Department of Architecture, Ann Arbor, Mich., Prof. Robert M. Darvas

Westinghouse Electric Corp., Pittsburgh, Pa., Mr. Perry Taylor

P. Robt. Young Associates, Mamaroneck, N.Y., Mr. P. Robt. Young

The Zlowe Company, Inc., New York, N.Y., Mr. John Mulholland

Irving Skeist
Summit, N.J.
July, 1966

CONTENTS

1 THE ROLE OF PLASTICS IN CONSTRUCTION

IRVING SKEIST

Skeist Laboratories, Inc.
Newark, New Jersey

Building has been with us ever since man moved out of the cave. The building industry is a huge one, utilizing a quarter of a trillion pounds of materials in the United States alone.

By contrast, the synthetic resins that go into plastics, coatings, adhesives and fibers are products of the twentieth century. At present, they comprise less than one per cent of the total tonnage of construction materials in the United States, but their usage and influence are growing rapidly. Not only are they supplanting older materials for many conventional applications, but they are also stimulating the architect and designer to innovate new types of structures and structural components.

ADVANTAGES OF PLASTICS

The plastics offer many advantages over other materials.[1-3] Of course, one must select the most appropriate material for the particular end use, since every material does not possess all of the following virtues:

(1) High light transmission, for glazing and lighting fixtures.

(2) Colorability and aesthetic appeal.

(3) Infinite texture possibilities; smooth surface if desired.

(4) Easy maintenance; permanence of color without painting.

(5) Infinite design possibilities. Sheets can be cast into either simple or compound curvatures and can be corrugated. Thermoplastics can be extruded in continuous lengths with intricate profiles. Complex shapes can be molded.

(6) Resistance to water, corrosion and weathering, making them suitable for facades, gutters, pipes, bathroom fixtures, waterproofing, etc.

(7) Light weight and high strength-to-weight ratio, an especially important feature in high-rise construction. Prebuilt components are easily transported, thus encouraging the use of prefabricated construction, with great savings in labor. The speeding up of on-the-site erection lowers capital investment requirements.

(8) High impact resistance. In the glazing of schools and public buildings, the replacement of glass by plastics has greatly reduced damage by vandalism.

(9) Excellent dielectric characteristics, making them suitable for electrical insulation.

(10) Low thermal conductivity, consequently warm to the touch and pleasant to handle. Plastic foams are outstanding for thermal insulation, especially against cold.

(11) Excellent adhesion (while still in liquid form) to wood, aluminum, concrete, glass and other building materials.

DISADVANTAGES

Several factors have impeded the utilization of synthetic resins in building. Fortunately, most of these can be overcome, at least by some plastics for some purposes:

(1) Cost per pound is high. However, because of their low density, the cost per cubic inch is comparable to or lower than

(4) Some plastics are subject to deterioration from ultraviolet light, or combinations of light and heat, making them unsuitable in hot climates. Improved formulation can mitigate environmental effects.

(5) Most plastics burn, in common with wood and other organic materials. However, many plastic materials are now available which are self-extinguishing or nonburning.

FIG. 1–1. Stone Mountain Mauna at Stone Mountain, Ga. The curtain walls are translucent structural sandwich panels with faces of "Panelux" acrylic-modified polyester reinforced with glass fiber, fused to a core of chemically treated reinforced cellulose. (*Courtesy Glidden Co., Atlanta, Ga.*)

that of other materials. Furthermore, the cost of synthetic resins has been coming down consistently, in opposition to the price trends of other materials.

(2) Plastics are not as strong as some other building materials. Consequently, while they make excellent facades, it has been found expedient to use them in conjunction with structural members of steel or reinforced concrete. But sandwich construction, with faces of fiber glass-reinforced plastics, results in panels that show promise as structural members.

(3) The scratch resistance of plastics is not as great as that of glass or porcelain.

(6) Building codes have in the past been based on specific materials, consequently they have tended to preclude the use of plastics simply because of their newness. Now, performance codes are becoming more widely accepted, and plastics are thus placed on a fairer competitive basis.

(7) Some building trade unions, e.g., plumbers and carpenters, have a vested interest in older materials, and therefore resist the introduction of plastics. The current trend toward greater prefabrication of building components has lessened the impact of these artisans' opposition.

(8) The architect and builder are wary of

FIG. 1–2. 103,900 sq ft of "Darvic" vinyl sheet is used to clad the walls of the Clyde Tunnel constructed for the City of Glasgow. (*Courtesy Imperial Chemical Industries, Ltd., England*)

FIG. 1–3B. Interior view of the partially opened dome from one end of the pool. Notice the "leafing" effect of the dome sections. The translucent, stationary segment is at the center. The transparent segment to the right leafs over it, the segment to the left leafs under. Space heaters are mounted in panel spaces in the stationary, translucent section. Lights for exterior and interior illumination are mounted on longitudinal beams.

FIG. 1–3A An exterior view of the transparent "Plexiglas" acrylic dome, from a terrace of the International Inn, Washington, D. C. The partially opened section of the dome has a cut-out portion. Closed, this fits over the entranceway leading from the hotel, permitting protected access to the pool in inclement weather. Neoprene weather flaps join the segments when closed.

plastics because of their newness and the sparcity of information about them. More engineering data must be published by both the raw materials suppliers and the fabricators of plastic components. Accelerated aging tests must be developed further to compen-

sate for the youth of the synthetic organic materials. Warrantees of satisfactory performance for periods of 15 years or longer will do much to encourage the architect to specify plastics more freely.

HISTORICAL

The first thermoplastic, cellulose nitrate (celluloid), was developed a hundred years ago by the Hyatt brothers in the United States and Parkes in England. Blended with fish scale to give it a pearlescent appearance, it was in vogue a generation ago as a covering material for wooden shelves and toilet seats,

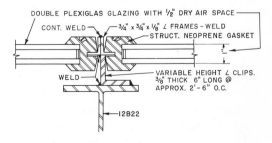

FIG. 1–3C. Section showing details of a typical glazing joint. Type 12 B22 steel beams are used for the framework. (*Courtesy Rohm & Haas*)

but its flammability precluded more extensive use in building.

Smooth-surface resilient flooring has also celebrated its centenary. Linoleum, the first of the yard goods, was made from linseed oil and other natural products. Sixty years later came the so-called asphalt tile, based essentially on coumarone-indene and petroleum resins. Vinyl tile and yard goods, with us a scant twenty years, are rapidly displacing older materials because of their superior color, resilience and abrasion resistance.

Paints and other coatings, like floor covering, were originally based on the unsaturated oils. With the development of alkyd resins in the 1920's, the superior oil-modified alkyds began to replace the all-natural binders. In our own generation, the latex coatings, especially styrene-butadiene, have become predominant for interior application, while vinyl acetate and acrylic-based latexes are rapidly achieving acceptance for outdoor usage as well.

The first synthetic thermosetting resin, phenol-formaldehyde ("Bakelite"), was developed by Baeklund sixty years ago. These hard, heat-resistant materials, with their excellent dielectric characteristics, soon showed their merit for electrical plugs, sockets and outlets. Later they proved to be superior adhesives for the bonding of plywood, capable of producing a laminate that could withstand exposure to heat and water, hence could be used for exterior applications as well as below grade.

For interior wood-bonding applications above grade, the cheaper urea resins, developed in the 1920's, became preferred. Phenolic and melamine resins achieved acceptance for the preparation of decorative laminates for counter tops and table tops, under such familiar trade names as "Formica," "Micarta" and "Textolite."

The main advances in plastics usage in building have come since World War II. Old materials have surged, and new polymers have shown their merit. Latex paints and vinyl tile have already been mentioned.

Polyethylene, a wartime development of Imperial Chemical Industries, Ltd. (England), now shares the wire coating market with polyvinyl chloride. In addition, polyethylene has been found to be a superior moisture barrier in the preparation of foundations. Both polyethylene and PVC are being utilized in pipe, along with newer materials such as ABS (acrylonitrile-butadiene-styrene). Most of the plastic pipe is used for the transport of water, gas and oil. However, it is being accepted more and more for indoor applications, such as DWV (drain, waste and vent) systems, especially in trailers and rural homes.

Because of their good light transmission, plastics have come into use in many lighting and glazing applications. The crystal-clear acrylics, the tough translucent glass-reinforced polyesters, and the economical styrene resins are the leading materials. Polyester shower doors encourage ingenuity of design while transmitting light and resisting heat and breakage.

Foamed plastics are a significant development for thermal insulation, especially perimeter insulation and the erection of

TABLE 1-1. Billion Pounds Produced, USA

Year	All Plastics	Plastics in Construction	Per Cent in Construction
1958	4.658	1.027	22
1959	6.022	1.407	23
1960	6.284	1.489	24
1961	6.856	1.581	23
1962	7.803	1.747	22
1964	9.6	2.3	24

TABLE 1-2. 1964 Estimate of Plastics in Construction

	Million Pounds
Surface coatings	535
Glues and caulking compounds	220
Wire and cable coatings	430
Decorative laminates	70
Electrical and lighting fixtures	90
Plumbing fixtures	25
Pipe and similar shapes	150
Insulation and vapor barriers	205
Wall covering (interior)	35
Light transmission (glazing, skylights, panels)	65
Floor covering	475
	2,300

TABLE 1–3. Consumption of Plastics in U. S. Construction for 1964[6]

End Uses	Acrylics	Urea and Melamine	Phenolics	Reinforced Plastics (Polyesters)	Polyvinyl Acetate	Polyethylene, LD	Polyethylene, HD	Polystyrene and styrene-butadiene	Polyvinyl Chloride	Coumarone-indene and Petroleum Polymers	Alkyd Resins	Miscellaneous	Total
End Uses													
Glazing, skylights	20			40					3				63
Building panels									10				10
Paints, coatings	50	5	2		105			90	40		230	10	532
Plywood, boards		100	110										210
Wire coating						200	20		200			12	432
Electrical devices		10	49										59
Lighting, fixtures	10	3						25	5				43
Decorative laminates		35	35										70
Wall tile, wall covering								20	15				35
Plumbing, fixtures			14					9				3	26
Floor covering									305	170			475
Moisture, insulation barriers			85			60		60					205
Pipe, profile extrusions				5		70	35	15	60			15	200
Total	80	153	295	45	105	330	55	219	638	170	230	40	2360
% of total plastics production in construction	36	32	36	16	36	16	9	13	40	52	40	4	24

Courtesy, Modern Plastics

cold-storage rooms and warehouses. Polystyrene foam is the leading material, followed by urethane.

Structural panels, wall covering, terrazzo flooring, and many other applications for plastics are still in an early stage of development.

PRESENT USAGE

For several years, the Monsanto Company has estimated the usage of plastics in construction in the United States at slightly less than one-fourth of all plastics.[4,5] Thus, approximately 2.3 billion pounds of plastics went into building in 1964.

Plumb[5] has broken down the 1964 figures by end use, as shown in Table 1-2. Out of this list of applications, polymers are used as shown below:

Uses for Polymers in Construction 1964

As a coating or glue	55%
As part of a fixture	5%
In pipe	7%
In the building shell itself	33%
	100%

A further breakdown according to type of plastic material, using much the same figures, is shown by Fisher[6] in Table 1-3.

The United States is by far the largest user of plastics in construction, accounting for

TABLE 1-4. World Production of Plastics, 1964[6]

	Total Production (million lb)	Estimated Total Consumption in Construction (million lb)
United States	9700	2400
West Germany	3700	825
Japan	2350	460
United Kingdom	2000	300
Italy	1500	350
France	1120	285
USSR	1200	250
Canada	440	110
East Germany	370	95
Holland	350	90
Sweden	220	55
Others (Poland, Czechoslovakia, Belgium, Australia, Argentina, India)	750	180
	23,700	5400

45 per cent of the total of 5.4 billion pounds. Plastics usage in other countries is given in Table 1-4.[6]

PROSPECTS

The United States consumption of plastics in 1970 is forecast at 4.4 billion pounds, if one projects present usage figures. However, the

TABLE 1-5. 1970 Estimate for Plastics in Building[5]

	Million Pounds As Now Projected	Possible
Surface coatings	750	750
Glues and caulking compounds	505	505
Wire and cable coatings	1000	1000
Decorative laminates	125	125
Electrical and lighting fixtures	125	125
Pipe and extruded shapes	450	550
Plumbing fixtures	58	300
Insulation and vapor barriers	475	700
Wall covering (interior)	50	100
Light transmission	150	200
Floor covering	670	1700
Wall covering (exterior)	25	250
Roofing	17	400
Total	4400	6705

TABLE 1-6. Opportunities for Chemical Products in Construction 1970–1975

		Million Pounds	
Walls	Residential exteriors—siding	300	
	Trim—gutters—windows	100	
	Non-residential curtain walls	100	
	Facings	100	
	Insulation	200	
	Total		800
Roofs	Single-membrane roofing	1000	
	Insulation	200	
	Residential shingle roofing	100	
	Total		1300
Floors	Resilient flooring	700	
	Synthetic fibers	1000	
	Synthetic terrazzo	100	
	Total		1800
Partitions	Sound-deadening and covering	150	
	Panels—unknown— (estimate)	50	
	Total		200
Plumbing fixtures			200
	Grand Total		4.3 billion lb

figure could reach 6.7 billion pounds, in the view of Plumb,[5] if plastics succeed in penetrating several markets to a greater extent: pipe, plumbing, insulation, wall covering (both interior and exterior), light transmission, floor covering and roofing.

A further breakdown of opportunities for expansion of plastics usage in construction is given in Table 1-6.[5]

By extrapolating a 15 per cent gain per year, Fisher[6] arrives at the estimates shown in Table 1-7 for usage of individual plastic materials. Many opportunities are seen for unusual growth.

TABLE 1-7. Forecast of U. S. Plastics in Construction[6]

	Million Pounds 1964	1970
Acrylics	80	200
Urea and melamine	153	600
Phenolics	291	500
Polyvinyl acetate	105	250
Polyesters	45	150
Polethylene	385	900
Styrene	230	600
Vinyls	638	1500
Coumarone-indene and petroleum polymers	170	400
Alkyd resins	230	600
Miscellaneous	40	500
Total	2367	6200

Bathtubs and other bathroom fixtures are available from reinforced polyester in the United States, and acrylic in the United Kingdom and continental Europe. The main obstacles to greater acceptance have been sensitivity to scratching and cigarette burns. The scratch resistance can be built up to some extent by formulation, while the burning cigarette problem has been overcome most ingeniously by leaving no horizontal surface capable of supporting a cigarette. In this case, however, a stainless steel or other metal tray must be provided.[7a]

If the cost of *plastic foam* can be reduced sufficiently, a tremendous market is available.[5,7b] A significant reduction in the price of isocyanates for urethane foam took place in mid-1965. Noncombustible foam will be required for many applications. Foam is expected to be used in ever greater amount as a form liner for concrete roofs, and in conjunction with various other building materials. Temporary shelters will be made to an increasing extent by spraying urethane foam upon an air-inflated film of polyethylene or other plastic.

Panels for exterior walls, both load-bearing and curtain walls, will be made more and more from polyester or rigid polyvinyl chloride.[5,7d] The price of PVC has been coming down steadily and drastically; meanwhile, the quality has been building up. Weatherability has been a problem, especially

FIG. 1–4. Garage. This ramp parking garage in Rochester, New York, uses FRP for entire side wall, providing a modern exterior and plenty of daylight for drivers inside. (*Courtesy Alsynite Division of Reichhold Chemicals, Inc., San Diego, Calif.*)

in the southern states, but improved rigid PVC formulations appear to have satisfactory resistance to degradation.

Windows and doors[5,8] offer another significant market for polyvinyl chloride, either alone or as a cover for wood. Wood frames are objectionable because they must be painted, while aluminum frames transmit heat and are easily corroded.

FIG. 1–5. Singing Gallery at the Second Presbyterian Church, Fort Lauderdale, Fla. The four modules shown, as well as many others, were each cast in reinforced concrete, from a single fiber glass-reinforced polyester mold. (*Courtesy George Krier, Jr., Inc.*)

In *roofing*,[5] the new single membrane construction has replaced the built-up roof in many non-residential installations. Neoprene/chlorosulfonated polyethylene ("Hypalon") and butyl rubber are among the materials being used. A huge potential is available for plastics.

Terrazzo flooring[5] is turning to synthetic resins—epoxies, polyesters, urethanes—in order to save on thickness and weight. Now that the objectionable load of thick inorganic terrazzo is no longer a problem, builders of some high-rise apartments are installing organic-bound terrazzo in the foyer of each apartment, and sometimes in the bathrooms as well. Other adhesives are becoming more widely used for the bonding of concrete, cinder block and brick, the application of decorative facings, and the manufacturing of laminated lumber.[9]

In *flooring*,[3] there will be a trend toward far greater use of synthetic fiber carpeting, as well as increased use of vinyl foam cushioned flooring.

The problem of changing *codes* is being attacked vigorously in the United States by the Society of the Plastics Industry. The SPI Construction Council is tabulating all data on durability. A program supported by the Manufacturing Chemists Association is being carried out at the National Bureau of Standards on the mechanisms of aging. The National Bureau of Standards also plays a part in the Voluntary Industry Standards drafted by industry under the auspices of the Department of Commerce. ASTM, the American Society for Testing and Materials, is continually engaged in devising and revising test procedures on plastics through its Committee D-20. It is interesting that European countries have similar problems with regard to local autonomy in building legislation.[7f]

The quality of plastics and their resistance to deterioration are steadily increasing, while prices and code restrictions are falling. The talents of the polymer chemist, the engineer and the architect are being combined to develop better raw materials, building components, and finished structures. Increasingly, plastics will be used in conjunction with other materials to produce composites having the best features of both. The future of plastics in building is bright.

REFERENCES

1. Skeist, I., "Plastics in the U. S. Building Industry," *Brit. Plastics*, **37**, No. 4, 190 (April, 1964)
2a. Skeist, I., "A Survey of Recent Developments in Reinforced Plastics," Paper #12, SPI Conference on Reinforced Plastics, Chicago, Ill., February 1964.
   b. Skeist, I., "Reinforced Plastics in Building," *The Indian Builder*, Builders Publications of India, Ltd., New Delhi-11 (1964 Annual).
   c. Skeist, I., "Verstaerkte Kunststoffe im Hochbau," *Kunststoff-Rundschau*, **10**, 615 (1964).
3. Conger, R. P., "Plastics in Building," *SPE J.*, **21**, 538 (1965).
4. Williamson, R. D., Monsanto Company, private communication.
5. Plumb, David S., (Monsanto Company), "Use of Plastics in the Building Materials Field is Surveyed," *The Journal of Commerce*, Paper 7A (June 3, 1965); also *Chem. Eng. News*, **43**(20), 26 (1965).

6. Fisher, J. R., "A Realistic Look at Plastics in Building," *Mod. Plastics*, **42,** No. 6, 72 (February, 1965). The figures originally printed have been amended slightly by the editor of *Modern Plastics* in a private communication.

7. Lien, A. P. and Shand, L. D., "Polymers and Plastics in construction," Preprints, Symposium sponsored by Division of Petroleum Chemistry, American Chemical Society, **10** (4-A), Atlantic City, N. J. (September 12–17, 1965).

   a. MacLeod, N. D., and deNormann, John, "Properties and Applications of Plastics Experiences in the United Kingdom," A-133.

   b. Einhorn, I. C., "Cellular Plastics in Building and Construction," A-55.

   c. Leeper, H. M., and Gomez, I. L., "Processing and Application of Rigid Polyvinyl Chloride for Exterior Construction Applications," A-69.

   d. Holtz, R. T., "Engineering of PVC Building Products to Meet End-Use Criteria," A-37.

   e. Akin, R. B., "Codes and Durability as Factors in Marketing Plastics for Construction Usage," A-49.

   f. Csillaghy, J., "Some Aspects of the Consumption of Plastics in the Building Industry in Europe," A-145.

8. Anon., "Is This the Final Word in Vinyl Windows?" *Mod. Plastics*, 102 (November, 1965).

9. Skeist, I., "Modern Structural Adhesives for Use in the Building Industry," *Adhesives Age* (April 1964).

10. Gutzeit, R., Society of the Plastics Industry, Inc., New York, N. Y., private communication.

2 THE PLASTIC MATERIALS

HAROLD A. SARVETNICK

Skeist Laboratories, Inc.
Newark, New Jersey

The plastic materials commercially available today represent a broad range of properties, forms and applications. These vary from foams for insulation, to elastomer sealants which cure in place, to strong rigid glass fiber-reinforced plastics. This chapter will be devoted to a description of the basic types available, their applications and properties.

In the past, the terms for plastics and resins have often been expressed as trade names. A more suitable approach to the selection of materials is based on (a) a knowledge of what to expect from a given chemical species and (b) data on the particular formulation.

Following are the names of most of the common plastics and the abbreviations suggested by ASTM.

Term	Abbreviation
Polyacrylonitrile	PAN
Polyamide (nylon)	PA
Polybutadiene-acrylonitrile	PBAN
Polybutadiene-styrene	PBS
Polycarbonate	PC
Polyethylene	PE
Polyethylene terephthalate	PETP
Poly (hexamethylene adipamide)	Nylon 66
Poly (methyl-α-chloroacrylate)	PMCA
Poly (methyl methacrylate)	PMMA
Polymonochlorotrifluoroethylene	PCTFE
Polypropylene	PP
Polystyrene	PS
Polystyrene-acrylonitrile	PSAN
Polytetrafluoroethylene	PTFE
Poly (vinyl acetate)	PVAc
Poly (vinyl alcohol)	PVAL
Poly (vinyl butyral)	PVB
Poly (vinyl chloride)	PVC
Poly (vinyl chloride-acetate)	PVCAc
Poly (vinyl formal)	PVF
Styrene-butadiene plastics	SBP
Styrene-rubber plastics	SRP
Urea-formaldehyde	UF
Urethane Plastics	UP

Recommended Abbreviations

(a) Plastics and Resins

Term	Abbreviation
Acrylonitrile-butadiene-styrene plastics	ABS
Carboxymethyl cellulose	CMC
Cellulose acetate	CA
Cellulose acetate-butyrate	CAB
Cellulose acetate propionate	CAP
Cellulose nitrate	CN
Diallyl phthalate plastic or resin	DAP
Epoxide	EP
Ethyl cellulose	EC
Melamine-formaldehyde	MF
Phenol-formaldehyde	PF
Poly (acrylic acid)	PAA

(b) Plastic and Resin Additives

Term	Abbreviation
Dibutyl phthalate	DBP
Dicapryl phthalate	DCP
Diisodecyl adipate	DIDA
Diisodecyl phthalate	DIDP
Diisooctyl adipate	DIOA
Diisooctyl phthalate	DIOP
Dinonyl phthalate	DNP
Di-*n*-octyl-*n*-decyl phthalate	DNODP
Dioctyl adipate	DOA
Dioctyl azelate	DOZ
Dioctyl phthalate	DOP
Dioctyl sebacate	DOS
Tricresyl phosphate	TCP
Trioctyl phosphate	TOF
Triphenyl phosphate	TPP

(c) Miscellaneous Plastics Terms

Term	Abbreviation
General purpose	GP
Single stage	SS
Solvent welded plastics pipe	SWP

The plastic materials fall into two major classifications: thermoplastic and thermosetting materials. *Thermoplastics* are materials which soften when heated, and resolidify upon cooling, like butter or wax. The process of melting by heat and hardening by cooling may be repeated many times. These plastics are made up of threadlike molecules which might extend to perhaps a millionth of an inch if stretched to full length. These tiny threads are intertwined to such an extent that they are hard to pull apart at room temperature. When heated, however, they slide past one another more readily and thus can be formed into the desired shape.

(A)

(C)

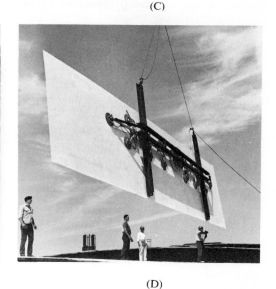

(B)

(D)

FIG. 2-1A–D. The Bell System's Exhibit Building at the New York World's Fair was constructed with a skin of nearly 500 large panels of fiber-glass-reinforced plastic. (*Courtesy Luna Laminates, Wyandanch, N. Y.*)
(A) Layers of fiber glass mat, saturated with resin, are shingled in over a "gel-coat" layer of pigmented plastic resin.
(B) Then another layer of resin is sprayed on. Hardening takes 1 hr.
(C) A steel framework is bonded to the fiber-glass-reinforced plastic panel.
(D) Despite its huge size—12 ft x 40 ft—the panel is sufficiently light in weight to be positioned with suction-cup lifter.

The two most common methods of processing these materials are injection molding and extrusion. *Injection molding* is similar to metal die casting. The plastic material is heated in a cylinder, then forced through a narrow aperture into the cavity of a mold, in which it cools. Then the mold is opened to permit extraction of the piece, and the cycle is repeated. The process is very economical if the cost of the mold can be amortized over a sufficiently large number of pieces— ordinarily at least 10,000. Injection molded plastics of complex shape often give a great savings of labor cost over their metal counterparts made by techniques involving assembly and/or machining.

In *extrusion*, the material is again heated in the cylinder, from which a turning screw forces it through a die. Thus, continual lengths of any shape can be extruded: sheet, film, pipe, or materials of irregular "profile" (cross section) for gasketing, in window frames, etc.

The great advantage of thermoplastics is easy processability. They usually lack the heat resistance and creep resistance of the thermosets, however.

Polyvinyl chloride and polyethylene are the thermoplastics most widely used in building. Other thermoplastics in construction include acrylics, polystyrene, polypropylene, cellulose esters, ABS, nylon, acetal resins, polycarbonates.

Other methods for processing thermoplastics include the vacuum forming of sheet, calendering, coating, blow molding, casting, organosol and plastisol techniques such as slush and rotational molding.

Thermosetting resins are materials which are hardened when heated, like an egg. They begin as tiny threads, but the heat causes chemical reactions to take place which *cross-link* the threads, tying them to other threads at various points so that they can no longer move freely. Consequently, once they have been "hardened" or "cured," they may no longer be melted. The cross-linked structure makes them more resistant to heat, solvents, chemicals, and creep. Thus, the thermosetting resins are generally

preferred for *structural* (i.e., load-bearing) end uses.

Phenolics (phenol-formaldehyde resins), melamines (melamine-formaldehyde resins), polyesters, and epoxies are the most important thermosetting resins used in building. Phenolics are brown-colored resins which are mixed with fillers and catalysts to be *compression molded* into the familiar wall outlets and plugs and other electrical fixtures. Phenolics surfaced with melamines are used in the form of sheets, heated under high pressure to make decorative laminates for kitchen counter tops and table tops under such familiar trade names as "Formica" (American Cyanamid), "Micarta" (Westinghouse) and "Textolite" (General Electric).

Polyesters are the principal resins which are combined with glass fibers, in one form or other, to give fiber glass-reinforced plastics (FRP or RP). Epoxy resins also are used as adhesives and binders. Both polyesters and epoxies may be cured at room temperature with the aid of suitable hardeners or catalysts, as well as at elevated temperatures. This feature can be very useful in on-site applications.

Through the use of diluents, plasticizers, fillers, reinforcing materials, extenders, and alloys with other plastic materials, a great multiplicity of properties and characteristics is possible. Additional modifications are obtained through selection of the basic raw materials (monomers), variation of molecular weights, or degree of cross-linking.

The distinction between thermoplastic and thermosetting materials was once sharply defined but is becoming increasingly blurred. Many of the thermoplastics are now being cross-linked for special purposes, e.g., acrylics for glazing, polyethylene for pipe to be used at high temperature, PVC (polyvinyl chloride) plastisols for structural adhesives. On the other hand, some of the resins which are cross-linked are also available in thermoplastic form, e.g., the phenoxies, closely related chemically to epoxy resins, and some of the polyurethanes.

In view of all of these variations, it is essential that the architect or designer have physical property data in order to characterize the grades of materials to be selected for a given application.

Plastic foams are utilized in building principally for thermal insulation, especially more elastomeric sealants are required for

high-rise buildings. These are based on such materials as polysulfides, polyurethanes, silicones, and a special acrylic.

The table which follows presents the range of values of physical properties for the most common plastics used in building.

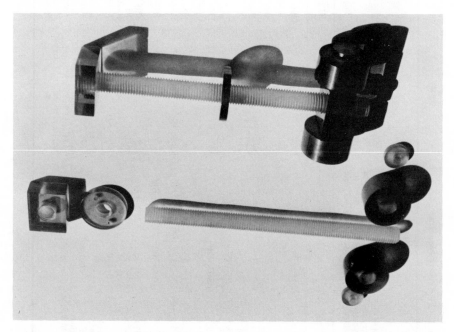

FIG. 2-2. Door hardware fabricated from polycarbonate resin is used to support a load of over 900 lb, on a metal-free wall in special aircraft fire control calibration hangars at Hamilton Air Force Base, California. (*Courtesy General Electric Co.*)

for insulation against cold. Their closed cell structure results in exceptionally low heat conductivity. The two most important foamed plastics for construction are polystyrene, which is inherently rigid, and polyurethane, which is specially formulated for insulation to make it rigid.

Sealants are materials used to exclude water and air at joints in windows, curtain wall panels, etc. The ideal sealant should have good adhesion, excellent aging characteristics (not becoming hard or brittle as the result of light or temperature exposure), and sufficient elasticity to enable the joint to withstand wind stresses as well as temperature fluctuation.

While oleoresinous putties and caulks are still used largely in home construction, the

Forms	Typical Materials Used
Rigids	PVC, ABS, acrylics, polystyrene, cellulosics, polypropylene polyesters, epoxies
Flexibles	PVC, polyethylene, polypropylene alkyds
Foams (rigid)	Polyurethanes, polystyrene
Foams (flexible)	Polyurethanes, PVC
Elastomers ("elastoplastics")	Polysulfide, polyurethane, acrylic
Films	Polyethylene, polypropylene, PVC
Coatings	Alkyd, polyvinyl acetate, SBR, acrylic
Adhesives	Neoprene, reclaimed rubber, SBR, epoxies
Fibers	Nylon, cellulosics, acrylics, polyester, polypropylene
Reinforced plastics	Polyesters, epoxies

TABLE 2-1.[2] **Physical Properties**

THERMOPLASTICS

Term	ASTM Test D 1600	ABS Acrylonitrile-Styrene-butadiene (High-impact)	Acetal	PMMA Acrylic (Polymethyl Methacrylate) (Cast)	CA Cellulose Acetate (H6 to H1)	CAB Cellulose Acetate Butyrate (H4)	Nylon 66 Poly(hexamethylene adipamide)	PC Polycarbonate	PE Polyethylene High-density	PE Polyethylene Low-density
Specific Gravity	D791	1.02–1.04	1.425	1.17–1.19	1.25–1.31	1.22	1.14	1.20	0.96	0.918–0.925
Coefficient of thermal expansion, 10^{-5} per °F	D696	5.5–6.0	4.5×10^{-5}	4.5	4.4–9.0	$6–9 \times 10^{-5}$	5.5	3.75×10^{-5}	8.3–16.7	8.9–11.0
Water adsorption, (24 hrs), %	D570	0.2	0.25	0.3–0.4	1.7–2.7	2.0	1.5	0.15	>0.01	>0.01
Flammability, ipm	D635	1.3	1.1	0.5–2.2	0.5–2.0	0.5–1.5	Self-extinguishing	1.1	1.0	1.0
Heat distortion temperature (264 psi) °F	D648	190–205	255	150–180	120–188	196	—	491	—	—
Tensile strength, × 1000 psi	D638	5.0–6.5	10.0	6–9	5.8–8	6.9	11.8	9.5	4.4	1.4–2.0
Hardness, Rockwell	D785	R95–105	M94, R120	M80–90	R103–120	R114	M79, R118	M78, R118	D68–70 (shore)	C73, D47–53
Impact strength (Izod), ft lb/in. notch	D256	3.0–6.0	1.4	0.4	1.1–3.9	3.0	0.9	14	1.2–2.5	—
Modulus of Elast in Flex, psi	D790, D747	$2.5–3.2 \times 10^5$	4.1×10^5	$3.5–4.5 \times 10^5$	$1.5–2.5 \times 10^5$	1.80×10^5	4.1×10^5	3.4×10^5	1.3×10^5	$12–30 \times 10^5$
Volume resistivity, ohm-cm	D257	$1–8 \times 10^{13}$	6×10^{14}	$>10^{15}$	$10^{10} – 10^{13}$	$10^{11} – 10^{14}$	—	1.7×10^{17}	$>10^{15}$	$10^{17} – 10^{19}$
Dielectric strength (short time) V/mil	D149	300–315	1900	450–530	250–600	250–400	385	400	480	480
Dielectric constant (60 cycles)	D150	2.9–4.2	3.7	3.5–4.5	3.5–7.5	3.5–6.4	4.0	3.17	2.3	2.3
Injection molding pressure psi		6–30	15–25	—	8–32	8–32	10–20	15–20	10–15	5–15
Temperature, °F		375–475	380–440	—	420–490	400–480	520–650	525–600	330–530	275–650
Common trade names (and manufacturers), partial listing		Cycolac (Marbon) Kralastic (US Rubber) Lustran (Monsanto)	Celcon (Celanese) Delrin (Du Pont)	Lucite (DuPont) Plexiglas Rohm & Haas	CA (Celanese) Tenite (Eastman)	Tenite (Eastman) Also Forticel (Celanese's cellulose propionate)	Zytel (du Pont) Also Plaskon (Allied Chemical's Nylon6)	Lexan (General Electric) Merlon (Mobay)	(Allied, Celanese, Dow Du Pont, Eastman, Goodrich-Gulf, W.R. Grace, Hercules, Koppers, Phillips, Shell, Union Carbide, U.S.I.)

TABLE 2-1.[2]

		THERMOPLASTICS			THERMOSETS			
Term	**ASTM Test D 1600**	**PP** Polypropylene	**PS** Polystyrene	**PVC** Polyvinyl chloride	**EP** Epoxide (Epoxy)	**MF** Melamine-Formaldehyde	**PF** Phenol-Formaldehyde	Polyester
Type		General-purpose	General-purpose	Rigid	General-purpose	General-purpose	General-purpose	Styrene Type Rigid
Specific Gravity	D791	0.903–0.907	1.04–1.07	1.32–1.44	1.1–1.4	1.47–1.52	1.32–1.55	1.12–1.46
Coefficient of thermal expansion, 10^{-5} per °F	D696	1.7×10^{-4}	3.3–4.8	2.8–3.3	$1.7–5.0 \times 10^{-5}$	$1.11–3.7 \times 10^{-5}$	1.66–2.50	$3.9–5.6 \times 10^{-5}$
Water adsorption (24 hrs), %	D570	0.03	0.03–0.05	0.03–0.40	0.1–0.5	0.1–0.6	0.3–0.8	0.15–0.60
Flammability, ipm	D635	0.7	1.0–1.5	Self-extinguishing	0.3 to self-extinguishing	Self extinguishing	Self extinguishing	—
Heat distortion, temperature (264 psi) °F	D648	30–150	165–205	140–170	to 250	350–410	260–340	120–420
Tensile strength, $\times$ 1000 psi	D638	5.2–5.35	5–8.5	5.5–9	4–13	7–10	5.0–8.5	4–10
Hardness, Rockwell	D785	R98–101	M68–80	R110–120	M75–110	M118–124 E110	M108–120	M65–115
Impact strength (Izod), ft lb/in. notch	D256	0.6–1.0	0.25–0.35	0.25–2.0	0.2–1.0	0.24–0.35	0.24–0.50	0.18–0.40
Modulus of Elast in Flex, psi	D790	$2.6–2.7 \times 10^5$	$4–5 \times 10^5$	$3.8–3.4 \times 10^5$	$0.4–1.5 \times 10^6$	15×10^5	$8–12 \times 10^5$	$3–9 \times 10^5$
Volume resistivity, ohm-cm	D747 D257	$10^{17}–9 \times 10^{16}$	$10^{18}–10^{19}$	$10^{14} - > 10^{16}$	$10^{12}–10^{14}$	$10^{12}–10^{14}$	$10^9–10^{13}$	$>10^{13}$
Dielectric strength (short time), V/mil	D149	520–800	>500	725–1400	350–550	310–330	200–425	340–570
Dielectric constant (60 cycles)	D150	2.26–2.49	2.5–2.6	2.3–3.7	3.5–5.0	8.4–9.4	5.0–9.0	2.8–4.4
Injection molding pressure psi	—	Wide range	10–24	720				
Temperature, °F	—	450–575	325–650	300–375				
Common trade names (and manufacturers), partial listing		(California Chemical, Dow, Eastman, Enjay, W.R. Grace, Hercules, Phillips, Shell, Union Carbide U.S.I.)	Styron (Dow) Fostarene (Foster Grant) Dylene (Koppers) Lustrex (Monsanto)	(Diamond Alkali, Dow, Escambia, Firestone, Goodrich, Monsanto, Union Carbide U.S. Rubber)	(Celanese, Ciba, Dow, Reichhold, Shell, Union Carbide)	(Allied, American Cyanamid)	(Borden, Hooker, Union Carbide)	(ADM, Allied, American Cyanamid, Atlas, Hooker, Marco, Pittsburgh Plate Glass, Reichhold, Rohm & Haas, U.S. Rubber)

THERMOPLASTIC MATERIALS

ABS Plastics (Acrylonitrile-butadiene-styrene)

Outstanding Properties: Tough and rigid; a good balance of heat resistance, dimensional stability, chemical resistance and electrical properties; readily molded; low cost.

Applications:
Drain, waste and vent piping
Sliding door and window tracks
Weather seals
Concrete forms
Appliance housings

Cellulosics

(Chiefly cellulose acetate (CA); cellulose propionate (CP); and cellulose acetate-butyrate (CAB).

Outstanding Properties: Lustrous colors, including transparents; ease of processing.

Deficiencies: Relatively high cost; questionable long-term outdoor aging; subject to dimensional changes due to cold flow and moisture pickup; heat sensitivity.

Applications:
Knobs

Light fixtures
Shades
Housings
Electrical appliance components
Lenses
Protective coatings and lacquers for wood and metals
Toilet seats
Tool handles

Acetal Resins

Polymers and copolymers of formaldehyde.

Outstanding Properties: High strength, stiffness and toughness. Suitable for replacement of metals in many applications.

Deficiencies: Relatively high cost; tendency to chalk on outdoor exposure.

Applications:
Gears
Bearings
Bushings
Snap fit assemblies
Light-duty springs
Appliance housings
Pump components

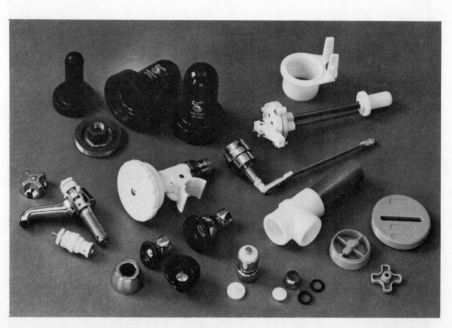

FIG. 2-3. Typical applications of acetal resin in faucet parts and showerheads (bottom), water line shock absorber (upper left), top and bottom views of drain plugs and waste line tee (lower right), toilet fixtures (upper right). (*Courtesy E. I. DuPont de Nemours & Co., Inc.*)

Acrylics

Outstanding Properties: Outstanding transparency and colorability; excellent outdoor weathering; intermediate cost.

Deficiencies: Scratch resistance and impact resistance not outstanding.

FIG. 2-4. Acrylic roof light weighing 17 pounds was injection molded on the Windsor AP.335 injection molding machine shown in the background. (*Courtesy Rollinx Ltd., Manchester, England*)

Applications:
Lighting shields and covers
Glazing
Building panels
Skylights
Screens and enclosures
Door knobs
Switchplates
Lighting fixtures
Towel bars
Toilet seats
Sinks
Tubs

Acrylic sealants, somewhat elastomeric in nature, are used in joints where movement is relatively small. Outdoor aging is excellent and adhesion is good.

Acrylic coatings are generally supplied as water-based emulsions. Adhesion and outdoor weathering are excellent.

Nylon

Outstanding Properties: Very low coefficient of friction; resistance to abrasion; toughness; chemical resistance.

Deficiencies: High water absorption.

Applications:
Gears
Bearings
Other mechanical parts
Latch parts
Wire connectors
Switches and relays
Wire coverings
Slides, rollers and tracks for cabinets

FIG. 2-5. Garfield Park Conservatory Palm House, Chicago, Ill., is enclosed with "Glasbord" acrylic-modified polyester, reinforced with glass mat. (*Courtesy Kemelite Corp., Joliet, Ill.*)

Polycarbonates

Outstanding Properties: High strength and toughness, dimensional stability. Their high maximum service temperature is exceptional for thermoplastics. Transparent grades are available.

Deficiencies: Slight yellowing and surface dulling on aging; high cost; high molding temperature.

(A) Trickling filter, Midland, Michigan

(B) Cherry City Playhouse

FIG. 2-6. Spiral generation of a dome structure from "Styrofoam" polystyrene foam. (*Courtesy Dow Chemical Co.*)

Applications:
  Switch components
  Appliance housings
  Filter bowls
  Lighting fixtures
  Glazing
  Hose couplings
  Fuse covers

Polyethylenes

These are subdivided into two major classes. The first, referred to as *low-density*, because of its lower specific gravity, is composed of branched chain molecules. The *high-density* type consists of linear chain molecules. Appearance is similar; however, the higher-density form exhibits greater rigidity and tensile strength and higher melting point.

Outstanding Properties: Easy processing, low cost, good barrier properties; chemical, solvent and water resistance; good flexibility; excellent electrical properties.

Deficiency: Poor outdoor aging unless pigmented black.

Applications:
  Wire and cable coatings
  Film and sheeting
  Pipe and tubing
  Tanks

Polypropylene

This material is similar to high-density polyethylene, but tensile strength, stiffness and heat resistance are greater.

Outstanding Properties: Low cost; serviceability at elevated temperatures; water, solvent and chemical resistance; easily processed; excellent electrical properties.

Deficiencies: Poor outdoor weathering unless pigmented black; embrittlement at low temperatures.

Applications:
  Pipe, tubing and fittings
  Rope and belting
  Wire coating
  Pump housings
  Tanks and tank liners
  Appliance housings
  Film and sheeting

Styrene Resins

This category includes both polystyrene (or homopolymer) and styrene copolymers made by "grafting" styrene onto a rubbery backbone.

Outstanding Properties: Low cost, transparency (of the homopolymer).

Deficiences: Poor impact resistance (with the exception of the copolymer impact grades); tendency to craze and crack; long-term outdoor weathering not good.

Applications:
  Wall tile
  Partitions and panels
  Knobs and drawer pulls
  Light fixtures
  Foam insulation for buildings, appliances and piping

PVC (Polyvinyl Chloride)—Rigid

Outstanding Properties: Low cost; can be stabilized to weathering; water, solvent and chemical resistance; self-extinguishing.

Deficiencies: Degrades in high-temperature service. Translucent grades may be sensitive to ultra-violet light.

Applications:
  Pipe
  Siding
  Ducts and vents
  Building panels
  Window components
  Rain gutter and downspouts
  Wall tile

Polyvinyl dichloride, which is now appearing in rigid applications, extends the service temperature 40 to 60°F. In addition, strength and chemical resistance are greater. Building applications projected are hot- and cold-water piping.

PVC—Flexible

Outstanding Properties: Low cost; wide range of processing possibilities, e.g., extrusion, organosol and plastisol techniques, etc.; compoundability to obtain a wide variety of end properties; good weathering.

Deficiency: Poor resistance to elevated service temperature.

Applications:
  Electrical insulation
  Floor coverings
  Pipe
  Corrugated sheets
  Weatherstripping
  Window frames
  Door jamb liners
  Upholstery coverings
  Wall coverings
  Decorative wallboard laminates
  Flexible film and sheeting

THERMOSETTING PLASTICS

Amino Resins

This class is composed of urea-formaldehyde and melamine-formaldehyde resins as well as various combinations. Melamine imparts higher strength, service temperature and water resistance, but at higher cost. Melamine resins exhibit the highest scratch resistance and surface hardness of the common plastic materials. UF and MF molded articles are generally highly filled with materials such as alpha-cellulose, wood flour, minerals, asbestos, and glass fibers.

Outstanding Properties: surface hardness; scratch resistance; heat resistance; colorability and color stability; adhesive and binder characteristics; electrical properties; low cost (urea-formaldehyde).

Applications:
  Drawer pulls and doorknobs
  Wiring devices
  Binders for particle board and plywood adhesives (urea-formaldehyde)
  Adhesives for furniture, laminations, etc. (urea-formaldehyde)
  Toilet seats
  Appliance housings
  Decorative laminates for table tops, countertops, etc.

Epoxies

Outstanding Properties: Water, solvent and chemical resistance; adhesion; impact resistance; electrical properties; curable at room temperature.

Deficiencies: Toxicity of some raw materials; cost; requires mixing of two components.

Applications:
  Flooring surfacing compositions
  Pipe linings
  Tank linings
  Electrical potting and encapsulation
  Concrete bonding agents
  Adhesive for ceramic and resilient floor tile

Phenolics

Phenol-formaldehyde resins, where employed as molding compounds, use wood flour, minerals, asbestos, carbon black and glass fiber for fillers. Selection of filler is dictated by end-use requirements. Other applications include adhesives for plywood and binder for fiber-glass thermal insulation.

Outstanding Properties: Low cost; excellent electrical properties; high heat resistance; dimensional stability; low moisture absorption; solvent and chemical resistance.

Deficiencies: High cure temperature; only available in dark colors.

Applications:
  Toilets seats
  Plywood adhesives
  Thermal insulation binder
  Hardboard binder
  Appliance housings
  Electrical components
  Handles and knobs

Polyesters

This is a large group of resins of which the unsaturated polyesters and the alkyds are the principal types used in building. *Unsaturated polyesters* are blended with styrene monomer and cured with the aid of a catalyst. Cure may be accomplished at room temperature, usually in the presence of an accelerator to hasten setting. Structural applications utilize fiber glass-reinforced polyesters. *Oil alkyds*, which are used primarily in coatings, cure in the presence of oxygen through the incorporation of various "dryers." Good adhesion and moderately good weather characteristics have made them standards for outdoor coatings. The following refers to the unsaturated polyesters.

Outstanding Properties: High strength, room-temperature curable; good electrical properties; water, solvent and chemical resistance.

Deficiencies: Outdoor weathering not outstanding.

Applications:

Structural sheet and facings for sandwich panels

Vents and ducts

Glazing

Room dividers

Protective coatings

Adhesives for structural applications.

Pipe

Transformer covers

Storage tanks

Appliance and industrial housings

Fluorescent light housings

Electrical laminates

Masonry coatings

Tabletop laminates and finishes

Fiber glass, which is the most important reinforcing filler for polyesters, is used in the form of pre-formed mats, cloth and woven roving, chopped strand, etc. Various finishes are employed on the glass fiber to improve adhesion between the polyester and the glass fiber. Asbestos, sisal, and other fibers are sometimes used as reinforcement. Fillers such as clays may be incorporated to reduce cost.

Polyurethanes

This versatile family of materials is used in the form of foams, elastomers, coatings and sealants. A wide range of flexibility can be obtained in urethane foams through selection of isocyanate, polyol and other raw materials. The highly cross-linked urethane foams, with closed cells, have exceptionally low thermal conductivity combined with rigidity, making them suitable components of insulating sandwich panels. They may be "foamed in place" by metering of the reactive ingredients through a specially designed mixing head. The cured foam adheres tenaciously to walls. In the production of foam core panels, pre-foamed slabs may be bonded to the outer surfaces or the foam may be generated between the surfaces, eliminating the need for adhesives.

Urethane sealants have high extensibility and good adhesion. They may be either two-component systems, consisting of a urethane pre-polymer and a polyol curing agent; or one-component, highly viscous liquids which are cured by atmospheric moisture.

Urethane coatings for building are usually one-component, oil-modified, hardened by exposure to oxygen in the air. The one-part moisture-catalyzed types are more expensive, but have better properties. For the most severe requirements, e.g., in chemical plants, two-component systems are employed. Urethane coatings exhibit exceptional abrasion resistance, fitting them for flooring and other applications where heavy wear will be encountered.

RIGID FOAMS

Outstanding Properties: Best thermal insulation properties of all plastic materials; good impact and dent resistance; may be formed in place; excellent adhesion to substrates; high tensile strength.

Deficiencies: High cost; not suitable for high-temperature service.

Applications: Insulation for walls, roofs, floors, appliances, mobile homes, pipe tank foam core panels, rug underlays, mattresses.

SEALANTS

Outstanding Properties: Toughness and abrasion resistance; tensile strength; high tear resistance.

Deficiencies: Ultraviolet light resistance not outstanding; tendency to form foamy surface; variable properties due to ambient temperature and humidity conditions.

Applications: Building sealants and caulks.

COATINGS

Outstanding Properties: Exceptional abrasion resistance and adhesion.

Deficiencies: Outdoor weathering of certain grades is poor; tendency to yellow; low maximum service temperature.

Applications: Coatings for floors, doors, panels, etc.

Polysulfides

These materials find their major use in building applications as pour-in-place sealants. Cure is generally accomplished by addition of catalyst prior to application.

Outstanding Properties: High extensibility; good adhesion.

Deficiencies: Resiliency decreases on aging; staining.

Applications: Building sealants.

Silicone Rubbers

These materials are supplied as one-part systems for application as sealants and caulks.

Outstanding Properties: Exceptional outdoor weathering; ease of application; one-part system; rapid cure; excellent performance at high as well as low temperatures; good color.

Deficiencies: High price; primer required.

Applications:

Building caulks and sealants

Gaskets

TABLE 2-2. Comparative Strength-To-Weight Ratios[a][2] (Specific Strength)

Material	Ratio
Reinforced plastics, filament wound epoxy	4300
Reinforced plastics, other epoxy	1600
Titanium and its alloys, heat-treated	1500
Reinforced plastics, phenolic	1000
Reinforced plastics, polyester	1000
Ultra-high strength steels	880
Nylon, glass-reinforced	570
Aluminum alloys, hard	530
Epoxies (cast)	370
Nylon 6,6	360
Polystyrene, glass-reinforced	340
Yellow brass (cast)	320
Acrylics, molded, extruded	290
Polycarbonate	280
Acrylics (cast)	280
ABS resins	270
Polyesters (cast)	250
Acetal	230
Melamines, general-purpose	220
Cellulose acetate	210
Polyvinyl chloride	210
Polypropylene	180
Phenolics (molded)	180
Polyethylene, high-density	150
Copper, hard	140
Polyethylene, low-density	90
Ingot iron, annealed	70
Lead and its alloys	4

[a]These values are obtained by dividing yield strengths (psi) of metals and tensile strengths (psi) of plastics by density (pounds per cubic inch.)

TABLE 2-3. Tensile Strengths[2]
($\times$ 1000 psi)

Material	High	Low
Alloy steels	345	98
Glass fibers	220	200
Cellulosic fibers	155	20
Nylon fiber	128	59
Polyester fiber	126	67
Nickel and its alloys, annealed	120	50
Aluminum and its alloys	60	22
Copper, hard	55	50
Yellow brass (cast) leaded	45	30
Copper, annealed	35	32
Nylon, glass-filled	31	19
Polyester film	28	17
Cellophane	19	7
Nylon 6 film	17	13.8
Epoxies (molded)	16	5
Nylon 6,6	12.6	7.1
Epoxies (cast)	12	0.1
Acrylics (molded, extruded)	10.5	5.5
Acetal	10	—
Melamines (molded)	10	3.5
Phenolics (molded)	10	3.5
Polyesters (cast)	10	0.9
Polycarbonate	9.5	9
Polyvinyl chloride	9	1
ABS resins	8.5	3
Cellulose acetate	8.5	1.9
Polystyrene, general-purpose	8	5
Wood comp. board (hardboard)	7.8	3
Lead and its alloys (cast)	7.4	21
Polypropylene	5	—
PVC film (nonrigid)	5	1
Particle board	5	0.5
Polyethylene, high-density	4.4	2.9
Polyethylene, medium-density	2.4	2

TABLE 2-4. Hardness of Plastics[2]

Rockwell M Hardness Material	High	Low
Melamines	M 125	M 110
Phenolics, general-purpose	M 120	M 108
Ureas	M 120	M 116
Polyesters (cast), rigid	M 115	M 65
Epoxies (cast)	M 110	M 76
Acrylics	M 103	M 80
Nylons, glass fiber-filled	M 95	M 85
Polycarbonates	M 90	M 78
Polystyrene, general-purpose	M 80	M 68

Rockwell R Hardness		
Cellulose acetate	R 121	R 39
Acetal	R 120	
ABS resins	R 118	R 95
Nylon 6 and 6, 6	R 118	R 103
Cellulose acetate butyrate	R 114	R 59
Polypropylene	R 101	R 77

TABLE 2-5. Comparative Prices of Common Engineering[2] Materials

Material	($/lb)	($/cu in.)
Platinum	1550	1200
Gold	612	428
Silver	22.50	8.50
Silicone rubber	2.50–4.00	0.08–0.11
Glass-melamine laminate	2.30–2.50	0.15–0.17
Urethane rubber	1.15–1.65	0.5–0.7
Polycarbonate	1.05	0.046
Asbestos-phenolic laminate	0.96–2.70	0.05–0.16
Nylon	0.90–2.18	0.04–0.09
Acetal	0.65	0.033
Epoxy	0.62	0.04
Acrylic	0.46–0.55	0.018–0.023
Alkyd	0.43–0.60	0.03–0.04
Melamine	0.42–0.45	0.022–0.023
Cellulose acetate	0.40–0.52	0.018–0.024
ABS resins	0.39–0.47	0.015–0.018
Austenitic stainless steels	0.38–0.60	0.11–0.16
Polypropylene	0.32–0.39	0.010–0.012
Copper	0.32	0.1
Aluminum (alloys)	0.28	0.03
Polyethylene, high-density	0.25	0.009
Vinyls	0.24–0.46	0.012–0.022
Polyester	0.23–0.29	0.009–0.013
Polyvinyl chloride (flexible)	0.20–0.45	—
Phenolic	0.20–0.35	0.01–0.02
Urea	0.19–0.34	0.01–0.018
Polystyrene	0.145	0.006
Low-density polyethylene	0.14–0.22	0.005–0.008
Zinc	0.135	0.003
Carbon steel	0.038	0.01

REFERENCES

1. "Modern Plastics Encyclopedia", New York, McGraw-Hill Book Co., 1965.
2. *Materials in Design Engineering*, Materials Selector issue, (October 1965).
3. Simonds, H., and Church, J., "Concise Guide to Plastics," second ed., New York, Reinhold Publishing Corp., 1963.
4. Simonds, H., "Source Book of the New Plastics," Vol. 2, New York, Reinhold Publishing Corp., 1961.

3 | BUILDING CODES AND REGULATIONS

HAROLD PERRINE*

Civil Engineer
New York, New York

BUILDING CODES

A building code is a collection of rules or regulations administered by an official who is required by his oath of office to see that buildings are constructed in a manner both safe and sanitary.

The building itself must be structurally adequate. Likewise, the various systems of service equipment and distribution, such as electrical wiring and fixtures, plumbing, elevators, heating plants, and air conditioning, must be safely installed. Materials must meet minimum requirements for structural safety and fire safety, and they must assure sanitary conditions, consistent with the building's use and occupancy.

Compliance with minimum requirements is assured by administering a "specification" type code or, more simply, a "performance" type code. However, as a rule, the responsibility of the official ceases on the completion of the building and its equipment. Maintenance rules are not set up under the administrative code. The official knows that the building's structural integrity is satisfactory before he issues the certificate of occupancy. He knows that the unobstructed exit facilities are adequate. He knows that the wall finishes are not hazardous to life and health. However, he is not sworn to see that these conditions are maintained. He revisits the building, in line of duty, only when an

*Deceased.

alteration is proposed; then the cycle is repeated. Continuing safe and sanitary conditions are policed by other departments of the political subdivision.

At the turn of the century there were comparatively few codes in existence. These were usually for the larger cities, although there were also a few state codes at that time. All of them were quite individual in character, mainly influenced by local conditions, and of the "specifications" type that allows little latitude for the builder and the producer of new materials or devices for the improvement of buildings.

However, during the past 20 to 25 years, more standardized codes have been appearing, prepared and sponsored by associations of building officials, fire insurance interests, and so on. Considering the vast amount of experience and research that has gone into the preparation of these standardized codes, it is easy to understand why cities lacking research facilities have found them attractive. With the passage of time, we can expect increasing adoption of standardized group codes for three main reasons: (1) they are all veering from the "specification" type to the "performance" type, (2) they continue to improve in character year by year as new materials become available and new methods are developed, and (3) it is cheaper for the municipality to adopt one of them than write its own.

There are now four major reference codes in existence, sponsored by the following groups:

(1) National Board of Fire Underwriters (N.B.F.U.)—National Building Code (N.B.C.)

(2) International Conference of Building Officials (I.C.B.O.), formerly Pacific Coast Building Officials Conference—Uniform Building Code (U.B.C.)

(3) Building Officials Conference of America (B.O.C.A.)—Basic Building Code and Abridged Building Code (B.B.C. and A.B.C.)

(4) Southern Building Code Congress (S.B.C.C.)—Southern Standard Building Code (S.S.B.C.)

These "regional" or "model" codes reflect the best thinking of responsible and knowledgeable professional men skilled in code writing and code administration. They have proved their value over the last quarter century. Municipal and state governments can select and adopt any one of them with confidence. They are all live documents, subject to annual amendment by democratic processes. Their sponsors are alert to the constant improvements in building products and assemblies. The availability of these model codes makes a Federal Building Code unnecessary, in the author's opinion.

National Board of Fire Underwriters (National Building Code)

The National Board of Fire Underwriters was a pioneer in code writing, having first produced its National Building Code more than 50 years ago. This code is quite different in significance from the other three group codes. It is written by the staff of the N.B.F.U. and periodically brought up to date by them. Code change procedures do not go through annual open hearing cycles as do the group codes controlled by building officials.

The N.B.F.U. code is written primarily for the purpose of minimizing property loss from fire. In spite of its name, the National Code has no federal connection or significance.

The aim of N.B.F.U. is to promulgate its code wherever possible, thereby reducing property losses from fires. To this end, copies are furnished to municipalities free or below cost. In the past, this practice influenced budget-conscious municipalities into adopting the N.B.F.U. Code. Now, however, the three other group codes are increasing in popularity.

International Conference of Building Officials

The International Conference of Building Officials, formerly the Pacific Coast Building Officials Conference, was initiated in the late 1920's by a small group of West Coast building officials, with the endorsement and support of building materials producers and other segments of the building industry, mainly in California. The objective was a uniform building code, to eliminate confusion in that area arising from conflicting laws or absence of laws. The resulting "Uniform Building Code of the Pacific Coast" has grown in importance and is now widely used in California as well as in Arizona, Colorado, Nevada, New Mexico, Montana, Oregon, portions of Texas, Utah, Washington, Wyoming, etc. The Uniform Building Code or "U.B.C." also has scattered acceptance in some middle western cities such as New Orleans, South Bend, Topeka, Jackson (Mississippi), and parts of Michigan and Minnesota. Notably, the U.B.C. is used by the Indiana State Government.

Where local or state laws permit, the U.B.C. has been adopted in hundreds of jurisdictions in the West, sometimes verbatim by reference, at other times utilizing the format but varying somewhat in detail. The list of adoptions grows each year. Even in the West, however, there are still numbers of large and important jurisdictions that are not affected directly by the U.B.C.

In the event that a building code problem in the Far West develops in one of the six larger nonconforming cities, it is recommended that one correspond with the appropriate department official of these cities (see Appendix A). In smaller cities, the Building Department can advise whether the U.B.C.* has jurisdictions.

Problems pertaining to the state of California should be taken up with the Senior Code Analyst, State of California, 1025 "P" Street, Sacramento, California. Matters pertaining to the Fire Laws of California should be taken up with California State Fire Marshal, 1025 "P" Street, Sacramento, California.

Southern Standard Building Code

In the early 1950's, a group of city officers—mayors, city architects and engineers, building officials, etc.—set up a Building Code Congress with mostly local building industry support. They produced the Southern Standard Code, or "S.S.B.C." This book now has wide distribution in some large cities and numerous medium sized and smaller ones in the southern states, ranging from Florida to Texas and north to Tennessee and Virginia. Unlike the U.B.C., the S.S.B.C. has little, if any, influence outside its designated territory.

While the S.S.B.C. is progressing actively, many large southern cities still maintain their own codes. These codes are holdovers from the period previous to the creation of the S.S.B.C. and are often difficult to change because of political situations peculiar to each. Some, however, show indications of being influenced by the regional code or codes. In Appendex 1B is a list of important southern cities with comments as to their respective code situations. Most code problems in the southern states involve the S.S.B.C.

A copy of the code may be purchased from Hubert N. Caraway, Executive Director, Southern Building Code Congress, Brown-Marx Building, Birmingham, Alabama. This office should also be contacted if information cannot be obtained from correspondence with officials of the larger cities listed in

*A copy of the U.B.C. is available from T. H. Carter, Executive Director, International Conference of Building Officials, 50 South Robles Street, Pasadena, California.

Appendix 1B or from the Building Inspector of the city in question.

Basic Building Code

Although there is one influential code-writing group of building officials in the Northeast and Middle West, this part of the country has many old cities proud of their reputations and achievements in code writing. Several states or groups of cities exert their influence. Old laws preclude drastic changes; but the codes keep up the progress to some extent by the addition of amendments. Usually, the larger the city, the harder it is to effect changes.

The Building Officials Conference of America was formed in 1915 by a group of eastern building officials. There was at first no attempt to write a standardized code. A group of cities including Boston and neighboring communities followed one style of code requirements, while New York City, Philadelphia, Washington, D. C., and cities in Connecticut worked out patterns of their own. The Industrial Commissions of the states of New York, Pennsylvania, Ohio, Wisconsin, and others pursued ideas in industrial safety in framing their codes. Code writing was thus approached from various viewpoints.

In the 1940's, B.O.C.A. wrote a group code, the "Basic Building Code," also with the support of the building industry. B.O.C.A. has an "Abridged Building Code" for smaller cities. The roster of members and committees with a list of cities and other governmental subdivisions that have adopted the B.B.C. is available to members of the B.O.C.A. Appendix C includes a list of the more important adoptions of the B.B.C. and code characteristics of other important cities in the region served by B.O.C.A.

GOVERNMENT REGULATIONS

A specification is a directive that the building and its equipment not only be constructed in a safe and sanitary manner, but remain so. Under the building code, the private architect designs the building in accordance with the private owner's budget to meet minimum requirements obtaining at time of the issuance of the certificate of occupancy. A study of the relative durabilities of competitive materials is a duty of the architect; the budget dictates their selection. The building official has no control or interest in this phase. Under the government specification, however, the government is owner, architect and official all in one.

Federal Government Construction Agencies*

The word "specification" has two meanings in federal construction. So-called "Federal and Military Specifications" are material and product "specs" followed by federal agencies in the *procurement* of supplies. The other meaning of the word is to be found in the *construction* specifications that constitute an essential part of the contract documents for most sizable building projects. There are four sets of such specifications—those of the Public Buildings Service, the U.S. Army Corps of Engineers, the Navy's Bureau of Yards and Docks, and the Veterans' Administration.

The producer of building components also must realize that architectural and engineering ("A&E") firms working under these federal agencies are strictly bound by the "guide-specifications" of each. They are not free to make decisions as to the acceptability of new products. The only way to gain acceptance is through the guide-specs, either by having the product incorporated in one or by having it established as an acceptable alternative.

The Public Buildings Service is a unit of the federal government's General Services Administration. It is responsible for the design and construction of a great many U.S. government buildings, the erection of each of which requires a complete set of working drawings and volume of construction specifications. The law requires that the construction specs for any building erected under any federal authority such as the PBS call

*This section prepared by William Demarest, formerly Architectural Director, Manufacturing Chemists' Association, 1825 Connecticut Ave., Washington, D.C.

for any such building products as conform with existing U.S. government procurement specifications, whether "Federal" or "Military." This is accomplished by providing the construction-spec-writer, whether on the PBS professional staff or an independent A&E firm retained for the job, with a thick volume of guide-specifications upon which he must draw.

This amounts to but a starting point, as it can readily be imagined that the U.S. government procurement specs, as officially promulgated, cannot encompass all the building materials and components needed for the economical construction of an efficient building. For instance, where a Federal or Military Specification for a certain kind of component has not been developed, the PBS need not wait. It simply sets up its own requirements for such a product, and compliance with these assures acceptability.

Gaining such recognition accomplishes two or three things for the producer of a new building component. The product has in all likelihood become eligible for the specific job which gave rise to the PBS's interest in and evaluation of it as a nonstandard item. In any case, it is—or is on its way to being— written into the guide-specs governing all PBS jobs for which it would be suitable. This constitutes a major first step toward recognition by the Federal Supply Service itself under a "Federal Specification."

Acceptance of a product for the Corps of Engineers' standards does not constitute approval of it for any particular construction project. Guide-specifications and standard technical specifications issued by the Corps of Engineers specify the materials, equipment and methods considered adequate to meet military construction requirements. Where several will satisfy these requirements, those that are economically competitive are permitted by the specifications as contractors' options. Field offices are required to use these specifications without change.

One over-all objective of the Bureau of Yards and Docks is to maintain uniform standards of quality throughout its area of responsibility but at the same time to utilize suitable local materials as much as possible. During the development of a guide-specification, industry comments are considered carefully. These are not initiated by industry, but are solicited by the Bureau. As far as practicable, the Navy uses the library of guide-specifications that is available, each of its design offices having an index of these. Where they do not apply, the specifying engineer develops the requirements in accordance with the "Armed Services Procurement Regulations" and other military directives.

The office that initiates changes in the VA's guide-specifications, according to which new VA medical facilities are built, is the Engineering Service of the Department of Medicine and Surgery, U.S. Veterans' Administration, Washington D.C. It should therefore be the first to be contacted by the producer whose building component is not recognized under the VA's guide-specs, although other VA offices may be the ones that actually need to be followed up regarding the new product submitted.

United States Government Specifications

Any question as to whether there is a U.S. government procurement specification governing the acceptability of a particular product must be resolved by consulting two references, not one. This is because there are two general categories of such specifications: (1) so-called "Federal Specifications" published by the agency that has been described as the government's housekeeper, the General Services Administration and (2) "Military Specifications" which are developed instead by the Army, Navy, or Air Force.

Consider first the role of the Public Buildings Service (PBS) of the General Services Administration. For the guidance of its architects and engineers, the PBS assembles "Guideline Specifications" books within which they must stay when selecting specific components to go into a building. The guide-specs will contain references to Federal, and perhaps Military, Specifica-

tions. In such instances, the manufacturer will find little latitude of decision on the part of the PBS technical people, but otherwise (and this is more likely to be the case with new products) it is for the PBS to draft its own specifications that will define acceptability.

For the manufacturer attempting to gain federal government recognition of his building product, this is all to the good since it may give him his initial opportunity to present the products on their merits. He or his representative is dealing with the PBS on much the same basis as with any architectural or engineering firm. In setting requirements of a "performance" type the PBS makes an effort to be open-minded about building components, including plastics products, that are new and relatively untried.

When considering a product not governed by Federal or Military Specifications, the PBS will normally require extensive test data indicating its characteristics that bear upon the proposed use. The General Services Administration, including the Public Buildings Service, is usually willing to accept data that are certified by an independent testing laboratory.

PLASTICS IN BUILDING CODES A NEW CODE PROBLEM

In the mid-fifties several segments of the plastics industry discovered the existence of code barriers as they reached larger and more widely diversified markets in the building construction field. As long as plastics in building construction was an experimental or developmental matter, as long as the total volume of plastics going into building was insignificant, and as long as plastic products for building had no particular identity, their occasional appearance on building plans raised few serious questions. However, with plastics frequently becoming an important functional part of buildings, e.g., as glazing or skylighting, building officials began to ask under what provisions of the building codes the new materials were being offered. The wide range of plastics presented a confusing picture, and the average building inspector or department head found himself unable or unwilling to judge the merits of any particular product. There were no coordinated reference data which might guide the industry and the building official in the problem of what plastics and how much should go into various types of buildings in this or that location. The easiest solution to the building department's problem was to refuse to approve or allow the installation.

Often a manufacturer of one plastic would obtain approval of his product in a city or area, and then a manufacturer of a totally different type of plastic would get approval of his product even though it had different physical characteristics and performance. The arrival of a third or fourth manufacturer in the city, seeking perhaps another use of plastic materials, or only offering a product competitive to the other two, would throw the building department into a turmoil.

In 1955, the Society of the Plastics Industry found that the number and nature of the problems which the industry faced before building departments around the country, and the number of products and companies involved, were so large as to require a special program aimed at obtaining fair building code legislation for plastic materials. The SPI Code Advisory Committee was organized.

In the mid-fifties, the Basic Building Code of the Building Officials Conference of America was the only one of the nation's principal building codes which even mentioned plastics. There was no standard procedure for acceptance, approval, or review of plastics as materials of construction. On advice of numerous building officials throughout the country, it became clear that it would be necessary to treat plastics in a separate chapter wherever building codes were involved, following the procedure used in codes regarding other materials such as wood, steel, reinforced concrete, masonry, etc.

In 1956, after many meetings, much study and data gathering, the SPI Code Advisory Committee felt that it could formulate a policy reconciling the public safety and welfare responsibilities of the building officials, called for in their codes, with the practical production offerings of the plastics manufacturers. This policy was set forth in a booklet entitled "A Model Chapter on Plastics for Inclusion in a Building Code," developed in collaboration with the Plastics in Building Committee of the Manufacturing Chemists' Association. It was circulated for review to over one thousand company members of the Industry, before release. The Model Chapter condensed a broad range of hundreds of prospective building materials to a small group of three or four readily identifiable classes and offered conservative uses of plastics in appropriate forms. Appendix D is the full text of the June, 1962, revision of The Model Chapter, with some changes adopted in 1963.

THE MODEL CHAPTER

The Model Chapter first sets up barriers against the introduction of inferior materials in building that (1) are not sufficiently standardized to be included in the listing appearing in the current edition of "Technical Data on Plastics" published by the Manufacturing Chemists' Association, Inc. (now out of print) and (2) do not pass one of two ASTM laboratory tests (ASTM D635 or ASTM D568). These ASTM tests set a barrier for the acceptance of any and all plastics materials which perform unsatisfactorily under these tests, but are not by themselves a guarantee of acceptance, nor were they so intended. Both the Chapter on Plastics of the Philadelphia Building Code, a document of several years existence, and the later Chapter 60 on Plastics in the Denver Code include these tests in their respective requirements.

In addition the Model Chapter recommends conditions of use:

(1) when fibrous glass or other noncombustible reinforcement is required, if used in sufficient percentage to insure safety;

(2) in roof panels, wall panels, skylights and domes, when the plastic is not to exceed in area or spacing, the safe recommended

practice of the plastics industry (also attendant installation precautions);

(3) as light-diffusing systems in ceilings and other areas, following recommended practice, including noncombustible hangers and electrical provisions;

(4) for other special applications, e.g., greenhouses;

(5) for plastic wall finishes conforming with the requirements of the local building code provisions as to flame spread.

The Model Chapter in Practical Use

Since its original publication in 1956, the Model Chapter has been in constant use as a reference medium by the SPI Code Advisory Committee, one of its co-authors, in the Committee's contacts with code writers nationally.

Rarely does a building code committee adopt a model code *in toto*. Usually it is adopted in principle but not literally. Local laws often preclude its use unamended.

An early adoption of the Model Chapter was effected by the Southern Building Code Congress, as Chapter XXVI of the Southern Standard Building Code. This group has made a few amendments to the original form which have improved its usefulness.

The Building Officials Conference of America had already written Article 20— Plastics—into the Basic Building Code before the publication of the Model Chapter. Article 20, while it conforms in principle to the Model Chapter, differs greatly in format. The Basic Building Code and, consequently, the plastics story in Article 20 enjoy wide usage. As for the West, the Model Chapter was developed almost coincidentally with the San Francisco Building Code as it now exists, and many of the references to plastics have carried over into the Uniform Building Code of the International Conference of Building Officials.

Most recently, more literal adoptions of the principle of the Model Chapter have been developed in Philadelphia, Washington, and Denver. Appendix 1-F is a reproduction of the Denver Building Code Chapter on Plastics.

Interior Finishes. Section 103.0 reads as follows:

"*Interior Finish and Trim.* Approved plastics may be used in all types of buildings for interior finish and trim provided that installations for other than light-transmitting purposes shall comply with Section — (Interior Wall and Ceiling Finish)."

The intent of the framers of the Model Chapter is that the highly important control of interior finishes and the life hazard involved under fire conditions is strictly a matter for decision on the part of the local building official. The dash in the last line of Section 103.0 should be filled with the numerical designation of the Section in the local code pertinent to Interior Finishes, calling for the Tunnel Test E-84 or its counterpart.

The Steiner Tunnel Test. The Eiffel Tower, built in 1889, demonstrated that steel could be erected to great heights. After the turn of the century, the first skyscrapers were built with steel frames protected by concrete, brickwork, clay tile, metal lath and plaster, etc. These were called "fireproof" buildings.

The Coconut Grove disaster occurred in a fireproof building. The occupants succumbed to smoke and poisonous gases produced by the combustion of the furniture, decorative hangings, and the wall finish. They were confined in this lethal atmosphere by blocked exits. To evaluate the hazards of wall and ceiling finishes, the Steiner Tunnel Test, ASTM E-84, was developed at the Underwriters' Laboratories, Inc., in Chicago. Most building codes use it. The Model Chapter of the Code Advisory Committee recognizes the prevalence of well-established Code Sections on Interior Finish and Trim almost exclusively on Tunnel Test Ratings. Other laboratories have also installed Tunnel Test equipment, e.g., Southwest Research Institute at San Antonio, Texas.

The SPI Code Advisory Committee recognizes the usefulness of the Steiner Tunnel Test for rating Interior Wall and Ceiling Finishes and Trim, but considers it inappropriate as a criterion for the acceptance of light-transmitting wall and roof panels of plastic or of plastic glazing in any form. The Tunnel Test was specifically designed to test interior surfacing. On the other hand, plastic light-transmitting panels are in normal use exposed to both the inside and outside air.

Many cities make use of the Building Code of the National Board of Fire Underwriters. In this Code, a rating of 200 by the Tunnel Method is required for plastics in wall openings. The New York State Construction Code requires a rating of 225 by the Tunnel Test for all plastics in buildings. In both cases the Tunnel Test is being misused, in the opinion of the SPI Code Advisory Committee.

GLAZING—SHATTER-RESISTANT MATERIALS

Vandalism is the chief source of breakage of glass windows. Other causes, in time of peace, include accidents and natural causes such as hail storms. Statistics on breakage of school windows are appalling. *The New York Times* of April 17, 1963, quoted Mr. Raymond Hudson, Chief of Custodians of the New York City Board of Education, on the amounts spent by the City to replace broken glass in its public school windows.

1960	$531,000
1961	818,680
1962	906,530

Additional amounts were spent for screening, etc., to protect windows from vandalism. Plastics can reduce this breakage. In 1961, New York City's Board of Standards and Appeals unanimously approved plastics for school glazing. In recommending approval, staff engineers pointed out that plastic panes installed in a test program at a Brooklyn school in 1958 had no breakage during the three-year period, although the glass breakage at the same school continued to be high.

Window breakage also results from baseball played adjacent to the school, as well as indoor accidents from janitors' broom handles and slammed doors. For example, a school in California experienced accidental glass breakage at the rate that repeatedly ran as high as five panes a day. In 1961, the school started using plastics as replacement glazing. Since then, not a single pane has been reported replaced. This has resulted in savings for the school district of approximately $15,000 a year.

Plastic glazing is also useful in industrial buildings. Lukens Steel Company, Coatesville, Pennsylvania, began replacing broken glass windows with plastic in 1960. The breakage rate has been reduced by 90 per cent—from 2500 panes a year to a current figure of 250 panes, with an annual saving in material and labor costs of $12,000 for reglazing.

Safety is another vital feature of plastic glazing. While plastics are exceptionally strong, they are not unbreakable. An extremely hard blow, such as would result from a thrown brick, can cause breakage. However, when fractured, the plastic glazing materials break into large, dull-edged pieces, rather than the sharp fragments which may fly from a smashed glass window. Moreover, the light weight of plastic imparts little momentum to the broken pieces, so that the injury hazard is further reduced.

In addition to being tougher than glass, an equal thickness of plastic weighs only half as much, and hence can be transported conveniently and safely in large sheets to the glazing area. It is easily cut with a circular saw in the shop or portable saw "on the job." Usually the plastic glazing is installed by caulking in the same manner as glass, but since the plastic is not readily broken by installation mishaps, reglazing is quicker and easier. Appendix 1E presents various approvals for the use of plastics for glass window panes.

PLASTIC PIPE AND FITTINGS

As a prerequisite to establishing uniform performance standards on plastic water piping, a system of pressure-rated standards has been developed by the Plastic Pipe Institute, and standards have been prepared covering these requirements. The significance of these standards is that all plastic pipe will be offered on a pressure-rated system regardless of the physical properties of the material. The pipe wall thickness is varied with materials to provide a nominal working pressure. The U.S. Department of Commerce standards covering pressure-rated piping are CS254, CS255 and CS256.

Commercial standards are being developed for drain, waste, and vent pipe from both ABS and PVC. The second draft of the standard will shortly be circulated by the Department of Commerce for approval. These standards are presently identified as TS5607 for ABS pipe, and TS5608 for PVC. Approval has been received from the Western Plumbing Officials Association for the use of ABS pipe for DWV (drain, waste, and vent) in mobile homes. The FHA has issued a "Use of Materials Bulletin," No. 33, covering ABS-DWV. The Southern Building Code Congress is considering adoption of ABS and PVC-DWV. Many local and group code bodies have already approved these materials for limited application in drainage systems. Plastic pipe, notably styrene rubber pipe, is being used for sewer and drain lines. Standards covering the product are CS222 and FHA's "Use of Materials Bulletin," No. 26.

CELLULAR PLASTICS AS INSULATION MATERIALS

Insulation is seldom delineated as a separate category in building codes except as it may be associated with wall, floor, or roof construction. Generally, the standards for wall, floor, or roof insulation require only that the insulation be noncombustible. The statement "Combustible insulation is permitted" or "Noncombustible insulation must be used" usually appears in association with the particular part of the building involved. No further effort is made in the code to define performance in terms of tests for other physical properties. Generally speaking, the type of construction (fire-resistive, non-fire-resistive, or other) will determine whether a combustible or non-combustible insulation is required. It is possible that the code may define the flame spread limitation by the Steiner Tunnel Test, ASTM E-84.

Approval by the regulatory groups of an assembly containing a cellular plastic core depends on the end-use of the assembly. It may go into a non-load-bearing wall, a load-bearing roof, or a wall or floor component. The performance requirements for each of these uses are clearly defined in the code, by building type. If the component conforms with the performance standards prescribed for the assembly in its final form, it will be accepted.

It is important that a well-thought-out and thorough engineering analysis be presented at the time the request for approval is presented. Proper product evaluation before presentation to building code agencies cannot be overemphasized. It is the best protection to the architect and builder.

Acknowledgments. W. Aikman, Owens-Corning Fiberglas Corp., Toledo, Ohio; F. X. Ambrose, La Jolla, California; J. Broslaw, Public Relations Consultant, West Hempstead, New York; C. I. Condit, Society of the Plastics Industry, New York City; Wm. Demarest, Architect, Guilford, Connecticut; E. A. Edberg, Koppers Co., Pittsburgh, Pennsylvania; Robert Gutzeit, Society of The Plastics Industry, N.Y.C., R. T. Holtz, B. F. Goodrich Chemical Co., Cleveland, Ohio; F. J. Rarig, Rohm & Haas Co., Corporation Secretary, Philadelphia, Pennsylvania.

REFERENCES

1. "A Model Chapter on Plastics for Inclusion in a Building Code"
   Society of the Plastics Industry
   250 Park Avenue
   New York, N. Y. 10017
2. "Basic Building Code" (Article 20 on Plastics)
   Building Officials Conference of America
   1313 East 60th Street
   Chicago, Illinois
3. Model Plumbing Code (163–10)
   "Suggestions for Inclusions of Plastic Pipe and Fittings in Governmental, State, Municipal and Other Regulatory Body Plumbing Codes"
   Society of the Plastics Industry
   250 Park Avenue
   New York, N. Y. 10017
4. "National Building Code" recommended by The National Board of Fire Underwriters
   85 John Street
   New York, N. Y. 10038
5. "N. F. P. A. Handbook"
   National Fire Protection Association
   60 Battery arch Street
   Boston, Massachusetts
6. "Ohio Building Code" (including Occupancy Pamphlets)

Ohio Board of Building Standards
Department of Buildings
Columbus, Ohio
7. "Chapter on Plastics"
Philadelphia Building Code
Department of Licenses and Inspections
City Hall Annex
Philadelphia, Pennsylvania
8. "Southern Standard Building Code" (Chapter XXVI—Plastics)
Southern Building Code Congress
Brown-Marx Building
Birmingham, Alabama
9. "Building Materials List"
Underwriters' Laboratories, Inc.
207 East Ohio Street
Chicago, Illinois 60611
10. "Uniform Building Code" (Chapter 52—Plastics)
International Conference of Building Officials
50 South Los Robles
Pasadena, California
11. Demarest, W., "Building Codes: Product Approvals," 1964
Ludlow-Bookman
P. O. Box 7037
New Haven, Connecticut

APPENDIX A

The following are the larger cities of the West that are not directly affected by the U.B.C.
Denver, Colorado
Los Angeles, California
San Francisco, California
Portland, Oregon
Seattle, Washington
Spokane, Washington
In seeking code information pertinent to the above cities, or to any other city for that matter, it is normally sufficient to address "Building Inspector, City Hall, (name of city)."

APPENDIX B

The following list of important cities of the southeastern portion of the country is given as a guide to their respective code characteristics.

Atlanta, Georgia	Independent
Birmingham, Alabama	S.S.B.C. (partially)
Charlotte	Independent
Corpus Christi	S.S.B.C.
Chattanooga	S.S.B.C.
Dallas	U.B.C.
El Paso	S.S.B.C.
Ft. Worth	N.B.F.U.
Jackson	U.B.C.
Jacksonville	N.B.F.U.
Memphis	Independent
Miami Beach	Independent
Nashville	S.S.B.C. (partial)

New Orleans	Substantially U.B.C. as amended by the city of New Orleans
Norfolk	Own code based on S.S.B.C
Richmond	Uses B.O.C.A. as reference
Shreveport	S.S.B.C.

APPENDIX C

In the Northeast and Middle West, the Basic Building Code of the Building Officials Conference of America enjoys many adoptions. Many cities, however, have their own codes which antedate the Basic Code. They remain ostensibly independent but are influenced by the U.B.C., N.B.F.U., etc., and especially the B.O.C.A.

State or City	Type of Code
Connecticut	The Connecticut State Building code is supplemental to B.B.C.
Bridgeport	Independent
Hartford	Substantially Natl. Board of Fire Underwriters
New Haven	Independent
Wilmington	B.B.C.
District of Columbia	Format and many provisions of the B.B.C. This is a new code and subject to continued loose-leaf revisions.
Indiana	U.B.C.
Illinois	
Chicago	Independent
Chicago Heights	B.B.C.
Evanston	B.B.C.
Rockford City and Township	Abridged B.C.
Peoria	N.B.F.U., B.B.C., and A.B.C.
Several additional communities	B.B.C. and A.B.C.
Iowa	
Cedar Rapids	B.B.C.
Kansas	
Hutchinson	B.B.C.
Wichita	Independent
Maryland	
Baltimore	Independent
Montgomery City	B.B.C.
Prince George's County	B.B.C.
Massachusetts	The State Board of Building Standards has approved the B.O.C.A. codes as acceptable rules governing the construction of buildings. An indeterminate number of local governments has exercised this privilege.
Boston	Independent; also recommend checking above ruling on Massachusetts

Brookline	do
Cambridge	do
Somerville	do
Springfield	do
Worcester	do
Waltham	B.B.C.

Michigan

Detroit — The City of Detroit has adopted B.B.C. with modifications.

Numerous cities, towns including all of *Wayne County* have either the B.B.C. or the A.B.C., perhaps 300 or more communities.

Flint	Independent
Grand Rapids	Independent

Minnesota

Minneapolis	Independent
St. Paul	Independent

Missouri

St. Louis — The newly produced code of the City of St. Louis has adopted B.B.C.

Joplin	B.B.C.
Springfield	B.B.C.

New Jersey — Approximately 75 cities and towns have adopted the A.B.C.

New York — New York State Building Construction Code, Housing Div., 270 Broadway, New York, N. Y. This code has been adopted in 35 cities, 102 towns and 170 villages. The cities include Binghamton, Elmira, Ithaca, Jamestown, Johnstown, Long Beach, Plattsburgh, Rome, Syracuse, etc. In addition to the Code itself, there is a Code Manual.

New York City — Independent but following B.O.C.A. philosophy

Ohio — The Ohio State Building Code adequated suitably to Tile Council recommendation.

Dayton	Adaptation of B.B.C.
Middletown	Independent

Pennsylvania

Allentown	A.B.C.
Altoona	A.B.C.
Bethlehem	A.B.C.
Philadelphia	The present independent type Philadelphia code is being revised.
Reading	B.B.C.

About 20 additional cities in Pennsylvania — B.B.C. and A.B.C.

Rhode Island

Providence — B.B.C. with modifications

Virginia

Arlington	B.B.C.
Charlottesville	B.B.C.

Richmond — B.B.C. used in conjunction with existing code

Wisconsin — Independent

Milwaukee — Individual code based on B.B.C. altered to suit local conditions

APPENDIX D

A Model Chapter on Plastics For Inclusion in a Building Code*

Purpose: This recommendation represents an effort by the Plastics Industry to discharge its responsibility to assist Building Officials by furnishing information and appropriate regulations to permit the use of plastics material in building construction.

Section 101.0 General

101.1 Scope. This chapter pertains to plastic materials for use in building construction and provisions for their intended applications.

101.2 Procedure. Where requested to insure compliance of the plastic material with the code, the manufacturer shall file with the building official such technical data as may be considered relevant. The data shall include the chemical classification and pertinent physical, mechanical, electrical and thermal properties such as coefficient of expansion, weather resistance and burning characteristics.

101.3 Identification. Each plastic material shall be identified by the manufacturer with a trademark, generic name and ASTM abbreviation, where available. Each piece or container of plastic material shall be adequately labeled with a mark, decal or sticker carrying the accepted identification.

101.4 Definition. *Plastic*—A material that contains as an essential ingredient an organic substance of large molecular weight, is solid in its finished state, and at some stage in its manufacture or in its processing into finished articles, can be shaped by flow.

Laminate—A product made by bonding together two or more layers of material or materials.

Reinforced Plastic—A plastic with some strength properties greatly superior to those of the base resin, resulting from the presence of high-strength fibers embedded in the composition.

Section 102.0 Installation

102.1 General. In addition to the provisions set forth in this article, all installations of approved plastics, for other than light-transmitting purposes, as wall or ceiling finish or as interior trim, shall comply with Section ————— (Interior Wall and Ceiling Finish).

102.2 Fastenings. Fastenings shall be adequate to withstand design loads as prescribed elsewhere in this

*Drafted by the Code Advisory Committee of The Society of the Plastics Industry, Inc., in cooperation with the Plastics in Building and Code Committee of The Manufacturing Chemists' Association, Inc.

Code. Proper allowance shall be made for expansion and contraction of plastic materials in accordance with accepted data on coefficient of expansion of the material and any material in conjunction with which it is employed.

102.3 Structural Requirements. All approved plastic materials and their assemblies shall be of adequate strength and durability to withstand the design loads as prescribed elsewhere in this Code. If required, substantiating data shall be submitted on allowable working stresses.

Section 103.0 Interior Finish and Trim

103.1. Approved plastics may be used in all types of buildings for interior finish and trim, provided that installation shall comply with ————.

103.2. Light-transmitting plastics need not comply with ————, provided that they conform to other requirements of this chapter.

Section 104.0 Wall Panels

104.1 General. A wall panel shall mean an area of one or more plastic sheets each of single thickness used as a light-transmitting medium in exterior walls.

104.2 Class A and B Plastics. Wall panels of Class A or Class B plastic sheets may be used in Types II, III and IV construction except in occupancy classifications 1, 3 and 4 provided:*

104.21. The wall in which such panels are installed is so located that openings are not required to be fire protected;

104.22. The total area of wall panels does not exceed 30 per cent of the wall area in any one story of the structure;

104.23. No section of wall panel shall exceed one hundred feet (100') in length horizontally and no section shall exceed twelve feet (12') in height;

104.24. In Types II and III construction, a wall panel up to forty feet (40') in length shall be separated longitudinally by a section of approved noncombustible siding equal in width to 20 per cent of the length of the section or four feet (4'), whichever is greater. Panels over forty feet (40') in length shall be separated by a section of approved noncombustible siding at least eight feet (8') in width;

104.25. In Types II and III construction, parallel panels shall be separated vertically by a section of approved noncombustible siding at least eight feet (8') in height;

104.26. Access panels shall be provided as required by the Code for structure and occupancy.

104.3 Class C and D Plastics. Wall panels of Class C or Class D plastic sheets may be used in locations and subject to the conditions specified in Section 104.2 provided the area of such panels does not exceed 20 per cent of the wall area in any one story of the structure and no section of such panels is over fifty feet (50') in length or eight feet (8') in height.

*See occupancy classification and types of construction on last page of these recommended practices.

Section 105.0 Glazing of Unprotected Openings

Doors, sash and framed openings may be glazed or equipped with transparent or translucent approved plastic materials, where such openings are not required to be fire protected, provided that the area so glazed shall not exceed 30 per cent of the wall area nor be located at a height greater than twenty feet (20') above grade level, unless greater areas and heights are approved by the Building Official.

Section 106.0 Proof Panels

106.1 General. Roof panels shall mean an area of one or more plastic sheets each of single thickness used as a light-transmitting medium in roofs. Transparent or translucent lighting panels of approved plastics may be used in roofs not required to have a fire-resistive rating and in all roofs where sprinkler protection is provided, except for Occupancy Classifications 1, 3 and 4, provided:

106.11. That on structures or over occupancies required to have fire-retardant or noncombustible roofing, the panels conform to the slope of the roof which shall be at least four inches in twelve inches (4" in 12") or steeper, and each area of plastic panels shall be separated from every other area of plastic panels by at least eight feet (8') laterally and ten feet (10') along the slope of the roof;

106.12. All plastic roof panels shall be attached directly to the building framework or shall be mounted individually in steel or other approved metal frames;

106.13. Corrugated panels shall be pitched in the direction of the corrugations.

106.2 Area Limitations. Plastic sections installed on roofs required to have a fire-retardant or noncombustible roofing shall conform to the following area limitations:

106.21 Class A Plastics. No section shall exceed three hundred square feet (300 sq ft) in area, and the aggregate area of such sections shall not exceed $33\frac{1}{3}$ per cent of the floor area of the room or occupancy sheltered by the roof.

106.22 Class B Plastics. No section shall exceed three hundred square feet (300 sq ft) in area, and the aggregate area of such sections shall not exceed 25 per cent of the floor area of the room or occupancy sheltered by the roof.

106.23 Class C and D Plastics. No section shall exceed one hundred square feet (100 sq ft) in area and the aggregate area of such sections shall not exceed 15 per cent of the floor area of the room or occupancy sheltered by the roof.

Section 107.0 Skylights

107.1 General. Approved plastics may be used in skylights, provided that the skylight is not installed over a shaft or stair well or over occupancy classifications 1 and 4, and provided that the plastic shall be mounted at least four inches (4") above the roof on a noncombustible or metal clad curb rising at least twelve inches (12") for industrial and commercial structures, and six inches (6″) for residential structures from the top surface of the roof covering, and provided that the units are installed on the roof with a minimum distance of five feet (5′) between units and not less than five feet (5′) from any exterior wall, and in no case shall such units be installed within the fire exposure separation required for fire protected openings in walls.

107.2 Class A Plastics. Class A plastics may be used for skylights provided:

107.21. That the maximum area enclosed within the curb of units equipped with flat or corrugated plastic sheets does not exceed three hundred square feet (300 sq ft) and the aggregate area of all such units does not exceed 33⅓ per cent of the floor area of the room sheltered by the roof in which the units are installed;

107.22. That for flat or corrugated units, the panel shall slope from the horizontal at least three inches in twelve inches (3″ in 12″) and the panel does not exceed ten feet (10′) from the bottom to the top of the inclined plane. Corrugations shall run with the inclined plane;

107.23. That the plastic, if dome-shaped, rises above the mounting flange a minimum distance equal to 10 per cent of its maximum span or five inches (5″), whichever is the greater.

107.3 Class B Plastics. Class B plastic sheets or domes may be employed in skylights under the same conditions as allowed in Sub-Section 107.2 except that the aggregate area shall not exceed 25 per cent of the floor area sheltered by the roof upon which it is erected.

107.4 Class C and D Plastics. Class C and D plastics may be used in skylights provided:

107.41. That the maximum area enclosed within the curb of units equipped with flat or corrugated plastic sheets does not exceed one hundred square feet (100 sq ft) and the aggregate area of all such units does not exceed 15 per cent of the floor area of the room sheltered by the roof in which the units are installed;

107.42. That for flat or corrugated units, the panel shall slope from the horizontal at least four inches in twelve inches (4″ in 12″) and shall not exceed eight feet (8′) from the bottom to the top of the inclined plane;

107.43. That the plastic, if dome-shaped, rises above the mounting flange a minimum distance equal to 10 per cent of its maximum span or five inches (5″), whichever is the greater.

Section 108.0 Light-transmitting Panels in Monitors and Sawtooth Roofs

108.1 General. Where a fire-resistive rating is not required for roofs, approved plastics may be used with or without sash. The lower edge of the plastic material shall be at least six inches (6″) above the horizontal surface of the roof. The areas of such plastic panels shall be separated from each other by a section of noncombustible material or by a section of the roofing material of the structure, said section to be equal in length to one-tenth (1/10) of the length of the plastic section, or five feet (5′), whichever is greater.

108.2 Class A and B Plastics. Class A and B plastics may be used provided that the maximum length of a section of plastic panels shall not exceed one hundred feet (100′), and the distance between the upper and lower edges shall not exceed ten feet (10′).

108.3 Class C and D Plastics. Class C and D plastics may be used provided that the maximum length of a section of plastic panels shall not exceed fifty feet (50′) and the distance between the upper and lower edges shall not exceed eight feet (8′).

Section 109.0 Light-diffusing Systems in Ceilings

109.1 General. Plastic light-diffusing systems in ceilings shall mean installations of plastic panels suspended below lighting fixtures for the purpose of diffusing light throughout a room or space and supported directly or indirectly from floor or roof construction.

All electrical work, lighting equipment, fixtures, wiring and installation of same, when they are installed in conjunction with these systems, shall comply with the requirements of the Electrical Code.

109.2 Installation Requirements. Plastic light-diffusing systems in ceilings shall not be installed in required fire exits or corridors or in occupancies 1, 3, and 4, unless the assembly employs Class A plastics and is approved for such installations by the Building Official. In other rooms or spaces, panels of approved plastics may be installed as light-diffusing systems in accordance with the following provisions:

109.21. Plastic diffusers installed in light-diffusing systems in which the aggregate plastic area exceeds 30 per cent of the ceiling area shall be deemed to be an interior finish and as such shall conform to the requirements of Section ———— (Interior Wall and Ceiling Finish), except that a plastic light-diffusing system, the plastic of which has a heat distortion temperature of 225°F or less (ASTM D648—45T) and the panels of which have been shown in appropriate tests by a recognized testing laboratory to fall from their mountings at an ambient temperature at least 200°F below the ignition temperature of the material, shall be exempt from this provision, provided the maximum length of plastic panels weighing more than two ounces per square foot shall not exceed ten feet (10′), the maximum length of plastic panels weighing two ounces or less per square foot shall not exceed twenty-five feet (25′), and provided that the weight of the plastic material shall not exceed eight ounces per square foot in any case.

109.22. Plastic diffusers of approved plastics may be installed in light-diffusing systems provided the aggregate plastic area does not exceed 30 per cent of the ceiling area.

109.23. Plastic diffusers installed in surface mounted or recessed fixtures shall not be subject to the requirements of this section unless the aggregate area of the diffusers exceeds 30 per cent of the area of the ceiling.

109.24. No plastic light-diffusing system shall be installed in areas required to be equipped with automatic sprinklers unless appropriate tests by a recognized laboratory have shown that such system does not prevent effective operation of the sprinklers or unless sprinklers are located both above and below the light-diffusing system to give effective sprinkler protection.

109.25. In Types, I, II and III buildings all hanging supports and fastenings shall be of noncombustible material. Hangers shall be at least No. 12 U.S. Standard Gauge galvanized wire, or equivalent.

109.26. The maximum anticipated service temperature in the space between the panel and the ceiling shall not exceed the manufacturer's recommended maximum service temperature for the plastics employed in the panel.

Section 110.0 Partitions

110.1 Construction. Where partitions are not required to be of noncombustible construction, Class A plastics may be used for the construction of the entire partition.

110.2 Light Transmitting Panels of Plastic in Partitions. Approved plastics may be used to provide the light-transmitting medium in partitions where plain glass is permitted, provided the area of plastic so installed does not exceed in the aggregate one-third ($\frac{1}{3}$) of the area of the partition in which installed.

Approved plastics may also be installed in openings in movable partitions made of metal or other noncombustible material, provided the area of plastic so installed does not exceed in the aggregate one-half of the partition in which installed.

Section 111.0 Exterior Veneer

Class A plastics may be attached to a backing of masonry, concrete or cement plaster in accordance with applicable requirements provided: that no plastic veneer shall be attached to any exterior wall to a height greater than thirty-five feet (35′) above grade, but shall be permitted only on the first story of buildings located in the fire limits.

Section 112.0 Awnings and Canopies

Class A and B plastics may be used in awnings and canopies, and all such awnings and canopies shall be constructed in accordance with provisions governing projections and appendages as provided elsewhere in this Code.

Section 113.0 Greenhouses

Approved plastics may be used in lieu of plain glass in greenhouses. Class A and B plastics may be substituted for wire glass.

Section 114.0 Signs, Fences and Similar Structures

The use of plastics in signs, fences and similar structures shall be governed by the specific sections of this Code applicable to these structures.

The following designations are for ready reference in this chapter recommendation only.

Occupancy Classification

Numerical Designation	Description
1	Theaters, Public Assembly
2	Schools
3	Institutions; e.g., jails, hospitals, orphanages, mental and rest homes, etc. Hazardous units; e.g., manufacturing, storage or handling highly flammable or explosive materials and liquids.

Types of Construction

Type Designation	Description
I	Fire-resistive Fireproof
II	Heavy timber and ordinary masonry
III	Light noncombustible frame
IV	Wood frame

APPENDIX E

Building Code of the City of Denver

Chapter 60

Plastics

Section 6001. General

(a) Approval. Plastic materials may be of any class as defined in this Chapter. Prior to approval of plastic material for use, the manufacturer of such plastic material shall file with the Department such technical data as may be considered relevant to the proposed use of the plastic material. This data shall include the physical properties of the material, its chemical composition and properties, weather resistance, electrical properties, fire resistance, burning and flame spread characteristics, products of combustion and coefficient of expansion.

(2) Upon review of the data furnished, the Department shall determine the adequacy of the material offered and if it is found that the material is satisfactory for the use intended, may approve the material subject to the limitations specified in this Chapter.

(b) Identification. (1) Each plastic material shall be identified by the manufacturer with a number, trade name designation or other means of identification satisfactory to the Department, including the fire classification.

(2) Plastic materials indicated on drawings or specifications shall be identified on such drawings or specifications by accepted designation.

(3) Each sheet, roll or container of plastic employed in buildings or structures shall be identified with a mark, or other device which will identify the material as that indicated in the drawings or specifications.

Section 6002. Definitions

(a) *Plastic Materials.* (1) Plastic materials are those made wholly or principally from standardized plastics listed and described in the Standards.

(2) An approved plastic material is one which the Department has found to be suitable functionally for the purpose for which it is intended, and which burns no faster than two and one-half (2½) inches per minute in sheets sixty-thousandths (.060) of an inch in thickness when tested in accordance with the American Society of Testing Materials standard specifications titled "Tentative Method for Flammability of Rigid Plastics over Fifty-thousandths of an Inch in Thickness," or which is not consumed in less than two minutes when tested in accordance with standard specifications titled "Tentative Method of Test for Flammability of Plastics Fifty-thousandths of an Inch and Under in Thickness" with the thickness of the plastic material determined by Method "B" of the standard specifications titled "Tentative Methods of Test for Thickness of Solid Electrical Insulation."

Section 6003. Classification

(a) *Class A Plastics.* Class A plastic materials shall be those reinforced or unreinforced approved plastic materials which are self-extinguishing when tested in accordance with the test procedures described in this Chapter.

(b) *Class B Plastics.* Class B plastic materials shall be those approved plastic materials which are reinforced with glass fiber or other incombustible material amounting to at least 1.5 ounces per square foot and at least 20 per cent by weight of the plastic panel or sheet.

(c) *Class C Plastics.* Class C plastic materials shall be those approved plastic materials which are reinforced with glass fiber or other incombustible material amounting to at least 10 percent by weight of the plastic panel or sheet.

(d) *Class D Plastics.* Class D plastic materials shall be those approved plastic materials other than Class A, B, or C, which meet the requirements of Section 6002.

Section 6004. Installation

(a) *General.* In addition to the provisions set forth in this Section, all installations approved plastics for wall, ceiling or interior finish, with the exception of those used for light transmitting purposes, shall comply with Chapter 42.

(b) *Fastenings.* Fastenings shall be adequate to withstand design loads as prescribed elsewhere in this Building Code. Proper allowance shall be made for expansion and contraction of plastic materials in accordance with accepted data on coefficient of expansion of the material and any material in conjunction with which it is employed.

(c) *Structural Requirements.* All approved plastic materials and assemblies shall be of adequate strength and durability to withstand the design loads as prescribed elsewhere in this Building Code. If required, substantiating data shall be submitted on allowable working stresses.

Section 6005. Interior Finish

(a) *Permitted Uses.* Approved plastics may be used in all types of buildings for interior finish provided that installations for other than light-transmitting purposes shall comply with Chapter 42.

Section 6006. Plastic Wall Panels and Glazing

(a) *Permitted Uses.* Plastic wall panels shall mean plastic sheets fastened directly to structural members, to structural panels or to sheathing of exterior walls.

(b) *Permitted Uses for Class A and B Plastics.* Class A and B plastic wall panels shall be permitted in walls which are not required to have a fire-resistive rating or in wall openings which are not required to be wire-glazed or have other fire-resistive protection. (See Section 6012 for other uses.)

(1) Panels shall not be installed at a height greater than twenty (20) feet above grade in buildings located within Fire Zone No. 1, unless as otherwise provided.

(2) The inside surface of panels shall not constitute more than ten (10) per cent of the exposed interior surface area of the wall of a public assembly area or required exit.

(3) In types other than Type V construction, the aggregate area of such panels shall not exceed thirty (30) per cent of the area of the wall in which the panels are installed. The panels shall be so distributed that the wall area of any story occupied by panels does not exceed thirty (30) per cent of the wall area of that story. The area of the wall of any room in the structure occupied by panels shall not exceed thirty (30) per cent of the interior surface of that wall.

(4) No single assembly consisting of wall panels or group of wall panels and no run of contiguously mounted panels shall exceed one hundred (100) feet in length or twelve (12) feet in height.

(5) In buildings of other than Type V construction, single assemblies or runs of contiguously mounted plastic wall panels up to forty (40) feet in length shall be separated longitudinally by a section of the required incombustible or fire-resistive wall construction equal in length to twenty (20) per cent of the length of the assembly of run or four (4) feet in length, whichever is greater. Assemblies or runs over forty (40) feet in length shall be separated by a section of the required incombustible or fire-resistive wall construction at least eight (8) feet in length.

(6) In buildings other than Type V construction, assemblies or runs of plastic wall panels shall be separated vertically by a section of required incombustible or fire-resistive wall construction of a height of at least four (4) feet or a height equal to fifty (50) per cent of the height of the highest panel in the next lower assembly or run, whichever is greater.

(7) In Type V construction, Class A and B panels

may be used wherever the installation of ordinary wood panels or plywood sheathing with the surface exposed is permitted.

(8) If sprinkler protection is provided for the plastic installation, the permissible percentage of area occupied by plastic panels and the area of a single assembly or a contiguous run may be doubled and required separations between assemblies or contiguous runs may be reduced by fifty (50) per cent.

(c) *Permitted Uses for Class C and D Plastics.* Class C and D plastic sheets may be used as plastic wall panels subject to the conditions specified for Class A and B plastics provided that

(1) In types other than Type V construction the aggregate area of plastic panels shall not exceed twenty (20) per cent of the area of the wall in which the panels are installed.

(2) The panels shall be so distributed that the wall area of any story occupied by panels does not exceed twenty (20) per cent of the wall area of that story.

(3) The area of the exterior wall of any room in the structure occupied by panels shall not exceed twenty (20) per cent of the interior surface of that wall.

(4) Single assemblies or runs of panels in such construction shall not be in excess of fifty (50) feet in length or eight (8) feet in height.

(d) *The Glazing of Unprotected Openings.* Doors, sash and framed openings not required to be fire protected may be glazed or equipped with transparent or translucent approved plastic materials subject to the height and percentage of wall area limitations and separation requirements specified in this Chapter. (See Chapter 38 for window requirements.)

(e) *Combination of Plastic Panels and Glazing.* Combinations of plastic glazing and wall panels shall be subject to the height and percentage of wall area limitations and separation requirements applicable to the class of plastics employed in the wall panel nstallation.

Section 6007. Roof Panels

(a) *General.* Transparent or translucent lighting panels of approved plastics may be used in roofs not required to have a fire-resistive rating and in all roofs where automatic fire sprinkler protection is provided throughout the entire building or structure except in buildings or structures of Group A through E occupancies, provided:

(1) That the roof is sloped at least four (4) inches in twelve (12) inches or steeper on structures, and that the panels conform to the slope of the roof.

(2) Plastic panel areas, limited as specified in Subsection 6007(b), shall be separated from each other by a distance of at least eight (8) feet measured laterally and by a minimum distance of four (4) feet measured along the slope of the roof, but the separation distance along the slope shall not, in any case, be less than fifty (50) per cent of the length of the longest plastic panel in the next lower assembly or run.

(3) All plastic roof panels shall be attached directly to the building framework or shall be mounted individually in steel or other approved metal frames.

(4) Corrugated panels shall be pitched in the direction of the corrugations.

(5) Panels shall not be installed in walls where openings in such walls are required to be fire protected.

(6) Exposed edges of plastic panels shall not project beyond the face of a building wall.

(b) *Area Limitations.* Plastic sections installed on roofs required to have a fire-retardant roofing shall conform to the following limitations:

(1) Sections of Class A plastics shall not exceed three hundred (300) square feet in area, and the aggregate area of such sections shall not exceed 33W per cent of the floor area of the room or occupancy sheltered by the roof.

(2) Sections of Class B plastics shall not exceed three hundred (300) square feet in area, and the aggregate area of such sections shall not exceed 25 per cent of the floor area of the room or occupancy sheltered by the roof.

(3) Sections of Class C and D plastics shall not exceed one hundred (100) square feet in area, and the aggregate area of such sections shall not exceed 15 per cent of the floor area of the room or occupancy sheltered by the roof.

Section 6008. Skylights

(a) *General.* In lieu of glass, approved plastics may be used in skylights provided that the skylight is not installed over a shaft or stair well or over public assembly areas and provided that the plastic shall be mounted above the roof on an incombustible or metal-clad curb rising at least twelve (12) inches for buildings of office (F-1) or commercial or industrial occupancies, and six (6) inches for buildings of other occupancy types. The curb height shall be measured from the top surface of the roof covering, and the plastic units shall be installed on the roof with a minimum distance of five (5) feet between them and not less than five (5) feet from any exterior wall. In no case shall such panels and units be installed within the fire exposure separation required for fire protected openings in walls.

(b) *Permitted Uses for Class A Plastics.* Class A plastics may be used for skylights subject to the requirements of this Section.

(1) The maximum area within the required curb shall not exceed three hundred (300) square feet for flat or corrugated plastic sheets nor shall the aggregate area of such units exceed 30 per cent of the floor area of any room sheltered by a roof in which the units are installed.

(2) Flat or corrugated units shall slope from the horizontal at least three (3) inches in twelve (12) inches and the high edge shall not exceed ten (10) feet from the bottom of the inclined plane. Corrugations shall be parallel to the inclined plane.

(3) Dome-shaped units shall rise above the mount-

ing flange a minimum distance equal to 10 per cent of its maximum span but in no case shall the rise be less than five (5) inches.

(4) The exposed edges of plastic domes shall be metal protected.

(c) *Permitted Uses for Class B Plastics.* Class B plastic sheets or domes may be employed in skylights under conditions specified in Subsection 6008(b) except that the aggregate area shall not exceed 25 per cent of the floor area sheltered by the roof upon which the skylight is erected.

(d) *Permitted Uses for Class C and D Plastics.* Except as provided in Subsections 1 and 2 of this Section, Class C and D plastics may be used in skylights under the conditions specified in Subsection 6008(b).

(1) The maximum area enclosed within the required curb shall not exceed one hundred (100) square feet for flat or corrugated plastic sheets nor shall the aggregate area of such units exceed 15 per cent of the floor area of any room sheltered by a roof in which the units are installed.

(2) Flat or corrugated units shall slope from the horizontal at least four (4) inches in twelve (12) inches and the high end shall not exceed eight (8) feet from the bottom of the inclined plane.

Section 6009. Light-transmitting Panels

(a) *General.* Where a fire-resistive rating is not required for roofs, approved plastics may be used with or without sash. The lower edge of the plastic material shall be at least six (6) inches above the horizontal surface of the roof. The areas of such plastic panels shall be separated from each other by a section of incombustible material or by a section of the roofing material of the structure, which section shall be equal in length to one-tenth (1/10) of the length of the plastic section, or five (5) feet, whichever is greater.

(b) *Permitted Uses.* Class A and B plastics may be used, provided that the maximum length of a section of plastic panels shall not exceed one hundred (100) feet, and the distance between the upper and lower edges shall not exceed ten (10) feet.

(2) Class C and D plastics may be used, provided that the maximum length of a section of plastic panels shall not exceed fifty (50) feet and the distance between the upper and lower edges shall not exceed eight (8) feet.

Section 6010. Plastic Light-diffusing

(a) *Definitions.* Plastic light-diffusing ceilings shall mean installations of plastic panels suspended below lighting fixtures for the purpose of diffusing light throughout a room or space. They shall not include plastic diffusers which are parts of electric or ventilating fixtures unless the aggregate area of the diffusers exceeds 30 per cent of the area of the room or space.

(b) *Installation Requirements.* (1) Plastic light-diffusing ceilings shall not be installed in assembly areas or in required exits or corridors or in buildings or structures of Group D or E occupancies. In other rooms or spaces, panels of any class of approved plastics may be installed as light-diffusing ceilings in accordance with the following provisions:

(A) Where the aggregate area of plastics in light diffusing ceilings exceeds 30 per cent of the ceiling area of the room or space, such plastics shall conform to the requirements of Chapter 42.

(B) Plastics which have a heat distortion temperature of 225 degrees F or less as established by the American Society for Testing Materials standard titled "Standard Method for Test for Deflection Temperature of Plastics under Load" and the panels of which have been indicated in appropriate tests by an approved testing laboratory to fall from their mountings at an ambient temperature at least 200°F below the ignition temperature of the material, shall be exempt from all finish requirements, provided the maximum length of plastic panels weighing more than two (2) ounces per square foot do not exceed six (6) feet, and the weight of the plastic materials does not exceed eight (8) ounces per square foot in any case.

(2) Plastic light-diffusing ceiling shall not be permitted below sprinklers unless tests by a nationally recognized laboratory indicate they will not interfere with the action of sprinklers, or unless sprinklers in the quantity required by Chapter 38 are also placed below the plastic ceiling.

(3) In building or structures of other than Type V construction, all hanging supports and fastenings shall be of incombustible material. Hangers shall be at least No. 12 U. S. Standard Gauge galvanized wire, or equivalent, and shall be spaced so as to support the weight of the ceiling assembly safely.

(4) The maximum anticipated service temperature in the space between the panel and the ceiling shall not exceed the manufacturer's recommended maximum service temperature for the plastics employed in the panel.

(5) Piping carrying gas or volatile combustible fluid shall not be located in the space above a plastic light-diffusing ceiling.

Section 6011. Partitions

(a) *Construction.* (1) Where partitions are not required to be of incombustible or fire-resistive construction, Class A plastics may be used for the construction of the entire partition.

(2) Approved plastics may be used to provide the light-transmitting medium in partitions where plain glass is permitted, provided the aggregate area of plastic so installed does not exceed one-third of the area of the partition in which it is installed.

(3) Approved plastics may be installed in openings in movable partitions made of metal or other incombustible material, provided the aggregate area of plastic so installed does exceed one-half of the area of the partition in which it is installed.

Section 6012. Exterior Veneer, Spandrel Facings and Decorative Panels

(a) *General* Approved plastics may be applied as veneers or installed as facings or decorative panels on walls, spandrels, or structural members as provided herein.

(1) In Fire Zone No. 1 spandrel wall sections meeting structural requirements of Chapter 16 may be faced with an approved plastic veneer or decorative panel on the exterior surface provided that no single plastic panel exceeds twenty-five (25) square feet in area and provided that the panel is located not less than thirty (30) feet from a party line or faces upon a street or alley or other open space not less than fifty (50) feet in width. Outside Fire Zone No. 1 approved plastics may be applied as veneers or decorative panels on walls, spandrels or structural members provided that on buildings or structures of other than Type V construction the plastic panels shall be separated vertically by a section of incombustible material at least four (4) feet in height and at least two (2) feet horizontally.

(2) Such veneers or decorative panels shall be attached to the building or structure with incombustible supports and in such a manner to withstand imposed wind loads. The distance between engaged edge of the panels and the exterior wall shall not exceed four (4) inches.

Section 6013. Awnings and Canopies

Class A and B plastics may be used in awnings and canopies and all such awnings and canopies shall be constructed in accordance with provisions governing projections and appendages.

Section 6014. Greenhouses

Approved plastics may be used in lieu of plain glass in greenhouses, in Fire Zone No. 3 only.

Section 6015. Signs and Similar Structures

The use of plastics in signs and similar structures shall comply with the requirements of Chapter 56.

Section 6020. Standards

Unless as specified in other Sections of this Building Code, the following standards shall apply:

Organization	Title of Publication
MCA	Technical Data on Plastics–1961
ASTM	Flammability of Rigid Plastics over 0.050 Inches in Thickness D635-56T
ASTM	Flammability of Plastics 0.050 Inches and Under in Thickness D568-56T
ASTM	Thickness of Solid Electrical Insulation D374-57T
ASTM	Deflection Temperature of Plastics Under Load D648-56

Legend

MCA—Manufacturing Chemists Association, Inc. 1825 Connecticut Avenue, N.W. Washington 9, D.C.

ASTM—American Society for Testing Materials 1916 Race Street, Philadelphia 3, Pa.

(Ordinance 284, Series of 1962)

APPENDIX F

Proposed Revision of Article 20 of the Basic Building Code of the Building Officials Conference of America

Submitted by The Society of the Plastics Industry, Inc., in 1965.

Delete present article and substitute the following:

Article 20
Plastics Construction

Section 2000.0 Scope

The provisions of this article shall govern the quality and methods of application of plastics for use in buildings and structures, when offered for one or more of such typical uses as:

Interior finish and trim
Light-diffusers in ceilings
Panels in interior walls and partitions
Glazing of unprotected openings
Roof panels
Skylights
Panels in monitors and sawtooth roofs
Exterior veneer
Awnings and canopies
Greenhouses
Signs, fences, and similar structures

Section 2001.0 Definitions

Glazing—Light-transmitting material set in a frame or sash. (As distinguished from roof or wall panels, defined in this section.)

Laminate—A product made by bonding together two or more layers of material or materials.

Light-diffusing Systems in Ceilings—Installations of plastic panels suspended below lighting fixtures for the purpose of diffusing light throughout a room or space and supported directly or indirectly from floor or roof construction.

Plastic—A material that contains as an essential ingredient an organic substance of large molecular weight, solid in its finished state, and at some stage in its manufacture or in its processing into finished articles, can be shaped by flow.

Reinforced Plastic—A plastic material with some strength properties superior to those of the base resin, resulting from the presence of high-strength fibers or other reinforcing materials embedded in the composition.

Roof Panels—Plastic sheets installed in the plane of the roof and attached directly to the structural members or to the roof sheathing without frame or sash, whether opaque or as a light-transmitting medium.

Self-extinguishing Plastic (check-test)—A plastic material which will not continue to burn when tested in accordance with the ASTM standard for flammability listed in appendix C.

Slow-burning Plastic (check-test)—A plastic material which burns no faster than two and one-half (2½) inches per minute when tested in accordance with the ASTM standard for flammability listed in appendix C.

Thermoplastic Material—A plastic material which is capable of being repeatedly softened by increase of temperature and hardened by decrease of temperature.

Thermosetting Material—A plastic material which is capable of being changed into a substantially infusible and insoluble product when cured under the application of heat or by chemical means.

Wall Panels—Plastic sheets fastened directly to structural members or sheathing, without frame or sash, whether opaque or as a light-transmitting medium in exterior walls.

Section 2002.0 Design, Installation, and Conditions of Acceptance

2002.1 General. In addition to the provisions set forth in this article, all installations of approved plastics, for other than light-transmitting purposes, as wall or ceiling finish or as interior trim, shall comply with applicable sections of Article 9.

2002.2 Fastenings. Fastenings shall be adequate to withstand design loads as prescribed elsewhere in the Basic Code. Proper allowance shall be made for expansion and contraction of plastic materials in accordance with accepted data on coefficient of expansion of the plastic and any material in conjunction with which it is employed.

2002.3 Structural Requirements. All approved plastic materials and their assemblies shall be of adequate strength and durability to withstand the design loads as prescribed elsewhere in the Basic Code. If required, substantiating data shall be submitted on allowable working stresses.

2002.4 Application for Approval. Where requested to insure compliance of the plastic material with the Basic Code, the manufacturer shall file with the building official such technical data as may be considered relevant. The data shall include the chemical classification and pertinent physical, mechanical, electrical, and thermal properties such as coefficient of expansion, weather resistance, and burning characteristics.

2002.5 Identification. Each plastic material shall be identified by the manufacturer with a trademark, generic name and ASTM abbreviation, where available. Each piece or container of plastic material shall be adequately labeled with a mark, decal, or sticker carrying such accepted identification.

2002.6 Plans and Specifications. Plans and specifications submitted to the building official and calling for use of a plastic material shall identify the material as in 2002.5.

2002.7 Qualification. Upon review, the building official shall determine the adequacy of the plastic material and if found satisfactory for the intended use, the building official may approve the material subject to the limitations specified by Article 20.

Section 2003.0 Approved Plastic Materials

2003.1. Only those plastic materials that have been found functionally suitable by the building official for the purposes for which they are intended and which meet the requirements of this section may be used in structures regulated by the Basic Code.

2003.2. Plastic materials which meet the requirements of the following classifications:

2003.21 Plastic Material Classification. Class A. Reinforced, unreinforced or laminated plastic materials which are self-extinguishing when tested in accordance with test procedures in appendix C and tabulated in section 2003.22.

Class B. Plastic materials which are reinforced with glass fiber or other noncombustible material amounting to not less than 1.5 ounces per square foot and not less than 20 per cent by weight of the plastic panel or sheet.

Class C. Plastic materials which are reinforced with glass fiber or other noncombustible material amounting to not less than 10 per cent by weight of the plastic panel or sheet.

Class D. Plastic materials other than class A, B or C which meet the requirements of section 2003.22.

2003.22 Approved Plastic Material. An approved plastic material is one which the Building Official has found to be suitable functionally for the purpose for which it is offered, which burns no faster than two and one-half inches (2.5″) per minute in sheets sixty-thousandths of an inch (0.060″) in thickness when tested in accordance with Standard Specifications for "Standard Method for Flammability of Plastics over Fifty-thousandths of an Inch (0.050″) in Thickness" (ASTM Designation D635-44), or which is not consumed in less than two (2) minutes when tested in accordance with Standard Specifications for "Standard Method of Test for Flammability of Plastics Fifty-thousandths of an Inch (0.050″) and under in Thickness" (ASTM Designation D568-43), the thickness of the plastic material to be determined by Method "B" (ASTM Designation D374-42).

2003.23. Plastic materials whose products of combustion are not significantly more toxic than those of wood or paper burned under similar conditions.

Section 2004.0 Interior Finish and Trim

2004.1. Approved plastic materials may be used in all types of buildings for interior finish and trim, provided that installation shall comply with applicable sections in Article 9.

2004.2. Light-transmitting plastic materials need not comply with Article 9, provided that they conform with other requirements of Article 20.

Section 2005.0 Exterior Wall Panels

2005.1 General. A wall panel shall mean an area of one or more plastic sheets whether opaque or used as a light-transmitting medium in exterior walls.

2005.2 Class A and B Plastics. Class A and class B plastic sheets may be used in wall panels in types 2, 3 and 4 buildings except in occupancy classifications A, F-1, F-2, F-3 and H provided the following requirements are met:

(1) The wall in which such panels are installed is so located that openings are not required to be fire protected;

(2) The total area of plastic panels in any story does not exceed thirty (30) per cent of the wall area in that story of the structure;

(3) No continuous section of plastic panels shall exceed one hundred (100) feet in length horizontally and no section shall exceed twelve (12) feet in height;

(4) In types 2 and 3 buildings, sections up to forty (40) feet in length shall be separated longitudinally by a section of approved noncombustible siding equal in width to twenty (20) per cent of the length of the section or four (4) feet, whichever is greater. Sections over forty (40) feet in length shall be separated by a section of approved noncombustible siding at least eight (8) feet in width;

(5) In types 2 and 3 buildings, parallel sections shall be separated vertically by a section of approved noncombustible siding at least eight (8) feet in height;

(6) Access panels shall be provided as required by the Basic Code for structure and occupancy.

2005.3 Class C and D Plastics. Class C and D plastics may be used as wall panels in locations and subject to the conditions specified for class A and B plastics provided the area of such panels does not exceed twenty (20) per cent of the wall area in any one story of the structure and no section of such panels is over fifty (50) feet in length or eight (8) feet in height.

Section 2006.0 Glazing of Unprotected Openings

2006.1 General. Doors, sash and framed openings may be glazed or equipped with transparent or translucent approved plastic materials, where such openings are not required to be fire protected, provided that the area so glazed shall not exceed thirty (30) per cent of the wall area nor be located at a height greater than seventy-five (75) feet above grade level, unless greater areas and height are approved by the building official.

Section 2007.0 Roof Panels

2007.1 General. Roof panels shall mean an area of one or more plastic sheets whether opaque or used as a light transmitting medium in roofs. Transparent or translucent lighting panels of approved plastic materials may be used in roofs not required to have a

fire-resistive rating and in all roofs where sprinkler protection is provided, A, F-1, F-2, F-3 and H, provided the following requirements are met:

(1) That on structures or over occupancies required to have fire-retardant or noncombustible roofing, the panels conform to the slope of the roof which shall be at least four (4) inches in twelve (12) inches or steeper, and each area of plastic panels shall be separated from every other area of plastic panels by at least eight (8) feet laterally and ten (10) feet along the slope of the roof;

(2) All plastic roof panels shall be attached directly to the building framework or shall be mounted individually in steel or other approved metal frames;

(3) Corrugated panels shall be pitched in the direction of the corrugations.

2007.2 Area Limitations. Plastic sections installed on roofs required to have a fire-retardant or noncombustible roofing shall conform to the following area limitations:

2007.21 Class A Plastics. No section shall exceed three hundred (300) square feet in area, and the aggregate area of such sections shall not exceed thirty-three and one-third ($33\frac{1}{3}$) per cent of the floor area of the room or occupancy sheltered by the roof.

2007.22 Class B Plastics. No section shall exceed three hundred (300) square feet in area, and the aggregate area of such sections shall not exceed twenty-five (25) per cent of the floor area of the room or occupancy sheltered by the roof.

2007.23 Class C and D Plastics. No section shall exceed one hundred (100) square feet in area, and the aggregate area of such sections shall not exceed fifteen (15) per cent of the floor area of the room or occupancy sheltered by the roof.

Section 2008.0 Skylights

2008.1 General. Approved plastics may be used in skylights, provided that the plastic shall be mounted at least four (4) inches above the roof on a noncombustible or metal clad curb and provided that the units are installed on the roof with a minimum distance of five (5) feet between units and not less than five (5) feet from any exterior wall, and in no case shall such units be installed within the fire exposure separation required for fire protected openings in walls. Approved plastics may be used in skylights of an approved fire-venting type (section 911.42) where venting is required.

2008.2 Class A Plastics. Class A plastics may be used for skylights provided:

(1) That the maximum area enclosed within the curb of units equipped with flat or corrugated plastic sheets does not exceed three hundred (300) square feet and the aggregate area of all such units does not exceed thirty-three and one-third ($33\frac{1}{3}$) per cent of the floor area of the room sheltered by the roof in which the units are installed;

(2) That for flat or corrugated units, the panel shall slope from the horizontal at least three (3) inches in

twelve (12) inches and the panel does not exceed ten (10) feet from the bottom to the top of the inclined plane and corrugations shall run with the inclined plane;

(3) That the plastic, if dome-shaped, rises above the mounting flange a minimum distance equal to ten (10) per cent of its maximum span or five (5) inches, whichever is the greater.

2008.3 Class B Plastics. Class B plastic sheets or domes may be employed in skylights under the same conditions as allowed in Section 2007.2 except that the aggregate area shall not exceed twenty-five (25) per cent of the floor area sheltered by the roof upon which it is erected.

2008.4 Class C and D Plastics. Class C and D plastics may be used in skylights provided:

(1) That the maximum area enclosed within the curb of units equipped with flat or corrugated plastic sheets does not exceed one hundred (100) square feet and the aggregate area of all such units does not exceed fifteen (15) per cent of the floor area of the room sheltered by the roof in which the units are installed;

(2) That for flat or corrugated units, the panel shall slope from the horizontal at least four (4) inches in twelve (12) inches and shall not exceed eight (8) feet from the bottom to the top of the inclined plane;

(3) That the plastic, if dome-shaped, rises above the mounting flange a minimum distance equal to ten (10) per cent of its maximum span or five (5) inches, whichever is the greater.

Section 2009.0 Light Transmitting Panels in Monitors and Sawtooth Roofs

2009.1 General Where a fire-resistive rating is not required for roofs, approved plastics may be used with or without sash. The lower edge of the plastic material shall be mounted at least four (4) inches above the roof on a noncombustible or metal clad curb. The areas of such plastic panels shall be separated from each other by a section of noncombustible material or by a section of the roofing material of the structure, said section to be equal in length to one-tenth (1/10) of the length of the plastic section, or five (5) feet, whichever is greater.

2009.2 Class A and B Plastics. Class A and B plastics may be used provided that the maximum length of a section of plastic panels shall not exceed one hundred (100) feet, and the distance between the upper and lower edges shall not exceed ten (10) feet.

2009.3 Class C and D Plastics. Class C and D plastics may be used provided that the maximum length of a section of plastic panels shall not exceed fifty (50) feet and the distance between the upper and lower edges shall not exceed eight (8) feet.

Section 2010.0 Light Diffusing Systems in Ceilings

2010.1 Installation Requirements. Plastic light diffusing systems in ceilings shall not be installed in required fire exits or corridors or in occupancies A, F-1, F-2, F-3 and H, unless the assembly employs class A plastics and is approved for such installations by the building official. In other rooms or spaces, panels of approved plastics may be installed as light diffusing systems in accordance with the following provisions:

(1) Plastic diffusers installed in light diffusing systems in which the aggregate plastic area exceeds thirty (30) per cent of the ceiling area shall be deemed to be an interior finish and as such shall conform to the requirements of applicable sections of Article 9, except that in a plastic light diffusing system, the plastic of which has a heat deflection temperature of two hundred twenty-five (225) degrees F or less as determined by standards for heat deflection of plastics listed in appendix G and the panels of which have been shown in appropriate tests by a recognized testing laboratory to fall from their mountings at an ambient temperature at least two hundred (200) degrees F below the ignition temperature of the material, shall be exempt from this provision, provided the maximum length of plastic panels weighing more than two (2) ounces per square foot shall not exceed ten (10) feet, the maximum length of plastic panels weighing two (2) ounces or less per square foot shall not exceed twenty-five (25) feet, and provided that the weight of the plastic material shall not exceed twelve (12) ounces per square foot in any case;

(2) Plastic diffusers of approved plastics may be installed in light diffusing systems provided the aggregate plastic area does not exceed thirty (30) per cent of the ceiling area;

(3) Plastic diffusers installed in surface mounted or recessed fixtures shall not be subject to the requirements of this section unless the aggregate area of the diffusers exceeds (30) per cent of the area of the ceiling;

(4) No plastic light diffusing system shall be installed in areas required to be equipped with automatic sprinklers unless appropriate tests by a recognized laboratory have shown that such system does not prevent effective operation of the sprinklers or unless sprinklers are located both above and below the light diffusing system to give effective sprinkler protection;

(5) In Types 1, 2 and 3 buildings all hanging supports and fastenings shall be of noncombustible material and hangers shall be at least No. 12 U.S. standard gauge galvanized wire, or equivalent;

(6) The maximum anticipated service temperature in the space between the panel and the ceiling shall not exceed the manufacturer's recommended maximum service temperature for the plastics employed in the panel;

(7) All electrical work, lighting equipment, fixtures, wiring and installation of same, when they are installed in conjunction with these systems, shall comply with the requirements of the National Electrical Code and Article 15 of the Basic Code.

Section 2011.0 Partitions

2011.1. Approved plastics may be used to provide the light transmitting media in partitions where plain glass is permitted, provided the area of plastic so installed does not exceed in the aggregate one-third (⅓) of the area of the partition in which installed.

2011.2. Approved plastics may be installed in openings in movable partitions made of metal or other noncombustible material, provided the area of plastic so installed does not exceed in the aggregate one-half (½) of the area of the partition in which it is installed.

2011.3. Where partitions are not required to be of noncombustible construction, class A plastics may be used for the construction of the entire partition.

Section 2012.0 Exterior Veneer

2012.1 General. Approved plastics may be attached to a backing of masonry, concrete or cement plaster in accordance with applicable requirements provided: that no plastic veener shall be attached to any exterior

wall to a height greater than thirty-five (35) feet above grade, but shall be permitted only on the first story of buildings located in the fire limits.

Section 2013.0 Accessory Structures and Miscellaneous Equipment

2013.1 Awnings and Canopies. Approved plastics may be used in awnings and canopies, and all such awnings and canopies shall be constructed in accordance with provisions governing projections and appendages as provided elsewhere in the Basic Code.

2013.2 Greenhouses. Approved plastics may be used in lieu of plain glass in greenhouses under the provisions of section 301 and 302.

2013.3 Signs, Fences and Similar Structures. The use of plastics in signs, fences and similar structures shall be governed by the specific sections of the Basic Code applicable to these structures.

4 CONSTRUCTION AIDS

J. A. Baumann

Union Carbide Corporation
Plastics Division
Bound Brook, New Jersey

INTRODUCTION

Plastics have found extensive use as aids in the construction of buildings. Plastic films serve as permanent moisture barriers preventing the deleterious migration of water through various building elements, and as temporary protection for men and materials. Some films, mainly reinforced ones, are fabricated into shapes which are subsequently inflated to become buildings in their own right. Other plastics serve to protect or modify concrete, or to free concrete design from the restriction of forming lumber's plane configuration. Silicones effectively prevent the entry of liquid water through porous brick, stone, and concrete; thermoplastic latices are added to concrete and mortars to improve adhesion and tensile strength; and concrete forms are made of molded or thermoformed plastics which permit design freedom, simple erection, fine surface texture, and compound curves.

I: MOISTURE BARRIERS AND PROTECTIVE COVERS

Water, both liquid and vapor, has plagued mankind and his structures for centuries, creating damp, unhealthful conditions, destroying the effectiveness of insulations, encouraging mildew and rot-inducing organisms, warping wooden elements, peeling off protective coatings, and causing deterioration of wood, metal and masonry. With the relatively recent availability of moisture-impermeable plastics films, the means are at hand—and much has been accomplished —to control the movement of water and reduce its deleterious effects.

MATERIALS

The plastic film used most extensively in construction is polyethylene, in thicknesses from .002 to .006 inch. Where exposed to sunlight, it is used in black. It is also obtainable reinforced with fabrics such as nylon, "Dacron," or burlap, or coated on paper for other special purposes. Plasticized vinyl film or sheet, somewhat thicker usually, is used under concrete slabs primarily for preventing liquid water movement, for vapor barriers in industrial built-up roofing, and where its better sealability and toughness make it the choice of engineers and architects. The newer ethylene-vinyl acetate copolymers now being marketed combine some of the advantages of both these materials. Other films offered, but not extensively used for the purposes of concern here, are polyester, e.g., poly (ethylene terephthalate), cast vinyls, and cellulose acetate butyrate.

Older materials being supplanted or supplemented by plastic films for vapor barriers, underlayments and protective covers include asphalt felts, roll roofing and laminates of paper and asphalt. Some paints have provided effective vapor barriers, especially rubber-base paints and paints with high varnish content.[15]

USES

Some of the common applications for plastic films in construction and allied areas are listed below, in four categories: vapor barriers, underlayments, temporary protective covers, and miscellaneous building uses. Almost all construction jobs use some plastic films; many of the larger jobs use films in all of these categories.

Vapor Barriers

(1) Wall and ceiling vapor barriers, 2 to 4 mil polyethylene.

(2) Film between rough and finished floor for barrier plus squeak, dust, and draft stop.

(3) Ground cover in crawl spaces to prevent rise of water vapor from damp ground, polyethylene 4 to 6 mil.

(4) Roof vapor barriers below insulation on industrial built-up roofing;[2,10] 4-mil vinyl which is flame-resistant and non-dripping.

(5) Cold storage room vapor barriers.

(6) Curing blankets for concrete to retard evaporation, polyethylene. Figure 4-1.

(7) Steam tents for curing precast concrete, fabricated polyethylene film.

Underlayments

(1) Beneath slab-on-ground, vapor and liquid barrier.

(2) Foundation wall waterproofing.

(3) Highway, airport runway and apron subgrade—vinyl or polyethylene.

(4) Liners for irrigation ditches, reservoirs, ponds, and aqueducts.

Temporary Protection

(1) Scaffold shelters, film stapled to movable wood frames.

(2) Temporary glazing or siding.

(3) Dust and dirt screens and temporary partitions during demolition, cleaning, and other dusty and dirty operations.

(4) Covers for materials and equipment, film held down with brick, block, or tie-downs.

(5) Drop cloths, 2 to 4 mil polyethylene.

(6) Silo caps, fumigation blankets in agricultural applications.

(7) Covers for earthen slopes for protection from rain to reduce likelihood of slides.[3]

Miscellaneous Building Uses

(1) Reduction of heated space by false ceilings of film in shops, sheds, barns.

(2) Insulation by double glazing storm sash with film.

(3) Concealed flashing around windows, doors, and masonry joints.

(4) Form liners (protecting wood from water, eliminating oiling of forms and providing smooth paintable finish).

(5) Polyethylene-coated paper tubes for column forms.

(6) Double film on wood frames as cover to insulate fresh poured concrete.

(7) Bond breakers for slip forms.

(8) Slip surface to allow expansion and contraction of concrete and minimize cracking; several layers of polyethylene between slab and base.[8,11]

Fig. 4-1. Polyethylene film curing blanket. (*Courtesy Union Carbide Corp., Plastics Div.*)

(9) Lift slab bond breaker.

(10) Greenhouse glazing.

(11) Moisture barrier pan under shower stalls, 20-mil polyethylene.[20]

ADVANTAGES AND DISADVANTAGES

Water barrier materials in general require light weight, low water vapor transmission, permanence, toughness and puncture resistance, ease of joining sheets in the field, and low cost. Many of the applications previously listed also require translucency.

Weight

Polyethylene film 2 mils thick weighs less than 10 lb/1000 sq ft. Vinyl, though heavier than polyethylene, still weighs only about one-tenth as much as equivalent barrier standard mopped felts for built-up roof construction.

Water Vapor Transmission

Polyethylene film has very low water permeability and in 2-mil thickness can readily meet FHA requirements for this property.

Longevity

Below-ground longevity of polyethylene is superior to any of the competitive materials, being completely unaffected by water, salts, or bacteria. Asphalt paper laminates may last only five to ten years during which their effectiveness is completely destroyed.

The alkaline conditions prevailing under concrete would be completely destructive to aluminum foil or its laminates. Roll roofing (55 pounds), while acceptable, is affected by soil burial conditions. Properties of vinyl change primarily by leaching action of soil and bacteria on the plasticizers. The vinyl is suitable, however, and is sometimes used in underslab application where its better puncture resistance is required. Above ground, exposed to the sun's rays, clear polyethylene has an expected life of only about one season; black pigmented film will last several.

Toughness

Superior toughness of plastics films is largely a result of their high elongation.

Vinyl is superior to polyethylene in puncture resistance except at low temperatures. There vinyl becomes stiff and more easily ruptured. The new copolymers are comparable to the vinyl films in these properties at ordinary temperatures, but they maintain the properties at temperatures approaching $-100°C$.

Joining

There are numerous excellent proprietary adhesives for vinyl films. Polyethylene is not as successfully joined by adhesives, but it can be joined by heat sealing, and 40-foot-wide films are available, thereby reducing the need for sealing.

Costs

Low price is a primary advantage of polyethylene film, selling for slightly more than half the price of vinyl films, about 0.5¢/sq ft for 2-mil thick film.

HISTORY

Polyethylene was introduced to the construction industry by Visking in 1954. Usage of polyethylene film in construction has climbed from 8 million pounds in 1956 to about 38 million pounds in 1963. There are many examples where this film has cut costs and improved the efficiency of building materials and operations. Each year has seen about 4 to 5 million pounds more used.[18]

The condensation problem in buildings was first recognized in 1923 at the Forest Products Laboratory during a survey of dwellings on which early paint failure had occurred.[4] It was in 1941 that the U.S. Department of Agriculture discovered the decay hazards in crawl spaces, and began investigations leading ten years later to the widespread use of roll roofing to hold down the water vapor.[17] Membranous covers are now required by FHA minimum property standards, but the roll roofing is almost completely supplanted by polyethylene for this use. Several government agencies and universities made major contributions to the understanding and control of water vapor in homes, but the problem was not solved until the introduction of the polyethylene films. Polyethylene as a vapor barrier is almost an absolute necessity with electrical heating due to generally higher humidities in electrically heated homes.

Polyethylene film has been used as a slip surface that permits movement of a concrete slab due to shrinkage and to temperature changes, thus allowing the number of expansion joints to be reduced. In the Pittsburgh auditorium,[11] where the concrete slab is covered with ice for hockey games and ice shows, the slip surface consists of three layers of film with powdered talc between each layer. At Gatwick Airport, England,[8] some 3 million square feet of film are laid under the runway, aprons, and service roads.

Almost half our state highway departments have published specifications on the use of film as a curing blanket for highway construction.[11] Many contractors prefer film to burlap or paper because of its light weight, excellent moisture retention, and durability (reported reuses average six times). On the Dallas–Fort Worth Turnpike, polyethylene film in 20-foot widths was used. Film was placed by two or three men. Edges were draped over the pavement and covered with dirt to hold the sheets down.

Vinyl film was used in 1962 to protect underground pipe conduits at the Penn Station South,[21] a cooperative apartment project in New York City. The project includes ten 22-story buildings having a total of 2820 housing units. Conduits for the project carry water at 42°F for summer cooling, water at 200°F for heating, and 125 psi steam for generating hot water. The water and steam pipes are encased in a lightweight insulating concrete which is then wrapped in a blanket of flexible vinyl sheeting which protects the entire system from water damage. The usual

FIG. 4-2. Vinyl film applied to concrete duct. (*Courtesy Union Carbide Corp., Plastics Div.*)

TABLE 4-1. Physical Properties of Plastic Films*

Property	ASTM Test	Ethylene-Vinyl Acetate Copolymer	Polyethylene	Vinyl
Tensile strength, psi	D–882	3100	2500	2000
Modulus of elasticity, psi	D–882	11,000	23,000	1600
Elongation, % D	D–882	600	450	350
Specific gravity	D–1505	.94	.92	1.2
Tensile impact, ft-lb/sq in.	D–1822	350	150	260
Tear Resistance, g/mil	D–689	280	150	200
Vicat softening point, °C	D–1525	68	90	60
Brittle temperature, °C	D–746	−100	−100	−24
Moisture vapor trans, perms.	E–96 (Proc. A)	.18	.14	.86
Hardness, Durometer A	D–1706	75		
D	D–1706	33		
Puncture impact, ft-lb/mil		.3	.1	.2
Yield sq ft/lb at .004 in. thickness		51	52	39

*Courtesy Union Carbide Corporation, Plastics Division.
Ethylene-vinyl acetate = 8 mil DQAA-1801
Polyethylene   = DFD-0600
Vinyl   = KAA-2030

concrete jackets coated with tar or other sealants are effective in dry ground with good drainage but perform poorly in wet soil. See Figure 4-2.

PROPERTIES

The film properties of most concern are tensile strength, elongation, tear resistance, impact resistance, and resistance to weathering and decay. Temperature influences the action of film—brittle temperature is one measure of the handling properties of film at low temperatures. Polyethylene and copolymer films are normally produced by extrusion, and are strongest in the longitudinal direction. Tensile strength may be 25 to 35 per cent less in the transverse direction. Calendered plasticized vinyls tend to have equal properties in both directions. Representative properties of polyethylene, an ethylene-vinyl acetate copolymer, and a plasticized vinyl film are listed in Table 4-1. Polyethylene film properties are strongly affected by extrusion conditions as well as differences in properties of the original extrusion resin.

Table 4-2 lists the permeability of polyethylene film as it varies with thickness.[22]

TABLE 4-2. Water Vapor Permeability of Polyethylene[22]*

Thickness (in.)	Perms**
.001	.67
.002	.33
.003	.22
.004	.17
.005	.13
.006	.11
.007	.095
.008	.08
.009	.075
.010	.07

*ASTM E-96 Procedure E.
**The unit of permeance called a perm is a

$$\frac{grain}{hr \; sq \; ft \; in. \; Hg}$$

Note that the permeability varies inversely as the film thickness. Even 2-mil film satisfies the basic requirement for most vapor bar-

riers. Additional thickness, where required, is to ensure maintenance of these properties after the necessary handling during installation. Table 4-3 lists the impact resistance,

TABLE 4-3. Impact Resistance of Polyethylene Film*

Thickness (mils)	Dart Drop (g)
1.0	40
2.0	85
4.0	165
6.0	260
10.0	475

*ASTM D-1709.

measured by dart drop test, throughout the range of thickness normally used.[14,16]

A recent study concerned with testing the decay resistance of vapor-retarding round cover[17] reported no change in weight or permeability of 4-mil polyethylene in soil burial tests covering periods as long as 78 weeks. Roll roofing (55 pounds) and two proprietary asphalted laminated felts, one of which contained a fungicide and had polyethylene on one surface, were also tested. The proprietary items showed maximum weight losses of about 40 per cent, the roll roofing 20 per cent. Due to deterioration of cellulosic reinforcements, properties of these materials would not be maintained during service as concrete underlayments.

Polyethylene is practically unaffected by solutions of common acids, alkali, salts, detergents and motor oils, whereas toluene, carbon tetrachloride, dry cleaning solvents, and gasolines cause weight gain when tested according to ASTM D-543 (test for chemical resistance of plastics). Vinyls are similarly resistant to the effect of inorganic solutions but are more susceptible to damage by solvents and to leaching of plasticizers by soils. Resistance of polyethylene, vinyl, and ethylene-vinyl acetate films to chemical attack is presented in Table 4-4.

Various codes, standards and tests control the use of film in construction. The pertinent commercial standard is CS-238-61. The ASTM tests of major concern for films are:[1]

TABLE 4-4. Chemical Resistance of Film Materials*
(ASTM D-543)

Reagent	Ethylene-Vinyl Acetate	PE	Vinyl
5% Acetic acid	+	+	−
Acetone	−	+	−
Carbon tetra-chloride	−	−	−
Water	+	+	+
Seawater	+	+	+
10% Hydrochloric acid	+	+	+
Methanol	+	+	+
Mineral oil	+	+	+
10% Sodium hydroxide	+	+	+
3% Sulfuric acid	+	+	+
Turpentine	−	−	+
1% Soap solution	+	+	−
1% Chlorox solution	+	+	+

*Courtesy Union Carbide Corporation, Plastics Division.
Ethylene-vinyl acetate copolymer = UCC DQAA-1801
Polyethylene = UCC DFD-0600
Vinyl = UCC KAA-2030

+ = resistant
− = attacked

Tensile Strength and Elongation (D-882-61T). The method covers the tensile properties of plastics in the form of thin sheeting, less than 40 mils thick. Two methods of testing are specified, but results of the two methods cannot be directly compared. Method A is preferred.

Tear Resistance (D689). The Elmendorf machine measures the force necessary to tear a partially slit film. The Graves tear resistance (ASTM D-1004-61) test measures the force to initiate tearing. Data from the two methods cannot be compared.

Brittle Temperature (D-746-57T). This is the temperature at which 50 per cent of specimens fail under impact. The test does not utilize film, and while it is useful for comparing one material with another, it does not necessarily measure the lowest temperature at which the material may be used.

Impact Resistance of Polyethylene Film (D-1709-62T). This test measures the energy to fracture the film by a free-falling dart with either a 1.5- or a 2.0-inch hemispherical head.

Water Vapor Transmission of Materials in Sheet Form (E-96-53T). This test is applicable to sheet materials in general including plastics films and paper. Five procedures are listed: A and C for tests in the low range of humidities, B and D for the high range of humidities and E at elevated temperature with very low humidity on one side and very high humidity on the other side of the test sample. Procedures C, D and E are conducted at elevated temperatures to shorten the time of testing highly impermeable materials. Procedures A and C approach the usual conditions of above ground vapor barriers; B and D more closely simulate conditions for underlayments.

The Building Research Advisory Board to the FHA has recommended tests specifically for vapor barrier materials for slab-on-ground or as ground cover in crawl spaces.[13] A vapor barrier under a slab should have and maintain a transmission rate not greater than 0.5 perm after each of the following treatments:

(1) "Alternating wet and dry" by immersing in water for 16 hours and drying at 140°F for 8 hours for a total of 10 cycles.

(2) "Prolonged soaking" (28 days) and a 90° bend.

(3) "Soil block test, or soil burial test" in which the material is subject for 28 days to soil rich in microbial life that decomposes cellulose.

(4) "Abrasion" by having the specimen sandwiched between ¾-inch washed gravel and a smooth surfaced 100 pound weight. The weight is turned 90° abrading the film between stone and weight.

(5) "Plastic flow and elevated temperature" by loading the film placed on ¾-inch washed gravel with a weighted (25 pound) square (6 × 6 inch) plywood slab. Loading is 28 days at 140°F and 30 per cent relative humidity.

Requirements for material as ground cover are the same except that water vapor transmission should not be greater than 1.0 perm. Underlayment should have sufficient strength to resist rupture during placement and subsequent application of concrete mix. After test the tensile strength should be not less than 10 lb/in. of width in either direction, unless the material has an elongation greater than 100 per cent in which case the tensile strength should be equal to or greater than 7 lb/in. width. With a 2000-psi tensile strength, a 3.5-mil polyethylene film meets this requirement.

DESIGN CRITERIA

Problems of water migration and condensation became aggravated with the widespread use of insulation in dwellings, with increased use of water within the building, and with newer constructions utilizing enclosed crawl spaces. The ordinary activities of a family—respiration, cooking and washing—may add 5 to 10 pounds of water per day. Drying clothes inside may add 30 pounds or more. A crawl space may contribute as much as 100 pounds of water per 24 hours to the air in a house.[4] This water may be removed by ventilation through open doors, leaks around windows, chimneys, exhaust fans, and by diffusion through walls and ceiling.

The most practical means to reduce this latter mode of water elimination is to provide interior surfaces impermeable to water vapor. The preferred vapor barrier is polyethylene film. It should be placed near the warm side of the building element in which it is installed so that its temperature is never below the dew point of the ambient vapor; otherwise the vapor will condense.

This vapor barrier should have a permeance not greater than 1.25 perms including joints, fittings and outlet boxes.[4] All joints should be overlapped on solid backing (studs, joists, etc.). Any openings in the film on walls or ceilings result in almost total ineffectiveness of the vapor barrier in that area.[9] No wood should remain exposed, for wood has a high permeance and is sensitive to atmospheric humidity.[25] Any outside sheathing paper should have a permeance of 5 perms or greater, which will allow it to pass any water vapor which gets past the barrier

on the inside. This precludes the use of polyethylene film as sheathing paper and is the reason for the rule *never use two vapor barriers*. For the vapor barrier, 2- to 4-mil polyethylene film is used stapled to studs and to the underside of ceiling joists before the finish ceiling and walls are applied. The same polyethylene is spread over the sub-floor. Protection of the crawl space is provided by the sub-floor barrier, a polyethylene ground cover, and ventilation of the space between.

A common use of polyethylene today is as *underlayment film* in slab-on-grade construction. The purposes of this underlayment are:

(1) Protect the slab from moisture and possible corrosion from sulfate salts.

(2) Permit ultimate drying of the slab.

(3) Serve as a capillary stop.

(4) Protect below-slab heating ducts and insulation. (Water entering heating ducts will be distributed throughout a house.)

(5) Act as a separator over porous fill preventing loss of water and cement from the fresh concrete.

(6) Protect flooring materials and adhesives.

Any film is subject to tearing and puncturing during installation, and this must be guarded against. Fortunately the consequences of holes here are primarily proportional to the percentage of area punctured—unlike the effect of a puncture in film over open studs. While the underlayment prevents loss of cement to porous fill, it also retards the cure of concrete. This retardation is enough to require finishing crews to work beyond normal hours, and some workmen have succumbed to the temptation to puncture the barrier after the cement was laid, thus hastening the water loss and drying of the slab. Though good slabs, in themselves, may have a permeance of only 0.5 to 2.0 perms, the Building Research Advisory Board[12] in their report stated that it was not satisfactory to omit the vapor barrier. Their recommendation was that an underlayment for slab-on-ground house construction have a permeance not greater than 0.3 perm as determined by ASTM-E96 procedure B. This is a wet-cup method which, of the five, most nearly corresponds with actual field conditions. Usual practice is to use wide polyethylene film, 4 to 6 mils thick. Vinyl sheet, which is more expensive, is more resistant to puncture during handling, and is used more often for large-scale industrial, commercial, and government installations.

The main purpose of film overlays for concrete is to improve ultimate physical properties, mainly abrasion resistance and compressive strength. It has been reported[8] that concrete cured with polyethylene-curing membrane has had compressive strengths 17 per cent greater than air-cured concrete and only 8 per cent less than concrete cured under ideal conditions. Polyethylene-cured concrete is much more abrasion resistant than damp sack or than air-cured concrete. Abrasion indexes measuring relative loss were:

Polyethylene cured concrete   100
Damp sack cure   123
Air-cured   182

Film thickness required is primarily dependent on handling characteristics—2 to 6 mil

and over is satisfactory. Where wind may cause problems with light material, or where a number of reuses are desired, use 4-mil or heavier material. On highway construction, an average of six reuses and as many as twenty have been reported.[11]

Polyethylene film is available in three colors—natural (clear or translucent), black for good weathering, and white. The usual construction thicknesses, 2, 4 and 6 mils, are available in continuous widths to 40 feet. Standard widths are 3, 4, 6, 8, 10, 12, 14, 16, 20, 24, 28 and 32 feet. Film can be obtained in 100 foot rolls in flat widths up to 12½-feet wide. Wider film comes folded on the roll in one of three types of folds.[5]

Most other films are available in widths from 3 to 4 feet and thicknesses from 1 to 10

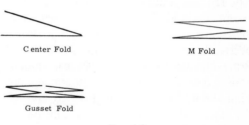

Center Fold   M Fold

Gusset Fold

FIG. 4-3.

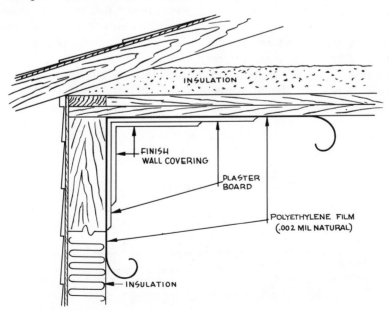

FINISH WALL COVERING

PLASTER BOARD

POLYETHYLENE FILM (.002 MIL NATURAL)

INSULATION

FIG. 4-4. Polyethylene vapor barrier on walls and ceilings. (*Courtesy Union Carbide Corp., Plastics Div.*)

mils and over. Vinyl sheet is easily solvent, adhesive, or heat-sealed, and fabricated wide sheeting is available.

Auxiliary items such as electric sealing irons, adhesive-backed plastic tape, and simple wire clips for plastic tarpaulin tie downs are obtainable from most film suppliers.

INSTALLATION

Exterior Walls and Ceilings

Use 2-mil polyethylene film in the widest practical width. All exterior walls and ceilings, of whatever material, should have a polyethylene film vapor barrier. Apply the film on the warm side after insulation is installed and before sheet rock or other finish material is applied. Apply the film horizontally, attaching it with staples 6 inches or less on centers. Stapling is not required on intermediate studs or joists except to hold film in place. Where film joints are required, use at least a 3-inch overlap over a solid continuous backing. Bring film up tight against electric outlets, door and window frames and other openings. Film should be wide enough to cover both the plate and sill and to overlap film on the ceiling and floor.

Sub-floor

Again use 2-mil polyethylene film in widest practical width. Be sure all surfaces are clean and dry. Lay film over sub-floor as in Figure 4-5. Any joints should overlap 4 inches or more. Staple film at the wall

line to anchor the film in place, lapping over the edges of film coming down from the walls. Apply finish floor in the conven-

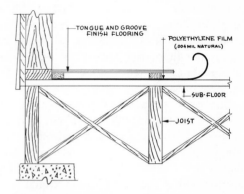

FIG. 4-5. Polytheylene film applied to sub floor. (*Courtesy Union Carbide Corp. Plastics Div.*)

tional manner. If finish floor is the type which is fastened by adhesive, conventional adhesives may be used but the film must first be adhered to the sub-floor.

Slab-on-grade

Use 4-mil polyethylene over coarse sand or 6-mil film over gravel or fines, Figure 4-6. Smooth the subgrade by any suitable method which will prevent protrusions that may puncture the film. Use the widest practical seamless widths of film laid over the sand or gravel base. Where joints are necessary, overlap at least 6 inches with the top lap in the direction that concrete will be spread. If no capillary break is provided, seal the film joints, using a manufacturer's recom-

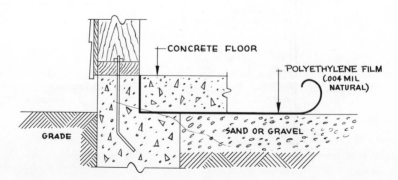

FIG. 4-6. Polyethylene film under slab-on-grade. (*Courtesy Union Carbide Corp., Plastics Div.*)

mended materials or methods. If insulation is used below the slab, apply it over the vapor barrier before pouring the concrete. Radiant heating pipes or perimeter heating ducts should be laid *on top of the film*, and concrete should be poured in the conventional manner. Great care must be taken to protect underslab hot-air ducts from water, as any moisture will be distributed throughout the building, Figure 4-7. Reinforcing mesh can

FIG. 4-7. Barrier film under ducts. (*Courtesy Union Carbide Corp., Plastics Div.*)

be laid directly over the film prior to pouring concrete, but care should be taken to avoid film punctures. Some commercial installations have used a layer of sand over the film to protect it during pouring of concrete and to hasten the drying of the cement. Any wiring outlets or pipes which penetrate the floor require the film to be cut carefully around and taped with pressure-sensitive tape to ensure maximum barrier effectiveness. At the perimeter, the film should be brought up to the top surface of the slab.

Concrete Curing Blanket

Use 2 to 6 mil polyethylene film depending on the amount of handling required. Smooth down the film to remove air and obtain all-around contact of film with the concrete. Leave in place for normal curing times.

Edges may be held down with sand, dirt, or boards where wind may be a problem. If film is placed while concrete is still soft, a very smooth, slippery concrete surface will result, hence delay is required for preliminary set to take place. A double layer of film on 2 × 2 frames can retard moisture loss and provide insulation in cold weather.

Temporary Shelters and Covers

For long-term use, black polyethylene or ethylene-vinyl acetate is preferred. Pad all corners or protrusions which might cause film wear or puncture. For covers, tie downs are available. Where film is tacked to frames, it should be covered with lath or batten strips to distribute the stress on the film. Greenhouse experience has shown it desirable to plane or otherwise smooth the strip to which the polyethylene is tacked and to use a cover strip wider than the framing lumber.[5] This strip apparently shades the edges of the film where stress is greatest and protects it from deterioration due to weather. Double up or lap the film at the edges of a frame, and leave some play in the film for shrinkage in cold weather. For 4-foot spans 4-mil film can be used; for 6-foot spans use 6-mil film.

TABLE 4-5. Prices of Plastic Film and Building Papers

Material	Weight	Price ($¢$/sq ft)
Polyethylene	2 mil	0.5
	4 mil	0.94
	6 mil	1.5
	4 mil black	1.05
Vinyl, clear cast	4 mil	4.81
Vinyl translucent calendered	4 mil	3.31
Cellulose butyrate	5 mil	6.24
"Mylar* (UV protected)	3 mil	11.24
"Mylar* (UV protected)	5 mil	12.49
Roll roofing	55 lb	2.8
Roll roofing	45 lb	2.5
Saturated felt	30 lb	1.27
Saturated felt	15 lb	.64
Cannon duck, single fill	8 oz	7.0

*Du Pont trademark, polyester film.

ECONOMICS

The outstanding success of polyethylene film in the construction field has been due to its excellent physical properties, light weight, convenient widths and low price. Table 4-5 lists prices of polyethylene film as of the end of 1963 together with prices of other plastics film[19] and roll roofing and saturated felts. The prices given were commonly listed retail prices. Wholesalers' and builders' discounts are available on all these materials, but except for published list prices, the costs to other than retail purchasers are difficult to ascertain. If you are buying, this is the most you should expect to pay.

II: FORMS FOR CONCRETE

Plastic materials are making important contributions to the pouring of concrete as forms, treamies, chutes, and tools—but especially as forms. Their primary attractions are ease of handling, design freedom provided to the architect, and cost. With such characteristics, plastics participation in this use may be expected to grow.

Materials

Glass fiber-reinforced plastic structures are much used for these forms. They may be made by hand layup, sprayup, or by matched-metal molding, depending on the size, complexity and number of pieces required. Such forms have a number of advantages over other materials, not the least of which is that the total cost may be lower.

Plastic-coated plywood and particle board have been used in place of plywood for concrete molds. Longer life, smoother finish, and as much as 20 per cent lower cost are reported advantages of the particle board.[24] The resin glaze from the particle board pressing operation provides excellent hold-out for the form oil, and large unmarred wall surfaces, smooth enough to paint, can be cast against single sheets as large as 5 feet × 16 feet.

Expanded polystyrene planks have been used as form boards for casting concrete. One such reported use was on a hyperbolic paraboloid shell roof for a gas station in Midland, Michigan.[28] There the styrene planks were confined between two layers of prestressed wires, one-half inch of mortar was applied to stiffen the plank and then a 3-inch concrete layer was cast to form the doubly curved roof. The planks were 3 inches thick and about 2 × 8 feet in lateral dimensions. The expanded polystyrene, left in place, provides thermal insulation for the completed building. A somewhat different use involved the facing of forms with carved polystyrene foam to obtain special architectural artistic effects in the wall surfaces of a church in Spokane, Washington.[26] Such applications are as yet not widespread, but the possibilities are intriguing, and increased use of polystyrene may be anticipated.

Thermoplastic sheets, in general, are available for concrete form work. Concrete will very closely match the surface of the form against which it is poured, whether it be a glass smooth or an embossed plastic surface—or whether it be the almost imperceptibly raised grain of a plywood surface. A British publication[30] describes the use of vacuum-formed vinyl sheet as lining for concrete molds to provide decorative relief patterns. Such vinyl-lined molds have been used for over 130 castings without noticeable deterioration. British practice apparently is to glue the formed vinyl sheet to wood or metal backing. Very thin sheets can be used, but the thickness required is dependent on the shape and size of the vacuum formed mold protrusions. Patterns with grooves 2 to 3 inches in diameter and 1 to 2 inches deep should not suffer from flattening due to concrete pressure; larger patterns might need support on the under side or might require heavier sheet. Similarly molds in the United States have been lined with thermoplastic sheet of $\frac{1}{16}$ to $\frac{3}{32}$ inch thickness. At the Fire Research Center of the Portland Cement Association in Skokie, Illinois,[32] 29 precast columns 35 feet high and weighing $11\frac{1}{2}$ tons each were cast against plastic-lined forms. In the lobby, a series of 12-inch square patterned panels form a mural in colored concrete. The ease of forming thermoplastic sheet makes it economically feasible to study various shapes and patterns before settling on a final design, or before making more molds, or molds of other more expensive materials.

Polyethylene has been used in plastic-lined fiber forms for round columns from 2 to 16 inches in diameter. Such forms are very lightweight and require minimum bracing. They are particularly useful for piers, posts, columns, and underpinning. These, of course, provide one-time-use forms which are easily removed leaving very smooth ready-to-paint concrete. Polyethylene has additional uses as accessories for reinforced concrete construction.[35] These include such items as continuous slab and beam bolsters, mesh bolsters, and plastic "donuts" for holding reinforcing away from forms. The bolsters prevent electrolytic action with reinforcing steel and prevent rust stains. Similar functions are performed by conventional wire accessories available with heavy plastisol coatings. A more spectacular item is the high-density polyethylene treamie such as was used to pour concrete for the Lincoln Center for the Performing Arts in New York City.[37] Treamies were fabricated of extruded sheeting and weigh about one-eighth as much as usual steel units. Concrete does not stick to their surface, and they do not rust; thus cleaning is less difficult and needs be less frequent.

Characteristics of Plastic Forms

The characteristics which make plastics useful aids in concrete construction are shared by many plastics, but their most favorable combination seems to have been achieved by the polyester fiber-glass forms.

Economy is the main reason for continued use of plastic forms. Initial cost of plastic forms is higher, usually, than for the conventional wood forms, but ability to reuse the plastic forms results in lower cost per casting. The fiber-glass forms are tough and nondenting. They do not rust as does steel, nor do they react with alkaline constituents of concrete as do aluminum molds. Molds which are broken or marred are easily repaired with more fiber glass and polyester resin. Evidence of such repair

is not visible in the finished concrete. As a result these plastic molds have been used for as many as 22 castings in construction of an apartment building in Pittsburgh[34] and 66 castings at Marina City in Chicago.[27,31] A report by the U.S. Naval Civil Engineering Laboratory in 1962[29] suggests that their fiber-glass forms might be useful for a total of 150 castings with an average of 20 uses between repairs.

Much greater freedom of design is accorded the architect, for designs can be molded in and compound curves can be accommodated easily. The much lower weight (plastic waffle-slab forming pans weigh less than half as much as their counterparts in steel) permits larger—and fewer—mold pieces to be handled and assembled. Joint lines are thus virtually eliminated.

Once the concrete has set, the forms are easily stripped. It is common for 8 to 10 per cent of waffle-slab pans to come loose with the staging. The concrete with forms removed is left with sharp smooth surfaces ready for painting without the usual costly finishing processes of grinding and patching.

Two notes of caution: Molds should be designed with sufficient draft for easy removal. Also, plastics have relatively high coefficients of thermal expansion so that drastic temperature changes after erection of forms can cause gaps or buckling.

Two Buildings using Plastic Forms

Plastic forms were utilized in a 5-building residence hall project at the Pennsylvania State University.[33,36] The contractor credits the waffle-slab forming pans with a 15 per cent saving in initial cost and a reduction in total stripping time to 5 sec. The trueness and smoothness of the exposed concrete ceilings made unnecessary any costly and time-consuming finishing prior to painting. Figure 4-8 is a closer view of the forming pans which illustrate their light weight (6¾ pounds), nestability, and method of installation. The pans here have flange dimensions of 24 × 24 inches with a void of 19 × 19 × 8 inches and a wall thickness of .110 inch. They weigh 6¾ pounds each. One nail at each intersection of 4 pans is sufficient to hold them in place. The construction schedule at Penn State called for only 7 to 9 pours, but pans were used for 25 or more pours.

FIG. 4-8. (a) Pans are strong, lightweight, nestable, easy to handle and to install.

FIG. 4-8. (b) Releasing molded pans.
(*Courtesy Molded Fiber Glass Co., Ashtabula, Ohio*)

Another job of interest utilized specially designed T-shaped fiber-glass forms to mold the exposed faces of load-bearing columns and spandrel beams. The building is the 22-story, $7 million, cast-in-place concrete Washington Plaza Apartments in Pittsburgh.[34] What was wanted—and accomplished—was columns with smooth unmarked surfaces and with a deep inset or rustication. The mold designed for this job consisted of a complex of molded fiber-glass, plywood, rubber stripping, and supporting steel framework. Each T-shaped form is 8 feet 7 inches long and contains an inset which is 5 feet 8 inches high, 2½ inches deep, 8 inches wide and beveled in four directions. The plan called for 21 castings each for the first 21 floors and then modification of the molds for casting the 22nd floor. Only one full set of forms plus four spares were made for this project. How the molds were used and the configuration of the column faces can be seen in Fig. 4-9.

Economics

Full consideration of the economics of plastic forms is too involved for consideration here. However, the experiences of certain projects may be of value.

For preliminary feasibility studies, recommended cost figures for molded polyester fiber-glass items are $0.60 to $1.25/sq ft of surface area for 0.125-inch thick material.[25] The waffle-slab pans described above cost initially roughly $0.71/sq ft for the Penn State job. This amounted to approximately $0.84 per pan pour, whereas the quoted price for steel pans amounted to $1.00/pan pour. On the basis of 7 pours/fiber-glass pan these costs amount to 10¢/sq ft. Additional costs of 6¢/sq ft for handling, erecting and stripping should be less—certainly not more—than equivalent handling of steel pans.

The set of forms for the Marina City development in Chicago were more expensive to fabricate, costing initially $4 to $5/sq ft.[35] These were larger forms constructed by hand layup. Wood and steel stiffeners were incorporated to reinforce the form sections.

Fig. 4-9. T-shaped form being removed. (*Courtesy Molded Fiber Glass Co., Ashtabula, Ohio, Concrete Accessories Corp., Zelienople, Pa.*)

One set of forms was used 68 times; thus despite the high initial cost, the net cost of this set of forms was only 7½ ¢/sq ft.

Hromadik and Bliss[29] have reported on experiments in precasting and setting up concrete panels to construct a military barracks-type building. Four types of molds were considered—plywood, plastic-coated plywood, structural plastic, and concrete. From data and estimates contained in their report, the structural plastic molds were equivalent in cost to the plastic-coated plywood molds at 40 reuses and to the plywood molds at 30 reuses. Their estimate was that the structural plastic molds would have a total life of 150 casts with an average of 20 casts between repairs which would cost, for their molds, about $100. The concrete molds were less costly than structural plastic molds above roughly 100 castings. These required the fabrication of relatively expen-

sive structural plastic masters from which concrete molds would be cast. It should be kept in mind, when anticipating using molds near their expected limit, that one step beyond causes a sudden increase in cost per casting. This new cost may be appreciably higher than that of an initially more expensive but longer-lived mold.

III: SILICONE-BASED WATER REPELLENTS

Silicone resins are used extensively to treat above-grade masonry structures. Usually the silicone resins are dissolved in solvents in 3 to 5 per cent concentration. Concentrated solutions containing 33 per cent solids are available for dilution. Water-based silicone compositions are also used, primarily for highway structures.

Silicone treatments are applicable to almost all masonry materials including stone, concrete, mortar, brick, tile, stucco, block and cement-based paints. The major exceptions seem to be limestone and marble, stones of calcareous origin, where staining might result from reaction with contained iron. Besides building faces, the treatment is useful for concrete shells, bridges, piers, floors, patios, masonry porches and precast and exposed aggregate concrete.

The function of the silicone is to make the masonry water-repellent without sealing the pores. Liquid water will not penetrate but internally generated water can be eliminated as vapor. Thus the silicone water repellents:

(1) Prevent or minimize spalling and cracking
(2) Reduce maintenance costs
(3) Keep the building clean longer
(4) Minimize efflorescence
(5) Prevent interior water damage
(6) Permit escape of internal moisture by "breathing"
(7) Prevent color change caused by wetting.

Silicones are also added to cement paints, typically styrene-butadiene paints with a high filler content, to make a "breathing" coating which does not allow water absorption.[39] Another system consisting of a water-based silicone in a latex has been used in Europe to create a dampproof course by injection into mortar courses, usually in older constructions built without membrane flashings.[40]

Alternate Treatments

Certain water-repellent *metallic stearates* in solvent solution serve much the same function as silicone-based repellents. These are reported to be of most use on limestone, marble, or other iron-bearing stones.[43] Care must be taken that such solutions do not "run" on the face of the building, and surfaces, once treated, cannot subsequently be painted without removing the stearate. Older coatings have been based on *waxes*, *resins*, or *oleoresinous varnishes*. Common paint coatings based on various latices (acrylic, vinyl), or alkyd or solvent-based vinyl paints are used as protective coatings.[39] But these are essentially different in their function providing a waterproof membrane which covers and hides the masonry.

The huge curved concrete roof of the Trans World Airline passenger terminal at Kennedy International Airport was coated with a silicone-based water repellent after careful consideration by Eero Saarinen, architect, and the Brisk Waterproofing Company.[46] Workmen applied the silicone solution with a sprinkling can and brushed it out with push brooms. Coverage was approximately 100 sq ft/gal. Silicones permitted fulfillment of the designers' intention to protect the shell surface while retaining the appearance and texture of normal concrete.

One well-publicized story of several years ago depicted the Mount Rushmore Memorial getting a silicone bath. Another well-known structure which has received "the treatment" is New York's Trinity Church.

Absorption of water is a common factor in most of the modes of failure of masonry walls. Water, penetrating the pores, freezes in cold weather, expanding and causing tiny cracks to form. These widen, and eventually portions of the masonry flake away. Water-borne salts from the mortars work their way to the surface where the water evaporates leaving ugly destructive efflorescence. Water works its way through the wall, wetting plaster, peeling paint, causing mildew, and creating other unsightly, unhealthy conditions. Rain hitting the surface contains small particles of dust, dirt and soot which are left behind, building up an unsightly deposit. Because water wets the masonry, its pores and hairline cracks act as capillaries and literally draw the water into the wall.

A silicone treatment coats the surfaces with a very thin layer of silicone resin which bonds tenaciously to the masonry but which is itself not wet by water. On such a surface, water does not spread out and penetrate but balls up. The capillaries now resist the entry of water, so that even a strong wind does not force it through the pores. While the silicone waterproofing is not recommended below grade and is really a water repellent rather than a waterproofer, a silicone-treated brick will float (Fig. 4-10).

The following are important general features of silicone water repellents:

Clear and invisible
One coat
Penetrating (as much as ¼ inch)
Nonsealing of masonry pores
Quick development of water repellency (as soon as solvent evaporates)
Useful on most types of masonry
Applied over wide temperature range (15 to 100°F)
Long lasting (estimating 10 years or more)
Paintable
Easy to apply

Since all silicone solutions for water repellents are not alike, treatment of perhaps 100 square feet of surface is advisable to establish coverage and reveal any adverse effects such as discoloration or noncompatibility. Composition and performance specifications for silicone water repellents include:

U. S. Federal Specificaton SS-W-00110a (GSA-FSS)

Canadian Specification 58-GP-1 for "Water-Repellent: Colorless, Silicone Resin Base (Hydrocarbon Solution)"

Port of New York Authority "Specification for Water-Repellent Silicone Resin Solution"

Philadelphia Board of Education "Specification S-82 Water Repellent"

fective should be raked out to a depth of about ½ inch, brushed clean, wetted down, and then repainted. Spalled or cracked masonry should be replaced, and any cracks wider than 1/64 inch should be filled.

Previous waterproofing compounds or loose or chalked coatings should be removed preferably by sand blasting. Effloresence can

FIG. 4-10. Water does not penetrate pores of the treated brick, therefore, it floats. (*Courtesy Union Carbide Corp., Silicones Div.*)

INSTALLATION

The following has been reported as good practice in applying silicone water repellents. [42, 44, 45]

Surface Treatment

At the time of application to new construction, any mortar or concrete should be well cured, either aged for 3 to 4 weeks, at normal temperatures or for 8 to 9 weeks if the temperature has bordered on freezing. In the case of precast concrete, equivalent cure may be reached by other means such as heating or autoclaving.

On old construction, all masonry joints should be tested and those found to be hollow, unsound, cracked, or otherwise de-

be removed in the usual manner by scrubbing down with muriatic acid, but the acid should then be rinsed off with copious quantities of water. For exposed aggregate concrete surfaces, it may be preferable to wash thoroughly with a detergent solution with mild scrubbing to ensure that all dust and dirt are loosened. Follow with a thorough rinse.

The building must be dry when treated. Three days drying time should be allowed following wash down or a rainstorm. Treatment should not be started if rain is expected within 36 hours of completing. Silicones can be applied at temperatures from 15 to 100°F, but treatment should be delayed if there is a chance that the masonry contains frozen trapped water.

Application

Treatment calls for a flood coat of clear silicone solution to be applied from the top down. Generally a run-down of 6 to 12 inches is suggested. Brushing or spray application is suitable. A garden-type sprayer, with a coarse spray, operating at low pressure to avoid ricochet is ideal.

Care should be taken to avoid getting the solution on asphalt or painted surfaces. Shrubs or other plant life should be covered. If windows are hit with the spray, it can be removed with mineral spirits while still wet. If the spray has dried, the silicones cling tenaciously to the glass, but they can be removed by wiping with "Cellosolve"* solvent.

Normal safety precautions for handling hydrocarbon solvents should be taken to prevent fires and to avoid excessive breathing of solvent fumes, and extensive contact with the skin.

Coverage

Table 4-6 presents coverage which may be expected with one type of silicone water repellent.[45]

TABLE 4-6. Estimation of Average Coverage; R-27 Based Water Repellent*

Type Surface	Approx. Porosity (%)	Silicone Concentration (%)	Coverage (sq ft /gal.)
Terra cotta block	1–3	3	250–400
Terazzo	1–3	3	250–400
Dense brick	2–4	3	150–200
Concrete	2–4	3	150–200
Mortar	6–10	3 or 5	100–125
Stucco	6–10	3 or 5	100–125
Common brick	6–12	3 or 5	100–125
Cement brick	8–11	3 or 5	60–100
Concrete block	8–12	3 or 5	60–100

*Courtesy Union Carbide Corporation, Silicones Division.

IV: RESINS FOR MODIFYING CONCRETE

Latices of polyvinyl acetate, styrene/butadiene, vinyldene chloride, and some acrylics

*Trademark of Union Carbide Corporation.

are added to cement to modify the properties of concrete and mortar. Added in proportions up to 0.2 part latex solids to 1 part cement, they improve adhesion, impact strength, flexural and tensile strengths flexibility, abrasion resistance, dry cure, and/or workability.

Other resins such as methyl cellulose and hydroxy ethyl cellulose[59] may also be added to mortars, particularly tile pointing mortars, to retard water evaporation thus permitting better cure of the cement.

Various filled epoxy resin systems have been used as mortars. Trowelable mortars made with epoxy resins, fine sand, and dry Portland cement have better adhesion, tensile strength, abrasion resistance, and dry cure than the modified cement mortars,[47] but they cost more, and their use in building has not been extensive, except for special terrazzo type flooring. Epoxy block mortars are used with ground blocks to minimize the amount of mortar needed.[55,56] These systems are made up without water and the cement is not necessary. Thus, for the purposes of this chapter, the epoxy resins are not considered additives for modifying concrete.

The premium prices of modified concretes can be justified for many applications.[49,50,58]

Ceramic tile grout and bedding
Coatings for industrial insulation
Portland cement plasters and stucco
Brick and cement block mortars
Precast concrete slabs, panels, beams
Flooring underlayments
Acid resisting cements
Terrazzo floors
Adhesives for building materials
Dust proofing for concrete floors
Resurfacing cement for cement floors, drives, and bridge decks

The principal disadvantages are increased cost and water sensitivity. The first problem is mitigated for some applications by adding only 8 to 12 per cent of acrylic latex solids,[52] and some recent latices have exhibited improved resistance to water.

HISTORY AND ECONOMICS

Addition of rubber latex to Portland cement to increase the resiliency of floorings was reported in 1937. An even earlier reference is Bond's specifications in British Patent 369561 (1930).[59] Significant commercial development is more recent. In 1953, J. M. Geist et al[50] made a fundamental study of the effects of a polyvinyl acetate emulsion additive in various concentrations on tensile strengths, elongation, modulus of elasticity workability, curing conditions, etc. In 1958 the Corps of Engineers published a review on polyvinyl acetate in admixture with concrete.[60] The chief drawback found was water sensitivity.

Though about a dozen resin producers offer polymer emulsions for use in Portland cement compositions, estimates of sales for this purpose vary from 5 to 20 million pounds per year. Sales of other concrete additives have been estimated at 40 to 50 million pounds.[59] Cost is the deterrent to greater sales.

$4.54/cu ft, a cheaper 4-inch brick wall could be made to outperform a conventional 8-inch brick wall. The 4-inch brick wall at $1.81/sq ft had a breaking load of 110 lb/sq ft while an 8-inch conventional wall at $2.27/sq ft withstood only 47.9 lb/sq ft. Eighteen free-standing walls 13 feet long × 6 feet 8 inches high were constructed in this manner for the Gas Industry Pavilion at the Century 21 World's Fair in Seattle.

A common use for acrylic emulsions is modifying mixes for terrazzo floors.[52] The greater adhesion, tensile strength, flexibility, and less-stringent curing requirements make possible major changes in construction. For instance, the modified terrazzo can be reduced to ½-inch thickness and can be laid directy on a concrete — or even a wood floor. Conventional practice requires ¾ inch of terrazzo laid on top of a 1½-inch sand layer. Even so the modified terrazzo probably amounts to only about 5 per cent of the total. Adherence to traditional family construction

TABLE 4-7. Latex Costs

	Cost		
	Wet		Solids
Latex Type	(¢/lb.)		(¢/lb.)
Stryene butadiene	12½	(48)	26
Acrylic	14¾	(46)	32
Polyvinyl acetate	15	(55)	27.3

If the latex is used in its optimum proportion (0.2 lb latex solids/lb cement), the cost of latex alone is from two to four times the cost of the cement. Even when the proportion of acrylic latex can be cut in half, as reported, the additive still costs more than the cement. For this reason, we should not expect to see emulsions used in formulas for massive concrete castings. Economic conditions dictate applications where conventional cements are unsuitable or give unsatisfactory service or where building methods can be modified to produce a net saving.

An example is cited in which a vinyl chloride/vinylidene chloride copolymer emulsion is used as a mortar additive.[51,53] Though mortar cost was increased from 68¢/cu ft to

methods is at least partly responsible for slow acceptance of the newer terrazzo systems.

In the home repair "do-it-yourself" kits sold in retail hardware stores, the latex is diluted to such an extent that it may be added directly to prepared sand-cement mixtures without additional water. The cost is high— $2.00 to $2.50 for 5 pounds of sand/cement mix and a pint of latex. But the mix bonds well to old cement, requires no wet cure, and has sufficient toughness to allow it to be used in thin sections.

HOW A LATEX WORKS

Microscopic examination of ground mortar specimens revealed to Geist et al.[50] that cured cement gel contained voids and that in latex-modified mortars these voids were filled with polymer particles. Cement particles are larger than polymer particles, about 80 per cent of them being larger than 5 microns.[55] The polymer particles studied by Geist ranged from 0.2 to 2 microns. The smaller size is typical of latex solids offered as concrete additives. At the optimum ratio of latex solids to cement of 0.2, these voids were completely filled. Less latex left unfilled voids, while more latex resulted first in considerable polymer directly in contact with sand grains ($L/C = 0.3$) and eventually in a continuous phase consisting of more than three-fourths polyvinyl acetate ($L/C = 0.4$).

Typical properties of three latexes offered as concrete additives are listed in Table 4–8.

TABLE 4-8. Typical Latex Properties

	Styrene/butadiene[49]	PVC	Acrylic[57]
Solids, %	48	48–51	45
Specific gravity	1.01	1.14	1.05
Weight per gallon	8.5	9.4	8.8
pH	10.5	7.5	9.4–9.9
Particle size, (A)	1900–2100	—	—
Viscosity, cp	10–12	14	—
Surface tension, dynes/cm²	30–32	—	—
Freeze thaw stability, cycles	1+	—	5

These latices are formulated for good stability in the presence of electrolytes. The S/B latex in Table 4–8 of typical latex properties is unaffected by dilution with 5 per cent solutions of NaCl, $CaCl_2$, $Al_2(SO_4)_3$, concentrated HCl, or 30 per cent $CaCl_2$ at 25°C. At 50°C, the 50 per cent $CaCl_2$ will coagulate the latex. The *latices are commonly not stable to most air entraining agents*, and, in fact, defoamers are generally added to the cement mixes to reduce air entrainment. The high strength requirements which justify the added cost of latex additions, require also the highest-density concretes.

Latex also increases the workability of cement mortars. Again the greatest workability is attained when polymer/cement ratio is 0.2. At this latex concentration a water/cement ratio of 0.35 in a laboratory mortar formulation is as workable as an unmodified mortar with a water/cement ratio 0.45. This again is advantageous since a workable cement already contains more than enough water to hydrate the cement. Excess water results in greater shrinkage and more voids, hence weaker mortars.

But the emulsion polymer provides still another valuable service. Under conditions of natural humidity, water may evaporate from an unmodified mortar before the slow hydration reaction can be completed. A weak mortar results. An unmodified mortar cures best when kept wet. On the other hand, modified mortars give even better properties when cured under normal atmospheric conditions, e.g. 35 per cent relative humidity. One hypothesis is that the polymer particles retard the evaporation of water because of their hydrophilic nature. Another, more plausible reason is that initial loss of water soon leaves a polymer skin at the surface that prevents or greatly reduces continued evaporation.

PROPERTIES

Latex addition usually improves tensile, compressive, flexural and bond strengths considerably. Results vary, however, depending on formulation, mixing techniques, testing, and especially cure conditions. When cured wet, the modified mortars do not develop their maximum properties. Mortars modified with polyvinyl acetate latex are especially water sensitive. When cured dry, they give the greatest property improvements, but when cured wet, properties are lower than those of unmodified mortars, perhaps because of hydrolysis of the polymer to the alcohol and acetic acid in the presence of free alkalis in cement.

Listed in Table 4-9 are ratios of properties of modified mortars compared to those of unmodified mortars compiled from the data of various investigators.

Abrasion resistance of properly formulated and cured modified mortars is 8 to 10 times better than that of unmodified mortars.

TABLE 4-9. Comparison of Latex Modified Unmodified Mortars*

	Cure Condition	Acrylic	Styrene / butadiene	Polyvinyl Acetate	Vinyl Copolymer	Vinylidene Chloride
Tension	7 days dry	1.3–2.2*	1.1–3.2	1.3–5.2	4.0	–
	7 days wet	.25–.6	.5–.9	.2–.6	1.6	–
Flexure	7 days dry	1.2–2.6	1.0–1.2	.6–1.5	–	1.3–1.5
Bond	7 days dry	2.2–4.5	2.1–4.7	1.2–6.7	5.4	–
Compression	7 days dry	.36–1.5	.34–1.5	.2–3.7	–	–

*Ratios are value for modified mortar /value for unmodified mortar.

Latex modified mortars contract considerably more upon drying and curing than do ordinary mortars. For example, Tyler[59] reports:

TABLE 4-10. Shrinkage of Latex Modified Mortars*

Latex Modifier	Shrinkage (in. /in.)
"Internally plasticized vinyl Copolymers"	.00138
Butadiene/styrene	.00225
PVA	.00290
Control	.00049

*Samples were cured at 70°F and 65% relative humidity. Water /cement ratio = 0.35; latex /cement ratio = 0.2.

Although shrinkage is 4 to 6 times as great as that of plain mortars, the *tensile elongations* of such modified mortars are 30 to 40 times as great as those of unmodified mortars, and thus cracks are prevented.

Latex-modified mortars have enhanced chemical resistance to certain materials which attack plain mortars, e.g., most dilute acids, emulsified cutting oils, motor oils, cola drinks, and beer. On the other hand, certain polymer solvents such as xylene, trichloroethylene, and ketones may drastically reduce the strength of modified mortars.

Typical material ratios used for laboratory mortars are:

Water/cement	0.35
Sand/cement	3.0
Latex solids/cement	0.20

Tests applicable to modified and unmodified mortars are:

	ASTM Procedure
Setting-time	C-254-52
Compressive strength	C-109-52
Tensile strength	C-190-19
Flexural strength	C-192-52T
	C-293-52T
Bond strength	C-321-54T
Abrasion resistance	C-241-51
Chemical resistance	C-109-52
	C-267-51T

INSTALLATION

Latex is usually furnished in 55-gallon drums. Store where the contents will not freeze. Mix thoroughly, and screen the latex as it is used to remove any skin or material which may have coagulated.

Mixing latex-modified mortars can be done in conventional equipment. Mix sand and cement. Separately, blend latex, antifoamer, and some of the required water. The wet mix is then added to the dry solids and mixing is continued for not more than 5 minutes. The antifoamer becomes ineffective with excess mixing, and air entrainment becomes excessive. Combine with additional water to obtain the desired workability. Note that latex mixes use less total water—ratios of only .25 to .35 water/cement for good workability compared to .45 to .55 for unmodified mixes. Also, modified mixes have high slumps, i.e., 8 to 10 inches. Working life is relatively short; the mix must be placed and finished with little delay. Latex-modified mortars adhere tenaciously to tools and mixers, so thorough and rapid cleanup with water is essential.

Any surface to which latex mortar is to be

applied should be free of grease, oil or loose materials such as dust, dirt, or rust. Water absorbent bases should be damp but not have puddles of water. Wood surfaces may be coated with clear latex before covering. Concrete surfaces give better bond if a thin layer of mortar is first broomed in. Mortar must be troweled lightly to prevent polymer drag. If tools drag, they or the cement can be wet with diluted latex. For best properties, the mortar can be left to cure without covering with plastic film or wet burlap, unless the atmosphere is exceptionally dry and breezy.

V: INFLATED BUILDINGS

An inflated building is an air-supported structure which consists of a strong flexible balloonlike envelope supported and stabilized by maintaining a small pressure differential within the envelope.[65] They are used primarily as a cover or temporary shelter where wide span cover with no columns and portability are needed.[64]

Because material properties, quality of fabric sealing, uses, sizes and shapes are so variable, most air shelters are custom engineered. Knowhow in design fabrication and installation is a valuable feature bought with a custom designed building. On the other hand, items in common use, e.g., swimming pool enclosures, may be available in standard sizes.

Inflated buildings for commercial uses are normally made of vinyl-coated nylon[62] of varying weight depending on design, but 2 to 4 oz/sq ft is common. They may also have transparent or translucent vinyl for windows or transmission of light. Military applications might also use "Hypalon" or neoprene-coated nylon or "Dacron."[61,64]

There are three main types of inflated buildings: (1) a single diaphragm balloonlike envelope, (2) a cellular dual-wall building with only the wall section pressurized, (3) structures in which the balloon is stabilized with auxiliary framing.[65]

Some competitive type buildings are:

(1) Large clear span tent structures supported by beams

(2) Wood domes with plastic sheet roofs
(3) Steel lamella roofs
(4) Geodesic structures.[62]

Advantages of Inflated Buildings:

(1) Lightweight—about ¼ the weight of the lightest other structures of comparable size.[2]

(2) Ease of erection—1/5 to 1/20 the time of competitive types.

(3) Easily heated—inside may be as much as 45° warmer than the outside temperature.[67]

(4) Low cost—perhaps $1.00/sq ft to $5.00/sq ft.

(5) Wide span with no columns.[4]

(6) Portability.

(7) Easily patched.

(8) Translucent walls.

Disadvantages:

(1) Relatively short life time—5 years, perhaps 10 years in special occasions.

(2) Need for a blower for continued inflation (but in storage buildings, the balloon may be allowed to deflate over the stored goods, and then inflated only when entering).

(3) The single balloon must be kept fairly air tight.[61]

(4) With air sandwich walls, the building need not be pressurized inside, but buildings use more materials and pressures are greater, requiring compressors.[61]

Uses

Military uses include radomes, towers, parabolic antennas, shelters, missile maintenance shops, hangars, hospitals, storage buildings. Among commercial uses are: store rooms, construction shelters, swimming pool enclosures, physical education arenas, theaters, exhibition halls, field classrooms, shops, reservoir covers, temporary banks, air inflatable molds, shelters for winter construction[67] reservoir covers.[69]

History: Inflatable buildings seem to have been first conceived in 1946 at Cornell Aeronautical Laboratories as a unique solution to U. S. Air Force requirements for lightweight portable weather-resistant radome shelters to house large early-warning radar antennas.

This program was under the direction of Walter W. Bird. In late 1955, Bird and some of his associates left Cornell to form an organization aimed at the development of civilian uses for inflated buildings.[63,65]

By 1960, Bird's business had grown to about $1,000,000.[61] The buildings looked so deceptively simple that about 50 companies had entered into the competition; these were mainly manufacturers of tents, awnings, tarpaulins and parachutes. But successful design of inflated buildings requires knowledge of materials, assembly knowhow and engineering sophistication; consequently, participation in the field has narrowed appreciably.

A few examples illustrate the wide range of building types and uses.

In 1960, the AEC had built the inflated buildings shown in Figure 4-11. This is an exhibition building designed to be transported from city to city in South America. The exhibit was part of the U.S. Atoms for Peace Program, a complete movable laboratory with technical facilities to show the atom at work in power, agriculture, medicine and industry. The structure encloses 22,000 square feet of floor space. It is 300 feet long, 126 feet wide and 53.6 feet high. Unlike the usual inflated building, this one has undulating sides and roof, but the ends are sealed by rigid end frames. The total weight of the building including hardware and frames, blowers, doors, etc., is about 28 tons; of this, the fabric weighs less than 6 tons. Time to erect the building is 3 to 4 days. Any other buildings considered by the architect would take 5 to 20 times as long to set up.

The world's largest air-supported structure was the construction shelter and radome built for the Telstar project in Maine.[65] Figure 4-12 shows the 210-foot spherical diameter 160 foot high construction shelter which permitted construction of the satellite communication antenna in Maine during the winter months.

An inflated spherical building was put up by City Federal Savings in Union, New Jersey, as a temporary bank while the new building was being erected just across the way.[68] The building was a unique and highly successful advertisement and permitted an earlier than usual start in business.

One of the largest selling items in the inflated building market is shelters for swimming pools erected for about $1.50/sq ft.[61]

Another interesting application was use of a small inflated building for a form on which glass fiber and polyester resin was sprayed to give a rigid structure about $12 \times 24 \times 6$ feet high. The inflated mold weighed only 25 pounds.[71] A somewhat similar but earlier application was use of inflated rubberized fabric as molds on which concrete was sprayed to form shells for some houses in Florida.

FIG. 4-11. "Telstar" construction shelter and radome shown above is the world's largest air supported structure, designed and manufactured by Birdair for the Bell Telephone Laboratories' Project Telstar. Measuring 210 ft spherical diameter, the 160 ft high construction shelter permitted "shirt sleeve" construction of the satellite communication antenna in Maine during the winter months. Upon completion of the antenna, the construction shelter was replaced by a Birdair-manufactured air supported radome of the same size and shape to provide permanent, year-round, all-weather protection for the antenna. (*Courtesy Birdair Structures, Inc.*)

Building Characteristics

Sizes and Shapes. Inflated buildings have ordinarily been built in the shape of spheres, or portions thereof, or cylinder halves. The main requirement is that the surface be a surface of revolution or combinations of

FIG. 4-12. AEC exhibit structure designed in collaboration with architect Victor A. Lundy, this Birdair structure is an integral part of the U. S. Atomic Energy Commission's "Atoms-for-Peace" South American tour. Providing 22,000 sq ft of theater and exhibit space, the 300 ft long structure is 126 ft wide and 54 ft high. Many special design features were incorporated to satisfy specific functional requirements and provide unquestionable occupant safety.

such surfaces. Thus, tapered cylinders, half cylinders with undulating sides, and spheres with hemispherical bay windows have been constructed. There seems to be no insurmountable limit to size of these buildings; they could cover large stadiums or conceivably even whole farms and cities.

Package Sizes. A structure such as the Atoms for Peace building, 126 feet wide and 300 feet long, could contain a volume of roughly 2 million cubic feet and yet be packed, as was that one, in a volume equivalent to 1 boxcar. Ratios of package size to inflated building size of 1/400 to 1/1000 are apparently easily achievable. This portability is an important advantage.

Internal Pressures. Internal pressures commonly used in these buildings are 5 to 10 lb/sq ft or roughly 1 to 2 inches of water. These pressures can be obtained with simple blower systems. A 1-horsepower centrifugal blower with a capacity of 6600 cu ft/min. is reported to keep a 40 × 80 foot building

inflated, such that it will withstand a 70 mile/hr wind or the weight of a man walking across the top.[67] The smaller swimming pool shelters can be supported at 5 lb/sq ft by small ⅓-horsepower blowers, the same power as a 100-watt bulb.[61] On the other hand, those structures constructed as air sandwiches may require pressures of 15 to 20 psi and greater; hence, blowers are inadequate and air compressors must be used. A compensatory feature is that the inflated wall constructions have much less leakage. The internally inflated buildings require that the blowers make up losses occasioned by entry and exit of men and machines.

Hold Down. While the usual building with which we are familiar requires a foundation to support the weight of the building, these new inflated structures must be held down! Though internal pressures are low, areas are great and the lifting forces are tremendous. For instance, at 5 lb/sq ft, the 40 × 80 foot building exerts a lift of about 7 tons, and this without any added lift by wind. Two methods of holding down the internally pressured buildings are commonly used. One is to fasten the bottom perimeter of the building to pipe which is anchored to the ground by stakes set into the ground or into concrete. The other is to sew a tube around the perimeter of the building and to fill this tube with sufficient water or sand to counter-balance the lifting forces. A typical 80 × 40 × 20 foot high building is weighted with 23,000 pounds of water contained in such a tube 15 inches in diameter.[66]

Conditions of the base therefore impose almost no limits on the erection of inflated buildings. Thus it has been possible to erect temporary banks in parking lots and emergency hospitals in open fields.

Stress and Loading. The internal pressures may be low; but the skin stresses developed can be quite high. For example, this 40-foot cylindrical building of 10-mil material would undergo, in still air, a hoop stress of about 580 psi or 70 lb/linear ft of perimeter. The simple static tensile forces can be approximated by the following formulas:

For hemispheres $\quad S = \dfrac{PD}{48t}$

For half cylinders with hemispherical ends

$$S = \frac{PW(L - 215W)}{13.7t[W + 1.75L]}$$

where

S = stress, psi
P = internal pressure, lb/sq ft
D = diameter of sphere, ft
W = width of half cylinder building, ft
L = total length of half cylinder building, ft
t = material thickness, in.

Superimposed on these stresses are those created by wind. These are proportional to the square of wind velocity, the actual values depending on building shape as well as size. Despite this, well-designed inflated structures will withstand strong winds, the Atoms for Peace exhibit building being designed to withstand steady winds of 70 miles per hour with gusts to 90 miles per hour.

Entry. Entry to internally inflated buildings is normally through some type of air lock. If only occasional personnel access is required, this can be provided by a simple zippered opening. In this case, opening may be accompanied by a noticeable slackening of tension in the top. More typical is use of a revolving door or a tunnel-like entrance with doors at each end. The inflated-wall buildings, of course, are usually not internally inflated and thus do not have entry restrictions.

Economics

Where inflated buildings will adequately perform, substantial savings can often be realized. For example, the aforementioned 80 foot × 40 foot × 20 foot high building[66] was reported in May 1957, to be available at under $1/sq ft, or roughly 6½¢/cu ft when comparable prefabricated metal buildings were selling for $3/sq ft. The AEC Atoms for Peace building[62] cost more—$4.50/sq ft—because of its size: 300 feet long by 126 feet wide and 53.6 feet high at the peak. Double-wall construction was used and the building was pressured both internally and between walls. Its costs (reported November 1960) were $99,870 plus $25,000 erection work at the site, excluding site preparation. Estimating the volume at 2 million cubic feet, the original cost was approximately 5¢/cu ft with erection costing about 3¼¢/cu ft more, including $40,000 for site preparation.

One of the latest reports concerns an inflated building owned by the Bonneville Power Administration.[70,72] This building is 200 feet × 100 feet × 58 feet high and is kept at a normal pressure of 7 lb/sq ft. Pressured to 20 lb/sq ft it will withstand a 100 mile/hr wind. It weighs 7000 pounds and cost as reported in February, 1964, $29,000. This is $1.45/sq ft, nearly one-third less than alternate structures. Its volume cost was less than 4¢/cu ft.

REFERENCES

Moisture Barriers and Protective Covers

1. ASTM, "Standards on Plastics," 13th Ed. Philadelphia, Pa. American Society for Testing Materials, November, 1962.
2. Curtis, F. W., "Vinyl Film as a Roof Vapor Barrier Building," Research Institute. Report of a Meeting at Washington University, pp. 16–18 (1957).

3. *Engineering News Record*, 25 (March, 1957).

4. Forest Products Laboratory, "Condensation Control in Dwelling Construction" Washington, D. C., Housing and Home Finance Agency, 1950.

5. Gering Plastics, Ger-Pak Polyethylene News, Informa Sheet No. 2, Kenilworth, N. J., 1961.

8. Imperial Chemical Industries Ltd. "Plastics in Building Welwyn Garden City, Hertfordshire, England," pp. 63–65.

9. Joy, F., Penn State University, private Communication, Nov. 8, 1963.

10. *Modern Plastics*, 218 (November, 1957).

11. Mooney, W. B. "Plastics, How Contractors Use Them," reprint from Construction Methods, New York, McGraw Hill Book Co., Inc., 1962.

12. National Research Council, Building Research Advisory Board "Protection from Moisture" Publication 707, Washington, D. C., 1959.

13. National Research Council, Building Research Advisory Board "Vapor Materials for Use with Slab-on-Ground Construction and as Ground Cover in Crawl Spaces" NRC Publication 445, Washington, D. C., 1956.

14. National Bureau of Standards, Commercial Standard CS-238-61 "Polyethylene Sheeting" (Construction, Industrial and Agricultural Applications), Washington, D.C.

15. Novak, W. J., "Electrical Construction and Maintenance," p. 95–96 (June, 1961); pp. 112–114 September, (1961).

16. Phillips Petroleum Company, "Handbook of Polyethylene Standards and Specifications," Bartlesville, Oklahoma.

17. Scheffer, T. C., and Clark, N. J., *Forest Products J*. 330–336, (August, 1963).

18. Schram, J. F., *Building Products*, 7, No. 11 17–20 (1961).

19. Sears, Roebuck, "Fall and Winter Catalog," Philadelphia, Pa., 1962.

20. Thor, C. J. B., and Rogers, T. S., "Plastic Film Vapor Barriers," Building 3 Research Institute, Report of Meeting at University of Michigan, pp 33–38, Washington, D. C., 1956.

21. Union Carbide Corporation, Bakelite Review, pp. 14–15, New York (October, 1962).

22. Union Carbide Corporation, Plastics Division, "Visqueen Film Water Vapor Barrier," Chicago, Illinois, 1959.

23. Whippo, H. M., and Arnberg, B. T., "Survey and Analysis of the Vapor Transmission Properties of Building Materials," PB. 131219, Washington, D. C., United States Department of Commerce, 1955.

Forms for Concrete

24. *Building Products*, 6 (September, 1963).

25. Cincinnati Milling Machine Company, "Cimastra FRP Publication," No. C-303, Cincinnati, Ohio.

26. *Construction Methods and Equipment*, 7, No. 2, 44–45 (February, 1962).

27. *Engineering News Record*, **168**, 30–32 (February 22, 1962).

28. *Engineering News Record*, **170**, 39 (March 28, 1963).

29. Hromadik, J. J., and Bliss, R. A., "Multipurpose Mobilization Building," Tech. Report R196, June 25, 1962, U. S. Naval Civil Engineering Laboratory, Port Hueneme, California.

30. Imperial Chemical Industries Ltd., Welwyn Garden City, Hertfordshire, England, *Plastics in Building*, 26.

31. Kirby, R. J., *Concrete Construction*, 7 (7) 203–204 (July, 1962).

32. *Modern Plastics*, **35**, 126–129 (November, 1957).

33. Molded Fiber Glass Company, Ashtabula, Ohio, "Molded Fiber Glass Waffle-Slab Forming Pans." (Prepared by Morrison and Gottlieb, New York.)

34. Molded Fiber Glass Company, Ashtabula, Ohio, "Molded Fiber Glass Forms Give Stone-Smooth Facade for Concrete Apartments," (Prepared by Morrison and Gottlieb, New York.)

35. Mooney, W. G., "Plastics—How Contractors Use Them," Construction Methods and Equipment, New York, Reprint, pp. 20–23, 1962.

36. *Plastics Technol*, **7**, 69 (November, 1961).

37. *Plastics World*, 62 (November, 1962).

Silicone Water Repellents

38. *Architectural Record*, **120**, 265 (October, 1956).

39. Cahn, H. L., *Paint Industry Magazine*, 18–22 (April, 1961).

40. Hurst, H., *Rubber Developments*, **14**, (4) 110–117 (1961–62).

41. Mitchell, W. B., *Journal of American Concrete Institute*, **29**, 51, 7 (July, 1957).

42. Sonneborn Chemical and Refining Corporation, Building Products Division, "Hydroxide S-X Trycon," New York, N. Y., April, 1960.

43. Sonneborn Chemical and Refining Corporation, Building Products Division, "Technical Data Guide No. 44," New York, N. Y., June, 1962.

44. Union Carbide Corporation, Silicones Division, "Union Carbide R-27 Silicone Water Repellent for Surface Treatment of Exposed Aggregate Concrete," New York, N. Y., June, 1963.

45. Union Carbide Corporation, Silicones Division, "R-27 Silicone for the Formulation of Silicone Masonry Water Repellents," New York, N. J.

46. Roofing, Siding and Insulation, "Weatherproofing the Free Form Roof with Waterproofing," pp. 15–17 (December, 1961).

Resins for Modifying Concrete

47. Adhesive Engineering, San Carlos, California, Technical Data Bull., No. AEX-118, February, 1962.

48. *Chemical and Engineering News*, "Semi Annual Report on Current Chemical Prices," 75 (February 3, 1964).

49. Dow Chemical Company, Midland, Michigan, "Dow Latex 560 for Portland Cement Compositions," January, 1960.
50. Geist, J. M., Amagna, S. V., and Mellor, B. B., *Ind. Eng. Chem.*, **45**, No. 4, 759–767 (1953).
51. *House and Home*, 181 (May, 1962).
52. Huff, L., Private Communication, January, 1964.
53. *Modern Plastics*, **32**, No. 9, 115 (May, 1962).
54. Monfore, *ASTM Bull.*, 30, (January, 1943).
55. Raybestos-Manhattan, Inc., Bridgeport, Connecticut, "Raybestos Threadline Mortar," R-100, 1961.
56. Raybestos-Manhattan, Inc., Bridgeport, Connecticut, "Raybestos Threadline Mortar Technical Bulletins, Nos. 1, 1a, 2, 3, 4, 5," 1961.
57. Rohm & Haas Company, Philadelphia, Pennsylvania, "Emulsion MC 4530," August, 1958 (Rev. April, 1960).
58. Rohm & Haas Company, Philadelphia, Pennsylvania, "Resin Review," Spring, 1963.
59. Tyler, O. Z., and Drak, R. S., *Adhesive Age*, 30–39 (September, 1961).
60. U. S. Army Engineer Waterways Experiment Station, "Review of Available Information on Polyvinyl Acetate as an Admixture for Concrete," Vicksburg, Miss., Technical Report No. 6-486, July, 1958.

Inflated Buildings

61. Allison, D., "Those Ballooning Air Buildings," *Architectural Forum* (July, 1959).
62. Allison, D., "A Great Balloon for Peaceful Atoms," *Architectural Forum* (November, 1960).
63. *Architectural Forum*, **156** 160–162 (April, 1957).
64. Bird, W., Private Communication, December, 1963.
65. Birdair Structures Inc., Buffalo, New York, "Air Supported Structures for Military, Commercial and Industrial Applications."
66. *Compressed Air Magazine*, **62**, 147 (May, 1957).
67. *The Constructor*, 30–32 (Augusta, 1960).
68. *The Daily Journal*, Elizabeth, New Jersey (June 3, 1960).
69. Kay, W. B., *Public Works*, 107 (October, 1962).
70. *Plastics World*, **22**, No. 2, 14 (February, 1964).
71. Schramp, J. M., Stabler, G. J., McCormick, J. E., and Gurdo, A. F., "15th Annual Technical and Management Conference; Reinforced Plastics Division," The Society of the Plastics Industry Inc., Sec. 17A pp. 1–10 (February, 1960).
72. United States Department of the Interior, Bonneville Power Administration, "Extra High Voltage Direct Current Test Center."

5 STRUCTURAL FIBER GLASS–REINFORCED PLASTICS FOR BUILDING APPLICATIONS

RICHARD E. CHAMBERS

Simpson Gumpertz & Heger Inc.
Consulting Engineers
Cambridge, Massachusetts

INTRODUCTION

Fiber glass–reinforced plastics* are structural composites comprised of components that, individually, have no particular attributes as structural materials. Bundles of fine, almost invisible, very strong glass fibers are bound in various controllable patterns within a matrix of moldable, fluid resin which can be hardened to a rigid state. The glass fibers, independently, have limited structural form except perhaps as fabrics. The resins, independently, offer little in the way of structural properties, and while they are basically moldable, when cast in large sections they warp, shrink and crack. However, when the components are combined, the resin imparts form and structural continuity to the filaments, and the filaments in turn provide strength and dimensional stability to the resin. The composite is crudely analogous to reinforced concrete, but because of the scale of the components, it more closely compares to the Ferro-Cementé—a mixture of fine wire and cement grout—introduced by Nervi in the early 1940's.

Fiber glass–reinforced plastics are well-known and respected engineering materials. Segments of the boat-building, automotive, aircraft, missile and electronics industries

* Fiber glass–reinforced plastics are abbreviated as RP and FRP by the industry. FRP will be used in this text.

now depend heavily on some of the unique properties or characteristics offered by glass-in-plastic structural systems. Indeed, the building industry has had some extensive exposure to FRP in interior decorative panels, in skylights and corrugated roofing panels, translucent sidewalls and in concrete formwork. Exciting structures such as the early Monsanto House of the Future, the American Pavilion in Moscow (1959), the American Pavilion at Brussels (1958), and a host of other imaginative structures at the Seattle (1962), and New York (1964) World's Fairs serve to demonstrate that FRP can be engineered to serve major structural tasks.

An immense amount of data have been generated, particularly in the last decade, on the behavior of reinforced plastics systems. The architect or building engineer, faced for the first time with the task of designing a reinforced plastic structure, not only must master the basic aspects of working with this unique material and its behavior; the designer is also faced with a formidable amount of literature from which to draw needed details. Thus, the purpose of this chapter is to set forth the important considerations that should be recognized and understood by the designer of fiber glass–reinforced plastic-based building structures. Even when the scope is narrowed to building applications, the degree to which components and hence properties can be varied is still so wide as to preclude detailed discussion of all possible parameters and their interactions.

Although an attempt is made to be as definitive and quantitative as possible, in many respects this section should be considered as an introduction to FRP materials as they apply to building structures. A selected bibliography is included for those who wish to pursue particular phases of the subject in further detail.

A distinction should be made between the kinds of components that can be considered for building applications. First, there are the proprietary, standard items of manufacture, such as flat and corrugated sheet, some sandwich panels and the like. Second, there are the "custom" structures designed for a given application by the architect or engineer. Structural capabilities and manufacturing processes for the proprietary items have usually been established in fair detail; hence, little difficulty should be encountered in incorporating them into a design. But if the building designer is to custom-tailor his own original structure, much more should be known of the basic characteristics and behavior of the material and the types of manufacturing processes that are available to him. While it is hoped that much of this chapter will be generally applicable to both types of components, the chapter is oriented specifically as an aid to the designer of original structures.

EXISTING STRUCTURAL APPLICATIONS

To provide the reader with some insight into fiber glass-reinforced plastics as engineering materials, some of the highly successful applications of the material will be reviewed. While some of these applications lie outside of the building field, they are particularly noteworthy because they demonstrate how fiber glass-reinforced plastics have offered unique solutions to a range of product demands. In the building field, too, fiber glass-reinforced plastics have made significant contributions. The list of major applications is growing so rapidly that only the historically significant ones will be discussed.

Military and Commercial Products

Marine Applications. Reinforced plastics are now the predominant materials of the pleasure craft market. They have been particularly effective in replacing wood because of the following factors:

(1) Design: Molding of hydrodynamic and aesthetic forms can be easily accomplished.

(2) Manufacture: Expensive operations of cutting, fitting, assembly, and finishing that are required in wood constructions are reduced or eliminated.

(3) Structure: Continuous shell forms can be developed with the stiff, strong, impact-resistant FRP systems.

(4) Customer appeal: Crisp, bright, colored auto-like finishes and forms encourage initial acceptance, while low maintenance, rot resistance, and built-in color provide long-term appeal.

Marine floats and decks are also gaining acceptance for many of the same reasons. Durability, low maintenance, and favorable economics have led to heavy use of reinforced plastics for large military craft and submarine components.

Automobile and Truck Bodies. Fiber glass-reinforced plastics are used regularly in the manufacture of certain sports car bodies and truck cabs. Strength, stiffness, toughness, corrosion resistance and high-quality finishes are the obvious functional needs that must be satisfied, but economics is the crucial consideration governing the choice of FRP over conventional formed steel.

Since FRP can be molded at low pressures, the tooling required can be much lighter and hence less expensive than that used to form sheet steel. Tooling costs become critical in the relatively small production runs involved in these specialty automotive products and can compensate for the increased raw materials costs of FRP over steel. The production level below which FRP is favored over steel will, of course, vary with the nature of the part and the

(a)

(b)

FIG. 5-1. Interior and exterior view of large diameter radomes. (a) Interior view shows geodesic type space frame in which FRP skins and ribs are integrally molded and subsequently bolted together in the field. (b) Exterior view shows geodesic-type aluminum space frame over which thin membranes of FRP have been placed.

FIG. 5-2. The Monsanto House of the Future, the first application in which FRP was used as a building structure. Free-standing FRP "U" bents are cantilevered from the foundation and form a monolithic floor–end wall–roof system.

production facilities available; the break-even point falls at yearly production levels on the order of thousands of units.[1]

Radomes. (Figure 5-1). Spherical radomes based on either the geodesic or sandwich shell structural framing system are fabricated in many cases exclusively of fiber glass–reinforced plastics. The domes range up to 150 feet in diameter and are designed to resist hurricane wind forces. Fiber glass–reinforced plastics are uniquely qualified for this application because they offer good structural properties and yet they permit passage of electromagnetic radar signals with little attenuation. In some geodesic designs, the moldability of the material allows integral rib and skin construction. In other sandwich shell arrangements, moldability allows the generation of doubly warped spherical segments.[2,3]

Rocket Motor Cases. Solid fuel rocket motor cases house the propellant for many of our existing missiles. These cases are fabricated in the form of a cylinder having dome ends

by the very efficient filament winding process Projected size of these units ranges up to 22 feet in diameter and 40 feet long. The crucial consideration is strength per unit weight, and in this application, fiber glass–reinforced systems offer the highest attainable values.[4]

Pipe and Tanks for Chemicals. The chemical industry has found that fiber glass–reinforced pipe, tanks, and stacks are superior to stainless steel in many applications. While the critical consideration is corrosion resistance under extreme environments, the ease of fabrication of complex tank shapes and simplicity of connection details enhances the competitive cost picture.

Recently, a full-size railroad tank car was developed for use in transporting corrosive materials.[4] The 9-foot-diameter tank is 55 feet long; wall thickness is 3/8 of an inch. The structure is made by the filament winding process and represents a direct extension of the rocket motor case developments to a commercial application.

(a)

(b)

FIG. 5-3. The entire "bicycle wheel" roof (a) of the American Pavilion at Brussels (b) was covered with translucent FRP stress-skinned panels to provide soft natural interior lighting.

Building Applications

Monsanto House of the Future; Disneyland, California, 1956 (Figure 5-2). The Monsanto House of the Future represents the earliest full-scale use of reinforced plastics in a building application.[5] This building was designed to illustrate that new design concepts could be exploited through the use of moldable, strong, stiff, fiber glass–reinforced plastics.

The American Pavilion in Brussels, 1958 (Figure 5-3). The American Pavilion in Brussels represents the first large-volume application of fiber glass–reinforced plastics in a building application.[6] The entire circular roof, 300 feet in diameter and constructed of suspended cables, was covered with stressed-skin structural panels consisting of a glass-reinforced plastic skins bonded to a core of light aluminum gridwork. The requirements for this structure were that the roof be light in weight, easily installed, and translucent to provide natural interior lighting.

Panels similar to the above have seen extensive use in schools, churches, office buildings, and exhibition structures.

The American Pavilion in Moscow, 1959 (Figure 5-4). This structure was intended to provide a light airy, open shelter under which

FIG. 5-4. An array of delicate FRP "tulip" structures provided shelter for visitors to the American Pavilion in Moscow. Note the patterns created by local reinforcement at the ribs and column capitals.

various functions could be held.[7] The repetitive tulip shape column units were prefabricated in the United States and assembled at the site. This application demanded a moldable material to permit dramatic form, a prefabricated structure to allow rapid on-site fabrication with a minimum of U. S. technical personnel, a translucent structure to provide opportunity for natural and artificial lighting.

This application represents a particularly good example of architectural expression of material and structure. For structural reasons, local reinforcement was required at the top of the column section and at the edges of the panels. When backlighted from the sky, this local reinforcement appears darker than the thin translucent skins and creates a pattern that fully expresses the structural demands.

M.I.T. School, Cambridge, Massachusetts, 1959. The M.I.T. School represents a prototype study of a totally prefabricated, self-sustaining, modular classroom unit.[8] The concept here is that of installing standard package units with a minimum of site preparation. The roof of this building is a hyperbolic paraboloid sandwich, 8 feet square in plan, comprised of fiber glass-reinforced plastic skins separated by a low-density plastic core. Obviously, the need here is for a panel system that is light in weight and easily erected. FRP is considered as one material that answers this need.

Holiday Inn Jr., 1964 (Figure 5-5). Motel units represent another application where large-scale prefabrication using FRP is contemplated.[9] Units of four rooms are fully prefabricated including utilities and plumbing. FRP is used as the outer skin of the wall sandwich panels. Other areas where FRP has been employed are in an arched roof having a 6-foot span, and in cornice and sill bands. To date, a prototype unit has been erected, and several others are under construction. If full production is undertaken, this will probably represent the largest integrated building application of FRP.

Proprietary Items. There exists a number of proprietary FRP items that are regularly used in the building field. Translucent panels are used as sky-lights, glazing panels, roofing panels or as decorative screening. These materials are provided in the forms of flat sheet, corrugated sheet or as sandwich panels.

Concrete Forms. The moldability, strength, durability and surface finish of fiber glass–reinforced plastics are leading to increased use of the material in concrete formwork.[10] Early uses were in pans for grid-slab construction. Larger custom forms of complex shape have been used in such major structures as the Marina City Towers, Chicago, Illinois, the University Apartments, Hyde Park, Illinois, and in the multistory buildings of the Technology Square complex in Cambridge, Massachusetts. FRP is also extensively used in forms for precast concrete panels, and as a durable surface for plywood forms.

CHARACTERISTICS OF FIBER GLASS–REINFORCED PLASTICS

The applications discussed in the preceding section should provide an idea of the characteristics of fiber glass–reinforced plas-

FIG. 5-5. Fiber glass–reinforced plastics are used extensively in this low-cost prefabricated motel unit.

FIG. 5-6. Commercially available corrugated translucent FRP sheet materials provide durable side-walls and natural interior lighting for this storage warehouse.

tics that can contribute to successful structural usage. This section will serve to summarize and extend the attributes of the material as they may affect building applications. Limitations will also be discussed in order to provide an objective, balanced, total picture of FRP systems. Only through knowledge of both can the material be engineered with purpose and confidence to the objective of any good design, that is, to produce a system that embraces every possible advantage while the limitations are held to a tolerable level.

Attributes

Fabrication. Perhaps the greatest advantages accompanying the use of fiber glass–reinforced plastics relate to the ease with which the material can be fabricated and the variety of fabrication methods that are available. Principal benefits that can be derived from the materials' excellent fabricating characteristics are the following:

(a) *Process:* Processes can be selected to fit the full range of production levels—from a few special components for a single building, to unlimited members of like pieces for repetitive modular construction. Little or no pressure is required in the molding process and hence light, relatively inexpensive molds and molding equipment can be used.

(b) *Geometry:* There are few restrictions on the choice of geometry of the product; flat, corrugated, singly or doubly curved shapes can be easily fabricated in a wide range of sizes. Specific limits do exist; they depend upon the form of reinforcement, type of resin, mold cost, and manufacturing process. Problems in transportation provide another limit on practical size.

(c) *Texture:* The mold surface can be patterned to produce variations in the texture of the surface, or indeed the entire panel may be molded to achieve gross textural variations to create shadow details and the like.

(d) *Structural Detailing:* Local, gradual changes in thickness may be made as required, and ribs, and box or channel sections may be added to provide strength or stiffness in localized areas.

Fabrication will be considered in more detail beginning on p. 91 of this chapter.

Strength and Stiffness. Short-term ultimate strength of reinforced plastics varies from 10,000 to over 200,000 psi, while modulus of elasticity varies from about 0.5 to over 7×10^6 psi. Strength and stiffness are strongly dependent upon the type and relative quantity of resin and reinforcement, the manufacturer, and the manufacturing process used. The section of this chapter beginning on p. 108 is devoted to considerations of these factors.

Low Weight. Density of fiber glass–reinforced plastics is on the order of 100 lb/cu ft. The low density of this strong, stiff material allows the use of light sections. In addition to the structural advantages offered by such

(a)

(b)

FIG. 5-7. Fiber glass–reinforced plastic sandwich construction permits the use of large lightweight sections in the Marina structures at the New York World's Fair (1964). In upper photo, roof section is supported by crane and "column" support is shown inverted at left.

lightweight sections, there are potential benefits in shipping, handling and erection.

Light Transmission. The light-transmission characteristics can be tailored from nearly transparent, although never as clear as glass, to totally opaque. The translucency is, of course, a unique property offered by no other truly structural material.

(c)

Fig. 5-7 (continued)

Color and Color Variations. Fiber glass-reinforced plastics can be dyed or pigmented to virtually any color or color intensity. In addition, random or regular colors or patterns can be obtained through spattering, mottling, or the incorporation of printed paper sheets into the laminate.

Corrosion and Chemical Resistance. While corrosion resistance depends to some degree on the resin formulation used, reinforced plastics can usually be considered inert to normal industrial atmospheres.

Insulation. Fiber glass–reinforced plastics are good thermal and electrical insulators.

Limitations

Fire and Temperature Resistance. The resinous component of fiber glass–reinforced plastics composites, being organic in chemical structure, will burn. While totally fireproof resins have not been forthcoming, the industry has been successful in reducing the degree to which resins will contribute to fire spread. This is done by molecular tailoring of the chemical structure of the resin molecule or by incorporating fire-inhibiting additives into the resin mixture. This subject will be considered in more detail in the section beginning on p. 89.

The glass-in-plastic systems will lose strength when exposed to high temperatures. Both the glass and the resinous components are responsible for this. Most systems will not suffer significantly under ambient temperatures normally found in buildings, but when heated to a few hundred degrees, the properties of the material degrade rapidly. Because of this, temperature rise due to fire, even though the material may not be ignited, may reduce the strength and stiffness of the structure.

Effects of Weather and Sunlight. Reinforced plastics systems vary considerably in their resistance to the effects of outdoor environment. There are tendencies to dull, discolor, lose translucency, or erode. These effects can be reduced substantially by proper choice and careful design of the components of the system; this will be discussed later in this chapter (see pp. 91 and 111).

Stress History. Many claims are made regarding the strength capabilities of FRP laminates which are based on conventional test values. But working stresses must be kept well below short-time test values if long-term or cyclic loads must be carried. The design section of this chapter deals with this subject in detail.

Cost. A number of factors such as type and quality of resin and reinforcement, and num-

FIG. 5-8. Gaily painted FRP shell roof structures of sandwich construction are used with a steel supporting framework to form the "7-UP" Pavilion at the New York World's Fair (1964).

ber and complexity of units, will obviously influence the cost of components. Judging from other similar applications, it would be expected that structural building components should cost about $1.25 to $1.50 per pound. For the unit cost to fall below this range, the component would have to be produced in a quantity sufficient to justify the setup and tooling of a highly automated manufacturing process, and inexpensive materials would have to be employed. The unit cost could easily exceed the price range given if details are complex, if the production run is small, or if expensive resins or reinforcements are used.

In comparing the cost of FRP systems with other materials, the density of the material must be taken into account. On a volume basis, the cost of the material falls into the price range of some forms of aluminum.

Acoustics. Fiber glass–reinforced plastics can be tailored into very efficient, lightweight, thin-skinned systems, that are highly elastic. These factors combine to yield a structure that efficiently transmits and radiates sound. Such light-weight elastic members provide little barrier to noise; hence, rain impinging on thin skins or wind fluttering a light membrane can create noise problems within a structure. The architect should consider acoustic treatment if reinforced plastics are to house sound-sensitive areas.

Compatibility of Attributes. The preceding sections deal with the often-quoted characteristics of FRP composites with particular emphasis on those that apply to building applications. Seldom, however, can a given component possess all of the attributes (or limitations) that have been mentioned. There are important compromises that must be struck when materials capabilities, aesthetics, choice of process, and economics are considered; insofar as is possible, these will be treated in detail in later sections of this chapter.

THE MATERIALS

There are three primary elements that comprise a fiber glass–reinforced plastic structural system. First, there is the fibrous glass element which reinforces and gives strength to the laminate. Next, there is the resinous component which is in itself a system that binds and forms the fibrous element into a useful structure. And finally, there is a finish, or coupling agent, whose precise role remains elusive, but whose intended role is to enhance adhesion between the resinous and the fibrous components of the laminate. This section is intended to acquaint the reader with these components, and the forms in which they are available.

There are other secondary components that may be present in FRP composites which usually take the form of fillers. Fillers are used sometimes to reduce cost by displacing a volume of more expensive materials, but this is seldom done in truly structural laminates. More often, fillers may be added to color a laminate or in some cases to harden the surface of a composite. Fillers can also be used to modify the viscosity and flow characteristics of the resin during processing or to control the quantity or quality of the light transmitted through a laminate. Since fillers are seldom used in high concentrations, they have little influence on structural performance. Therefore, they will not be considered in detail as a component of structural laminates.

Fibrous Glass

"E" Glass. The basic glass composition usually used in common glass-fiber reinforcements for structural laminates was decided upon early in the history of fiber glass-reinforced plastics. The bulk material from which fibers are drawn was first developed for electrical applications and thus the term "E" (electrical) glass has been applied to it, and the fibers made from it. "E" glass is a lime-alumina borosilicate composition which is low in soda content. The demands of certain military applications have resulted in the development of glasses of higher strength and/or modulus than "E" glass, but their premium costs presently exclude them from consideration in building applications.

Manufacture. The usual process used to

manufacture glass fibers is simple and highly automated. Molten glass is allowed to flow from a heated reservoir through an array of small orifices or "bushings." The melt is attenuated into a filament by drawing the molten material from the bushing at high velocity. At some point in the continuous process, the attenuated material "freezes" into the solid fiber form. Fiber diameter is controlled to within close limits by control of the drawing speed, melt temperature and other variables. Usually 204 filaments are combined to form a bundle("strand," "end"). Bundles are then combined to form multi-end continuous roving, or they are twisted together and used as a yarn in the manufacture of fabrics.

Properties of Fibrous Glass. Glass fibers that are used as reinforcement for plastics are extremely fine; they range from 20 to 75×10^{-5} inches in diameter. The modulus of elasticity of fibers is 10.5×10^6 psi which is near that of bulk glass. If extreme precautions are taken in handling, preparing and testing glass fibers, observed strength can exceed one-half million psi; this is orders of magnitude above the strength of the bulk glass.

The reason for the high strength of fibrous glass has not been clearly established—primarily because it is difficult to control simultaneously all of the parameters that can affect strength. It has been shown that the molecular structure is not oriented in the drawing process; hence, this can be discounted as a contributing factor. A second theory proposes that a favorable molecular structure is frozen into the fiber because of the rapid cooling rate that the fiber undergoes during drawing. There is some evidence to bear this out. A third postulation does not account for all observed phenomena relating to the strength of fibrous glass, but does appear to be a rational explanation for many. This theory proposes that the marked difference in strength between bulk and fibrous glass is due to the relative number and severity of flaws existing in the two cases. It is reasoned that glass, being brittle, should be highly sensitive to flaws or stress

concentrations that are caused by abrasion, corrosion or other damage of the surface. It is further reasoned that a statistical distribution of flaw severity must exist, and thus, the chances of a severe flaw occurring in a given surface area must be a function of the size of that area. Thus, chances are that as fiber length is increased (diameter fixed), or as fiber diameter is increased (length fixed), a corresponding decrease in strength should be observed. These effects have been noted experimentally. It can also be reasoned that if extreme precautions are taken such that no flaws are present, there should be no effect of fiber size. This, too, has been verified experimentally.

When glass is used in fiber form, it is more sensitive to environment than is bulk glass. Water or humidity, abrasion, and attack by chemicals caused marked decreases in strength. These effects of exposure are not seen on bulk glass because the density of flaws is so great that the already low strength is not appreciably lowered by environmental attack. Clearly, care in handling and storage of fibrous glass prior to lamination and subsequent protection by the resin after fabrication are essential if the initial high strength of the glass component is to be preserved.

Forms of Reinforcement

The fabricator and, hence, the designer has a generous selection of forms of fiber glass-reinforcement from which to choose. The number of types is so great that they cannot all be considered here. Rather typical representative forms that should be of greatest interest have been selected for discussion.

There are several considerations that should govern the choice of specific reinforcements. While the criteria for selection will rest with the particular application, the following are usually critical:

(a) *Strength and stiffness:* Strength and stiffness of a laminate can easily vary by an order of magnitude depending upon the choice of reinforcement.

(b) *Directional properties:* Reinforcements

can be selected or arranged to best fit one-dimensional, two-dimensional, or isotropic states of stress.

(c) *Structure:* Open, loosely packed types of reinforcements permit the usually viscous resins to saturate the fiber network and provide channels for the escape of air that is entrapped during laminating. Thus, the effort expended in fabrication is much lower than that required for tightly bound fiber systems.

(d) *Drape:* Supple, loose reinforcements are desired because they can be easily shaped to meet sharp single, or double curvatures.

(e) *Bulk:* A given laminate thickness can be built up rapidly if heavy, bulky reinforcements are employed. Hence, savings in labor and time are gained if such reinforcements can be used in place of thin, fine-textured varieties.

(f) *Economics:* All of the above considerations will have their influence on the economics of the reinforcement for a given application, and in addition, there is over a 3 to 1 difference in per pound price among the common types of reinforcements.

filament winding, sprayup or other processing methods (these methods will be discussed in detail beginning on p. 94).

Woven Roving. Woven roving is made by weaving bulky, multi-end, continuous roving into the form of a simple heavy fabric. The material is supplied in both "balanced" and unidirectional constructions; the balanced construction has approximately equal quantities of material in the warp and fill directions,* whereas the unidirectional weaves have the majority of the fibers lying parallel to the warp direction.

Woven roving is an attractive reinforcement for several reasons. First, the material is inexpensive because the size of the strand and the simplicity of the weave permit rapid economical manufacturing processes to be used. The bulk of the material contributes to further economies during fabrication. And finally, the mechanical properties of woven roving-based laminates are reasonably high.

The principal disadvantages of woven roving are associated with the heavy coarse texture of its weave. Molding of the material over sharp, single or double curvatures

TABLE 5-1. Typical Fiber-Glass Reinforcements

Type of Reinforcement	Tensile Strength* (lb/in. of width) Warp	Fill	Thickness (in.)	Weight (oz/sq yd)	Cost** ($/lb)	Structure	Drape
Roving (continuous strand)	—	—	—	—	0.32	—	—
Woven roving	1000	900	0.040	24.2	0.46	Tight	Fair
Mat	—	—	Varies	18	0.46	Open	Good
10-oz fabric	440	405	0.013	9.7	1.23	Open	Excellent
181 fabric	340	330	0.0085	8.9	2.00	Tight	Excellent
143 fabric	675	56	0.009	8.9	2.12	Tight	Excellent

* This is a calculated value, and as such it merely indicates the relative quantity of material in each direction.
** Cost is based on quantity order in mid-1966. Since costs will vary, the figures quoted should be considered as approximate.

Table 5-1 summarizes pertinent data on the selected typical reinforcements, and the following sections provide a brief description of other pertinent characteristics.

Continuous Roving. Continuous roving is the least expensive form of glass reinforcement since it is essentially a raw material. It can be used directly by the fabricator in

becomes difficult and some trouble is encountered in impregnating the tight-knit weave with viscous resins. Also, the coarse texture of the fabric will be evident on the

*The "warp" direction indicates the direction of manufacture or the continuous direction of a fabric. The "fill" direction is perpendicular to the warp direction in the plane of the fabric.

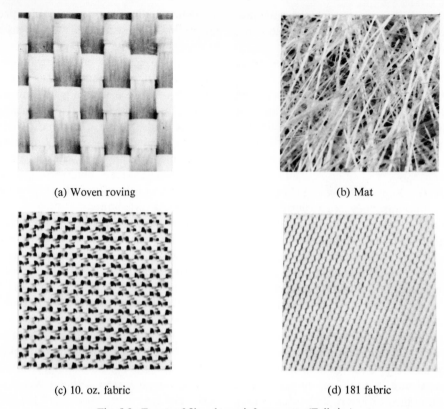

(a) Woven roving

(b) Mat

(c) 10. oz. fabric

(d) 181 fabric

Fig. 5-9. Forms of fiberglass reinforcement. (Full size)

surface of laminates unless special surface reinforcements are used. And finally, the gross geometry of the weave creates weak shear planes in woven roving-based laminates that are reflected in relatively low interlaminar strength.

Mat. Mat is a nonwoven reinforcement that is built up from a deposition of randomly oriented continuous or chopped strand. For handling purposes, the mat is lightly impregnated with an organic resin binder which serves to "tack" neighboring fibers together. This mat-making process is simple and well automated; hence, mat is an inexpensive reinforcement. Mat finds heavy use in structural applications because it is easy to work, it conforms reasonably well to contours, and it is inexpensive. It also leaves a reasonably smooth and even-textured laminate surface. Many times, mat will be alternated with plies of woven roving to increase interlaminar shear strength and to enhance surface appearance and quality. Properties of mat-reinforced laminates fall

on the low end of the range available in fiber glass–reinforced plastics.

Very thin surface or "veil" mats (developed from continuous strand) are often used for surfacing of laminates. These continuous mats create a resin rich surface layer that is free of fiber ends. The result is an attractive fine-textured surface that is more chemical and weather resistant than surfaces created by the coarser structural reinforcement.

Nonwoven-Unidirectional-Fabric. Nonwoven-unidirectional-fabric,[11] a proprietary reinforcement,* is a sheet material that is developed from parallel continuous strand. Transverse strands are bonded at 3-inch intervals across the sheet to keep the filaments in place during handling and fabrication. Cost of this material is said to be in the range of mat reinforcements, and this is probably due to the low cost of conversion of inexpensive continuous strand into this fabric form.

* NUF—A product of Ferro Corp., Nashville, Tennessee.

The principal advantages of nonwoven-unidirectional-fabric relate to cost and to rather respectable mechanical properties. Properties are said to lie in the range of those attainable with the more exotic fabric systems (e.g., 181 and 143 fabrics—see following discussions). Disadvantages of the material pertain to fabrication. Nonwoven-unidirectional-fabric does not drape as well as other fabrics, and it does not have the "give" of mat reinforcements; therefore, some difficulty should be encountered in forming the material to sharp double curvatures. Some other fabrication problems are introduced since the strands are unsupported between cross bands.

10-ounce Fabric—"Boat Cloth." Ten-ounce fabric, which is also termed "boat cloth" or "1000 cloth," is a plain, reasonably fine, balanced, open-weave fabric made from twisted multi-end strand. Since the fabric has a fine weave, manufacturing costs are increased over those of mat and roving reinforcements. The 10-ounce fabric has better handling characteristics than most other fabrics; its open weave allows rapid resin penetration and wetting during fabrication, and the looseness of weave and drapability allow it to conform to almost any curvature. The strength and stiffness of 10-ounce fabric-based laminates fall in the intermediate range of properties available with FRP reinforcements.

Principal disadvantages of 10-ounce reinforcement are its cost and its lack of bulk.

181 Fabric. 181 fabric is a very fine-textured, balanced woven fabric that is made in a special weave to minimize crimps and bends in the filaments. It is an expensive reinforcement because of the cost involved in producing the fine-textured pattern.

181 fabric has good draping qualities, but it lacks bulk (e.g., 12 layers are required to develop a ⅛-inch thickness). The mechanical properties of 181 fabric-reinforced laminates approach the maximum that can be obtained with balanced fabric based systems.

The 181 fabric is of interest for another reason. This material has been adopted as an unofficial standard reinforcement for the evaluation of variables that affect laminate properties, and in many cases, the literature will contain information on a particular parameter using only this reinforcement as the reference.

143 Fabric. 143 fabric is similar to 181 cloth in weight, "feel," general appearance, cost and fabricating characteristics. There is a major difference in construction, however, since 143 cloth is highly directional rather than balanced. More than 90 per cent of the fibers are oriented in the warp direction. When plies are laminated parallel to each other, very high-strength unidirectional laminates result. Such laminates may possess the highest mechanical properties (in one direction) that can be achieved with fabric-based systems.

Practicality of the Reinforcements. Not all of the reinforcements listed above can be considered as practical for major reinforcement in building structures. Fabrics of the 181 and 143 variety are of high quality and produce laminates having optimum strength and stiffness-to-weight ratios, but their cost eliminates them from major use in building structures where these ratios are not usually critical; such fabrics may have application as local reinforcement in zones of high stress. Boat cloth is somewhat less expensive than other fabrics, and yet it yields laminates of reasonably high quality. In building applications, it is probably practical to use this material as local reinforcement or as perhaps the outer skins of a laminate made up from the cheaper, lower-quality reinforcements. Generally, continuous roving, woven roving, nonwoven continuous strand, and mat reinforcements can be considered as most practical for major reinforcements in building applications where cost must be a critical parameter.

Resin Systems

The only reason that fiber glass–reinforced plastics can be considered for building applications is that there are resins available which possess a unique set of properties and characteristics before, during and after processing. Such resins are fluid enough to penetrate into the network of fiber bundles, and after impregnation, they can be polymerized ("hardened," "cured") to a rigid state—little or no heat or pressure is required. When cured, these resins are strong and stiff enough to effectively transfer and distribute stress throughout the fibrous reinforcement, and they can provide a myriad of other features relating to the performance of the composite. The polyesters, epoxies, and thermosetting acrylics are the principal resin systems that meet the requirements for building applications.

Although there are just three resin systems that will be considered here, there is a boundless spectrum of variations in handling and fabrication characteristics and in end properties that can be achieved by various modifications of these formulations. Some of these modifications are built into the resin system by the resin supplier; others can be made, locally, in the shop of the fabricator. This capability of tailoring resin systems contributes greatly to the success of fiber glass-reinforced plastics in many widely divergent applications.

The following sections should serve to introduce the reader to the resin systems that may find application in building components and to acquaint the reader with certain of the major modifications that can be achieved through manipulation of formulations. It should be recognized at the outset of this discussion that the range of end products available is so broad, that a detailed treatment is not possible and that further restrictions exist because knowledge of the influence of each possible variation on all properties of interest is seldom available.

Polyesters

The Liquid Resin. Polyester resins of the rigid, general-purpose category are provided as liquids consisting of unsaturated polyester blended with styrene monomer. (Typically polyester concentration is 60 to 70 per cent.) The polyester provides the principal molecular chain or backbone, and the styrene serves as the cross-linking agent that interconnects the polyester molecules to form a rigid three-dimensional structure.

Since the cross-linking action tends to proceed at ambient temperature, an inhibiting agent is provided in the supplied mixture to prevent premature reaction during shipment and storage. The unreacted liquid resin is syrupy, and viscosity will vary from 300 to 2000 centipoise, depending upon the molecular weight of the polyester and the amount of styrene monomer present in the formulation.

Curing the Liquid. Prior to laminating, the liquid resin is formulated to produce the desired curing characteristics. If it is desired that the material remain workable for periods of up to a few hours, an organic peroxide catalyst and an accelerator are usually used to initiate polymerization. The material will remain liquid for the approximate predetermined time, then the effects of progressive cross-linking will become apparent. Progressive cross-linking or polymerization is evidenced by a stiffening of the liquid resin to a gel-like state ("cheesey" and rubbery) and subsequent hardening of the gel to a rigid state. This reaction will usually last for a few hours to a few days, depending upon the concentration of catalyst and the temperature. If polymerization proceeds rapidly, considerable heat of reaction (exotherm) will be developed, which, if not removed, further accelerates cross-linking.

If longer working life prior to gel is important, heat-activated catalysts can be used. Polyesters so catalyzed will remain liquid at room temperature for several hours or days, but the material must be heated to produce cross-linking in a reasonable length of time. On heating, such systems will progress through the liquid, gel, and rigid stages in minutes or hours depending upon the temperature and the catalyst.

By manipulation of catalyst and temperature, the fabricator can tailor the single base resin to cure on a schedule that best suits his process. The specific cure schedule selected will depend upon the size and thickness of the laminate, the resin system, and the type of equipment available.

The Cured Resin. The rigid general-purpose variety of polyester resin will cure to a rigid, glassy transparent, pale amber solid. (Cobalt naphthenate, which is a common accelerator, will impart a purple cast instead of an amber color.) Typically, such resins will have. a modulus of elasticity of about 0.5×10^6 psi and a tensile strength of about 8000 psi. Compressive and flexural strengths are about 16,000 psi and 23,000 psi respectively. Specific gravity of general-purpose resins is about 1.2.

Fiber-glass laminates made from the general-purpose polyester resins will give respectable performance in many applications. Mechanical properties are high at normal temperatures, and the material is generally compatible with environments found in building applications. The general-purpose resins are easy to work with in most fabrication operations, they are not toxic, and they are among the cheapest laminating resins available at a cost of about $0.30 per pound (quantity price, in mid-1966, for good quality resins). Rigid general-purpose polyesters are regularly and successfully used in marine applications, and this alone is reasonable testimony to their economics and their durability to abuse and to hostile environments.

Modifications of Polyester Formulations

Seldom does a general-purpose product exist that cannot be improved to fit a given service application, and indeed, this is the case for the polyesters. There are a number of modifications in formulation that can be made to enhance performance under certain conditions. The following sections will deal with such modifications and, insofar as possible, will indicate the important "side effects" that may arise as a result.

Styrene Dilution. It is common practice to dilute "as-supplied" general-purpose polyester systems with styrene monomer. This is done to reduce cost and to enhance fabricating characteristics by lowering viscosity. As this is done, the resin takes on more of the characteristics of the thermoplastic polystyrene—cracking and crazing tendencies, in-

creased shrinkage, and lowered mechanical properties may result. Military specifications MIL-R-7575 A (12) require that polyester concentration be held to a minimum of 60 per cent for structural aircraft laminates, and this should be a good guide as to the degree of dilution permissible without adverse results.

Flexibility. Rigid general-purpose polyester resins are relatively brittle; ultimate elongation of such materials usually does not exceed 5 per cent. Thus, visible microcracking and crazing may occur on impact or in regions of overstress. Even though in some cases the laminate strength may not be significantly affected, microcracking may be visually objectionable, and since it usually occurs at the surface, microcracking bares the glass fibers for subsequent attack by moisture. Microcracking can be reduced or eliminated through the use of "flexibilized" resins, which are supplied or blended with rigid resins to ultimate elongations of up to 300 per cent. Because strength and stiffness (and presumably temperature and creep resistance) decrease with degree of flexibility, it is usually necessary to limit the degree of "flexibilizing" such that the ultimate elongation of the resin is about 10 per cent. Such resins are usually termed "semirigid" and are frequently used in such applications as structural boat hull laminates.

Fire Retardance. The resin industry has not yet been able to produce nonburning compounds. However, a number of approaches have been developed to reduce the burning tendencies. The extent to which these measures have been effective depends upon the evaluators' concept of the critical aspects of fire in buildings.

There are several ways in which polyester resin systems can be altered to reduce the effects of fire. One common approach is to add antimony trioxide (5 per cent concentration) and/or chlorinated waxes to general-purpose resins. These waxes are not reactive with either the polyester or the styrene component of the resin; because of this, they tend to act as plasticizers (which must have deleterious effects on creep and temperature resistance) and they tend to leach out of the resin. Another approach involves substitution of all or part of the polyester component in the general-purpose resins with coreactive chlorendic acid (HET* acid) or tetrachlorophthalic based polyesters. These resins are heavily chlorinated, and it is this chlorine that imparts resistance to fire. This approach is considered to yield the most stable and fire-retardant products, since the chlorine-containing ingredient is a chemically bound within the molecular structure of the resin and, further, no sacrifice in mechanical properties is involved.[13]

There are, of course, a variety of test methods available to evaluate the burning behavior of plastics materials. Some are empirical comparative evaluation tests; others are more closely related to performance. While these cannot be treated in detail here, representative tests of particular interest will be discussed to provide some insight into the fire-resistance problem. One empirical test involves placing a sample in an oven under a standard set of conditions and observing the length of time (t_1) that is taken to ignite the material. An index of self-extinguishing capability is provided by noting the time (t_b) taken for the flame to cease once the heat source has been removed. G. W. Burton[14] has developed substantial test data using this type of test which is reasonably close to Method 2023-2 of Federal Specification LP 406 B. Table 5-2 summarizes some of these data.

While the results shown in Table 5-2

* Trademark, Hooker Chemical Co.

should be self-explanatory, two observations seem particularly pertinent. First, little change in burning characteristics occurs with the addition of antimony trioxide. Second, very marked reduction in burning tendencies can be achieved through proper formulation with chlorinated coreactive polymer systems.

A test that relates more closely to performance of panels under exposure to fire has been developed by Underwriters Laboratories. The arrangement for this test, commonly called the "Tunnel Test," consists of a duct 25 feet long whose top surface is made up of the test panel. Gas burners are used to provide a flame which is induced to travel down the duct under carefully controlled draft conditions. The distance that the fire propagates in a given length of time is one measure of performance, and on this basis, a flame-spread scale is set up in which asbestos is given a rating of zero and red oak is assigned a value of 100. Some unmodified polyester laminates will fail this test with a flame-spread rating of over 200, which is considered highly combustible. Depending upon the amount of coreactive chlorine-based compound that is added, laminates can be produced that fall into the slow-burning (flame-spread 50 to 75), retardant (flame-spread 25 to 50) or noncombustible (flame-spread 0 to 25) categories. Note should be made that only the flame-spread ratings are established by Underwriters Laboratories; classification is done by other agencies.

While resins cannot as yet be formulated

TABLE 5-2. Effect of Resin Formulation on Resistance to Fire[14]

Type of Retardant Added to General-purpose Polyester	t_1*	t_b*	Rating	Classification
NONE	90	400	Combustible	Poor
5% antimony trioxide	80	350	Self-extinguishing	Poor
25% "HET" acid	75	74	Flame-retardant	Good
100% "HET" acid	88	21	Flame-retardant	Excellent
25% tetrachlorophthalic	100	100	Flame-retardant	Good
100% tetrachlorophthalic	130	15	Flame-retardant	Excellent

* See text for explanation of symbols.
Note: All laminates contain glass, resin, and filler in approximately equal proportions by weight. Results will vary depending upon relative proportions.

to be fireproof, considerable reduction in burning tendencies can be achieved through proper selection of resin components.

Weather Resistance. Like most other building materials, fiber glass-reinforced plastic systems are subject to degradation under long-term outdoor exposures. Changes in the following properties may occur.

(a) Color: Laminates will tend to yellow on aging.

(b) Gloss: The exposed surface may erode, and in some cases this can proceed so far that the reinforcement is bared to the elements.

(c) Translucency: Incompatibility of expansion and contraction of resin and fibers with temperature and moisture changes will cause an increase in fiber prominence; this is reflected in a lowering of the light transmitting capabilities of translucent laminates.

(d) Strength: Mechanical properties will be lowered.

The changes in these properties can be linked, either directly or indirectly, to the resinous component of the FRP laminate system. Fortunately this component can be tailored to minimize these effects.

Methods of tailoring for weather resistance, and performance resulting from such modifications, can best be discussed if general-purpose polyester resins are taken as the frame of reference. Ultraviolet stabilizers can be added to such resins, and these will reduce color change, but they do not contribute significantly to reduction of the other forms of degradation. Total performance under outdoor exposures can be substantially improved by the substitution of methyl methacrylate (acrylic) monomer for one-half of the styrene monomer in an otherwise general-purpose polyester resin. (A typical weather-resistant formulation is: 60 per cent polyester/20 per cent methyl methacrylate/20 per cent styrene).

Tables 5-3 and 5-4 show the dramatic improvements in weather resistance that result from use of the acrylic-modified formulation. While changes in color, gloss, translucency and tensile strength with outdoor exposure are still evident, the magnitude

TABLE 5-3. Weather Resistance of General-purpose (Light-stabilized) and Acrylic-modified Polyester Based Mat-reinforced Laminates (Exposure — 4 Years at Bristol, Pa)[15]

Resin Type	Gloss*	Color**	White Light Transmittance
General-purpose (UV-stabilized) polyester			
Control	69.3	14.6	77.0
Exposed	12.5	37.5	51.6
Acrylic-modified polyester			
Control	72.3	0.0	84.2
Exposed	64.5	17.7	79.1

* High value indicates good gloss.
** Low value indicates low yellowing.

TABLE 5-4. Influence of Resin Type on Laminate Strength After Exposure to Weather[15]

Laminate Type	Exposure	Ultimate Flexural Strength (psi) General-purpose Polyester Resin	Acrylic-modified Polyester Resin
12-ply glass fabric	None	69,300	69,500
	Bristol, Pa.—2 yr	59,200	64,100
	Florida—2 yr	46,700	60,300
25% glass mat	None	17,500	21,500
	Bristol, Pa.—3 yr	16,700	22,200
	Florida—3 yr	12,400	20,600

of these changes is notably smaller than those observed in an ultraviolet-stabilized general-purpose resin.

While the fire-retardant resin systems discussed in the previous section can be light stabilized, their resistance to weather does not compare to that offered by the acrylic-modified blends. The principal drawback of the fire-retardant formulations is their tendency toward excessive erosion. To circumvent this, commercial fire-retardant translucent panels are usually coated with polyvinyl fluoride film* or with a weather-resistant lacquer which does not detract significantly from resistance to flame-spread. A variety of paints and resinous coatings have been used successfully to protect fire-retardant panels in radomes,[16] and such structures must service the range of climates from arctic to tropic.

Where translucency is not a factor, weather-resistant "gel coats"** may be used to improved weathering of general-purpose or fire-retardant laminates. Early experience with gel coats as weather protection for radomes was that cracking occurred in areas where the gel coat was excessively thick. Great advances have been made in tailoring of gel coats to meet severe environments; if reasonable precautions are taken in thickness control and formulation selection, they should provide satisfactory weather protection.

Epoxies

Epoxy resins differ markedly in chemical structure from the polyester systems just discussed. The basic epoxy backbone polymer can be reacted with a great variety of compounds to produce a cross-linked structure. For example, there are catalysts such as tertiary amines and boron trifluoride that produce cross-linking solely within the epoxy backbone polymer, and there are a host of amines, polyamide/amines and

* Tedlar, a product of E. I. du Pont de Nemours, Inc.
** A "gel coat" is a thin, non-reinforced resin layer which is allowed to partially cure (gel) before the reinforcement is laminated to it.

anhydrides that cross-link by coreacting with the epoxy chain molecules. Some of the latter cross-linking agents (curing agents, hardeners) are so reactive with the epoxy that they need not be heated to initiate the cross-linking. Such systems are usually termed "room-temperature" curing agents. Other hardeners are more sluggish at room temperature and, therefore, heat or catalysts are used to induce and sustain cross-linking. In addition to these variations, the epoxies can be flexibilized with nonreactive or coreactive agents and modified to improve fire resistance and ultraviolet resistance. Indeed, the epoxy systems offer greater freedom of choice in chemical structure, and hence in curing and fabrication characteristics, and physical and mechanical properties, than perhaps any other polymer.

Epoxy resins are well known for their outstanding adhesive characteristics and their low shrinkage on curing. These properties are reflected in the behavior of epoxy-based fiber-glass composites, where the inherent adhesion of the resins to glass creates a well-bonded system that is stronger and stiffer than laminates based on polyester resins having similar mechanical properties. This superiority is particularly noticeable in the property of compressive strength, where good bonding prevents buckling and ultimate collapse of the minute fibers. Epoxy-based laminates are also notably superior to polyster-based systems in strength retention after exposure to water; this too, can probably be traced to the high integrity of the glass-epoxy bond. The characteristic of low cure shrinkage also implies the desirable characteristics of low internal stress and high dimensional stability. The attributes of strength, water resistance and stability combine to place epoxy-based laminates at the highest level of quality available with low-pressure laminating systems.

The majority of epoxy resins with their curing agents cost about twice as much as polyester systems, and therefore, they have difficulty competing in the building component market. There are other disadvantages of many of the systems that limit their use for large structural panels that would be suitable for buildings. First, the majority of the optimum quality resins are highly viscous and are difficult to work into the usually tightly bound fiber network. (There are diluted versions available, but some sacrifice in properties occurs on dilution.) Second, because a large number of curing agents are toxic or irritating, precautions must be taken to protect personnel from contact and exposure to vapors. This is particularly critical in spray operations and in the fabrication of parts that require a large amount of hand labor. And finally, if a particular curing agent is selected to yield specific properties, the resulting cure schedule may be excessively long. Certainly, these factors contribute to the expense of epoxy laminates.

Epoxy-based laminates can be considered for building applications if one or more of the following factors are critical:

(1) Adhesion: It may be desirable to laminate the composite to other structural materials during manufacture.

(2) Dimensional accuracy and stability.

(3) Mechanical properties—wet, dry, or at high temperature.

(4) Sandwich "skins" over polystyrene foams: the styrene monomer present in polyester-based laminates dissolves polystyrene foam.

(5) Processing: In some manufacturing operations, particularly those that are highly automated such as the filament winding process, the problems of toxicity and viscosity are not as critical as with methods involving extensive hand labor. Also, in filament-wound structures, resin content may be so low as to render the cost of the resin component a small part of total cost of the product.

Epoxy resins cannot be considered as competitive in the "general-purpose" applications that the polyester systems satisfy so well; rather they are premium or special-purpose resins that can satisfy the demands of certain critical or unique applications.

Acrylics

Thermosetting acrylics have essentially the same properties as the familiar thermoplastic acrylics that have been used so successfully in such outdoor applications as automobile taillights, aircraft canopies and windows, signs, decorative panels, and "bubble" skylights. Weather resistance has been adequately proved in service, and in addition, mechanical properties compare to those of general-purpose polyester and epoxy resins. Thus, thermosetting acrylics are natural candidates as matrices for structural laminates for buildings—particularly when outdoor exposures are contemplated.

While the curing characteristics of the thermosetting variety of acrylics may be less rigorous than required by their thermoplastic counterparts, they are still more difficult to handle than general-purpose or acrylic-modified polyesters. In addition, thermosetting acrylics are fairly volatile and viscous, and the reaction is moisture sensitive. As a result, thermosetting acrylics require considerable sophistication in processing; special care must be taken to insure proper impregnation of the fiber network, to exclude moisture from the reaction, and to control temperature such that volatilization of the monomer does not occur. Consequently, fabrication and processing of acrylic-based laminates is more expensive than that of conventional systems; a premium must be paid to gain the superior weathering characteristics offered by the acrylic family of resins.

Considerable differences of opinion arise over the relative weathering characteristics of acrylic and acrylic-modified polyester-based laminates. There is little question that straight acrylics are more light stable and more resistant to erosion than acrylic-modified polyesters. However, acrylics shrink and swell more on outdoor exposure than do the acrylic-modified polyesters; thus, debonding occurs between the resin and the more dimensionally stable fibrous glass. Debonding spoils the optical match between resin and fibers; the result is increased fiber prominence as evidenced by decreased translucence. Comparison of straight acrylics with acrylic-modified polyesters depends upon the relative importance that is attached to erosion, discoloration, and loss in translucency. Clearly, if translucency is not a requirement, or is not critical, as must be the case in some building applications, straight acrylics will offer better weathering characteristics than the acrylic-modified polyesters. Note should also be made that the tendency for debonding can be reduced if certain forms and arrangements of reinforcement are chosen and special finishes are used. (Finishes will be discussed in the following section.)

In summary, straight thermosetting acrylics can be considered for building applications when the following criteria govern the design:

(a) Quantity is sufficient to warrant setup of sophisticated processing techniques and controls

(b) Minimum loss in color and gloss.

(c) High initial costs balance possible savings in maintenance.

Like epoxies, the acrylics must be considered as special-purpose systems. By some standards, the acrylics will contribute optimum weathering properties, but at the same time, substantial loss in flexibility and ease of processing, with a corresponding increase in manufacturing expense, will result.

Coupling Agents—Finishes

It is highly desirable to protect glass fibers from exposure to water, for water will degrade short-term strength and creep rupture strength of the fibers. Although in the usual sense, the resinous matrix of an FRP laminate provides a barrier to moisture, in fact, resins will absorb a small percentage of water on soaking. This absorbed water can reach the surface of the imbedded fibers. Water can also penetrate from exposed edges of a laminate, as it can follow fibers whose ends have been exposed by erosion due to weathering, or water can enter a laminate through microcracks in the resin caused by shrinkage or overstressing. Finishes or coupling agents are applied to the glass fibers by the glass manufacturer, or processor, to reduce the effects of this moisture on the strength and stiffness of the laminate.

There are a number of coupling agents on the market, and each has its particular effect on such properties as:

(a) Wet strength retention,

(b) Compatibility with specific resins,

(c) Optical match between resin and glass,

(d) Stiffening effects on the reinforcement (thereby affecting handling),

(e) Wetting of resin to glass (which has its effect on amount of working necessary to impregnate a fiber network),

(f) Cost.

The role of the coupling agent is a vital one, and in building applications where strength must usually be maintained under humid or wet conditions, the use of quality systems seems in order. The "vinyl silane" type finishes are generally considered most effective,[17] and although they cost more than some other types, they should not affect the total cost of the end product by a significant amount.

FABRICATION

One of the principal advantages of fiber glass-reinforced plastics is the inherent ease of forming and fabrication. Moldability is a significant plus factor, which in certain instances may result in savings in tooling or may allow freedom of structural form not possible or practical with other structural materials. By now, another equally critical facet of fabrication should be strikingly clear; that is, the designer has full control of the type and arrangement of components that comprise the laminate. In order to render a competent design, it is important to know the processes by which the elements of the fiber-glass composite can be manipulated into the final product; the following sections are intended to familiarize the reader with these techniques.

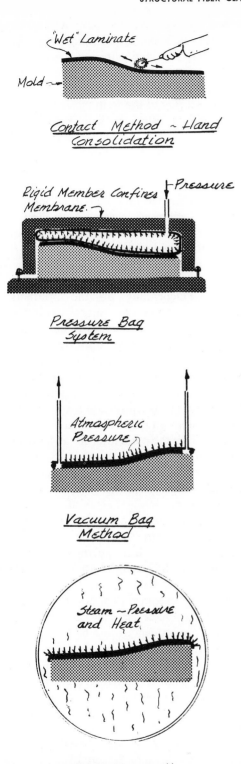

FIG. 5-10. Common methods of consolidation and molding.

Hand Layup

Lamination. The hand layup method of fabrication, while perhaps the most unsophisticated, is also the most versatile manufacturing technique available. In this process, a layer or layers of reinforcement, pre-cut to the desired pattern, are positioned on the mold, and the reinforcement is impregnated with the liquid resin either before or after placement. In the latter case, which is more common, the resin is either brushed, poured or sprayed onto the reinforcement as the buildup progresses. In this way, sections can be developed to the desired thickness, and additional amounts of reinforcement can be placed as required for local strengthening.

When gel coats are used, they are applied to the mold surface prior to the laminating operation. They are brushed or sprayed onto the mold to the required thickness, and curing is allowed to proceed until the material gels. At this point, the material is firm enough so that it is not displaced by the subsequent laminating operations, and yet it is tacky enough to permit intimate and thorough bonding with the next application of resin.

Consolidation (Figure 5-10). Once the layup is complete, it is necessary to consolidate or compact the laminate to eliminate air entrapped during impregnation. Several alternative techniques are available for this compaction operation. The technique that involves no further equipment or tooling is the "contact" method in which the laminate is hand worked by kneading with squeegees or rollers. This displaces the entrapped air and helps to compact and densify the composite.

A second method, the "vacuum bag" technique, utilizes a membrane of rubber or plastic that conforms to the contours of the outer surface of the layup. A vacuum is drawn between the membrane and the mold; this compresses the laminate and evacuates the entrapped air. Many times, the laminate will be kneaded, through the membrane, to assist the action of the vacuum.

The third compaction process is the "pressure bag" system. This method utilizes a pressurized rubber bag that conforms to the outer surface of the laminate. The bag is placed between the outer laminate surface and a rigid support. When pressurized, the bag fills the void between the laminate and the support, thereby exerting a pressure on the laminate. This, of course, consolidates the laminate and forces entrapped air to the free edges of the panel.

A fourth process involves the use of an autoclave, which simultaneously pressurizes the laminate and provides a source of heat for curing.

There are, of course, other consolidation processes that can be used, but the ones given above are of principal importance.

The type of consolidation that is employed has important bearing on the quality and economics of the resulting laminate. The contact method involves no accessory apparatus and equipment; hence, capital expenditure is low. Maximum densification of the laminate will not be achieved under the compaction effort normally employed in the contact method. Glass contents will be low, and hence strength and stiffness will be lower than can be obtained with other methods. (There is an important paradox here that will be discussed on p. 115.)

Contact molded laminates are inclined to have small pockets of entrapped air that will be visible on close inspection, and usually only one surface, on the mold side, is smooth; these characteristics may or may not be found objectionable depending upon the application. Because of the amount of hand effort involved, reproducibility of laminates will vary unless strict supervision and control are maintained. The process imposes no limit on the size of the component; in fact, very large boat hulls have been made using this method. The other processes involve the application of pressure which increases the glass content and reduced the amount of entrapped air. These factors combine to produce laminates of higher mechanical and visual quality, and there is inclined to be better part-to-part reproducibility. They do require accessory apparatus, and therefore, they add to the cost of the part; in addition, the size of the part is limited. Generally, the contact molding process is sufficient for building application, and it has been the principal method used thus far in the "custom" type of FRP building structures.

Cure. Curing of the resinous component is accomplished after the consolidation has taken place. The schedule used depends upon the resin system, the catalyst, and the size of the component. The simplest cure is obtained by formulating the resin to harden at ambient temperature. Thus, the compacted laminate is allowed to remain on the mold until the material has hardened to a point where the product can be handled; this usually takes a few hours. This, of course, requires molds to be idle for long periods of time. Depending on the production schedule, it may be more economical to use elevated temperature cures using heated molds, infrared units, or ovens to hasten the cure. If heating is feasible, systems can be used that give long working life during the consolidation operation. In either the room-temperature or the heat curing systems, it may be practical to remove the part from the mold after it has hardened, and then "post-cure" the part in an oven until cure is complete. This step reduces the idle time of the mold and improves production efficiency.

Whatever cure method or schedule is adopted, the critical consideration is that the product be fully polymerized before leaving the fabricator's shop. Optimum properties—mechanical, weathering, dimensional and chemical—cannot be achieved without complete cure. The time and temperature sequence must be scheduled to achieve this end. Resin suppliers usually have or can obtain extensive data on the time/temperature/catalyst parameters for any given resin formulation.

Sprayup (Figure 5-11)

The sprayup process lends itself particularly well to the manufacture of large structural polyester based panels. In this process, chopped fibers and resin are deposited simultaneously against a mold surface. The unit used for this deposition consists of a chopper and dual spray nozzles. Continuous strand is fed into the chopper where it is cut to length. Fiber length can be varied from about ½ to 2 inches. (The longer fibers are desirable for structural panels because they impart higher mechanical properties.) The accomplished using any of the methods discussed above. Usually, the contact method is employed.

The sprayup laminating method is a semiautomatic process which proves economical in many manufacturing operations. It is presently used in the manufacture of

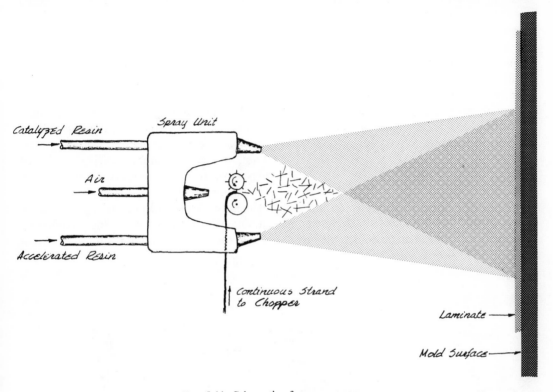

Catalyzed Resin
Spray Unit
Air
Accelerated Resin
Continuous Strand to Chopper
Laminate
Mold Surface

FIG. 5-11. Schematic of sprayup process.

fibers are fed into the path of the dual spray nozzles. Separate reservoirs supply one nozzle with catalyzed resin and the second nozzle with accelerated resin. The resin formulation is tailored such that neither component is highly reactive, and therefore, each may remain in the reservoirs for at least several hours. When the products leave the dual elements of the spray gun, they intersect and intersperse, and pick up the chopped fibers before striking the mold. The resin mixture is then ready to cure at a convenient rate as predetermined by the concentration of catalyst and accelerator.

After the sprayup operation has been completed, consolidation and curing may be

such items as housings, bathtubs and boats. It is inherently economical, since it uses the reinforcement in its least expensive form—continuous roving. There are no limitations on the size of the component that can be produced, and the chopped fibers can be made to fit almost any practical contour. For these reasons, the sprayup process is a practical method for producing structural building panels.

There are several limitations to the sprayup process. First, the laminate produced is of the chopped fiber or mat form (although alternate layers of sprayup and woven roving can be deposited). As will be shown in later sections of this chapter, properties of this type of laminate fall at the low end of the range attainable with FRP materials. A second limitation is that the sprayup process is generally limited to polyester systems. Most epoxy systems present problems in toxicity of the fine vapor spray, in catalysis, and in viscosity. There is also the consideration of workmanship. The thickness of the laminate must be judged by the operator of the sprayup unit; and hand consolidation methods that are usually employed introduce human error and subsequent part-to-part variation. If adequate quality control measures are instituted, these disadvantages should not be of significance in limiting the use of sprayup method for building structures.

Filament Winding (Figure 5-12)

Filament winding is a highly automated process that can be used to generate extremely efficient structures. In the usual

the quantity and orientation of the fiber deposition can be varied to best fit the stress levels and directions that will occur in the structure.

Consolidation of filament wound laminates is usually unnecessary. The roving is wound under some tension which tends to force air out of the resin matrix as the wrapping progresses.

Curing can be accomplished at either room or elevated temperatures. As has been discussed, this is a function of the resin system used and the demands of the production schedule.

Filament winding has several advantages that make it an attractive technique for the manufacture of certain types of structures. First, it uses continuous roving, the least expensive form of reinforcement. Second, the filaments can be oriented to take stresses efficiently, thereby producing highly efficient laminates with a resulting savings in material. Then too, molds are not subject to great

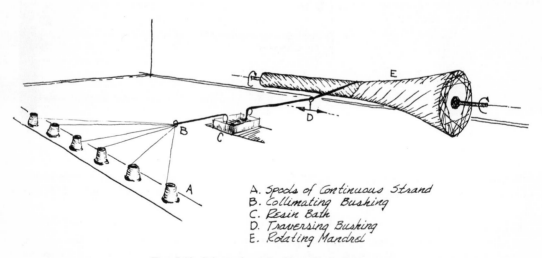

A. Spools of Continuous Strand
B. Collimating Bushing
C. Resin Bath
D. Traversing Bushing
E. Rotating Mandrel

FIG. 5-12. Schematic of the filament winding process.

filament winding process, several strands of continuous roving are fed through a liquid resin bath and wound onto a rotating mandrel or mold. When generating large structural shapes, the mandrel rotates about a fixed axis, as the glass feeding mechanism travels the length of the mandrel in a programmed motion. By adjusting the rate of traverse relative to the rate of rotation,

pressures, so tooling costs are reasonable And finally, since laminates made by this process are self-consolidating, there is little need for hand labor. The elimination of hand labor reduces both fabrication expense and part-to-part variation. These factors combine to yield a highly efficient product having sometimes unequaled ratios of strength to weight.

One of the major limitations imposed by the filament winding process concerns the geometry of the part. Obviously, the first requirement of the process is that the surface must be developable by winding. This limits, for example, depression of the surface in the direction of the wrap, since the taut roving would tend to span the cavity. Also, the angle of wrap with respect to the curvature of the surface must be such that the taut winding will not slip out of position. Thus, for example, while no problems exist in winding an equatorial wrap on a sphere, it becomes progressively more difficult to wrap smaller parallel circles as the poles of the sphere are approached. (It is clear that a sphere would be best developed by wrapping with meridional bands). Even with these limits, substantial freedom in the shape of components is possible. Certain surfaces of revolution are ideal (for example, cylinders, spheres, saddle forms, ellipsoids), but it is also possible to generate boxlike and prismoidal forms. Geometry of the structure will also have great influence on mandrel cost and complexity. Rocket casings, which are essentially cylinders with closed ends, are wound on disposable mandrels of salt or plaster. The expense of such forms probably could not be justified in building components, therefore, the most practical shapes are those having open ends, or those that can be cut along certain axes to permit removal from the mandrel.

The filament winding process is best suited to items where moderate to high production runs are anticipated. Tooling costs will, of course, vary with the complexity of the part, and they need not be high if open-ended molds and easily generated shapes are used, but considerable setup time and expense are involved in test runs, and in the programming of the winding schedule.

While there are no known applications where filament winding has been used to produce building components, it is the author's belief that filament winding can be employed to great advantage in the manufacture of certain types of building structures. It is conceivable, for example, that large dome-ended cylinders or saddle forms could possibly be generated as full cylinders and then bisected along a plane passing through the axis of rotation. The resulting shells might then form barrel-vault or saddle-type roof structures, or serve as formwork for similar structures in sprayup concrete. It is also possible to use filament winding as an intermediate process in producing efficient laminates for structures of other shapes. Material can be wrapped on a cylindrical form to the desired orientation, and then cut from the mandrel and placed, for example, on a hyperbolic paraboloid mold for subsequent curing. The formation of such structures using the simple efficient, automated filament winding process may prove to be an economic means of utilizing fiber glass-reinforced plastics in buildings.

Matched Metal Molding

Matched metal molding becomes an economical process when high-volume production levels are required. In this process either mat or fabric is pre-cut to shape, or if the form is complex, a "preform" reinforcement is prepared by making a chopped fiber mat to the approximate shape of the finished product. The tailored reinforcement is then placed in a press bearing heated, mating metal dies. A measured quantity of resin is poured over the reinforcement, and the press is closed. The pressure forces the resin through the fiber network, and curing of the resin at the high mold temperature is initiated and completed within a few minutes. The materials can be inexpensive, labor is minimized, and the production rate is high. If production levels are high enough, these factors will balance the high capital cost of the metal molds, and the unit price of the product will be lower than can be achieved by other fabrication methods. Other than mold cost, the principal disadvantage of matched metal molding is limited size of product. For example, some facilities are presently available that can produce boat hulls up to 17 feet in length; but the preponderance of equipment for matched metal molding is for sizes 4 feet by 8 feet, or less.

Other Processes

It is easy to envision a variety of processes that can be developed to fabricate the versatile resins and reinforcements of FRP systems. Centrifugal casting and a host of continuous molding techniques are now commonplace. The author has chosen to limit the discussion to the more standard types of fabrication, but this by no means implies that a special process cannot be developed to meet the needs of a particular application.

DESIGN CONSIDERATIONS

Unfortunately, there are no codes governing the use of FRP; the designer cannot yet take the considered opinion of code committees and confidently incorporate their recommended safety factors and design approaches into his design. Consequently, it is vital that materials behavior, and the influence of major parameters on this behavior, are well understood. Some particularly pertinent aspects of laminate mechanics will be presented here,* and then realistic properties will be given along with some quantitative measure of the influence of major parameters on these properties. This should lend some perspective to the capabilities of fiber glass-reinforced plastics in building structures, and some background should be provided for judging other data that may be encountered in technical or manufacturers' literature.

Behavior of Unidirectional Laminates in Tension

The simplest arrangement of reinforcement in a composite is one in which all fibers are parallel to each other. Such unidirectional, orthotropic,** laminates can be produced by the filament winding process, or by laminating parallel layups of nonwoven unidirectional fabrics. Parallel layers of 143 fabric

---

* Reference 18 contains more detailed discussions of laminate behavior and laminate mechanisms.
** An orthotropic body is one that possesses three discrete principal axes of elasticity (and strength). Wood serves as a classic orthotropic material because of the differing properties found in the longitudinal radial and circumferential directions.

---

will also yield essentially unidirectional material, although a few per cent of the fibers are oriented in a transverse direction.

Stress-deformation behavior of these unidirectional materials is described in Figure 5-13(a). Behavior is characterized by a nearly linear stress-strain relationship to failure.

A good portion of the stress-strain behavior of unidirectional laminates can be described by the simplified, one-dimensional, transformed section theory that is used to approximate the behavior of reinforced concrete (i.e., strains in reinforcement and matrix are assumed equal, and Poisson effects are neglected; this forces stress in each component to become a function of its modulus). One point of difference between FRP and reinforced concrete is the reinforcement/matrix modulus ratio. In FRP composites, the modulus ratio is 20 or greater, depending on the stiffness of the resin, whereas in reinforced concrete the ratio lies between 6 and 15 depending on the strength of the mix. A second point of contrast is in the percentage of cross-sectional area that the reinforcement occupies in the two systems. Reinforcing steel usually occupies a maximum of a few per cent of the gross area, whereas fiber glass will occupy perhaps 10 per cent to a theoretical maximum of about 90 per cent of the gross area. Because of the larger modulus and area ratios, fiber glass plays a relatively greater role in composite behavior than does the steel in reinforced concrete.

The theoretical maximum packing of fibers is about 90 per cent of the laminate volume with a hexagonal close-packed array. The transformed section theory would predict a modulus of elasticity of such a laminate to be slightly above 9×10^6, which represents the maximum modulus that could be expected in an "E" glass-based laminate. In practice, it is not feasible to achieve such high glass loadings, and thus, under the best of conditions, a maximum modulus of about 7×10^6 psi is attainable with very carefully prepared unidirectional materials. Carefully prepared 143 laminates yield moduli of about

5 to 6 × 10⁶ psi—the fibers in the fill direction do not permit dense packing. The modulus of elasticity will decrease with fiber loading, which of course, in the limit, approaches the modulus of elasticity of the resin.

Although it should be possible to compute the tensile strength of a unidirectional laminate by transformed section theory, in practice, precise correlation is difficult to obtain. This is most probably due to the substantial scatter associated with the strength of fibrous glass. In a laminate, there may be a weak point in one fiber, and

it may fracture, but statistically, other fibers at the same cross section are stronger. Thus, stress from the broken filament may be transferred (in a manner analogous to the mechanism of stress transfer in lapped reinforcing steel) to neighboring fibers that are stronger (statistically) at that particular location. Because of this fracture mechanism, the stress in the glass as computed by transformed section theory can be significantly above the average strength of a group of fibers tested singly, or as a strand. (No such phenomenon is observed in

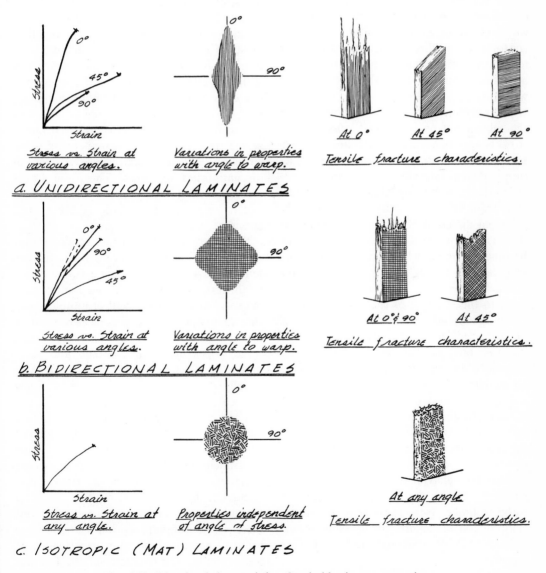

FIG. 5-13. Directional characteristics of typical laminate constructions.

concrete reinforcing steel because of the very low scatter found in the yield stress of a given steel). While a quantitative prediction of the strength under this simple stress condition and material arrangement is not yet available, a conservative estimate of the strength may be gained by using the average strength of a group of fibers in the transformed section calculations. It is interesting to note that the fiber stress at failure, as computed from transformed section theory, can be 260,000 psi[11] or greater, in practical laminates.

Tensile rupture of unidirectional laminates is characterized by splitting, splintering and delamination in much the same manner as wood. However, because much more energy is stored in unidirectional laminates prior to failure, the rupture zone is inclined to be more extensive than that observed in wood.

The characteristics described above cover the behavior of unidirectional laminates, as stress is applied parallel to the fibers. When such laminates are stressed at other angles (in plane), considerable degradation in properties result. Stiffness and strength decrease with angle of stress, until at 90° from the principal direction, the material approaches the characteristics of the resin. The material becomes frangible when stressed "off axis," and fracture usually takes place by splitting parallel to the fibers at stress levels comparable to the strength of the resin.

Unidirectional materials are only practical in bar or rod form where stresses are applied in directions parallel to the fibers. It is unrealistic to consider the use of unidirectional laminates as simple span plates for example, because the secondary transverse bending stresses would tend to cause cracking across the "grain." The common sense rules that apply to the use of wood should also govern the use of unidirectional laminates, because the behavior of the two materials is strikingly similar (in kind). For example, wood in timber form is efficient in tension, compression or flexure but cross-laminated plywood is the obvious solution for plate-like members.

Bidirectional Laminates in Tension

A more practical arrangement of fibers for a plate-like structure is that offered in a bidirectional laminate. For simplicity, let us assume for discussion a balanced laminate in which there are equal quantities of reinforcement oriented at right angles in the plane of the laminate. Such laminates can be produced from parallel laminations of balanced fabric, from crossed laminations or unidirectional fabrics, or from filaments laid down at 90° to each other in the filament winding process.

Complications arise when the theory of transformed sections is applied to bidirectional laminates because of two effects. First, the fibers perpendicular to the direction of stress prevent normal Poisson's contraction of the system; hence, they provide a stiffening effect not accounted for by simple one-dimensional theory. The other complication is caused by the crimping of fibers of woven fabrics; these crimps are particularly severe in plain-weave woven-roving construction, and they can cause substantial discontinuities in stress. Thus, the transformed section theory can yield only first-order approximations of stiffness and strength.

Stress-strain curves for bidirectional laminates are given in Figure 5-13(b). Under tensile stress parallel to either axis, the stress-strain relationship is linear to a point usually between 30 and 50 per cent of ultimate, and then there is a decrease in slope as the sample approaches failure. For obvious reasons, these slopes define an "initial" and "secondary" modulus, respectively—the two usually do not differ by more than a few per cent.

There is no fully quantitative explanation for the change in modulus with stress level. The author's opinion, based on some experimental work, is that the fibers oriented transverse to the direction of stress, cause stresses to arise that will fracture the resin around them. This would· indicate that there is microfailure within the laminate prior to reaching the ultimate strength of the laminate. The character of the fracture that occurs on ultimate tensile rupture of fabric-based laminates in some ways resembles torn cloth fabric, and this may be accompanied by delamination of neighboring plies. Cross-plied unidirectional materials will fail by splintering and delamination.

The preceding discussion covers the case of stressing a bidirectional laminate in its principal direction. If the laminate is truly balanced, the laws of symmetry dictate that the properties at 90° to the principal direction should duplicate those of the principal direction. They do in some systems; but in glass fabrics, for example, there may be a slight difference in construction that causes small but measurable differences in the properties in the two perpendicular directions.

In the case of balanced bidirectional laminates, tensile properties degrade as the angle of stress (in plane) is varied from the principal directions. Minimum properties are reached at 45° to the principal axes. When stressed at this angle, the laminate will deform, neck down, and stretch many per cent before ultimate fracture. Judged by the stress-strain diagram alone, the material describes a ductile type of behavior. Actually, substantial degradation of the resin occurs early in the stress history, and therefore, the behavior should not be considered as ductile. The deformation and fracture characteristics in the 45° direction are analogous to those of common fabric that is stretched on a bias.

Isotropic Laminates in Tension

Unidirectional and bidirectional laminates display in-plane directional properties. In contrast, mat-based constructions display isotropic behavior within the plane of the laminate.

While it is easy to rationalize that randomly deposited chopped or wandering fibers will produce a laminate having the nondirectional characteristics of an isotropic material, it has not yet been possible to describe the tensile behavior of mat-based laminates in terms of the properties of the principal components. Analysis for stresses and deformations becomes difficult because of the randomness of the system and because of the extreme complexity of the stress transfer between the reinforcement and the matrix. Qualitatively, however, laminate behavior tends to reflect the characteristics of the resin [see Figure 5-13 (c)]; resin content is usually high in mat-based laminates because the crisscross pattern of the fibers does not permit close packing of the reinforcement.

Laminates in Compression

The compressive behavior of a unidirectionally reinforced fiber glass-based composite differs from that observed in tension. The stress-strain relationship in compression is also approximately elastic to failure, but the compressive modulus is usually slightly lower than the tensile modulus. It is not significantly lower, and therefore transformed section theory can be applied to give reasonable estimates of compressive modulus based on the fiber area.

Since surface flaws should have little effect on compressive strength, the strength of a fiber in compression should be higher than that observed in tension. The obvious, but erroneous, conclusion would be that the compressive strength of a laminate should be greater than that found in tension. In fact, the compressive strength of highly loaded laminates is usually less than the tensile strength. The reason for this appears to be buckling instability; that is, either the resin is not stiff enough, or the resin-to-glass bond is not strong enough, to support the very fine, highly stressed fibers (or fiber bundles) against buckling. This can be seen on examination of fractures of laminates where the fibers split apart in a splintering fashion or where the laminate fails by sliding along a plane at 45° to the thickness. The former failure is probably a function of instability due to direct compression, whereas the latter may be initiated by shear as well as compressive instability. Since these forms of failure exist, simple transformed section theory cannot be used to predict compressive strength of laminates, and a more applicable theory remains evasive.

Compressive modulus and strength of unidirectional laminates will decrease as the angle of stress is varied from the principal direction of reinforcement. The pattern of the variation in properties with angle of stress is similar to that observed in tension.

Bidirectional laminates that are subjected to compression along either of their principal axes undergo a reasonably linear stress-strain relationship to failure. No dual modulus is observed in compression, and according to the author's theory none should; since the stress state around transverse fibers is compressive, microcracking should not be favored.

Compressive failure of bidirectional laminates will take many forms depending on the type and texture of the reinforcement. Fine-textured fabrics and cross-laminated unidirectional materials will usually fracture along a diagonal plane through the thickness. Coarser woven roving may fail by progressive "pop-out" buckling of the crimped strand, or an interlaminar cleavage plane may form, resulting in the splitting and buckling of individual plies.

"Off-axis" compressive properties of bidirectional laminates show the same general trend with angle as is observed in tension.

Compressive stress-strain behavior of mat-based isotropic laminates tends to reflect resin characteristics. Compressive rupture of mat-based materials will usually take the form of a diagonal fracture through the thickness of the laminate.

Laminates in Flexure

In flexure, behavior of the unidirectional laminate is reasonably elastic to failure. The modulus in flexure is often reported as being lower than that stated for either tension or compression. The author has shown that this is merely a function of the test method (ASTM or Military), and that true flexural modulus of the material is the average of the tensile and compressive moduli—as would be expected. The lower modulus in flexure that is usually reported neglects a shear deflection that can contribute substantially to the total deflection of the member under test. Although precise determination of deflection is usually not required, if high shear stresses do exist, they can be conservatively accounted for by conventional shear deflection formulas, providing the shear modulus of the resin is used.

Flexural strength of unidirectional laminates will always exceed the compressive strength of the material, and it can be greater than the tensile strength as well. There is no quantitative explanation as to why flexural strength should be so high, although this same result is observed in a variety of plastics and other materials. Perhaps the reason why flexural strength exceeds uniaxial compression strength can be explained by a theory that has been applied to wood, which shows similar behavior; that is, the stress gradient on the compression side allows only a few extreme fibers to be stressed highly, and the inner, low stressed fibers restrain these highly stressed fibers from the premature and massive buckling that exists in direct compression. An explanation for the observation that flexural strength exceeds uniaxial tensile strength has not yet been found. It is known that at span/depth ratios greater than those used in standard tests (span/depth ratio 16 to 18), the flexural strength will decrease and approach the tensile strength. It should also be noted, however, that substantial deflections occur, prior to failure at high span/depth ratios, and thus it is difficult to envision a practical case where such deflections would be tolerable. Hence, reduction in strength to account for the length effect is probably not necessary except in unusual cases.

Rupture in flexure will take either of two forms. One is similar to that found in compression where a diagonal failure will occur within the compression zone. The other form of failure is evidenced by progressive tensile rupture (splintering and delamination) starting at the extreme fibers and progressing through the thickness of the laminate. There appear to be no clear-cut criteria by which the exact type of failure can be predicted.

The preceding discussion that applies to unidirectional laminates in flexure is generally applicable to flexural behavior of bidirectional and isotropic laminates.

In-Plane Shear

In-plane shear, also known as plate shear, is defined here as the condition in which the plane of the applied shear stresses coincides with the plane of the laminate. Although in-plane shear properties are often critical in practical structures, such properties are usually neglected in the literature. This section will touch upon some of the more important aspects of in-plane shear behavior.

Shear properties of unidirectional laminates are strongly dependent upon angle of the applied stress relative to the axis of the

fibers [see Figure 5-14(a)]. When shear is applied parallel and perpendicular to the fiber axis, rupture will occur at a low value of stress, because only the weak resin prevents the sliding of neighboring fibers past each other. If the direction of shear stress is rotated to a position 45° to the fiber axis, the shear strength will also be low if the stress causes diagonal tension across the fibers. Here, again, only the relatively weak resin prevents the separation of the fibers under this diagonal tensile stress. If the 45° shear stress leads to diagonal compression transverse to the fibers, the resin will support substantial compression, while the diagonal tension is taken efficiently by the fibers.

Bidirectional laminates also display significant variations in shear properties with direction of stress [refer to Figure 5-14(b)]. When stress is applied parallel and perpen-

Shear at 0° & 90° permits sliding parallel to warp

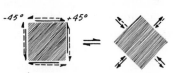

Shear at +45° causes compression across grain. Shear at -45° causes tension across grain.

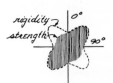

Variations in shear properties with angle to warp.

a. UNIDIRECTIONAL LAMINATES

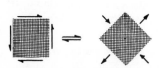

Shear at 0° & 90° causes direct stresses at 45° to act on bias.

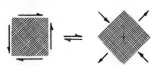

Shear at 45° causes direct stresses to act in direction of fibers.

Variations in shear properties with angle to warp.

b. BIDIRECTIONAL LAMINATES

Random fibers are effective at any angle.

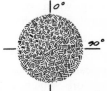

Shear properties do not vary with angle of stress.

c. ISOTROPIC (MAT) LAMINATES

FIG. 5-14. Directional characteristics of typical laminates under in-plane shear stress.

dicular to the warp direction, shear strength is low. This may best be understood, perhaps, if the shear stress is converted to diagonal tension and compression components, which lie at 45° to the warp direction. It should be clear that the diagonal tension stresses the laminate "on the bias"—the weak axis of the laminate. The action of the accompanying diagonal compression is to further increase the deformation caused by the diagonal tension. When the shear stress is oriented at 45° to the principal axis, the bidirectional laminate becomes an extremely efficient shear resisting structure. The diagonal tension and compression components, in this case, act along the warp and fill directions—the strong directions of the laminate.

Isotropic, mat-reinforced laminates, of course, show no directional effects with respect to in-plane shear stress [see Figure 5-14(c)]. These laminates are reasonably efficient in shear, because the randomness of the fibers renders some fibers available to resist diagonal tension and compression at any angle.

For simplicity, the in-plane modulus of rigidity was not included in the preceding discussion. In general, the modulus of rigidity will vary with angle from the principal axis in much the same manner as does the strength.

Brief note must be made of the types of tests that are used in the determination of shear properties. One test method[19] used at the Forest Products Laboratory involves stressing a 3-inch square test section in approximately "pure" shear. The method involves elaborate test fixtures, and specimen preparation procedures are time consuming when compared to uniaxial and flexural test techniques. Even after great care is taken in testing, results are often inconsistent. It has long been recognized that testing for shear properties is a difficult procedure which cannot be classified as suitable for routine quality control types of evaluation.

The Johnson-type shear test (Method 1041 of Federal Test Method Std. No. 406, October 5, 1961) is often used as an expedient over more complicated shear tests such as those developed at the Forest Products Laboratory. It is the author's view that the "punching" type of shear strength that is determined by the Johnson-type shear test has little relevance to the state of two-dimensional stress that exists, for example, in beam webs, plates, or flexural members. Reference 19 contains data that confirms this point. Caution is urged in using punch-type shear data in a structural design.

There is substantial evidence[19,20] that shear strength can be computed from simple tensile test data. The following equation governs this relationship:

$$\frac{1}{F_{\alpha\beta}{}^2} = \frac{4}{F_x{}^2} - \frac{1}{F_\alpha{}^2} - \frac{1}{F_\beta{}^2}$$

where

$F_{\alpha\beta}$ = shear strength with shear stress applied parallel and perpendicular to the warp

F_x = tensile strength at 45° to warp,

F_α = tensile strength parallel to warp,

F_β = tensile strength perpendicular to warp.

Although this equation in the form given does not provide values of shear strength at angles to the principal axis of the laminate, F_x is all that is required to predict ultimate strength under combined stress. (Failure under combined stress is treated in Reference 21). Because there is reasonable verification that the shear strength can be calculated, it is probably more advisable to use such values in a structural design. If this is done, simple tension tests at 0, 45 and 90° to the warp can replace the cumbersome plate shear test and the questionable punch-type shear test.

Interlaminar Characteristics

Fiber glass–reinforced plastics are particularly weak in shear whenever planes of unreinforced resin occur. Such planes may exist parallel to the reinforcement in a unidirectional laminate, and shear behavior of such systems has been discussed in the preceding section. Similar weak shear planes exist between layers of reinforcement. Since no interlayer reinforcements exist, the interlaminar strength is governed either by the strength of the resin or by the adhesion between the resin and the surface of the reinforcement. In either case, the interlaminar strength is low when compared to in-plane properties, and hence, interlaminar stress may become critical where shear stresses are high.

Interlaminar strength may prove critical in cases where tension exists normal to the plane of the plies, e.g., in a sharp corner subject to bending. But more commonly, interlaminar strength may prove to govern when laminates are subjected to shear stress in beams and plates.

Orthotropic and Layered Theories

Much of the in-plane behavior of laminates can be treated quantitatively by orthotropic theory. The strict definition of "orthotropic" implies a system in which there are three mutually perpendicular axes of elasticity; however, for simplicity, the theory for laminates neglects* the axis which is normal to the plane of the laminae. Orthotropic theory is well developed, and since it is presented in a number of references,[18,19,21–23] it will not be treated here in detail. The theory applies to the unique but common arrangement of reinforcement—that in which all layers are laminated parallel to each other. In essence, orthotropic theory can be used to predict modulus of elasticity, shear modulus and Poisson's ratio at any angle to the principal axes of the laminate (warp and fill), if these properties are known (measured) in the two principal directions. There has been reasonable verification of this theory as it applies to FRP laminates.[19]

There are also analytical expressions available that describe the in-plane behavior of laminates that are built up from laminae having different properties, and having their principal axes oriented in any way.[18,21–24] This layered theory assumes that in-plane strains of each orthotropic layer of the composite are equal, since the layers are, in fact, bonded together with the interlaminar resin. Analysis for stresses and strains using this theory can become complex

if there are a great number of differing plies or if there are a great number of orientations to be considered. It has been verified[24] that the layered theory provides reasonable estimates of the variations in properties with angle of loading. Because the theory is cumbersome to apply, it is common practice to use test values in cases where laminates are built up from a complex arrangement of layers.

The theories described above apply to laminates that are subject to stress lying within their plane. There are analytical expressions developed to cover the case of flexure,[25] but these are extremely complex in application. As a result, flexural test data are used in most practical designs.

"Pseudo-brittle" Behavior

The extent to which a material shows brittle or ductile tendencies will have great influence on the way it is used in a design. Brittleness implies rapid crack propagation from a local overstress, and hence the potential of catastrophic collapse; to be conservative, high safety factors and extreme care in stress analysis must be taken. There are, of course, several reasons why ductility is the desired feature. Ductility can be relied upon to relieve high stress concentrations in local areas, and in some cases, it permits excessive deflections to occur without total failure—giving visible warning of impending failures. Indeed, ductility allows the full utilization of sections or structures that are otherwise inefficient (e.g., plastic design in steel). When judged by some standards, fiber glass-reinforced plastics appear brittle; by others, they are not. It is important, then, to consider these measures of brittleness and determine their implications in a structural design.

Stress-strain curves of fiber glass-reinforced plastics will vary depending upon reinforcement and orientation of stress. However, most stress-strain curves taken along the natural principal axes are reasonably straight up to failure. There is certainly no yield domain such as occurs, for example, in structural steel. By one definition—the

---

* This is equivalent to the assumption made in common plate theory, where normal stresses are assumed small compared to in-plane stresses.

lack of yield deformation—fiber glass-reinforced plastics must be considered brittle. But fiber glass-reinforced plastics do not demonstrate other types of behavior common to the classical brittle materials, e. g., glass, concrete and cast iron. Brittle materials shatter on impact and rupture, forming clean, sharp surfaces; FRP materials are impact resistant and the rupture is more like tearing or splintering. Brittle materials have tensile strengths on the order of one-tenth of their compressive strengths; FRP materials have tensile strengths that are one-half to over two times their compressive strength. Brittle materials are sensitive to stress concentrations and fail when the magnitude of the stress concentration exceeds the ultimate strength of the material, even though other portions of the section are under markedly lower stress; FRP systems show relatively small sensitivity to stress concentration, such as small holes and notches. Although fiber glass-reinforced plastic systems lack ductility, their behavior does not reflect all of the common undesirable features that nonductile materials usually display. Therefore, FRP may be termed "pseudo-brittle."

It is the author's belief that the composite nature of the material leads to many of the "pseudo-brittle" characteristics of fiber glass-reinforced plastics. Take, for example, impact resistance, which is a function of the ease of crack propagation within a material. If a crack is initiated in a fiber glass composite, its path will not be long before a fiber or a fiber bundle is intercepted. Considerable energy will be absorbed in the rupture of this bundle, and thus there is a tendency to hinder the further progression of the crack. In a sense, local microfracture at the tip of a crack serves to inhibit crack growth in much the same manner as does yield deformation in ductile steel. Similar reasoning can be applied to explain the behavior that occurs at the tip of a sharp notch or at the edge of a small hole where stress concentrations exist. Adjustments in stress level at such points of stress concentration can occur through local microfracture, again simulating the behavior of ductile steels. This microfracture mecha-

nism appears to be a reasonable explanation for "pseudo-brittle" behavior.

It is critical to point out that fibers must be present to resist the tendency of crack propagation. There are two important conditions that arise in which reinforcement is not available to inhibit crack growth. One such condition is found in highly directional laminates, where cracks can (and do) easily propagate parallel to the fibers. The second case is in the interlaminar resin layers where cleavage can be initiated rather easily. For these cases, the material must be considered brittle.

In light of the foregoing discussion, the following considerations appear applicable:

(a) The linear stress-strain characteristics require the use of the elastic approach to analysis and design.

(b) Although the stress-strain curve is linear to fracture, high safety factors need not be employed as is required for other linear materials such as glass and concrete (in tension). This is reasonable providing fibers are present to inhibit crack growth.

(c) The material must be considered as brittle in certain weak planes where the resin is not reinforced.

(d) Gross overstress cannot be relieved by the local "microfracture" mechanism proposed and, thus, the designer cannot count on yielding to adjust for inaccuracies of design—analysis must be as accurate as possible.

Consideration of these points should lead to a realistic approach to a structural design with "pseudo-brittle" fiber glass-reinforced plastics.

ENGINEERING PROPERTIES

The purpose of this section is to provide reasonable working values for the engineering properties of "typical" fiber glass-reinforced plastic laminates that may find application in building structures. Before values are given, it is necessary to impose certain conditions in order that the presentation be kept to a manageable level, and to establish a frame of reference for the later discussion of the influence of major parameters on the quoted test values. The restrictions imposed are the following:

(1) Only the more typical reinforcements that were described in the section beginning on p. 84 will be considered.

(2) Principal axes of the reinforcements coincide with the principal axes of the laminate—random orientations of layers are not considered.

(3) The resin is a rigid or semi-rigid (maximum of 10% flexible component) general-purpose polyester. (Data are probably valid for acrylic modified and coreactive fire-retardant resin grades.)

(4) The coupling agent is a quality, silane type.

(5) Hand layup process is used, and consolidation is achieved without the use of pressure (contact method).

(6) Complete cure has been achieved by proper choice of time and temperature schedule and catalyst concentration.

(7) Good fabrication practice has been followed in storage and handling of materials, workmanship, and quality control.

With these restrictions applied, it is possible to quote some "typical" laminate properties and such are given in Table 5-5.

Typical Properties

The properties given in Table 5-5 should be typical of values that may be obtained from laminates that are prepared with normal care. Properties could easily be higher than those noted if great care is taken in workmanship and if positive pressure is applied during consolidation and curing of the laminate, but in general, such steps would involve fabrication expense that could not

TABLE 5-5. Properties of General-purpose Polyester Resin-based Laminates Reinforced With Various Fiberglass Constructions

		Main Reinforcement		Local Reinforcement	
	MAT (2 oz/sq ft)	WOVEN ROVING	10-oz FABRIC	181 FABRIC	143 FABRIC PARALLEL LAMINATED
PROPERTY					
% glass by weight	25	50	45	60	60
Specific gravity	1.4	1.6	1.6	1.8	1.8
Elastic Properties					
Modulus of elasticity (in plane) psi $\times 10^6$	0.82	2.40	2.20	2.5	4.5
Direction ratio (0°/45°/90°)	(1/1/1)	(1/0.4/0.9)	(1/0.5/1)	(1/0.6/0.9)	(1/0.3/0.3)
Shear rigidity (in plane), psi $\times 10^6$	0.40	0.45	0.52	0.57	0.48
Direction ratio (−45°/0°/45°)	(1/1/1)	(2*/1/2*)	(2*/1/2*)	(2/1/2)	(2/1/2)
Shear rigidity (interlaminar), psi $\times 10^6$*	0.16	0.16	0.16	0.16	0.16
Poisson's ratio	0.32	0.14	0.14	0.12	0.25
Direction ratio (0°/45°/90°)	(1/1/1)	(1/4.5/0.8)	(1/4.5/0.8)	(1/4.5*/0.9)	(1/—/0.24)
Strength Properties					
Tension (in plane), psi	11,000	33,000	24,000	33,000	65,000
Direction ratio (0°/45°/90°)	(1/1/1)	(1/0.3/0.9)	(1/0.5/0.8)	(1/0.5/0.9)	(1/0.2/0.1)
Compression (in plane), psi	22,000	17,000	21,000	26,000	39,000
Direction ratio (0°/45°/90°)	(1/1/1)	(1/0.6/1)	(1/0.7/0.9)	(1/0.6*/1)	(1/0.3*/0.4)
Flexure (in plane), psi	20,500	31,000	31,000	39,000	68,000
Direction ratio (0°/45°/90°)	(1/1/1)	(1/0.6/1)	(1/0.8/1)	(1/0.5*/0.9)	(1/0.2*/0.2)
Shear (in plane), psi	7,800**	5,100**	6,540**	8,000	6,500
Direction ratio (−45°/0°/45°)	(1/1/1)	(—/1/—)	(—/1/—)	(2/1/2.2)	(1.1/1/2.3)
Shear (interlaminar), psi	1,500*	1,500*	1,500*	4,100	3,000*

* Estimated values.
** Shear strength calculated, see p. 106.

normally be justified in "custom" types of building structures.* On the other hand, the properties could be much lower than the values quoted if workmanship is substandard and adequate quality control measures are not followed during fabrication. Thus, the term "typical" as applied to the data, implies an end product of reasonable or average quality.

Published data were used and modified freely in the preparation of Table 5-5. In particular, reference 26 was used as the source of data for the mat, woven roving, and 1000 cloth laminates. This excellent source reports considerable variations in properties depending upon thickness of the laminate and quality of fabrication (laminates from four fabricators were studied). In this case, a rounded-off average value for a thickness of $5/16$-inch was used, and the values that were representative of two or more fabricators were assumed as typical. Reference 20, another excellent reference for designers, was used as a source for data on the 181 and 143 fabric-based laminates. Since the latter source is intended as a guide to design of flight vehicles, the author's view is that the quality of the laminates described might be too high for building structures, where optimum laminates may not be economically justified. Thus, the values reported in the reference were rounded off at 15 per cent below quoted values. In some cases, it was necessary to use calculated values for directions other than the principal directions of the laminate. There were other cases in which the author used his considered judgment in estimating values, and these data are so designated in Table 5-5. It should also be noted that no reductions were taken in Poisson's ratio values. It is the author's best judgment that the data given in Table 5-5 are reasonable and that they represent values that can be achieved when quality materials are fabricated with reasonable care.

Further note must be made of the condi-

tions of test under which the source data are valid. First, test samples were submersed in water for at least 30 days prior to test. Next, tests were performed under standard conditions of 73°F and 50 per cent relative humidity. And finally, duration of test was on the order of a few minutes. The test conditions, being standard, are those usually used to determine most data that appear in the literature.

As has been noted in earlier discussions there are usually some differences found in modulus of elasticity, depending upon whether the sample is stressed in tension, compression or flexure. For simplicity, only one value is quoted, and this is the average value of the tensile and compressive modulus of the material. Modulus for any given stress condition should not vary by much more than 10 per cent of the value quoted. If modulus is a critical factor in design, test values on the actual laminate under consideration should be obtained.

A new term, direction ratio, has been introduced in Table 5-5. The direction ratio is merely the ratio of properties at 45 or 90° to the properties in the warp direction. In the case of in-plane shear properties, the direction ratio defines the ratio of properties at −45 or +45° to the principal direction of the laminate (see Figures 5-13 and 5-14). It is believed that the direction ratio permits a clearer presentation of the significant characteristics of each material than it is possible to give if properties in each direction are listed separately.

Influence of Major Parameters

Discussion in earlier sections of this chapter has implied, in varying degrees of detail, that a great number of parameters will affect the engineering properties of fiber glass-reinforced plastic laminates. Materials, environment, stress and stress history, and variations in fabrication methods and control will all have their influence on the ultimate performance of a structure. Space does not permit the detailing of all possible variations that can occur, and indeed in many cases, the interaction among variables

---

*Recent improvements in finishes may account for 10 to 20 percent increases in properties given in Table 5-5.

is complex, and not well understood. The effects of some of the major parameters that may be encountered in building applications have been studied however, and these will be treated in the following sections.

Effect of Water. It is generally felt that a high percentage of the ultimate degradation due to water will occur after 30 days exposure to water (or after a 2-hour boil period, as is called for in some specifications). Thus, it is common practice to take no further reduction in "wet" test values, such as are quoted in Table 5-5, for situations where FRP materials are subject to normal moisture conditions.

Effects of Weathering. Some of the effects of weathering on the strength of polyester-based laminates have been noted on p. 91. and in Table 5-4. There are several other sources of data on the effects of weathering,[27–30] perhaps the most significant of which is reference 29. In this reference, data are presented for the loss of strength of general-purpose polyester resin reinforced with 181 fabric that had been stressed *during* exposure for three years in Florida. (Florida exposure is considered the most severe environment for FRP laminates.) In the tests described, control samples were kept at normal laboratory conditions, while a second set of samples was exposed to the Florida environment. A third set of samples was held, during exposure, at a constant deformation that was equivalent to 25 per cent of the short-term ultimate deflection of the sample. All samples were tested at the end of the exposure period. Results of the tests are given in Table 5-6. There was permanent set in the stressed samples which indicated that stress was not constant during exposure, but nonetheless, certain implications are clear. Severe weathering causes a reduction of up to 40 per cent of initial short-term strength, and this reduction occurs whether or not the laminate is stressed to modest stress levels.

The foregoing results consider weathering degradation on a percentage basis, but it is critically important to note the effects of weathering on the absolute reduction in strength. The materials and fabrication procedures used in preparing the samples were essentially those prescribed in military standards. The data in Table 5-5, as derived from reference 21, were also based on laminates prepared according to military standards. The critical fact to note is that the absolute strength values reported in reference 21, as obtained after wet conditioning, differ by only a few per cent, in the worst case, from the values reported after 3 years exposure in Florida. Data in the other sources mentioned show similar trends. Thus, a reasonable conclusion is that test data based on standard wet conditioning procedures adequately reflect the degradation to be expected after extended and severe outdoor exposure.

In the foregoing experiments, no special care was taken in formulating or in otherwise protecting the laminate surface from attack by weather. It has been noted on p. 91 that

TABLE 5-6. Effects of Three Years of Florida Weathering on the Strength of General-purpose Polyester Resin-based 181 Fabric-reinforced Laminates

Stress Mode	Control Strength[30] (psi)	Strength after Exposure[30] (psi)	Wet Strength of Equivalent Laminates[21] psi)
Tension	56,000	44,000 U 45,400 S	38,000
Compression	47,000	34,600 U 30,500 S	30,000
Flexure	72,100	45,600 U 42,400 S	⁻45,000

Note: U = Unstressed during exposure.
　　　S = Stressed during exposure.

acrylic-modified polyester systems show better strength retention than do general-purpose polyester systems.* Weather-resistant coatings or gel coats would also prevent the surface erosion and subsequent fiber exposure that occurs in general-purpose polyester systems. Thus, if some special precautions are taken to increase weather resistance, the strength retention under severe weather conditions can be improved. In any event, it seems reasonable that the data in Table 5-5 have been sufficiently reduced (for the effect of moisture) to account for the effects of severe outdoor exposure.

at 160°F. This may be taken as an indication that ambient temperatures existing in buildings will probably not have significant effect on laminate properties.

Effects of Duration of Stress. The duration of stress has a marked effect on the strength and stiffness of fiber glass-reinforced plastic laminates. The general trend is that of an increase in strength (perhaps 15 per cent) and stiffness (about 5 per cent) when loads last a few seconds rather than the few minutes required for standard tests. If, however, loads are applied for long durations relative to the conditions of standard tests, laminate

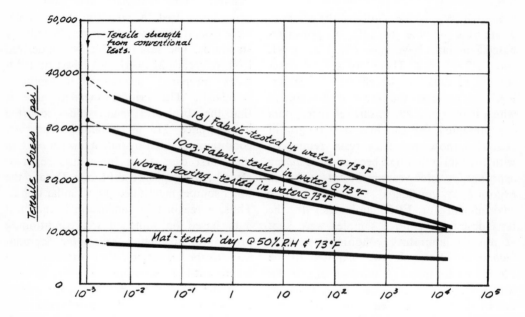

FIG. 5-15. Tensile stress-rupture characteristics of general-purpose polyester-based laminates having various styles of reinforcement.[31]

Effects of Temperature. There are little data available on the effects of temperature on engineering properties. Generally, properties will increase at temperatures below normal test temperature (73°F) and decrease above this temperature. One requirement of Mil-R-7575A (12) is that 181 fabric-based general-purpose rigid polyester resins retain 80 per cent of their strength and 92 per cent of their stiffness after one-half hour exposure

strength and stiffness may be much lower than the values quoted in Table 5-5.

Figure 5-15[31] illustrates this point for prolonged tensile stress for several laminates under wet conditions. At the end of 10,000 hours (1.15 years) the stress is between 39 and 48 per cent of short time standard test values which are shown at time = 0.0015 hour. The relationships between time and stress are linear on a semilog scale, and the trend is confirmed in some cases for stress durations up to 3.3 years. An empirical relationship describing the stress-rupture

*Recent advances in finish technology have also lead to improved strength retention after exposure to weather.

characteristics has been derived from these and similar plots. That is:

$$\sigma_R = \sigma_0 - M \log t$$

where

σ_R = stress (psi) that can be maintained for a given time interval,

t = time interval (hours),

σ_0, M = constants from stress-rupture plot.

Constants are given in Table 5-7. (The short-term strength of the mat laminate seems to be unusually low when compared to data

tain a reasonable estimate of the strains occurring for any duration of stress and stress level.

Effects of Cyclic Fatigue. FRP laminates are sensitive to the effects of cyclic stressing. Data are not available for fatigue effects on all types of laminates, but data on a number of reinforcements (mat and fine fabrics) in polyester resins, indicate that stress levels of ½ to ⅔ of short time strength can be supported for up to 1000 cycles.[32,33] There appears to be no well-defined endur-

TABLE 5-7. Constants Describing Stress-Rupture and Strain/Time/Stress Characteristics of Polyester-based Laminates[31]

Material	For Stress-Rupture			For Strain/Time/Stress			
	σ_0 (psi)	M (psi)	ϵ_0 (in/in)	σ_ϵ (psi)	m' (in/in)	σ_m (psi)	n
181 fabric	27,700	3050	0.033	80,000	0.00017	13,000	0.210
181 fabric (FR)*	26,300	3300	—	—	—	—	—
10-oz. Fabric	22,500	2620	0.280	80,000	0.00011	6,500	0.190
Woven roving	17,700	1800	0.206	40,000	0.0146	40,000	0.230
Mat**	6,400	275	0.0067	8,500	0.0011	8,500	0.190

* FR indicates general purpose resin with 10% flexibilizer; all other materials are based on general-purpose polyester resins.
** Mat laminates were tested dry; all other materials were stressed while submersed in water.

from other sources.) The stress level that can be maintained by a laminate for any time interval may be predicted by use of the Table and the equation.

Similar data have been developed for the change in strain with duration of stress. The equation governing the strain/time/stress relationship is as follows.

$$\epsilon_t = \epsilon_0 \sinh \frac{\sigma}{\sigma_m} + m't^n \sinh \frac{\sigma}{\sigma_m}$$

where

t = time of stress application (hours),

ϵ_t = strain (inches per inch) occurring in time t,

σ = stress level (psi) that is applied for time t,

$\epsilon_0, \sigma_m, m', n$ = empirical constants from strain/time/stress plot.

Table 5-7 contains values for the constants in the above equation, which apply to rigid general-purpose polyester resins reinforced with a number of fabric constructions. With such information, it is possible to ob-

ance limit in fiber glass-reinforced plastics, as there is in many metals, however, most degradation due to fatigue occurs by at least 10^6 to 10^7 cycles. Polyester-based laminates will support stresses of 20 to 30 per cent of short-term strength in the few million cycle range, and this is independent of type of reinforcement (mat, fine fabric or woven roving.)

Effects of Stress Concentrations.

Stresses around Notches and Holes. In the discussion of pseudo-brittleness of FRP (p. 107) it was noted that the material is less sensitive to sharp notches and small holes than are perfectly brittle materials. Sensitivity is shown to be small by data presented in reference 21, where the effects of "V" notches and holes of ⅛-inch diameter are noted. Ultimate failure stresses on the net section were 70 to 100 percent of laminate strength—in contrast, brittle materials would fail at 40 per cent or less of the strength of the bulk laminate. There is also evidence that the effects of such concentrations on cyclic and static fatigue are not great. A microfracture mechanism has been proposed as the mode of relief of small stress concentrations. It has also been noted (on p. 108) that stress concentrations cannot be relieved by microfracture if a large zone of overstress exists. Thus far, analytical or empirical expressions have not been developed to define the point of transition between "small" and "large" stress concentrations. Some experimental studies have been made[34] which indicate that the transition lies somewhere between the 1/8-inch diameter and a 1-inch diameter hole size. Tests on a 1/8-inch thick 181 fabric-based general-purpose polyester laminate show that a 50 per cent reduction in bulk laminate strength will occur on the net section of a 3-inch plate having a 1-inch diameter hole. This reduction approaches the 60 per cent reduction expected for a circular hole in an infinite plate, and so, holes of 1-inch diameter or greater should be expected to produce stress concentrations close to theoretical. Concentrations arising from holes of this diameter or greater cannot be relieved by the mechanism of microfracture.

Stresses in Bolted Connections. Significant stress concentrations can arise as a result of the complex stress condition existing in bolted connections. Laminate failures in bolted connections can take the following forms:

(a) Crushing in bolt bearing,
(b) Fracture across a row of bolt holes,
(c) Pullout of the bolt through the end of the laminate.

It is, of course, desirable to design a connection such that failure occurs in by crushing in bolt bearing, since some visible warning of impending failure may be given by excessive joint deformation. In addition, crushing in bolt bearing may provide a mechanism for adjustment of stress if an unequal distribution of stress occurs, for example, along a row of bolts.

Proper spacing of bolts in a connection should insure that failure does not occur by laminate fracture or pullout. Reference 26 provides data for the required edge and side distances and bolt spacing such that failure will occur by bolt failure or crushing in bolt bearing (see Table 5-8). Data are also given for bearing strength for 1/4-inch diameter bolts in laminates of 1/4-inch thickness. The use of bolt diameter to thickness ratios of 2, will reduce these values by 70 per cent; therefore, it is desirable to keep bolt diameter small relative to laminate thickness. More extensive bolt bearing data are presented in the literature.[22,26,35]

Many of the problems arising from the use of bolted connections can be reduced or eliminated through the use of adhesive-bonded joints. In some respects adhesive bonding is the more efficient joining method because it is compatible with the continuous structure offered by FRP. Adhesive bonding is a field in itself and, as such, it cannot be treated here. Reference 36 is an excellent source covering the practical aspects of adhesive bonding of FRP materials. In general, the greatest problem encountered in using adhesive-bonding techniques is that of insuring quality of the bond.

Effects of Thickness. There is much contradictory evidence concerning the variation of laminate strength with laminate thickness. Some sources report increases in strength with thickness whereas others claim that the opposite trend exists. Empirical relationships which support the latter hypothesis have been proposed in reference 21. These are similar to form factors used in timber design for the reduction of the allowable extreme fiber stress in bending due to increase in beam depth. The author's belief is that there are many interrelated factors that can affect the strength/thickness relationship and that the application of a simple empirical formula may prove tenuous.

Data reported in reference 26 show some effect of thickness (in the range of 1/2 to 1/8 inch) but this effect varies with the style of reinforcement and the mode of stressing. Data are given for mat, woven roving and 10-ounce cloth-based laminates. The major variations in properties with thickness were found in the mat laminates. Also, variations in properties of "identical" materials made by four fabricators were noted. In general, the greatest variations found among fabricators were in the mat-based materials. The variations observed are probably due to the constant, strength and modulus of elasticity will increase with decreasing thickness (increased compaction), but moment resistance and stiffness may well decrease with

TABLE 5-8. Characteristics of Bolted Connections of General-purpose Polyester-based Laminates[26]

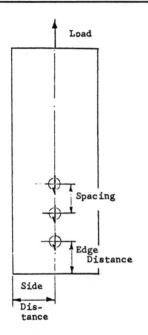

| | Fabric Style | |
	Woven Roving or Cloth	Mat
Edge distance (bolt dia.)	2.5	2.0
Side distance (bolt dia.)	2.5	2.0
Spacing (bolt dia.)	3.0	3.0
Bearing strength* (% of tensile strength)		
No permanent deformation	64	187
At Failure	91	289

* For ¼-in. diameter bolt in ¼-in.-thick laminates. Bearing strength will change for other relative proportions.

fact that mat materials can be compressed during fabrication to varying degrees depending upon the starting thickness and the amount of compactive effort expended. Certainly some of the variations found with thickness and fabrication can be attributed to degree of compaction.

There is another point that must be made regarding thickness. It must be remembered that FRP is built up from layers and that a significant portion of layer strength is governed by the amount of glass area present. The author's experience has been that the tensile strength, for example as expressed by pounds per ply per inch width will be essentially constant whereas tensile strength as expressed in pounds per square inch will vary widely. Thus, compactive effort, and hence laminate thickness, may vary widely, but the tensile *force* capacity of the laminate will remain unchanged. Similar effects can be seen in flexure. If quantity of glass is held decreasing thickness. Since moment resistance and stiffness are the critical factors in structural design, it should be apparent that optimum compaction methods do not necessarily yield the most effective laminate. Reference 37 presents an excellent discussion and extensive data in support of this view.

Effects of Fabrication Variables. The properties of an end product made from FRP will be strongly dependent upon the care, talents, equipment and materials offered by the fabricator. Unfortunately, it is difficult to specify and control all of the variables that may be introduced by the fabricator, because so many of them are interrelated.[38] Certainly, the results given in reference 26 give adequate testimony as to the variations that can be expected among fabricators who use the same materials prepared according to the same specifications. In some instances, properties differed by a factor of two, and in many cases, the ratio was three to one depending upon the fabricator. The author's experience has been that "name" of the fabricator has little to do with the quality of his product, and yet some small, local fabricators have produced laminates over a period of years with remarkably consistent results. With such possible variations among fabricators, the best course is to specify the materials to be used and then verify the results with performance tests. Before a fabricator is selected, it should be required that representative coupons *made under realistic conditions* be provided for test.

An excellent list of specifications covering materials and performance requirements is given in reference 39.

CONCLUDING REMARKS

An attempt has been made to familiarize the potential designer of fiber glass-reinforced plastic structures with an objective picture of the materials' capabilities as they now stand. Applications, materials and processes as they presently exist have been treated, and particular attention has been given to materials' behavior and the influence of significant parameters of process, stress and environment on them. There are those who would say that we do not know enough about these materials to apply them to a structure in a building. The author must admit that much of the information contained here was not at his fingertips at the outset of this work, but his confidence in this material has multiplied with study of the vast amount of information that has been developed. True, we will probably never know or understand all of the intricate interrelationships that govern the performance of this complex material, but neither do we understand completely the behavior of timber, concrete or steel—they too remain subjects of intensive research. It is the author's hope that this presentation has placed FRP in its proper perspective, that is, that FRP is an engineering material that can be designed with reasonable confidence to meet major structural tasks.

Acknowledgments. Mr. Herbert B. Ailes of Owens-Corning Fiberglas, Dr. Frank J. Heger of Simpson Gumpertz and Heger, Inc. and Mr. Arthur L. Smith, Consultant, have added considerably to the content of this chapter by their helpful comments and discussions, and my wife, Ann, has contributed immeasureably in many ways; their help is deeply appreciated.

This chapter was witten while the author was a research staff member of the Materials Division, Department of Civil Engineering, Massachusetts Institute of Technology, Cambridge, Massachusetts; the services provided by this organization during the preparation of the manuscript are greatfully acknowledged.

Photos were supplied by Owens-Corning Fiberglas Corp.

REFERENCES

1. Chapman, H. H., Jr., "The Economics of Fiberglas Reinforced Plastic in Automotive Bodies," Proceedings of the 18th Annual Technical and Management Conference, Reinforced Plastics Division, SPI Inc., 1963.*

2. Nilo, S. C., "Ground Radomes," *SPE J.*, **19**, No. 2 (February 1959).

3. Fretz, G. C., "Design, Fabrication and Erection of 140-ft. Diameter Honeycomb-Sandwich Radome," Proceedings of the 15th Annual Technical and Management Conference, Reinforced Plastics Division, SPI Inc., 1960.*

4. Rosato, D. V., and Grove, C. S., Jr., "Filament Winding: Its Development, Manufacture, Applications and Design," New York, Interscience Publishers, 1964.

5. Dietz, A. G. H., Heger, F. J., and McGarry, F. J., "Engineering the Plastics House," *SPE J.*, **13**, No. 5 (May 1957).

6. Dietz, A. G. H., "Plastics in the Construction of the U. S. Pavilion, Brussels World's Fair," Proceedings of the 13th Annual Technical and Management Conference, Reinforced Plastics Division, SPI Inc., 1958.*

7. "U. S. Pavilion in Moscow," *Mod. Plastics*, **37**, No. 4 (December 1959).

8. Goody, M. E., "Design and Prototype Construction of Flexible, Segmental School Building," Proceedings of the 17th Annual Technical and Management Conference, Reinforced Plastics Division, SPI Inc., 1962.*

9. "Modular Motel," *Mod. Plastics* (February 1964).

10. Turner, W. F., and Banks, J. H., "Reinforced Plastics Forms in Poured Concrete Building Construction," Proceedings of the 18th Annual Technical and Management Conference, Reinforced Plastics Division, SPI Inc., 1963.*

11. Boyd, A. R., and Moore, L. D., "Properties and Application of Non Woven Unidirectional Materials," Proceedings of the 18th Annual Technical and Management Conference, Reinforced Plastics Division, SPI Inc., 1963.*

12. Military Specification, "Resin, Low Pressure Laminating," MIL-R-7575A, 27 April 1953.

13. Hammerl, A. J., "Designing Fire Retardance into Reinforced Plastics Structures," Proceedings of the 18th Annual Technical Conference, Society of Plastics Engineers, January, 1962.

14. Burton, G. W., "Flame Retardant Laminates," Proceedings of the 16th Annual Technical and Management Conference, Reinforced Plastics Division, SPI Inc., 1961.*

15. Smith A. L., and Lowry, J. R., "Long Term Durability of Acrylic Polyesters vs. 100% Acrylic Resins in Glass Reinforced Construction," Proceedings of the 15th Annual Technical and Management Conference, Reinforced Plastics Division, SPI Inc., 1960.*

16. Lampman, J. R., and Damon, G. F., "Protective Coatings for Electronic Laminates," Proceedings of the 14th Annual Technical and Management Conference, Reinforced Plastics Division, SPI Inc., 1959.*

17. Elliot, E. C., and Hoffman, K. R., "Results Illustrating the Effect of Silane Coupling Agents on the Properties of Reinforced Plastics," Proceedings of the 18th Annual Technical and Management Conference, Reinforced Plastics Division, SPI Inc., 1963.*

18. Baer, E., Editor, "Engineering Design for Plastics," New York, Reinhold Publishing Corp., 1964.

19. Werren, F., and Norris, C. B., "Directional Properties of Glass-Fabric-Base Plastic Laminate Panels of Sizes that Do Not Buckle," Reports No. 1803 and Supplement, U. S. Forest Products Laboratory, Forest Service, U. S. Department of Agriculture, Madison, Wisconsin, April, 1950.

20. Werren, F., "Mechanical Properties of Plastic Laminates," Report No. 1820, U. S. Forest Products Laboratory, Forest Service, U. S. Department of Agriculture, Madison, Wisconsin, February, 1951.

21. MIL-HDBK-17, "Plastics for Flight Vehicles," Part I, Reinforced Plastics, Armed Forces Supply Support Center, Washington, D. C., November, 1959.

22. Dietz, A. G. H., Editor, "Engineering Laminates," New York, John Wiley & Sons, Inc., 1949.

23. Sonneborn, R. H., "Fiberglas Reinforced Plastics," New York, Reinhold Publishing Corp., 1954.

24. Erickson, E. C. O., and Norris, C. B., "Tensile Properties of Glass-Fabric Laminates with Laminations Oriented in Any Way," Report No. 1853, U. S. Forest Products Laboratory, Forest Service, U. S. Department of Agriculture, Madison, Wisconsin, Nov. 1955.

25. Stavsky, Y., and McGarry, F. J., "Investigation of Mechanics of Reinforced Plastics," WADD Technical Report No. 60–746, July, 1961.

26. Gibbs and Cox, Inc., "Marine Design Manual for Fiberglass Reinforced Plastics," New York, McGraw-Hill Book Co., 1960.

27. Werren, F., "Weathering of Glass-Fabric Base Plastic Laminates," WADC Technical Report 55–319, Supplement I, ASTIA Document No. 208316,** Wright Air Development Center, Air Research and Development Command, U. S. Air Force, Wright-Patterson Air Force Base, Ohio, January, 1959.

28. Werren, F., "Weathering of Glass-Fabric-Base Plastic Laminates," WADC Technical Report 55–319, Supplement 3, Wright Air Development Division, Air Research and Development Command, U. S. Air Force, Wright-Patterson Air Force Base, Ohio, March, 1961.

29. Kimball, K. E., "Weathering of Glass-Fabric-Base Plastic Laminates Under Stress," ASD Technical Report 61–145, Aeronautical Systems Division, Air Force Systems Command, U. S. Air Force, Wright-Patterson Air Force Base, Ohio, June, 1961.

30. Kimball, K. E., "Effects of Weathering on the Mechnical Properties of Four Reinforced Plastic Laminates," Technical Report No. WADC–TR–55–319, Supplement 4, Directorate of Material and Processes, Aeronautical Systems Division, Air Force Systems Command, Wright-Patterson Air Force Base, Ohio, October, 1962.

31. Boller, K. H., "Effect of Long-Term Loading on Glass-Reinforced Plastic Laminates," Proceedings of the 14th Annual Technical and Management Conference, Reinforced Plastics Division, SPI Inc., 1959.*

32. Boller, K. H., "Fatigue Properties of Glass-Fiber Reinforced Plastic Laminates Subjected to Various Conditions," Proceedings of the 12th Annual Technical and Management Conference, Reinforced Plastics Division, SPI Inc., 1957.*

33. Fried, N., "Fatigue Strength of Reinforced Plastics," Proceedings of the 12th Annual Technical and Management Conference, Reinforced Plastics Division, SPI Inc., 1957.*

34. Strauss, E. L., "Effects of Stress Concentrations on the Strength of Reinforced Plastic Laminates," Proceedings of the 14th Annual Technical and Management Conference, Reinforced Plastics Division, SPI Inc., 1959,*

35. Strauss, E. L., "Design of Mechanical Joints for Reinforced Plastic Structures," Proceedings of the 15th Annual Technical and Management Conference, Reinforced Plastics Division. SPI Inc., 1960.*

36. Perry, H. A., "Adhesive Bonding of Reinfocred Plastics," New York, McGraw-Hill Book Co., 1959.

37. Moore, L. D., and Lahde, P., "Evaluation of Laminate Construction for Boats," Proceedings of the 13th Annual Technical and Management Conference, Reinforced Plastics Division, SPI Inc., 1958.*

38. Sonneborn, R. H., Isham, A. B., and Dennen, F. W., "Control of Variables in Heat Resistant Glass Reinforced Plastics," Proceedings of the 15th Annual Technical and Management Conference, Reinforced Plastics Division, SPI Inc., 1960.*

39. Beach, N. E., "Defense Specifications and Standards for and Relating to Reinforced Plastics," Plastics Technical Evaluation Center, Picatinny Arsenal, Dover, New Jersey, March, 1963.

* Preprints of the Proceedings containing these papers are available from The Society of the Plastics Industry, Inc., 250 Park Avenue, New York 17, New York. 10017.

** ASTIA Documents may be obtained from Armed Services Technical Information Agency, Arlington Hall Station, Arlington, Virginia.

6 DESIGN OF REINFORCED PLASTIC SHELL STRUCTURES

Frank J. Heger

Simpson Gumpertz & Heger Inc.
Consulting Engineers
Cambridge, Massachusetts

INTRODUCTION

Fiber-glass-reinforced plastics (FRP) may be molded to form large curved shell elements with relative ease; consequently they are appropriate structural materials for shell structures. For applications such as roof structures, liquid containers and pressure vessels, shell construction often provides an effective means of minimizing quantity of structural material required for enclosure and load transfer. In such applications, FRP materials may be economical solutions to the problem of structural enclosure.

In addition to their easy adaptability to molding, they are strong and light. They are relatively stiff compared with most other materials with similar adaptability for molding, but have low stiffness compared to more traditional structural materials such as steel, aluminum, and reinforced concrete.

FRP materials provide significant benefits beyond their structural qualities. They have inherently high corrosion resistance. They can be fabricated with integral finishes of various colors and textures, translucency for light transmission, designs laminated integrally with the material, and good thermal insulation when combined with low-density core materials. With proper resin formulation, they will not support combustion, but they can never be made immune to destruction by fire. Again, with different resin formulations, they can have improved resistance to ultraviolet degradation although experience is lacking concerning very long term weathering effects. Where opacity is acceptable, weathering resistance can be improved with the use of a gel-coated exterior surface.

The high unit cost of FRP places a premium on efficient design and demands economical fabrication techniques with these materials. Their use can only be justified by design for minimum weight of material in a form susceptible to economical fabrication. Shell structures offer a means of attaining this efficiency; fabrication experience with large roof shells, tanks and pressure vessels is relatively limited. Thus, economic analysis of FRP potential for such structures still requires considerable judgment, engineering experience and innovative skill.

This chapter will focus attention on design methods and design concepts which lead most directly to optimum structural design for FRP shell structures in building construction. Structural properties and fabrication techniques of FRP differ markedly from traditional structural materials; thus, some new methods and new concepts that may be unfamiliar to engineers used to working with wood, metals, or reinforced concrete will be required for effective design with the FRP family of structural materials.

EFFECT OF MATERIAL PROPERTIES ON DESIGN

Because of the variety of glass and resin components available in FRP laminates, structural and other properties can be tailored over a range of values to best meet design requirements. Strength and stiffness properties are derived from the orientation and quantity of glass fiber components of the laminate. See Table 5-5 for some typical mechanical properties of commonly used laminates. Note that strength properties are high, but stiffness is low, compared with other structural materials. In particular, the ratio stiffness to strength is much lower than similar ratios for traditional structural materials. This will prove to be a significant consideration for the design of FRP shell structures.

Mechanical properties of reinforced plastics are substantially altered by the conditions under which they are used. Commonly reported short-time strength values are reduced by:

(1) Long duration load.
(2) Cyclic loading—fatigue.
(3) Unfavorable environment—wet conditions or increased temperatures.

Creep deformation or loss of stiffness may also result from long-duration loading, particularly at stress levels above about 50 per cent of ultimate short-time strength. See References 1 and 2 for more complete data on material strength properties and for quantitative data on the effect of strength reducing factors.

Selection of working stresses must take these factors into account. As yet there are no authoritative specifications or codes which establish allowable working stresses for FRP. Therefore the choice of working stress is left to the designer.

In spite of the wide range of properties available with FRP materials, some worthwhile generalizations can be stated regarding their use for shell structures:

(1) Because of the low ratio of stiffness to strength, stability is usually the governing design criteria whenever compressive stresses exist in an FRP shell structure.

(2) To utilize the high strength of FRP efficiently, shapes and arrangements which transmit load primarily by tension are best. Unfortunately, shell roof structures must usually be designed to support both downward snow load and upward wind load. Thus, roof shells will be subjected to compressive stress under at least one loading condition. On the other hand, some tanks and pressure vessels which are designed for a single type of load, such as gas or water pressure, may be designed solely as tension shells.

(3) For structures subject to long-term tensile loads, allowable working stresses must be reduced drastically below published short-time strength values to preclude excessive creep deformation and stress rupture. More data are needed concerning the long-term strength of FRP materials. Maximum allowable long-term stress values may be as low as 10 per cent or less of short-time tensile strength.

(4) For structures subject to compressive stresses, economical design for stability usually requires one or more of the following:

(a) Stiff shell configuration and proportions, which produce low compressive stresses and high buckling resistance.

(b) Sandwich construction.

(c) Rib stiffened construction.

(5) Strength and stiffness properties of FRP are usually approximately proportional to unit cost of laminate. Laminates reinforced with fiber-glass mat and woven roving are at the lower end of the strength, stiffness and cost range of available FRP laminates. These laminates are often the most suitable types for shell structures because:

(a) For uniform thickness shells, wall thickness is a more significant parameter than modulus of elasticity. Thicker walls are feasible with lower unit cost materials.

(b) For sandwich shells, proportions for minimum cost of sandwich section usually require the thinnest and lowest cost FRP facings that are practical to fabricate.

(6) Higher strength reinforcing materials often may be effectively used to reinforce highly stressed local areas of stress concentration from connections, edge reactions or concentrated loads.

(7) Under some conditions, it is econom-

ical to combine FRP shell elements with structural edge members of steel, aluminum, wood, or reinforced concrete.

SHELL CONFIGURATION

For analysis and design purposes it is convenient to classify shell structures in four basic configurations:

(1) Cylindrical shells.
(2) Shells of revolution.
(3) Translational shells.
(4) Free form or general shells.

These configurations are illustrated in Figures 6-1 through 6-4.

Cylindrical surfaces (Figure 6-1) are formed by translating a plane curve in a direction

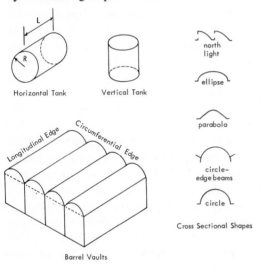

FIG. 6-1. Cylindrical shells.

orthogonal to its plane. The circular cylinder, formed when the defining curve is circular, is the most common type of cylindrical shell. Complete circular cylinders are used for tanks and pressure vessels. Cylindrical shell segments are used for barrel shell roofs, corrugated sheet, etc.

Surfaces of revolution (Figure 6-2) are formed by rotating a plane curve around a fixed axis in the plane of the curve. Most commonly, the axis of rotation is an axis of symmetry for the rotating curve. The spherical shell, formed when the rotating curve is circular with the axis of rotation through the center of the circle, is the most

frequently used shell of revolution. Spherical shells and other surfaces of revolution are used for domes, segments of domes, tops,

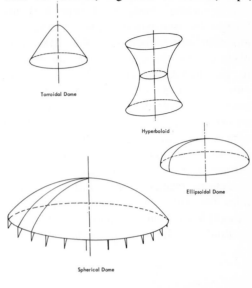

FIG. 6-2. Shells of revolution.

bottoms and ends of pressure vessels, and other types of rotationally symmetric structures. Shells which cover square, rectangular,

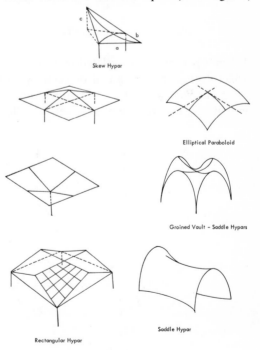

FIG. 6-3. Translational shells.

or other shapes of non-rotationally symmetric plan areas may be cut from surfaces of revolution.

Translational surfaces (Figure 6-3) are formed by translating a plane curve in a direction which forms another system of plane curves which are orthogonal or skew to the translating curve. The hyperbolic paraboloid (hypar) shell, developed by translating a parabola in a direction which forms an orthogonal or skew system of parabolas with reverse curvature, is a frequently used type of translational shell. This remarkable surface is in the form of a doubly curved anti-clastic (saddle) configuration, yet contains two orthogonal or skew systems of straight lines. Thus, patterns for molds may be built up with narrow straight elements.

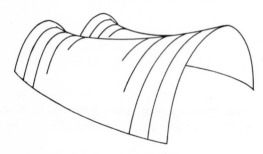

FIG. 6-4. Free-form shells.

When a parabola is translated in a direction which forms an orthogonal or skew system of parabolas with the same direction of curvature, the resulting surface is called an elliptical paraboloid. This type of shell surface is also useful for covering square or rectangular areas but is more difficult to form than the hypar surface.

Shells with *free form surfaces* (Figure 6-4) have no particular generic geometry and cannot be readily defined by simple mathematical expressions. Because they have no easily defined geometry and are difficult to analyze for stress and stability, they are not often used in structural applications.

STRESS ANALYSIS

Much information is available in the literature for the stress analysis of the more common shell configurations. This section will briefly indicate the method of approach that may be used for the stress analysis of each of the previously described shell configurations. For specific methods and summary solutions, reference will be made to pertinent technical publications.

In the general case, eight unknown stress resultants exist at a point on a thin shell (Figure 6-5) while only six equilibrium equations are available. Consequently, the general problem of shell analysis is indeterminate and can be solved accurately only by inclusion of deformation compatability relations in addition to equilibrium equations. While it is not too difficult to set up the differential equations of equilibrium and deformation for general bending shell behavior, solutions of the equations are either

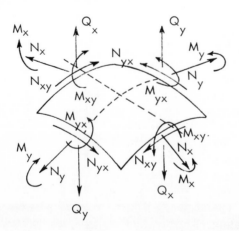

Note: For thin shells:

$$M_{yx} = M_{xy}$$

$$N_{yx} = N_{xy}$$

FIG. 6-5. Internal stress resultants at a point in a shell.

not available or too lengthy for practical application.

Fortunately, for most doubly curved shell structures, it has been shown that bending, twisting and radial shear stress resultants are relatively unimportant compared to normal force and tangential shear stress resultants. If bending, twisting, and radial shear stress resultants are assumed to be zero, there exist only three unknown stress resultants at any point on a shell surface. These stresses are termed the "membrane stresses" because the assumption of zero bending means that the shell is acting as a pure membrane, subjected only to tension, compression, and in-plane (tangential) shear stresses.

The membrane stress problem is statically determinate within the shell because three equations of equilibrium are available for every point in the surface; however, for a complete membrane solution, edge support forces and deformations must be provided which exactly meet the membrane solution requirements. Often, these support requirements cannot be entirely met; consequently, in such cases, bending stresses will exist in the vicinity of supports. Again, fortunately, these bending effects usually damp out rapidly in directions into the shell from the edge, so that approximate bending solutions for the portions of the shell near the edge supports often are sufficient for shell design.

The approach usually taken for shell analysis is as follows:

(1) Assume membrane solution is valid, and tabulate membrane stresses at significant points in the shell.

(2) Determine edge reactions and deformations required for membrane analysis.

(3) Apply unknown, or redundant, edge reactions at points where membrane edge supports and/or deformations cannot be provided in the actual structure. This constitutes removal of nonexistent membrane reactions and addition of any edge reactions needed to permit compatible deformations between shell edge and support structure. An approximate bending stress and de-

formation analysis for the region of the shell in the vicinity of the support is usually required to account for the effect of the unknown edge reactions.

(4) Determine unknown (redundant) edge reactions from compatibility of shell edge and support structure deformations. Shell edge deformations are the sum of membrane plus bending deformations.

(5) Superimpose stresses due to redundant edge reactions with membrane shell stresses.

Cylindrical shells have been treated more extensively in the literature than any other type. Because they have only single curvature, membrane solutions are easy to obtain for many types of loading. Full cylindrical shells under distributed load, such as pressure vessels and tanks, have edge bending disturbances only in the vicinity of circumferential edges. Generally these circumferential edge disturbances produce longitudinal bending moments which damp out rather rapidly in a longitudinal direction into the shell. This is particularly true for long shells. Membrane solutions and circumferential edge bending analyses are given in References 3 and 4. Also see Table 6-3 for a summary of applicable edge bending formulas. Equations for membrane stresses are tabulated in Reference 5 for many load types and cylinder configurations.

Partial cylinders, such as barrel vault roofs, usually have significant transverse bending effects which result from longitudinal edge disturbances. For long shells, transverse bending moments extend over the entire width of the shell. These bending moments must be evaluated in order to design the shell. Practical stress analysis for many barrel shell structures may be carried out with the aid of the tables given in Reference 6. Approximate methods for preliminary design purposes are discussed in References 7 and 8.

Shells of revolution have also been treated extensively in the literature. For continuous loading conditions on all but very flat shells, bending moments may be ignored except in the vicinity of edges. Note, however, that a certain amount of bending stiffness must be provided for stability. This will be discussed in detail in the next section. Equations for membrane stresses are tabulated in Reference 5 for many load types and shapes of revolution. Equations for membrane deformations at the edges are given in Reference 3.

The usual approximate method for evaluation of edge bending effects is termed the "Geckler" approximation. The approach used is to simulate the edge region of a shell of revolution with the end of a circular cylinder which is tangent to the edge of the actual shell. The bending solution for axisymmetric edge loading on the end of the tangent cylinder readily gives approximate bending moments and deformations for the edge region of the shell of revolution. This approximation gives very good accuracy for shells of revolution subject to axi-symmetric loading and edge supports provided they are not too flat. See Reference 3 for a detailed discussion of approximate and exact analysis of edge bending in shells of revolution. A summary of applicable formulas for approximate edge bending analysis is given in Table 6-3 (see p. 132).

The hyperbolic paraboloid (hypar) has been a popular type of *translational shell*. Membrane stress analysis of the hypar is given in Reference 9. Membrane stress analysis for both the hypar and elliptical paraboloid are given in Reference 10. No practical analysis is available for edge bending evaluation. Rough approximations[10] indicate that, except in very flat regions, edge bending effects die out rapidly in hypar shells if the edge ribs and supports are properly designed.

Free form shells can only be mathematically analyzed by numerical methods based on "finite difference" solutions of differential equations, lattice analogy, and other similar methods. For shells of practical size these methods require the use of high-speed electronic computers. Considerable progress has been made on development of such methods for general shell analysis. Several computer programs now show promise for practical analysis in the near future.

Design of free form shells may also be approached via model analysis techniques. However, it is a major undertaking to obtain accurate stresses from small scale model testing. Shell models are easier to develop for stability studies than for stress analysis.

Shell structures subjected only to a single loading distribution may be shaped to permit construction by filament winding with the direction of filaments (fibers) oriented so as to maximize strength-to-weight ratio. For a particular pressure distribution, this is accomplished if the structural shape and arrangement of fibers results in the same uniform stress in all fibers. A special type of membrane analysis called a "netting" analysis has been developed to determine shape of structure, arrangement of fibers and uniform fiber stress for such filament-wound structures. See Reference 11 for a detailed discussion of analysis methods for filament-wound structures. Shells subject to a single condition of loading and fabricated by the filament winding process are not often used in building structures; consequently, further discussion of structural analysis methods for optimum filament-wound structures is outside the scope of this chapter.

STABILITY ANALYSIS

Stability analysis is particularly important for the design of FRP shell structures. The high strength-to-stiffness ratio of FRP materials and the economic need to minimize thickness of these materials in a structure both result in designs governed by stability rather than strength considerations. Methods of stability analysis for shell structures, particularly with ribbed or sandwich construction, are not widely treated in the literature. However, approximate methods have been developed[12,13] which are probably sufficiently accurate for practical design of the basic shell configurations described on p. 121. Such approximate methods for stability analysis of uniform thickness, sandwich, or ribbed shells will be summarized in this section.

Stability of most shells may be evaluated approximately by considering two basic types of structural action of a cylinder:

(1) Axially loaded cylinder—longitudinal stress is compressive.

(2) Radially loaded cylinder—circumferential stress is compressive.

Figure 6-6 shows the axially loaded cylinder divided into longitudinal strips around the entire circumference, and circumfer-

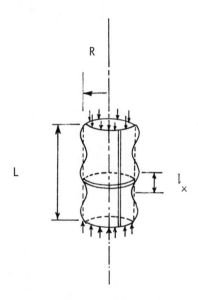

FIG. 6-6. Axially loaded cylinder buckling.

ential hoops along the entire length. Each longitudinal strip behaves as a slender end-loaded bar with continuous elastic support from the circumferential hoops. Cylinder buckling resistance is a function of both the longitudinal bending rigidity, $E_x i_x$, and the circumferential hoop rigidity, $\frac{E_\theta a_\theta}{R}$. This same model may be used as an approximate representation of the buckling resistance in either of the two principal stress directions in any doubly curved shell structure. Consequently, buckling relations for an axially loaded cylinder may be used to evaluate the stability of a large number of doubly curved shell configurations. For these shells, the direction of principal stress for which buckling strength is desired corresponds to the longitudinal direction in the axially loaded cylinder. Radius of curvature in the orthogonal direction corresponds to the axially loaded cylinder radius.

Figure 6-7 shows the radially loaded

cylinder divided into circumferential hoops along the entire length. For very long cylinders in the regions away from the ends of the cylinder, these hoops behave like slender radially loaded rings. These rings derive little support from the end diaphragms which are too far away. Buckling resistance of the ring is a function of length of circumference or radius, R, and the circumferential flexual rigidity, $E_\theta i_\theta$. However, for cylinders of moderate length, the circumferential rings derive elastic support against buckling from tangential or membrane shear stiffness because the cylinder behaves as a shell with diaphragm end supports. Consequently, a moderate length cylindrical shell has a significantly higher buckling resistance under radial pressure loading than a long cylinder with the same radius and wall construction. Very short cylindrical shells under radial pressure or circumferential stress act approximately as long, narrow plates with supported edges parallel to the direction of stress.

Formulas for critical buckling stress for the basic cylindrical shell configuration under either axial load or radial load are summarized in Table 6-1. Cases involving solid

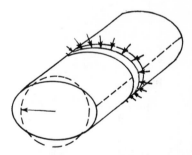

FIG. 6-7. Radially loaded cylinder buckling.

uniform thickness walls, ribbed construction and sandwich construction are included. Formulas are also given in Table 6-1 for critical buckling stress in spherical shells and hyperbolic paraboloid (hypar) shells with solid uniform wall thickness or sandwich construction. Similar formulas for approximate critical buckling stress with other shell shapes may be derived from the basic cylindrical shell case.

For many shell forms, the approximate

TABLE 6-1. Formulas for Approximate Stability Analysis for Various Basic Shell Types

Shell Configuration	Type Construction	Type Load or Stress Direction	Critical Buckling Stress	Critical Buckling Load	Remarks
(1) Cylindrical	Isotropic, uniform wall	Axial or longitudinal	$C\dfrac{Et}{R}$	—	(1) $R/t < 50 : C = 0.45$ $R/t = 100 : C = 0.35$ $R/t = 500 : C = 0.2$ $R/t = 1000 : C = 0.12$ (2) $l_z = 1.72\sqrt{Rt}$
(2) Cylindrical	Orthotropic, ribbed	Axial or longitudinal stress	$C\dfrac{E_z h_e}{R}$	—	(1) $i_\theta a_z > i_z a_\theta$ (2) $h_e = 2\sqrt{3}\sqrt{\dfrac{E_\theta i_z a_\theta}{E_z(a_z)^2}}$ (3) $w_{ez} = 0.5 d_z \sqrt{\dfrac{\sigma_{cr\theta}}{\sigma_{cr}}} < 0.5 d_z$ (4) $l_z = \pi\sqrt[4]{\dfrac{E_z i_z R^2}{E_\theta a_\theta}}$ (5) Must be 3 circumferential ribs in length, l_z (6) C from Case 1 with h_e replacing t
(3) Cylindrical	Sandwich, $t_f < < t_c$ $E_c < < E_f$	Axial or longitudinal stress	$2\sqrt{3}\,k_s C \dfrac{E_f}{R}\sqrt{\dfrac{i_f}{a_f}}$ or approx.: $\sqrt{3}\,k_s C \dfrac{E_f}{R}(t_c + t_f)$ or: $k_s C E_f \dfrac{h_e}{R}$	—	(1) $h_e = \sqrt{3}(t_c + t_f)$ (2) $l_z = \pi\sqrt[4]{\dfrac{R^2 i_f}{(1 - \nu^2)a_f}}$ (3) $k_s = 1$, if shear deflection of core is neglected (4) $k_s\alpha \dfrac{E_f t_f}{G_c R}$; see Reference 18 (5) C from Case 1 with h_e replacing t
(4) Cylindrical, long shell	Isotropic, uniform wall	Lateral pressure or circumferential stress	$\dfrac{E}{4(1 - \nu^2)}\dfrac{t^2}{R^2}$	$\dfrac{Et^3}{4(1 - \nu^2)R^3}$	(1) $\dfrac{L}{R} > 20$ when $\dfrac{t^2}{R^2} = 240 \times 10^{-6}$ to $\dfrac{L}{R} > 50$ when $\dfrac{t^2}{R^2} = 12 \times 10^{-6}$

TABLE 6-1. (Cont.)

Shell Configuration	Type Construction	Type Load or Stress Direction	Critical Buckling Stress	Critical Buckling Load	Remarks
(5) Cylindrical, moderate length	Isotropic, uniform wall	Lateral pressure or circumferential stress	$\dfrac{0.855\,E\,t^{3/2}}{(1-v^2)^{3/4}LR^{1/2}}$	$\dfrac{0.855\,E\,t^{5/2}}{(1-v^2)^{3/4}LR^{3/2}}$	(1) For sandwich shells use: $E_{f\theta}$, $i_{f\theta}$ and $a_{f\theta}$
(6) Cylindrical, long shell	Ribbed or sandwich	Lateral pressure or circumferential stress	$\dfrac{3E_\theta i_\theta}{R^2 a_\theta}$	$\dfrac{3E_\theta i_\theta}{R^3}$	
(7) Cylindrical, moderate length	Ribbed or sandwich	Lateral pressure or circumferential stress	$\dfrac{5.5E_\theta}{LR^{1/2}}\left[\dfrac{E_z a_z}{E_\theta a_\theta}\right]^{1/4}\left[\dfrac{i_\theta}{a_\theta}\right]^{3/4}$	$\dfrac{5.5E_\theta}{LR^{3/2}}\left[\dfrac{E_z a_z}{E_\theta}\right]^{1/4}(i_\theta)^{3/4}$	(1) For sandwich shells use: $E_{f\theta}$, E_{fz}, $i_{f\theta}$, a_θ, and a_{fz} (2) $w_{e\theta} = 0.5d_\theta\sqrt{\dfrac{\sigma_{cr\theta}}{\sigma_{cr}}} \leqq 0.5d_\theta$
(8) Spherical	Isotropic, uniform wall	All stresses, Radial pressure	$C\dfrac{Et}{R}$	$2CE\left\{\dfrac{t}{R}\right\}^2$	(1) $C = 0.275 - 0.000365\,\phi\sqrt{R/t}$ or $C = 0.11$ whichever larger
(9) Spherical	Ribbed	All stresses	Same as Case 2	$4\sqrt{3}k_s C\dfrac{E_f}{R^2}\sqrt{i_f a_f}$	(1) See Reference 15 for more accurate solution
(10) Spherical	Isotropic Sandwich	All Stresses Radial pressure	Same as Case 3		
(11) Hypar	Isotropic, uniform wall	Principal stress, long diagonal (c is $+$)	$\dfrac{Ec}{2ab\sin^2\frac{w}{2}}\dfrac{t}{\sqrt{3(1-v^2)}}$		$w \leq 90°$
		Principal stress, short diagonal (c is $-$)	$\dfrac{Ec}{2ab\cos^2\frac{w}{2}}\dfrac{t}{\sqrt{3(1-v^2)}}$		
		Load normal to plane a-b		$\dfrac{2Ec^2}{a^2b^2\sin^2 w}\dfrac{t^2}{\sqrt{3(1-v^2)}}$	

TABLE 6-1. (Cont.)

Shell Configuration	Type Construction	Type Load or Stress Direction	Critical Buckling Stress	Critical Buckling Load	Remarks
(12) Hypar	Isotropic Sandwich	Principal stress, long diagonal (c is +)	$\dfrac{E_f c}{ab\sin^2\frac{w}{2}}\sqrt{\dfrac{i_f}{a_f(1-v_f^2)}}$		
		Principal stress, short diagonal (c is −)	$\dfrac{E_f c}{ab\cos^2\frac{w}{2}}\sqrt{\dfrac{i_f}{a_f(1-v_f^2)}}$		
		Load normal to plane a-b		$\dfrac{4E_f c^2}{a^2 b^2 \sin^2 w}\sqrt{\dfrac{i_f a_f}{(1-v_f^2)}}$	

NOMENCLATURE:

a_f Cross-sectional area per unit width of facings of sandwich shell

a_z, a_θ Average cross-sectional area per unit width for stress in longitudinal (x), and circumferential (θ) directions

a Length of one edge, hypar shell

b Length of other edge, hypar shell

c Vertical rise, hypar shell

C Shell buckling constant

d_z, d_θ Distance between ribs for stress in longitudinal (x), and circumferential (θ) directions

E Modulus of elasticity

E_f Modulus of elasticity of facing material, sandwich shell

E_z, E_θ Modulus of elasticity in longitudinal (x), and circumferential (θ) directions

G_c Shearing modulus of rigidity of sandwich shell core

h_e Equivalent thickness of sandwich or ribbed shell

i_f Moment of inertia of transformed cross section per unit width of sandwich shell, based on facings modulus of elasticity

i_z, i_θ Moment of inertia of cross section per unit width for stress in the longitudinal (x), and circumferential (θ) directions

k_s Buckling constant for effect of core shear rigidity in sandwich shell

L Length of cylindrical shell

l_z Half wave length of buckled cylindrical shell in longitudinal direction

R Radius of shell

t Thickness of shell

t_f Thickness of facing in sandwich shell

t_c Thickness of core in sandwich shell

w Angle between director planes in hypar shell

$w_{ez}, w_{e\theta}$ Effective width of skin on each side of ribs for stresses in longitudinal (x), or circumferential (θ) direction

x Longitudinal direction, cylindrical shell

σ Stress in shell

σ_{cr} Local buckling stress in skin between ribs

σ_{crg} General instability stress for shell

v Poisson's ratio

v_f Poisson's ratio for facing material

θ Circumferential direction

φ Meridional direction in spherical shell

formulas presented in Table 6-1 may be used with a suitable factor of safety for final design for FRP shell structures. However, until more service experience is available with a wide variety of FRP shell structures, the stability behavior of many shell configurations, particularly those with unusual edge conditions or compound curvature, should be checked by model tests or full scale prototype tests. Model tests are particularly useful for investigation of stability because necessary test data can be obtained from relatively small scale models with simple instrumentation for measuring deformations. Note, however, that models must be carefully made to accurate shape and scale and must be properly loaded in order to represent correctly design conditions. In situations where a large number of identical units will be constructed, approximate design methods and model testing may be used for prototype design; then full scale load tests should be carried out on one or more prototype units to permit use of an accurate factor of safety, and development of any necessary design revisions for maximum economy and safety.

SANDWICH CONSTRUCTION

Under certain conditions it is advantageous to combine structural materials in a layered composite or sandwich construction, which is designed to utilize each structural component in its most effective location in the sandwich. Most commonly, the concept of a sandwich structure, consisting of thin, strong, relatively stiff facings bonded to a thick, lightweight core of relatively low strength and stiffness (although possessing adequate shear rigidity) is used to achieve sufficient depth and efficiency of section for bending strength, buckling resistance, or deflection requirements without excessive thickness of facing materials. FRP laminates are used as sandwich facings over extremely lightweight foam plastic or resin impregnated paper honeycomb core construction.

The concept of sandwich construction permits the selection of materials and section proportions in such a way as to minimize the cost of structural materials for a given type and configuration of structure. Although

there are an infinite number of sandwich proportions that provide the required structural properties for any one combination of materials and structural configuration, only one "optimum proportion" provides the required structural properties for the minimum combined cost of the particular materials being considered. Thus, each "optimum" or "minimum cost" design for various combinations of different materials may be compared to determine the best materials to use for a particular structural function.

Formulas for optimum proportioning of certain common types of sandwich structures to meet various structural criteria are summarized in Table 6-2. Formulas are given to calculate the following information about the optimum section design:

(1) "Optimum" proportions of sandwich section (i. e., facing thickness and core thickness) which produce the required sectional property, such as moment of inertia, for minimum cost of materials.
(2) Minimum material cost per unit of sandwich panel surface area for a given combination of materials to produce a required sectional property.

The formulas in the Table are applicable only to sandwich structures with two symmetrical facings which are both thin and stiff relative to core structure. They were developed from approximate expressions for cross-sectional area, section modulus and moment of inertia as a function of facing thickness and core thickness. Unit sandwich panel cost was then related to the required facing and core thickness and unit material costs. Panel cost was minimized with respect to facing thickness by setting the first derivative of the panel cost equation equal to zero.

Note from the formulas for critical buckling load given in Table 6-1 that the structural parameter associated with buckling strength of shell structures which buckle like an axially loaded cylinder is $E_f\sqrt{i_f a_f}$. For a given shell configuration, design load, and design factor of safety, there is a certain required $E_f\sqrt{i_f a_f}$ obtained using the equations in Table 6-1. The sandwich proportions which produce the minimum materials cost

TABLE 6-2. "Optimum" Design of Sandwich Sections

Required Section Property	"Optimum" Proportions for Minimum Materials Cost		Minimum Combined Materials Cost
	Facing Thickness t_f (in.)	Core Thickness t_c (in.)	($/in.²)
(1) Section modulus per unit width, s_f, in.³/in.	$\sqrt{\dfrac{c_c s_f}{2c_f}}$	$\dfrac{2c_f}{c_c}\,t_f$	$\sqrt{8c_f c_c s_f}$
(2) Moment of inertia per unit width, i_f, in.⁴/in.	$\sqrt[3]{\dfrac{c_c^2 i_f}{2(c_f - c_c)^2}}$	$\left(\dfrac{4c_f}{c_c} - 3\right) t_f$	$\sqrt[3]{27 c_c^2 \left(c_f - \dfrac{c_c}{2}\right) i_f}$
(3) Product of area of facing and radius of gyration, $\sqrt{i_f a_f}$, in.³/in.	$\sqrt{\dfrac{c_c \sqrt{i_f a_f}}{2c_f - c_c}}$	$\left(\dfrac{2c_f}{c_c} - 2\right) t_f$	$\sqrt[2]{c_c(2c_f - c_c)\sqrt{i_f a_f}}$
(4) a_f, and $\sqrt{a_f i_f}$ or i_f, are both required as in Cases: (1) Strength determines facing thickness, stability determines core thickness (2) Minimum practical thickness determines facing thickness, stability determines core thickness	$\dfrac{a_f}{2}$	$\dfrac{2\sqrt{i_f a_f}}{a} - \dfrac{a_f}{2}$	$\left(c_f - \dfrac{c_c}{2}\right) a_f + 2c_c \dfrac{\sqrt{i_f a_f}}{a_f}$

Nomenclature:

c_c Unit volume cost core material, $/in.³
c_f Unit volume cost facing material, $/in.³
t_c Thickness of core in sandwich section, in.
t_f Thickness of one facing in symmetrical sandwich section, in.
a_f Cross-section area of unit width of facings of sandwich section, in.²/in.
i_f Moment of inertia of transformed cross section per unit width of sandwich section, based on facings modulus of elasticity, in.⁴/in.
s_f Section modulus of transformed cross section per unit width of sandwich, based on facings modulus of elasticity, in.³/in.

for this type of sandwich shell structure are given in Table 6-2, Case 3, for required $\sqrt{i_f a_f}$.

For cylindrical shells under radial load, the structural parameter associated with buckling strength is $E_f i_f$. Thus, sandwich proportions given in Table 6-2, Case 2, for required i_f (required i_f obtained from Table 6-1) are the optimum or minimum cost proportions.

Note also that, with FRP sandwich shells, required facing thickness for optimum proportioning is often too thin for practical manufacture with currently available fabrication techniques. When this occurs, the minimum practical facing thickness should be used. Then core thickness is determined from the equations given in Case 4, Table 6-2.

The technique of sandwich construction makes it feasible to design rather large shell roof structures with FRP facings between about 0.08 to 0.20 inch thick, the approximate range of practical facing thickness. However, structures with maximum width greater than about 8 to 12 feet must be fabricated in several pieces because shop fabrication is required for FRP sandwich construction. Thus, for proper shell behavior, field joints must be used between prefabricated sections of the shell, and must provide continuity of the sandwich facings. Use of adhesive bonded splice plates is perhaps the most obvious way to accomplish this; however, it is usually too difficult to control environmental conditions to achieve the careful quality control necessary for successful use of adhesives under field conditions. Another obvious solution—use of splice plates and metal bolts—produces unsightly connections which are difficult to make watertight and expensive to erect.

Field connections have been accomplished

on some sandwich shell structures using cam operating locking devices* preset in the core area along the connecting edges of the shell units during shop fabrication. In the field, the abutting edges are securely locked together by turning the cam locks with an "Allen Head" wrench from below. The locking action prestresses the joint so that it may effectively resist tension and small bending moments as well as compression. Most significantly, this type of connection maintains the integrity of the shell stability because of rigidity obtained by prestressing the joint. As an alternative to the use of cam-operated locking devices, bolt pockets can be left in the inside facing and core at the required spacing along adjoining edges. The sandwich panels can then be fastened with bolts placed with axes tangential to the shell curve at mid-depth of the core and tightened to prestress the joints. The adjoining edges must be properly reinforced in the vicinity of the connection to take the localized stresses resulting from the prestressed bolts. The bolt pockets can be covered with cover plates, tape, or some other finish element on the inside of the shell.

The edges of the shop-fabricated shell panels must be reinforced for the local stresses around the connection points. Protection must also be provided for the lightweight core and their facings along panel edges. This can be accomplished with molded FRP edge members. Edge reinforcing also is necessary at the support regions of the shell to permit connection to the supporting structure. See p. 133 for further discussion about connections and support requirements.

Several different techniques have been used to date for fabrication of FRP sandwich shell roof structures. Perhaps the simplest is to fabricate both skins in separate molds, apply a paper honeycomb or premolded foam core to one skin while the resin on the inside surface is still wet, and finally to adhesive bond the other skin, after it is cured, to the previously laminated core

and skin. Bonding pressure is obtained from air pressure using a large air bag over the shell surface. By this process the shell will have two smooth finished mold surfaces. A gel-coat finish may then be used on both sides. Where only one smooth finished surface is required, the second skin may be laid up wet over the core, thereby eliminating the second molding operation and the problem of handling a thin unstiffened skin.

Foam-in-place techniques are available for fabricating a foam plastic core[14]. However, foaming-in-place between two premolded facings is a sophisticated operation which requires the proper combination of mold design, foam material formulation, foam equipment, and foam handling techniques. It should not be attempted without proper equipment and careful process development. It is essential for the structural integrity of the sandwich shell that the thin skins be *continuously* bonded to foam plastic or paper honeycomb cores.

EDGE SUPPORTS AND EDGE BENDING EFFECTS

Efficient structural action associated with shell behavior demands adequate support at the edges of the shell. If possible, edge structure should be strong enough to provide the required membrane stress reactions. In addition, it should be stiff enough to minimize deformations in excess of those required by the membrane solution. Even if edge members have sufficient strength to support membrane stresses, in general their deformation will not be exactly in accord with the requirements of pure membrane behavior. Consequently, bending stresses almost always must be expected in the vicinity of shell edges.

Whether or not the edge bending moments are significant to the design of the shell depends on the relative strength and stiffness of the edge supports provided. In doubly curved shells, these moments usually die out very rapidly in a direction away from the edge of the shell. With adequate edge ribs, it usually is sufficient to gradually increase the thickness of a doubly curved single thickness FRP shell to a maximum of about double the primary thickness over a very short region near the edge of the shell (approximate edge distance affected by bending is 0.76 $\sqrt{Rt}$ in from edge).

Doubly curved FRP *sandwich* shells usually have sufficient bending strength to take edge bending effects.

Formulas for approximate analysis of edge bending effects are summarized in Table 6-3. The formulas in the Table are for deformations and moments due to axisymmetric edge moment and shear on the circumferential edges of a cylindrical shell

TABLE 6-3. Axi-symmetric Circumferential Edge Loads and Deformation for Cylinders and Shells of Revolution

Note:
$R\psi = x$ in cylinder

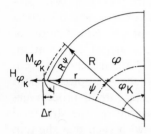

Shell of Revolution

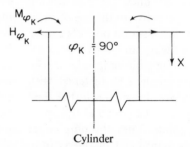

Cylinder

$$\text{Shell constant } \lambda = \sqrt[4]{\frac{E_\theta a_\theta R^2}{4 E_\psi i_\varphi}} = R\beta \quad (\text{see Reference 3})$$

	Edge Load, $H_{\varphi K}$	Edge Moment, $M_{\varphi K}$
Radial deformation in base plane, Δr	$+\dfrac{2\lambda R \sin^2\varphi_K}{E_\theta a_\theta} H_{\varphi K}$	$+\dfrac{2\lambda^2 \sin \varphi_K}{E_\theta a_\theta} M_{\varphi K}$
Edge rotation	$-\dfrac{2\lambda^2 \sin \varphi_K}{E_\theta a_\theta} H_{\varphi K}$	$-\dfrac{4\lambda^3}{E_\theta a_\theta R} M_{\varphi K}$
Meridional moment	$\dfrac{R \sin \varphi_K H_{\varphi K}}{\lambda}\left[\dfrac{\sin(\lambda\psi)}{e^{\lambda\psi}}\right]$	$\sqrt{2}\, M_{\varphi K}\left[\dfrac{\sin\left(\lambda\psi + \frac{\pi}{4}\right)}{e^{\lambda\psi}}\right]$
Maximum meridional moment	$\dfrac{0.322\, R \sin \varphi_K H_{\varphi K}}{\lambda}$, at $\lambda\psi = 0.8$	$M_{\varphi K}$, at $\lambda\psi = 0$
Meridional thrust	$\sqrt{2} \sin \varphi_K H_{\varphi K}\left[\dfrac{\cot \varphi \sin\left(\lambda\psi - \frac{\pi}{4}\right)}{e^{\lambda\psi}}\right]$	$\dfrac{-2\lambda \cot \varphi_K M_{\varphi K}}{R}\left[\dfrac{\sin \lambda\psi}{e^{\lambda\psi}}\right]$
Circumferential thrust	$-2\lambda \sin \varphi_K H_{\varphi K}\left[\dfrac{\sin\left(\lambda\psi - \frac{\pi}{2}\right)}{e^{\lambda\psi}}\right]$	$\dfrac{-2\sqrt{2}\lambda^2 M_{\varphi K}}{R}\left[\dfrac{\sin\left(\lambda\psi - \frac{\pi}{4}\right)}{e^{\lambda\psi}}\right]$

NOMENCLATURE:

a_θ	Average cross sectional area per unit width for stress in circumferential (θ) direction	$M_{\varphi K}$	Edge moment per unit length of edge circumference
E_θ, E_φ	Modulus of elasticity in circumferential (θ) and meridional (φ) directions	R	Radius of shell
e	Naperian logarithms base	β	Cylindrical shell constant (see Reference 3)
$H_{\varphi K}$	Horizontal edge load per unit length of edge circumference	λ	Shell constant
		φ_K, φ, ψ	Angles
i_φ	Moment of inertia of cross section per unit width for stress in meridional direction		

(Figure 6-8). They may be used to approximate edge bending effects in any symmetrically loaded shell of revolution by considering the edge region as a cylinder. These formulas

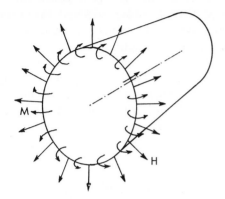

FIG. 6-8. Moment and shear on circumferential edge of cylinder.

may also be used as rough approximations for estimating edge effects in shells of revolution under unsymmetrical loads and for other types of shells.

In long- and intermediate-length cylindrical barrel shells, edge bending effects along the longitudinal edges are of a different nature and do not damp out quickly. They usually cause significant bending moments over the entire transverse direction of the shell. This behavior was discussed on p. 123. Stiff supports along the longitudinal edge help to minimize these transverse bending moments. However, it is never possible to develop the required membrane deformations along these edges; thus, transverse moments are almost always significant in barrel shells. On the other hand, bending moments due to restraints along the circumferential edges of a barrel shell usually damp out rapidly in a longitudinal direction.

With sizable FRP shell structures, it is frequently most economical to construct edge supports with one of the conventional structural materials such as steel, aluminum, wood, or reinforced concrete. Since these materials have an appreciably higher ratio of modulus of elasticity to unit cost than FRP, they are often more suitable for ribs than molded FRP edge construction. The

FRP shell elements can be connected to the edge members either in the shop or in the field.

Shop connection can be accomplished either by adhesive bonding between completed shell panels and edge ribs, or by inserting the edge ribs into the mold before the wet lay-up of the FRP shell panels. However, if FRP elements are laminated to other materials, extreme care must be taken that adequate bond strength is available, not only for computed edge transfer stress due to design load, but also for temperature and shrinkage stresses between FRP and rib materials. Experience has shown that contact surfaces must be absolutely clean (i.e., sandblasted steel surfaces, etc.) and that the proper adhesives must be selected to meet environmental conditions. Frequently, the resin used in the FRP laminate is also the adhesive. However, this adhesive may be brittle; its adequacy should be checked for the worst environmental conditions expected in the life of the structure. More research is needed concerning temperature and other environmental effects in order to properly design adhesive-bonded or resin-laminated composite structures of FRP and other structural materials.

Field connections are carried out with metal bolts, lag bolts, special clips, or various other types of special mechanical connectors. See Reference 1 for data on bolt bearing strength and edge distance requirements for various types of FRP laminates. Note that allowance must always be provided for ample tolerance with field connections. Adhesive bonding is usually not suited to field connections because controlled environmental and pressure conditions are necessary for proper fabrication of adhesive joints.

Frequently edge ribs constitute the primary elements in the load capacity of a shell structure. As much care should be taken to correctly conceive and design these elements as the shell structure itself. The structure doesn't know where the shell stops and edge ribs begin. Proper design of both shell and edge ribs is necessary to the safety and economy of the complete structure.

DESIGN EXAMPLES

The complete design of an FRP shell roof structure usually involves the following process:

(1) Selection of trial shell size and configuration based on functional requirements, aesthetic qualities, inherent stability and fabrication, shipping, and erection considerations.

(2) Determination of design loadings. These are often established by local code requirements.

(3) Membrane stress analysis for the various design loading conditions. Membrane stresses are "statically determinate" and, hence, not dependent on material properties, section thickness or type construction, or edge restraints.

(4) Trial selection of type of construction, type of FRP laminate, material thickness, rib spacings, etc. Determination of allowable stress based on strength.

(5) Approximate evaluation of stability. Consideration of both over-all shell stability and local buckling of plate elements. Determination of critical buckling stress or allowable stress based on stability.

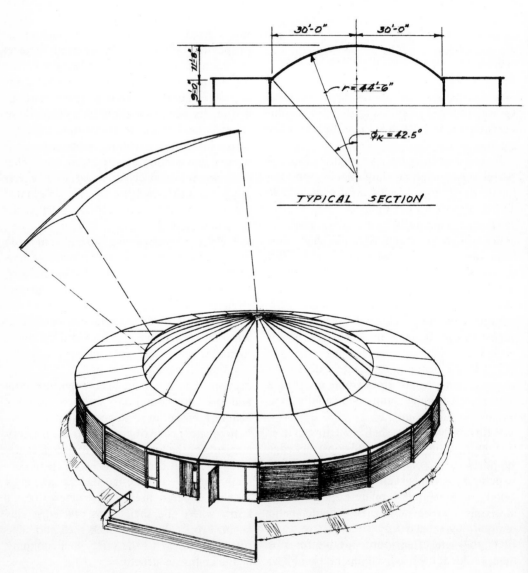

FIG. 6-9. Sixty-foot diameter spherical sandwich dome–perspective.

(6) Revision of trial configuration or trial design to meet stability and strength requirements.

(7) Trial design of edge support system. Arrangments of supports, material selection and support proportioning for strength and stiffness.

(8) Approximate evaluation of edge bending effects in the shell due to interaction between shell and supports. Superposition of stresses due to edge bending and membrane stresses. Evaluation of edge bending effects on support system.

(9) Design revisions for shell edge region and support system as required.

(10) Review of final design from viewpoint of aesthetics and economics of materials and fabrication.

Design Example 1:

The development of an FRP sandwich shell design for a 60-foot diameter spherical dome is discussed first to illustrate some of the design methods presented in this chapter. Figure 6-9 indicates the general arrangement and geometry for this simple dome structure.

Design Concept

Sandwich construction was selected for this structure in order to obtain the necessary buckling resistance with an economical quantity of FRP materials. With a single skin, uniform thickness, mat-reinforced laminate, required shell thickness would have been $1\frac{1}{8}$ inches. Such a laminate would be impractical and uneconomical.

The sandwich shell concept is a desirable solution for this dome because in addition to minimizing the quantity of high cost FRP materials, it provides suitable insulation and both exterior and interior surfaces are smooth. The skins can be constructed with a colorful gel-coated surface and a "self-extinguishing" fire-retardant resin. Phenolic impregnated paper honeycomb was chosen as the core material in order to facilitate economical fabrication of the doubly curved sandwich panels.

The spherical dome structure may be fabricated in 24 or more identical pie-shaped panels. Individual panels can be connected in the field with cam operating connectors, such as Simmons "Roto-Lock" or "Dual Lock" connections. These connectors provide a prestressed connection capable of taking either circumferential compression or tension forces. The connection can also take meridional shear forces in the plane of the shell. With this type of connection, no bolt heads or nuts mar the smoothness of the inner surface or impair the weather resistance of the shell. A $\frac{1}{4} \times \frac{1}{4}$ inch recess for polysulfide caulking is provided at the top surface of the joint to insure weathertight performance.

Design Process

(1) Architectural requirements indicated a circular structure of 60 foot clear diameter. Width of individual shell units was limited to about 8 feet by shipping considerations. Cost of structure, erected, should not exceed about $4.00 to $4.50 per square foot. Maximum speed of erection was desirable. The structure should be demountable with a minimum loss of parts and cost to dismantle. The circular spherical dome constructed from pie-shaped sandwich elements is a practical, relatively economical, and straightforward solution to this problem.

(2) Design loading was (see Figure 6-10):

Downward: $p_s = 30$ psf snow

$\qquad\qquad p_g = 3$ psf dead load

Wind: $\qquad p_w = 25$ psf

(3) Membrane stress analysis was carried out using the following well-known equations for spherical shell analysis (see Reference 5):

Uniform downward load:

$$N_\phi = -\frac{p_g R}{(1 + \cos \phi)} - \frac{p_s R}{2} \tag{1}$$

$$N_\theta = p_g R\left[\frac{1}{1 + \cos \phi} - \cos \phi\right] - \frac{p_s R}{2} \cos 2\phi \tag{2}$$

Wind load:

$$N_\phi = -\frac{p_w R \cos \theta \cos \phi}{3 \sin^3 \phi}(2 - 3 \cos \phi + \cos^3\phi) \tag{3}$$

$$N_\theta = \frac{p_w R \cos \theta}{3 \sin^3 \phi}(2 \cos \phi - 3 \sin^2 \phi - 2 \cos^4 \phi) \tag{4}$$

$$N_{\phi\theta} = -\frac{p_w R \sin \theta}{3 \sin^3 \phi}(2 - 3 \cos \phi + \cos^3 \phi) \tag{5}$$

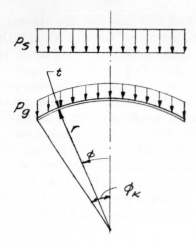

GRAVITY LOAD

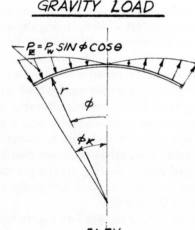

$$P_z = P_w \, SIN \, \phi \, COS \theta$$

ELEV.
WIND LOAD

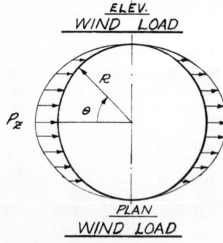

PLAN
WIND LOAD

FIG. 6-10. Design loading on 60-foot diameter spherical sandwich dome.

The following are maximum membrane stress resultants:

Downward load:

$$\text{Base: } N_\phi = -736 \text{ lb/ft}$$

$$N_\theta = -78 \text{ lb/ft}$$

$$\text{Peak: } N_\phi = N_\theta = -733 \text{ lb/ft}$$

Wind load:

$$\text{Base: } N_\phi = \pm161 \text{ lb/ft}$$

$$N_\theta = \pm566 \text{ lb/ft}$$

$$N_{\phi\theta} = \pm238 \text{ lb/ft}$$

(4) The trial design was assumed as sandwich construction with polyester resin fiber glass mat-reinforced laminate skins and phenolic impregnated paper honeycomb core. Allowable skin stresses based on strength considerations alone would be (for downward load—snow load duration):

tension: $\sigma_a = 2000$ psi

compression: $\sigma_a = 2800$ psi

shear in plane of laminate: $\tau_a = 1600$ psi

(5) For this structure, trial design should be based on stability. Equations for stability analysis of shells of revolution are summarized in Table 6-1.
For a spherical sandwich dome:

$$N_{cr} = \sigma_{cr} a_f = 2\sqrt{3} \, kC \frac{E_f \, a_f}{R} \sqrt{\frac{i_f}{a_f}} \qquad (6)$$

For a sandwich shell with a relatively thick and rigid core assume:

$k = 1$

$C = 0.125$ (should be quite conservative)

Using a factor of safety of 3 against buckling:

required $N_{cr} = 736 \times 3 \div 12 = -184$ lb/in.

$$N_{cr} = 0.25\sqrt{3} \, \frac{E_f \sqrt{i_f a_f}}{R}$$

required $\sqrt{i_f a_f} = \dfrac{2.3 \, N_{cr} R}{E_f}$

$$= \frac{2.3 \times 184 \times 535}{0.9 \times 10^6} = 0.252$$

Proportions for minimum cost (see Table 6-2):

Assume following unit costs:

Facings: Mat reinforced FRP at 80¢/lb or 3.8¢/cu in.
Core: Phenolic impregnated honeycomb at 12¢/bd ft or 0.084¢/cu in.

$$t_f = \sqrt{\frac{c_c}{2c_f - c_c}} \sqrt{i_f a_f} \qquad (7)$$

$$t_f = \sqrt{\frac{0.084 \times 0.252}{2 \times 3.8 - 0.084}} = 0.053 \text{ inch}$$

$$t_c = \left(\frac{2c_f}{c_c} - 2\right) t_f \qquad (8)$$

$$t_c = \left(\frac{2 \times 3.8}{0.084} - 2\right) 0.053 = 4.77 \text{ inches}$$

Unit cost of materials in sandwich shell:

$$c = 2 \times 0.053 \times 3.8 + 4.77 \times 0.084$$

$$= 0.404 + 0.494 = 0.81¢/\text{sq in.} = \$1.17/\text{sq ft}$$

However, assume that minimum practical $t_f = 0.09$ inch.

$$\text{required } t_c = \frac{\sqrt{i_f a_f}}{t_f} - t_f \qquad (9)$$

$$t_c = \frac{0.252}{0.09} - 0.09 = 2.71 \text{ inches}$$

Unit cost of materials in sandwich shell:

$$c = 2 \times 0.090 \times 3.8 + 2.71 \times 0.084$$
$$= 0.684 + 0.226 = 0.91¢/\text{sq in.} = \$1.31/\text{sq ft}$$

For practical design use:

$$\text{minimum } t_f = 0.09 \text{ inch}$$

$$t_c = 3.00 \text{ inches}$$

Check membrane stress in skin:

$$\sigma = \frac{N}{a} = \frac{736}{12 \times 2 \times 0.09} = 342 \text{ psi} < 2800 \text{ psi}$$

Check factor for shear deformation of core:

$$\frac{E_f t_f}{G_c R} = \frac{0.9 \times 10^6 \times 0.09}{10,000 \cdot 535} = 0.015 < 0.1$$

Conclusion: $k = 1.0$ is satisfactory, no reduction is needed because of core shear deformation.

(6) No revisions are indicated for the trial configuration.

(7) The dome is supported at its base on a steel ring girder. The ring girder is supported on 16 pipe columns at approximately 11.8 feet circumferential spacing. The edge loads produced by membrane conditions with maximum uniform downward load on the shell are:

Vertical: 504 lb/ft + wt girder

Horizontal: 550 lb/ft

The horizontal load produces a ring tension of 16,500 pounds. The vertical load produces a maximum bending moment of approximately 6,200 foot-pounds in the ring. Select a box section constructed from 2-7[9.8 welded continuously for a trial base ring design. The box section provides both good bending and torsional resistance.

(8) Radial movement of the base ring due to radial tension causes bending moments in the edge regions of the shell. These bending moments may be evaluated by superimposing a solution for edge loading on the membrane solution. See Table 6-3 for the required formulas for edge deformation and maximum bending moment.

Radial edge deflection in the plane of the base due to a horizontal edge load, ΔH is (see Figure 6-11):

$$\Delta r_e = \frac{2\lambda R}{E_f a_f} \sin^2 \varphi_k \Delta H$$

For a sandwich shell:

$$\lambda^4 = \frac{a_f R^2}{i_f} = \frac{2t_f R^2}{4t_f d^2/2} = \frac{R^2}{d^2} \qquad (11)$$

$$\lambda = \sqrt{\frac{R}{d}} \qquad (12)$$

Radial edge deflection in the plane of the base due to membrane loading condition is:

$$\Delta r_m = \frac{(N_\theta)_m R \sin \varphi_k}{a_f E_f} \qquad (13)$$

When the centerline of the shell intersects the centroid of the steel base ring, the radial deflection of the ring centroid is (see Figure 6-11):

$$\Delta r_r = \frac{(H_m - \Delta H) R^2 \sin^2 \varphi_k}{E_r A_r}$$

$$\Delta r_r = \frac{(-N_{\phi k} \cos \varphi_k - \Delta H) R^2 \sin^2 \varphi_k}{E_r A_r} \qquad (14)$$

The unknown horizontal edge load may be found from the compatibility of ring and shell radial deflections. Thus:

$$\Delta r_r = \Delta r_e + \Delta r_m \qquad (15)$$

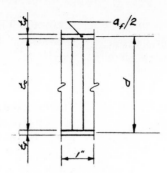

SANDWICH SECTION

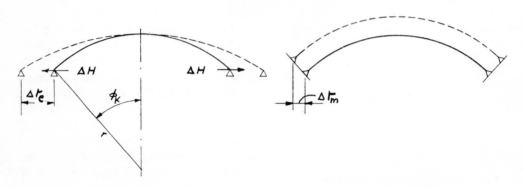

EDGE LOAD   _MEMBRANE CONDITION_

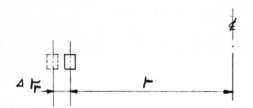

RING LOAD

Fig. 6-11. Spherical sandwich dome edge conditions.

For the specific shell under discussion:

$$\lambda = \sqrt{\frac{R}{d}} = \sqrt{\frac{535}{3.09}} = 13.2$$

$$\Delta r_e = \frac{2 \times 13.2 \times 535 \times (0.675)^2 \Delta H}{0.9 \times 10^6 \times 0.18} = 0.040\Delta H$$

$$\Delta r_m = \frac{-78 \times 535 \times 0.675}{12 \times 0.18 \times 0.9 \times 10^6} = -0.015$$

$$\Delta r_r = \frac{(736/12 \times 0.738 - \Delta H)(535 \times 0.675)^2}{30 \times 10^6 \times 5.64}$$

$$= 0.035 - 0.00077\Delta H$$

$$0.035 - 0.00077\, \Delta H = -0.015 + 0.040\Delta H$$

$$\Delta H = 1.2 \text{ lb/in.}$$

Bending moment due to edge load, ΔH. From Table 6-3:

$$\max M = \frac{0.322\ R(\sin\varphi_k)\Delta H}{\sqrt{R/d}} \qquad (16)$$

For the shell under discussion: $\sin\phi_k = 0.675$

maximum $M = 0.218\sqrt{535 \times 3.09} \times 1.2$
$$= 10.6 \text{ in.-lb/in.}$$

maximum $\sigma_b = \dfrac{M}{s_f} \approx \dfrac{M}{t_f d} = \dfrac{10.6}{0.09 \times 3.09} = 38$ psi

Maximum facing stress due to combined membrane and edge bending conditions:

$$\text{maximum } \sigma = -342 - 38 = -380 \text{ psi}$$

Conclusion: Edge bending effects are not of much significance in this particular sandwich shell design.

The effect of a difference in coefficient of expansion between steel edge ring and FRP shell also causes edge bending in the shell and may be evaluated as follows:

(a) Assume the difference in coefficient of expansion between steel and FRP, $\Delta\alpha = 6.0 \times 10^{-6}$ in./in./°F.

(b) Assume a maximum change in temperature from the temperature existing when shell and edge ring were first connected = 40°F.

Maximum radial "free" temperature movement:

$$\Delta r_T = \Delta\alpha R \sin \varphi_k \Delta T \qquad (17)$$

$$= 6 \times 10^{-6} \times 535 \times 0.675 \times 40 = 0.086 \text{ inch}$$

$$0.086 - 0.00077\Delta H_T = 0.040\Delta H_T$$

$$\Delta H_T = 2.1 \text{ lb/in.}$$

Maximum bending stress in the shell due to restraint of temperature change:

$$\text{maximum } \sigma_T = \frac{2.1}{1.2} \times 38 = 67 \text{ psi}$$

Conclusion: Temperature effects are not of much structural significance in this particular sandwich shell design.

(9) No design revisions are required either in shell or base ring design because of edge bending conditions.

(10) Review of design gives the following average material quantities:

Fiber-glass mat-reinforced polyester plastic facings	1.5 lb/sq ft horizontal floor area
Phenolic impregnated 99-lb kraft paper honeycomb core	3.5 bd ft/sq ft horizontal floor area
Base ring and pipe columns	1.9 lb/sq ft horizontal floor area

Design Example 2:

The proportioning of a uniform thickness skew hypar shell (unit 2—Figures 6-12 and 6-13) will be developed as a second example illustrating the use of the design methods presented in this chapter. The structure shown in Figures 6-12 and 6-13 was originally designed as part of a study for optimum utilization of FRP materials for large-span roof construction carried out for Owens-Corning Fiberglas Corporation. The basic structural configuration was developed to meet the following general criteria:

(1) For maximum economy FRP shell construction should be a single thickness, mat-reinforced laminate.

(2) For a roof structure of 100-foot diameter, a single thickness mat laminate shell construction is only feasible as a sub-element supported on a primary structural framework.

(3) In order to minimize site labor costs, it is desirable to fabricate portions of the primary framework and FRP sub-shells as composite units. Units should be as large as possible, considering shipping restrictions. It should be possible to erect units with a minimum of temporary falsework.

(4) In order to provide for maximum size of thin shell units, the individual units should have an inherently stiff configuration. Length should be substantially greater than width, which is limited to about 8 to 10 feet maximum because of shipping requirements.

(5) The shape of FRP units should be easy to fabricate. Geometry should be readily defined, and molds should not be too complex.

(6) The structure should have aesthetic interest.

Design Concept

The "skew hypar" space dome shown in Figures 6-12 and 6-13 is a steel skeleton space frame with FRP "skew hypar" panels as a covering skin. FRP shells are formed from a uniform thickness mat-reinforced laminate. The "skew hypar" shape is easy to fabricate because mold patterns can be developed from straight line translation (see Figure 6-3). Consequently, the geometry is simple to define and molds are relatively easy to construct. Moreover, this shape is an extremely stiff shell configuration because:

(1) It permits sharp curvature in directions normal to the long diagonal which is the direction of maximum principal stress. This maximizes buckling strength.

(2) Regardless of whether roof load is up or down, one principal stress is always tensile.

The tensile stresses stabilize the structure against compressive stresses in the orthogonal direction and thereby increase the critical buckling stress compared with cylinders or spheres of similar curvature.

Furthermore, this shape provides long narrow shell elements which cover a large area within fairly narrow width limitations for shipping. These shapes are suitable to transport and erect.

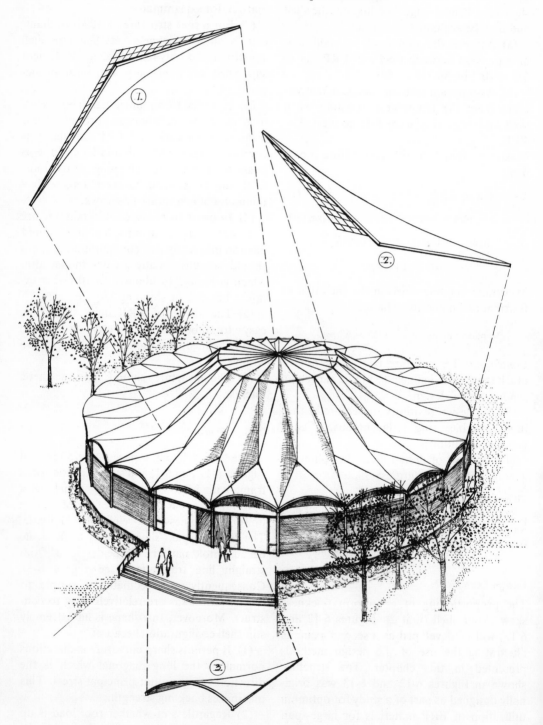

FIG. 6-12. Skew Hypar roof—perspective.

Design Process

Only that portion of the design process relating to the design of FRP shell unit 2 will be discussed here. See Reference 13 for a more complete discussion.

(1) Design loading for shell membrane:

Downward: $p_s = 30$ psf snow

$p_g = 2$ psf dead

Upward: $p_w = 20$ psf wind

(2) Approximate membrane stress analysis for the skew hypar shells: *

Maximum shear: $\tau = \dfrac{pab}{2tc} \sin w$ (18)

Principal normal stresses: $\sigma_I = \tau \tan \dfrac{w}{2}$

$\sigma_{II} = \tau \cot \dfrac{w}{2}$ (20)

*See Reference 9 for development of membrane stress equations.

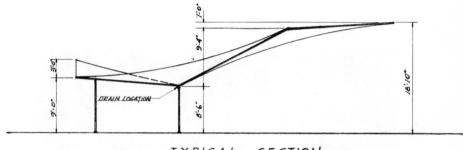

TYPICAL SECTION

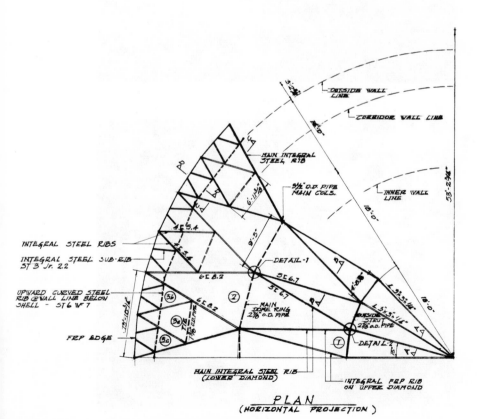

PLAN
(HORIZONTAL PROJECTION)

FIG. 6-13. Skew Hypar roof—plan and section.

For downward load on shell 2 (Figure 6-13):

$$\tau = \frac{32 \times 18 \times 16^2 \sin 30°}{2 \times t \times 118} = \frac{22.4}{t} \text{ psi}$$

$$\sigma_1 = -\frac{22.4}{t} \tan 15° = \frac{6.0}{t} \text{ psi, compression}$$

$$\sigma_{11} = \frac{22.4}{t} \cot 15° = \frac{83.4}{t} \text{ psi, tension}$$

(3) A single uniform thickness, polyester resin, mat-reinforced, laminate may be used: Allowable stresses, based on strength considerations alone, for this material would be:

Tension: $\sigma_a = 2000$ psi

Compression: $\sigma_a = 2800$ psi

Shear in plane of laminate: $\tau_a = 1600$ psi

It is evident that shell thickness required by strength considerations is very thin and that stability must be considered. Minimum tensile and compressive modulus of elasticity for this material is about 900,000 psi.

(4) An approximate evaluation of stability can be carried out using Case 11 in Table 6-1:

$$p_{cr} = \frac{2Et^2c^2}{\sqrt{3(1 - \nu^2)}a^2b^2 \sin^2 w} \quad (21)$$

When thickness is governed by stability:

$$\text{required } t = \frac{ab \sin w}{1.1c} \sqrt{\frac{p_{cr}}{E}} \quad (24)$$

If a factor of safety of 3.0 is used for de-

Fig. X–14 – Skew Hypar Roof – Views of Model

FIG. 6-14. Skew Hypar roof—views of model.

sign based on stability, the required critical uniformly distributed load capacity is:

$$p_{cr} = \frac{32}{144} \times 3 = 0.67 \text{ psi}$$

The required thickness for shell 2, Figure 6-13, is:

$$\text{required } t = \frac{218^2 \sin 30.1}{1.1 \times 118} \sqrt{\frac{0.67}{0.90 \times 10^6}} = 0.16 \text{ in.}$$

With this value of t, membrane stresses are:

$$\tau = \frac{22.44}{0.16} = 140 \text{ psi}$$

$$\sigma_\mathrm{I} = -\frac{6.0}{0.16} = -38 \text{ psi}$$

$$\sigma_\mathrm{II} = \frac{83.4}{0.16} = 522 \text{ psi}$$

The value of σ_I above is exactly ⅓ of the critical buckling stress for shell 2.

A complete design for the roof structure shown in Figures 6-12 and 6-13 resulted in the following average material quantities:

Skin structure—fiberglass mat-reinforced polyester plastic	1.6 lb/sq ft of horizontal floor area
A36 steel ribs, struts and columns	3.5 lb/sq ft of horizontal floor area

CONCLUSION

A number of FRP shell roof structures constructed in the past few years have been designed following the methods presented in this chapter. See Figures 6-15 to 6-18 and

Fig. 6-15. FRP sandwich shells, 7-Up Pavilion, N. Y. World's Fair. (*Courtesy Owens Corning Fiberglas Corp.*)

Reference 19 for examples of some of these shells. Experience with these prototype FRP shell structures indicates that even with presently available materials and fabricating

FIG. 6-16. FRP sandwich dome, West Virginia Pavilion, N. Y. World's Fair.

FIG. 6-18. FRP "Parasol" shells, American National Exhibition, Moscow, Russia.

methods, there are situations where such structures are economical and practical solutions to specific esthetic and functional design problems.

FIG. 6-17. FRP sandwich Hypar shells, M.I.T. Demonstration Schoolroom, Cambridge, Mass.

NOMENCLATURE*

A_r	Area of base ring
d	Depth of sandwich section between center-lines of facings
E_r	Modulus of elasticity of base ring

*Nomenclature for Design Examples in addition to that shown in Tables 6-1, 6-2, and 6-3.

H	Edge load per unit of circumference in plane of base due to membrane load
ΔH	Change in edge load due to compatible deformation of shell edge and ring
ΔH_T	Change in edge load due to temperature effects
N_θ, N_ϕ	Axial force per unit width in circumferential (θ), and meridional (ϕ) directions
$N_{\phi\theta}$	Tangential shear force per unit width of shell
M	Bending moment per unit width
N_{cr}	Axial force per unit width which causes buckling
p_s	Snow load per unit horizontal projected area
p_g	Gravity load per unit surface area
p_w	Wind load per unit surface area
p_{cr}	Buckling load on unit area of shell surface
Δr_m	Radial edge displacement in base plane due to membrane stress
Δr_e	Radial edge displacements in base plane due to edge loads
Δr_r	Radial displacement of edge ring
Δr_T	Radial displacement in base plane due to temperature effects
α	Coefficient of expansion
σ_a	Allowable normal stress
σ	Shear stress
σ_a	Allowable shear stress
σ_b	Bending stress

σ_T Temperature stress

σ_I, σ_{II} Principal stress in each of two orthogonal directions

ϕ Meridional angle

θ Circumferential angle

REFERENCES

1. U. S. Defense Department, "Plastics for Flight Vehicles, Part 1—Reinforced Plastics," Military Handbook 17, U. S. Government Printing Office, Washington, D. C., 1959.

2. Gibbs & Cox Inc., "Marine Design Manual for Fiberglass Reinforced Plastics," New York, McGraw-Hill Book Co., 1960.

3. Timoshenko, S., and Woinowsky-Krieger, S., "Theory of Plates and Shells," 2nd Ed., New York, McGraw-Hill Book Co., 1959.

4. Flügge, W., "Stresses in Shells," Berlin, Springer-Verlog, 1960.

5. Pflüger, A., "Elementary Statics of Shells," New York, F. W. Dodge, 1961.

6. ASCE, Manual No. 31—"Design of Cylindrical Shell Roofs," 1952.

7. Lundgren, H., "Cylindrical Shells," Copenhagen, Danish Technical Press, 1951.

8. Callari, C. E., "Méthode simplifié de Calcul de Voiles Minces Cylindriques Soumis à des Charges Nonsymétriques," Proceedings of a Colloquium on Simplified Calculation Methods of Shell Structures, Brussels, September 1961, p. 260, Amsterdam, North-Holland Publishing, 1962.

9. Candela, F., "General Formulae for Membrane Stresses in Hyperbolic Paraboloidical Shells," *ACI Journal*, 353 (October 1960).

10. Parme, A. L., "Hyperbolic Paraboloids and Other Shells of Double Curvature," *ASCE Trans.*, 989 (1958).

11. Plastics Evaluation Center, Plastec Report 10—"A Survey of Filament Winding Materials Design Criteria, Military Applications," May 1962, Picatinny Arsenal, Dover, New Jersey.

12. Heger, F. J., Chambers, R. E., and Dietz, A. G., "On the Use of Plastics and Other Composite Materials for Shell Roof Structures," Proceedings of a World Conference on Shell Structures, October 1962, Building Research Advisory Board, 1964.

13. Heger, F. J., "Engineering Concepts in the Design of Two FRP Shell Structures," Proceedings of the Annual Technical and Management Conference, Reinforced Plastics Division, The Society of the Plastics Industry, New York, February, 1964.

14. Swenson, S. B., "Buildings in Barrels, Part II," Proceedings of the Annual Technical and Management Conference, Reinforced Plastics Division, The Society of the Plastics Industry, New York, February 1964.

15. Klöppel and Roos, "Beitrag zum Durchschlag Problem Dunnwandiger ver Steifter und Unversteifter Kugelschalen for Vollund Halbseiteitige Belastung" Der Stahlbau, March 1956.

16. Timoshenko, S. and Gere, J. M., "Theory of Elastic Stability," 2nd Ed., New York, McGraw-Hill Book Co., 1961.

17. Gerard, G., "Introduction to Structural Stability Theory," New York, McGraw-Hill Book Co., 1962.

18. U. S. Defense Department, "Composite Construction for Aircraft, Part III—Design Procedures," Military Handbook 17, U. S. Government Printing Office, Washington, D. C., 1961.

19. Heger, F. J., and Chambers, R. E., "Design, Analysis and Economics of Fiberglass Reinforced Plastics Worlds Fair Structures," Proceedings of 21st Annual Technical Conference, SPI Reinforced Plastics Division, N. Y., 1966.

7 PLYWOOD, PARTICLE BOARD AND OTHER RESIN-BONDED WOOD STRUCTURES

Charles B. Hemming

United States Plywood Corporation
Lawrence Ottinger Research Center
Brewster, New York

PLYWOOD AND PARTICLE BOARD

Plywood, or at least veneering, is said to have been invented by the ancient Egyptians. Particle board is of more recent ancestry, owing its development to the continual search by man for ways to utilize waste products.

Whatever the ancestry and the reason for being, modern forms of plywood and particle board could not exist without plastics. The plastic resin used in the manufacture of plywood is only about 4 per cent by weight of the panel. In the case of particle board, resin content is about 10 per cent or less. Clearly, with these low plastic contents, the wood is dominant. Nevertheless, neither structure would be what it is or perform as expected without the benefit of the plastic resin used as the adhesive or binder. If you don't have a bond, you don't have a product.

For example, plywood made of all birch veneers and glued with a phenol-formaldehyde resin will have 1.5 times the strength-weight ratio of mild steel considered in tension at the proportional limit, and 1.8 times the strength-weight ratio of hard drawn aluminum alloy considered in the same manner.

Many adhesive substances are suitable for bonding veneers in plywood and binding particles of wood in particle board. The preponderance of adhesives for plywood are based on synthetic resins, and the use of natural-based adhesives is steadily dwindling. In the case of particle board, the binders are almost exclusively synthetic resin based.

A plywood panel is an interesting mechanical structure. Its chief virtue, from a structural standpoint, is high strength-to-weight ratio. Plywood made of all birch veneers and glued with a phenol-formaldehyde resin is superior to metals in strength-weight ratio. Plywood has additional properties that distinguish it from other materials of construction. It has almost equal strength in either direction, in contrast to lumber, which is weak across the grain. It has much greater stiffness at the same weight than steel or aluminum alloy. It is almost impossible to split, whereas lumber is easily split along the grain.

Plywood is self-balancing. The normal construction always contains an odd number of plies, and all adjacent plies have the grain directions lying at right angles to each other. This accomplishes physical restraint; although wood expands and contracts with variations in its moisture content induced by changes in atmospheric humidity, movement is sharply limited. As a rough rule of thumb, plywood is considered to be 75 per cent dimensionally stabilized in the plane of the panel simply by this cross-banding action.

Plywood is no more an ideal product than other materials of construction. It has less stiffness for a given thickness along the grain than lumber and therefore is somewhat less desirable for heavily loaded shelving. On the other hand, its trapezoidal shear strength or diaphragm action is superior to lumber. Sheathing and sub-floors have long been made of plywood in earthquake areas where resistance to shearing forces is of critical importance. Plywood shrinks and swells perpendicular to the plane of the panel. On this axis, there is no restraint resulting from the configuration and its movement is practically identical with that of the same species of lumber.

Plywood, like lumber, has a very low coefficient of thermal expansion, has a high heat capacity and is a reasonably good heat insulator. The last two features combined give wood and plywood their well-known warmth to the touch.

The exposed-face ply of plywood can be a decorative veneer instead of a utilitarian species. This seldom has any effect on strength except possibly to increase it if dense hardwoods are substituted for softwoods.

Plywood can be finished in any manner suitable for the finishing of lumber and, in fact, is better equipped to hold the finish because of the stabilizing action, so that likelihood of checking is reduced. There is one notable exception. Plywood made from Douglas fir is notorious for checking and is generally considered not suitable for finishing in the usual manner. Douglas fir lumber is little better except for certain cuts which are relatively expensive; the weakness is inherent in the species and not due to construction.

Particle board may be viewed as man's first feeble attempt to create lumber. In fact, it has been called reconstituted wood. Assuming carefully controlled manufacture and uniformity in the product, one can achieve useful strength values with as little as 10 or 15 per cent excess in weight over that of the same species in lumber form.

While particle board does not have the same strength/weight ratio as lumber or plywood of the same species, it has merit of its own. Particle board can be very uniform in strength in all directions in the plane of the panel. Variations in grain, knots, grain deviation and other problems in nonuniformity, found particularly in lumber but also often in plywood, can be minimized or eliminated. Particle board can be made species-insensitive within broad limits, and is not dependent upon the quality of the wood from which the particles are made, assuming there is no decay and the particles are clean. It can almost be claimed that wood fit for no other purposes than burning under boilers can be made into good particle board if excessive fines and foreign matter can be eliminated.

Particle board is seldom designed for intrinsic beauty, but when overlaid or reveneered, it becomes one of the most useful core materials available at reasonable cost. It is capable of receiving plastic surface sheets of various kinds (decorated or in plain color), overlay surfaces which have excellent paintability, and metal surfaces like those on metal-clad plywood. With properly designed fillers, the surface of the particle board devoid of an overlay can be made paintable.

The weaknesses of particle board include a lack of stiffness which is not remedied by increase in thickness. Tensile strength in the normal (perpendicular) direction, a measure of the internal bond, is considerably weaker than wood of most species. Screw-holding power is limited, although recent developments have sharply improved this property.

Resin Adhesives

The choice of adhesive controls the durability and performance of the plywood. The adhesive has two functions. The obvious one is to hold the plies together; the less obvious one is to keep them from moving with respect to each other. This is no simple task. The expansion and contraction forces due to changes in moisture content of wood across the grain can approach 10,000 psi. These forces can be demonstrated simply. Polyvinyl butyral resin, a thermoplastic, is a very strong adhesive for wood. However, if plywood is made with it and subjected to expansion stresses by increasing the moisture content of the wood, the face plies will exert sufficient force to cause flow in the glueline and will protrude an appreciable distance over either edge across the grain. The core ply will appear to have shrunk in this direction but will protrude in a direction 90° to the first. All this occurs without any sign of delamination. Therefore adhesives for plywood should be thermoset to avoid flow or creep.

In the manufacture of particle board, the adhesive binds the particles together so that the panel acts as a uniform plate of material. There are internal stresses similar to those of plywood, but they exist between the particles. If one cycles the particle board through varying moisture contents, an inadequate glueline can be ruptured. If the binder is adequate and the changes are severe, the particles themselves will be ruptured. This effect can be measured by determining changes in internal strength; it can often be seen in the form of "core checks." It is this phenomenon which has made it so difficult to produce an exterior grade particle board.

Effect of Choice of Adhesive on Performance and Grade. Anyone who has worked with plywood knows there are exterior and interior grades. Less well-known, but of increasing importance, are the intermediate, highly moisture-resistant grades which, while not fully exterior, are chosen for severe interior work. These distinctions are attributable largely to the adhesive.

Phenol-formaldehyde resins produce plywood of such quality that the last thing to fail under conditions of severe exposure is the glueline. However, these resins are expensive and perhaps more durable than necessary for interior work. Furthermore, phenolic resin adhesives, having considerable color, often give trouble with staining. Melamine-formaldehyde resins can be substituted for phenol-formaldehyde in the adhesive for exterior grade board, eliminating the problem of staining; unfortunately, they are even more expensive.

The workhorse adhesives used in interior work are based on urea-formaldehyde resin, and for most purposes the performance is adequate. If greater durability is required,

fortification is obtained with varying amounts of melamine-formaldehyde resin.

Special adhesives comprising resorcinol-formaldehyde or melamine-formaldehyde resins may be utilized for splicing two or more pieces of plywood together, or in the assembly of veneer faces and cores before the final step in making the plywood.

There is no true exterior grade particle board and, consequently, no point in changing the adhesive to gain exterior durability or increased moisture resistance. The two common binders for particle board are urea-formaldehyde resin and phenol-formaldehyde resin. The principal advantage of the latter is increased heat resistance. Since this requirement seldom has to be met, most particle board uses urea-formaldehyde as a binder. Special adhesives are not significant. There have been attempts to make floor tiles out of wood particles, using vinyl adhesives for better resilience, but no substantial amount has been produced.

Methods of Manufacture

Most plywood utilizes rotary cut veneer. The log peeling operation, which has been compared to unwinding the log, produces rotary veneers equivalent in grain structure to flat cut lumber. This method of producing veneer, while fast and economical and giving maximum utilization of the veneer log, produces sapwood and heartwood. Sapwood, the outer few inches of the log, often has little or no defects and seldom has knots. It produces the most uniform-looking panel and is structurally quite adequate. However, sapwood of any species is not resistant to decay, and this can be significant in the choice of plywood for some structures. In building, it is seldom important unless the plywood is used decoratively. Here, peculiarly enough, heartwood is often preferred in spite of its lesser uniformity because of its greater color and richness. For decorative use, defects found in the heart of the log of any normal tree are clipped out immediately after peeling and before drying. This operation is most important in setting the quality and appearance of the final product.

The manufacture of particle board has been less well described than that of plywood. While the production of consistently good particle board with a maximum strength-cost ratio requires high-grade equipment and constant attention to detail, it is basically a simple process. Scrap wood of all sorts is ground, chipped or flaked into particles generally coarser than sawdust, the fines and dirt are removed, and the clean particles are dried if necessary. The particles are coated with an appropriate adhesive which is partially dried; they then go to a machine which forms a mat containing the desired weight of glue-covered particles. The length and the width of the mat at this point are set but the thickness is not. In order to avoid excessive bulk, the mat is pre-pressed in a cold press so that it can readily be fed into the opening of a hot press. Here, the mat is compressed to its final thickness, and the binder is cured by heat. After removal, cooling and trimming, it may be surface sanded as is plywood, then it is ready for inspection and shipment. There are other commercial processes with sharply different techniques, but the great bulk of present-day production in this country and in Europe follows some variation of the method described above.

Fields of Utilization

Plywood End Uses:

Concrete forms
Siding
Sheathing
Sub-floors
Roof decks
Gusset plates
Wall decoration and construction
Ceiling panels
Cabinet work
Furniture
Shelving
Soffits
Doors
Floor underlayment

The above list contains many old uses and some that are less well-known. Concrete forms are used in the casting of foundations, walls and concrete floors which are not slabs on grade. Plywood serves well here because it is strong, economical, dependable and convenient. The plastic resin bond insures integrity during construction under exposure to the alkaline concrete, the large quantities of water, the weather, mud and the general deteriorating influences that surround the building site.

Siding is perhaps the newest application for plywood in the building of homes. Its use in this manner has been accelerated by simple modular constructions that go in place quickly, are interlocking, and can be had preprimed or prefinished.

Sheathing and sub-floors are made of plywood in earthquake areas to benefit from the diaphragm action. Some such construction is mandatory. Roof decks are stronger and more economical when plywood is used.

With the possible exception of floor underlayment, the rest of the list of uses is obvious. Floor underlayment is beneficially made of plywood, even when strip flooring is desired, because of the rigidity it introduces as a result of its excellent diaphragm action. The trend toward wall-to-wall carpeting and exotic resilient vinyl floor coverings and tiles has accelerated the use of plywood as a stiffening underlayment

Particle Board End Uses:

Floor underlayment
Work surface underlayment
Cores for table tops and furniture stock panels
Partitions in storage cabinetry
Shelves and store fixtures
Displays
Sliding and folding doors

Particle board is newer than plywood and does not have as long a list of uses in building. Its fields of usefulness in the building industry overlap somewhat, but particle board has been so successful in work-surface underlayment for kitchens that it has largely supplanted plywood. To an increasing extent, this is also true of dinette tables.

The product is still somewhat controversial as a core in the manufacture of stock from which furniture is produced; but good particle board properly reveneered does produce excellent case goods if the furniture has been designed with the limitations of particle board in mind.

In sliding and folding doors, particle board is superior to plywood because of its uniformity and its excellent behavior as a free-standing, vertically oriented panel.

Despite its shortcomings, particle board is often the material of choice where both economics and uniformity or homogeneity of construction are important.

FINISHING, OVERLAYS AND LAMINATES

Finishing

Finishing utilizes substantial additional quantities of plastics and resins. The general rules for finishing plywood are similar to those for finishing metal and lumber. For the finishing system to stay in place, the first coat applied must have high adhesion for wood and subsequent coats must have good adhesion for each other. This is not automatically obtained and is occasionally overlooked with disastrous results.

Wood expands and contracts to some degree with changes in moisture content induced by changes in relative humidity. The finish must be sufficiently hard to give adequate mar resistance, but not so rigid that expansion and contraction would result in checking or crazing. It is not possible to stabilize woods or plywoods by means of surface-applied finishes, although it is true that a good finish can slow the rate of change of moisture content with changes in humidity and reduce the shock effect, giving the plastic in the finish a chance to follow the dimensional changes without failing by cracking. The balancing of mar resistance against this necessary flexibility is sufficiently important that it must be related to the expected exposure. If the exposure is severe, as in outdoor work, the flexibility must be attained even if it is necessary to forego mar resistance.

Other problems peculiar to wood and therefore plywood have to do with obtaining adequate smoothness, adequate color and, in the case of transparent finishes, adequate contrast to bring out the beauty of the grain.

Problems peculiar to particle board finishing do not differ greatly from those of finishing plywood with one exception. Particle board by its very nature contains unavoidable pits on the surface even of the smoothest types. In so-called sawdust-faced boards or more properly, fines-faced boards, the pits are very fine; but cyclic exposures generally cause loss of smoothness, so there is a question about the value of this approach. An overlay of plastic or resin-impregnated fiber is often applied where the finish is important. However, the same results can also be achieved by filling the pits with an adequate glazing compound—a highly filled oleoresinous putty—followed by smooth sanding. Regardless of which of these techniques is used, the procedure is then the same as for finishing plywood, but transparent finishes are rarely used.

The two methods of finishing either type of material are (1) liquid application and (2) the newer laminating techniques in which the finish is a film of plastic, applied generally by roller.

Overlaying

Although finishing has always been with us, *prefinishing* in the plywood or particle board mill is new. The last decade has seen a tremendous growth in the production of prefinished plywood. Particle board will probably follow suit in the next. Plant equipment can produce a higher-grade, more uniform finish at lower cost than field finishing. The balance is further tipped in the favor of mill finishing because the necessary skill can be concentrated in a few locations. There are not enough skilled finishers in many localities to satisfy the demand, and the production of a high-grade, durable, good-looking finish is not for the casual artisan.

Bringing finishing into the manufacturing plant gives impetus to the idea of overlaying as a means to this end. The oldest overlay is a phenolic resin *impregnated paper* of high-density grade, i.e., with high phenolic resin content. It was originally developed as a concrete form stock, but since the surface resulting is very smooth, it can, by proper means, be painted with excellent results out of doors, e.g., for signs.

A medium-density impregnated paper has given us an overlay which is softer and helps hide the grain of the wood or particle board where that is desired. This type of overlay is highly paintable and has given rise to improved forms of siding which are easier to finish on the job but which can also be prefinished economically at the mill.

Fiber overlays are mentioned for the sake of completeness, and considerable development work has been done. Production is still low.

Hardboard has been used as a veneer, and in a sense is an overlay. The product has been around for a long time and its use is slowly increasing. Hardboard overlaid plywood combines the uniform, smooth, relatively grainless surface of hardboard with the lightness and strength of plywood.

The newest and most important overlays are the *plastic films*. The list includes vinyls, polyester-fiber glass preformed sheet, liquid polyesters, polyvinyl fluoride, cellulose-ester foils, diallylphthalate resin on a paper carrier, melamine-formaldehyde resin on a paper carrier and, more recently, so-called colorless phenolic resins on paper carrier

With this wide range of choices, the designer can satisfy almost any specific physical property requirements; all of them can be made adequately protective, highly decorative, and varied in effect. Choice is governed by end use. None of these is an exact duplicate in performance for any other; the strong points and weaknesses must be considered along with economics.

Wet cast overlay, almost a contradiction in terms, is the technique of finishing with the liquid polyesters, either alone or modified with glass fiber and other resins. Furniture and doors have been produced in limited quantity in America; but the only substantial and sustained production has come from Europe. The present state of this art is such that the final material requires considerable rubbing and polishing for passable results. Our labor costs are too high to permit economical production, and adequate machinery has not been developed. There has been considerable work directed toward avoiding the necessary rubbing and polishing, but no process thus far revealed has become both adequate and economical. There also exist serious adhesion problems which, while soluble, add to the cost. We see wet cast overlays as successful ultimately, but there is still much work to be done. The reason for persisting, even in the face of the extensive availability of plastic films, is the unmatched brilliance and beauty which result from the wet casting process.

Before leaving the subject of overlays, one must mention *metal foils*. Their use in connection with building construction is increasing, they require resins as adhesives, and they solve problems not easily solved by other means.

Metal and glass are impermeable membranes. If one wants a high moisture vapor barrier, metal foil should be seriously considered (it is too difficult to utilize glass in the same manner). Metal foil can be used as a surface layer (overlay) or it can be buried, in the case of plywood, in one of the gluelines. Metal foil also is utilized as a reflective insulator. For this purpose, it is most effective as an outside layer.

Metal foil is also used to increase the heat resistance of the plywood surface. The heat conductivity of metal is utilized to carry the heat away and prevent surface damage. In such a construction, the glueline immediately under the surface veneer also carries the metal foil. If a heat-resistant plastic finish is chosen, the decorative veneer is kept to a minimum thickness, and the metal foil is of adequate thickness, almost complete cigarette burn resistance can be achieved.

Laminates

These are structures with a core of one material faced on both sides with another material. *Metal-clad plywood* is a laminated structure which so far has found little use in housing, somewhat greater use in fascia work and substantial use in special buildings, special-purpose rooms within buildings and in transportation structures. Metal-clad plywood behaves as a true structural sandwich and brings to the laminate the well-known properties of the metal of choice but the tremendous stiffness of a thick structure at a weight penalty only slightly greater than that of plywood. Since almost all metals can be bonded to plywood, the designer has considerable choice.

A variant of metal-clad plywood is *porcelain-enameled steel* or *porcelain-enameled aluminum-clad plywood*. Present use is limited to some fascia work and some special structures. This laminate brings to the structure the well-known properties of porcelain enamel, but there is a difficult adhesion problem involved, and panels must be mounted to insure the complete exclusion of moisture from the edges.

Hardboard-faced plywood has been mentioned above. Its principal uses are cutting tables in the garment industry, checkout counters in shopping centers and wherever a relatively grainless, smooth, nonmetallic surface, with the stiffness of plywood, is required.

High-pressure plastic-clad plywood touches almost all of us. This laminate is the familiar work surface of the kitchen, the dinette table, many restaurants tables and many food counters in restaurants. Again the advantages of the plywood or particle board — stiffness with economy and light weight — are enhanced for the specific use by the hardness, decorative quality and wear resistance of the high-pressure plastic outer layer.

Reveneered particle board is not too likely a choice for primary building construction. However, it is increasingly used in furniture of all kinds and in shelving where the uniformity of construction and economy of particle board make an excellent core for a high-grade, decorative wood veneer.

In some cities and in most public buildings, the use of plywood is limited because of its combustibility. In order to circumvent this limitation, plywood is impregnated with *fire-proofing* compounds. This is acceptable to codes, and ratings have been issued. However, such plywood is not attractive from a decorative standpoint and is generally reveneered to produce a laminate

with all the attractiveness of an untreated piece of plywood of the same species. This is also permissible so long as the thickness of the surface veneer is held to a specified limit.

A laminate which involves wood and in a sense is plywood that has become very important is comprised of a *core* of *cellular calcium silicate* with appropriate veneers adhered to either side of the surface. Such a construction permits the manufacture of doors with the appearance of wood but with incombustibility ratings up to and including an hour and a half. These laminates make excellent front doors or exterior opening doors since the tendency to warp in severe weather is very small and they become neither excessively loose in winter nor excessively tight in summer. Partitions are also made of this construction.

The newest member of this family of "incombustible" laminates is *wood-veneered cement asbestos hardboard*. In thin constructions approximating those of decorative plywood, the designer has the freedom to select the decorative properties of the wood veneer of choice and at the same time can comply with codes requiring incombustibility or very low rates of flame spread.

Conductive layers have been proposed which would then be able to carry a current and furnish a simplified warm-wall heating system. Patents in this field have been granted and considerable work has done, but there are design and safety problems which must be overcome.

A laminate of increasing importance in schools and laboratories is *chalk board*. Most of these have a normal plywood core of a grade suitable for interior use and a face of porcelain-enameled steel or porcelain-enameled aluminum. The porcelain is quite special and carries a dull, satiny surface rough enough to take chalk but smooth enough to erase. Such chalk boards are light in weight, can be cut in the field and are of top durability.

Sandwich Constructions

Perhaps the most potentially useful but controversial building module that makes use of plywood is the sandwich construction. Where controversy exists, it generally stems from one or two factors: the more common is economics; the other is the attachment or joint problem.

During World War II, substantial amounts of sandwich construction were based on

FIG. 7-1. An experimental sandwich construction of high strength-weight ratio involving a very low density foam.

panels with plywood faces and honeycomb cores. The more stringent economic requirements of nonmilitary use have retarded wide use of the construction. It has a further handicap which is also a challenge.

Post and beam, or window wall (curtain wall) construction, is presently used only in large buildings and commercial construction. For such structures, plywood-faced panels are not suitable. Smaller structures and housing which could use this construction seem to be too tightly bound by convention to make the change.

The initial success of plastic foams in insulation and flotation fields has encouraged the idea of sandwich construction in small buildings, and plywood sandwich constructions with *foam cores* are being produced. The laminated foam sandwich has many of the problems of honeycomb-cored sandwiches—adhesive bonding, edge-sealing, telegraphing. The foamed-in-place variation avoids these troubles. In this procedure, the module is formed as part of the building and the resulting space is filled with foam formed within the construction. Of course, either this or the assembled foam-core panel can be produced in the factory. In contrast, honeycomb-core sandwich panels cannot be produced in the field.

Doors represent a form of sandwich construction although the common adaptations do not behave as true sandwiches because the core is simply a filler between two skins which are held in place by stiles and rails. Some filler, however, is an advantage over a stressed skin, for without increasing the weight appreciably, the cores or fillers prevent drumming and add a little to the stability.

Stressed frame structures are not necessarily sandwich in nature. When properly designed, the stressed frame does all of the work of supporting the structure of which it is a part. It may or may not be self-supporting, and it needs some type of face for closure and decoration. Stressed frame structures with plywood faces, utilized in smaller buildings, are somewhat akin to hollow-core wooden doors.

Modern buildings, even those of large size, are steadily becoming lighter and more rigid. Meanwhile, the machinery required by modern living, whether it be a home, an office or a factory, has become more extensive. Thus, we have more noise producers with less resistance to noise. In the older buildings, sound was controlled by sheer mass. Foundations were heavy, walls were heavy and machinery was isolated to certain areas. Mass and physical isolation are no longer available. *Soundproofing* has thus turned to sandwich constructions for a partial answer. Properly designed, sandwich constructions can accomplish significant attenuation of sound passing through them.

A sandwich construction which has been commercially used in the erection of small factories is *plywood-faced fiberboard*. Sheathing grade fiberboards have improved in quality, durability and structural performance over the years to the point where they are widely used in the construction of homes. Going one step farther, small buildings are built with walls in which the structure and the insulation are integral by attaching sandwiches made of plywood faces and fiberboard cores. Such a construction needs only to be protected from leaks that would wet the core and a stiff, well-insulated, wind-tight construction is economically obtained. The future of this construction for small buildings is clouded because of resistance to change, despite the unit's better in-place economics than separately applied sheathing and siding.

Modules

A late starter as compared to sandwiches is the building module—the pre-built sub-structure. The industry has been much quicker to adopt the module principle, and use is expanding rapidly. Structures of this type utilize much plywood, but particle

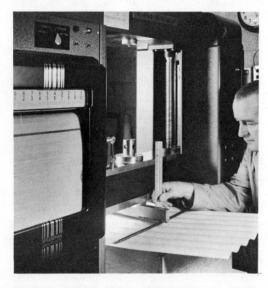

FIG. 7-2. Checking for rigidity in a translucent, reinforced plastic building panel.

board has had only a limited application. *Glued trusses* are an excellent example. The gusset plates are almost always plywood, and where face plates are desired or required, they too are thin plywood.

Glued, laminated wooden beams are slowly establishing themselves as allowing new beauty in construction, and time and again are continuing to prove that while made of

combustible material they withstand fires better than other materials. Their use of plywood is generally limited to decorative housings or boxing-in. Resins form an important part of the construction; not only is the plywood glued to the beam with an adhesive, but increasingly the beams themselves are glued together with adhesives.

Built-up modular floors such as the American Plywood Association's "2-4-1" and other combined sub-floor finished floor constructions have plywood as a main component. While they can be nailed, they are even better in terms of rigidty and performance if resin glued.

Modular roofs are in their infancy but the solutions to basic problems of producing modular floors are available here, and the only essential difference is the exposure to exterior conditions. Unit constructions can go up in sections quite rapidly and carry a complete plastic finish of known exterior performance. Experimental houses of this type have been built and found satisfactory.

Special Combinations

A product which comes from the plywood industry, but which is not in itself plywood, is veneered metal. Several examples illustrate its use in modern construction: elevator cab interiors, incombustible lamp shades, and opaque lighting cove covers, automobile trim and doors for dishwashers. These look like wood and thus harmonize with the modern, increasingly popular, all-wood kitchen. Veneered metal uses adhesive in two places. A highly specialized, multi-component adhesive is required, for example, a phenol formaldehyde–polyvinyl butyral blend. The finish for the veneered metal has to have special durability and is likely, therefore, to be based on one of the newer light-stable, chemically resistant, synthetic resins, e.g., acrylics or special polyesters.

ENGINEERING THE CONSTRUCTION

The natural evolution in building construction from logs to lumber to plywood was greatly accelerated by the development of durable adhesives based on synthetic polymers. Too often, convenience or economics has dictated the choice of adhesive, with insufficient consideration to physical and mechanical properties. Urea-formaldehyde was used instead of the more durable but more expensive phenol-formaldehyde, for example.

Plywood and its resin components should be chosen carefully as to construction, dimension, species, type of adhesive, type of finish and how it is combined with other materials when that is desired.

Much modern construction requires balanced modules or units. This is particularly true of plywood. The very panel itself must be of balanced construction as outlined in the introduction. It is a general rule with few exceptions that anything that is done to one side of the plywood (or particle board panel) must also be done to the other. In other words, building a module from a piece of plywood requires construction details that will not disturb the balance. The module in turn must have balance within itself, or the building will have unnecessary weaknesses. An unbalanced door, no matter how well glued and constructed, will warp and twist far more than a balanced one.

Partitions behave similarly, as do floors; when roof modules become popular, those which are balanced for the position they will occupy will be the most successful. Balancing a unit does not necessarily mean identical construction on either side of a neutral axis. It does mean that changing ambient conditions must cause like changes in either side. For wood and plastics, heat has some effect; but the principal disturbance arises from changing relative humidity.

There are designers who would forget these physical facts and secure the units so they cannot distort. This means stresses are built up which the unit must resist but which are of no benefit in giving strength to the whole structure. Efficient, economical construction requires that the unit must of itself be relatively stress-free for average conditions of surface temperature and relative humidity. Temporary excursions or differentials will cause temporary stresses and perhaps temporary distortions, but when equilibrium returns, the properly designed unit again becomes stress-free or resumes its original configuration if it has been distorted.

In modern materials, engineering the

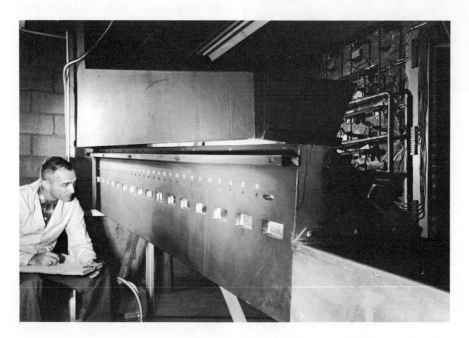

Fig. 7-3. Tunnel test for measuring the rate-of-flame spread across the surface of a building panel.

construction includes deciding on the finish required and whether it will be applied in the mill or on the job. No one finish is right for all purposes; neither is there a uniform decision as to mill finishing versus field finishing.

Installation requirements can give rise to serious problems. Sometimes, the very nature of the structure or the materials is such as to dictate the choice. At other times, inertia and stubbornness in accepting change are handi-

FIG. 7-4. Vertical furnace for measuring the resistance to fire penetration of fire doors and fire resistant partitions.

caps to be overcome. The materials engineer or the designer must know the installation problems; new materials of construction in the building industry are wisely first examined in actual practice before they reach the marketplace. Such procedures as field trials and time and material studies together give data on durability and the economics of erection, but they also show how to avoid pitfalls and to make the best use of the building material. The designer would do well to obtain this information where available and to give proper emphasis to it.

Evaluating The Construction

Evaluation of a material of construction or a modular unit is carried out by a test or quality control laboratory. The materials engineer will become an increasingly important co-worker of the construction designer and the architect. The materials engineer makes a business of knowing what the evaluation results are. From them, he can choose between several alternatives in the composition and makeup, whether it be selecting a type of plywood or a more complicated structure such as a window-wall panel or a roof deck. From the durability results, he knows the extent to which he may expose the structure. From the physical properties, he can calculate the performance of the structure as a whole.

While it is primarily the province of the design engineer to solve attachment and joint problems, those who utilize plywood or any panel material in the design of a substructure would do well if they also furnished, as part of their development, workable means of bringing substructures together and of attaching them to other parts of the building. For example, in a movable partition, perhaps the most important problem to be solved is the hardware required to hold it in place. Certainly in fireproof and soundproof modular constructions, the joint or attachment cannot be a source of weakness, or the entire unit is without much value. Thus, in ordering plywood, lacquer or paint or other plastic adjuncts, one must know how they combine and what can be expected of them in service

REFERENCES

1. ASTM Standards, Philadelphia, Pa.
2. American Plywood Association, "Plywood Handbook," Portland, Oregon.
3. Dietz, A. G. H., "Engineering Laminates," New York, 1949.
4. Meyer, L. H., "Plywood—What It Is—What It Does," New York, McGraw-Hill Book Co., Inc., 1947.
5. Perry, T. D., "Modern Plywood," New York, Pitman, 1942.
6. Skeist, I., Ed., "Handbook of Adhesives," New York, Reinhold Publishing Corp., 1962.
7. Wood, A. D., and Linn, T. S., "Plywoods," New York, Chemical Publishing Company, 1943.

8 OTHER PLASTICS FOR WALLS, ROOFS AND DOORS

R. C. HESS AND J. A. BAUMANN

Union Carbide Corporation
Plastics Division
Bound Brook, New Jersey

PART A: Vinyls*

RIGID VINYL SHEET

Physical Properties

Rigid vinyl sheet is a relatively new structural material now available to the engineer and designer. It provides a wide range of attractive physical properties. Rigid vinyl compounds consist essentially of polyvinyl chloride homopolymer or vinyl chloride–vinyl acetate copolymers suitably formulated with stabilizers, lubricants and pigments. The normal-impact material, usually referred to as Type I, is compounded to the minimum extent necessary to obtain good processing. Type I rigid vinyl compounds have notched Izod impact values in the range of 0.40 to 0.60 ft lb/in. of notch. They are most noted for superior chemical inertness. High-impact rigid vinyl, referred to as Type II, is compounded during manufacture to increase impact resistance. Izod impact values as high as 15 ft lb/in. of notch can be developed. This is accompanied by a slight loss in chemical resistance and physical properties (lower modulus and strength properties).

As noted above, rigid vinyl sheet may be formulated using either a vinyl chloride homopolymer (commonly referred to in the industry as PVC) or a vinyl chloride–vinyl acetate copolymer. Each has its advantages,

the homopolymer from a use standpoint, the copolymer from a manufacturing standpoint. The homopolymer is inherently more heat and light stable. It also has a 10 to 15°C higher heat distortion temperature, thus permitting a higher use temperature. The copolymer, on the other hand, has a lower softening temperature but is easier to process.

Physical properties of rigid vinyl copolymer and the two types of rigid PVC are given in Table 8A-1.

Plastics, particularly thermoplastics such as rigid vinyl, are subject to considerable creep under continuous loads. Hence, strength values as shown in Table 8-1 apply only to short-term tests. These plastic materials are unlike metals in this respect. This plastic flow dictates decreased loading for long-term applications. Tests conducted by the Firestone Plastics Co.[1] to determine the tensile strength and related values under long-term loads have shown that with increasing loading periods, the ultimate tensile strength decreases to a minimum value of 5500 psi at room temperature. This finding was confirmed in work performed by Union Carbide Plastics Division. The evaluation of polyvinyl chloride sheeting for stress rupture in water showed an upper working stress limit of about 5000 psi at 23°C and 1800 psi at 60°C.[2]

*This part by R. C. Hess.

157

Chemical Properties

Rigid vinyl plastics offer exceptional resistance against a great number of corrosive media, in many cases surpassing that of high-grade steels and alloys. These materials

Forming and Fabrication

Rigid vinyls can be machined, formed and joined by a wide variety of fabrication methods. The methods are either identical to those used with conventional construction

TABLE 8A-1. Physical Properties of Rigid Vinyls

	ASTM Method	Rigid Vinyl Copolymer	Rigid PVC Type I	Rigid PVC Type II
Specific gravity	792–60T	1.37–1.51	1.38–1.45	1.35–1.45
Tensile strength, psi	638–61T	8000	9000	7000
Tensile modulus, 10^5 psi	638–61T		415	350
Flexural strength, psi	790–61	13,400	14,000	10,500
Flexural modulus 10^5 psi	790–61	4.4	5.1	4.5
Izod impact, ft lb/in. of notch at 73°F	256–56	0.4–0.6	0.4–0.6	15
Izod impact, ft lb/in. of notch at −20°F	256–56	0.2–0.5	0.3	1
Heat distortion, °F at 264 psi	648–56	135–150	160	155
Rockwell hardness	785–62		R110	R105
Moisture absorption, % in 24 hr at 73°F	570–59aT	0.08	0.05	0.10
Thermal expansion, 10^{-5}/°C	696–44	7	5	10
Thermal conductivity, 10^{-4} cal/cm²/sec/°C		3.7	3.5	4.5
Flammability, in./min.	635–56T		Self-extinguishing	
Ultraviolet resistance		Good	Good	Good
Heat formability		Excellent	Good	Good

resist attack by most mineral acids (including sulfuric and nitric acids), bases and salts through a broad range of concentrations, with a maximum temperature of up to 165°F at which they can be satisfactorily employed. Maximum temperature varies with the concentration of the corrosive medium. Rigid vinyls are not recommended for use with ketones, ethers, esters, aromatic hydrocarbons and chlorinated hydrocarbons. In the event that mixtures of two or more chemicals are encountered, special exposure tests should be carried out to determine the resistance. Determination of temperature limits is often important. It is frequently advisable to carry out tests under actual operating conditions to determine the ability of the plastic to perform satisfactorily in a specific corrosive environment.

Corrosive attack on rigid vinyls results in the penetration of the corrosive medium into the bulk of the material rather than a chemical reaction with the surface. Consequently, rigid vinyls like most other plastics show an increase in weight and volume rather than a loss as shown by metals undergoing corrosion.

materials or slight modifications that allow for or take advantage of some of the particular properties of rigid vinyls.

TABLE 8A-2. Fabrication Methods for Rigid Vinyls

Machine	Form	Join
Saw	Bend	Cement
Drill	Roll	Nail, bolt, screw, rivet
Mill	Deep draw	Weld, by
Turn	Vacuum form	(a) Hot gas
Shear		(b) Friction
Plane		(c) High frequency
Rout		
Sand		

Applications

Vinyl Building Panels. Advances in rigid vinyl formulation and in processing equipment design have made available to the U.S. building industry a new dimension in building panels. These panels lend themselves admirably to use for roofing, siding, various shelter and enclosure constructions and interior paneling. Domed roofs covered with attractively colored corrugated sheets, and unpainted sidings in colors pleasing to the eye, represent a major breakthrough in the building industry. They have already caused some revolutionary changes in building concepts.

Rigid PVC building panels have made their debut in the United States. This came after approximately five years of actual use experience in Europe, spurred by a shortage of more traditional materials. Results overseas have been most encouraging. Five or six companies in the United States are now in commercial production or soon will be. Some companies in this field estimate an annual consumption of about 125 million pounds of PVC resin within a few years.[3] This represents approximately 250 million square feet of sheet. Future markets, for which PVC sheet panels are eminently suitable, include:

Roofing and siding for factories, warehouses, barns, etc.
Porch enclosures
Sports arena enclosures (tennis courts, swimming pools, etc.)
Bus stop shelters
Cabanas
Carports
Terrace fencing
Patio roofing and fencing
Marquees
Translucent ceilings
Interior paneling (decorative and others).

Advantages of Rigid Vinyl Panels. Rigid vinyl panels provide a combination of price and properties unequaled by the current competitors — glass, corrugated aluminum, galvanized steel, canvas and fiber glass-reinforced polyester.

(1) Attractive Appearance: Rigid vinyl panels are available in a rainbow of hues, translucent or opaque. This has both decorative and functional value. For example, when used as roofing or siding, light intensity can be adjusted by using panels of different colors or opacities in any one installation (see Figure 8A-1). (The opaque materials have the best resistance to ultraviolet light; see below.)

(2) Weatherability: Accelerated weathering tests and five-year actual performance data from Europe have indicated that the

vinyl panels do not lose their structural integrity over long periods of time. A slight loss in light transmission has been reported after several years of use in the case of translucent panels, but further aging has little, if any, additional effect. Slight color changes have been reported, but these are uniform throughout the entire installation and are difficult to

Fig. 8A-1. Factory roofing on European industrial plant consists of two differently colored panels to provide the proper balance of illumination on the inside. This installation is in Italy. (Photo L. M. P.). (*Courtesy Modern Plastics and L. M. P.*)

detect except by comparison with a standard panel. Rigid vinyl is moisture resistant and is unaffected by salt air; therefore, it can be used along the seashore. In Europe, panels have been installed all the way from the Scandinavian countries to southern Italy without any reported failures.

(3) Flexibility: Rigid vinyl sheeting can be installed with appreciable radius to produce arch-type structures not easily producible with other covering materials (see Figure 8A-2).

(4) Light Weight: Rigid vinyl weighs about one-half as much as aluminum, one-sixth as much as galvanized steel and four-fifths as much as reinforced polyester panels. Shipping and handling economies are obvious. In several case histories reported by Lavorazione Materie Plastiche (L. M. P.), Turin, Italy, construction costs for support structures were also materially reduced when

rigid vinyl panels were specified over conventionally used roofing materials.[3]

(5) Corrosion Resistance: Rigid vinyl is immune to industrial atmospheres and to

While rigid vinyl plastic has many outstanding properties which qualify it for the building panel application, it is extremely important that its limitations be understood.

FIG. 8A-2. Bus stop shelter made of corrugated sheet, represents a typical application. Note that the sheet is curved, making all horizontal seaming unnecessary. (Photo, Allied Chemical Corp., Barrett Div.). (*Courtesy Modern Plastics and Allied Chemical Corp.*)

most chemical reagents, acids and alkalies, common detergents, oils, greases and bacteria. It is unaffected by such common building materials as cement and plaster. The use of rigid vinyl sheeting in corrosion service ductwork has long proved the ability of the material to resist corrosive attack.

(6) Fire Resistance: Rigid vinyl burns, but does not support combustion. It is self-extinguishing.

(7) Cleanability: Rigid vinyl panels are easy to keep clean. Their smooth surface does not accumulate dirt. Periodic refinishing is not required.

(8) Easy Installation: The panels are light in weight and easy to handle. No special tools or techniques are required. Panels can be cut, sawed or drilled with conventional equipment.

Limitations of Rigid Vinyl Building Panels.

Rigid vinyl *softens at elevated temperatures*. Above its heat distortion temperature, 135 to 160°F, sheet will sag between its supports and will not return to its original state. Consequently, it is imperative that in any installation the material not be subjected to heat levels above the heat distortion temperature. It is important to note, also, that a sheet exposed to the weather may reach temperatures well in excess of ambient air temperature, especially if the color is dark.

Strain release can also be a problem. However, this should be obviated or at least minimized if the sheet is produced according to good manufacturing practice. Certain processing strains are induced in a sheet which has been formed at a temperature too low for that formulation. Subsequently, these strains are released when the sheet is subjected to elevated temperatures lower than the normal heat distortion temperature, and change in dimension and/or warping takes place. A reputable supplier is the best assurance against trouble from strain release.

FIG. 8A-3. Rigid vinyl gutter and leader developed by A/S Plastmontage, Kastrup, Denmark. (*Courtesy Plastics World.*)

The relatively *high coefficient of thermal expansion* (compared to metals) must not be overlooked, although it is no higher than for other plastic materials. Proper design can offset any problems which might otherwise result from this inherent property.

While results of exposure to the weather have thus far been encouraging, it must be realized that tests in this country have gone on for only a limited number of years. Weathering exposure is more stringent in the United States than in northern Europe. For example, although New York City and Rome have the same latitude, choice of color and degree of opacity must be made only after exacting consideration of location and its environmental character.

Polyvinyl chloride building panels are in an early commercialization stage in this country. Significant progress has already been made, and it is reasonable to assume that further advances in technology are in store. At the same time, all due consideration must be given to the possible limitations.

Rain Gutters and Leaders. Rigid vinyl plastic is being used for rain gutters and leaders in Europe, particularly in Denmark, Sweden, Germany and Great Britain. A/S Plastmontage, Kastrup, Denmark was among the first to develop a plastic product for this application. The field of plastic material candidates was narrowed down to two possibilities. Both a glass fiber-reinforced polyester and polyvinyl chloride with ultraviolet absorbers would withstand low freezing temperatures and long exposure to sunlight.[4] The Danish firm decided on the rigid polyvinyl chloride plastic (PVC) on the basis of its lower cost.

The design is a half-round gutter with a lip on one side to grip the metal mount and protect it from the weather. The metal support is designed with a small tooth (protected by the roof overhang) so that the plastic gutter is simply snapped into place firmly and requires no special tools, screws or holes. The roof mounts are made of

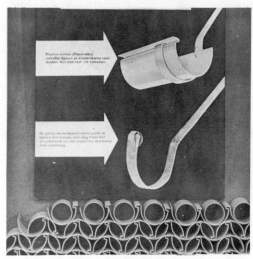

FIG. 8A-4. Rigid vinyl gutter by A/S Plastmontage is designed with a lip that grips the roof mount but still allows movement caused by expansion or contraction. (*Courtesy Plastics World*)

galvanized metal or stainless steel (see Figures 8A-3 and 8A-4).

The gutters are available in three sizes with corresponding drain pipes, and they come in four colors. A complete line of elbows, joints, ends, flanges, corners (both inside and out), metal mounts, bends and expansion joints is available. Expansion joints are necessary on runs of over 100 feet. The large coefficient of expansion for PVC makes it necessary for the gutters to be hung, not nailed, so that they are free to move in the roof mounts.

Installation is simple. The gutters are cut to correct lengths, the ends are wetted with acetone, a special adhesive (supplied by the company) is applied, and the pieces are stuck together.

There has been product development activity along similar lines in this country by a number of companies. Any commercialization of such a product will be considerably slower here than abroad, for several reasons:

(1) The more stringent weathering conditions in the United States as compared to Europe are cause for a more conservative approach. It is necessary to collect weathering results over longer periods of time to evaluate the practicality of such a product.

(2) The cost ratio of PVC to other plastic materials and to other traditional materials is less of an advantage in this country than in Europe.

(3) The greater availability of traditional building materials in this country makes for less incentive to develop such a product.

The outstanding properties of rigid vinyls, as well as their limitations, as discussed earlier relative to building panels, apply equally well here.

Doors, Sash and Frames. Another fast-growing building market for rigid vinyls, particularly rigid PVC, is in the production of doors, window sash and frames, where aluminum and wood are presently predominant. Rigid PVC used as framing for doors, windows and screens aims for markets presently estimated at 20 million units per year of which 40 percent is aluminum.[5]

Figure 8A-5 shows a rigid PVC window unit. The white frame weathers well, does not chip or peel and requires no painting. Should a color change be desired, paint will adhere. Recommendations relative to the type of paint should be obtained from the manufacturer. Rattling from metal-to-metal contact is eliminated. Condensation is low. No lubrication is necessary.

FLEXIBLE VINYL SHEETING

Physical and Chemical Properties

Flexible vinyls are compounds of vinyl resins with stabilizers, lubricants, colorants and plasticizers such as high-boiling liquids,

Fig. 8A-5. Rigid PVC window unit. (*Courtesy Crestline Co., Wausau, Wis.*)

soft resins or elastomers. Suitable vinyl resins include polyvinyl chloride and those copolymers which are predominantly vinyl chloride. Among the principal copolymers are those containing vinyl acetate and vinylidene chloride. These vinyl polymers and copolymers are made with a wide range of properties by controlling the polymerization conditions, the co-monomer selection and concentration, and combinations thereof. The plasticizers provide flexible or rubber-like characteristics, the extent of the flexibility being dependent upon the amount and type of plasticizer.

The flexible vinyls are among the most versatile thermoplastics and can readily be converted to products of varying shapes and flexibility. Within this range of products is flexible vinyl sheeting which is of particular interest here.

Flexible vinyl sheeting can be produced

in essentially any color, clear, translucent or opaque. The sheeting offers advantages of toughness, excellent abrasion resistance and outstanding resistance to acids, alkalies, alcohols, most solvents, oils, fats and waxes. The properties of fire, water, and moisture resistance are inherent in these materials and can be preserved and enhanced with proper choice of compounding materials such as plasticizers, stabilizers and pigments. Essentially any sheeting surface texture may be produced by embossing, providing almost unlimited styling possibilities.

The principal limitation of flexible vinyl sheeting is exposure to heat. At elevated temperatures the sheeting will show a decrease in tensile strength. Depending on the formulation, flexible vinyl sheeting is satisfactory for service at temperatures ranging from -65 to $+175°F$.

Applications

The physical and chemical properties of flexible vinyl sheeting make it eminently adaptable to wall coverings and folding doors.

Wall Coverings. Wall coverings constitute a well-established application for flexible vinyl sheeting. Distinction must be made between two vinyl sheeting materials that are quite different—unsupported vinyl sheeting and supported, which is backed by a substrate such as paper or cloth. The supporting fabric provides added strength and installation advantages. Supported wall coverings have better dimensional stability than unsupported wall coverings. Less trouble with seams can be expected. Supported materials are generally regarded as having the better all-round properties for this use.

Wall coverings are generally classified as: Light weight, Medium weight, Heavy weight. These weights might be further defined by an example of what one wall covering manufacturer produces:

The lightweight wall covering is backed by a cotton Osnaburg or sheeting fabric yielding between 2.10 and 2.40 yd/lb and is generally coated to a total finished weight range of 18 to 23 oz/lineal yd (54-inch width — 1½ square yards). Medium-weight wall covering has a 1.85 drill backing and is generally coated to a total finished weight range of 22 to 33 oz/lineal yd (54-inch width — 1½ square yards). Heavy-weight covering is on a 1.06 broken twill and is generally coated to a total finished weight range of 30 to 40 oz/lineal yd (54-inch width — 1½ square yards).

In general, lightweight material is limited in its use and should be considered a maintenance-free covering for areas not subjected to heavy abrasion or traffic. In effect, this material replaces paint or other finishes to eliminate maintenance.

Medium-weight material should be considered for any normal use where there is average traffic and scuffing.

The heavy-weight material should be used for corridors, where there is excessive traffic such as that involving movable hospital equipment, pushcarts and the like. There are some flocked heavy-weight materials which are comparable in quality to the heavy-weight fabric-backed sheetings. A line of strong, durable wall coverings is made by fusing color to the underside of a clear vinyl sheet with a flock (short fibers such as rayon or nylon) applied to the back to protect the color. When viewed from the top surface, the color is underneath the heavy vinyl, protected against scratching, scuffing and other wearing action. These materials provide excellent wall coverings where rough treatment is encountered—in hospitals, hotels, schools, restaurants, theaters, stores, lobbies, etc.

The leading aspects of vinyl wall coverings are their durability, toughness and beauty. Most manufacturers offer a guarantee that their products will not chip or scratch, and will resist most scuffing and abrasion. Ease of maintenance and resistance to soil and stains also are important advantages. Vinyl wall coverings are much more easily cleaned than are ordinary wall surfaces without the use of strong detergents or hard scrubbing. The use of white or light colors thus becomes practical. Essentially any color can be had, and a wide variety of textures and designs is available, including reproductions of bamboo, straw, wood, linen and silk.

Today's vinyl wall coverings are so versatile that it is possible to use them to advantage in any room with plaster, masonry or dry-wall construction. There is wide acceptance for institutional use and for service areas where durability is required. Recent progress in styling has resulted in rapid acceptance for residential interiors as well.

Several considerations are important in selecting the right vinyl wall covering for the job.

(1) The greatest widths available (usually 50 to 54 inches) should be used to minimize seams and shading.

(2) Flexible vinyl sheeting with knit backs, stretch backs or other jersey backs should not be used. These fabrics are manufactured especially for upholstery applications.

(3) Heavy texture patterns are not recommended for installations where frequent washing is necessary.

(4) The wall coverings here considered are generally for interior applications, not exterior.

(5) Selection of the wall covering should not be made from small samples. These can be quite misleading in providing a preview of the finished installation.

Installation costs of the various qualities of wall covering vary considerably. Heavy-weight, flock-back materials and stiff fabrics are the more costly to install.

Hanging techniques are generally the same with vinyl wall coverings as with canvas or any other similar type of wall covering. No special tools are needed. The regular procedures of trimming, elimination of bubbles, seam rolling, etc., are employed. Special care must be exercised over painted surfaces to ascertain that no water-sensitive paints have been used. If such is the case, and the paint cannot be removed, it is necessary to apply an impervious barrier coat of chlorinated rubber-base paint. A primer coat of the recommended paste, thinned down, is recommended on very absorbent walls. Special adhesives are required for glass, metals, ceramic tile and any other impervious surfaces. Suppliers should be consulted for detailed information.

Folding Doors. Flexible vinyl sheeting is finding increasing use in folding doors. Several types of doors are available:

(1) A popular low-cost line of doors features flexible vinyl sheeting laminated to steel slats which are then constructed to provide an accordion folding-type action. These are used primarily in residential houses. Standard door sizes are available at retail prices as low as $5.95. The vinyl-steel construction provides strength, durability and smooth operation.

(2) Another type of folding door is made from heavy-weight supported vinyl sheeting in a dual-wall construction. This is designed for heavier duty requirements than type (1). It too provides an accordion-like folding action. While such doors are used in residences, they lend themselves particularly well as room dividers in all types and sizes of buildings.

Whether the doors are of type (1) or (2), the flexible vinyl sheeting provides essentially the same advantages as were noted for this plastic material in the wall-covering application. The vinyl sheeting provides durability, toughness and beauty. Attractive colors and a wide variety of textures and designs are available. Matching valances are available to provide the ultimate in decor. The washable vinyl sheeting makes for ease of maintenance. Resistance to soiling and staining is also an important advantage.

Resilient floor covering, plumbing and electrical insulation of vinyl are discussed in later chapters.

REFERENCES

1. Huscher, J. L., "Fabrication and Use of Rigid Polyvinyl Chloride Plastics," *Materials and Methods*, **39**, 119 (1954).
2. Carey, R. H., Weekly Report—Union Carbide Plastics Division, January 10, 1955, unpublished.
3. "Builders Discover Rigid PVC Sheet," *Modern Plastics*, **39**, No. 10, 80 (1962).
4. Sachs, H. L., "PVC Rain Gutters in Dennark," *Plastics World* (September 1962).
5. "A Critical Analysis—Plastics 1962—Applications in New Markets," *Modern Plastics*, **40**, No. 5, 115 (1963).
6. "Plastics in Roofing," *British Plastics* (October, 1960).

PART B: Honeycomb*

Honeycomb is a fabricated cellular structure made of sheet material assembled to form nested hexagonal voids (Figure 8B-1). In structural applications it is commonly used as a low-cost, low-density core in

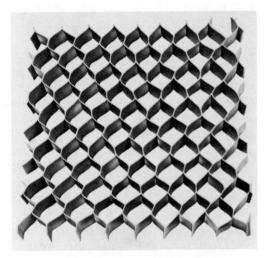

FIG. 8B-1. Honeycomb structure.

sandwich construction (Figure 8B-2). Honeycombs fabricated of aluminum, stainless steel, reinforced plastics, and paper are available, but the most common for building applications is kraft paper honeycomb, plain or impregnated with phenolic resin.

HISTORY AND APPLICATIONS

A major and continuing interest developed in paper honeycomb about 20 years ago. Tuttle and Kennedy[1] published results of tests in 1946. At about this same time, work was in progress at Forest Products Laboratory on phenolic resin-impregnated paper honeycomb, and an experimental house was built there in 1947, which utilized sandwich panel construction with paper honeycomb

*This part by J. A. Baumann.

cores[2,4]. The following year the famous Acorn House was completed in Concord, Massachusetts.[3] This used sandwich panels of waterproof plywood on paper honeycomb, but the panels were hinged so that the house could be folded up, tracked to the site, and again unfolded for occupancy. Previously, in 1945–1946, Lincoln Industries Incorporated had built some 10 homes with aluminum-faced paper honeycomb panels. Of these, 9 were still in service in November, 1959.[4] Fifty other homes, built in 1947 by Southern California Homes Incorporated, were reported to still be in service in 1959—30 in California and 20 in Venezuela where they had been erected for housing oil company representatives.[4]

Paper honeycomb was also used in commercial building, portions of the General Motors Technical Center having been built with such panels as early as 1950.[5] These had porcelainized steel faces bonded to impregnated paper honeycomb whose hexagonal voids were filled with granular material for improved insulating properties. Problems encountered in the early curtain wall construction were solved with constructions utilizing the same type cores but with improved adhesives, rubber moldings, sealants, and welded aluminum frames. These and many other commercial installations have performed satisfactorily over the years. Thus, phenolic resin-impregnated paper honeycomb has a history of successful performance in both residential and commercial construction which extends back almost 20 years.

Paper honeycomb is also utilized in many other building applications. The transportation, furniture, and building industries make extensive use of this core in such applications as partitions, baggage racks, tables, doors, floors, missile fins, and other lightweight structures.

DESCRIPTION OF THE PRODUCT

Paper honeycomb is normally designated by specifying paper basis weight, per cent of impregnating resin, and cell size, the latter being the average distance across flats of the hexagonal voids. The product is available as whole pads, unexpanded slices, expanded sheets, or expanded and faced panels. These may be impregnated or not.

Standard honeycomb with paper weights of 60, 80, 99 and 125 pounds is available, but other weights and paper types can be provided. Impregnated papers usually contain from 11 to 20 per cent resin. Greater resin impregnation contributes to strength and to water and fungus resistance, but cost and brittleness are increased. Sheet sizes vary among manufacturers, one supplying sheet 15 inches wide and 6 to 9 feet long,[6] while some supply sheet as much as 6 feet wide in continuous unexpanded lengths. Packaging and handling are the limiting factors in length of expanded sheet. Thicknesses vary from ¼ inch to 3 feet, but most use is made of sheets ⅜ to 6 inches thick. Up to this dimension, the usual thickness tolerance is ±.010 inch. Cell sizes most used are ½, ¾ and 1 inch.

Phenolic resins are commonly used for impregnating the paper. These are mostly liquid, water-soluble, one-step resins or resoles. These are especially formulated and manufactured to have low molecular weight for high solubility and high penetration. (Union Carbide's BRL-1100 is typical.) Alcohol soluble one-step resins are also used; these have higher molecular weight and provide better impact resistance and less embrittlement of the paper structure. (Representative is Carbide's BLS-2700.) Where sheets are provided impregnated but unexpanded, the resin has been dried to a B-stage or solid but uncured condition. The sheet can subsequently be expanded and heat cured.

MANUFACTURING PROCESSES

Several processes are in use for making paper honeycomb. In one, glue strips are continuously applied to paper which is then folded back and forth to form a pad. Glue strips are so spaced that when the pad or slices thereof are expanded, hexagonal cells will be formed (Figure 8B-3). The pads are expanded by being pulled out with metal fingers. As the pad is expanded, the width decreases about 25 per cent. This expanded pad is dropped into a frame whose sides restrict the width, maintaining this 25 per cent reduction and hence the expanded

TABLE 8B-1. Paper Honeycomb[a] Properties

Type	Thickness (in.)	Price (¢/ft²)	(¢/bd ft)	Density (lb/bd ft)	(pcf)	Compressive Strength (psi)	(load/$)[b]	Shear Strength (psi)	(load/$)[c]	Shear Modulus (Gc psi)	(Gc/$)[d]
80–(18)–½	1	11.3	11.3	.187	2.25	135	172,000	110–60	530	5100	45000
	2	19.8	9.9			117	170,000	70–40	405	4100	41500
	3	28.3	9.4			105	160,000	55–30	320	3300(8)	36000
	4	36.8	9.2			100	156,000	44–25	270	2750	30000
99–(18)–¾	3	23.2	7.7	.156	1.87	70	130,000	42–26	340	2500	32500
99–(11)–¾	1	8.15	8.15	.144	1.73	91	160,000	37–24	295	—	—
99–(11)–1	1	7.05	7.05	.108	1.30	53	108,000	25–16	225	—	—
80–(0)–½	1		6.59	.156	1.87	71	155,000				
99–(0)–¾	1		5.07	.130	1.56	54	154,000				
99–(0)–1	1		4.19	.096	1.15	33	113,000				
Styrene bead foam			6–8		.9	14	33,500	16	265	475	7900
Styrene extruded			10		1.8	40	57,600	27	270	600	6000
Urethane board			17		1.9	30	25,500	24	140	400	2350

[a]Expanded cured.
[b]Compressive load lb/ft² ÷ price ($/bd ft).
[c]ULT shear strength, minimum value ÷ price ($/bd ft).
[d]Shear modulus ÷ price ($/bd ft).

shape. The whole is immersed in impregnating solution for a timed period and then sent through a drying, curing oven at temperatures from 350 to 450°F. Another process expands and cures the sheets continuously.[7] Unexpanded slices are edge glued, then sent through two sets of rollers which stretch the sheet by their differential speed and by the effect of a constriction created by side guides. Some grades are moistened by a spray of wet steam, which facilitates setting of non-impregnated cores in the drying section and softens impregnated grades, thereby reducing the force necessary for expansion. The expanded core is carried forward by side conveyor chains which hold the expanded core to desired width. Force drying sets the non-impregnated honeycombs; the impregnated grades are heated to 350 to 450°F for full cure of the phenolic resin.

PROPERTIES

Paper honeycomb is an important structural material because of its excellent combination of physical properties, maintenance of those properties under adverse conditions, and auxiliary characteristics which contribute to its over-all value.

The physical properties of most importance when paper honeycomb is used as the core of a panel are compressive or crushing strength, shear strength, and shear modulus. These are affected by paper weight, cell size, amount of resin impregnation, and core thickness. Typical values for a number of paper honeycombs are presented in Table 8B-1 together with values for some commercial foams. Included are compressive loads per dollar of core, shear strength divided by price per board foot, and shear modulus divided by this same price. The apparent superiority of impregnated paper honeycomb in shear modulus is important, for in many panel designs, core shear modulus rather than shear strength is the limiting design factor. In foam cores, shear deflection, due to low shear modulus, can easily equal or exceed bending deflection for spans up to 10 to 15 feet. The higher the shear modulus, the less is the shear deflection of a sandwich panel. The advantage of the five- to tenfold

greater modulus of the paper honeycomb is obvious.

If core physical properties are important, maintenance of these properties under adverse conditions is of equal importance.

One test subjects a panel or core section to six cycles:

(1) Immerse in water at 122°F for 1 hour;
(2) Spray with wet steam for 3 hours;
(3) Hold at 10°F or less for 20 hours;
(4) Dry at 212°F, 3 hours;
(5) Spray with wet steam (194 to 200°F) 3 hours;
(6) Dry at 212°F, 18 hours.

Well-made impregnated paper honeycombs will undergo such testing with 10 per cent or less deterioration in physical properties. Submersion in hot water may cause a temporary diminution of 20 to 40 per cent in physical properties—recovered on drying. Humidity creates no problem, and one manufacturer, in a usually dry climate, regularly stores impregnated paper honeycomb outside. Resistance to decay fungi is greatly enhanced by impregnation with phenolic resin. Tests by the U. S. Forest Products Laboratory[9] have demonstrated that at above 15 per cent resin impregnation,

FIG. 8B-2. Sandwich panel with honeycomb core.

loss in tensile strength of paper exposed to decay fungi culture for two months is approximately 5 per cent or less.

The useful temperature range for this

material is from at least −65 to +250°F, a range which covers all except the most unusual conditions in building. Although honeycomb is not classified as incombustible

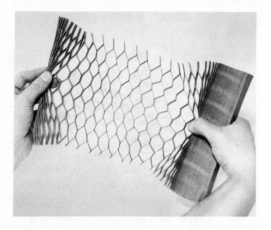

FIG. 8B-3. Expanding slice. (*Photos Courtesy of Union Bag–Camp Paper Corp.*)

in its raw state, it does not support combustion when completely enclosed by facings and framing which are themselves incombustible.

Of the auxiliary properties which enhance the value of paper honeycomb, probably the most important is the high strength-to-weight ratios which can be obtained in structures utilizing the material. Honeycomb panels also have substantial resistance to sound transmission which is reported to be satisfactory for most common installations. Where greater resistance is required, heavy face sheets, interlaminations, or double wall construction may be used. Typical transmission losses are presented in Table 8B-2.[10]

If one face of a honeycomb core panel is

TABLE 8B-2. Average Transmission Loss in Decibels

Panel Facings 1-in. cell size	Panel Thickness 1¾ in.	3 in.
Steel 16 gage	34.5	30.3
Steel 20 gage	29.6	25.9
Hardboard ¼ in.	25.4	24.6
Gypsum board ⅜ in.	26.6	25.9

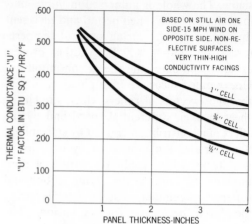

FIG. 8B-4. Thermal insulation values. Typical honeycomb panels–cells not filled. (*Courtesy Penn State University*)

perforated, it becomes an efficient sound absorbing structure.

Although not intended as a thermal insulating medium, the cellular construction of honeycomb in panels does provide substantial thermal resistance. This resistance can be increased by filling the cells with foamed resins, or with powdered or granular insulation; or the honeycomb can be made up with one or more paper interlaminations.[8] Typical values are shown in Figure 8B-4.

REFERENCES

1. Tuttle, O. S., and Kennedy, W. B., "Honeycomb Core Structures," *Modern Plastics* (1964).
2. U. S. Housing and Home Finance Agency, *Technical Paper No. 7* (February 1948).
3. *Architectural Record* (May 1950).
4. Markwardt, L. J., and Wood, L. W., "Sandwich Panel Design Criteria," *Natl. Acad. Sci.—Natl. Res. Council*, *Publ.* **798**, 104–123 (1960).
5. Hastings, R. F., "Sandwich Panel Design Criteria," 99–103, *Natl. Acad. Sci.—Natl. Res. Council*, *Publ.*, **798**, (1960).
6. Douglas Aircraft Co., Inc., "Aircomb," Santa Monica, California, February, 1957.
7. Union Bag–Camp Paper Corporation, "The Core of the Job," Technical Service Bulletin H-1, New York, New York, 1961.
8. Panelfab Products, Inc., "Technical Paper No. 1 Panelfab," Miami, Florida, 1957.
9. U. S. Forest Products Laboratory report R 1796
10. Union Bag–Camp Paper Corporation, "Versatile Kraft Cores," New York, New York, 1963.

9 PLASTIC FOAMS IN THERMAL INSULATION

ROBERT N. KENNEDY AND PAUL HARSHA

The Dow Chemical Company
Midland, Michigan

In the years since World War II, plastic foams have won their spurs as thermal insulation. An estimated 400 million board feet of foam found its way into building construction in 1962. And market research by one large manufacturer indicates that this figure can double in another five years.[1-5]

The largest use to date has been as insulation for refrigerated storage rooms and equipment. However, foamed plastics are making rapid strides as insulation in "comfort" temperature ranges in commercial structures and, to a lesser extent, in homes.

Although most plastics can be foamed, few have been serious contenders in the mass building market.[6] Polystyrene foams are far and away the front runners; urethanes are second.

Foams have entered construction first by direct replacement of conventional materials. Successful service records, improved technology, and designers' imagination have set the stage for future growth. Most foams can be made in a spectrum of properties, densities and shapes.

A problem both to producer and user is classification and identification of a specific plastic foam. Some 125 manufacturers of rigid plastic foams utilize over 150 different trade names. Polystyrene foam alone is produced by more than two dozen manufacturers.

FOAMS: EXPANDED PLASTICS

Foam plastics are made from the same resins that give us solid plastics. The difference is that in the manufacturing process, air or some other gas is introduced so that gas filled cells are distributed throughout the mass (Figure 9-1). Polystyrene, for example, is expanded 40 times in the foaming process. The result is a very low-density material. Many names are used interchangeably for these products—expanded plastics, cellular plastics, foam plastics.

The various plastic foams can be hard or soft, rigid or flexible, or intermediate between the two extremes. There can be varying degrees of open, interconnecting cells or closed, non-interconnecting cells. Some foams are only available in the form of boards or shaped objects for use at the job site, while others come as liquids or particles that can be foamed or sprayed in place.[7-9]

With any specific plastic, the foam density and the proportion of interconnected cells generally control the physical strength properties. Thermal conductivity is a function of density, cell size, and gas within the cell. Water absorption and water vapor transmission vary with the water susceptibility characteristics of the base plastic and the proportion of open cells.[10-12]

Basic Properties

Rigid foam plastics, the leaders in thermal

insulation, have several common properties. They are strong and lightweight. When closed celled, they are buoyant and water

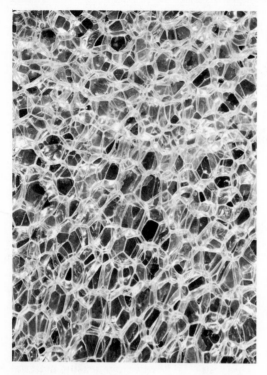

FIG. 9-1. Cellular structure of a plastic foam.

resistant. They are easy to cut and fabricate, are good thermal insulators and have high resistance to attack by bacteria, rot and fungus.

The "ideal" foam insulation would be:
Competitive in cost
Structurally strong
Thermally efficient
Fire resistant
Easy to fabricate
Durable
Light in weight.

Cellular products have been made from most of the basic plastic materials, but lack of some of the above characteristics has limited or proscribed their use. In the highly competitive and price-conscious construction industry, cost is a prime consideration. High cost of foams may be the result of expensive base material, processing or high density. As insulation, however, installation costs become an important factor in over-all

consideration. Other important assets of closed cell foams are permanence of insulation value and excellent water and water vapor resistance.

Nine major types of plastic foams that have been considered as construction materials are vinyl, polyurethane, polystyrene, polyethylene, epoxy, silicone, phenolic, cellulose acetate and ureaformaldehyde. Of these, only polystyrene foams are highly developed and in wide use. The rigid polyurethanes, just entering the field, show great promise. Among the semi-rigid foams, only polyethylene and vinyl so far have had commercial success, and their construction potential appears small.[6]

Foamed Polystyrene. Polystyrene, at present the leading cellular plastic, is an excellent insulator, low in cost, readily available, easily fabricated, strong, durable and resistant to degradation or attack. Cellular polystyrene is produced by expanding polystyrene with a gaseous blowing agent. One type of polystyrene foam is extruded on special equipment in the form of planks from which boards are cut (U. S. Patents 2,669,751; 2,740,157). Successful service records for this extruded foam have paved the way for foam plastics in widespread building usage. Extruded polystyrene is available in the form of boards of various thicknesses, widths and lengths, and as special board forms for such uses as perimeter masonry wall and roof insulation.[3] Another type of polystyrene foam is molded into boards. Often termed "beadboards," these are available in a large variety of sizes that can be cut from billets as large as $2 \times 4 \times 12$ feet. The boards are made from polystyrene beads containing a gaseous hydrocarbon blowing agent, e.g., pentane. They are foamed by placing partially foamed beads into a mold and applying heat generally in the form of steam, causing the beads to expand and knit together. The molding operation is relatively simple but requires a steam source and fairly heavy molds to withstand the internal pressures developed. Thus, it is impractical to foam expandable polystyrene at the job site, for example, in a cavity wall or on a roof. However, it is possible in a manufacturing plant to foam expandable polystyrene directly between skins or facings to form structural sandwich panels for the building trade.[14,15]

Urethane Foam. The urethane class of products, which has been the subject of interest and intense research and development by the plastics industry, consists of polymeric materials resulting from the condensation-polymerization of isocyanate and polyols. Urethanes derive their name from the chemical linkage formed when the isocyanate radical reacts with the active hydrogen of the polyol. Although the name "urethanes" has been recommended by the Society of the Plastics Industry for use in the plastics industry, these polymers are also known as isocyanates, polyurethanes, polyester isocyanates, and polyether-isocyanates.

Polyurethane foams are composed of two main constituents—the isocyanate portion and the polyol portion. Both are subject to a large number of variations in their chemical properties, on which the versatility of the physical properties of the finished polyurethane foam depends.

The most widely used isocyanate is toluene diisocyanate. The commercial product is a mixture of 80 per cent 2,4 and 20 per cent 2,6 isomers.

2,4-isomer   2,6-isomer

Other isocyanates used primarily for rigid urethane foam are modified TDI (a special controlled crude form of toluene diisocyanate) and polyisocyanates made from aniline-formaldehyde reaction products.

The most characteristic reaction of isocyanate is that of condensation with compounds containing active hydrogen atoms. The chemistry of polyurethane foams is based on the reaction of isocyanates with three types of compounds:

(1) Alcohols to give urethanes, R—NH—CO—O—R.

(2) Organic acids to give urethanes and and $CO_2 \uparrow$.

(3) Water to give substituted ureas and $CO_2 \uparrow$.

The alcohols may be diols, triols, hexols, octols, etc., derived from either polyesters or polyethers.

Depending upon the functionality and the polymer chain length between the reactive OH groups, the resulting foam will be either rigid or flexible. Rigidity increases with functionality and decreases with chain length.

Both flexible and rigid foam products were first developed to market acceptance with formulations based on a so-called prepolymer and/or semi-prepolymer basis. In these cases, the disocyanate is reacted with part of the polyol in a prior step to produce a buildup polymer of controlled molecular weight to form the "prepolymer." A final reaction between the prepolymer and polyol blended with blowing agent, H_2O (if CO_2 is to be generated), catalyst, cell control agents and other desired additives produces the final foamed product.

The trend, however, in the urethane industry for better economics is toward the "one-shot system" for preparing both flexibles and rigid foams based on polyethers. This system utilizes the direct reaction step of the isocyanate and polyol containing the required additives to produce foam. This system is well established for flexible urethane foam. The technique for using "one-shot" for rigid foam has taken longer to develop. Present technology permits consideration of "one-shot" for many low-density rigid foam applications.

Rigid foamed urethanes are not one material but a variety of different plastics. They are generally foamed in place, but they can also be foamed into boards at a plant and marketed as such (Figure 9-2). Most rigid urethane foams for insulation are made by expanding with a fluorinated hydrocarbon. This gas remains permanently in the closed celled rigid urethane, resulting in a foam with a very low k factor.* Al-

*k = thermal conductivity (Btu-in./hr-sq ft-°F).

though the fluorocarbon remains in the cells, air can permeate into the foam rather rapidly. Thus, thermal conductivity rises until internal equilibrium is established, at

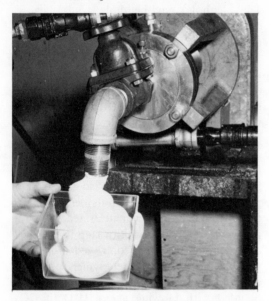

Fig. 9-2. "Froth" foaming of a urethane.

which time the insulation value is stable and is reported as the "aged" k factor.[16-22]

Polystyrene and rigid urethane foams have similar properties with a few exceptions, as shown in Table 9-1. Both of these ma-

TABLE 9-1. Properties of Foamed Plastics

	Polystyrenes	Rigid Urethane
Density, lb/cu ft	1–4	1.5–4
Compressive strength*	15–40	35–60
Shear strength*	25–35	20–30
Modulus of rigidity*	600–1500	300–600
Flexural strength*	40–60	40–60
Thermal conductivity (k), Btu-in./hr–sq ft–°F at 70° mean temperature	0.24–0.30	0.11**–0.16***
Water vapor transmission, perm-in.	0.5–3	1–3
Water absorption, lb/sq ft of surface area	0.15	0.15
Heat distortion temperature, °F	160–185	175–275
Burning characteristics	May be made self-extinguishing	

*lb/sq in. at 2-lb/cu ft density.
**When foamed between air impermeable skins.
***"Aged" or stabilized.

terials can be made in a wider range of densities than shown; however, these are the densities normally used as insulation in buildings. It may be noted that the strength properties and the excellent water resistant characteristics are very similar. The first major difference is in thermal conductivity. Rigid urethanes have a k factor of approximately ½ to ⅔ that of the polystyrene foams. The lower k factor value shown for rigid urethane foams results when the material is foamed in place between skins that are impermeable to air. The higher figure is for board stock or sprayed type of insulation where the air can permeate into the material and raise the factor. The other major difference in characteristics is heat distortion where the urethane foams average 50°F higher than the polystyrene foams. In addition, the urethanes have higher resistance to many solvents.[20-22]

Fire Safety. Fire safety of plastic foams as of any other building material—relates to conditions of storage and use as well as to inherent characteristics. For example, the safety of foam insulation installed in a finished building so that it is protected by plaster, masonry, or earth has been borne out by years of experience and use of many millions of board feet of material. On the other hand, direct exposure to a large fire can damage or destroy foam insulation as well as other building components.[23]

Fire considerations involving foams are measured by a variety of standard tests. Some of the major tests are discussed here.

Typical thermal and flammability properties of plastic foams as compared to old oak wood are shown in Table 9-2.

Resistance to Accidental Ignition. Damaging fires at the site of a building under construction usually occur because of lack of proper understanding in the storage and handling of combustibles. Causes of these fires are usually small localized sources of ignition such as welding torches, sparks, or carelessly thrown matches.

Self-extinguishing or flame-retardant foams provide an added safety factor by resisting ignition from such common sources. Such foam will extinguish itself after exposures to lighted matches and other small flame sources or even an intense gas flame. If a flame is held stationary against the foam, the foam will melt back and ex-

tion of bitumen and plastics is essentially the same, about 18,000 Btu/lb. However, the asphalt accounts for 30,000 Btu/sq ft where a nominal thickness of one inch of

TABLE 9-2. Typical Thermal and Flammability Properties

Property	Polystyrene	Urethane	Polyethylene	Wood
Heat of Combustion				
Btu/lb	16,000	11,000	16,000	8,000
Btu/ft^3	32,000	22,000	32,000	320,000
Btu/bd ft	2,660	1,840	2,660	26,600
Ignition Temperature (ASTM D 1929–62T)				
Flash ignition temperature, °F	650–700	600	650	500
Self-ignition temperature, °F	735–900	975	660	500
Surface flame spread (ASTM E 84–61 "tunnel test")	10–25	40–80	Non FR	100

tinguish itself. Foams classified as "self-extinguishing" when tested in accordance with ASTM D 1692-59T, a standard flammability method for plastic foams and sheeting. The foams must extinguish themselves within 10 seconds.

Flame Spread. Flame spread is usually determined by testing a product according to ASTM E 84-59T, more commonly known as the "tunnel test." This test is intended to predict the relative rate at which fire might spread across the surface of a material.

For reference, red oak flooring has a flame spread index of 100 and asbestos board of zero. Flame spread rate of foam is applicable under circumstances where the foam is installed with its surface exposed.

Data obtained on extruded polystyrene foam establish a flame spread of 10 to 25 in one-inch thickness. A rating of 25 or less is classed as "noncombustible" by many code authorities.

Fuel Contribution. In the event of a large-scale building fire, the foam in areas of prolonged fire exposure would be expected to melt and be consumed. However, fuel contribution would be relatively minor as is indicated by the low density of most foam insulation board (approximately 2 lb/cu ft. The Btu content of this density foam is about one-tenth that of an equivalent volume of wood.

In the case of roofs, the heat of combus-

foam accounts for 3000 Btu/sq ft. The energy available in the complete destruction of the foam is not to be neglected, but it is well to have it in perspective with the entire roof structure. Special tests developed for roof decks include the White House test in which a 20 × 100 foot structure is covered by the roof deck system under test. A standard exposure fire is maintained in one end, and the resulting distance of flame spread is noted over a 30-minute period.

Fire Endurance Time—ASTM E 119-61. Although foams by themselves do not exhibit high fire endurance times, generally, when a building component is required to exhibit a certain degree of fire endurance, the plastic foam which may be present as plaster base, cavity wall insulation, etc., is considered to neither add to nor detract from the endurance time of the basic masonry portion of the structure.

Smoke Evolution. Plastic foams, like many other organic materials, burn with a yellowish flame and generate black smoke. For this reason, flame-retardant foams are used to minimize combustion.

Toxicity of Combustion Products. The products of combustion of polystyrene have been thoroughly investigated. An independent research laboratory, after exposing animals to polystyrene combustion products, concluded that the effects were no worse than those expected from exposure to common combustibles used in building construction. A private study of the nature and composition of the products of combustion of polystyrene similarly concluded they were essentially the same as those of other building materials.

Less data are presently available on urethane foams; however, intermittent exposure to combustion products has caused no problems to laboratory personnel during developmental testing.

Research data and many years of development experience indicate that flame-retardant plastic foam building products constitute no more fire or toxicity hazard than other organic materials in common use in the building industry when:

(1) Properly stored in sprinklered warehouses,

(2) Used according to recommended procedures and with good housekeeping practices during construction,

(3) Installed in properly designed structures.

Foam Applications in Building

The present uses for foam as thermal insulation in building may be grouped into low-temperature space insulation, pipe and equipment covering, wall insulation, perimeter insulation, roof insulation, backerboard for metal siding, panels, thin shell concrete, flexible foam and miscellaneous. Large markets virtually untouched by foam plastics are wall sheathing, acoustical tile, formboards, and window walls.

In these markets, plastic foams may compete with many types of insulation: fill types (fibers and granular), batts and blankets (fibers, organic and inorganic), and rigid boards (foam glass cork fibers). Rigid plastic foams more completely fulfill the property requirements for moderate- and low-temperature insulations than most of the existing insulation products. However, they are usually higher in raw material cost.

Table 9-3 compares the cost of polystyrene and urethane foams with other insulations. The figures show the spread within each material and also the cost difference per pound between polystyrene and urethane The board stock costs in dollars per board foot which present a comparative picture of the plastic foams with various competitive insulations in the building field, on a volume basis, are very important.

When plastic foams are evaluated for thermal insulation, several advantages

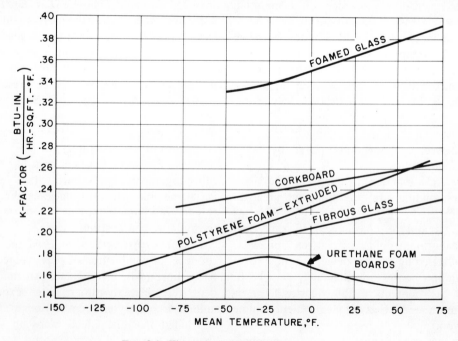

FIG. 9-3. Thermal conductivity (K-factor).

should be considered—structural strength, thermal efficiency, resistance to water and handleability (light weight, foam-in-place, etc.)

TABLE 9-3. Comparative Material Costs

Expanded Plastics	Raw Material ($/lb)	Board Stock ($/bd ft)
Expanded Plastics		
Urethanes—rigid	0.35–0.75	0.15*
Polystyrenes	0.20–0.45	0.08**
Nonplastics		
Insulation		
Fill type (fibers and granular)		0.02–0.05
Batt and blankets (fibers, organic and inorganic)		0.02–0.08
Boards (foamed glass, cork, fiber)		0.05–0.18

*Preexpanded board, 2 lb/cu ft.
**Preexpanded board, 1.5–2.0 lb/cu ft.

The thermal efficiency and resistance to water along with other properties of plastic foams as compared to other insulations may be seen in Table 9-4. The inherent resistance of plastic foams to water allows the plastic foams to be used with minimum protection against water and water vapor.

Figure 9-3 details the thermal conductivity properties with curves for the various insulations showing *K* factor as a function of mean temperature. Often the strength properties, particularly compressive strength, of plastic foam insulation can be used advantageously. Figure 9-4 shows the compressive strength as a function of strain for various insulating materials.

Refrigerated Rooms. The first major entrance of foamed plastics in the construction field was by foamed polystyrene as insulation in refrigerated spaces. Over a period of approximately ten years, polystyrene has displaced cork as the industry standard. Today approximately 80 per cent of all the refrigerated rooms in the United States are insulated with foam polystyrene.

Freezers and coolers in the dairy and meat industries, sharp freezers, storage and cooler rooms in the fruit producing and distributing fields, and refrigerated locker plants in rural communities are examples of this end use, estimated to be 200 million bd ft/yr. Refrigerated spaces require an insulation with long life to give efficient operation. Low

TABLE 9-4. Average Properties of Competitive Insulations

	Density (lb/cu ft)	Compressive Yield Strength (psi)	Compressive Modulus (psi)	Thermal Conductivity Btu-in./hr sq ft-°F	Heat Distortion (°F)	Water Absorption (% by volume)	Water Vapor Transmission (perm-in.)	Flammability
Polystyrene foam, extruded	1.8	30	1000	.26	170	<.25	1.5	B-FR
Polystyrene foam, molded	1.0	12	400	.24	175	1–5	2–5	B-FR
Urethane foam	2.0	40	750	.11* .15**	250	1–4	1.0–2.5	B-FR
Corkboard	7	15	370	.27	250	15	3–7	FR
Expanded glass	8	100	3000	.38	800	.2	.1	FR
Expanded rubber	4.5	70	4350	.22	150	.275	.1+	B-FR
Fibrous glass batts***	0.5	—	—	.19–.29	600	Large	100	FR
Fibrous glass PF (pre-formed)	2.1	3	30	.23–.26	600	Large	100	FR
Fibrous glass AE (asphalt enclosed)	2–9	5	80	.26	150	Large	3	B
Mineral wood board***	15	8–24	225–350	.27–.34	150–300	Large	High	FR

*When foamed between air-impermeable skins.
**"Aged" or stabilized.
***Products vary considerably.

water vapor transmission is necessary to keep out water and ice and to enable the insulation to function properly. Cellular

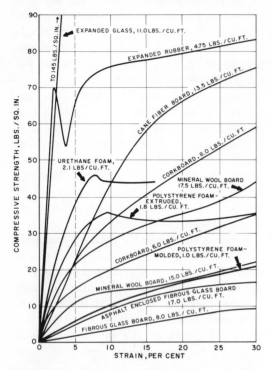

FIG. 9-4. Compressive strength properties.

polystyrene and polyurethane, with their excellent low-temperature insulating characteristics and retention of insulating efficiency during prolonged use, are displacing other natural insulations which are in the same cost range but lack the desired property retention.[24]

Piping and Equipment Uses. Insulation characteristics for piping and equipment are like those for refrigerated spaces except that an additional requirement of solvent or chemical resistance may be necessary. Insulation supplied to this field is either prefabricated pipe covering shapes or blocks and boards. With the preexpanded plastic material, shaping and fitting for pipes and equipment must be done in the field or precut by a fabricator. Cutting and fitting foam boards to complicated shapes may result in a high percentage of waste. Large cylindrical tanks and vessels may be insulated with foamed plastic boards by actually bending the boards around the tanks.[25]

Pipe and equipment insulation may be divided into two classes: hot and cold. From 100°F down to liquid hydrogen temperatures is generally considered the cold range. Current usage is in the order of 50 million bd ft/yr. It is expected to double in the future. Plastic foams would be used here in fabricated sections, poured-in-place formulations for valves and fittings or sprayed onto tanks and equipment.

Recently techniques have been developed for spraying polyurethane (Figure 9-5) foam on walls of cylindrical tanks. This method offers attractive economic possibilities in comparison with fibrous batt and blanket type insulations. In the field of piping and equipment, flexible closed cell foams such as polyurethanes and polyethylenes manufactured into tubing and sheeting are becoming of interest.

"Comfort" Insulation with Foams. In "comfort" insulation, plastic foams compete primarily with the fibrous fill or batt-type insulations. Plastic foams are not always the best choice. For example, foams are not

FIG. 9-5. Application of urethane foam insulation to a tank by spraying.

competitive at present for use in the side walls or ceilings of frame structures where batt or blanket material can be used. This underlines the fact that plastic foams are higher in cost on a volume basis; thus maximum use must be made of their properties.

While they are preferred for low-temperature space applications, expanded plastics are not penetrating residential construction. Residential wall and ceiling insulation is usually based on low cost–fill, batt and blanket, and reflective types. In many areas, present building codes limit the use of plastic foams for residential construction, and relatively few building codes will as yet allow sandwich construction with plastic cores. Foam plastic materials will at best obtain only a small portion of this market, estimated as high as 2.5 billion sq ft/yr. At present, cavity wall and insulation plaster-base have potential for only about 60 million board feet.[26]

Perimeter Insulation. In some comfort applications, however, polystyrene foam has been successful in both residential and nonresidential fields. It is ideally suited to foundation perimeter insulation and floor slab insulation since it resists water and does not deteriorate when placed on or underground. It is the best material for the application at a competitive cost.

Plastic foam perimeter insulation is used similarly to conventional materials. The boards around the perimeter are applied either vertically, horizontally or a combination of both next to the foundation. Special products have been developed for perimeter insulation with thicknesses giving "R" factors* conforming to Federal Housing Administration standards. These thicknesses are based on a slab edge heat loss of approximately 40 Btu/hr/linear ft of slab; however, for economy and comfort the heat loss should be less than 30 Btu/hr/linear ft of slab. To meet the latter requirement in the coldest temperature zone ($-30°F$ and colder) a 2-inch thickness of polystyrene foam or 1¼-inch thickness of rigid urethane foam is required. Figure 9-1 shows the placement of polystyrene foam boards as perimeter insulation.

Insulating Walls. Plastic foam as wall insulation is generally confined to masonry

construction. Since 1946, when the first homes were insulated with polystyrene foam in the walls, the market has grown steadily—chiefly in low-temperature buildings and non residential construction such as institutional buildings. Plastic foam boards are applied to a masonry wall with a suitable adhesive, generally portland cement mortar or some type of mineral cement (Figure 9-6),

FIG. 9-6. Applying plastic foam board to masonry wall with portland cement mortar.

and then are plastered directly with gypsum plaster or covered with wall board. The development of a new adhesive with high wet strength has allowed spot bonding of the foam to the masonry wall. It is also used for applying wall board by spot bonding. This technique of applying wall board instead of plastering is competitive with accepted dry wall practices. It has the advantage of providing solid backing material and eliminates problems of "nail popping." Two inches of polystyrene foam board on masonry construction are adequate even for buildings heated electrically. This gives a "U" factor* of approximately 0.09. In cases where wall thicknesses are important, rigid urethane boards may be employed with a reduction of

*"R" factor (resistance to heat flow) is the reciprocal of the thermal conductance.

*"U" factor is the over-all heat transfer of the composite including air surface coefficients.

30 per cent in insulation thickness. As an example, by using low-factor rigid urethane foam board stock, a thermal resistance R of 14 (recommended for frame construction) can be achieved in masonry walls with only 1½ inches of insulation. The foam boards are placed between the inner and outer wythes of masonry. They may or may not be bonded to the inner wall.

A trend to slab-on-the-ground homes should greatly expand usage of perimeter insulation. Tri-level homes and living areas in full or partial basements call for floor slab insulation and moisture-proof plastic foam insulation for walls. One inch of insulation in a 70°F heated below-grade area can change floor temperature from 50°F to approximately 68°F, providing a tremendous difference in comfort especially for children playing on the floor.

Roof Insulation. The total potential for roof insulation has been estimated to be over a billion board feet per year. Of this, the potential for rigid board insulation might be in the range of 200 million board feet. Present volume in foam is very small. Insulation for this application must have sufficient struc-

tural strength in thin sections to withstand normal roof traffic over a built-up roof, must be able to span corrugations in roof decks, and must meet handling requirements. The thickness conventionally used ranges from ¾ inch through 2 inches. One third of the market needs a "*C*" factor* of less than .24. This is where a quality insulation has its greatest use. A disadvantage of polyurethane may be that, because of cost, it would have to be used in too thin a thickness to be readily handled. Polyurethane does have the advantage that hot built-up roofs may be mopped directly to the surface of the foam without protective materials or methods that are required with polystyrene foam.

The insulation of roofs deserves greater attention. The roof is one of the greatest sources of heat loss, particularly in large buildings. It is also subjected to greatest variation in temperature and climatic conditions. Proper installation of the insulation is a necessity. Foam plastic hoards have entered this field primarily as an over deck insulation. They can be installed on any

*C factor is the thermal conductance of a given thickness of a homogeneous material or a composite.

FIG. 9-7. Applying conventional roofing over plastic foam insulation using a coated base sheet.

structural deck surface using hot asphalt, nails, fire-resistant adhesives or non-piercing clips. Expanded polystyrene can be covered

eliminates any damage of melting the foam due to direct contact with the hot bitumen. The same technique can be used on larger

FIG. 9-8. A felt laying machine is used to place the roofing felts and hot bitumen to plastic foam insulation boards.

with a hot applied built-up roof by making use of special techniques to protect the foam against the melting from the hot bitumens used in built-up roofing. The first method giving ample thermal protection was the application of ¼-inch or more of portland cement grout over the foam. In a later development, a special polystyrene foam wrapped in a protective heat barrier of paper and asphalt was produced. The latest method, employing a special foam polystyrene board, uses a coated base sheet of conventional 15- or 30-pound saturated felt, coated heavily on one side with asphalt and on the other side with a slip agent such as sand, talc or mica. This sheet (Figure 9-7) is laid dry with the asphalt coating adjacent to the foam. The top surface is then mopped with hot bitumen and a standard built-up roof applied in the conventional manner. The heat from these successive layers of asphalt melts the asphalt in the base sheet, bonding the base sheet to the foam insulation. This

installations with the aid of modified felt "layers," i.e. laying machines. The equipment used applies asphalt to a saturated felt rather than to the insulation. The coated felt is then applied directly to the insulation with hot bitumen acting as adhesive as well as the waterproofing membrane (Figure 9-8).

Built-up type roofs are expected to grow most rapidly because of their adaptability to low pitch roofs and their moderate cost. But this system of multiple layers of asphalt or pitch and roofing felts is woefully inefficient. To replace it, plastics engineers and chemists have developed a combination sprayed polyurethane insulation-sprayed plastic surfacing system (Figure 9-9).[27-28]

Backing for Siding. One of the fastest-rising stars in the building industry is aluminum siding. In the past years, aluminum siding has been used almost exclusively for renovation of older homes. This pattern is expected to change. The FHA communication on backed aluminum siding should be a tremendous impetus to specify this material for new homes.

FIG. 9-9. Spraying urethane foam insulation on a roof deck.

Backing is required for dent resistance, longitudinal stiffness, some sound-deadening, appearance, protection from corrosion, water resistance and thermal insulation. Backing permits use of thinner aluminum than normally required.

Panels. Building panels are a popular subject with manufacturers and suppliers for the construction industry, as well as the industry itself. Workable integrated systems are needed. Some major metal and chemical companies have recognized a basic design and manufacturing concept and have instituted long-range development programs. Building material manufacturers are also active. The Research Institute of the National Association of Home Builders has devoted a large portion of its budget to research houses mostly constructed of panels. The Institute is convinced that sandwich building panels constitute a fundamental building system and is seeking to obtain broad acceptance of the system.

The concept of panels has been developed by architects to permit wider use of factory made and finished components. Thus far these are mainly non-load bearing, curtain-wall types and most of the installations are in the "monumental building." For the most part, each building requires a custom-made panel. These panels include three types of construction: (1) two shallow pans fitted at the edges forming a kind of closed rectangular, thin box, (2) stressed skin panel, (3) sandwich panel.

In the sandwich panel, the core is continuous and structural and may contribute significant insulation value. Skins or faces are bonded to this core. This panel utilizes practically 100 per cent foam plastic cores and should be the most functional panel available. Increased production should make it competitive to the first type panel.

The curtain wall concept is not new. In the past decade, the building panel has been refined to include insulation and sophisticated finishes (Figure 9-10). In its present-day design, the panel replaces masonry, and incorporates fenestration and frequently includes services. The acceptance of panels over masonry can be attributed to a number of factors. Because of their light weight,

FIG. 9-10. Sandwich curtain wall panel on a school building

there is a reduction in resultant structural frame and foundation requirements (Figure 9-11). Additional floor space is gained as the result of using a thinner exterior wall. There

is that the weather does not affect construction as drastically.

Here are examples of recent panel developments:[29]

FIG. 9-11. Panelized roof structure.

is a reduction in on-site construction time, hence earlier occupancy and return on investment (Figure 9-12). Another advantage

FIG. 9-12. Roof sandwich panels to be raised in place.

(1) A multideck sandwich of alternate layers of polystyrene foam and kraft paper bonded together with a phenol-resorcinol-formaldehyde adhesive and made in thicknesses from 1½ to 4 inches. The core is bonded to exterior plywood or metal faces to which vinyl film is applied for the finish. The manufacturers envision use from exterior walls to roof deckor flooring and say that attachment over 12-foot spans is possible.

(2) A vinyl skin and urethane foam core is made by several companies, using urethane foamed in place. The skin offers weather and flame resistance and colorful appearance.

(3) A paper skin with urethane foam core designed as insulation for built-up roofs.

(4) A skin of precast concrete with molded polystyrene foam or extruded polystyrene foam.

(5) Acrylic skin with urethane foam core.

(6) Acrylic skin with styrene-acrylonitrile foam core which is both insulating and 65 per cent light transmitting.

(7) Sheet metal skin with urethane foam core.

The architect can specify a broad range of performance properties, whether they relate to load bearing, insulation, transparency, weight, ease of installation, cost, or appearance. For all but the polystyrene foams, however, only limited service records are available.

Building panels for the nonresidential market are an accepted commercial product which account for nearly 40 million square feet of wall area, of which about one-half is glass. This is small considering an estimated total potential for curtain walls of 600 million square feet. However, it is expected that rigid core materials should capture 125 million board feet in the future.

Residential construction is an exceedingly difficult market to enter with panels. It has more controlling influences than other markets, but it also has more dollar volume. The evolution of a panel system is imminent but mass acceptance may be five to ten years in the future. Many large companies are spending much research money on the development of panels and other products that will capture a share of the housing market. Present volume is small even though the wall area available is much larger than for nonresidential.[30,31]

Low-temperature space storage is a promising market for a true sandwich panel. A panel would provide a portable, completely insulated walk-in freezer or cooler which is ideally suited for retail stores and institutional buildings.

Shell Structures. One of the latest advances in a combined structural and architectural use of plastics has to do with plastic foams in thin shell construction. More and more, architects are letting their thoughts and plans wander along unlimited horizons of shape and surface and are emphasizing an aesthetic approach to modern architecture. Already domes, scalloped domes, barret vaults and hyperbolic paraboloids stand in testimony.

Conventional construction of thin shell roofs involves the creation of elaborate forms, the erection of extensive supports, and the casting of adequately reinforced concrete. After the concrete obtains sufficient strength, removal and, in many cases, destruction of the form work supports have been necessary. Further steps are often involved, particularly with the application of vapor barrier and thermal insulation as well as additional interior decoration. A simplified construction technique for thin shell roofs appears, therefore, to be of prime interest (Figure 9-13).[32,33]

For many shell configurations, the plywood forms and much of the false work can be eliminated through the use of the plastic foam as a form board that serves structurally while the cement is wet, then remains permanently as insulation. In the construction

FIG. 9-13. Plastic foam board used as form liner in the construction of concrete hyperbolic paraboloid roof.

of a scalloped dome, for example, boards of polystyrene foam are arched and placed between steel angles, covered with wire mesh, and sprayed with concrete. The arched

FIG. 9-14. Plastic foam used as a form liner over contoured earth. Reinforcing steel is in place ready to receive the structural concrete that will form the shell.

boards have adequate strength to support the weight of wet concrete during a curing cycle.

A variation of this form liner concept involves the use of polystyrene in "tilt-up" or "life-slab" construction where large flat or contoured sections are cast from concrete in horizontal forms or even contoured earth (Figure 9-14) and then tilted or lifted into position with the plastic foam remaining on the underside.

Miscellaneous Uses. Many miscellaneous applications for foam plastics in the construction industry can be enumerated. Plastic foam boards perform excellently as blow-out walls in areas where explosions might occur. They are lightly fastened to a framework and painted on the outside with a weather-resistant coating. One unusual plastic foam application is in the construction of large dams. Polystyrene foam boards are placed against the curing concrete of a large dam. The foam acts as an insulation to control the moisture and temperature during the curing period. A higher-density foam has been utilized for forming a contraction joint in

highway construction. Other miscellaneous construction applications are: foamed cores in mobile homes, structural core and insulation in flush doors, home insulation, core material in interior partitions, do-it-yourself uses, etc. Miscellaneous usage is estimated conservatively at 20 million board feet for the future.

Flexible Foams. Closure strips and roof expansion joints are applications worthy of mention for flexible foams (Figure 9-15). Volume is small and market is small, though the function performed is very important. Vinyl and polyethylene are fabricated into corrugated strips for sealing junctures of corrugated siding and roofing to prevent air from entering and heat from traveling out. A new and novel roof expansion joint incorporating polyethylene foam and plastic

FIG. 9-15. Polyethylene foam roof expansion joint ready to receive the waterproofing membrane.

flushing solves many of the failure and maintenance problems inherent in conventional metal joints. Thin tubes of polyethylene foam also are used as insulating filler back-up for caulking and as frames and gaskets for glass windows. Plastic materials allow flexibility in all directions.

Future Developments

The large volume conventional building materials are due for increasing competition from plastic foams.

Today in most frame houses, the skeleton is covered with a sheathing material (e.g., wood, insulation board) before the siding or exterior skin is applied. Sheathing acts as a brace, minimizes penetration of weather and wind, and in some cases has a specific insulation value. It also serves as a base for applying shingles, wood, bricks and stucco. Foams are being used today in this application only as a base for stucco. Present foams would have to be reinforced in a manner to add stability to the frame structure and they would need to have some nailability. The problem, however, is to be able to do it at a cost per square foot that would not add measurably to the cost. Total potential here is estimated at ¾ billion square feet. If the rigid foam could double as interior sheathing–plaster base, the market would double.

With the increasing demand for noise control and consequent use of acoustical ceilings, it appears that the plain painted concrete ceiling of the past will prove unsatisfactory for office applications and most other nonresidential use. Where expense is not an overpowering consideration, it is expected that the drop ceiling will be the accepted type of ceiling finish. It is good looking, leaves room for service lines, and is efficient in sound control. There is little doubt that acoustical systems are being considered in practically all nonresidential buildings today. Several different types of acoustical systems and materials are on the market; these include acoustical plaster, acoustical tile, panels, and perforated metal pans.

Since none of the currently available acoustical materials meet all of the property requirements desired, the field is open to improvement by the chemical industry. One new possibility is the use of acoustical materials which can double as an insulation material.

A molded polystyrene ceiling tile has been introduced in the shape of a square, with installation the same as conventional tile. It has many of the properties of conventional tile in addition to improved insulation value —high light reflectance, improved dimensional stability, better water resistance, and a surface that offers many advantages over the conventional ones. It is competitive. Some of the markets in which it should receive acceptance are: air-conditioned buildings where combined insulation-acoustical-decorative features are desired; engineering offices and showrooms where high light reflectance is important; textile plants and laboratories where high humidities are present; and dairies, meat processing plants and hospitals where ceilings must be washed frequently.

Formboards could be another important use for a foamed plastic board or panel wherein the formboard would incorporate a built-in vapor barrier, interior ceiling finish, acoustical abilities, water resistance and permanent thermal insulation.

The decorative translucent window wall is becoming more and more popular to the new home builder, the remodeler, the do-it-yourselfer and the architect. A light-transmitting insulating decorative panel combining a large-celled, light-stable foam with ordinary panes of glass and conventional edgings has been introduced. The foam, a copolymer of styrene and methyl methacrylate, can also be used with plastic skins.[34] It can retail for less than half the cost of the present conventional systems—glass blocks, insulated window panes, translucent window walls, and insulated skylights. The development is significant as a portent of novel property combinations.

New Vistas for Polyurethanes. The versatility and promise of polyurethanes, particularly foam-in-place rigid urethanes, pose a variety of possibilities worth exploring. The significant difference to the architect and contractor may be that his order for insulation will be delivered by the gallon instead of the board foot. Urethanes are available as liquids which, after mixing, can be cast into cavities or spray-applied to the desired surface. Thus, the contractor will need equipment capable of mixing the liquid components and applying them to the structure.

There are three basic techniques which may be employed to apply urethane foam—

fabricated boards, foam-in-place and spray. Rigid urethane foams can be foamed in place by either pouring the mixed liquids directly into the cavity and allowing the foaming to occur entirely there, or by frothing the mixed liquids through the incorporation of a low-boiling liquid. In the latter case, partial expansion of the urethane foam reactants occurs as the volatile liquid is vaporized when it is discharged from the mixer into the cavity. The froth foam then further expands to its final density. Sprayed urethanes are applied with special guns which allow the application of 1-inch foam thicknesses per pass on either horizontal or vertical surfaces. These application methods require proportioning equipment to accurately meter and pump the reactant components to the mixing head for either spraying or dispensing into a cavity. In order to produce satisfactory urethane foam, experienced operators are required to operate precision equipment. In addition, operators must be aware of the many variables such as tempera-

The possibility of eliminating sheathing in the brick veneer house is being studied. The foam would be sprayed from the inside against the brick wythe, filling the complete cavity between the framing and the wall.

Another example of the versatility of urethane foams is the filling of a cavity wall by using the foam-in-place froth technique (Figure 9-17). The cavity can be filled in one continuous application with low average densities and low internal pressures on the

FIG. 9-16. Spraying rigid urethane foam.

ture, humidity, and application techniques which govern urethane foam properties. Finally, consideration must be given to the toxic vapors which are given off during the foaming reaction. Operators must work in well-ventilated areas or use face masks (Figure 9-16).[35]

FIG. 9-17. Filling a cavity wall with pour-in-place rigid urethane foam.

cavity walls. It has been found that an experienced operator can fill a cavity as rapidly as with loose fill insulating materials.

Filling the cavity with foam adds to the strength of walls. Tests indicate that a 10-inch brick cavity wall with a 2½-inch cavity filled with urethane foam has double the transverse strength of the non-filled wall. Thermally this amount of foam in a cavity

tion of the structure, or its cost. Applications to date have been hardly more than an initial entry, and a market of one billion board feet is foreseeable by the late 1960's. Low-cost polystyrene foams will remain very important in the areas of perimeter insulation, as insulation plaster base, and as roof insulation. It is a good possibility that the rigid urethane foams will take over prefab

Fig. 9-18. Air-supported structure rigidized with sprayed-on urethane foam.

wall will give a "*U*" value of 0.06—very adequate for the most demanding heating applications. This type of wall also is very water resistant and resists air infiltration. While initial costs may be higher, it has been estimated that a savings in fuel due to the increased thermal efficiency will more than pay for the additional material costs.

Many other possibilities exist for these versatile foam-in-place and spray types of rigid urethane foam. (Figures 9-18 and 9-19). Other applications being considered are placing insulation between dry wall and solid masonry walls, panels and the application of insulation to existing structures which are difficult to insulate with conventional materials.

The Growth of Foams

Plastic foam materials have entered many segments of the building industry in the last 15 years. By doing so they have improved either the method of construction, the opera-

panel applications and other structural insulating applications, mainly because of their ability to be foamed in place and their excellent thermal characteristics. The foam-in-

Fig. 9-19. Interior of sprayed foam structure.

place advantage will also lead to innumerable new applications as an insulation material for new and old structures. In short, plastic foams will find wide utility as building insulation. Healthy competition among both producers and foams assures architects and builders of more and better products.

REFERENCES

1. Tallman, J. C., *Chem. Eng. Progr.*, **57**, No. 10, 60 (1961).
2. Dworkin, D., *SPE J.*, **17**, 1269 (1961).
3. Goggin, W. C., *Mod. Plastics*, **37**, No. 5, 124 (1960).
4. Waite, H. J., "Abstracts of Papers, 139th Meeting," p. 6H, St. Louis, Mo., American Chemical Society, March, 1961.
5. Shedd, Daniel P., "Accomplishments of Today—Promise of Tomorrow of Cellular Plastics," 7th Annual Technical Conference Proceedings, "Cellular Plastics—Today's Technology," Cellular Plastics Division, Society of Plastics Industry, April, 1963.
6. Kennedy, R. N., "The Utilization of Foams," *Progressive Architecture*, 160 (June, 1960).
7. Brenner, Walter, "Foamed Plastics," *Mater. & Methods*, 143 (June, 1956).
8. Society of the Plastics Industry, Inc., "Cellular Plastics," in "Plastics Engineering Handbook," No. 3, Ch. 12, New York, Reinhold Publishing Corp., 1960.
9. Riley, M. W., "What's New in Foamed Plastics," *Mater. Design Eng.*, 119, (March, 1961).
10. Guenther, F. O., *SPE Trans.*, **2**, 243 (1962).
11. Doherty, D. J., Hurd, R., and Lester, G. R., *Chem. Ind.* (London), **1962**, 1340 (1962).
12. Cooper, A., *Plastics Inst. (London), Trans.*, **26**, 299 (1958).
13. "Styrofoam: Expanded Polystyrene," Technical Bulletin No. 171–188A, The Dow Chemical Company, Midland, Michigan.
14. "Dylite," Technical Manual, Koppers Company, Inc., Pittsburgh, Pennsylvania.
15. "Pelaspan," Technical Bulletin No. 171-90, The Dow Chemical Company, Midland, Michigan.
16. Stengard, R. A., "Properties of Rigid Urethane Foams," E. I. du Pont de Nemours and Company, Inc., Wilmington, Delaware, June, 1963.
17. Frisch, K. C., and Robertson, E. J., "Advances in Technology in Uses of Rigid Urethane Foams," *Mod. Plastics*, **40**, No. 2, 165 (October, 1962).
18. Harding, R. H., *Mod. Plastics*, **37**, No. 10, 156 (1960).
19. Harding, R. H., and James, B. F., *Mod. Plastics*, **39**, No. 7, 133 (1962).
20. Knox, R. E., *Chem. Eng. Progr.*, **57**, No. 10, 40 (1961).
21. Patten, G. A., and Skochdopole, R. E., *Mod. Plastics*, **39**, No. 11, 149 (July, 1962).
22. Knox, R. E., *ASHRAE J.*, **4**, No. 10, 43 (1962).
23. Manufacturing Chemists Association, Inc., "Plastic Foams—Storage, Handling and Fabrication," Safety Guide SG5, September, 1960.
24. "Low Temperature Insulation: Styrofoam," Technical Bulletin No. 157–201, The Dow Chemical Company, Midland, Michigan.
25. "Styrofoam: Low Temperature Pipe Covering," Technical Bulletin No. 157–204, The Dow Chemical Company, Midland, Michigan.
26. "Building Insulation Products and Systems," Technical Bulletin No. 157–243, The Dow Chemical Company, Midland, Michigan.
27. Sheahan, J. P., "Foamed Plastic Roof Insulation," *Performance of Plastics in Building*, **1004**, Building Research Institute (1962).
28. "Roofmate FR Plastic Foam Roof Insulation," Technical Bulletin No. 157–205, The Dow Chemical Company, Midland Michigan.
29. "Sandwich Panels," *Mod. Plastics*, **40**, No. 9, 100 (May, 1963).
30. Dow, Alden B., "Ten-Year Performance of Plastics in Residences," *Performance of Plastics in Building*, **1004**, Building Research Institute (1962).
31. Waidelich, A. T., "Plastics in Structural Panels," *Performance of Plastics in Building*, **337**, Building Research Institute—April, NAS-NRC, 51–56 (1955).
32. "Forming Thin Shells," Technical Bulletin No. 171–191, The Dow Chemical Company, Midland, Michigan.
33. Ziegler, E. E., "Foamed Polystyrene in Thin Shell Construction," *Structural Foams*, **892**, Building Research Institute (1961).
34. "Styrocel," Technical Bulletin No. 157–250, The Dow Chemical Company, Midland, Michigan.
35. "More Versatility in Rigid Urethanes," *Mod. Plastics*, **40**, No. 11, 74 (July, 1963).

10 SEALANTS

GORDON E. HANN

The Tremco Manufacturing Company
Cleveland, Ohio

Sealants are elastomeric materials that have been developed within the past two decades for the sealing of joints against wind and water in construction, automobiles, refrigerators, truck bodies, aircraft and rockets. Caulks (calks) are less extensible materials, adequate only for less critical end uses.

Three centuries ago, the word caulk (calk) referred to the action of driving tarred oakum, cotton twist or wicking into the seams between the planks of a ship or boat. This method of sealing openings was subsequently improved through the development of asphaltic compounds made from residual asphalt mixed with asbestos fiber and other pigments.

Linseed oil putties for windows were introduced around 1800, and oil-based caulks a century later. In the past quarter of a century, improved caulking compounds were developed from vegetable or marine oil or oleoresinous vehicles. Tremendous volumes of caulking compound of this type have been used to seal openings around windows in homes and similar openings in other types of building construction. This type of caulking took place after the building was erected and was usually a remedial action taken to reduce or eliminate the infiltration of air or moisture through openings left inadvertently. The need for sealants has increased with the size of windows; a $\frac{1}{15}$-inch crack around a 4 × 6 foot picture-frame window has an area of 15 square inches.

With the advent of thin curtain wall construction, employing highly effective materials to provide the heat insulation, the physical space between the exterior and the interior has diminished so that there is no longer a thick wall reservoir for water that may leak through open joints on the outside. Likewise, there is no effective baffling system to prevent air coming directly to the inside in the event of open joints. Permanently adhesive and elastic sealants must be used in order to make this type of construction practical. In attempts to lower the cost of the construction of automobiles, mobile homes, truck trailers, etc., fewer fasteners are employed to hold sections of the side panels together. These fasteners may be rivets, individual nuts and bolts, self-threading screws or even spot welding. Effective sealants are needed to fill the space between the fasteners, and these sealants must have high adhesion to the specific surfaces employed and sufficient elasticity to withstand movement in the joint (Figure 10-1). In addition to excluding moisture and air, the sealants must provide satisfactory appearance at the junction of individual panels of which these devices are composed. Standard caulking compounds of ten years ago or longer do not provide satisfactory answers to these problems.

SEALANT FORMULATION

Sealants are composed of three fundamental parts—the basic nonvolatile vehicle, the pigment portion, and in most cases a solvent or thinner to make application easier.

The basic vehicle can vary from a vegetable oil such as linseed to an exotic specially

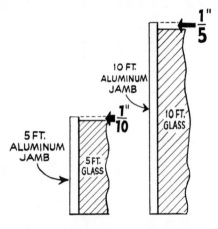

Thermal Movement

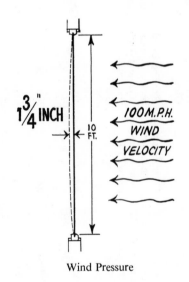

Wind Pressure

FIG. 10-1. The need for flexible sealants.

synthesized elastomer. These will be discussed later, and it will become clear that there is no universally superior vehicle. Each has its own peculiar properties—some suitable for certain specific situations and not for others.

The pigment portion is introduced for rheological or flow control and to impart opacity or color to the mass where desired. A broad range of pigments is available to the

formulator, making the formulation of sealants much more of a science today than ten years ago.

The solvent, when added to a sealant composition, has the sole purpose of reducing the viscosity to a point at which the sealant may be easily applied in its proper thickness and position. After application, the solvent evaporates, causing the sealant to shrink by an amount equivalent to the volume loss of solvent and reach its desired final, higher viscosity.

Five basic types of sealants will be discussed:

(1) Oxidizing vehicle type which gradually increases in viscosity upon exposure to air, usually containing solvent, which leaves the mass causing some increase in viscosity.

(2) The solvent release type of sealant which attains its final increase in viscosity solely through the loss of solvent.

(3) The chemically curing type of sealant which attains its final viscosity through a chemical reaction between a curing agent and the prepolymer vehicle incorporated in the formulation.

(4) The thermosetting sealant which attains its final viscosity through exposure to an elevated temperature for a sufficient time for the sealant to cure.

(5) The non-drying type of sealant which does not change in viscosity, retaining its original consistency and tack throughout its life.

There is a wide range of consistency variation in each of the five major classifications described above. Following is a description of each, with some generalizations given in Table 10-1.

Oxidizing Vehicle Sealants

Into this group fall the older type of caulking compounds. Up until the early fifties, the only type of quality sealant available was that made from oxidized and polymerized vegetable oils. When compounded with pigment such as asbestos fiber, solvent such as mineral spirits and a small amount of drier, this resulted in a reasonably satisfactory caulking compound, depending upon the amount of vehicle present. In recent years,

TABLE 10-1. Comparison, of Mastic Joint Sealants

(Warning: These are generalizations and may not apply to a specific compound)

	Oxidizing vehicle Sealants	Solvent Release Sealants Butyl	Solvent Release Sealants Acrylic	Chemical Curing Sealants	Gun Consistency	Non-Drying Mastics Hand Consistency	Extruded Tape	Thermosetting Sealants
1. Chief ingredient	Vegetable oils, synthetic oils, calcium carbonates, fiber	Butyl rubber, calcium carbonates, fiber	Acrylic polymer, calcium carbonates, fiber	Polysulfide, silicone or urethane polymers, fillers, resins	Polybutene, stabilizer, fiber, calcium carbonates	Polybutene, special stabilizer, fiber, pigments	Polybutene, butyl, polyisobutylene, asbestos and other inert fillers	Vinyl resin, plasticizers, fillers
2. Package forms	Bulk, cartridges	Bulk, cartridges	Bulk, cartridges	Bulk, cartridges, base and accelerator separate for 2 part	Bulk, cartridges	Bulk	Tapes and beads (rolls or cut lengths)	Bulk
3. Consistency	Heavy paste gun consistency	Heavy paste gun consistency	Heavy paste gun consistency	Heavy paste gun consistency	Heavy paste gun consistency	Soft putty	Stiff putty	Heavy paste gun consistency
4. Per cent solids volume	70–80	70–80	90	95–100	85–95	98–100	99–100	80–100
5. Application: cleaning surfaces	For good results all surfaces must be free of oil, grease, water, dust, and foreign matter	Same	Same	Same	Same	Same	Same	Same
6. Resealing	No	No	Yes	No	Yes	Yes	Yes	No
7. Method of application	Gun	Gun	Gun	Gun	Knife or gun	Knife	Hand	Knife or gun
8. Handling characteristics	Requires careful protective measures and skillful application	Requires careful protective measures and skillful application	Cartridges should be heated when temperature is below 75°F	Requires careful protective measures and skillful application	Easily handled by experienced glazier	Easily handled by experienced glazier	Easily handled by inexperienced labor	Requires careful protective measures and skillful application
9. Adhesion	Fair	Fair	Excellent	Good	Good	Fair	Good. Must be under compression	Poor to excellent
10. Colors available	All	All	All	All	Gray to black	Gray to black	Gray to black	All
11. Elongation, %. At break, 75°F 24 hr cure	25–200	200–600	200–600	200–600	200–600	25–50	25–300	25–200
At rupture, weathered seal	0–125	100–350	100–350	100–350	100–350	10–20	10–300	25–100
Max. usable for 10 effective seal		25–50	100	100	100	5–10	10–50	25–50

TABLE 10-1. Continued

Property								
12. Max. width, in. (channel ½ in. deep without sag)	1	½	½–¾	½–¾	¾	1	—	⅜
13. Hardness Shore A								
72-hr cure	0–10	0–5	0–5	10–60	0	0	0–10	20–40
10-yr cure	65+	45–60	55–60	Initial plus 30	Initial plus 10	5–30	10–50	55–60
14. Normal storage life	1 year	1 year	1 year	3 to 9 months temperature under 90°F	1 year	1 year	2 years	6 months
15. Pot life (mixed compound)	Does not apply	Does not apply	Does not apply	2 part—3 to 6 hr at 70°F; 1 part—does not apply	Does not apply	Does not apply	Does not apply	Does not apply
16. Curing	Skins overnight; firm set 4–8 weeks	Skins over 2–4 hr; firm set 6 weeks to one year, normal temperature	Skins over 2–4 hr; firm set 4–6 weeks normal temperature	Dependent on weather conditions, humidity Initial cure: 2 part 6 days 40°F, 10–15 hr 70°F, 1½–6 hr 100°F Final cure: 3 to 8 times longer 1 part 1–3 days 50% R.H. 77°F, 7–90 days 10% R.H. 32°F	Does not apply	Becomes firm 6–8 months; very little change after that expected.	No curing action involved	15 to 60 minutes at 250–350 °F
17. Temperature range for application °F	60–100	40–100	75–110	40–80	40–100	40–100	40–100	40–100
for service, intermittent, °F	−20 to 150	−20 to 200	−30 to 200	−60 to 200	−60 to 200	−40 to 175	−40 to 175	−20 to 150

TABLE 10-1. Continued

	Oxidizing vehicle Sealants	Solvent Release Sealants Butyl	Acrylic	Chemical Curing Sealants	Gun Consistency	Non-Drying Mastics Hand Consistency	Extruded Tape	Thermosetting Sealants
18. Effect of weathering	Hardness increases with age; loss of adhesion as hardness reaches 80–90	Hardness increases with age; loss of adhesion as hardness reaches 50–60	Hardness increases with age; probable max. Shore A 55–60	Hardness increases with age; loss of adhesion as hardness reaches 80–90	Slight stiffening, otherwise unaffected	Surface crusts; bulk firms but remains plastic	Hardness increases with age; loss of adhesion as hardness reaches 80–90	Hardness increases with age; loss of adhesion as hardness reaches 80–90
19. Life expectancy, yr	5–10	10	20	20	15–20	10–15	10–20	5–10
20. Chief limitations	Should be used in joints of maximum movement of 10%	Often remains slightly tacky—ultimate poor adhesion	Must be heated for application; pungent odor during application	2 part: Requires thorough mixing; qualified applicator; cost is high; possible under some conditions to cause staining 1 part: Requires proper ambient conditions for satisfactory cure; requires primer	Non-drying, non-skinning; can be used only in hidden nonporous joints not subject to severe air or water pressure	Non-drying; might collect dirt in some areas	Non-skinning; permanently tacky; exposed surfaces collect dirt; compressive confinement required for effective sealing	Requires heat to cure
21. Pounds per gallon	10–14	10–14	11–13	9–16	11–15	12–16	12–16	10–15
22. Cost, $ per gallon	1.90–2.50	5.00–6.00	13.50–15.00	9.00–30.00	2.50–3.00	1.75–2.50	1.80–4.00 per 100 lineal foot ($\frac{1}{8}$" x $\frac{1}{2}$")	4.00–9.00

these vehicles have been specially treated so as to slow down the oxidation of the vehicle once a reasonable cure has been obtained. Additives such as the chlorinated paraffins and the polybutenes have been incorporated as plasticizers to lengthen the flexible elastic life of the sealant. While these sealants have been considerably upgraded in recent years, they are still not satisfactory for many of the critical joints in current construction or original equipment manufacture. However, they did and still do satisfy the basic needs for certain simple joints. These materials are made in consistencies that can be brushed; they may also be applied by caulking guns (hand or air-power operated) and in a higher consistency requiring that they be hand-smoothed with a tool such as a glazing knife.

Depending upon the consistency, these materials have flexibilities permitting 25 to 100 per cent static elongation at break, after final curing, but they generally are not applicable for use in joints where there is more than 10 per cent continual variation in the joint width.

Immediately after initial cure these compounds usually are soft, with a Shore "A" Durometer Hardness of 0 to 10, but they can be expected to arrive at a Shore "A" Hardness of 65 to 80 after approximately 10 years, cure.

They have a life expectancy of 5 to 10 years, usually requiring maintenance or replacement after that length of time.

Solvent Release Sealants

A large variety of sealants fit into this classification; it is a very popular method of formulation. The sealant "cures" solely by the release or evaporation of the solvent, causing the consistency to increase. Into this group fall the butyl rubber solution types, the polyisobutylene solution types, neoprene rubber solution types, and the newer acrylic copolymer solution type. Polymers of moderate molecular weight can be used in sealants of this class to obtain inherent adhesive ability. This is a heterogeneous group of sealants, with great differences in the results obtained, depending on the type and amount of the specific basic vehicle employed. However,

in general these sealants are superior to the drying oil type.

These materials are produced in consistencies ranging from a brushing or pouring through the heavier consistencies applicable by hand-gun or air-pressure gun. They are not normally supplied in hand or knife consistencies. All of this class exhibits shrinkage upon release of the solvent. The amount of shrinkage depends upon the amount of solvent and varies from 5 to 50 per cent, which provides a further reason to invalidate any attempt to attribute common characteristics to this class.

Depending on the type and amount of the basic polymer employed and the degree of extension of the vehicle through the use of fillers, these sealants may be expected to have a static elongation of from 100 to 600 per cent at break. After weathering or curing to the final consistency, the better sealants in this group may be expected to withstand up to 100 per cent elongation continually without failure. While there is a large variation, this class of sealant will average an initial Shore "A" Hardness of 5 to 10 in 14 days and will reach 50 to 60 in 10 years.

The life expectancy of the better sealants in this group is considered to be 20 years if properly applied in typical joints.

Chemically Curing Type Sealant

Into this group falls a large variety of sealants. The oldest and most standard is probably the "Thiokol" polysulfide type. This is composed of one of the polysulfide polymers manufactured by the Thiokol Corporation, compounded with other ingredients. It is necessary to include ingredients to assist in the cure and also to control its speed, so that cure will take place in a reasonable time while allowing a reasonable pot life. It is also necessary to add tackifiers or adhesive agents, since these high polymers do not normally have inherent bonding ability. A curing agent is added at the job site, resulting in a cure to the consistency of soft rubber within a few hours after application, under normal conditions. This fast cure is their prime advantage.

These polysulfide compounds do not ordinarily contain much solvent. As they are approximately 95 to 100 per cent solids, there is little shrinkage during curing.

The initial cure of the polysulfide sealants results in an average Shore "A" Hardness of from 15 to 50 in about 24 hours, with a cure in about 10 years of approximately 40 to 70 depending on the initial cure. The curing agent is normally provided in some excess to force an adequate cure even if not exactly measured and mixed. This results in a slow, continual increase in cure over the years above the initial value. The static elongation at break after the initial cure of polysulfide compounds ranges from 200 to 600 per cent, whereas the elongation after the final cure and that which can be considered usable as, an effective seal, is approximately 100 per cent.

Into this class also fall the silicone base and the so-called one-part polysulfide sealants which in reality are two-part sealants inhibited or retarded so that until actually exposed as a bead, the chemical cure does not take place. This eliminates the necessity of mixing the curing agent and the base material on the job site and any inaccuracies possible there. However, there exists a variation in the rate of cure depending on the local weather conditions after exposure. If humidity or temperature is too low, these compounds may require extremely long curing periods. If the ambient humidity and temperature are proper for a sufficient period of time and with a substantial portion of the bead exposed to the atmosphere, the physical characteristics of the cured one-part sealant of this class are approximately the same as for two-part polysulfide compounds. There have been some polyurethane compounds put on the market to a limited extent but not in sufficient quantity to form any accurate opinion as to their general characteristics.

One characteristic is apparent in practically all of the compounds in this general class that are available to date: they require adhesion additives in order to bond reasonably well to the surfaces to which they are applied. After cure, the cohesive strengths are extremely high in comparison to com-pounds of the solvent release type. Stresses placed upon the sealant, as a result of joint movement, are transferred to the adhesive bond, and there is little inherent adhesion in these polymers. Properly formulated, however, sealants of the chemically cured class provide excellent solutions to many sealant problems. They can be effective for 20 years if properly applied.

Thermosetting Sealants

Original equipment manufacturers have found certain types of thermosetting sealants to be very applicable to joint sealing problems. While not particularly applicable to the construction industry, these sealants are suitable for the exterior coach joints in automotive assembly, the drip rail joint in automotive assembly, the joints in the "can" or the exterior box of refrigerators to prevent ingress of moisture-laden air into the insulation, and other similar joints wherein the unit is to be heated during the process. These sealants are in general plastisols or organosols designed with rheological and curing characteristics for the specific system involved. It is possible to develop adhesion without primers where these sealants are employed, but in severe cases, primers have been found necessary. These vinyl sealants produce an excellent appearing joint with a Shore "A" in the neighborhood of 20 to 40 and elongations permissible in the neighborhood of 25 to 100 per cent, depending upon the amount and type of vinyl used. The curing required depends upon the formulation, but will range from 15 to 60 minutes at temperatures from 250 to 350°F. The life expectancy is equal to that of the product on which it is used.

Non-drying Sealants

Some joints requiring sealing have so little exposure to view or to the weather that it is unnecessary for the sealant to cure, skin over, or increase in viscosity. Providing that the sealant does not allow any of its vehicle to migrate, this type of non-drying sealant is highly effective. Sealants of this class are manufactured largely from poly-butenes, polyisobutylenes, and butyl rubber. They range in consistencies from thin pourables through gun consistency and into the heavy extruded elastomeric rubberlike tapes supplied in rolls or pre-cut lengths. Sealants of this class are used in male-

Fig. 10-2. Gun consistency sealant.

female joints of building panels, for example. They are found in lap joints in all types of boat construction. The extruded tapes are found in insulated glass construction, window setting in sash, truck trailers and mobile home assembly, automotive assembly and many types of overlap joints in original equipment manufacture assembly.

Depending upon the composition, these sealants reach an initial Shore "A" Hardness upon cure of 0 to 25, and change little upon exposure over their lifetime. The corresponding static elongation immediately after cure varies from 300 to 25, and maximum usable elongation after final cure varies from about 100 to 10 per cent. They have a life expectancy approaching 20 years.

Some Formulation Problems

Excessive filler and solvent is the major difficulty with ordinary caulking compounds. Very superior sealants can be made from the older types of caulking compound vehicles simply by building up the percentage of basic vehicle which provides the flexibility and adhesion. The polysulfides and other sealants are superior to the best that could be developed with the oleoresinous type in *elasticity* or elastomeric properties. However, poor *adhesion* is still the main cause of failure of the sealant and resultant leakage of moisture and air. This is apparent even with the newer exotic types of sealants. Many sealants are very flexible and elastic but still can be easily pulled away from the joint.

Sealants must be formulated that do not require excessive cleaning, priming or surface conditioning of the sides of the joint, since these procedures rely too much upon expert workmanship. It is currently

Fig. 10-3. Extruded tape.

recommended generally that sealant application not be attempted at temperatures below 40°F since very few sealants will obtain a grip to the sides of a joint covered with a layer of ice. Most skinning and/or curing sealants will cure at the ice-sealant interface, and therefore never develop satisfactory adhesion to the metal. A sealant must have specific resealing ability that permits it to obtain complete adhesion after the ice has dissipated, for application when ice may be present.

JOINT SHAPES

The shape of the joint has considerable effect on the success of the joint sealant. As a joint moves, stresses are imposed on the sealant that may be more or less severe, depending on the natural or original shape of the joint. The deeper a sealant is in a given joint for a given width, the more "necking" and internal stress occurs in the sealant as the joint opens. As is seen in Figure 10-4, a joint ½ inch wide × 1 inch

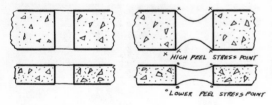

FIG. 10-4. Effect of joint shape on necking.

deep "necks" or pulls up within itself far more than a joint ½ inch wide × ½ inch deep. Consequently, there is a greater chance for cohesive failure with the deeper joint.

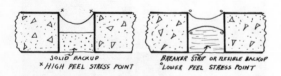

FIG. 10-5. Reducing stresses with a breaker strip.

A similar problem is involved when a sealant is used in a joint in which there is no breaker strip at the bottom or back of the joint, so that the sealant is in contact with

three sides of the joint with only the face of the joint exposed. This, again, puts a greater strain on the cohesive strength of the sealant. The obvious recommendation here is to employ a breaker strip or type of backing which will not restrict or restrain the sealant, but will move with it as the joint moves (Figure 10-5).

Table 10-1 presents a comprehensive comparison of the main sealant materials. Some of the polymeric components are shown in Figure 10-6.

JOINT DESIGN AND INSTALLATION

Vision Light Sealant Recommendations

All of the improvements in sealant technology that have occurred, and all of them that will occur, will not solve joint sealing problems alone. The increased demand upon sealants for modern construction is closely paralleled with the demand upon the designers themselves. They must determine the amount and kind of movement that occurs in the joints, so that sealants with given characteristics can be matched to joints with defined movements.

Many joints in modern construction must be studied individually and sealant procedures recommended specifically for them. There are, however, certain fundamentals that may be applied to the sealing of vision light sash.

Glazing Aluminum Sash; Minimum Standards: (1) Sealant Thickness. Minimum designed space for sealant thickness shall be ⅛ inch (in bed for face glazing; either side of glass for angle or channel glazing).

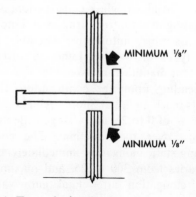

(a) Face glazing space

Solid Types

Polysulfide   Butyl   Neoprene   Chlorosulfonated
                                                       Polyethylene

An Acrylic Liquid Type

FIG. 10-6. Some typical high molecular weight basic polymers.

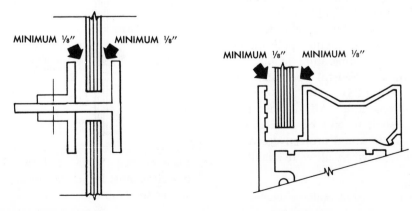

(b) Angle glazing space   (c) Channel glazing space

(2) Bite or Lap of Glass Edge on Stop. Glass shall be cut or manufactured to size as per glass manufacturer's directions. One glass manufacturer recommends the following: "On glass thickness up to a ¼ inch, the bite on the glass should be a minimum of ½ inch. On hermetically sealed double glazed windows, the bite on the glass should be a minimum of ⅞ inch and preferably 1 inch.

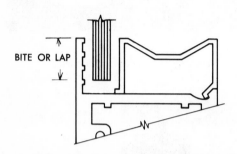

BITE OR LAP

Up to 50 united inches*	¼ in.
50-100 united inches	⅜ in.
Over 100 united inches	½ in.

(3) Centering Glass. Maintain centered position of glass in glazing rabbet and minimum ⅛-inch thickness of sealants as above on all glass over 50 united inches. Transmit wind loads from glass to sash through the use of setting blocks at the sill. Center by shims on both faces and all four sides, spaced as per glass manufacturer's directions and kept ¼ inch down from sight line to allow for continuous seal of the sealant. All glass in ventilating sections under 50 united inches must also be centered by shims.
(4) Application Temperatures. No sealants to be applied below 40°F unless the contractor takes necessary steps to elevate the temperature in the immediate application area. The minimum temperature of 40° is set up under Interim Federal Specification TT-G-00410C (GSA-FSS).
(5) Cleaning—Preparation. All surfaces to receive sealants shall be free of dust, dirt, foreign matter, or unsound protective coatings. Usually a xylol wipe will remove faulty coatings.

*United inches (U. I.) equals width + height.

Installation. Aluminum Sash:
(1) Lights of Glass Under 50 United Inches

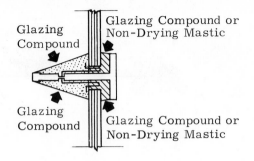

Glazing Compound

Glazing Compound or Non-Drying Mastic

Glazing Compound

Glazing Compound or Non-Drying Mastic

(a) Face glazing (indoors or out). Bed glass in glazing compound or non-drying mastic. Set clips and face glaze with glazing compound.

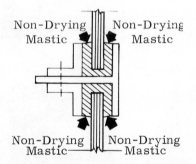

Non-Drying Mastic

Non-Drying Mastic

Non-Drying Mastic

Non-Drying Mastic

(b) Angle glazing (indoors or out). Bed glass in non-drying mastic. Set glass. Finish non-drying mastic and embed angle.
(2) Lights of Glass 50 to 100 United Inches

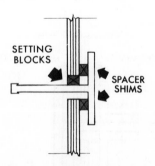

SETTING BLOCKS

SPACER SHIMS

(a) Face glazing. Same as 1 (a) above, but glass must be set on blocks, using spacer shims in bed.

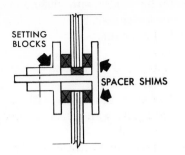

(b) Angle glazing. Same as 1(b) above, except glass must be set on blocks and spacer shims must be used to insure centering of glass.

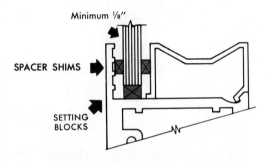

(c) Channel glazing. Same as angle glazing 1(b) but glass must be set on setting blocks and spacer shims must be used to insure centering of glass.

Note: Where a superior job is desired and lights are from 50 to 100 United Inches, any of the following recommendations for lights over 100 United Inches may be used.

(3) Lights of Glass Greater Than 100 United Inches. Because of the much greater demands placed on the sealants through greater movement and other factors previously referred to, the sealant manufacturer should be consulted for specific recommendations.

The following are examples of jobs completed without any leakage, and where recommendations were based on individual job situations. The previously outlined "minimum standards" apply. Before setting any glass, all four corners where vertical members joined horizontal members were sealed with an elastomeric gunnable sealant to in-

sure an elastic seal (unless this had already been done in shop fabrication).

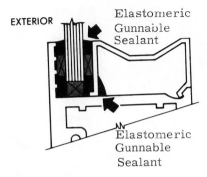

EXAMPLE 1: Set glass in an elastomeric gunnable sealant, filling entire glazing channel to sight line.

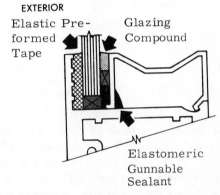

EXAMPLE 2: Bed glass in an elastic preformed tape. Apply heel bead of elastomeric gunnable sealant, lapping on glass edge a minimum of ¼ inch. Set molding and back fill with glazing compound or elastomeric gunnable sealant after overnight set of heel bead.

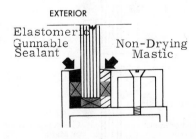

EXAMPLE 3: Bed glass in an elastomeric gunnable sealant to sight line. Back fill with non-drying mastic to interior sight line.

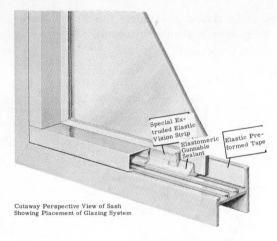

Cutaway Perspective View of Sash
Showing Placement of Glazing System

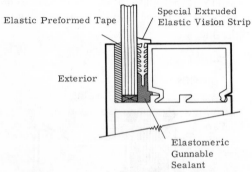

EXAMPLE 4: Bed glass in elastic preformed tape. Apply heel bead of elastomeric gunnable sealant, lapping on glass edge a minimum of ¼ inch. Set molding. Cut extruded elastic vision strip about 1 inch longer than stops. Insert strip into space between stop and glass.

Steel sash: Angle Glazing

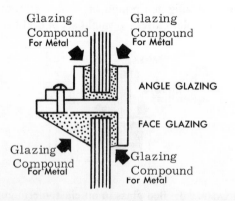

(1) Apply bed of glazing compound for metal sash.
(2) Bed glass.

(3) Butter angles with glazing compound for metal sash.
(4) Install angles.

Face Glazing
(1) Apply bed of glazing compound for metal sash.
(2) Bed glass and secure with clips.
(3) Face glaze with glazing compound for metal sash.

Note: Where superior face glazing job is required, follow recommendations given below for Detention Sash.

Detention Sash: ¼-inch stock steel—outside face glazed.

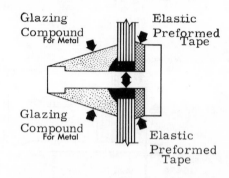

(1) Bed glass in elastic preformed tape.
(2) Run a heel bead of elastomeric gunnable sealant on exterior side, to provide a positive seal between glass and sash.
(3) Face glaze with glazing compound. (The face glazing bead hides the elastomeric gunnable sealant).

Note: When glass exceeds 50 united inches, consult sealant manufacturer for specific recommendations.

Wood Sash: With Molding

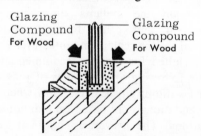

(1) Apply bed of glazing compound for wood sash to the permanent stop.
(2) Bed glass and secure with glaziers points.

(3) Butter moldings with glazing compound for wood sash.

(4) Install moldings.

Face Glazing

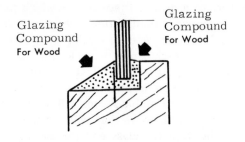

(1) Apply bed of glazing compound for wood sash to the permanent stop.

(2) Bed glass and secure with glaziers points.

(3) Face glaze, using glazing compound for wood sash.

Note 1: All wood surfaces to receive glazing compound for wood sash shall be thoroughly primed and sealed.

Note 2: When glass exceeds 50 united inches, consult sealant manufacturer for specific recommendations.

Insulating Glass in Aluminum and Steel Sash:

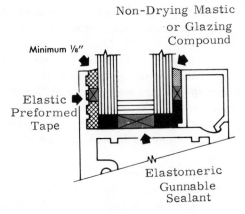

(1) Use spacer shims and setting blocks.

(2) Bed glass in elastic preformed tape with squeeze-out beyond sight line.

(3) Apply a heel bead of elastomeric gunnable sealant completely around the perimeter of the glass making a minimum ¼ inch contact on glass and metal leaving void around edge of glass at jambs and head.

(4) At sill, fill under glass edge solidly with elastomeric gunnable sealant.

(5) Secure inside molding.

(6) After sealant sets, back fill interior molding to sight line with glazing compound or non-drying mastic.

Note: When a superior job is required, follow recommendations given under Example 4 for aluminum sash over 100 United Inches as shown on p. 000.

Insulating Glass in Wood Sash:

(1) Shop or In-Plant Glazing. In addition to an enduring seal and economy, shop glazing of heavy insulating glass units, i.e., studio windows, must provide for:

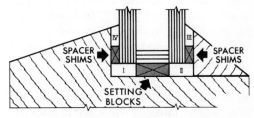

(a) Possibility of displacement of sealants thru movement or shifting of glass in handling, shipping and erection—design and extent of shimming and blocking provided by manufacturer.

(b) Type of equipment available for pneumatic, mechanical or hand applications of sealants.

(c) Speed of mass production line and time allowable for glazing operation.

(2) Job Site or Field Glazing. Oleo-resinous type compounds should never be used as a primary sealant for insulating glass.

Where oleo-resinous sealants or polybutene elastic preformed tapes are used in combination with other sealants, all wood rabbets should be thoroughly paint primed and sealed to prevent migration of vehicles.

Where two part polysulfide liquid polymers or one part acrylic terpolymer compound is to be used, contact can be made directly to virgin wood.

Considerations of size, bite, detail of rabbet will govern but in general the following might apply.

(1) Use spacer shims and setting blocks.

(2) A heel bead of elastomeric gunnable sealant at I.

(3) A heel bead of elastomeric gunnable sealant at II, completely filling at sill only. (On jambs and head, fill rabbet to sight line but leave a void around the glass edge.)

(4) Set inside wood molding and back fill with glazing compound for wood sash at III.

(5) Needle glaze exterior with elastomeric gunnable sealant, filling space solidly to meet heel bead and tapering up $\frac{1}{16}$ inch on glass to form a natural water table shed at IV.

Alternatively, substitute elastomeric preformed tape at position IV flush with sight line and $\frac{3}{8}''$ up from table of rabbet.

Elastomeric gunnable sealant at position I is applied after glass is set so that it meets bottom edge of elastomeric preformed tape and completely fills under glass at sill. Pressing glass into bed will force elastomeric preformed tape above sight line on exterior approximately $\frac{1}{16}$ inch. Instead of cutting off, if possible, leave to shed water.

Recommendations for Glass Glazing Applications. The oldest sealant common to the construction industry is the putty or glazing compound still used in a large majority of the wood and metal sash windows. Glazing compounds have been improved and new ones have been developed. While the older ones fitted completely in Classification (1) described previously, some of the newer ones qualify for Classification (5) (see p. 000). In any event, they all have been improved and are far superior to the old hard-setting putties.

However, methods of application have not changed materially over the years. Glaziers still employ the old practices satisfactory for commercial sidewall sash for factories, but completely unsatisfactory when the glass is to be placed in a modern metal sash for residential or office buildings. A few of the causes and the remedies for difficulties with glazing compound follow.

General Recommendations for All Glazing Jobs. (1) Wipe the surfaces to be glazed with a clean, dry rag to ensure removal of all dust and dirt. If there is any oil, grease, or moisture present, wipe the sash with a clean rag dampened with xylol and allow the surface to dry before proceeding. No adhesive material with the high consistency of a sealant can adhere to a dusty surface or one which has been coated with moisture, oil, or grease.

(2) Use two setting blocks at quarter points from each corner, when length dimension is over 30 inches. Glass must not be allowed to set on the metal sash at one corner or the other, or undue strains will result and movement will occur that will rupture the bond between the glass and the glazing. If glass is firmly supported by two setting blocks, there is less likelihood of excessive movement at certain points because of extension and contraction of the sash and transmission of windloads from glass and sash.

(3) All glazing or sealing of sash shall be done with the sash above 40°F, to avoid frost or ice.

(4) All openings shall be checked to make certain that they are square, plumb and secure in order that uniform face and edge clearances will be maintained. Otherwise, later movement of the sash will cause excessive movement of the glass, if, for example, one point of the glass touches the sash. If the sash is not secure, subsequent movement of the sash will cause a rupture of the glazing bond.

(5) The glazed sash must be protected against handling or operation of the sash until compound has set as prescribed by the manufacturer of the compound. Otherwise, the seal between the compound and the glass, or the sash, may be broken and never regained.

(6) Apply the glazing compound or sealant as directed by the manufacturer, especially in regard to the applicator to be used, the volume to be installed and details such as tooling, brushing, etc. A fast skin bead, untooled, will not produce the results predicted by the manufacturer who assumes that a deep set, tooled bead is to be applied.

Special Recommendations for Channel or Bead Glazing Installations. (1) Ensure $\frac{1}{8}$ inch minimum clearance between both faces of the glass and the sash, using spacers recommended by the glass manufacturer. This is considered the minimum thickness of a glazing compound or sealant that will have adequate volume to stand up under the requirements of a glazing seal. It must be recognized that movement of as little as $\frac{1}{16}$ inch represents 50 per cent movement of a $\frac{1}{8}$-inch seal, either in tension, compression, or shear. There are few compounds, available at any price, that will stand continual elongation of even 25 per cent either in compression, tension or shear; therefore, it is obvious that bead widths of less than $\frac{1}{8}$ inch are extremely hazardous and almost certain to produce failures in time.

(2) Maintain the following bites or overlaps on the glass edge without exception:

$\frac{1}{4}$-inch bite under 50 united inches
$\frac{3}{8}$-inch bite under 50 and 100 united inches
$\frac{1}{2}$-inch bite over 100 united inches

No glass or sash is perfectly true and, of course, the larger the lights the greater the tolerance. The larger the lights the greater the movement, as well.

(3) Leave an air space around the edge of the glass at both jambs and the head where the glass is over $\frac{1}{4}$ inch thick. Otherwise, where thick glass such as insulating glass is used, and the entire space around the edge of the glass is filled, unless a chemical curing, two-part component has been installed, there is likelihood of pressures forcing compound out of that pocket onto the face of the glass as the glass expands into the channel formed by the sash.

(4) Fill the sill of all glazing jobs completely full under the glass edge and up to the sight line. In the event there is a fault in the seal above the sill, it is necessary to make sure that water does not collect under the bottom edge of the glass at the sill.

(5) When striking the surplus compound from both sides of the glass, leave the remaining bead with a slight angle sloping away from the glass. In this way, water will not lay at the joint between the compound and the glass, but will be shed.

Special Recommendations for Face Glazing.
(1) Ensure a minimum of $\frac{1}{8}$ inch for the backbedding through the use of a spacer shim. Otherwise, it is almost impossible to obtain a uniform width of bedding during manual installation. Furthermore, any pressure clips applied to the outside will inevitably force the glass, in due time, and reduce the width of the bed if there are no shims.

(2) Apply the specified number and type of spring clips as specified by the sash manufacturer, to ensure uniform pressure. Otherwise, stange movement of the glass may result, causing rupture of the seal if it occurs before the sealant has thoroughly cured.

(3) Face glaze the rabbet to the sight line to form a neat, trim line, applying proper pressure to the glazing tool to ensure bond to the glass. Unless a fast, firm stroke is made on most glazing compounds, when applying them to the glass, there is a tendency for the glazing compound to adhere to the putty knife and pull slightly away from the glass. This often is not noticeable unless very close scrutiny is made of the junction between the glazing compound and glass.

(4) Face glazing corners should be neatly turned with a smooth, slightly round shape rather than a sharp cut. A sharp cut in the corner produces a weak point in the glazing compound.

(5) Cut the surplus back bead off at an angle sloving away from the glass, to permit water to shed.

(6) Paint the face of the compound to extend its life expectancy. (Some glazing compounds do not require painting.)

Recommendations for Porcelain Veneer Sealants. One of the most imposing problems facing the sealant manufacturer is the one of obtaining and retaining adhesion to porcelain enamel veneer such as is found in many buildings today. Gas stations, porcelain enamel veneer curtain wall construction and porcelain enamel veneer commercial building construction all provide small moving joints with surfaces literally of glass to which the sealant must adhere. The older oleo-resinous caulks were inadequate; but polysulfide compounds have proved reasonably satisfactory. Sealants with extremely high adhesive ability are required. One type of sealant has been developed for this type of work from acrylic copolymers specifically synthesized for maximum adhesion and fairly permanent elasticity. This has been accomplished by completing the polymerization reaction so that there are no monomers left that could react with air moisture or polymerize as a result of exposure to ultraviolet, ozone, etc. This is a sealant in the solvent release class, but other inherently adhesive sealants not requiring fugitive tackifiers will no doubt be developed.

Specific Recommendations for Original Equipment Manufacturers. The joints found in this area are too numerous to cover in any few simple recommendations. There are, however, some generalizations that can be made. "Coach joints" or exterior joints, requiring sealant primarily for appearance and also to provide an absolutely tight seal, are usually best handled by one of the plastisols or organosols which will cure in a subsequent baking operation to which this piece of equipment is probably exposed. Otherwise a two-part chemically curing sealant is required in order to obtain a heavy rubberlike consistency necessary for satisfactory appearance on this equipment. Hidden joints, i.e., overlap joints, are best sealed by one of two general classes of extruded tapes currently available. Polybutene tapes are the least expensive and provide satisfactory sealing for joints where a slight edge of non-drying material is not harmful or where there is no necessity for the sealant to aid in holding the

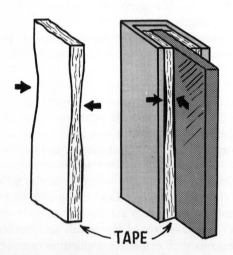

FIG. 10-7. Irregular tape thicknesses may produce voids.

joints together by acting as an adhesive. Many of these joints, however, are better sealed by using the high molecular-weight polyisobutylene or butyl rubber tapes, cured or uncured, which have high tensile adhesive strength. These more elastomeric tapes are practically permanently elastic, and aid materially in holding the sides of the joint together, reducing the number of fasteners required. This type of tape must be of exactly the proper size and shape for the specific joint to be sealed (Figure 10-7).

The polyisobutylene tapes generally have the greatest amount of inherent adhesion and

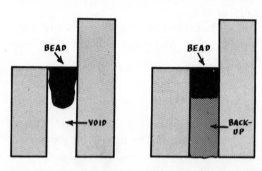

FIG. 10-8. Need for joint backing. Unless properly backed up before application, the sealant is not pressed against the sides of the joint so that only superficial adhesion is obtained.

ultimate flexibility although they exhibit a slight amount of cold flow. The butyl tapes, cured or uncured, as a general rule are higher in molecular weight and do not have quite the amount of adhesion of the polyisobutylene tapes, but they do have much less tendency to cold flow and they have a higher degree of recovery. It is not uncommon to find tapes made of blends of polyisobutylene and of butyl rubber, both of which come in quite a range of molecular weights.

PROPERTIES OF SEALANTS

All sealants are a compromise. There is no one sealant that has the best adhesion, the greatest amount of permanent elasticity, the lowest rate of hardening, the lowest rate of shrinkage, etc. Sealants have been developed in recent years with improved adhesion, elasticity, etc., but there still is no single sealant superior in all properties.

Adhesion

Practically all sealant failures are adhesion failures. When high elasticity or elastomeric characteristics are built into a sealant, this means chemically that the molecular weight is very high or the cross-linking is very great within the molecule, resulting in high cohesive forces or strengths which give good elastic recovery or rubberlike characteristics. But this same internal strength defies the sealant to adhere to the sides of the joint by transferring any strain on the sealant directly to the surfaces with which the sealant is in contact. Assuming two sealants with equal adhesive ability, one with a higher recovery characteristic and the other with a lower recovery characteristic and a greater stress relaxation ability, the latter will appear to have higher adhesive ability. Thus, while adhesion

FIG. 10-9. Needle glazing loose lights.

is not directly related to recovery or molecular weight, it is lacking in the extremely high molecular-weight types of sealants. Adhesion problems are aggravated when sealants are applied over construction dust, forming oils on the metal, protective greases on bronze sash, protective lacquers on aluminum sash, highly alkaline plaster dusts on sash, moisture condensation on aluminum sash, and even over a slight film of ice normally found on construction projects during the season the greatest majority of them are "closed in."

Elasticity

Elasticity is another characteristic which is difficult to evaluate. Extensibility (elongation) can be measured by simple single pulls on the sealant to determine the amount of stretch before rupture. However, building joints do not stretch just once. Rather, their movement is dynamic—repeated strains, usually of low magnitude. A straight single pull on a sealant does, of course, give a comparative evaluation between two sealants, but may not reveal that one sealant has a high susceptibility to fatigue upon constant movement of a lower order of magnitude. Because of the difficulty in setting up dynamic test procedures, there is no sealant specification available today except for one included at the end of this chapter which provides for such a test. Elasticity should not be improved at the expense of adhesion, since the latter is the more vulnerable property and most high-quality sealants of today have far more elasticity than they require.

Rate of Hardening

How long will it stay soft? How long will it last? Is this sealant good for 25 years? The user is thinking of the rate of hardening when he asks these questions. Ideally, the sealant should not change, but a small amount of hardening from the time of application may not be critical. Preferred Shore "A" hardnesses range from about 15 to 50. Under 15, the material is so soft that it is easily displaced; over 50, the material becomes so cohesive that it may fail in adhesion.

Shrinkage

Shrinkage is another characteristic whose importance varies with the use of the sealant. If the sealant is applied in a corner joint as a fillet, shrinkage actually may be desirable in order to have the joint become concave. On the other hand, a sealant put in the $\frac{1}{4}$-inch joint between two adjacent porcelain enamel panels cannot have excessive shrinkage or it will shrink into the joint providing an unsatisfactory appearance and also reducing the amount of sealant in the joint, possibly to an unsatisfactory amount. Sealants are available with shrinkage rates ranging from practically 0 to 50 per cent. If a very low order of shrinkage is required, a two-part chemically curing compound will provide shrinkages in the order of 0 to 2 per cent. If a modest amount of shrinkage is permissible and other characteristics unique in the compound are desired, solvent-release type compounds are available with shrinkages ranging from 10 to 20 per cent. For certain applications, sealants with 40 to 50 per cent solvent, providing about that amount of shrinkage eventually, may be entirely satisfactory, e.g., for needle glazing and other small joints where a concave finished joint is not harmful.

Oil Migration

A characteristic normally important only to the non-drying sealants, but occasionally escaping the notice of the formulator in other types of sealants, is oil migration. Occasionally sealants are compounded with an ingredient that is not tied in sufficiently well, so that in time, especially under some exposures of heat or vibration, a portion of the vehicle migrates out on to the surfaces adjacent to the sealant to provide a sticky, tacky surface that will collect dirt. This situation can be avoided by proper compounding.

Dirt Retention

Dirt retention is often overemphasized. Some compounds are more tacky than others, hence they will hold dirt which is blown upon them to a greater extent. In some applications, dirt retention must be minimal. It is obvious that a non-drying mastic would have a very high order of dirt retention and should not be used in white marble joints. However, in no situation is it necessary to have less dirt retention than the surfaces adjacent to which the sealant is applied. But the dirt retention of a sealant is often criticized only to find later that the stone or coated aluminum surface actually retained more dirt than the sealant.

Workability

Far too much emphasis has been given to the workability of sealants by the glaziers or caulking contractors who were the early appliers and to this date still constitute the largest number of appliers. These tradesmen have long placed workability at the top of the list of the important characteristics of a compound, with little regard for ultimate durability beyond the time necessary for them to be compensated for their work, namely, about one year. Fortunately, an increasingly large number of responsible contracting firms today take the long view, but they find it difficult to obtain cooperation from the tradesmen when a new radical technique is introduced. When first introduced, two-part polysulfide compounds, which had to be mixed on the job, were regarded as a hilarious absurdity by most of the tradesmen for several years. It is to the credit of some applicators that they adopted the new materials, compelling the others to follow suit. However, the majority still resist any different application procedure even though it may result in a better job. Consequently, it is nearly impossible to get a satisfactory priming job to the sides of a joint prior to the application of a sealant, making it necessary that compounds not requiring priming be developed and made available. Also, it is necessary to have compounds that will obtain adhesion through a reasonable amount of dust, moisture and other material interfering with the bond of the sealant because of the inability of the applier to understand the need for a laboratory clean joint.

SPECIFICATIONS

There are today available only a few specifications for sealants:

United States Government Specifications

TT-C-598	Caulking Compound, Oil and Resin Base Type (For Masonry and Other Structures)
TT-G-00410c	GSA-FSS Interim Federal Specification Glazing Compound, Sash (Metal). For Back Bedding and Face Glazing (Not for Channel or Stop Glazing)
TT-S-227b	GSA-FSS Sealing Compound; Rubber Base, Two Component (For Caulking, Sealing and Glazing in Building Construction)
TT-S-00230	(Comm.-NBS) Sealing Compound, Synthetic-Rubber Base; Single Component, Chemically Curing (For Caulking, Sealing and Glazing in Building Construction

Canadian Government Specifications

19-GP-1	Putty; Linseed-oil Type for Glazing
19-GP-2	Glazing Compound; Elastic, for Metal Sash Face and Channel Glazing.
19-GP-3	Compound; Caulking and Glazing, Elastomeric, Chemical Curing Type, Gun Grade
19-GP-4	Compound; Caulking, Elastomeric, for Marine Use
19-GP-5	Compound; Caulking and Glazing, Elastomeric, Solvent Release Type, Gun Grade, One Component
19-GP-6	Compound; Caulking, Oil Base, Gun Grade
19-GP-9	Compound; Caulking and Glazing, Elastomeric, Chemical Curing Type, Gun Grade, One Component
19-GP-7	Compound; Primer, for use with Two-component Elastomeric Caulking Compounds
19-GP-10	Compound; Primer, for use with One-component Elastomeric Caulking Compound
19-GP-11	Compound; Caulking, Elastomeric, for Underwater Use on Wooden Hulled Vessels

American Standards Association

ASA 116.1	Polysulfide Base Sealing Compounds for Building Trade

There are several committees working on test methods and specifications. American Society for Testing Materials, 1916 Race Street, Philadelphia, Pennsylvania, Committee C-24 on Joint Sealants, is interested in sealants of all types. The American Standards Association Incorporated, 10 East 40th Street, New York, New York, has released the specification indicated above which was developed largely through the efforts of the Adhesive and Sealant Council, 1410 Higgins Road, Park Ridge, Illinois. The National Paint, Varnish and Lacquer Association, 1500 Rhode Island Avenue, Washington, D. C., Caulking and Glazing Division, has an active technical group working on specifications for caulking and glazing compounds and did much of the development work on TT-G-00410C, for example.

A proposal for a broad specification for gun-applied sealants can be found in the Appendix to this chapter. This specification covers the solvent release and two-part chemically cured types of sealants with recommendations as to the specific parameters and limits for each characteristic. Note, particularly, the dynamic elongation test procedure.

GLOSSARY

Adhesion Failure—Failure of a compound by pulling away from surface with which it is in contact. (See *Cohesive Failure*.)

Affidavit, Performance—A statement in writing by a manufacturer or an independent testing laboratory, stating that a submitted product performs according to some specification against which the product has been tested.

Air Pockets—Bubbles of air formed within a compound or between two adjacent beads of compound applied successively in a joint.

Angle Bead or Joint—A bead of compound whose cross-section is triangularly shaped with the hypotenuse side exposed.

Angles—Short lengths of metal angle used to secure glass in some rabbets or channels that do not have a removable stop.

Bake Test—A laboratory test in which the elasticity and adhesion of compounds are tested by subjecting them to prolonged periods of heat.

Base—The general composition of a compound, such as vegetable oil, polysulfide, polybutene, etc. Also, in a two-part compound, the major unit of compound to which a curing agent or accelerator is added before use.

Bead—A sealant or compound after application in a joint, irrespective of the method of application, such as caulking bead, glazing bead, etc. Also a molding or stop used to hold glass or panels in position.

Bed or Bedding—The bead of compound applied between light of glass or panel and the stationary stop or sight bar of the sash or frame, and usually the first bead of compound to be applied when setting glass or panels.

Bedding of Stop—The application of compound at base of channel, just before the stop is placed, or buttered on inside face of stop.

Bevel of Compound Bead—Bead of compound applied so as to have a slanted top surface so that water will drain away from the glass or panel.

Bite—Amount of overlap between the stop and the panel or light.

Buttering—Application of compound to the flat surface of some member before placing the member in position, such as the buttering of a removable stop before fastening the stop in place.

Channel—A three-sided, U-shaped opening in sash or frame to receive light or panel as with sash or frame units in which the light or panel is retained by a removable stop. Contrasted to a rabbet, which is a two-sided, L-shaped opening, as with face glazed window sash.

Channel Depth—The measurement from the bottom of the channel to the top of the stop, or measurement of sight line to base of channel.

Channel Glazing—The sealing of the joints around

lights or panels set in a U-shaped channel employing removable stops.

Channel Width—The measurement between stationary and removable stops in a U-shaped channel at its widest point.

Clips—Wire spring devices to hold glass in rabbetted sash, without stops, and face glazed.

Cohesive Failure—Failure of a compound when placed under a strain, in which, because of insufficient elasticity and elongation to absorb the strain, the compound splits open.

Compound—A formulation of ingredients, usually grouped as vehicle and pigment, to produce some form of sealant such as a glazing compound, caulking compound, elastomer joint sealer, etc.

Compression—Pressure exerted on a compound in a joint, as by placing a light or panel in place against bedding, or placing a stop in position against a bead of compound.

Concave Bead—Bead of compound with a concave exposed surface.

Consistency—Degree of softness or firmness of a compound as supplied in the container, and varying according to method of application, such as gun, knife, tool, etc.

Convex Bead—Bead of compound with a convex exposed surface.

Cover Plate—A plate that is used to cover joining sections, such as mullions.

Curing Agent—One part of a two-part compound which, when added to the base, will cause the base compound to set up by chemical action between the two parts.

Elastomer—An elastic, rubberlike substance, as natural or synthetic rubber.

Elongation—The amount of stretch exhibited by a compound, before rupture.

Exterior Glazed—Glass set from the exterior of the building.

Exterior Stop—The removable molding or bead that holds the light or panel in place when it is on the exterior side of the light or panel, as contrasted to an interior stop located on the interior side of the light.

Face Glazing—On rabbetted sash without stops, the triangular bead of compound applied with glazing knife after bedding, setting and clipping the light in place.

Filler—A material such as cotton mop yarn, cotton wicking, or glass-fiber insulation, which is pressed into an opening or joint so that compound applied to seal the joint will exert pressure and form good contact against the sides of the opening,

Flange (Sash)—The projection around the perimeter of some sash, which extends back into the masonry.

Flush Joint—Compound applied in an opening or joint so that it is even with the top edge of the joint.

Gassing—Addition of a slight amount of white gasoline to an oleoresinous glazing compound by the glazier to soften its consistency.

Gun Consistency—Compound formulated in a degree of softness suitable for application through the nozzle of a caulking gun.

Hand-operated Pressure Gun—A caulking-gun operated by hand and extruding the compound under pressure.

Hand Tool—A tool with a narrow, blunt blade used to press tool consistency compounds into joints and finish off the surface.

Head—In sash, the topmost horizontal member of the sash.

Heel Bead—Compound applied at the base of channel, after setting light or panel, and before the removable stop is installed, its purpose being to prevent leakage past the stop.

Interior Glazed—Glass set from the interior of the building.

Interior Stop—The removable molding or bead that holds the light in place, when it is on the interior side of the light, as contrasted to an exterior stop which is located on the exterior side of a light or panel.

Jambs—In sash, the two vertical members of the perimeter of the sash.

Gasket—Preformed shapes, such as strips, grommets, etc., of rubber or rubberlike composition, used to fill and seal a joint or opening, either alone or in conjunction with a supplemental application of a sealant.

Knife Consistency—Compound formulated in a degree of firmness suitable for application with a glazing knife such as used for face glazing and other sealant applications.

Light—Another term for a pane of glass used in a window.

Manufacturer's Label—Label applied to container of compound by its manufacturer, stating the name and location of the manufacturer of the compound.

Mastic—Descriptive of compounds that remain elastic and pliable with age.

Migration—Spreading or creeping of oil or vehicle from a compound out onto adjacent nonporous surfaces, as contrasted to bleeding which refers to absorption into adjacent porous surfaces.

Mitered Corners—The 45° butted flush joints produced in some sash where vertical jamb members meet horizontal head and sill members.

Mullion—The vertical member that holds together two adjacent units of sash or sections of curtain wall.

Muntin—In sash having horizontal and vertical bars that divide the window into smaller lights of glass, the bars are termed muntins or muntin bars.

Needle Glazing—Application of a small bead of compound at the sight line by means of a gun nozzle about ¼ inch × ⅛ inch in opening size.

Non-drying—Descriptive of a compound that does not form a surface skin after application.

Non-migratory—Freedom from spreading or creeping of oil or vehicle content onto adjacent nonporous surfaces. (See *Migration*.)

Non-oxidizing—Descriptive of a compound that withstands accelerated weathering the equivalent of 30 years of normal weathering without oxidizing.

Non-skinning—Descriptive of a product that does not form a surface skin after application.

Non-staining—Characteristic of a compound which

will not stain a surface by bleeding of migration of its oil or vehicle content.

Oakum—Hemp-like fibers in loose, ropey strands such as used by plumbers for packing pipe bell joints, and formerly used as joint filler before caulking where deep joints were present. Since superseded by materials such as glass-fiber insulation, cotton wicking, mop yarn, etc., because of their greater freedom from ingredients that would stain masonry.

Operator (*Sash Detail*)—Device for opening and closing the ventilator portion of sash.

Peeling—The failure of a compound whereby the skin curls away from the remaining compound under the skin.

Points—Thin, flat, triangular or diamond shaped pieces of steel used to hold glass in wood sash by driving them into the wood rabbet.

Polybutene Base—Compounds made from polybutene polymers.

Polysulfide Base—Compounds made from polysulfide synthetic rubber.

Priming—Sealing of a porous surface so that compound will not stain, lose elasticity, shrink excessively, etc., because of loss of oil or vehicle into the surface. Frequently the sign of inferior formulation when compound requires priming of surface before application.

Pulling Away—Failure of a joint sealant by loss of adhesion to surfaces.

Rabbet—A two-sided L-shaped recess in sash or frame to receive lights or panels. When no stop or molding is added, such rabbets are face glazed. Addition of a removable stop produces a three-sided U-shaped channel.

Racking—Movement and distortion of sash or frames because of lack of rigidity or caused by adjustment of ventilator sections. Puts excessive strain on the sealant and may result in joint failure.

Raking Out—Removal of a portion of the compound already in a joint in order to apply a second and supplemental bead, as in the case of needle glazing.

Sagging—Caused by compounds not capable of supporting their own weight in joint, or by application in joints larger than compound is designed for, or by improper application.

Sash—The frame including muntin bars when used, and including the rabbets to receive lights of glass, either with or without removable stops, and designed either for face glazing or channel glazing.

Sash Member—Any part of the sash such as head, jamb, or sill portions, muntins, etc.

Screw-on Bead or Stop—Stop, molding or bead fastened by machine screws as compared with those that snap into position without additional fastening.

Sealant—Compound used to fill and seal a joint or opening, as contrasted to a sealer which is a liquid used to seal a porous surface.

Sealed Containers—Compound as received from manufacturer and not previously opened.

Setting—Placement of lights or panels in sash or frames. Also action of a compound as it becomes more firm after application.

Shear—Strain put on a compound between two surfaces when there is a slipping movement of the two surfaces, parallel to and in opposite directions along the length of the joint.

Shims—Small blocks of composition, lead, rubber, etc., placed under bottom edge of light or panel to prevent its settling down onto bottom rabbet or channel after setting, thus distorting the sealant.

Shore "A" Hardness—Measure of firmness of a compound by means of a Durometer Hardness Gauge. Range of 20–25 is about the firmness of an art gum eraser. Range of 40–50 is about the firmness of a rubber heel.

Shrinking—Deficiency of a compound, when it occurs excessively, in which the applied bead loses volume and contracts, by evaporation of solvent, or loss of oil or vehicle into a porous surface, etc.

Sight Line—Imaginary line along perimeter of lights or panels corresponding to the top edge of stationary and removable stops, and the line to which sealants contacting the lights or panels are sometimes finished off.

Sill Member—The bottom horizontal bar of a sash or frame next to the sill.

Size of Bead—Normally refers to the width of the bead, but there are many situations in which both the width and depth should be taken into account in design, specification, and application.

Skinning—Formation of a dry film on the surface of compound upon exposure, resulting from oxidation of oil or vehicle near the surface of the compound.

Snap-in Bead or Stop—A stop, molding, or bead that snaps into place without any additional fastening, as compared with a screw-in stop that is fastened by machine screws.

Spacers—Small blocks of composition, wood, rubber, etc., placed on each side of lights or panels to center them in the channel and maintain uniform width of sealant beads. Prevent distorting the sealant excessively.

Spacer Shims—Devices that are U-shaped in cross section and an inch or more in length, placed on the edges of lights or panels to serve both as shims to keep the lights or panels centered in the sash or frames, and as spacers to keep the lights or panels centered in the channels and maintain uniform width of sealant beads. Usually made of rubber.

Spalling—Being forced off in pieces, as from some pressure underneath, such as a bead of compound forced off by freezing water under the bead, masonry forced off by freezing of water trapped in porous surfaces, etc.

Staff Mold—Wood molding fastened around perimeter of wood window frame or casing to cover opening between causing or frame and adjoining masonry.

Staining—Discoloration of a porous surface that has absorbed oil or vehicle from a compound in contact with the surface.

Stain Test—A laboratory test usually performed on filter paper to determine and measure the degree to which a compound will darken or discolor porous surfaces by bleeding.

Stationary Stop—The permanent stop or lip of a rabbet on the side away from the side on which lights or panels are set.

Stop—Either the stationary lip at the back of a rabbet, or the removable molding at the front of the rabbet, either or both serving to hold light or panel in sash or frame, with the help of spacers.

Stain Test—A laboratory test to measure the amount of elasticity or stretch a compound exhibits before failure when the two sides of a joint in which the compound is applied are pulled apart.

Striking Off—The operation of smoothing off excess compound at sight line when applying compound around lights or panels.

Tolerance of Glass—The plus or minus variation in dimensions, thickness, and contour of glass.

Tolerance of Sash—The plus or minus variation in dimensions of sash compared with drafting board measurements.

Tool Consistency (*See Consistency.*)

Tooling—Operation of pressing in and stroking a compound in a joint in order to press compound against sides of joint and secure good adhesion. Also the finishing off of the surface of a compound in a joint so that it is flush with the surface. A narrow, blunt bladed tool is used for this purpose.

Tracery—In setting stained-glass windows, tracery is an interlacing pattern of stone metal or wood into which the leaded panes or panels of stained glass are sometimes set.

Uniform Bead—Compound applied in a joint, with uniform width and appearance.

United Inches—Length plus width of a light of glass.

Vegetable Oil Base—Formulated with a vehicle of vegetable oils usually processed with resins by application of heat.

Vehicle—The liquid portion of a compound.

Ventilator—In some sash, the movable portion which can be opened and closed.

Weeping—Failure of a compound to support its own weight in a joint, but less pronounced than sagging.

Wrinkling—The formation of wrinkles in the skin of a compound during the formation of its surface skin by oxidation after application.

APPENDIX

Proposed Specification for Elastomeric Sealing Compounds (One- and Two-component) For Caulking, Sealing, and Glazing in Building Construction

1. Scope

1.1. This specification covers the properties of elastomeric (rubber like) sealing compounds, including curing agents in the case of two-component products, for sealing, caulking or glazing application in buildings and other types of construction. Use of a primer under certain conditions, when recommended by the manufacturer, is acceptable. Where a primer is recommended by a manufacturer for a specific surface, all tests on that surface shall include a primer.

2. Applicable Specifications, Standards, and Other Publications

2.1 Specifications and Standards. The following specifications and standards of the issues in effect on date of invitation for bids, form a part of this specification.

Federal Test Standard #141—Methods 1011 and 1021 and /or 1031.

Federal Test Method for Rubber, No. 601, Method 3021.

Federal Specification SS-R-406, Method 223.11, paragraphs 7.1 and 7.2.

ASTM Standard D-529-59T, section 2.

ASTM Standard D-1191-52T, paragraph 6(a).

American Standard Specification A 116. 1-1960, paragraph 7.4.4.4.

3. Requirements

3.1 Material. The sealing compound shall be furnished as single-component or two-component product. The base polymers, fillers and other components shall be optional with the supplier, but shall be suitable for the application intended. They shall be homogeneous as supplied, or as mixed in the case of two-component products, and suitable for hand gun operation or for pressure extrusion as recommended by the manufacturer. The procedures and suggested equipment for mixing two-component products shall be included in the manufacturers instructions. The compound when completely cured shall form an elastomeric, rubberlike solid capable of maintaining a seal against water, wind and dirt.

3.2 Classes. The sealing compound shall be available in the following classes:

3.2.1 Class A (*One-component, Self-sealing or Light Skinning, Solvent Release Type*). The compound shall be so formulated that it will penetrate through dusty or moist surfaces and attain satisfactory adhesion to the substrate to which it is being applied. If for any reason, such as excessive movement of the joint, the sealer should lose adhesion, it shall have the ability to readhere to the sides of the joint when such joint assumes its normal position. It shall be of such consistency that permits application to vertical or horizontal joints in a vertical plane without sagging or weeping at temperatures between 40 and 122°F. It shall develop elastomeric characteristics by loss of solvent.

3.2.2 Class B (*One-component, Non-self-sealing, Skinning, Solvent Release Type*). The compound shall have the same basic properties as the Class A product except that it is not required to possess self-sealing properties, that is, it would not be expected to obtain a bond through a film of dust or moisture or to readhere should its original bond be broken. It shall be of such a consistency that permits application to vertical or horizontal joints in a vertical plane without sagging or weeping at temperatures between 40 and 122°F.

3.2.3 Class C (*One-component, Chemical Curing Type*). The compound shall be so formulated that it will develop elastomeric characteristics by interaction of components within the base compound and will permit application to vertical or horizontal joints in a vertical plane without sagging or weeping at temperatures between 40 and 122°F.

3.2.4 Class D (Two-component, Chemical Curing, Self-leveling Type). The compound shall be formulated consisting of two separate portions, a base compound and a curing agent, which, when intimately mixed together just prior to application, will develop elastomeric characteristics by chemical reaction between the two components. It shall be of such a consistency that when properly mixed it has sufficient flow to give a smooth, level surface when applied in a horizontal joint in a horizontal plane at temperatures between 40 and 122°F.

3.2.5 Class E (Two-component, Chemical Curing, Non-sag Type). The compound shall be so formulated to have the same basic properties as the Class D product except to permit application in vertical or horizontal joints in a vertical plane without sagging or weeping at temperatures between 40 and 122°F.

3.3 Stability. The compound, furnished as one or two component in the original unopened container, or containers, shall be stable for at least 6 months from the time of delivery, when stored at a temperature not exceeding 80°F. When tested at the end of 6 months after time of delivery, the compound shall meet the requirements herein specified.

3.4 Toxicity. Under normal application conditions and adequate ventilation, the compound shall not be considered toxic.

3.5 Detail Requirements. *3.5.1 Color.* The color of the sealing compound, after curing 14 days in air at 73.4± 2°F, shall be any specific color agreed upon by the purchaser and the supplier provided formulation of such color does not adversely affect the physical properties of the compound.

3.5.2 Rheological Properties. 3.5.2.1 Class D (Self-leveling) Compound. The flow of a properly prepared Class D compound shall be such that when tested as prescribed in section 4.3.3.1, it shall exhibit a smooth level surface.

3.5.2.2 Classes A, B, C and E (Non-sag) Compounds. The flow of a properly prepared non-sag compound shall be such that when tested as prescribed in section 4.3.3.2, it shall not sag or flow more than 3/16 inch in vertical displacement.

3.5.3. Application Life or Extrudability*. 3.5.3.1 Class D (Two-component, Self-leveling) Compound. The properly conditioned and mixed compound, three (3) hours after mixing, shall have an extrusion rate of 4 fluid ounces in not over 30 seconds when tested as prescribed in section 4.3.4.1.

3.5.3.2 Class E (Two-component, Non-sag) Compound. The properly conditioned and mixed compound, three (3) hours after mixing, shall have an extrusion rate of 4 fluid ounces in not over 1 minute when tested as prescribed in section 4.3.4.2.

*Where recommended by the supplier it shall be permissible to warm the compound prior to application in the field. Procedure and equipment shall be included in the suppliers instructions.

3.5.3.3. Classes A, B, and C (One-component) Compounds. The properly conditioned compound shall have an extrusion rate of 4 fluid ounces in not over 1 minute when tested as prescribed in section 4.3.4.3.

3.5.4 Hardness. A compound when properly cured, as recommended by the supplier, shall show a hardness reading of not less than 20 and not more than 50 when tested for Shore "A" Hardness (Shore Durometer—instantaneous method) as prescribed in section 4.3.5

3.5.5 Tack-free Time. The compound when properly applied, as either a one- or a two-component product, shall cure to a tack-free condition in not more than 72 hours from the time of application, when tested as prescribed in paragraph 4.3.6.

3.5.6 Staining and Color Change. (1) (2) The compound when properly applied, as either a one or a two-component product, shall not cause any visible stain on the top surface of a white cement mortar base, when tested as prescribed in section 4.3.7. The compound itself shall not show a degree of color change that is unacceptable to the purchaser, when tested as prescribed in section 4.3.7.

(1) Compounds that are to be used exclusively for metal or glass or both, without any contact whatsoever to porous masonry such as concrete, brick, stone, etc., need not be refected because of staining. However, the complete staining and color change test shall be performed as prescribed and the results included in the test report.

(2) Extremely slight tan or gray stains shall not be regarded as cause for failure.

3.5.7 Durability (Bond Cohesion). When tested as prescribed in section 4.3.8, the total loss in bond area (or cohesion) among the three specimens tested (for each type of accessory material) shall be less than 2 square inches after the completion of 3 test cycles. The losses in area shall be estimated to the nearest 0.1 square inch.

3.5.8 Shrinkage. The compound when tested as prescribed in section 4.3.9 shall have a shrinkage of not over 15 per cent.

3.5.9 Resistance to Sun Lamp Exposure. The compound when tested as prescribed in section 4.3.10 shall show no loss of adhesion.

3.5.10 Dynamic Extension and Compressibility. The compound when tested as prescribed in section 4.3.11 shall show no evidence of adhesive failure or cohesive failure more than $1/32$ inch deep in the body of the bead.

3.5.11 Oil Migration. The compound when tested as prescribed in section 4.3.12 shall show a stain index of not over 6.

3.5.12 Self-sealing (Class A Type Only). The compound when tested as prescribed in section 4.3.13 shall show satisfactory adhesion to the metal plate.

4. Sampling, Inspection and Test Procedures

4.1. The supplier is responsible for the performance of all inspection requirements as specified herein. Except as otherwise specified, the supplier may utilize his own or any other inspection facilities or services acceptable to the government. Inspection records of the examination and tests shall be kept complete and available to the government as specified in the contract or order. The government reserves the right to perform any of the inspections set forth in the specification where such inspections are deemed necessary to assure that supplies and services conform to prescribed requirements.

4.2. Sampling and inspection should be in accordance with Methods 1011 and 1021 and/or 1031 of Federal Test Standard No. 141, as applicable.

4.3 *Laboratory Tests.* *4.3.1 Standard Conditions for Laboratory Tests.* The standard conditions of temperature and relative humidity referred to in the following sections are defined as 73.4± 2°F and 50± 10 per cent, respectively.

4.3.2 Curing of Test Specimens. Where laboratory test procedures require testing of a cured bead of compound, the curing schedule shall be as recommended by the supplier, however, such curing schedule shall not exceed 14 days.

4.3.3 Rheological Properties. 4.3.3.1. Class D (Self-leveling or Flow Compound). Accessory material required for this test is one aluminum channel (approximately #16 gauge), ¾ inch wide, ½ inch deep, 6 inches long and closed at both ends Figure 10A-1a.

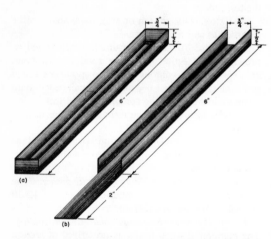

FIG. 10A-1. Channels used or determing rheological properties, (a) for self leveling or flow type compound (class A), (b) for non-sag type compound (class B)

The channel shall be cleaned with a detergent solution followed by a cleaning with methyl ethyl ketone or similar solvent. Before preparing the test assembly, 100 grams of base compound and the appropriate amount of curing agent shall be conditioned at 40 ± 2°F for 16 to 24 hours. The metal channel shall also be conditioned at 40 ± 2°F for 1 to 2 hours. At the end of the required conditioning period, the base compound and curing agent shall be removed from the conditioning chamber and hand mixed for

5 minutes. The mixed compound shall be returned to the chamber at 40 ± 2°F for 30 minutes after which it shall be poured into the conditioned channel, held horizontally at 40 ± 2°F and then maintained for 1 hour. At the end of this period, the compound shall be examined for flow properties.

4.3.3.2. Classes A, B, C and E (Non-sag) Compounds. Accessory materials required for this test are two aluminum channels (approximately #16 gauge) with inside dimensions ¾ inch wide, ½ inch deep, and 6 inches long with the top end open and the back surface extended 2 inches (Figure 10A-1b). Before preparing the test assemblies, 200 grams of one-component compound, or in the case of two-component compounds, 200 grams of the base compound and the appropriate amount of curing agent, shall be exposed at standard conditions for 16 to 24 hours and the two channels shall be exposed for 1 hour, one at 40 ± 2°F and the other at 122 ± 2°F. At the end of the conditioning period, two-component products shall be hand mixed for 5 minutes. One-component products require no mixing. The conditioned channels shall be removed from their respective conditioning chambers and both filled by spatula or gun, with either one-component product directly from its container or mixed two-component compound within 12 minutes. The filled channels shall then be returned to their respective conditioning chambers and set in a vertical position with the 2-inch extension in the base position. At the end of 4 hours, the channels shall be removed from the chambers and the sag of the compound at the lower ends, measured to the nearest ¹⁄₁₆ inch.

4.3.4 Application Life or Extrudability. 4.3.4.1. Class D (Two-component, Flow Type) Compound, Only. Accessory materials required are a Semco 6 ounce capacity air-powered caulking gun (or equivalent) with 6-ounce cartridge, 50-psi air line, gill (4-ounce) capacity can, and a stopwatch. The test shall be performed on the two components that have been conditioned at least 16 hours at standard conditions. At the end of the conditioning period, about 250 grams of base compound with appropriate amount of curing agent shall be mixed for 5 minutes and a sufficient amount placed into a 6-ounce cartridge, to fill the cartridge. The filled cartridge (with no nozzle added) and gun shall be set aside at standard conditions for 3 hours. At the end of 3 hours, the compound shall be gunned at 50-psi pressure into an empty gill (4-ounce) capacity can with friction rim previously removed. A stop watch shall be used to time the extrusion.

The compound meets the requirement for 3 hours application life if the time required to extrude 4 fluid ounces does not exceed 30 seconds.

4.3.4.2. Class E (Two-component, Non-sag Type) Compound, Only. The test procedure is the same as described under paragraph 4.3.4.1. The compound meets the requirements for 3 hours application if the time required to extrude 4 fluid ounces does not exceed 1 minute.

4.3.4.3. Classes A, B, and C (One-component) Compounds. The test procedure is the same as described under paragraph 4.3.4.1, except that single-component products require no mixing prior to testing. The three (3) hour hold period may also be eliminated. The compound meets the requirement for extrudability if the time required to extrude 4 fluid ounces does not exceed 1 minute.

NOTE: In cases where it is more convenient to determine the amount of compound extruded on a weight basis rather than a volume basis, or due to its physical properties it is difficult to fill the 4-ounce (fluid) container without voids or air pockets, convert 4 ounces (fluid) to weight by use of a predetermined specific gravity or weight per gallon and perform the determination on a weight basis.

4.3.5 Hardness. Accessory materials required are (1) Shore Durometer (Model "A"); (2) polyethylene form (or similar device) with inside dimensions of $4 \times 1\frac{1}{2} \times \frac{1}{4}$ inch; (3) aluminum plate, 3×6 inches (16 to 24 gauge).

The instrument used to measure hardness shall be the Shore Durometer (Model "A"), described in Federal Test Method for Rubber, No. 601, Method 3021. All readings shall be taken by the instantaneous method and the procedure carried out at standard conditions.

Condition approximately 200 grams of one-component compound—or in the case of two-component compounds, 200 grams of base compound and the appropriate amount of curing agent, at standard conditions for 16 to 24 hours. At the end of the conditioning period, two-component products shall be hand mixed for 5 minutes. One-component products require no mixing. Place portions of the compound being tested into two polyethylene forms with inside dimensions of $4 \times 1\frac{1}{2} \times \frac{1}{4}$ inch previously centered on a 3×6 inch aluminum plate. *Condition or cure the specimens as recommended by the supplier.* After the conditioning period, by means of a sharp knife or razor blade, cut along the inside edges of the form down to the metal plate and lift off the form carefully and store in the laboratory at standard conditions for 16 to 24 hours. Hardness measurements shall be made with the Shore Durometer, Model "A," at standard conditions. A total of three readings shall be taken on the two specimens, and the average of the 6 readings regarded as the accepted value.

4.3.6 Tack-free Time. Accessory materials required are (1) brass weight 30 grams, approximately $1\frac{5}{8} \times 1 \times \frac{1}{8}$ inch; (2) polyethylene strip approximately $4 \times 1 \times 0.004 \pm 0.002$ inch, polyethylene form same as that used for hardness test or any suitable form with the same dimensions. After exposing about 100 grams of single-component compound, or in the case of two-component compound, about 100 grams of base compound and the appropriate amount of curing agent—for 16 to 24 hours at standard conditions, mix the two-component compound for 5 minutes. One-component compound does not require mixing. Place a portion of the compound being tested into the form and strike off flat with a spatula. The specimen shall be exposed in air for 72 hours at standard conditions.

At the end of the applicable tack-free time (72 hours), the polyethylene film shall be pressed on to the top surface of the compound for 30 seconds with the brass weight (30 grams). The film shall then be progressively withdrawn at right angles to the compound. The sample meets the requirement for tack-free time if the film pulls off without any compound adhering to it.

4.3.7 Staining and Color Change. Accessory materials required are (1) white portland cement; (2) hydrated lime; (3) graded white Ottawa sand; (4) two aluminum plates $6 \times 2\frac{3}{4}$ inches, approximately #16 gauge; (5) rectangular brass frame, $\frac{1}{4}$ inch thick with inside opening slightly larger than aluminum plate. Test shall be made in laboratory at standard conditions, or as specified.

The test specimen shall consist of a test slab of a mortar mix upon which is placed either a one-component compound as furnished in its container or a properly mixed two-component compound. The mortar mix shall be prepared by combining 1 part white portland cement, $\frac{1}{2}$ part hydrated lime, and 3 parts graded Ottawa sand (by volume) with sufficient water to form a smooth workable paste. The mixture should be spread over the entire surface of an aluminum plate (about #16 gauge) $6 \times 2\frac{3}{4}$ inches to a depth of about $\frac{1}{4}$ inch and struck off flat with a spatula. The mix is spread with the aid of a rectangular brass frame, $\frac{1}{4}$ inch thick with an opening slightly larger than the aluminum plate. The mortar is allowed to cure in air for 4 hours at standard conditions. At the end of the curing period, about 30 grams of one-component compound or properly mixed two-component product (unopened sample of one-component or base compound and curing agent having previously been held at standard conditions for 16 to 24 hours) shall be spread over the mortar leaving a $\frac{1}{2}$-inch margin of mortar uncovered by the sealant. Two such specimens shall be prepared.

After both specimens have been exposed in air for 16 to 24 hours at standard conditions, one specimen shall be placed on the drum of an accelerated weathering machine (single or double arc, with 51-9 water cycle) for 200 hours.* The second specimen shall be exposed in the laboratory at standard conditions for 14 consecutive days and shall be immersed in distilled water for 1 minute once a day (working days only). At the end of the exposure periods, both specimens shall be examined for color changes and stains. (Note: Where a primer is submitted with the sample, the primer shall be applied to half the surface of the mortar of each specimen before application of the compound.)

---

*Described in ASTM D-529-59T, section 2. Specimen temperature shall be $140 \pm 5°F$ and water spray temperature, $75 \times 4°F$.

4.3.8 Durability (*Bond Cohesion*). 4.3.8.1. Extension Machine. The machine used in this test shall be so designed that the test specimen while at a temperature of $0 \pm$ 2°F can be extended to 150 per cent (to $\frac{9}{16}$ inch) of its original depth ($\frac{3}{8}$ inch) at a uniform rate of $\frac{1}{8}$ inch per hour. The machine shall be similar in design to the one described in Federal Specification

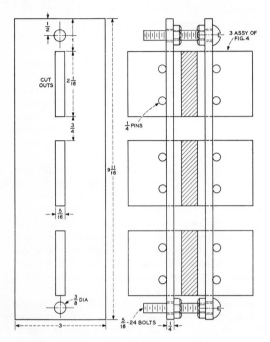

FIG. 10A-2. Alternate assembly for testing adhesive strength at low temperatures.

SS-R-406, Method 223.11, paragraph 7.1 or in ASTM Standard D1191-52T, paragraph 6(a).

Where a constant speed tester is not available, it shall be permissible to use extension equipment similar to that described in American Standard Specification for Polysulfide Base Sealing Compounds for the Building Trade, A 116, 1, 1960, paragraph 7.4.4.4, Adhesive Strength after Cycling at −20°F and 77°F (Figure 10A-2). When such alternate equipment is used it shall be so stated in reporting results. Elongation shall be in increments of $\frac{1}{32}$ inch every 15 minutes.

4.3.8.2. Accessory Materials. The accessory test blocks used in the Durability test shall be (a) portland cement mortar; (2) plate glass; (3) aluminum alloy. (Note: Additional accessory materials such as brick, wood, stainless steel, anodized aluminum, etc., may be specified for use in the Durability test at the request of the purchaser.)

4.3.8.2.1 Mortar blocks. Cement mortar blocks, $1 \times 2 \times 3$ inches shall be prepared as prescribed in Federal Specification SS-R-406, Method 223.11, paragraph 7.2, or in ASTM Standard D1191-52T, paragraph 6(a), except that each block shall be surfaced by wet grinding with No. 80 silicon carbide or

aluminum oxide abrasive grain. Type I portland cement shall be used rather than Type III specified in the ASTM test.

4.3.8.2.2 Plate glass. Glass accessory plates shall be $3 \times 2 \times \frac{1}{4}$ inch plate glass. Prior to use, the plates shall be washed with a detergent solution, rinsed with clear water, and finally cleaned with methyl ethyl ketone solvent and wiped dry.

4.3.8.2.3 Aluminum. The aluminum plates shall be $3 \times 2 \times$ approximately $\frac{3}{16}$ inch aluminum alloy 5052-H34, or any noncoated aluminum alloy used in the building trade. Prior to use, the plates shall be washed with a detergent solution, rinsed with clear water and finally cleaned with methyl ethyl ketone solvent and wiped dry.

4.3.8.3 Preparation of Test Specimens. Three test specimens shall be prepared for each accessory material that is used with the sample under test. After conditioning the sample for 16 to 24 hours at standard conditions, either 200 grams of one-component compound or 200 grams of base compound and appropriate amount of curing agent mixed for 5 minutes shall then be applied in a bead $\frac{3}{8} \times 1 \times 2$ inches between parallel 3×2 inch faces of two similar accessory blocks or plates as shown (Figure 10A-3a, b, c). Metal spacer bars $\frac{3}{8} \times \frac{1}{2} \times \frac{1}{2}$ inch shall be used to give the proper size of bead (Figure 10A-3d). Paraffin, mold release agent, or polyethylene sealed to the inside surfaces of the spacers shall be used to prevent adhesion. Heavy rubber bands or

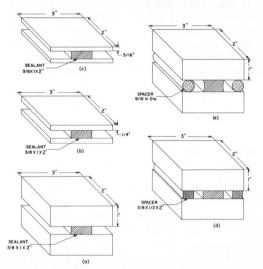

FIG. 10A-3. Test specimens used in durability test (a) concrete, (b) plate glass, (c) aluminum alloy, (d) specimen with $\frac{3}{8}$ inch spacers (e) specimen with $\frac{9}{16}$ inch spacers after extension.

clamps shall be used to hold the test assembly together before and after filling with compound. In the case of a flow-type compound, masking tape or melted paraffin may be used to retain the compound in place during the curing period.

The test assemblies shall be cured as recommended by the supplier prior to further testing. (Note: Porous test blocks—concrete, stone, etc.—shall be primed with the suppliers recommended primer before application of the compound, only when the use of such a primer is specified by the seller and agreed upon by the purchaser. In such cases, a duplicate set of specimens shall be tested without the primer.)

4.3.8.4 Cycling Procedure. Following the curing period as recommended by the supplier, the spacers shall be separated from the compound and the specimens put through the following cycle three times.

(a) Specimens (with spacers between blocks but not in contact with compound) shall be heated for 24 hours in an oven at 158 ± 2°F.

(b) Specimens shall be allowed to cool to room temperature and then immersed in distilled water (without spacers) at 73.4 ± 2°F for 7 hours.

(c) Specimens shall be surface dried and placed in a cold box held at 0 ± 2°F for not less than 8 hours.

(d) Specimens shall be placed (frozen) in the grips of the extension machine and extended to 150 per cent of the original width (to $\frac{9}{16}$ inch) at 0 ± 2°F as described in paragraph 4.3.8.1.

(e) Specimens shall be held in the stretched position with $\frac{9}{16}$-inch diameter spacers for 3 hours at standard conditions. (At this stage of the treatment, the specimens shall be examined for bond and cohesion breaks. Failures shall be measured to the closest 0.1 inch (see Figure 10A-3).

(f) To start the second cycle the specimens shall be placed with the original $\frac{3}{8}$-inch spacers, in the oven at 158 ± 2°F, so that the 2 × 3 inch face of each specimen rests on the oven shelf. (Note: The joint usually recovers to the original $\frac{3}{8}$-inch width. If necessary, a small weight (about 2 pounds) may be placed on the upper block to hasten recovery of the joint.)

4.3.9 Shrinkage. Accessory materials required are (1) a brass ring (metal about $\frac{1}{32}$ inch thick) approximately $2\frac{5}{8}$-inch diameter and $\frac{1}{2}$ inch deep, (2) two ground glass cover plates 3-inch diameter, (3) a slab of limestone, $3\frac{1}{2}$ inches square by $\frac{3}{4}$ inch thick, and (4) a leveling tool for spreading the compound. One surface of each cover plate and both edges of the ring shall be ground with a fine abrasive on a ground glass surface. The volume, V, of the ring is determined by weighing the ring and two ground glass cover plates to the nearest 0.01 gram. The ring is then centered on one plate and poured full of water at a temperature of 73.4 ± 2°F and covered with the second glass plate adding or removing water with a dropper until there are no air bubbles when the cover plate is centered on the ring. Overflow water or moisture on the outside of the ring or cover plates is removed and the weight of the water required to fill the ring is obtained by weight difference. In this test test, it is sufficiently accurate to consider 1 gram of water as 1 ml volume; therefore, the volume of ring, V, is recorded as the difference between the second and first weights.

The shrinkage of the compound is determined as follows: Weigh the slab of limestone, the brass ring, and a ground glass cover plate to the closest 0.01 gram and record the combined weight as W_1. Then center the ring on the limestone slab and spread a $\frac{1}{4}$-inch layer of the compound on the stone inside the ring, leveling with the tool to form good contact with ring and stone. The combined weight of the slab, ring, compound, and cover plate, W_2, is then determined to the nearest 0.01 gram. The portion of the ring above the compound is then filled with water at 73.4 ± 2°F so that no air bubbles are present when the cover plate is in position and the total weight, W_3, is determined. The volume of the compound is $V_c = V - (W_3 - W_2)$. The water is then poured off and the sample exposed for 15 days at standard conditions. After which determine the weights W_2^1 and W_3^1 corresponding to W_2 and W_3. The shrinkage is computed by the formula:

$$S = \frac{(W_3^1 - W_2^1) - (W_3 - W_2)\,100}{V_c}$$

4.3.10 Resistance to Sunlamp Exposure. Accessory materials required are (1) A piece of plate glass 4 × 7 inches; (2) 4 × 6 inch Grade A airplane fabric, 4.28 ounces per square yard, 80/84 thread count, available at Wellington Sears, 12 South 12 Street, Philadelphia, Pennsylvania; and (3) a General Electric RS Sunlamp. The compound to be tested shall be conditioned for 16 to 24 hours at standard conditions, 100 grams of one-component compound or 100 grams of base compound and the appropriate amount of curing agent. The two-component product shall be hand mixed for 5 minutes. One-component compounds do not require mixing. The plate glass panel previously washed with a detergent solution, rinsed with clear water, and finally cleaned with methyl ethyl ketone is coated with a $\frac{1}{8}$-inch layer of the compound. Then airplane fabric, approximately 4 × 6 inches is smeared with the compound and forced into the cloth using a spatula. Sufficient strike through should result so that there is discoloration on the reverse side of the fabric. The impregnated fabric is then laid over the covered surface without entrapping air. Then, the assembly is placed between spacer bars, and the top surface of the fabric is compressed so that the thickness of the compound between the fabric and glass is $\frac{1}{16}$ inch. The assembly is allowed to cure for 3 days at standard conditions. At the end of this cure period, the glass side of the assembly shall be exposed to ultraviolet radiation from a General Electric RS Sunlamp at a distance of 12 inches from the lamp. The sunlamp strength during the test shall be between 15 and 30 E-vitons per square centimeter, when tested with a General Electric RS Sunlamp tester. The air temperature at the surface of the test specimen shall not exceed 150°F during the exposure period. Exposure period shall be for 7 days. Allow the specimen to condition at standard conditions for a minimum of 2 hours. The surface of the

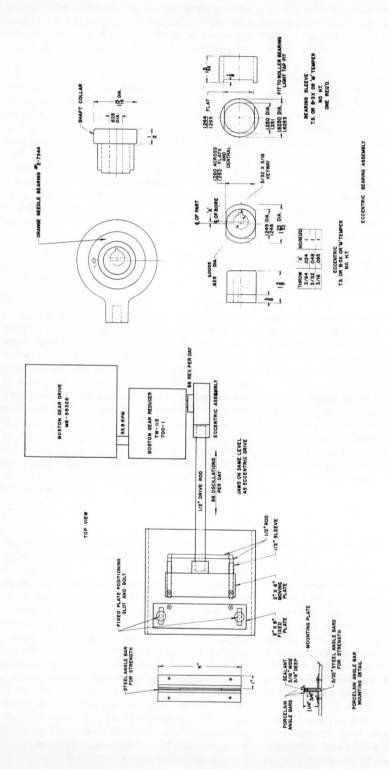

Fig. 10A-4 Apparatus for dynamic extension and compressability.

fabric is cut through to the base surface with a sharp razor blade on lines 1 inch apart. Undercut 1 inch of compound clean from the glass, and peel the compound and cloth from the glass at an angle of 180° at a rate of 2 inches per minute. Failure shall be entirely cohesive.

4.3.11 Dynamic Extension and Compressibility. Accessory materials required for this test are (1) aluminum panel $6 \times 4 \times \frac{1}{16}$ inch, (2) two porcelain enamel coated angle bars, 6 inches long by $1\frac{1}{4}$ inch high, with a 1-inch base leg, all projections being $\frac{1}{16}$ inch thich. (Davidson Porcelain Enamel Company); (3) General Electric RS Sunlamp; and (4) a flexing machine which will supply extension and compression at a rate of 86 cycles per 24 hour period (Figure 10A-4). The compound to be tested, either 100 grams of single-component compound or 100 grams of base compound and appropriate amount of curing agent are conditioned for 16 to 24 hours at standard conditions. The two-component compound shall be hand mixed for 5 minutes. The two porcelain enamel bars are mounted $\frac{3}{16}$ inch apart on the aluminum panel using two bolts on 5-inch centers on the base of each bar to hold the bars to the aluminum mounting plate. A piece of closed cell backing cut to dimensions of $\frac{3}{16} \times \frac{3}{4} \times 6$ inches is placed in the bottom of the joint formed by the two bars leaving a $\frac{3}{16}$ inch wide $\times \frac{1}{2}$ inch deep $\times 6$ inch pocket between the bars for application of the compound. Apply the compound to be tested to the joint between the porcelain bars by means of a spatula making sure that no air is entrapped. Wipe the joint with a rag or tissue soaked with a solvent sush as xylol or toluol to leave a smooth, level surface. Cure the specimen for 3 days at standard conditions. Then condition for an additional 15 days as follows: Place the specimen in a pan or similar receptacle that will hold water and add water until the surface of the compound is covered by a $\frac{1}{16}$ inch layer. Mount a General Electric RS Sunlamp at a distance of 8 inches from the surface of the assembly. Each 24 hours, add sufficient water to again cover the assembly with $\frac{1}{16}$ inch of water. At the end of the conditioning period, carefully remove the aluminum mounting plate and mount the assembly in the flexing machine. The machine shall be fitted with a $\frac{3}{32}$-inch eccentric and the machine set so that the bead is stretched to $\frac{9}{32}$ inch and compressed back to $\frac{3}{16}$ inch and operated in this manner for 24 hours. Then replace the $\frac{3}{32}$-inch eccentric with a $\frac{3}{16}$-inch eccentric and set the machine so that the compound in the joint extends and compresses between $\frac{3}{16}$ and $\frac{3}{8}$ inch for another 24 hours. Observe for evidence of adhesive failure or cohesive failure more than $\frac{1}{32}$-inch depth in the body of the compound.

4.3.12 Oil Migration. Accessory materials required for this test are (1) a $\frac{3}{4}$-inch inside diameter brass ring, $\frac{3}{4}$ inch high, approximately $\frac{1}{8}$-inch wall thickness with the wall at one end beveled to minimum diameter; (2) ten filter papers, No. 1 Whatman, 9-cm diameter; (3) a square inch piece of aluminum foil or Saran Wrap; and (4) a 300-gram weight (may

be obtained by nearly filling a $\frac{1}{2}$-pint can with water). The compound to be tested, either 50 grams of single-component compound or in the case of two-component compound, 50 grams of base compound and appropriate amount of curing agent, shall be conditioned for 16 to 24 hours at standard conditions. The two-component product shall be hand mixed for 5 minutes. Sufficient filter paper shall be dried for a minimum of 5 hours in an oven maintained at 215 to 240°F. From the oven, immediately place the filter paper in a desiccator. When the test is ready to proceed, remove 10 filter papers and staple them together. Place the brass ring centrally on top of filter papers, beveled edge in contact with the paper. Carefully fill the ring with the compound, taking care to incorporate as little air as possible. Place the aluminum foil or Saran Wrap on top of the filled ring and the 300-gram weight on top of that. Allow to cure at standard conditions for 72 hours. Then slide a thin spatula or knife under the brass ring and remove the ring and contents from the filter papers. Hold the top filter paper up to a light with a glass panel under it. Mark with a pencil point the diameters of maximum and minimum stain on the top side of the filter paper. Measure in millimeters this maximum and minimum stain marked with a pencil. Subtract 19 from the maximum and minimum diameters and divide by two. Record the average of these results as "Width of Stain." Examine the individual papers for oil stain by holding them up to light. Record the number of papers showing any evidence of oil staining as "Number of Papers Stained." The sum of "Width of Stain" and "Number of Papers Stained" shall be reported as "Stain Index."

4.3.13 Self-sealing (Class A Type Only). Accessory materials required are; (1) a metal plate about 6×6 inches; (2) fine particle size calcium carbonate pigment ("Atomite"* or equal); (3) a brass ring of $\frac{3}{4}$-inch inside diameter, $\frac{3}{4}$ inch high, approximately $\frac{1}{8}$-inch wall thickness with the wall at one end beveled to a minimum diameter (same as for the Stain test, paragraph 4.3.12); and (4) a roll-type doctor blade, $\frac{3}{4}$-inch diameter, 6 inches long with the center 4 inches machined out to cast a film of 0.003 $\pm$ 0.005 inch.

Clean the aluminum plate with a detergent solution, rinse with clear water and finally clean with methyl ethyl ketone. Approximately 25 grams of "Atomite" (or equal) are mixed with enough water to form a paint consistency mix. With a spatula, spread about a $\frac{1}{8}$-inch layer of the pigment-water mix about 3 inches wide on the aluminum panel. Using the doctor blade, roll out a film of the mix about 3×3 inches. Transfer the panel to an oven controlled at 215 to 240°F and allow to remain for 2 hours. Remove the panel from the oven, and condition at standard conditions for a minimum of one hour. Set the brass ring on the dried pigment-coated portion of the metal panel. The compound to be tested, previously conditioned for

*Thompson-Weinman Company.

16 to 24 hours at standard conditions, shall be carefully filled level into the brass ring with a spatula so as not to introduce air pockets. Allow the application to cure for 24 hours at standard conditions. After the cure period, lift the filled ring from the panel using the fingers and pulling in a vertical direction without any twisting motion. The compound being tested shall adhere to not less than 75 per cent of the contact area. With a fingernail or spatula, check the adhesion of the compound through to the metal plate. The compound shall adhere tenaciously and shall not be easily pulled clean from the metal.

11 ADHESIVES IN BUILDING*

GEORGE J. SCHULTE

Adhesives, Coatings and Sealers Division
Minnesota Mining and Manufacturing Company
St. Paul, Minnesota

ADHESIVES FOR BONDING PLASTIC BUILDING MATERIALS

This chapter covers the majority of adhesives that are used by the building trades industry to bond plastic materials. New technology is constantly being developed which will add adhesives and applications to this list. In many instances, these changes are slow; consequently most of the building adhesives mentioned will be in use for some years.

Plastic Wall Coverings

Plastic Tile Adhesives. Plastic wall tile is usually made from polystyrene. Several other types of plastic tile such as melamine have been marketed but have not attained popularity. Adhesives may be:

(a) Oil-resin,
(b) Resin,
(c) Rubber base with water vehicle.

There have been many varieties of oil-resin type mastics used for plastic tile. Many have been satisfactory, but a few have failed to perform well. A satisfactory plastic tile adhesive must have excellent adhesion to the tile and remain permanently soft or plastic. The U.S. Department of Commerce Commercial Standard for both plastic and metal tile adhesives is No. 168-50.

Application. Generally, the floating method is used to apply the adhesive directly to the wall with a notched trowel having ⅛-inch "V" notches, ⅛ inch apart. Many adhesive manufacturers recommend that the wall be primed with a special primer. The tile is left ungrouted, or it may be grouted with the tile adhesive itself. When cleaning the adhesive from the tile, care must be taken to avoid using a solvent that will attack the tile. Alcohol or a special tile cleaner is usually satisfactory.

The resin-type mastics such as the polyvinyl acetates are applied similarly; they may have a shorter bonding time. These types can usually be washed off with water. Some of these adhesives are unsuitable for application in areas which will be exposed to moisture because of their water sensitivity. The rubber-base type mastics have similar application properties.

Plastic Yard Goods Wall Covering Adhesives. Several types of plastic wall coverings in roll or sheet form are in use today. Flexible vinyl plastic coverings in rolls may be "supported" with a paper or fabric backing, or they may be unsupported, in which case the vinyl itself is the bonding surface on the back side. Rigid or decorative plastic laminate (melamine-phenolic plastic) is being used in tile as well as in sheet form for walls.

*Much of the information in this chapter is taken from the chapter "Adhesives in the Building Industry," by George J. Schulte in "Handbook of Adhesives," I. Skeist, Editor, New York, Reinhold Publishing Corp., 1962.

Another type (polyester plastic) is semi-flexible and comes in rolls. Adhesives are:

(a) Starch wallpaper pastes,

(b) Resin-base mastics,

(c) Rubber-base mastics,

(d) Linoleum pastes,

(e) Contact adhesives.

Starch pastes are sometimes used for paper- or cloth-backed vinyl wall covering.

Resin-base mastics for vinyl wall coverings may be the oil-resin type similar to that used for bonding plastic tile or the polyvinyl acetate type usually preferred because it may be washed off. Both of these have more water resistance than starch paste or linoleum paste.

The rubber-base mastics are slightly more difficult to use because they are quick drying and require solvents to remove excess adhesive from tools and surfaces. However, they have quick strength and are often preferred. The natural or synthetic rubber latex type is popular because of its light color. The reclaim rubber type, gray or black, is often used because of good strength and low cost. High-strength rubber-base adhesives may also be used.

For cloth- or paper-backed vinyl, linoleum paste is sometimes used. This is a by-product liquor of sufite paper manufacturing, inexpensive and easy to clean up with water. It is satisfactory on interior wall surfaces where moisture will not be a problem, but is not recommended on unsupported vinyl because of poor adhesion. Linoleum paste may also cause discoloration of the vinyl.

The plasticizers in vinyl may migrate, plasticizing or softening some adhesives. The synthetic rubber or linoleum paste types resist this action best.

Plastic laminates, either in tile or sheet form, may be bonded with a neoprene rubber-base contact bond adhesive. Contact bond adhesives are fast drying and permit bonding 5 to 10 minutes after adhesive application. The adhesive will still provide an excellent high-strength bond after 1 hour or more open time.

Application. For vinyl wall coverings, the mastics are usually applied to the wall surface with a very fine notched trowel having notches approximately $\frac{1}{32}$ inch deep. The subsurfaces must be clean, dry and very smooth. The adhesive is troweled on the wall. The wall covering is usually bonded soon after application of the adhesive to prevent "ridging" or "showing through" of the mastic.

For plastic laminates, contact bond adhesives are applied by brush, roller or spray gun to both surfaces. The decorative plastic laminate panel is carefully aligned, pressed into position and rolled down. Rubber-base mastics are used on plastic laminates by application with a notched trowel to the back of the panel or to the wall surface. These permit positioning. In most cases, it is necessary to shore or brace the panels until the mastic has set.

Plastic Floor Coverings

Resilient Floor Tile Adhesives. More common plastic resilient floor tile includes vinyl asbestos tile, solid vinyl tile and vinyl-covered cork tile. Other types are also used; thin vinyl tile with an asphalt paper backing, and various kinds of vinyl-coated linoleum tile. Also appearing on the market are simulated terrazzo tile made from epoxy or polyester plastic resins. The same types of adhesives may usually be used with each of these tiles:

(a) Rubber-base mastics with water vehicle,

(b) Resin-base mastics with alcohol solvent,

(c) Linoleum paste,

(d) Epoxy resin mastics.

Several types of rubber-base mastics are in use, one of which is a low-cost black reclaim rubber type which has high water resistance and flexibility. A new, light-colored synthetic rubber-type mastic with a water vehicle has excellent water and alkali resistance and is becoming popular for on-grade and below-grade concrete applications.

The resin-alcohol mastics are popular for rubber tile and vinyl tile; moreover they may also be used for vinyl cork tile and vinyl linoleum tile. These adhesives are reasonably water resistant and usually light in color. Linoleum paste is used where water resistance is not a problem. It is not usually recommended for vinyl tile however because of poor adhesion to some vinyl products. Epoxy resin adhesives are used over on-grade concrete and below-grade concrete floors where moisture is likely to occur. They are quite expensive.

Application. Most of these various types are spread with a notched trowel having notches approximately $\frac{1}{16}$-inch deep. Some adhesives may be brushed or rolled on the floor surface; subsequently the floor tiles are

FIG. 11-1. Resilient floor tile being installed with rubber-base mastic. Adhesive is spread with notched trowel. Floor tile is then pressed in wet adhesive.

laid into the wet mastic before it becomes too dry to effect a bond. It is important, particularly with vinyl tile, to lay the tile before the ridges of the adhesive have set up so that all of the ridges will be pressed out smoothly, thus eliminating any "telegraphing" or setup ridges showing through the tile. This is not so much of a problem with rubber, cork and linoleum tile. A floor roller, used to roll the tile securely to the floor, assists in flattening the ridges.

It is important to use only recommended adhesives over on-grade or below-grade level concrete slabs since moisture in the concrete can cause some adhesives to dissolve and/or lose strength. *Caution:* Apply these adhesives only over a dry, well-seasoned concrete floor. Of course, above-grade plywood or particle board provides a satisfactory surface too.

Vinyl Linoleum and Vinyl Sheet Goods Adhesives. Ordinarily the same adhesives used for resilient tile are satisfactory for vinyl linoleum and various types of vinyl sheet goods. Because sheet linoleum has so very few seams, linoleum paste is used despite its poor water resistance. In bathrooms and in other areas of extreme moisture concentrations, it is desirable to use one of the rubber-base or resin-base adhesives mentioned under Resilient Floor Tile Adhesives. The same methods of application are used as for resilient floor tile.

Asphalt and Vinyl Asbestos Tile Adhesives. These two types of tile are classified together because of their semirigid nature. The same types of adhesives may be used for both:

(a) Asphalt emulsion,

(b) Asphalt cut-back,

(c) Rubber-base mastics with water vehicle.

The asphalt or bituminous emulsion is most popular because it is inexpensive and generally satisfactory. The asphalt cut-back type, which contains very slow drying solvents, is losing favor because of difficulty in application and cleanup. The reclaim rubber and synthetic rubber-water types may be used in areas of high moisture content.

Application. The asphalt emulsion is spread with a fine notched trowel on the clean, dry and warm (room temperature, if possible) floor surface. In areas of extreme dust, a brushable primer is often used to provide better adhesion to the concrete. The adhesive is allowed to dry completely until all the moisture has escaped. This may require from 2 to 24 hours, depending on the temperature and humidity; then the tile is laid without rolling. The edges may not lie flat for a few days or even weeks if the temperature is low. However, they will gradually conform to the floor. This is particularly true of asphalt tile. Asphalt cut-backs are applied in the same manner.

The rubber-water types are applied in the same manner as for resilient floor tile. It is important to lay the tile in those mastics before the adhesive is dry.

Cove-base Adhesive. This is a thick mastic which is used for cementing vinyl, rubber or asphalt cove base to wall surfaces. It is usually composed of resins with a solvent vehicle. This product is applied to the back side of the cove base with a notched trowel having notches approximately $\frac{3}{32}$ inch deep. It can be applied over most wall surfaces with little or no preparation if they are clean and dry. Where it is applied around columns or curved surfaces, it may be necessary to brace the cove base in position until the adhesive is set.

Sink and Counter Tops

Decorative Plastic Laminate Adhesives. There are several types of decorative plastic laminates in use. One contains a paper impregnated phenolic plastic backing with a melamine plastic top sheet; another type is a solid polyester plastic. The decorative laminates are available mostly in sheet form. Some manufacturers are testing tiles, but these are not yet standard because of difficulty in holding them flat.

Two types of adhesives are used:
(1) Contact bond adhesives,
(2) Rubber-base mastics.
The typical contact bond adhesive may

FIG. 11-2. Applying contact bond adhesive to particle board prior to bonding decorative plastic laminate in the manufacture of sink and counter tops.

be applied by spreading with a notched trowel or spreader, rolling with a paint roller, brushing, or spraying. The adhesive is applied in a smooth even film to both the laminate and the other surface to be bonded.

Contact bond adhesives are used to bond all types of decorative plastic laminates to plywood and particle board in the manufacture of sink, counter, table, desk, vanity and bar tops.

These synthetic rubber-based adhesives permit bonding of the laminate within 5 to 30 minutes after adhesive application under normal conditions of temperature and humidity. However, the adhesive will still provide an excellent high-strength bond after one hour or more open time.

The contact bond adhesives require only contact pressure, as achieved with a hand roller, to effect a high-strength bond. Their strength is sufficient immediately after completing the bond to hold down edges of even badly warped plastic laminates and to permit routing or trimming of laminate edges immediately after the bond is completed. Bond strength increases with age due to a curing of the neoprene rubber or to an agent incorporated in the adhesive itself.

High heat resistance of the adhesive overcomes edge lifting and seam buckling that might occur in areas of sunlight or on counters exposed to boiling water or hot pans.

Extremely thin glue lines can be obtained. Water based contact adhesives reduce objectionable odor, are completely resistant to water when dry, are nonstaining on decorative plastic laminates and withstand exposure to oxidation, oils and greases.

Most contact adhesives become glossy when dry. If they do not dry with a gloss, more adhesive should be applied. With many of the contact adhesives, the applicator has up to 2 hours to complete the installation, during which time the adhesive on the mating surfaces will bond only to itself.

Application. The plastic laminate is pre-cut and fitted before spreading the cement. After spreading and drying, the laminate is positioned carefully and pressed into place. The paper slip sheet method, in which heavy kraft paper is used between the plastic laminate and the base surface, makes proper alignment of the laminate easy. The paper is placed on the dry adhesive on the base surface, and the laminate is carefully positioned on top of the paper to get one corner and one side properly in place. Then the paper is pulled out and the laminate is carefully pressed into position, by working from one side to the other to prevent entrapment of the air. The laminate is rolled firmly over the entire area with a wood or metal hand roller. A rubber mallet or a hammer and a small block of wood may be used to apply pressure if desired. For cleanup of excess, many contact bond adhesives may be rolled off the surface by hand; others require a solvent.

FIG. 11-3. Laying plastic laminate on paper between the plastic and the adhesive coated subsurface.

When a brush is used, care must be taken not to brush over the cement after it has dried as this may cause unevenness in the film.

Some adhesives, particularly the water-vehicle types, may be sprayed. Paint spray equipment is generally satisfactory.

The rubber-base mastics are spread with a notched trowel on the base surface. After the laminate is carefully aligned, it is pressed into place with a twisting motion. With most mastics, it is possible to manipulate the panel. The laminate is then rolled with a hand roller. It may be necessary to apply additional pressure to shore or brace the panels until the mastic has set.

FIG. 11-4. Applying pressure to plastic laminate after paper is removed and laminate is bonded to subsurface.

Resilient Covering Adhesives. Resilient coverings include vinyl, rubber, and linoleum sheet goods. It is important to use a waterproof-type adhesive on counter tops. Some of the waterproof types of adhesives that may be used are:

(a) Rubber-base mastics with water vehicle,

(b) Resin-base mastics with alcohol solvent.

These products are discussed under Resilient Floor Tile Adhesives.

Application. For counter tops, these adhesives are applied in much the same way as they are applied as resilient floor tile adhesives, but with a small hand roller. On vinyl, particularly, it is important that the adhesive be used only over a clean, dry surface. When vinyl is installed over a surface that previously had a counter-top covering, all of the old adhesive must be removed by scraping and sanding to obtain satisfactory adhesion.

Roof Adhesives

Nonflammable Roof Deck Adhesives. Since a disastrous automotive plant fire a few years ago, the nonflammable roof adhesives have been gaining in popularity. They bond the insulation to the roof deck. If a vapor barrier is used, they adhere the vapor barrier to the roof deck and the insulation to the vapor barrier. When hot, they will not burn, soften or drip through the joints of the deck onto the floor below, thus minimizing the possibility of a fire spreading. Most of these adhesives will only char at high temperatures.

There are two main types of adhesives used:

(a) Rubber-base liquid adhesives with nonflammable solvents and a fire-snuffing ingredient.

(b) Asphalt-base mastics and a fire-snuffing ingredient.

Application. The rubber-base liquid adhesives are semiviscous so that they may be applied either by brushing with a push broom or by spreading beads with an applicator cart. Carts much like large hopper-type garden spreaders are available which will spread adhesive in the proper size beads continuously along the deck. The vapor barrier or insulation is placed directly into these beads of adhesive as soon after spreading as possible. The vapor barrier may be coated by applying adhesive with a special portable roll coating machine or by hand with a brush or a paint roller.

The asphalt adhesive is usually applied with a push broom or mopping technique, and the insulation or vapor barrier is pressed into the adhesive within the time recommended. The asphalt adhesives generally give longer working time than do the rubber-base mastics. The vapor barrier film is rolled with a heavy roller after application to the deck. The insulation, depending on its type, is generally rolled also.

Flammable Roof Deck Adhesives. The conventional types of adhesives that have been used for many years are usually the coal tars. These are hot melts, applied ordinarily by mopping or push-brooming across the roof deck. The insulation is dropped into place while they are still tacky.

Several new plastic roofing materials in sheet form are appearing. These are adhered with neoprene-latex and urethane type adhesives. These are very new and further adhesive developments may be expected.

Ceiling Materials

Acoustical Tile Adhesives. There are many types of acoustical tile, including the vinyl-faced vegetable-fiber and glass-fiber types. The same adhesives may be used to install most of these various types of tile:

(a) Resin-base mastics,

(b) Rubber-base mastics,

(c) Contact bond adhesives.

Of these, the resin-base mastics are most popular because of low cost and high initial strength. The rubber-base mastics are used for specialty applications, where some special surface such as plastic or glass is involved or where extra strength is needed for large panels. Rubber-base mastics have better adhesion to a greater variety of surfaces, good ultimate strength, and high shock resistance. Similarly the contact bond adhesives are used for special applications where quick strength is desired and where the surfaces are very flat and smooth.

Application. The base surface must be clean, dry and solid. All old adhesives or loose paint must be removed. The resin-base mastics and the rubber-base mastics are usually applied by pressing a portion of adhesive approximately the size of a golf ball about 2 inches in from each corner of the tile. The tile is then immediately pressed into position with a sliding motion to the proper level. The base surface, in some cases, should be primed or sized as recommended. This usually applies to bare plaster which may draw some of the oils from certain resin-base mastics and which also may be very dusty. On dusty tile such as some of the mineral asbestos types, the area on the back of the tile to receive the adhesive is first primed. This is done by drawing the edge of the trowel or putty knife applicator across this area of the tile, spreading a thin film of the adhesive to wet down the dust; then the gob of adhesive is placed over the primed area. For large panels, the mastic may be applied to the joists in a bead form.

The contact bond adhesive is applied as described in previous sections of this chapter.

Of course, tile bonded with this adhesive cannot be manipulated. It is essential that the ceiling should not be disturbed for at least 48 hours. Some tile failures have resulted from premature installation of lighting, heating and air-conditioning equipment after the tile is installed.

Insulation

Insulation materials such as fibrous glass, plastic foam, cellular glass or cork are frequently bonded with adhesives to heating or cooling ducts, concrete walls, ceilings, etc. Adhesives include:

(a) Rubber-base liquid with solvent vehicle,

(b) Rubber-base liquid water dispersion,

(c) Rubber-base mastics with solvent vehicle,

(d) Rubber-base mastic water dispersion.

The rubber-base liquid adhesives with a solvent vehicle are most popular because they are easily applied by brush or spray gun and provide high strength. There are some rubber types based on synthetic rubber (rather than reclaimed rubber) which have higher heat resistance and are consequently preferred on heating ducts. Although the rubber water dispersions have lower initial strengths, they are used where fire hazard is great. Rubber-base mastics are used on irregular surfaces such as concrete block walls.

Synthetic rubber-base liquid with solvent vehicle insulation adhesives have been developed to be applied with low-cost, low air pressure spray equipment that prevents messy overspray, reduces cleanup requirements and provides good adhesive coverage. The adhesive can be spray applied quickly; this reduces bonding time requirements, increases profits, lowers worker fatigue and prevents delays.

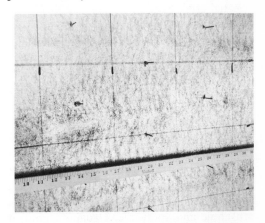
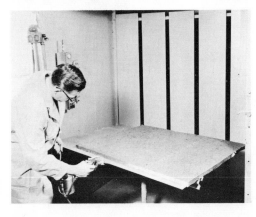

Fig. 11-5. Top left: Spray applying insulation adhesive to metal duct. Top right: Spray pattern of adhesive Bottom left: Edge sealing insulation with adhesive. Bottom right: Insulation pulls apart before adhesive bond fails.

These materials have a high fire-resistance rating, and exceed city and government building codes for installing low-density fibrous-glass insulation to duct work, furnaces and air-conditioning units.

These synthetic elastomer-based adhesives have quick aggressive tack with a good tack range, maintain high bond strength at temperatures between -20 and $+250°F$ and provide high-strength bonds between insulation and aluminum, galvanized steel, building board and similar base surfaces.

The adhesive accomplishes two jobs in one. Not only does it bond the insulations, but it can be used to edge-seal low-density insulation.

The long "open time" of the adhesive permits adhesive application on large areas for the bonding of large pieces of insulation. Long "open time" also eliminates dry spots, allows for production delays and reduces rejected assemblies.

The fast strength buildup of the adhesive permits the insulation to be applied immediately after adhesive application. This, in turn, permits quicker handling of the bonded insulated assembly, eliminates time required for drying and promotes high volume production operations.

The adhesive has good aging properties and resists oxidation. This prevents the adhesive film from becoming brittle after continued exposure to elevated temperatures.

Application. The liquid adhesives are brushable and sprayable. Usually a coat of adhesive is applied to the base surface and to the insulation; then, within a few minutes, the surfaces are joined with a firm hand pressure. The mastics are usually troweled or daubed on the base surface, after which, within a short time, the insulation is pressed into the wet adhesive. *Caution: Most solvent-vehicle adhesives attack plastic foam. Some can be used safely if manufacturers's directions are followed.*

Sandwich Panels

Most of this chapter has referred to adhesives that are used on the job. Some adhesives, important to the building industry, are used in the factory, e.g., in making sandwich or laminated panels. These panels may fill a space in a curtain wall construction or, in some cases, support a structural load such as in roof panels. Usually they have some insulation value. They are often used for decorative purposes on the exterior or interior of buildings.

There are many adhesives that may be used for making sandwich panels, the choice depending of the facings and cores involved. Also there are panels composed of plastic, metal or porcelain enamel facings and insulated cores such as cellular glass foam, glass fiber or a phenolic plastic paper or metal honeycomb. Some panels have ceramic tile or portland cement facings with various types of plastic or other core materials. Some of the decorative plastic laminates with plastic facings such as polyester fiber glass have been introduced for interior panel work. These, however, are but a few of the possibilities. The following are some of the adhesives that may be used with these combinations:

(a) Synthetic rubber adhesives with volatile solvents (contact bond adhesive is one type),

(b) Synthetic rubber adhesive with water vehicle,

(c) Rubber-base mastics with solvent vehicle,

(d) Synthetic resin-water vehicle type,

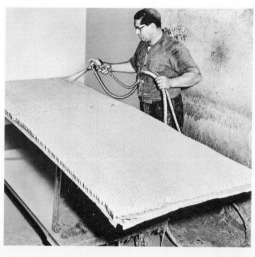

FIG. 11-6. Applying adhesive by the spray method to honeycomb core. Core is then bonded to metal facings to produce a honeycomb sandwich building panel.

(e) Synthetic resin, one or two part heat curing type, bonding films or liquid adhesives.

One synthetic rubber-base solvent vehicle adhesive with high strength and high heat resistance can be spray applied in a relatively dry form, permitting application directly to polystyrene. It requires only contact pressure for bonding a variety of materials including polystyrene, sheet plastic, steel, aluminum, wood, particle board and formed glass. Because of a new spray technique, excellent filleting properties are obtained; therefore, it is used extensively in fabrication of honeycomb sandwich panels. Other applications include bonding building panels and metal assemblies.

Component parts coated with this adhesive can be assembled, positioned and repositioned, if necessary, without the components adhering together. After proper assembly, a momentary application of pressure, as achieved with a nip roll, will immediately bond the two component parts together with a strong bond.

Tests performed on panels exposed to sunlight show that glue line temperatures may be much higher than ambient temperatures. For example, at ambient temperatures of 75 and 100°F, the glue line temperatures are 130 and 180°F, respectively.

One contact bond adhesive maintains extremely high dead load strength at these elevated temperatures and will provide dead load shear strengths of 175 psi at 200°F. In addition, it has a long bonding range, rapid rate of strength buildup, excellent resistance to heat and plastic flow, and good sprayability properties.

Application. The synthetic rubber-solvent type is applied usually by spraying both surfaces with a paint-type spray gun to give a continuous even film. After waiting the specified time for the solvent to evaporate, the bond is made by bringing the surfaces together with pressure applied with a rubber nip roll arrangement or with a cold press. Care must be taken not to exert more pressure than the facing or core will withstand, i.e., approximately 3 to 5 psi or 0.25 to 0.5 lb/in. These adhesives may also be applied by brushing or by applying with a paint roller to both surfaces. In some cases, large roll coating equipment is used to apply a smooth even film to a complete facing sheet. This technique has also been used on some core materials, such as aluminum or paper honeycomb, but it is most satisfactory on flat sheet metal or board. The synthetic rubber-water vehicle type may be applied in a similar fashion. The roll coating technique is particularly useful. The rubber-base mastics are almost always applied with a notched spreader similar to those used for bonding ceramic tile.

The synthetic resin-water type, e.g., polyvinyl acetate, is limited to interior partitions by its poor water resistance. This adhesive may be applied by rolling with a paint roller, brushing, or spraying. The bond must be assembled quickly since the resin sets quite rapidly. The bond is usually held under pressure for some period of time until all of the water has evaporated and the bond has reached full strength.

Some newer types of adhesives such as the one- or two-part synthetic resin (epoxy) types are being used where considerable structural strength is required. These may or may not require heat curing. They are usually applied with a roll coater or a knife coating arrangement. Many may be brushed, but a few can be sprayed. After assembling a panel, pressure is usually required for some time until the bond sets. In some cases, heaat cure is necessary to develop optimum strength.

As this chapter is written, other new plastic materials are being brought to the construction market. Vinyl and other plastics are being applied to wood siding and plywood in the factory to upgrade lumber and plywood and to provide a more durable surface than paint. New synthetic elastomer adhesives are being used which have weather resistance and durability.

ADHESIVES FOR BONDING OTHER MATERIALS

Wall Coverings

Ceramic Tile Adhesives. Four main types of adhesives are used for the so-called thin-bed-setting of ceramic tile.

(a) Rubber-base mastics with volatile solvent vehicle,

(b) Rubber-base mastics with water vehicle,

(c) Oil- and resin-base mastics,

(d) Portland cement with resin binder. The rubber-base solvent-type mastics were the first to be used, and they have been steadily improved from the standpoint of ease of application, strength and water resistance.

The ruber-base type with water vehicle is a newer product which is also being rapidly improved. It has won some favor because of its advantages of reduced odor, simple application, and easy cleanup with water. Its principal deficiency is in reduced water resistance as compared to the solvent types. Some of the water-vehicle ceramic tile adhesives should not be used in high-moisture areas such as shower stalls.

The oil-resin type is employed because of easy application and a long bonding time. Adhesives of this type generally have less strength than the rubber-base types; furthermore since they are relatively new, not much is known about their aging durability.

One new development is the use of a binder such as a polyvinyl acetate resin which is mixed with portland cement and sand. This is similar to the conventional mortar method of setting tile except that this mix may be applied with a notched trowel over a variety of surfaces. The binder is mixed on the job or premixed in the cement. The applicator merely adds sufficient water to bring the mix to the proper consistency.

Application. All the above-mentioned adhesives are thick or mastic in consistency, permitting two general methods of application:

(1) Floating method—adhesive is applied directly to wall with a notched trowel or spreader.

(2) Buttering method—small part of adhesive is applied to the back side of the tile.

Ceramic tile may be installed with adhesive to almost any sound, strong, dry and clean wall surface including brown coat plaster, finish coat plaster, gypsum wall-board, cement asbestos board, concrete, waterproof plywood and painted surfaces. When it is applied over a painted surface, the paint must be securely bonded to the subsurface. Paint should be scraped to test for adhesion.

In moisture areas, the base surface must be completely waterproofed. This is accomplished by applying a skim coat of the

Fig. 11-7. Applying ceramic tile adhesive to wall of bathroom by the floating method. Adhesive is applied directly to wall with notched trowel.

adhesive with the flat side of a trowel or by brushing on a waterproofing primer as recommended by the adhesive manufacturer. It is important to caulk or seal all open edges with the adhesive or a caulking compound. This includes all seams and corners of wallboard, plaster, plywood, etc., and is accomplished by packing the adhesive or caulking into the openings with a putty knife or caulking gun.

The adhesive is then applied either by the notched trowel or buttering method. Generally, the trowel should contain ridges about $\frac{3}{16}$-inch deep and about the same distance apart. This provides a sufficient volume of fresh soft mastic so that a long bonding time is attained. The wall should be completely covered with adhesive.

Tile is then set into the mastic with a slight twisting motion to break any skin coating on the adhesive. With most mastics, tile may be presoaked in water if desired. This provides moisture for proper curing of the grout cement if grouting of the joints is to be done the same day. After waiting at least 4 hours for the adhesive to dry, the tile may be sponged down to provide more moisture and grouted in the usual manner.

If the buttering method is preferred, the wall is skim coated or primed for water-proofing as before and a small pat of adhesive is placed on the back side of each tile. The tile is then immediately pressed into place with a twisting motion.

Specifications. The U.S. Department of Commerce has issued Commercial Standard No. 181-52 covering the performance of organic adhesives for installing ceramic tile. Products meeting this specification must provide strength of at least 40 psi under high moisture conditions.

Metal Tile Adhesives. Metal wall tile may be enameled aluminum tile, enameled steel tile, porcelain enameled steel tile, stainless steel tile and copper tile. The same types of adhesives are utilized for installing metal tile as are used for installing plastic tile, except that not all plastic tile adhesives are recommended for metal tile. The same floating or buttering techniques of application are also used.

Hardboard Adhesives. Hardboard or resin-impregnated fiberboard is adhesive bonded to existing walls to form a decorative wall covering. This material has either a pre-finished or unfinished surface, of which the former has an enamel coating applied to one side of the board. It is important with the prefinished hardboard to use an adhesive which will not stain through or discolor the paint. Adhesives in most common use are:

(a) Rubber-base mastics with solvent vehicle,

(b) Resin-base mastics,

(c) Oil-resin base mastics.

The rubber-base mastics with volatile solvent vehicles are the most satisfactory from the standpoint of easy application, high strength, and good water resistance.

The resin-base types are easy to apply, but they have less ultimate strength and reduced

water and heat resistance. Since the resin types have high initial strength, they are occasionally used where this property is desired but where final strength is not an important factor.

Oil-resin base mastics similar to the plastic tile adhesives have also been used successfully for hardboard.

Application. All of these types of adhesives may be applied by the "floating" method with a notched trowel, having notches approximately ¼-inch deep and ¼-inch apart. A primer is recommended in high-moisture areas to seal the wall. The adhesive is applied to the back of the board with a notched trowel, and the hardboard is immediately pressed against the wall. The board is firmly pressed over its entire area to effect a bond. The wall surface must be clean, dry and free of contaminating material. In some instances, failure has occurred where mastics were used over old linoleum cement or bituminous adhesive which previously secured a wall covering material.

While the use of hardboard is recommended in moisture areas, it is important that all seams be carefully sealed to eliminate moisture penetration and possible swelling of the board. It is also important to fit the board loosely in moldings so that moisture will not cause buckling of the board.

The second method of application is the buttering method. The adhesive is placed in spots (or "gobs") about 2 inches in diameter and 1 inch deep, spaced approximately 1 foot apart across the back side of the board. The board is then pressed to the wall with a sliding action to smooth the adhesive. This method is often used on an uneven wall to provide a smooth surface, but it does not provide as solid a surface as the troweling method.

Plywood or Wood Paneling Adhesives. Adhesives may be used in several ways to install plywood or wood paneling to wall surfaces. A mastic may be used in similar fashion to those used in applying hardboard. A contact bond-type adhesive may be preferred to fasten the plywood to wooden furring strips or to the wall itself. Types include:

(a) Rubber-base mastics with solvent vehicle,

(b) Synthetic rubber with solvent or water vehicle known as contact bond adhesive.

The rubber-base mastic should have high initial strength and good ultimate strength. The adhesive should dry to a flexible film to absorb any dimensional changes in the plywood. The bonding of plywood on exterior surfaces is generally not recommended because moisture can penetrate plywood to cause swelling, which may fail the adhesive bond. Adhesives may be used on the exterior if supplementary nails or screws are employed.

Contact bond adhesives should have high ultimate strength with good resistance to creep or flow.

Application. Rubber-base mastics are applied with a notched spreader of approximately the same size as that used with hardboard. The application is similar to that for hardboard except that batten strips or wood moldings may be nailed over the joints instead of metal moldings. Care must be taken not to restrict the edges of the plywood since some expansion can occur resulting from a change in moisture content.

Contact bond adhesives are used in two ways, the first of which is with furring strips. The usual precautions of having clean, dry, dust-free surfaces are important; moreover the furring strips must be plumb and in line. Any shimming must be done behind the furring strip. The contact bond adhesive is then applied by brush, spreader or roller to the surface of the furring strips and to the back side of the plywood. The adhesive should be allowed to dry for the specified time, and the board is aligned and pressed into place. A few nails are often used at the corners and at the center of the plywood. These may be finishing nails covered with wood filler or wood plugs. It is difficult to manipulate the board once it is pressed into position using this method.

The contact bond method may also be used in installing plywood over a solid flat surface such as plaster, cement-asbestos board or gypsum wallboard. The adhesive is applied to both surfaces and allowed to dry the specified period; then the board is carefully aligned and pressed into place. Usually no nails are necessary with this method if sufficient bond contact area (at least one-half of the area) is obtained.

Gypsum Wallboard Adhesives. There are two principal applications of adhesives for gypsum wallboard (drywall) installation. One is the laminating of two layers of wallboard, which is frequently done to eliminate nailheads in the finished surface. The second use of adhesive is for bonding gypsum wallboard directly to studs or joists to reduce the number of nailing operations. This also reduces the number of nailheads to fill and finish. Some nails are used to apply pressure between the wallboard and stud so that the adhesive will spread out to give complete contact between the stud and the back of the wallboard. Because the adhesive helps hold the drywall in place, fewer nails are required in the final installation. In many instances, the use of drywall adhesive reduces the required number of nails by as much as 50 per cent. Types include:

(a) Casein or dextrin adhesives which come either in powder form or in premixed, semimastic form,

(b) Rubber-base mastics—solvent or water type,

(c) Contact cements.

The caseins and dextrins are primarily used for double-laminating drywall although rubber-base mastics and contact cements may be used for the same purpose. Rubber-base mastics are used for bonding wallboard (drywall) directly to studs to strengthen the wall and reduce nail usage and nail popping.

Application. The casein or dextrin adhesives of the powder type require mixing with water to form an adhesive with a paste consistency. This is applied with a fine notched trowel or by brush to the already installed drywall base surface; then the second sheet of drywall is placed on the adhesive-coated base surface. Slight sliding action provides best contact. The premixed adhesives are applied in a similar fashion, after which the joints are taped as in the usual manner. Rubber-base mastics, which are premixed, may be used in the same fashion for laminating drywall or for application directly to studs. This adhesive has high adhesion, strength and water resistance and is often utilized where moisture could occur.

Contact cement is applied by brush or roll coater to both surfaces, dried, and bonded with roller pressure.

When used on studs for minimizing nail popping, rubber-base mastics are applied with caulking guns in approximately ⅜-inch diameter continuous beads to the centers of the studs or joists. On joists where two adjacent pieces of drywall join, the bead is applied in a zigzag fashion to give best contact. Drywall is pressed into place as soon as possible after complete application of the adhesive over the area that the board is to cover. The drywall is applied with a slight sliding action to break any skin that may develop on the adhesive. Some supplementary nails are required to anchor the board to the wall until the adhesive sets. There is varying opinion as to how many nails are required; however the trend is toward the use of fewer nails, e.g., one nail in each corner and two nails in the "field." Some building codes today require a minimum of ½ the number of nails that were formerly used without adhesive. The usual methods of taping joints and finishing the board are then used.

Metal and Plastic Wall Clips and Furring Strip Adhesives. There are a variety of special metal and plastic clips for attaching such materials as furring strips, insulation or various types of wallboard including plywood. These clips are attached with mastic or heavy liquid adhesives to walls, ceilings, air-conditioning ducts, and other surfaces. They may be made of galvanized steel, aluminum, or plastic. They are used mostly where it is difficult or impractical to attach either the clip or the wall-surfacing material by mechanical means such as nailing, etc. They are especially useful on masonry and metal heating ducts. Adhesives are:

(a) Rubber-base mastics with solvent vehicle,

(b) Liquid contact cement types.

The rubber-base mastics, which are the most commonly used types, are of the very high initial strength variety. They are applied in small dabs or preferably smeared over the back side of the clip in a film ⅛ inch thick. The clip, which contains a series of perforations or holes in the bonding surface, is then pressed in place with a sliding motion so that the mastic squeezes through the holes to provide a high-strength bond. The mastic is allowed to set for 2 to 18 hours depending on the drying rate. The furring strips, which are pre-drilled, are then placed over the protruding screw or nail of the clip and fastened into position. The same general method of installation applies where insulation or other wall and ceiling surfacing material is being attached. On heating ducts an adhesive with sufficient flexibility and strength at elevated temperatures should be employed.

The contact cement types are occasionally used on very smooth surfaces such as metal or wood or where very high initial strength is desired. A coat of the adhesive is applied liberally to the back of the clip and another to the wall or ceiling surface. When the adhesive has dried as specified, the two surfaces are joined with as much hand pressure as possible.

Cementitious Materials Adhesives. Adhesives have been developed for bonding cementitious materials such as concrete and plaster to themselves as well as to many sound subsurfaces. This technique now enables the building industry to repair existing surfaces more easily and to build new buildings with greater versatility of design. Types include:

(a) Epoxy resin mastics,

(b) Synthetic rubber-water emulsions,

(c) Vinyl-water dispersions.

The epoxy resin adhesives are two-part materials requiring mixing of an amine or polyamide curing agent to cure or "set" the product. They are used primarily for applying new concrete to old concrete.

The synthetic rubber emulsions are used as admixes in cement to bond new concrete to old concrete.

The vinyl-water dispersions are employed principally for bonding new plaster to a concrete base or to other wall or ceiling surfaces.

Application. (a) The epoxy resin mastics are mixed and applied immediately to the wall by brushing or troweling. It is important that the existing concrete be clean, dry and sound. While the epoxy is still "wet" (un-cured), the new concrete is poured into place.

(b) The synthetic rubber emulsions are mixed into the concrete as recommended. A second method is to make a thin cement paste containing the rubber emulsion which is brushed or troweled on the old surface before applying the new concrete.

(c) The vinyl-water dispersions are sprayed over the new concrete. When dry, the wall is plastered.

Floor Coverings

Woodblock Flooring Adhesives. There are three main types of woodblock flooring in-stalled with adhesives. One is the block made up of strips of regular strip flooring. These are held together with a steel spline or other device usually in 9 inch × 9 inch tile form. Another very popular type is the laminated plywood tile block. Both types have tongue-and-groove edges so that they lock together. The third type, which is the single-ply or solid-sheet tile, is occasionally composed of little squares of hardwood that are glued or fastened together. In other blocks, it is a rather flexible, veneer-type tile. The adhe-sives used for these three types of blocks vary considerably. Types include:

(a) Rubber mastic-solvent vehicle,

(b) Rubber mastic-water dispersion,

(c) Asphalt cut-back,

(d) Asphalt emulsion,

(e) Hot asphalt or coal tar.

The rubber base-solvent type adhesive is used with plywood block and also to some extent with the solid veneer and the strip flooring type. The rubber-base water emul-sion is employed with the plywood-type block. The asphalt cut-back is used primarily with the strip floor block. The asphalt emul-sion is utilized with the plywood block. Where extreme moisture may occur, it is usually best to use a rubber-base product with a solvent vehicle. If there is water in a concrete

floor, no adhesive should be used since expansion of wood due to moisture may break the bond.

Application. All of these adhesives may be applied with a notched trowel having notches approximately ¼ inch deep. The asphalts are frequently troweled or spread to form a flat bed of mastic. The thinner veneer tile will not require such deep notches. The rubber-base mastics require that the tile be bonded within a certain time after spreading. The asphalt cut-back and emulsion types usually require a longer waiting time with virtually no restriction upon the maximum length of time before bonding. Hot asphalt or hot coal tar is often delivered hot to the job; otherwise drum or pail heaters must be used to soften it for application.

The blocks are laid into the adhesives at the recommended time. Blocks should be rolled with at least a 100-pound roller soon after installation.

Ceramic Floor Tile Adhesives. Adhesives may be used for laying various types of ceramic floor tile, either the small unglazed or glazed ceramic mosaics or the larger quarry-type tile.

(a) Rubber-base mastics with solvent ve-hicle,

(b) Rubber base mastics with water vehicle,

(c) Portland cement with resin binder.

The rubber-base solvent-type mastics have gained in popularity for setting floor tile because they permit tile to be placed, in many cases, where mortar cannot be used. They are particularly good for installing floor tile over smooth concrete floors and in buildings that are being remodeled, and over plywood or underlayment board in new residential construction.

The rubber-base mastics with water vehicle generally do not have as high a water resist-ance; therefore they should not be used in areas of extreme moisture.

Portland cement with resin binder is a new product for installing floor tile. It has su-perior leveling properties and smooths out irregularities in the floor surfaces. It can be used over a number of floor surfaces such as concrete, but is not as versatile in this re-spect as the rubber-base mastics.

Application. The rubber-base mastics are spread with a notched trowel having notches approximately $\frac{1}{16}$ inch deep over clean, dry and smooth floor surfaces. In moisture areas, a skim coat of adhesive or brush coat of sealer is recommended on plywood and other water-sensitive surfaces. After this dries, the adhesive is troweled over this primer film. The tile, whether it be ceramic mosaic or quarry tile, must be laid before the adhesive dries. Frequently the ceramic mosaics must be manipulated to straighten the small tiles; then the tile is pounded with a wooden beating block. After installation, the tile should be covered with boards to prevent the small tiles from sliding out of position. After the adhesive has set, which usually requires at least 4 hours, the tile may be grouted in the conventional method except that it should be covered with building paper or plastic film to hold the moisture and ensure a proper cure of the grout.

The portland cement–resin binder type is sometimes troweled on using a deeper notched trowel, or it may be used in a $\frac{1}{2}$ to 1-inch-thick bed similar to laying tile in mortar.

Carpet Tack Strip Adhesive. This is a synthetic rubber, thick liquid adhesive that is brushed or spread on the wooden carpet tack strip and the concrete or wood floor. When adhesive surfaces are tacky, but not completely dry, the strip is placed firmly to the floor to effect a bond. A wait of at least one hour is recommended before the carpet is stretched over the tacks.

Sink and Counter Tops

Ceramic Tile Adhesives. Ceramic tile may be laid on counter tops with adhesive, providing that the base surface is suitably waterproof and that a waterproof adhesive is used. Because of the many joints, it is most important to have the tile joint cement, i.e., grout tight and free of cracks or openings. The rubber-base mastics with volatile solvents are preferred on counter tops because of their superior water resistance.

These mastics are applied with a $\frac{1}{16}$-inch-deep notched trowel similar to the procedure for installing ceramic floor tile. The same general procedure is recommended including a skim or brush coat of adhesive for waterproofing. All edges of the plywood or underlayment base should be sealed against moisture with the adhesive or a primer.

TABLE 11-1. Approximate Adhesive Applied Costs Per Square Foot

Group	Approximate Material Cost per Square Foot (cents)*
Contact adhesives	1–3
Resin adhesives	2–4
Resin-base mastics (water vehicle)	3–5
Resin-base mastics (solvent vehicle)	2–4
Rubber-base mastics	2–4
Rubber-base liquid (solvent vehicle)	1–4

*Material cost will be affected by the method of application. The most commonly used application method was used in determining these figures.

12

RESILIENT FLOORING AND CARPETING

ROBERT P. CONGER* AND LEONARD MOZER†

PART A: Resilient Flooring

ROBERT P. CONGER

Congoleum-Nairn, Inc.
Kearny, New Jersey

INTRODUCTION

Smooth-surface resilient flooring is just past its hundredth year. Some installations have been in use for over 50 years and are still in good condition. Most installations are removed today because of the desire by the housewife for the latest fashion or for a more beautiful and more highly aesthetic product. Where failures have occurred, they probably could have been prevented by proper maintenance and more careful consideration of the basic principles of selection and installation.

There are many types of smooth-surface resilient flooring and several subtypes within each group (not counting color or pattern). This large number of choices has evolved because of the desire on the part of the manufacturers to meet the specific needs of architects, flooring contractors, and building owners. In some cases, cost is of prime importance; in others, certain physical or chemical characteristics dictate the type of flooring to be specified. Sometimes moisture problems exist; at other times, severe traffic problems. In certain places, the over-

riding need is for a highly aesthetic product. Several tables have been included at the end of this chapter as aids in selection of flooring.

Smooth-surface resilient flooring will be discussed under the following headings:

Yard Goods
Printed Felt Base
Linoleum
Rotogravure Printed Vinyl Laminates (Loose-lay)
Vinyl Yard Goods
Foam Cushion Vinyl Yard Goods

Tiles
Asphalt Tiles
Vinyl Asbestos Tiles
Linoleum Tiles
Cork Tiles
Rubber Tiles
Vinyl Tiles

Special
Static Conductive Linoleum Yard Goods and Vinyl Tiles

Where possible, the published data of the various manufacturers have been correlated in the Tables. In the cases of the safe static load limit, the thermal conductivity (K factor) and the thermal conductance (C factor), the values given are as comparable as possible. These may not agree with some

*Congoleum Nairn, Inc., Kearny, New Jersey
†American Carpet Institute, New York, N. Y.

published values because of variations in testing procedures and techniques.

For each product, the following topics are discussed:

(1) Background—with sales volume
(2) Composition
(3) Manufacturing methods
(4) Properties—with sizes and decorations available
　　(a) Advantages
　　(b) Disadvantages

Details about bases and adhesives for smooth-surface flooring and the installation and maintenance of these resilient products are covered in the excellent manuals put out by the various manufacturers. Use of the adhesive recommended by the manufacturer of the flooring purchased is strongly urged. One should also consult "Installation and Maintenance of Resilient Smooth-Surface Flooring." *National Academy of Sciences— National Research Council Publication* 597, based on a 1958 conference of the Building Research Institute; and "The Care, Cleaning and Selection of Floors and Resilient Floor Coverings," written by B. Berkeley and C. S. Kimball of Foster D. Snell for the American Hotel Association in 1961.

TILES VERSUS YARD GOODS

Tiles have the advantage that their modular size permits rapid and simple installation with minimum disturbance of the normal routine. With yard goods, it is definitely recommended that an expert installer be hired for the job.

When excessive abuse or severe accident makes a repair necessary, tile products have some advantage over yard goods (roll types of floor coverings) and significant advantage over the terrazzo and other composition floors. In the case of asphalt tile, however, it is very difficult to obtain a good match even with tiles left from the original lot. The changes which occur in shade are caused by light and by soil ground into the tile surface. Vinyl asbestos (VA) tiles have greater resistance to light discoloration and to soiling than asphalt tiles; nevertheless, it is still difficult to match unused tile with those that have been on the floor for any

length of time. Yet the large users replace damaged tiles as a standard procedure, the color differential becoming less with time.

Yard goods have the advantage of far fewer seams. In a room 12 × 12 feet, yard goods would have only 12 feet of seams, while 9 × 9 inch tiles would have 360 feet. Each of these seams is a dirt catcher. In rooms where a high order of cleanliness is essential, the footage of seams should be kept to a minimum.

YARD GOODS

Printed Felt Base

The forerunner of printed felt-base flooring covering was floor oilcloth, patented in England in 1627, a coarse fabric coated with multiple layers of oil paint. A printing machine for this material, patented in 1790, used a hand-block printing method.

By 1911 the United Roofing and Mfg. Company, later the Congoleum Company, had perfected a method whereby a complete pattern and bordered rug could be printed by a wood-block machine. This plant produced enamel printed asphalt-impregnated felt-base flooring called "Congoleum."

This type of inexpensive floor covering reached its peak sales in 1948 and 1949 when over 2500 million square feet were sold annually. From that time, it has declined continuously to about 1800 million square feet in 1957 and 585 million in 1962. It is expected to decline further as people begin to use longer-lasting products.

Printed felt-base floor covering consists of a base of asphalt-impregnated felt which has been sealed with coating paint and decorated with an enamel wearing surface. The felt is prepared from rags, wood, old newspaper, or other fibers. It is impregnated as it passes through large kettles of molten asphalt. Coating paints made up of inert pigments and an oleoresinous solvent cut or a latex vehicle are applied to both sides of this felt to seal in the asphalt and to provide a smooth surface for the top coating. This coating serves both as the decorative and the wearing surface. It is usually of an oleoresinous type such as linseed, dehydrated castor or other drying oils, but it may be a synthetic resin type such as alkyd or vinyl. It is generally applied by a flat-bed printing machine made up of a series of carriages, inking rolls and wooden blocks, each applying paint in its own particular color and design.

This product is made in 6-, 9- and 12-foot-wide yard goods plus many rug sizes. The "heavy weight" is about .060 inch thick with a decorated wear surface of about .004 inch. This inexpensive product should not be expected to last much more than five years under residential traffic and is not recommended for areas other than in the home.

Linoleum

Linoleum was invented by Frederick Walton in 1864. It is a thermoset material (unlike asphalt tiles and the vinyls) and has to be cured with heat. Because of this, it is more resistant to temperature changes and to indentation at higher temperatures. Of course, until the 1920's when asphalt and rubber tiles came into production, linoleum had the higher-priced market to itself and even outsold the inexpensive printed felt base around 1920. Now, about 100 years since its discovery, its hold on the medium-priced yard goods market has been largely displaced by vinyl products. Still, about 240 million square feet were sold in 1962; this compares to 675 million at its peak in 1948 and 450 million sold in 1957. In the last five years, it has held its portion of the yard goods market (about 15 per cent). This is an indication of its good service and low cost, the lowest cost per unit thickness of any resilient flooring product except asphalt tile.

Linoleum in its simplest form is about 33 per cent binder, 33 per cent organic fillers and 33 per cent inorganic fillers. The binder usually consists of oxidized linseed oil, natural gums and rosin. During times of linseed oil shortages, other more plentiful vegetable drying oils of lower unsaturation were used to replace part or all of the linseed oil with essentially no loss in important physical properties. The organic fillers have been ground cork and wood flour while the inorganic ones have been chiefly limestone and color pigments. It usually has a burlap or flooring grade felt as a carrier backing.

The different types of linoleum that have been made recently are listed below. The types which are still made today are underlined.

(I) Burlap backing
    (A) Calendered
        (1) Battleship
        (2) Plain
        (3) (a) Decorated effects
            (b) Jaspe
            (c) Marbelized
    (B) Static conductive linoleum
(II) Felt backing
    (A) Calendered
        (1) (a) Decorated effects
            (b) Jaspe
            (c) Marbelized
        (2) Plain
    (B) Molded inlaid
        (1) Decorated (repeating patterns)
        (2) Decorated and embossed
    (C) Straight-line inlaid
        (1) Decorated (repeating patterns)

Federal Specification LLL-L-315-b covers the heavy-gauge, ⅛-inch, battleship linoleum on burlap backing. LLL-L-367 covers plain, jaspe, marbelized, etc., linoleum which is ⅛-inch thick and on burlap backing while LLL-F-471 covers the .090-, 070-, and .0625-inch linoleum on felt backing. At this writing a new specification to consolidate and replace the above documents is being prepared for promulgation in 1966.

The manufacture of linoleum begins with the oxidation of the drying oil or oil and rosin. Originally, two processes were used. The initial, natural process (no longer used) involved pouring the oil over cotton sheets which had been suspended from racks in tall sheds. The oil was slowly oxidized as it dripped down the sheets at 100° to 125°F over a period of several months. When the oil had been oxidized to the desired hardness and thickness, the sheets or skins were cut up and ground. The ground skins, plus the mechanically oxidized oil, natural gums and rosins, were cooked in kettles to form the binder. Old-timers claim the skins imparted added toughness, durability and resilience to the finished product. However, today all linoleum is made by the newer mechanical oxidation process in which the raw oil plus rosin is agitated at high temperatures with air until solidified to a rubbery mass of the right toughness. At that point, it is poured into pans and cooled. This process is called *cement making*. The fillers and pigments are dispersed into the cement or binder in a Banbury mixer.

The calendered plain or battleship (using finely ground cork for added resilience) linoleum is formed by dropping ground composition onto the backing and passing this through the nip of two large, heated, differential-speed calender rolls. These rolls consolidate the granules to a dense sheet and adhere them to the backing, at the the same time producing a smooth surface. Jaspe linoleum is characterized by its longitudinal striation which is produced by using granules of two or more colors in a similar manner. Marbelized linoleum has a non-repeating veining made by mixing different colored granules and forming them into a sheet. The sheet is cut, folded, turned at right angles, passed through calender rolls, and then adhered to a backing.

A regular and repeating design with somewhat blurred joinings is characteristic of molded inlaid linoleum. Here granules of smaller particle size are aged carefully under controlled conditions to allow them to be used in the molding operations. Stencils of a great variety of designs are used to lay down the granules on the backing sheet. The patterned mix is then consolidated in a series of hot hydraulic presses with chromium-plated platens. An embossing stencil may be used in the last press to indent the face of the linoleum slightly, particularly along the color lines of the pattern. Today, this is the most popular type of household weight linoleum.

The most interesting type of linoleum, as far as manufacturing is concerned, is no longer being made. This was called straightline inlaid linoleum in which the repeating

geometric design had sharply defined joinings. This occurred because it was made by a huge 6-foot-wide, automatic, high-speed rotary machine which cut figures from four separate sheets of linoleum composition. It then placed these figures in exact position on a continuous web of backing material and passed this component through calendar rolls which continuously consolidated it into the finished floor covering with its geometric design. The first of these machines was built in 1908, and two others were made in the 1920's. Anyone who saw these "million dollar" giants at work could not help but be impressed by the four large sheets of linoleum composition being cut, apparently at random, and then placed on a web to form a continuous sheet with no blurred joinings and 6 feet wide. All of this was done at 130 ft/min.

Linoleum has to be cured—a process which causes the oleoresinous binder to cross-link and form an insoluble thermoset product. Oil-based paints cure in a similar manner at room temperature. Linoleum is normally cured in very large stoves at 175°F for periods of 14 to 21 days. The length of the cure depends on the thickness of the linoleum sheets and on the number of layers placed in the stove. After curing, the linoleum is protected with a factory sealer and a wax finish.

Linoleum is available for residential and other moderate to light traffic areas in .0625-, .070-, and .090-inch thicknesses on felt backing. These have minimum wear layers of .022, .030 and .050-inch, respectively. It is also sold for commercial, industrial, and other heavy traffic areas in .125 (⅛) inch thickness on burlap backing. Both are made 6 feet wide. A special static conductive type is available in .125-inch thickness, 6 feet wide, and is described fully below.

Linoleum is produced in several plain and marbelized colors, with numerous variegated designs, several of which contain metallic decorations, and quite a number of embossed inlaid (repeating) designs. If desired, quite pretty and striking floors can be custom-tailored by creative persons.

However, since linoleum is an opaque material, the aesthetic possibilities are limited.

Since linoleum is heat cured, it has quite a high resistance to indentation from long-time static loads. With the cork filler and blown oil binder, its resilience or underfoot comfort and its quietness underfoot are very high. However, it is surpassed in both these respects by full-thick cork, rubber and homogeneous vinyl tiles. Its resistance to grease and oil is excellent, and its shrinkage resistance is very good. When it is properly installed on suspended floors and maintained according to recommendations, the .125-inch linoleum has lasted in good condition for over 50 years. The .090-inch material should last a minimum of 15 to 25 years. Linoleum is quite easy to maintain, being better in this respect than asphalt, rubber and cork tiles. Because it is a good insulating material and is used in thicker sections, linoleum feels quite warm to the touch. Only cork tile and the new Cushionflor are superior.

Most complaints about linoleum seem to involve indentation and nailheads showing through. It must be remembered that linoleum is quite vulnerable to attack by alkali because of the nature of the binder. Degradation and leaching of the binder occur when strongly alkaline cleaning agents are used, especially in areas with hard water. The calcium and magnesium salts of hard water have a synergistic action with alkalies on degradation. Linoleum is also quite sensitive to moisture and so should not be used over on- or below-grade concrete unless the slab is well protected by a waterproof membrane. It also should not be used in humid localities. When it has absorbed moisture from cleaning solutions or high humidity, it becomes soft and plastic and then shows poor resistance to indentation and abrasion. This absorbed moisture also tends to slowly degrade the oxidized oil-resin binder. However, when the moisture dries out, the linoleum once again becomes a tough and abrasion-resistant floor covering—unless degradation has already occurred.

The installation and the maintenance of linoleum flooring are normal. Each company has its own installation instructions and its own adhesives. See Tables 12A-6 and 12A-7 for helpful ideas on maintenance and stain removal problems.

Rotogravure Printed Vinyl Laminates (Loose-lay)

Rotogravure vinyl laminate is one of the later entries into the resilient flooring field. In price, it is one step up from the printed felt base and is used in much the same way—loose-laid as yard goods or borderless rugs. It was introduced in 1950. Today several companies produce it. Sales reached a peak of 810 million square feet in 1960 and declined to about 675 million square feet by 1962 and 600 million in 1965.

The product consists of a rotogravure printed design on a suitable base covered with a wear surface of clear, transparent vinyl. In some cases, the printing is done on a thin sheet of specially impregnated paper. This is then coated with a vinyl organosol or plastisol, and the coating is fused into a durable continuous film. Finally, it is laminated to the supporting felt backing. In the second method, the printing is done directly on specially coated felt backing. Then the vinyl organosol or plastisol wearlayer is formed as before.

Currently, there are two types of bases available: (1) the inorganic or asbestos fiber felt saturated with rubber latex and usable in all grade locations, and (2) the organic fiber (high rag-kraft) felt saturated with resins or asphalt and usable only in above-grade or suspended floor locations.

In the case of plastisols, wearlayers are made from emulsion grade vinyl chloride resins, suitable plasticizers and stabilizers. In the case of organosols, a non-solvent such as toluene or naphtha is added to decrease the viscosity of the solution. The wearlayer normally contains from 30 to 50 parts plasticizer per hundred parts of resin.

Rotogravure vinyl laminate flooring is offered in 6-, 9- and 12-foot widths and in several sizes of borderless rugs. It usually has an over-all thickness of about .055 inch and a vinyl wearlayer of .003 to .004 inch. Some permanently installed versions have been made—these are discussed under Vinyl Yard Goods.

Since the printing rolls are made by a photographic process, the design possibilities of this product are practically unlimited—the cost of the big 12-foot-wide printing cylinders being an important factor. The product has the good resistance of a plasticized vinyl to fats, oils, greases, acids and alkalies. It is flexible and easy to handle.

Because of its relatively thin wearlayer, its durability is not great; printed felt base is the only product it surpasses in this important property.

Vinyl Yard Goods (over .006-inch wearlayer)

Vinyl yard goods, quite naturally, appeared on the market shortly after the homogeneous or flexible vinyl tiles. In about 1947, they were produced in 6-foot widths with an asphalt saturated felt backing. Today they are produced with resin-impregnated felt (organic base), asbestos (inorganic base) and vinyl backings. However, we are considering only those yard goods with wearlayers of over .006-inch thickness; thus we eliminate the large volume of inexpensive rotogravure printed felt-backed products which are briefly described on p. 235. These vinyl yard goods are produced as (1) the less expensive (and larger-volume) calendered products and (2) the more expensive (more highly aesthetic) press-molded products. Some rotogravure printed yard goods are available with a clear wearlayer (.006 to .015 inch thick).

Because the vinyl is made just soft enough for good handling properties, these vinyl yard goods have excellent resistance to stains, grease and indentation. They are quite comfortable underfoot and have very good wearing qualities. However, the ones with transparent areas present in moderate to large quantities tend to show scratches more than the filled ones and are very definitely damaged by having a lighted cigarette allowed to burn out or be stepped out on them. Even the filled patterns can be marked badly by burning cigarettes.

These yard goods sell in larger volume than linoleum because of their more beautiful designs and better colors. Their principal uses are in kitchens, entrances, and other rooms in the home and several commercial applications where burning cigarettes are not likely to be dropped on the floor. The price is in the medium to high range—up to $1.10/sq ft.

The volume of vinyl yard goods is still climbing each year. In 1958 and 1959, the volume was about 80,000,000 square feet. In 1960, it soared to 225,000,000 square feet and kept climbing fast. By 1962, sales had grown to 250,000,000 square feet, outranking linoleum. In 1965 they reached 450,000,000 square feet.

Vinyl yard goods comprise (a) a backing, (b) a tie or color layer, and (c) the vinyl layer. The backing can have an organic, inorganic or vinyl base. The exposed vinyl layer can be made from filled, or a combination of both filled and unfilled stocks. The tie or color layer usually contains a modified styrene-butadiene latex or a modified acrylic. It prevents migration of colors into the vinyl layer and also hides the color of the base in transparent vinyls.

The organic backings are prepared from felts which are made from combinations of rags, kraft and newsprint. The amount of each of these ingredients and the type of rags employed depend greatly on the use that will be made of the end product. The highest-priced line uses a high rag stock of good quality rags. These felts are then impregnated with a special indent-resistant resin in order to make them into suitable backings for vinyl yard goods.

The relatively new inorganic backings are based on asbestos. The fibers are held together by means of an elastomeric binder such as neoprene or styrene-butadiene rubber. This felt needs no additional impregnating step; nonetheless, it is expensive because of the high cost of the materials. Its greatest advantage is that it can be installed above, on, or below grade since it does not rot when exposed to moisture as do the organic felts.

Vinyl backings are also available. They consist of highly filled and/or scrap vinyl compounds—as inexpensive as possible while still retaining the necessary physical properties needed in this type of goods.

(1) The tie or color layer must hide the color of the base by its own color in the case of transparent or translucent sheets. (2) It must adequately bond the base to the vinyl wearlayer. (3) It must prevent the migration of the dyes used in the rags in the organic bases; prevent the migration of the resins, their reaction by-products, and the rag dyes from the resin-impregnated organic bases; and prevent the migration of the rubber antioxidants and curatives or their by-products in both the organic and the inorganic bases. They are not necessary in the case of vinyl bases. Some of the tie layers must be able to allow air and moisture to pass out through them because of certain processing conditions. Most of these coatings are based on modified styrene-butadiene latices or modified acrylics.

The top vinyl layer is usually made up of a continuous vinyl sheet decorated in various ways with large, medium or small chips. Both the layer and the chip compositions contain from 30 to 50 per cent binder when filled. Sometimes the chips are clear, especially when they contain metallics. Some of the most popular, high-priced yard goods have the continuous sheet made of a clear vinyl so one gets the feeling of depth. Of course, both of these clear compounds are essentially 100 per cent binder.

The binder consists of medium or high molecular weight polyvinyl chloride polymer, plasticizers, pigments, stabilizers and any processing aids needed. The PVC homopolymer is usually used because its physical properties are superior to those of vinyl chloride/vinyl acetate copolymer. In a few cases, a small amount of a rubber is added to the PVC. These polymers require higher temperatures to become thoroughly fused and, thus, are processed at temperatures close to their decomposition points. PVC by itself is a very hard and quite brittle plastic, but it can be softened to any desirable degree by the addition of plasticizer.

The chief plasticizers in use in this type of flooring today are dioctyl phthalate (DOP), butyl benzyl phthalate (BBP), and tricresyl phosphate (TCP). Each of these has certain advantages and disadvantages. DOP has the advantage of low cost and imparts the best low-temperature properties of the three. Quite often these yard goods are installed at temperatures below the recommended 70°F; therefore, low-temperature cutting and handling properties should be maintained. This requirement can be achieved through the use of small to moderate amounts of special plasticizers, such as dioctyl adipate, didecyl adipate or dioctyl sebacate. DOP is the least volatile of the three. Since these stocks are mixed and processed at high temperatures, low volatility is an important characteristic, for the plasticizer should not cause even moderate fuming during the manufacturing steps. BBP is almost as low in cost as DOP, but it is somewhat more volatile, though still within the usable range. One of its greatest advantages is its excellent rubber heel stain resistance. Staining in traffic areas caused by the antioxidants used in rubber heels has become an increasingly important problem in the past few years because of the extensive use of clears, whites, and pastel colors in resilient flooring. BBP has mitigated this problem but has by no means conquered it. Besides being somewhat volatile, BBP imparts poor low-temperature properties to its stocks. However, it causes fast fusion of the PVC resin at lower temperatures than required for DOP; for this reason alone, large quantities of BBP have been used.

TCP is also a fast-fusing plasticizer, but it is expensive when compared to the other two. Also, it becomes quite yellow on exposure to light. Previously, when the dark or full-bodied colors were very popular, this tendency to yellow slightly was not very important, but today it is a serious drawback in some transparent or light-color formulations.

Some new plasticizers are trying to gain a foothold into this market in spite of their high prices. Their outstanding property is resistance to household and rubber heel stain. Since the trend is toward products which require this resistance, the use of these special plasticizers should increase.

The physical properties of the product are

determined by the resin/plasticizer ratio and—in opaque sheets—by the amount of filler added. If the ratio is kept high and, thus, a lot of polymer is used, then the clear part of the product will be hard and inflexible, will scratch easily and will be less comfortable underfoot. Its stiffness would cause difficulty in making and especially in installing the yard goods. If a high plasticizer content is used, the product would exhibit unacceptable indentation characteristics, ready soiling and easy staining. By the time this ratio is down to 2:1 (50 parts of plasticizer per hundred parts of resin), soiling usually becomes a serious problem. For opaque or filled portions of these vinyl yard goods, the physical properties can be altered further by the addition of various amounts of fillers. Since the filler absorbs some of the plasticizer, the binder portion (polymer + plasticizer) is usually made softer than for clear compounds. The filler then "stiffens" the final product and makes it less susceptible to soiling, etc.

Calcium carbonate (whiting) is by far the most widely used filler, because of its extremely low cost and its good color. Small amounts of other fillers have been used in vinyl yard goods for special reasons. Precipitated whiting is usually preferred because its considerably finer particle size causes it to "stiffen" the product more. The refined natural whiting and larger-sized particles of calcium carbonate are used to lower the cost of the product, to help entrapped air to escape, etc. The latter are less expensive, costing well under one cent a pound.

Stabilizers are an essential part of every flooring formulation made of PVC since they prevent or minimize the breakdown of the polymer during the high temperatures of processing. The correct stabilizers will allow the manufacturers to maintain the vinyl up to 400°F for several minutes so it can be decorated and formed correctly. Other stabilizers will protect the product from discoloration caused by the breakdown of the polymer (or some other ingredient) due to the "bombardment" of light. Ultraviolet radiation in sunlight is the major offender, even through glass where most of the ultraviolet rays are filtered out. High-priced chemicals are incorporated to absorb the damaging ultraviolet rays and convert them into harmless energy. The manufacturers must also be careful of the near-ultraviolet light and even of the light given off by the common fluorescent lights.

Yard goods flooring is made either clear or filled with non-discoloring materials. These may be opaque, translucent or transparent. The pigments used in vinyl today have been vastly improved in the last few years. It is no problem to obtain bright, clear colorations, beiges, and pastel colors.

Other processing aids are used as needed. Some lubricating materials that aid in manufacturing these products include low molecular weight polyethylene, waxes, and stearic acid.

The Federal Specification which covers these vinyl yard goods flooring materials is L-F-475a(1).

Vinyl yard goods may be calendered, molded or rotogravure printed. In calendered vinyl goods, the mixture of materials is fed into a Bunbury mixer and converted into a homogeneous mass by means of heat and vigorous mixing. This is dropped to a hot two-roll mill and either broken up into small pieces or sheeted off to the calender. Here, it is made to the desired thickness and width. Next, the decoration in the form of various types of chips, metallic, etc., are added and fused into the sheet. Finally this sheet is adhered to a backing. The goods are trimmed, finished, inspected and packed ready for shipment.

For molded vinyl yard goods, the expensive product made with large chips in a clear vinyl background will be described. The chips are made separately by calendering a stock as above, giving it character by adding another stock and cross-rolling it or by other means, and then breaking up the finished sheet. The organic felt base or the inorganic asbestos backing has been coated with a cement. The chips are packed into a random design by special vibrators and conveyors and then are placed on the cement and thus stuck to the backing. The voids between the chips are filled with small chips or powdered clear vinyl. After heating, this unit is then consolidated in a press using as short a cycle as possible. In some cases, the product is fused further by subsequent heating and smoothing. The yard goods are then trimmed, finished, inspected and packed.

The rotogravure printed vinyl yard goods can be made either by printing onto the backing sheet or by reverse printing the clear wearlayer (over .006 inch thick for this category). In the second method, the vinyl back sheet is calendered in a manner similar to the wearlayer except that this sheet is usually more highly loaded with filler. The clear wearlayer is also calendered to the desired thickness, and the underside is printed (in the reverse pattern, of course) on a rotogravure press. These two plies are then laminated together using a Rotocure, probably with some method for preheating the stocks as they enter the "curing drum." The goods are then trimmed, inspected and packed. The finished width of the product is currently limited to 6 feet because of equipment limitations.

Vinyl yard goods are normally offered in 6-foot-wide rolls which are 90 feet long, a total of 60 square yards. Half rolls and other sizes are available. In some cases, short lengths (under 30 square yards) are sold at a lower price. Thickness ranges from .050 to .090 inch depending on the type and the pattern. Generally, the rotogravure and the calendered patterns are the thinner ones and the molded patterns are the thicker ones. Designs vary from simple printed rotogravure products and chip designs on a colored background for calendered products to highly aesthetic molded materials with fancy, multicolored chips in a clear or highly tinted clear matrix. These molded vinyl yard goods are a match for all but the extremely high-style (and high-priced) homogeneous or flexible vinyl tiles.

The finished vinyl yard goods are attractive products, resistant to severe service conditions, comfortable to walk on, and quiet underfoot. Many of them can stand heavy loads for long periods of time without any noticeable permanent indentations. Their wear resistance is exceedingly good,

and their colors remain bright and clear throughout their lifetime. Resistance to surface moisture, alkali or detergents, grease, fats, oils or household cleaners is excellent. Those made with asbestos backing can be used below grade, but the vinyl backed products are recommended only for on-grade installation.

The biggest problem with regard to the use of vinyl yard goods is their susceptibility to cigarette burns and surface scratching. All types of vinyl flooring can be damaged to a greater or lesser degree by lighted cigarettes. The filled vinyls (opaque) are marred badly enough, but the clear, high-style yard goods (as well as the clear, highly aesthetic tiles) are even more severely damaged, often beyond repair.

Vinyl floorings can be scratched by pieces of grit, ash, etc., brought in on the soles of shoes. In fact, after a time, the highly polished surface of a product will become dull because of the great number of small scratches. The desired sheen or gloss can be recaptured by a thorough cleaning (to get the dirt out of the cracks) and a good waxing. Of course, if a proper coating of wax has been maintained on the floor, the scratching would be minimized. Many manufacturers apply a factory finish of acrylic resins on the surface of their higher-grade products to help retain the initial gloss for a longer period and to protect the surface until such time as the proper maintenance schedule can be initiated. Good maintenance would make these floors last as long as desired.

The problem of traffic staining occurs more often in the filled compounds and especially in the white, beige or pastel colors. This discoloration is caused by amine antioxidants used in the manufacture of rubber heels and soles. Often, this stain can be lessened by the use of fine steel wool or other abrasive cleaning materials. The problem has been ameliorated by the introduction of new, highly stain-resistant plasticizers, but these are expensive.

Vinyl yard goods have little or no trouble with permanent indentation as long as the floor has not been abused and improper installation techniques have not been used.

Nailheads seldom show through because the felt tends to hide them. However, attention should be paid to obtain a smooth, uniform and properly secured underlayment. The use of Underlayment Grade DFPA plywood secured with special high holding power nails is recommended. The use of the proper furniture rests (as recommended by the various flooring manufacturers) is added insurance against permanent indentation.

Foam Cushion Vinyl Yard Goods

This is the newest type of resilient flooring on the market, introduced in 1962. Its special design, incorporating a layer of vinyl foam between the felt and the wearlayer, gives it many advantages over the other types. In the future, a product of this construction will undoubtedly be offered with as much as ¼ inch of foam covered by .014 to .030 inch of clear wearlayer. This will be in direct and fierce competition with woven and tufted carpeting, thus opening up another big market for resilient flooring.

This cushioned flooring is made up of three layers. The backing can be an organic felt (resin-impregnated rag felt) or an inorganic (asbestos) felt. The manufacturer recommends loose-lay installations for the standard-weight material and permanent installations below, on, or above grade for the asbestos backed middleweight yard goods.

The foam is a blown vinyl formulation with little or no filler present. It has been pigmented to a white with titanium dioxide.

The clear wearlayer is made from a regular, stain-resistant formulation by ordinary techniques.

The design of this product is printed between the clear wearlayer and the vinyl foam. The newest designs in both weights are now embossed in register with the printing—no small feat when one considers that this product is made 6, 9 and 12 feet wide. With printing and embossing combinations, a large number of designs are possible.

Foam cushion yard goods are made in two weights. The standard-weight material (organic felt backing) is offered in rolls 6, 9 and 12 feet wide and 90 to 110 feet long. It is about .095 inch thick; the wearlayer is about .008 inch. The medium-weight material (organic or inorganic felt backing), offered in rolls 6 feet wide and about 90 feet long, is close to .090 inch thick; the wearlayer is about .015 inch.

A large number of attractive designs are possible using the rotogravure printing technique plus in-register embossing. Pebbles, stones, tiles, bricks, etc., are easily outlined by their grout which is embossed to a lower level to produce three-dimensional effects. Other decorations such as glitter, metallic flakes, chips, etc., can also be used for special effects.

Foam cushion vinyl yard goods have several advantages. They have by far the highest underfoot softness and thus are very comfortable to stand on, even surpassing cork tile. They exhibit the lowest noise level, whether from things dropped on them or people walking on them; they are also lowest in noise transmitted through to the room below. The vinyl foam acts as an insulator, and thus the floor feels warm even when placed on a concrete slab. There can be as much as a 10°F difference in temperature between vinyl foam material and the concrete it is on. Because the feet sink into the foam somewhat, the chances of skidding or slipping are greatly diminished. The foam also cushions the wearlayer against abrasive wear and scratches; therefore, this product lasts longer than would be predicted from its wearlayer thickness.

As with all smooth-surface flooring with clear, unfilled wearlayers, these cushioned products are very easy to mop clean. The embossings have gently sloping sides which present no cleaning problems.

The resistance of these products to permanent indentation has been exceptionally good; however, indentations caused by heavy furniture or appliances do not come out at once. Imperfections in the subflooring have great difficulty in showing through this product because both the felt and the foam tend to hide them; nonetheless, care should be taken when laying the subfloor as with any other resilient or smooth-surface flooring.

The main disadvantage of these cushioned yard goods is cigarette burn damage.

When a lighted cigarette is dropped onto a vinyl flooring, the intense heat causes the vinyl to melt in the neighborhood of the burning tip. This heat and the weight of the cigarette cause it to penetrate into the clear vinyl for several mils. When the cigarette is stepped out, of course, it and its ashes are pushed physically into the softened vinyl for 10 to 15 mils. The area around the burn is blackened by the cigarette ashes and by the actual charring of the vinyl. These burned areas are extremely difficult to remove. In the case of the standard-weight foam cushion vinyl yard goods, the lighted cigarette must be recovered immediately or it will melt its way through the 8-mil wearlayer into the foam layer. With the 15-mil wearlayer of the medium-weight product, it takes the cigarette an appreciably longer time to penetrate to the foam, but as with all clears, a burned spot will soon develop.

When a heavy object with a relatively sharp edge (e.g., a full can, a plate, an iron, etc.) lands on the floor on its edge, it is almost certain to make an indent or a gouge in the flooring material. This is usually accompanied by a permanent indentation in the subflooring. In the case of the standard-weight product, this gouge will be somewhat larger than for other types of resilient flooring; conversely, an object of lighter weight will gouge the standard-weight floor covering while only denting some other products. Medium-weight cushioned product is just slightly more susceptible to gouges than other types of resilient flooring—it is a definite improvement over the corresponding standard-weight product. However, both materials tend to heal themselves so that in most cases it is very difficult to find the gouge in a few days (especially if it is cemented shut carefully with a vinyl cement); with other floorings, the gouge is permanently visible.

It is simple to repair burned spots in these products. A new piece is laid over the damaged spot so that the patterns match. Then a sharp, straight blade utility knife is used to cut through both pieces, the damaged piece is cut out, and a new matching piece is made. The new piece is then put in place, smoothed over, and the wearlayer is carefully cemented together.

TILES

Asphalt Tile

Commercial production of asphalt tiles began in 1922. United States industrial production was 25 million square feet in 1930 and 90 million in 1941. By 1960 it had risen to its peak of about 900 million square feet, declining to 600 million square feet in 1965. Asphalt tiles gained immediate acceptance because in the early days they were the only resilient floor covering which would perform satisfactorily in basements or on concrete slabs in direct contact with the ground. Linoleum and rubber tile, the most widely used floor coverings at that time, could not withstand the alkaline moisture generally present in these on-grade or below-grade locations. Another reason for their popularity was and still is their low cost. Today they are the least expensive commercial grade tile on the market (as far as the initial installation costs are concerned).

The early tiles were approximately 50 per cent asbestos fiber, 25 per cent mineral filler and 25 per cent gilsonite asphalt by weight. Some of today's Group A and B (dark) colors are still formulated in this manner. This product gained real recognition in the early 1930's with the development of light colors and marbelizing techniques through the use of hydrocarbon resins to replace the dark asphalt binders. Today the light-colored (C and D) asphalt tiles are semiflexible products comprising approximately 35 per cent binder, made up of coumaroneindene type resin, plasticized with animal, vegetable, or petroleum pitches; 60 per cent inorganic fillers, mainly asbestos fibers and limestone; and 5 per cent inorganic color pigments. The dark colors use asphalt or gilsonite as their resin portion. As far back as the 1930's, the Asphalt Tile Institute (now the Asphalt and Vinyl Asbestos Tile Institute) cooperated with the National Bureau of Standards in Washington, D. C. and arrived at what is now Federal Specification SS-T-306-b. This specification has been accepted as the yardstick of asphalt tile quality. SS-T-307, now cancelled, covered the grease-resistant variety of this tile. Most manufacturers have ceased production of these grease-resistant tiles.

In the production of these tiles, the ingredients are blended in a Banbury or other type of mixer or in differential-speed two-roll mills. While the mixture is hot, it is passed through a series of cool calender rolls which reduce the thickness of the sheet in steps down to the required gauge of the final product. These cool rolls also produce the desired surface finish. The sheets are then continuously cut into tile form by die presses or other suitable equipment. Selvage composition or rejected tiles are returned to the Banbury as rework.

Asphalt tiles are usually offered in 9×9 inch (some in 12×12 and 18×24 inch) sizes and in $\frac{1}{8}$- and $\frac{3}{16}$-inch thicknesses. They are made in a few plain colors, many marbelized or striated designs, many chip, cork, and textured patterns, and in some other variegated designs. As would be expected from an opaque material which is easier to produce in dark colors, the aesthetic possibilities are quite limited. However, by using a lot of imagination, many interesting flooring designs can be achieved. Presently, there are three color groups, plus certain other decorations, produced. Group B comprises the least expensive tiles with dark brown or black background plus a small amount of lighter-colored decoration. The Group C Tiles contain those with the background in the greys, dark and light greens, light browns and beiges—those colors which do not require the more expensive, almost colorless resins or a large amount of titanium dioxide. The Group D tiles include those with truer light color, cream and white backgrounds; these, of course, are the most expensive of the three. The special, more highly decorated asphalt tiles run slightly higher per square foot.

Asphalt tiles have good abrasion resistance under normal conditions. This would be expected since they are made principally of two materials naively thought to be almost indestructible—asbestos fiber and hydrocarbon resin. However, the abrasion resistance of these tiles drops drastically under gritty conditions, e.g., near entranceways from areas where sand, cinders, crushed stone or even dirt can readily be picked up by shoes. Because of their high density and the fact that some designs go all the way through the tiles, they can be worn quite thin under severe traffic conditions without changing the general appearance of the floor. In today's market this usually does not happen because of improved maintenance. Their inherent high resistance to moisture and their composition prevent rotting and drying out after installation. This moisture and rot resistance makes them the only low-cost floor covering, other than $\frac{1}{16}$-inch vinyl asbestos tiles, that performs satisfactorily in basement or other below-grade areas. Accidental surface flooding of below-grade areas covered with asphalt tiles has been numerous. The tiles have usually been found in excellent shape once the flood waters have receded and the dirt has been cleared away. Most other types of resilient flooring have had to be replaced under these conditions. Because of their high asbestos fiber and limestone content, they will not support combustion when installed. They are resistant to cigarette burns. With these qualities and their low price, asphalt tiles have been quite popular in commercial applications. They are recommended for most areas but are used primarily over suspended, on-grade or below-grade concrete floors.

Because of their thermoplastic nature and their lack of recovery from indentation under prolonged load or under light load at elevated temperatures, asphalt tiles have received more complaints about residual indentation than any other resilient flooring material. They are noisy and have poor comfort value because of the hard and brittle nature of their composition. They have poor solvent and grease resistance. Their tendency to buckle or crack is greater than for the other types. They soil easily and are hard to clean or polish when compared to other types.

Vinyl Asbestos Tile

The first vinyl floor covering was a semi-flexible vinyl asbestos (VA) tile made in 1931. An installation was made at the Chicago World's Fair in 1933. Since their introduction in 1948, these tiles have been the fastest-growing product in the resilient flooring tile field. By 1958 they were selling at the rate of 400 million square feet annually. In 1961, their volume had surpassed that of asphalt tile; in 1962, it rose still further to 950 million square feet and by 1965 reached 1,250,000,000 square feet. During the first ten years of sales growth (1948–1957), the price of VA tiles actually declined by over 50 per cent, while that of asphalt tiles remained practically constant and that of other flooring products increased substantially. In the face of constantly rising labor costs, this was made possible through continued improvements in the highly mechanized, continuous production process, lower raw material prices, and lower-cost recipes. In the 5-year period 1958–1963, the cost remained almost constant while that of practically everything else increased because of inflation.

The VA tiles consist of about 30 per cent binder, 65 per cent mineral fillers such as asbestos fibers and limestone, and 2 to 8 per cent stabilizers and color pigments. The binder is made up of vinyl resins of the vinyl chloride/vinyl acetate type (usually containing 15 per cent vinyl acetate) of moderate molecular weight and plasticizers such as dioctyl phthalate, butyl benzyl phthalate, dipropylene glycol dibenzoate, etc. Since they are composed of clear synthetic vinyl resins and colorless synthetic plasticizers, cleaner, clearer colors are possible with VA tiles than with most other resilient flooring materials containing natural resins and plasticizers which tend to be amber colored. The only limitation on VA coloration is the definite grey tint caused by the use of asbestos fibers. In addition, this binder formulation results in a tile which does not oxidize, harden or soften with age. The color stability of this product on aging is quite good. The 1/8-inch thick tiles are covered by Federal Specification L-T-00345 (COM-NBS).

Vinyl asbestos tiles are made in much the same way as asphalt tiles using a Banbury or other type of mixer and a series of cool calender rolls.

Vinyl asbestos tiles are offered in 9 × 9 and 12 × 12 inch sizes and in 1/16, 3/32- and 1/8-inch thicknesses. They are made in a few plain colors and in many marbelized, feather-veined, terrazzo, metallic chip and other variegated designs. The opacity of the product and its grey tint limit its aesthetic possibilities.

These tiles have surpassed asphalt tile in sales volume because they have all the desirable performance characteristics of asphalt tiles plus many more. They are more resistant to abrasion, as they have the same types and similar amounts of mineral fillers and a tougher, stronger binder resin. They have very good rot resistance and will not support combustion. Not only does the high filler content prevent its burning, but the resin itself is self-extinguishing because of its high chlorine content. Like asphalt tiles, they are very resistant to cigarette burns. However, the burns are generally more noticeable, especially in the light colors. Vinyl asbestos tiles are considerably less affected by alkaline moisture whether it comes from strong detergents or other harsh cleaning materials or from on-grade or below-grade concrete slabs. This permits their use in damp basements or slab houses. However, no resilient flooring is recommended where excessive moisture conditions exist, particularly where hydrostatic pressure is a factor.

Vinyl asbestos is also specified for areas requiring severe maintenance procedures. The true life of a flooring material so often depends on its complete resistance to alkalies present in even the mildest cleaning solutions. Despite the maintenance recommendations of manufacturers, harsh cleansers and detergents are used and they tend to break down the binders in most resilient floorings other than those based on vinyl resins. The dimensional stability of VA tiles is outstanding, though not as good as that of the thermoset polymers. The two major causes of shrinkage or expansion in flooring are (1) extremes in temperature and (2) excessive moisture. Since VA tiles are highly resistant to both, they can be safely recommended in problem floor areas such as automobile showrooms where the direct rays of the sun cause shrinkage of many other materials. Floor areas that are frequently flooded with soapy water from showers and washstands have stood up for years.

Unlike asphalt tiles and many other types of resilient tiles, vinyl asbestos is unaffected physically by oil and grease. Thus it can be recommended in manufacturing or other areas subject to tracking of mineral oils, fats or greases. However, one must remember that when vinyl asbestos becomes oil soaked, it cannot be restored by normal cleaning. It is improved by a hard cleaning with steel wool. It can also be recommended for commercial and institutional kitchens if one doesn't mind the dirt-filled seams that are present in great volume with any normal tile installation. Vinyl asbestos is also resistant to mild acids and many other reagents and so performs very adequately in laboratories, hospitals, etc., as long as solvents such as ketones and cyclic ethers are not used. Strong acids will cause the limestone filler to decompose and thus ruin the tile. Vinyl asbestos tiles have the necessary flexibility and durability to be used in large quantities on subway cars, ferry boats, steamships and railroad cars. Many installations are over 15 years old and still in good condition. After testing many types of resilient floors, the New York City Transit Authority found that only VA tile stood up to their severe service conditions—these floors seldom get washed and are never waxed.

The maintenance costs of VA tiles are claimed to be the lowest of the various types of resilient flooring. The records of a New York office-building superintendent showed that VA tiles cost about half as much as asphalt tiles or linoleum to maintain and about one-fourth as much as higher-priced resilient tiles. Of course, the level of cleanliness and appearance was undoubtedly much higher for the more aesthetic, high-priced tiles.

Like asphalt tiles, VA tiles are thermoplastic in nature. However, they are markedly superior to asphalt tiles in resistance to indentation. The greatest number of complaints about VA tiles seem to be from nail heads showing through. This is probably due to the use of thinner gauge tiles—$\frac{1}{16}$-inch vinyl asbestos versus $\frac{1}{8}$-inch asphalt tiles. Though it is better than asphalt tile in relative quietness and comfort underfoot, vinyl asbestos is quite inferior in these respects to the other present-day resilient flooring products.

Linoleum Tile

The history of linoleum tile follows very closely that of linoleum itself. It is estimated that sales amounted to 60 million square feet in 1958 and have fallen off to about 25 million in 1965.

Its composition is that of calendered linoleum. The residential tiles have felt backs while the special $\frac{1}{8}$-inch tiles have no backing.

Linoleum tile is available in 9×9 inch size (a few patterns in 4×27, 4×36, 6×12 inches) and in .0625, .070- and .090-inch thicknesses. They are made in marbelized, spatter and a sort of wood-grain effect.

Their advantages and disadvantages follow those of linoleum with the added ease of installation of tile and the more difficult maintenance caused by the seams.

Cork Tile

Cork tiles have been used in this country since about 1900. They are made from the outer bark of the cork oak tree found mainly in Spain and Portugal but also in the rest of southern Europe. Cork's unique cellular structure gives it the structural advantages of resilience, sound-deadening ability and insulative value, all of which are desirable and important characteristics of smooth-surface flooring. However, this same structure and the lack of proper adhesives gave rise to the problems of installation and maintenance (due to the porosity and the expansion and contraction of cork) which originally held down the volume of cork tile in use for many years. From the early 1900's until 1920, sales of cork flooring grew only to 200,000 sq ft/yr. By 1927 production had increased slowly to about 3 million sq ft/yr. Sales grew much more rapidly after World War II with the use of additive resins to improve properties. The peak sales of all types of cork flooring reached 36 million square feet in 1957. Since then sales have dwindled, until in 1962 only 3 million square feet of cork tiles were produced (other types of cork flooring are not listed).

There are four categories of cork tiles, some of them no longer produced. The original type consisted of cork granules baked under high heat and pressure. This caused the natural resins to flow out and become the necessary binder to form blocks. Tiles were then sawed from these blocks. Since those cork products had relatively low tensile strength, the cork tiles were furnished in heavy gauges ranging from $\frac{5}{16}$-inch upward without a factory finish. Once installed, they were quite durable but difficult to maintain.

The second category consisted of cork sheet which had been impregnated with a molten wax composition at the factory. This type of tile was also difficult to maintain and so is not used much today.

In the period following World War II domestic manufacturers started adding phenolic or other resins or plasticized glue as the binder to the granulated cork. The mixture is then placed into molds in large hydraulic presses and baked at elevated temperatures under compression. The binder is melted around the granules which are then compressed into a solid block. Finally, the binder cures or sets, and the block is removed from the mold and cooled. It is then continuously sliced into tile. The use of resin binders allows the use of lower baking temperatures and shorter baking time, and it produces tile with greater tensile strength, more resiliency (the natural cork resins are retained), more uniform color, and less porosity. All tile is now sanded to gauge and sealed at the factory.

The last category involves a marriage of cork and vinyl. Here the cork is bound together by vinyl resins, and a clear vinyl is applied to the surface as the wearlayer. This circumvents many of the drawbacks of the former types of cork tiles but also reduces their strongest points—relative quietness and underfoot comfort.

Cork tiles are covered by Federal Specification LLL-T-431b in two classes: class 1 includes cork tile with wax, lacquer or resin finish; class 2 includes cork tile with clear plastic film finish.

Cork (resin reinforced) and vinyl cork tiles are offered in 6 × 6, 9 × 9, 12 × 12, and up to 36 × 36-inch sizes. The cork tiles are available in thicknesses ranging from $\frac{3}{32}$ to $\frac{1}{2}$ inch including $\frac{1}{8}$, $\frac{3}{16}$, $\frac{5}{16}$ and $\frac{1}{4}$-inch. The vinyl cork comes in only $\frac{1}{8}$- and $\frac{3}{16}$-inch thicknesses. Though originally there were only three colors—light, medium and dark brown—some additional colors and effects have been added especially in the vinyl cork line. The color and design selection is very limited.

These tiles are recommended chiefly for above-grade application. The use of cork over on-grade concrete floors is permitted if a special adhesive is used and if the floor is one foot above grade drainage or has an efficient waterproof membrane installed. They are not recommended for below-grade installation.

The two principal advantages of cork tiles are their relative quietness and their underfoot comfort. In both these properties, they are better than any resilient flooring except the new Cushionflor. The *raw cork* and *resin tiles* are the least durable of those discussed. They have poor grease and surface alkali resistance and are difficult to maintain. Their resistance to permanent indent due to static loads is only moderate. It must be remembered that the degree of resistance to abrasive wear, water, grease, staining, dirt ingraining, etc., is directly related to the degree to which the pores of the cork tiles have been sealed and to the smoothness of the surface. There may be differences in the porosity and the surface smoothness of the same categories as supplied by the different manufacturers.

The *vinyl cork tiles* have the cork protected by a layer of clear vinyl. As would be expected, the relative quietness and the underfoot comfort are not as good as for regular cork tile. These vinyl cork tiles are not quite as good as linoleum or rubber tile in these properties, but they are better than flexible vinyl tiles and vinyl sheet goods and far superior to vinyl asbestos and asphalt tile. Of course, the vinyl surface improves the durability and the surface alkali resistance greatly. It also makes the vinyl cork tiles more resistant to grease and quite easy to maintain.

Since the installation and maintenance of cork tiles involve steps unlike those used generally, they will be described here. Cork is composed of about 55 percent air in its cellular structure; therefore, the factor of expansion and contraction must be given more consideration. As with other floorings, the cork tiles are preconditioned for approximately 24 hours prior to installation at the temperature of the area where they are to be laid—ideally at 70°F. Tiles should never be installed in a warm area after being brought in from the cold.

Prior to spreading the adhesive, the preparation of the sub-floor demands that only a latex type patch or underlayment should be used over worn or uneven concrete. A harder underlayment would eventually break away from the surface of the concrete due to the impacts from the traffic being transmitted through the highly resilient cork tile.

The lignum paste or alcohol-base water resistant cement used on cork tile should have a high solids content. Any large amount of liquid in the adhesive may cause the tile to swell initially because of the absorptive characteristics of the cork. In laying the tiles, care must be taken not to unduly compress them—a fairly easy thing to do in the thin gauges because of the flexibility and resiliency of the material. It is recommended that each 100 square feet be rolled and cross-rolled as it is laid.

The maintenance of the resin saturated cork and the vinyl cork tile is quite similar to that of other resilient floorings with the exception that a minimum amount of water and detergent should be used. This is a far cry from the periodic program needed for the natural cork tile (prewaxed or not): (1) remove the wax finish, (2) sand to level the floor surface, (3) seal with equal parts of clear shellac and alcohol, and (4) wax, using several coats of wax plus buffing.

Rubber Tile

Variegated rubber tiles, in practically their present form, have been manufactured here since the early 1920's. Some rubber matting (ribbed, etc.) and interlocking solid rubber blocks were made almost 20 years earlier, but these are not dealt with in this chapter. Until World War II (1941), natural rubber was used exclusively. By 1946, almost all the rubber tile was being produced from synthetic SBR (styrene-butadiene rubber). The SBR tiles have better aging and better oil and grease resistance than natural rubber tiles. They are equal in other respects. Some flooring has been made of other types of synthetic rubbers, but high costs or processing difficulties have limited their use to specialty items. The latest of these are "Hypalon" rubber tiles for which claims of excellent cigarette burn resistance are made. Some tests indicate they are much better than the homogeneous vinyl tiles in this respect, but only about equal to VA tile.

Rubber flooring reached its peak sales of about 100 million square feet (all types of flooring) in 1952. In 1958 and 1959, production of rubber tile was about 65 million square feet. Since then it has declined steadily until, in 1962, its sales were only 35 million. Most of the general line companies have now ceased production of rubber tiles.

Rubber tiles contain from 15 to 30 percent binder and 70 to 85 percent mineral fillers. The binder is made up of the synthetic rubber (perhaps with some natural rubber), processing aids such as certain resins, oils and waxes (softeners and plasticizers), color pigments, and small amounts of sulfur curatives plus special accelerators (e.g., mercaptobenzothiazole, diphenyl guanidine). The mineral fillers consist of various clays and ground limestone or whiting. The Federal Specification which covers rubber tiles is ZZ-T-301a; that for rubber sheeting is ZZ-F-461a.

The ingredients are thoroughly mixed in a Banbury and/or a differential-speed two-roll mill. Usually the Banbury-mixed chunks are dropped onto a two-roll mill and sheeted out by a couple of passes around the forward roll. A strip wide and thick enough to feed the calender is cut off and fed over to the top nip. During this part of the processing, the rubber is not cured; it acts like any thermoplastic material, becoming soft when heated and tough (hard) when cooled. At processing temperatures, it has the consistency of putty. It will flow under stress and does not return to its original shape. It can readily be calendered into sheet form. Here, any marbelizing that is desired is done. The sheets are cut into slabs and vulcanized or cured in hydraulic presses for 10 to 20 minutes at about 300°F using chrome-plated or stainless steel coated platens. Each press holds several slabs of rubber stock. The vulcanized material has lost its thermoplastic character and has become a rubbery, resilient, dimensionally stable product which will stretch but will return to its original shape when the stress is removed. It is then cut to the proper size, and its back is sanded to the desired thickness. Rubber cove base is also made in two styles and thicknesses.

Rubber tiles are normally offered in 9 × 9 and 12 × 12 inch sizes (other sizes up to 36 × 36 inches being available) and in .080-, ⅛- and 3⁄16-inch thicknesses. Rubber flooring is also offered as roll goods. The tiles are made in a number of marbelized patterns, but that is about all. The surface is smooth and glossy.

Rubber tiles have excellent resistance to permanent indentation under load. In this respect, no other resilient flooring product comes near them except the new homogeneous vinyl tiles which are their equal. However, they have poor resistance to stiletto heels—these cut into rubber tiles easily. They have good resilience or underfoot comfort and are quiet underfoot—equal to homogeneous vinyl but not as good as cork tiles. The moisture resistance of these tiles is good, and their alkali resistance is quite satisfactory. Their durability is also very good—about like the vinyl tiles. They are recommended for installation over suspended wood and concrete floors and over on-grade concrete floors. They can also be used over below-grade concrete floors provided no hydrostatic pressure is present.

The oil and grease resistance of rubber tiles is poor. This means they should not be used in kitchens or in industrial areas where these conditions may be encountered. They are also attacked by solvents and by certain rubber poisons such as the soaps of copper and manganese. These last two soaps will dissolve in the rubber compound and cause it to become soft and tacky. Following this stage, a rapid oxidation takes place and the rubber becomes hard and brittle and thus shows surface cracking. The reaction tends to be autocatalytic. In the case of oil, grease and solvents, they make the rubber tiles swell and become soft. In this state, the tiles may easily have dirt embedded in them and they abrade quite rapidly. This also means one must be careful about what products are used to maintain rubber tile floors. Cleaners and waxes containing solvents should never be used, nor should lacquers, varnishes, shellac or similar finishes. Oily dust mops and sweeping compounds (containing oil or sand) should be avoided. The Rubber Manufacturers Association publishes a list of cleaners and waxes which have been tested and approved for use on member companies' rubber tiles.

These rubber products are also degraded by ozone and by ultraviolet light. Ozone produces fine cracks in the surface of the rubber; this can be controlled by the use of special rubber chemicals, but these are usually not incorporated in tile. When exposed to the direct rays of the sun (through air doors or French windows), the rubber tiles ozone-crack quite rapidly due to the activation of this chemical reaction by the "intense" ultraviolet rays present in direct sunlight. Ultraviolet light will also cause fading of the colors in these tiles.

Maintenance of rubber tiles is easier than for cork and perhaps asphalt tile. It is generally considered more difficult nowadays than for linoleum and vinyl products.

Solid Vinyl Tile

The homogeneous or flexible vinyl tiles made their appearance commercially in 1945. This marked the first flooring use of polyvinyl chloride (PVC) resin since VA tiles used the vinyl chloride/vinyl acetate copolymer. The use of this homopolymer, or pure PVC, required higher processing temperatures which created many problems, but it produced exceedingly tough, flexible tiles—considerably softer and more pliable than VA tiles. These tiles are practically indestructible and have many exceptional properties. However, they are not perfect and have some disadvantages as described below. These flexible tiles are relatively expensive. They are usually selected on the basis of outstanding beauty and attractiveness, though their durability is important. The price range is the widest of all the categories studied: from $.35 to $3.50/sq ft. Some of the higher price is related to thickness and amount of filler, but most of it is applied toward obtaining the highly aesthetic decorations characteristic of the expensive vinyl tiles.

Sales of flexible vinyl tiles are still rising. The volume has increased at a fairly steady rate from 1958 when about 85 million square feet were sold. By 1962 sales had grown to 180 million square feet with indications of considerable additional growth for the future. In 1965 sales were still close to 180 million square feet.

Flexible vinyl tiles contain from 35 to 50 percent binder for the filled, opaque type and up to 100 percent binder in the case of the higher-priced translucent or transparent vinyls. The rest of the recipe is filler plus a small amount of pigmentation.

The binder consists of high molecular weight polyvinyl chloride polymer, plasticizers, stabilizers and any processing aids needed. Straight PVC resin is generally used in these tiles because of its superior physical properties, while the vinyl chloride/vinyl acetate copolymers are generally used in VA tiles. These resins, however, require high processing temperatures to achieve correct mixing and gelation, and this in turn imposes severe nonvolatility limits on the plasticizers.

Low volatility is an important plasticizer characteristic since the plasticizer must not cause even moderate fuming during the manufacturing process. Low volatility is important in service, too, along with good compatibility, since this flooring should exhibit no shrinkage due to plasticizer loss even after many years of use.

Resistance to staining caused by rubber heels and household ingredients has become increasingly important in the past few years because of the extensive use of white, light pastel colors, and clears in the wearlayer. This staining is now an extremely important problem which has not been entirely solved. Some degree of low-temperature flexibility and good resistance to extraction by detergents and household solvents are properties which must also be considered. The main plasticizers used in flexible vinyl flooring are the dioctyl phthalates, butyl benzyl phthalate and tricresyl phosphate. As indicated above, the use of "nonstaining" plasticizers is increasing—these are relatively new plasticizers and thus are generally more expensive.

The ratio of resin to plasticizer determines the physical properties of the binder and governs the limits within which satisfactory formulas can be developed. A high polymer content makes the product hard and prevents the use of much filler without serious loss of flexibility. Conversely, a high plasticizer content will cause unacceptable indentation characteristics of the tiles unless large quantities of filler are used; this amount of filler would bring us to the stiff, brittle formulations of VA tiles. The degree of soiling of the vinyl tiles during service is also influenced greatly by the resin/plasticizer ratio. When this is reduced below 2:1, soiling usually becomes a serious problem. For opaque (less-expensive) tiles, soft binders with high mineral filler contents give the most attractive compromise for production and service properties. In the case of the translucent and the transparent (moderate to very expensive) tiles, the resin/plasticizer ratio is increased until the proper stiffness is attained, for these recipes contain essentially no filler.

Though small amounts of other fillers are used in flexible vinyl tiles, calcium carbonate [limestone] is by far the most important filler present. Precipitated whiting is the preferred form of calcium carbonate because it has a considerably finer particle size than the refined natural whiting. The binder/filler ratio primarily determines the physical properties and the cost of the vinyl tiles. A careful study of the effect of changes in this ratio on flexibility, indentation and stain can lead to the development of the best available balance of these properties. In the luxury tiles, the raw material cost becomes unimportant and the main effort goes toward excellent properties plus a very pleasing, exciting design.

The vinyl binder per se is a clear, colorless material. The addition of certain stabilizers may cause it to become hazy or translucent but normally does not affect its color. Many fillers cause some or moderate discoloration, though most calcium carbonates (unless they are coated) merely make the material more opaque. Therefore, these tiles can readily be pigmented with a wide range of organic and inorganic materials to give products with bright attractive colors. These pigments must have high heat stability, good light stability and good resistance to acidic mediums. The popularity of the translucent and transparent tiles has brought about the use of transparent pigments or dyes in order to achieve the depth of color needed for these designs.

Stabilizers are an essential feature of every flooring formulation since their use prevents or minimizes the effect of the breakdown of PVC polymer during processing. In addition, certain ones give additional protection to the tiles during service since they prevent the breakdown of the polymer due to sunlight and, thus, prevent the changing of color of the product. Today, there are special chemicals which absorb the damaging ultraviolet rays of light and change these into energy which is harmless to the vinyl and the chemical.

The pigments used today in vinyl flooring products are vastly improved over those employed only a few years ago. These new pigments do not fade or change color under normal usage. They also are not harmed by the high processing temperatures needed to manufacture the products or by the acidity of the vinyl resin.

Small amounts of other materials are added to the formulations, mainly to help processing. These include the fatty acids (i.e., stearic acid) and their metallic salts, certain waxes, low molecular weight polyethylene, etc. All of these are used as lubricants and tend to make recipes easier to process.

The Federal Specification which covers the $\frac{1}{8}$-inch thick molded vinyl tiles is L-F-00450.

The processes used to manufacture the filled flexible vinyl tiles vary considerably among manufacturers, but the basic principles are the same. The materials are mixed in some manner under heat and pressure until they are soft and moldable. Then they are calendered, pressed or otherwise processed at elevated temperatures or pressures. Upon cooling, the product hardens into its finished form; no curing is needed to complete the process.

For roto printed tiles, a flexible, moderately filled back sheet is made first. A thin, clear PVC sheet is made for the wearlayer and then it is usually printed by rotogravure on the reverse side using vinyl inks. Quite often, an inner layer of the desired background color is also prepared. These are then usually laminated together in a rotary pressing unit, e. g., a Rotocure.

The calendered .050-inch tiles are produced in different ways by the various manufacturers. Striated decorations are made by taking thick sheets with chips of decorative stock in them and calendering them into thin sheets, thus drawing out the chip into a striation. When long, thin striations are desired, the reduction in thickness is great. If short, square striations are to be produced, the reduction taken is much smaller. In the marbelized decorations, these sheets are then cross-calendered. This means the sheets are cut into square pieces, turned 90°, and fed into the calender rolls so they are double thickness. The edge of a new sheet is put into the nip when the previous sheet is halfway through. The terrazzo or chip-type decoration is made by putting the desired decorative chips onto the hot calendered sheet and pushing them into the sheet. If the product has a plain backing, another calendered vinyl sheet is then laminated to the decorated top layer.

The molded or pressed tiles have to go through slower, more expensive processes. These processes usually turn out tiles with excellent dimensional stability (if annealed), perfect squareness and tight seams. The steps described below illustrate the stages necessary in one process used to form a homogeneous, flexible vinyl tile of the terrazzo design. (a) The vinyl resin, plasticizers, fillers and stabilizers are put into large blenders and mixed to a uniform, soft, powder-like substance. (b) The pre-blended material is charged into a Banbury—a very heavy-bladed intensive mixer. Color pigments and minor amounts of other additives may be added at this stage. The Banbury subjects this mixture to heat and pressure until it becomes a soft dough-like mix at temperatures over 300°F. (c) This hot vinyl compound is transferred into a heated open mixer where, if desired, color chips are added and mixed under carefully controlled conditions. If desired, chips are added to form the striated contrasting colors in the decorative chip stock. (d) The batch is then passed between heated calender rolls which squeeze it down to a sheet of the desired thickness. (e) Granulating machines rapidly break up the colored plastic sheet into granules of the desired sizes. (f) Different-colored granules are mixed in a blender in large quantities to insure uniformity. (g) These granules are then automatically charged into 37- to 38-inch square flat molds. The correct amount and distribution of granules is very important. (h) The molds are closed and automatically positioned in elevators for loading in multiple opening presses. (i) In the presses, heat and pressure fuse the granules into uniform, solid sheets. (j) These sheets are put on racks and then passed through an annealing oven which removes residual strain, thus elimi-

nating or minimizing shrinkage in service. (k) The annealed sheets are sanded to achieve the desired gauge and to roughen the back for better adhesion. (l) The surface of the sheet is polished to remove dust and to protect against scuffs and scratches. Some manufacturers factory-apply wax finish at this stage. (m) The sheets are fed to a die press which cuts them into sixteen 9×9 or nine 12×12 inch slightly oversized tiles. The four sides of these tiles are then sanded or sawed to give tiles of the exact size desired with perfect fit. (n) Finally, the tiles are inspected and packed into cartons.

Flexible or homogeneous vinyl tiles are normally offered in 9×9 and 12×12 inch sizes (other sizes up to 36×36 inches being available) and in thicknesses of .050, $\frac{1}{16}$, 0.080, $\frac{3}{32}$ and .125 inch. They are made in a greater variety of patterns than any other resilient flooring material. This is possible because in the inexpensive roto printed tiles, the design possibilities are very great and a number have been produced. The filled calendered and pressed tiles offer a large number of possibilities because of the bright clean colors available with vinyl. All sorts of filled chips, metallic flakes, metallic in clear chips, etc., can be added to enhance or enliven designs. These vinyl tiles can also be made with translucent and transparent areas which give them warmth and depth of color. They can be made with the decoration deeply imbedded or floating in clear colored wearlayers of any thickness. The design possibilities of these highly aesthetic, three-dimensional tiles are truly unlimited. Naturally, the price of these beautiful luxury tiles is high (see Table 12-1).

The finished flexible vinyl tile is an attractive product with a smooth and lustrous (or matted) surface. The vinyl resins which form the backbone of the product contribute far more than clean colors and good appearance. They are highly inert and tough materials and are very resistant to the severe service conditions most floors must withstand. They impart outstanding wear resistance to the tiles and enable them to withstand heavy loads for long periods of time without permanent indentation. Vinyl floors are very quiet and comfortable to walk on (highly resilient). They are almost equal to cork flooring with regard to noise level. They are practically unaffected by moisture, alkali or detergents, by grease, fats or oils, and by most of the common household cleaners or solvents. This means freedom from damage due to alkaline moisture in concrete, long contact with grease in kitchens, accidental spillage or strong cleaning compounds. The tiles do not harden or soften from aging or from the effects of light and moisture. Colors remain bright and clear, whether on the floor or in the box.

However, the lustrous or slightly matted surface of the new tile does not stay that way under constant traffic. It soon has its surface gloss dulled by small scratches and scuffs— the higher the initial gloss, the greater is the contrast. The choice of a satin finish tile will help alleviate this problem, and proper floor maintenance, including periodic waxing, will overcome it entirely. The wax will either prevent scratches or fill them in so they are not noticeable. Sometimes in light or pastel colors (especially in filled compounds), a discoloration develops in heavy traffic lanes. This is usually caused by certain materials used in the manufacture of rubber heels and soles. These stains can generally be removed by the use of very fine steel wool or other abrasive cleaning materials. The use of new, stain-resistant plasticizers in the luxury lines will help overcome this problem.

The problem of nailheads showing through the tiles is probably aggravated by the increased use of the thinner-gauge products and the subsequent transfer of underfloor blemishes to the surface. However, if more attention is paid to obtaining smooth, uniform and properly secured underlayment, this problem is readily solved. This involves the use of high-grade plywood fastened with special high holding-power nails, i.e., screw nails, etc. The strength and the serviceability of flexible vinyl makes it unnecessary to use heavy 1/8-inch tiles in many applications, and so the thinner-gauge products are coming into wider use for residential and other light traffic areas.

There should be little or no trouble with permanent indentation in flexible vinyl tiles, unless the floor has been abused or improper installation methods have been followed. If too much adhesive has been laid down, or heavy loads have been moved onto the floor before the paste has time to set-up, the adhesive can be displaced and indentation can result. Naturally, the thinner-gauge tiles are more susceptible to this type of abuse.

Conductive vinyl tiles are sold by several companies. A description of these tiles follows.

SPECIAL

Static Conductive Linoleum Yard Goods and Vinyl Tile

Static conductive linoleum is manufactured in 6-foot-wide yard goods 1/8 inch thick on burlap backing. It is available in plain black only. The nominal weight is 7.4 lb/sq yd. A roll contains from 12 to 62 square yards and comes packed with an electrical grounding kit. It is manufactured in two types to meet the requirements of two distinctive users: (1) "U" type for hospital use has a resistance of 25,000 ohms minimum to 1,000,000 ohms maximum. It is used in hospital operating rooms, anesthetic rooms, minor surgery rooms, emergency rooms, etc. (2) "G" type for industrial use has a resistance of 0 ohms minimum to 250,000 ohms maximum. This is the required conductive range for arsenals, powder plants, shell loading rooms or tables, explosive powder loading rooms or tables, or other areas where explosive materials are used, packed or stored.

Static conductive linoleum has all the advantages of regular linoleum—good wear resistance, flexibility, resiliency, smoothness and freedom from cracking. Because it is installed in 6-foot-wide sheets, the floor is free from multiple joints which may harbor dirt and germs. Since it contains a high percentage of linseed oil in its formulation and linseed oil has a high anti-germ value, the flooring maintains germicidal quality at all times. It meets the specifications of, or as approved by, Underwriter Laboratories Inc., U. S. Army Ordnance and National

Fire Protection Association. When compared to static conductive tile, linoleum's 6-foot width means that (1) no special underfloor grid is needed because the conductivity is built right into the linoleum, (2) there are almost no dirt catching seams to aid in bacteriological growth, (3) coving from floor to wall is made possible for easier maintenance, and (4) installation is easier and less expensive. A 12 × 12 foot floor would have only 12 feet of seams if covered by 6-foot-wide linoleum. It would have 360 feet of seams if covered by 9 × 9 inch tiles.

Conductive vinyl tiles are made in 9 × 9 inch size and in thickness of ⅛ and 3/16 inch. They are black with background colors of grey, green, black and white. The conductivity is obtained through special formulation.

The conductive vinyl tiles have the same advantages of homogeneous or solid vinyl tiles. Since conductive floors should not be waxed, any wear and maintenance tests should be run without waxing. Care should also be taken that no soap or detergent films are left on the surface after cleaning. Tests indicate that vinyl tiles are somewhat easier to maintain than linoleum under these conditions.

The vinyl tiles must have a conductive grid laid beneath them in order to meet the requirements and to connect all the tiles electrically. This means that an extra step must be taken when laying the floor. In practice the adhesive is spread, and copper or brass foil ribbons are then laid in both directions across the floor, spaced about 9 inches apart and crisscrossing approximately in the center of each tile. This entails laying down 384 feet of foil, taking care that no adhesive gets between foil and tile to act as an insulator. Foil strips are usually run up to cove height, and the ends are connected with one final strip around the top.

Conductive flooring should be installed according to the manufacturer's specific instructions. The finished installation must meet all conductivity requirements of the National Fire Protection Association and the National Board of Fire Underwriters as set forth in their Bulletin No. 56.

"Conductive Flooring for Hospital Operating Rooms," by Thomas H. Boone, Francis L. Hermach, Edgar H. MacArthur and Rita C. McAuliff, covers the National Bureau of Standards tests on conductive flooring. The data are applicable to other areas where there is a chance of an electrostatic spark setting off an explosion. The article was published in the October–December 1959 issue of *Journal of Research of the National Bureau of Standards—C. Engineering and Instrumentation*, **63C**, No. 2.

Acknowledgment. This chapter could not have been written without the able assistance of Mr. Donald J. Boone, Manager of Technical Services, Congoleum-Nairn, Inc., who not only corrected the body of the text but also helped immeasurably in correlating the tables.

TABLE 12A-1. Smooth-surface Resilient Flooring—Approximate Costs, Suggested Uses and Specifications

Type of Flooring and Guage	Approximate Installed Price/sq ft	Wear Layer Thickness, inch	Grade	Location	Traffic	Federal Specifications	Kitchens	Bathrooms	Bedrooms and Nurseries	Living Rooms	Entrances	Below-grade Rooms** (1)	Offices and Libraries	Light Traffic** Stores	Corridors of Public Buildings**	Dining Areas	Kitchens (Commercial)	Schools**	Hospital Corridors	Hospitals Bedroom
			Suggested Use				Residential					Commercial					C-I	Institutional		
	a	b	c	d	e	f	g	h	i	j	k	l	m	n	o	p	q	r	s	t
Yard Goods																				
I Linoleum																				
(1) .065–.070 in. residential	$.30–.40	.018 to .030	A	R	Light	LLL-F-471(1)	G	VG	G	G	P*	NR	NR	NR	NR	NR	NR	NR	NR	NR
(2) .090 in. light commercial regular	.35–.50	.050	A	R	Med	LLL-F-471(1)	VG	VG	VG	G	F*	NR	VG	F	NR	NR	NR	NR	NR	NR
(3) .090 in. light commercial premium	.50–.60	.050	A	R	Med	LLL-F-471(1)	VG	VG	VG	VG	G*	NR	VG	F	F	NR	NR	NR	NR	NR
(4) .125 in. marbelized	.55–.65	FT	A	RCI	Heavy	LLL-L-367(3)	VG	VG	VG	G	G*	NR	E	VG	VG	E	GVG	E	E	E
(5) .125 in. battleship	.40–.50	FT	A	RCI	Heavy	LLL-L-351B(1)	NR	NR	NR	NR	NR	NR	NR	E	E	E	GVG	E	E	E
(6) .125 in. conductive	.90–1.10	FT	A	RCI	Heavy	LLL-L-367(3)	For special use only													
II Vinyl Yard Goods																				
(1) .055 in. vinyl back	$.40–.50	.008	AOB	R	Light	None evolved	G	E	VG	G	P*	NR	NR	NR	NR	NR	NR	NR	NR	NR
(2) .065 in. felt back	.45–.50	.020	AO†	R	Light	L-F-475a(1)	G	E	VG	G	F*	NR	G	G	NR	NR	NR	NR	NR	NR
(3) .065 in. asbestos back	.60–.65	.020 to .030	AOB	R	Light	L-F-475a(1)	G	E	VG	G	F*	E	G	G	NR	NR	NR	NR	NR	NR
(4) .070 in. felt back	.50–.55	.030	AO†	RC	Med	L-F-475a(1)	VG	E	E	E	FG*	NR	VG	G	NR	NR	NR	NR	NR	NR
(5) .070 in. asbestos back	.70–.85	.030	AOB	RC	Med	L-F-475a(1)	VG	E	E	E	FG*	E	VG	G	NR	NR	NR	NR	NR	NR
(6) .090 in. asbestos back—regular	.90–.95	.050	AOB	RCI	Heavy	L-F-475a(1)	E	E	E	E	VG*	E	E	E	E	E	E	E	E	E
(7) .090 in. asbestos back—premium	1.05–1.20	.050	AOB	RCI	Heavy	L-F-475a(1)	E	E	E	E	VG*	E	E	E	E	E	E	E	E	E
III Foam Cushion Vinyl Yard Goods																				
(1) 0.90 in. felt-back residential	$.30	.008	loose	R	Light	None evolved	VG	VG	E	G	P*	NR	NR	NR	NR	NR	NR	NR	NR	NR
(2) 0.90 in. felt back residential	.45	.014	AOB	R	Light	None evolved	E	E	E	G	G*	NR	NR	NR	NR	NR	NR	NR	NR	NR
(3) 0.10 asbestos-back residential	.75	.015	AOB	R	Med	None evolved	E	E	E	G	G*	E	NR	NR	NR	NR	NR	NR	NR	NR

TILES

Item	Price	Gauge	Binder	Install	Traffic	Fed. Spec												
IV Asphalt Tiles																		
(1) ⅛ in. B Group	$.23	FT	AOB	RC	Med	SS-T-306b	NR	G	VG	P*	E	FG	G	F	NR	NR	F	F	P
(2) ⅛ in. C Group	.28	FT	AOB	RC	Med	SS-T-306b	NR	G	VG	P*	E	FG	G	F	NR	NR	F	F	P
(3) ⅛ in. D Group	.32	FT	AOB	RC	Med	SS-T-306b	NR	G	VG	P*	E	FG	G	F	NR	NR	F	F	P
(4) 3/16 in. B Group	.30	FT	AOB	RCI	Heavy	SS-T-306b	NR	G	E	FG*	E	G	VG	G	NR	NR	G	G	P
(5) 3/16 in. C Group	.37	FT	AOB	RCI	Heavy	SS-T-306b	NR	G	E	FG*	E	G	VG	G	NR	NR	G	G	P
(6) 3/16 in. D Group	.42	FT	AOB	RCI	Heavy	SS-T-306b	NR	G	E	FG*	E	G	VG	G	NR	NR	G	G	P
(7) ⅛ in. special decoration	.32	FT	AOB	R	Light	SS-T-306b	NR	G	VG	P*	E	FG	P	P	NR	NR	P	P	P
V Vinyl Asbestos Tiles																		
(1) 1/16 in. regular	$.35	FT	AOB	RC	Med	L-F-00345	GVG	G	VG	FG*	E	NR	NR	NR	NR	NR	NR	NR	NR
(2) 1/16 in. premium	.40	FT	AOB	RC	Med	L-F-00345	GVG	G	VG	FG*	E	NR	NR	NR	NR	NR	NR	NR	NR
(3) ⅛ in. regular	.55	FT	AOB	RCI	Heavy	L-F-00345	GVG	G	E	G*	E	G	E	E	E	E	E	G	G
VI Linoleum Tiles																		
(1) .0625 in.	$.25–.30	.018	A	R	Light	LLL-L-471(1)	F	FG	FG	P*	NR	NR	NR	NR	NR	NR	NR	NR	NR
(2) .070 in.	.30–.35	.030	A	R	Light	LLL-L-471(1)	FG	FG	G	P*	NR	NR	NR	NR	NR	NR	NR	NR	NR
(3) .090 in.	.40–.45	.050	A	RC	Med	LLL-L-471(1)	FG	FG	G	F*	NR	NR	NR	NR	NR	NR	NR	NR	NR
VII Cork Tiles																		
(1) ⅛ in.	$.65	FT	AOt	R	Light	LLL-T-431b	P	P	E	P*	NR	G	P	P	NR	P	P	P	NR
(2) 3/16 in.	.75	FT	AOt	R	Med	LLL-T-431b	P	P	E	P*	NR	VG	P	P	NR	P	P	P	G
(3) ⅛ in. vinyl cork	1.85	FT	AOt	RC	Med	LLL-T-431b	GVG	G	E	P*	NR	E	G	G	G	P	P	P	VG
VIII Rubber Tiles																		
(1) .080 in.	$.60	FT	AO	RC	Med	ZZ-F-301a	P	G	E	G*	E	E	F	G	NR	NR	NR	E	E
(2) .125 in.	.75	FT	AO	RCI	Heavy	ZZ-F-301a	P	G	E	G*	E	G	G	G	VG	P	E	G	E
X Vinyl Tiles																		
(1) .050 in. roto printed	$.40	.006 to .008	AO	R	Light	None evolved	G	G	VG	P*	NR	G	NR	NR	NR	NR	NR	NR	NR
(2) .050 in. calendered—regular	.35–.50		AO	R	Light	None evolved	G	G	VG	F*	NR	G	NR	NR	NR	NR	NR	NR	NR
(3) .050 in. calendered—premium	.60–.70	FT	AO	R	Light	None evolved	G	G	VG	F*	NR	G	NR	NR	NR	NR	NR	NR	NR
(4) 1/16 in. molded—regular	.60–.70	FT	AOB	R	Light	None evolved	G	G	E	FG*	NR	VG	VG	E	NR	NR	NR	NR	NR
(5) .080 in. molded—regular	.70–.80					None evolved	VG	G	E	G*	NR	E	VG	E	NR	NR	NR	NR	NR
(6) .080 in. molded—premium	.80–.85					None evolved	VG	G	E	G*	G	E	VG	E	NR	NR	NR	NR	NR
(7) .080 in. molded—luxury	.85–1.10	FT	AOB	RC	Med	None evolved	VG	G	E	VGE*	VG	E	NR	E	NR	NR	NR	NR	NR
(8) .080 in. molded—high luxury	1.10–1.50					None evolved	VG	G	E	VGE*	E	E	NR	E	NR	NR	NR	NR	NR

TABLE 12A-1. Smooth-surface Resilient Flooring—Approximate Costs, Suggested Uses and Specifications (Continued)

Type of Flooring and Gauge	Approximate Installed Price/sq ft (a)	Wear Layer Thickness, inch (b)	Grade (c)	Location (d)	Traffic (e)	Federal Specifications (f)	Kitchens (g)	Bathrooms (h)	Bedrooms and Nurseries (i)	Living Rooms (j)	Entrances (k)	Below-grade Rooms**(1) (l)	Offices and Libraries (m)	Light Traffic Stores (n)	Corridors of Public Buildings (o)	Dining Areas (p)	Kitchens (Commercial) (q)	Schools** (r)	Hospital Corridors (s)	Hospitals Bedroom (t)
							Residential					Commercial					C-I	Institutional		
(9) 3/32 in. molded	.85-.95	FT	AOB	RC	Med	None evolved	E	G	E	VGE	G*	GVG	GVG	G	NR	E	NR	NR	NR	NR
(10) .125 molded—regular	.75-.90	FT	AOB	RCI	Heavy	L-T-00450	E	G	E	VGE	VGE*	E	E	VG	G	E	E	VG	E	E
(11) .125 molded—premium	.90-1.15	FT	AOB	RCI	Heavy	L-T-00450	E	G	E	E	VGE*	E	E	VG	G	E	E	VG	E	E
(12) .125 molded—luxury	1.15-2.00					L-T-00450	E	G	E	E	E*	E	E	VG	G	E	E	VG	E	E
(13) .125 molded—high luxury	2.00-3.50					L-T-00450	For special uses													
(14) .125 in. conductive	2.40-2.50	FT	A	CI	Heavy	None evolved	E	G	E	E	E*	E	E	VG	G	E	E	VG	E	E

† = On grade under certain conditions as specified in floor manufacturers literature.
FT = full thick, A = above grade, O = on grade, B = below grade R = residential, C = commercial, I = institutional, E = excellent, VG = very good, G = good
F = fair, P = poor, NR = Not recommended. In-between values are given by combinations: i.e., GVG is between G and VG.
*These values correspond to the sandy, gritty wear values since these conditions many times exist at entrances.
**Values for areas away from entrances—for entrance ratings see column k.
(1) Below grade area must have absence of hydrostatic pressure.

EXPLANATION OF TABLES
12A-1, 12A-2, 12A-4, and 12A-5

Table 12A-1

The various smooth-surface resilient flooring products have been subdivided into their major classes. This is a purely arbitrary division by the author, but it does help distinguish between the degrees of wear values and the degrees of aesthetic values available.

Column c—Grade. ABOVE GRADE. Typically a floor of wood or concrete suspended over a ventilated air space. Here moisture is no problem. Of course, the floor surface should be smooth, dry and clean. Suspended concrete floors may be either standard construction, finished with a smooth cement topping, or solid slab construction which should be smooth troweled (not float finished).

ON GRADE. This is a concrete slab laid at ground level. It is very much in evidence today in modern ranch-type homes and basementless schools and business establishments. Although alkaline moisture is not as prevalent here as with below-grade floors, it is still a possible hazard.

BELOW GRADE. A typical example is the concrete basement floor. Such floors are in contact with the earth and may be subject to a destructive alkaline moisture condition at the surface. This is caused by ground moisture combining with alkaline salts in the concrete as it works its way upward. In such cases, special resilient floors and adhesives designed for the purpose should be used.

TABLE 12A-2. Smooth-surface Resilient Flooring—Physical Properties and Sales Volume

Type of Flooring and Gauge	Backing Material	Safe Static Load Limit (psi)*	Relative Underfoot Comfort	Relative Quietness Value	Surface Grease Resistance	Surface Alkali Resistance	Household-type Solvent Resistance	Dry Wear	Sandy Gritty Wear	Ease of Maintenance	Thermal conductivity K Factor*	Thermal conductance C factor*	Sales Volume (in millions of sq ft)				
	a	b	c	d	e	f	g	h	i		k	l	1958	1960	1962	1964	1965
Yard Goods																	
I Linoleum																	
(1) .065–.070 in. residential	FB	75	FG	GVG	VG	PF	G	FG	P	G	1.2	18.5	305	315	240	200	150
(2,3) .090 in. light commercial	FB	75	G	GVG	VG	PF	G	G	F	G	1.2	13.5					
(4) .125 in. commercial	Burlap	200	VG	GVG	VG	PF	G	GVG	G	G	2.3	18.5					
(5) .125 in battleship	Burlap	200	VG	GVG	VG	PF	G	GVG	G	G	2.1	17					
(6) .125 in. conductive	Burlap	200	VG	GVG	VG	PF	G	GVG	—	G	2.2	17.5					
II Vinyl Yard Goods																	
(1) .055 in. residential	VB	150	F	G	E	E	E	FG	P	G	4.5	82	80	225	250	340	450
(2) .065 in. residential	FB	75	G	G	E	E	E	GVG	FG	G	1.4	22					
(3) .065 in. residential	AB	75	G	G	E	E	E	GVG	FG	G	2.3	35					
(4) .070 in. light commercial	FB	75	G	G	E	E	E	VG	FG	G	1.5	21					
(5) .070 in. light commercial	AB	75	G	G	E	E	E	VG	FG	G	1.9	27					
(6,7) .090 in. commercial	AB	100	GVG	G	E	E	E	VG	G	G	1.8 to 2.6	20 to 30					
III Foam Cushion Vinyl Yard Goods																	
(1) .090 in. residential (loose lay)	FB	—	E+	E+	E	E	E	FG	P	E	1.1	11	None	None	NA	NA	NA
(2) .090 in. residential (installed)	FB	75	E+	E+	E	E	E	GVG	FG	E	1.2	11					
(3) .090 in. residential (installed)	AB	75	E+	E+	E	E	E	GVG	FG	E	1.4	11.5					
Tiles																	
IV Asphalt Tiles																	
(1,2,3) 1/8 in.	—	40	P	P	P	VG	P	G	P	F	5 to 5.5	40 to 44	800	900	750	650	600
(4,5,6) 3/16 in.	—	40	P	P	P	VG	P	GVG	P	F	5 to 5.5	27 to 30					
V Vinyl Asbestos Tiles																	
(1,2) 1/16 in.	—	100	P	P	E	VG	E	GVG	FG	VG	5 to 6	74 to 96	400	850	950	1150	1250
(3) 1/8 in.	—	100	P	P	E	VG	E	VG	G	VG	5 to 6	40 to 48					

TABLE 12A-2. Smooth-surface Resilient Flooring—Physical Properties and Sales Volume(Continued)

Type of Flooring and Gauge	Backing Material	Safe Static Load Limit (psi)*	Relative Underfoot Comfort	Relative Quietness Value	Surface Grease Resistance	Surface Alkali Resistance	Household-type Solvent Resistance	Dry Wear	Sandy Gritty Wear	Ease of Maintenance	Thermal conductivity K Factor*	Thermal conductance C factor*	Sales Volume (in millions of sq ft) 1958	1960	1962	1964	1965
	a	b	c	d	e	f	g	h	i		k	l					
VI Linoleum Tiles																	
(1,2) .0625–.065 in.	FB	75	FG	G	VG	PF	G	FG	P	G	$1.2-$	18.5	90	50	40	35	25
(3) .090 in.	FB	75	G	G	VG	PF	G	G	F	G	1.2	13.5					
VII Cork Tiles																	
(1) ⅛ in.	—	75	E	E	F	F	P	PF	P	P	1.3	10.5	11	4	3	3	2
(2) 3⁄16 in.	—	75	E	E	F	F	P	PF	P	P	1.3	7					
(3) ⅛ in. vinyl cork	—	150	G	GVG	E	E	G	FG	P	E	1.6	13					
VIII Rubber Tiles																	
(1) .080 in.	—	200	VG	VG	FG	G	G	VG	G	G	5.0	62.5	65	55	35	25	20
(2) .125 in.	—	200	VG	VG	FG	G	G	VG	G	G	5.0	40					
IX Vinyl Tiles																	
(1) .050 in. roto printed	VB	150	F	G	E	E	E	FG	P	E	4.5	90	85	120	180	200	180
(2,3) .050 in. calendered	VB	150	F	G	E	E	E	GVG	FG	E	2.2	44					
(4) 1⁄16 in. molded	VB	200	FG	G	E	E	E	GVG	FG	G	4.5	72					
(5–8) .080 in. molded	VB	250	G	G	E	E	E	VG	FG	G to VG	2.2 to 5.0	27.5 to 62.5**					
(9) 3⁄32 in. molded	VB	300	G	G	E	E	E	VG	G	G to VG	5.0	53					
(10–13) .125 in. molded	VB	300	G	G	E	E	E	E	G	G to VG	2.2 to 5.0	17.5 to 40**					
(14) 3⁄16 in. conductive (also ⅛ in.)	VB	300	G	G	E	E	E	E	—	G	4.5	36					

NOTES: FB = felt back, VB = vinyl back, AB = asbestos-back, E = excellent, VG = very good, G = good, F = fair, P = poor. In between values are given by combinations: i.e. GVG is between G and VG.

*Different companies run these tests in various ways and so obtain different values. These values are as comparable as possible.

**Depends on the amount of clear vinyl present. K-value of 2.2 is for transparent tiles, 5.0 for all opaque (filled) tiles. The translucent or tiles with some clear areas lie between these.

NA = Not available.

Table 12A-2

The same classification of the products as used in Table 12A-1 has been used in abbreviated form in Table 12A-2. Here are presented some of the physical properties of these flooring products. It must be remembered that tests such as the safe static load limit, the durability, the thermal conductivity (K factor) and the thermal conductance (C factor) are run in various ways by different companies. Thus many of them obtain values quite different from those presented in Table 12-2. We have endeavored in this Table to make these values as comparable as possible.

Column b—Safe Static Load Limit. The safe static load limit is that load in pounds per square inch which may be applied to the floor without causing noticeable permanent indentations. Protective cups should be placed under heavy, infrequently moved furniture. Where casters are required, they should be made with nonstaining rubber and not less than 2 in. in diameter and ¾ in. wide or guarded with suitable cups.

This property is influenced greatly by the resiliency of the product. From the standpoint of the consumer, resilience is perhaps one of the most important characteristics to be considered when specifying smooth-surface flooring. Basically, resilience is a measure of the ability of a material to recover or return to its original shape after an external load has been removed. Certain floor coverings such as rubber tile have what might be termed an "elastic memory," recovering their indentation almost entirely. Asphalt tile, on the other hand, is without this "memory" and shows virtually no recovery when subjected to heavy load.

Column c—Relative Underfoot Comfort. To be truly resilient, the flooring must possess the ability to "give" under impact. This ability of the flooring to depress readily underfoot is a direct measure of personal comfort in walking. Thus, the proper choice of flooring will aid in reducing fatigue of people who are required to be on their feet for long periods of time in the course of their work.

Column d—Relative Quietness Value. It should be kept in mind that floors play an important part in the acoustics of rooms and corridors. Walking on floors generates sound in direct proportion to their hardness. This ability of a flooring to absorb impact sounds from walking or dropping objects is a measure of relative quietness. When an object is dropped on the floor, part of the noise is absorbed into the floor, part is transmitted through the floor to the room below, and part is reflected back to the ear of the observer. The latter determines the degree of quietness of a floor.

Absorption of airborne noises by smooth-surface flooring is negligible. This type of noise requires other absorbents such as acoustical ceiling tile, draperies, and upholstered furniture.

Column e and f—Surface Grease and Alkali. Resilient floors can encounter grease and alkalies from these three sources:

(1) A common source is accidental spillage of liquids or solids containing grease or alkali. In this case, where contact with the floor is usually brief due to prompt cleanup of spills, damage to the floor is minimized or completely eliminated. Of course, if the floor has been properly maintained with a wax film over the surface, spills are removed so much easier and so much more completely.

(2) A greater problem occurs where there is a slow accumulation of grease or alkali on the floor over an extended period of time. This can happen in a kitchen where there is entrainment of cooking vapors on the floor. Another cause is faulty maintenance—where cleaning materials are not properly removed by adequate rinsing or where wrong cleaning materials are used.

(3) The most serious alkali problem is alkaline moisture in on-grade and below-grade concrete slabs. *To solve it satisfactorily, the architect should insist upon the following:*

(a) Selection of a product that gives adequate resistance to alkaline moisture.

(b) Installation according to specifications for materials and procedure.

(c) Installation of a suitable membrane, i.e., 6-mil polyethylene sheeting, prior to pouring of concrete subfloor.

Knowing the sub-floor and the projected usage for the finished floor, the architect can easily specify the product that will give the most satisfactory service under any or all of these three conditions.

Column h and i—Durability. Dry wear is the normal wear a floor is subjected to. The shoes are free of gritty, abrasive substances.

Sandy, gritty wear usually occurs at entrances and in a few cases is extended throughout the floor area. The abrasive material brought into the area on the soles of the shoes wears through the resilient floor covering rapidly, just as it does in the case of other flooring products.

Column j—Ease of Maintenance. One of the principal reasons for the growing popularity of resilient floors in residential, commercial and institutional buildings is ease of maintenance. With regular sweeping and occasional washing and waxing, resilient floors require little more care. For exceptionally rugged maintenance problems, select from the product types that give outstanding resistance to abrasion, moisture, chemicals and greases.

Ease of maintenance provides savings in labor and materials over other types of floors. And a resilient floor is never "out of service" for cleaning purposes—an important factor in commercial, institutional and industrial installations.

Column k and l—Thermal Properties. Thermal properties of the various types and gauges of resilient flooring are important when considering design characteristics of radiant heated sub-floors. Thermal conductivity and thermal conductance factors listed in the Table represent average values of the various floorings. These values were derived in accordance with the procedure listed in Military Specification MIL-I-16923D.

K factor = BTU/hr/sq ft/°F/in.

C factor = BTU/hr/sq ft/°F/for the nominal product thickness.

Sales Volume. The sales volumes listed in millions of square feet are estimated values.

TABLE 12A-3. Products by Increasing Costs with Suggested Uses

Approximate Price Range	Table I No.	Flooring Product	Above Grade	On Grade	Below Grade	Residential	Light Commercial	Commercial	Institutional
$.20–$.30	IV 1,2	1/8 in. asphalt tiles, B and C Group	X	X	X	X	X	X	
	VI 1	.0625-in. linoleum tiles	X			X			
$.30–$.40	I 1	.065–.070 in. residential linoleum	X			X			
	III 1	Felt back residential foam cushion vinyl yard goods	X			X			
	IV 3	1/8 in. asphalt tiles, D Group	X	X	X	X	X	X	
	IV 7	1/8 in. asphalt tiles, special decoration	X	X	X	X			
	IV 4,5	3/16 in. asphalt tiles, B and C Group	X	X	X	X	X	X	X
	V 1	1/16 in. regular vinyl asbestos tile	X	X	X	X	X		
	VI 2	.070 in. linoleum tiles	X			X			
$.40–$.50	I 2	.090 in. light commercial regular linoleum	X			X	X		
	I 5	.125 in. battleship linoleum yard good	X			X	X	X	X
	II 1	.055 in. vinyl-back vinyl yard goods	X	X	X	X			
	II 2	.065 in. felt-back vinyl yard goods	X	+		X			
	III 2	.090 in. felt-back foam cushion vinyl yard goods	X	+		X			
	IV 6	3/16 in. asphalt tiles, D Group	X	X	X	X	X	X	X
	V 2	1/16 in. premium vinyl asbestos tile	X	X	X	X	0		
	VI 3	.090 in. linoleum tiles	X			X	X		
	IX 1,2	.050 in. vinyl tiles, roto-printed and calendered—regular	X	X		X			
$.50–$.60	I 3	.090 in. light commercial premium linoleum yard goods	X			X	X		
	I 4	.125 in. marbelized linoleum yard goods	X			X	X	X	X
	II 4	.070 in. felt-back vinyl yard goods	X	+		X	X		
	V 3	1/8 in. regular vinyl asbestos tile	X	X	X	X	X	X	X
	VIII 1	.080 in. rubber tile	X	X		X	X	X	
$.60–$.70	II 3	.065 in. asbestos back vinyl yard goods	X	X	X	X			
	VII 1	1/8 in. cork tile	X	+		X			
	IX 3	.050 in. calendered vinyl tiles, premium	X	X		X			
	IX 4	1/16 in. molded vinyl tiles, regular	X	X	X	X			
$.70–$.80	II 5	.070 in. asbestos back vinyl yard goods	X	X	X	X	X		
	III 3	asbestos back foam cushion vinyl yard goods	X	X	X	X			
	VII 3	3/16 in. cork tiles	X	+		X			
	VIII 2	.125 in. rubber tiles	X	X		X	X	X	X
	IX 5	.080 in. molded vinyl tiles, regular	X	X	X	X	X	X	
$.80–$.90	IX 6	.080 in. molded vinyl tiles, premium	X	X	X	X	X	X	
	IX 9	3/32 in. molded vinyl tiles	X	X	X	X	X	X	
	IX 10	.125 in. molded vinyl tiles, regular	X	X	X	X	X	X	
$.90–$1.10	II 6	090 in. asbestos-back-regular vinyl yard goods	X	X	X	X	X	X	X
	IX 7	.080 in. molded vinyl tiles, luxury	X	X	X	X	X	X	
	IX 11	.125 in. molded vinyl tiles, premium	X	X	X	X	X	X	X
$1.05–$1.20	II 7	.090 in. asbestos back premium vinyl yard goods	X	X	X	X	X	X	X
$1.10–$1.50	IX 8	.080 in. molded vinyl tiles, high luxury	X	X	X	X	X	X	
$1.15–$2.00	IX 12	.125 in. molded vinyl tiles, luxury	X	X	X	X	X	X	
$1.85	VII 3	1/8 in. vinyl cork tile	X	X	X	X	X	X	
$2.00–$3.50	IX 13	.125 in. molded vinyl tiles, high luxury	X	X	X	X	X	X	X

+ = On grade under certain conditions as specified in floor manufacturers literature.
0 = Some decorations are recommended for this usage, some are not.

TABLE 12A-4. Light Reflectance Table by Colors

Light Reflectance (%)	Asphalt Tiles	Vinyl Asbestos Tiles	.050-in. Calendered Vinyl Tiles	Linoleum	.070-in. Vinyl Yard Goods
70–80 60–70		White (med. to dark colors) White (black)	White White (lt. and med. colors) Lt beige (lt. colors) White (deep and dark colors) White (black)	White [lt. colors] (M) Lt. beige (med. colors) White (med. and deep colors) Off-white (med. colors) (M)	White (lt. colors) (M) White [med. colors] (M) Sand (med. colors) (M) White (marble med. colors) Beige (beige) (M)
50–60		Ivory (med. colors) Blonde Beige (white) Lt. yellow (beige)	Lt. beige (med. and deep colors) Lt. and med. beige	Cream (lt. and med. colors) Lt. beige (lt. color) (med. color) Lt. tan (lt. color) Lt. colors (white) (M) Lt. color mixtures	Lt. beige (white) (M) Pearl white (lt. and med. color) Ivory white (lt. and med. color) Pink and white (M) Lt. colors (lt. and med. color)
	Beige (lt. colors)	Lt. beige (med. to deep colors) Med. colors (white)	Lt. colors (deep to dark colors) Lt. beige (deep to dark colors)	White (black) Cream (deep colors)	Med. beige (M) Beige [med. to deep colors]
40–50	White (deep colors) White (dark colors)	Yellow (white) Lt. green Lt. mocha Lt. colors (white) Lt. colors (lt. to med. colors)	Lavender (white) Med. colors (white) Lt. blue (white)	Lt. beige (deep colors) Lt. beige (med. color) (med. color) Lt. tan [lt. to med. color] Lt. tan (deep color) Tan (med. colors) Tan (lt. tan) (brown)	Med. colors [med. to deep colors] Lavender Med. colors White [med. color] [med. color] Lt. green
35–40	White (black) Beige (med. colors) Gray (med. colors)	Lt. sand (white) Lt. beige and beige Pink Lt. med. colors Gray, olive	Lt. green (white) Oak Lt. and med. beige Birch	Lt. gray (lt. color) (gray) Med. colors (deep colors) Beige (lt. beige) (dark beige)	Dark beige [beige] (M) Med. deep colors Dark beige Deep colors

TABLE 12A-4. Light Reflectance Table by Colors (Continued)

Light Reflectance (%)	Asphalt Tiles	Vinyl Asbestos Tiles	.050-in. Calendered Vinyl Tiles	Linoleum	.070-in. Vinyl Yard Goods
30–35	Lt. med. colors Yellow Mocha Med. colors Taupe, lt. cork	Blue, mocha Deep colors (lt. colors) Med. colors Med beige		Beige (med. beige) Gray (med. gray) Olive green (cream) Deep colors [lt. colors] Med. beige (beige) Med. colors (deep to dark color)	
25–30	Lt. beige (dark colors) Beige (med. colors)	Gray beige Blue, lt. green		Lt. brown (tan, brown) Lt. green (dark green, white) Yellow (lt. gray) Med. colors [dark colors]	
20–25	Gray (med. colors) Med. dark colors Deep gray Med. cork Gray (black)	Coppertone, taupe Med. dark colors Med. tan, med cork Med. green Med. gray	Med. dark colors Reddish brown Lt. walnut	Beige [brown] Beige (pink) (turquoise) Lt. colors [black] Cream [black]	
15–20	Lt. brown Dark cork Dark green	Red (white)	Slate green Red (white)	Tan [brown] Blue [white] Red (white)	Brown [lt. brown]
10–15	Red	Dark cork Dark green (white)	Walnut, terra cotta Slate gray Brown (white)	Black (white) (brown) Brown, deep gray Brown-black	
5–10	Dark brown (lt. colors) Very dark green Brown (black, white) Black (white)	Black (white)		Dark green Terra cotta Black (white)	
0–5	Black (green, white) Black (gold)	Black (gold)	Black (gray, white)	Black	

NOTES: (color) = Decoration in this color covers about 2-10% of pattern.
(color) = Decoration in this color covers about 10-30% of pattern.
(M) = Metallized chips in clear: silver, gold, etc. (2-10%.)
Floors with higher reflectance (whiter whites) can be made on special order. Floors with lower reflectance

Table 12A-4

The term "light reflectance" is defined as the percentage of total light falling on a surface which is reflected back to the eye of the observer. Reflectance of floors, as measured by the Hunter Multi-Purpose Reflectometer using a standard light source is not influenced by the nature (smoothness) of the surface, but it is dependent upon color of the surface. Pure white, the highest reflective value, is rated 100; pure black, the lowest reflective value, is rated zero. Reflectance thus refers to the lightness or darkness of any given color or combination of colors having specific reflective values falling between the extremes of black and white. Obviously, the reflectance of marble or multicolored patterns will vary depending upon the distribution and amount of the different decorative colors falling within the area of measurement. The reflectance values listed are average values over areas representative of the average color in the pattern tested.

TABLE 12A-5.   Tile and Yard Goods Calculator

12 in. × 12 in. Tiles
(1) Increase any fractional feet to the next higher unit.
(2) Multiply the length by the width to get the number of tiles needed.

> EXAMPLE: Room 9 ft 3 in. × 11 ft 9 in.: 9 ft 3 i n.→10 ft; 11 ft 9 in.→12 ft 10 ft × 12 ft = 120 sq ft = 120 12 in. × 12 in. tiles

9 in. × 9 in. Tiles (Simple Estimation)
(1) Increase any fractional feet to the next higher unit.
(2) Multiply the length times width of room.
(3) Double the answer.
(4) This total less 10% equals number of tiles needed.

> EXAMPLE: Room 9 ft 6 in × 11 ft 9 in.: 9 ft 6 in.→10 ft; 11 ft 9 in.→12 ft 10 ft × 12 ft = 120, 120 × 2 = 240, 240 (less 10%) = 216 9 in. × 9 in. tiles

Tile Equivalents
(1) Square feet (see above) × 16/9 (or divided by .5625) equals number of 9 in. × 9 in. tiles.
(2) Number of 9 in. × 9 in. × $\frac{9}{16}$ (or .5625) equals square feet.
(3) 16 9 in. × 9 in. tiles = 9 square feet.

Yard Goods (6 ft wide)
(1) Determine how many strips are needed.
(2) Determine the length of each strip.
(3) Compute total lineal feet (total af all sheets). Multiply this by $\frac{2}{3}$ to obtain the number of square yards of 6-ft material needed.
(4) To convert square yards into feet, multiply by $\frac{3}{2}$.

Room Size	Number of 9 in. × 9 in. Tiles	Lineal Feet of 6 ft Wide Yard Goods
6' Wide		
6'	64	6
6'9"	72	6¾
7'6"	80	7½
8'3"	88	8¼
9'	96	9
9'9"	104	9¾
10'6"	112	10½
11'3"	120	11¼
12'	128	12
6'9" Wide		
6'9"	81	13½
7'6"	90	13½
8'3"	99	13½
9'	108	13½
9'9"	117	13½
10'6"	126	13½
11'3"	135	13½
12'	144	13½
12'9"	153	20¼
13'6"	162	20¼
7'6" Wide		
7'6"	100	15
8'3"	110	15
9'	120	15
9'9"	130	15
10'6"	140	15
11'3"	150	15
12'	160	15
12'9"	170	22½
13'6"	180	22½
14'3"	190	22½
15'	200	22½
8'3" Wide		
8'3"	121	16½
9'	132	16½
9'9"	143	16½
10'6"	154	16½
11'3"	165	16½
12'	176	16½
12'9"	187	25½
13'6"	198	24¾
14'3"	209	24¾
15'	220	24¾
15'9"	231	24¾
16'6"	242	24¾
9' Wide		
9'	144	18
9'9"	156	18
10'6"	168	18
11'3"	180	18
12'	192	18
12'9"	204	25½
13'6"	216	27
14'3"	228	28½
15'	240	30
15'9"	252	27
16'6"	264	27
17'3"	276	27
18'	288	27
9'9" Wide		
9'9"	169	19½
10'6"	182	19½
11'3"	195	19½
12'	208	19½
12'9"	221	25½
13'6"	234	27
14'3"	247	28½
15'	260	30
15'9"	273	30
16'6"	286	30
17'3"	299	30
18'	312	29¼
10'6" Wide		
10'6"	196	21
11'3"	210	21
12'	224	21
12'9"	238	25½
13'6"	252	27
14'3"	266	28½
15'	280	30
15'9"	294	31½
16'6"	308	33
17'3"	322	34½
18'	336	31½
18'9"	350	37½
19'6"	364	39
20'3"	378	40½

TABLE 12A-5. (Cont'd.)

Room Size	Number of 9 in. × 9 in. Tiles	Lineal Feet of 6 ft Wide Yard Goods
11'3" Wide		
11'3"	225	22½
12'	240	22½
12'9"	255	25½
13'6"	270	27
14'3"	285	28½
15'	300	30
15'9"	315	31½
16'6"	330	33
17'3"	345	34½
18'	360	33¾
18'9"	375	37½
19'6"	390	39
20'3"	405	40½
21'	420	42
12' Wide		
12'	256	24
12'9"	272	25½
13'6"	288	27
14'3"	304	28½
15'	320	30
15'9"	336	31½
16'6"	352	33
17'3"	368	34½
18'	384	36
18'9"	400	37½
19'6"	416	39
20'3"	432	40½
21'	448	42
12'9" Wide		
12'9"	289	38¼
13'6"	306	38¼
14'3"	323	38¼
15'	340	38¼
15'9"	357	38¼
16'6"	374	38¼
17'3"	391	38¼
18'	408	38¼
18'9"	425	51
19'6"	442	51
20'3"	459	51
21'	476	51
13'6" Wide		
13'6"	324	40½
14'3"	342	40½
15'	360	40½
15'9"	378	40½
16'6"	396	40½
17'3"	414	40½
18'	432	40½
18'9"	450	56¼
19'6"	468	58½
20'3"	486	54
21'	504	54
21'9"	522	54
22'6"	540	54
14'3" Wide		
14'3"	361	42¾
15'	380	42¾
15'9"	399	42¾
16'6"	418	42¾
17'3"	437	42¾
18'	456	42¾
18'9"	475	56¼
19'6"	494	58½
20'3"	513	60¾
21'	532	57
21'9"	551	57
22'6"	570	57
23'3"	589	57
24'	608	57
15' Wide		
15'	400	45
15'9"	420	45
16'6"	440	45
17'3"	460	45
18'	480	45
18'9"	500	56¼
19'6"	520	58½
20'3"	540	60¾
21'	560	63
21'9"	580	65¼
22'6"	600	60
23'3"	620	60
24'	640	60
24'9"	660	74¼
15'9" Wide		
15'9"	441	47¼
16'6"	462	47¼
17'3"	483	47¼
18'	504	47¼
18'9"	525	56¼
19'6"	546	58½
20'3"	567	60¾
21'	588	63
21'9"	609	65¼
22'6"	630	67½
23'3"	651	63
24'	672	63
24'9"	693	74¼
25'6"	714	76½
16'6" Wide		
16'6"	484	49½
17'3"	506	49½
18'	528	49½
18'9"	550	56¼
19'6"	572	58½
20'3"	594	60¾
21'	616	63
21'9"	638	65¼
22'6"	660	67½
23'3"	682	69¾
24'	704	72
24'9"	726	74¼
25'6"	748	76½
26'3"	770	78¾
17'3" Wide		
17'3"	529	51¾
18'	552	51¾
18'9"	575	56¼
19'6"	598	58½
20'3"	621	60¾
21'	644	63
21'9"	667	65¼
22'6"	690	67½
23'3"	713	69¾
24'	736	72
24'9"	759	74¼
25'6"	782	76½
26'3"	805	78¾
27'	828	81

18' Wide		
18'	576	54
18'9"	600	56¼
19'6"	624	58½
20'3"	648	60¾
21'	672	63
21'9"	696	65¼
22'6"	720	67½
23'3"	744	69¾
24'	768	72
24'9"	792	74¼
25'6"	816	76½

26'3"	840	78¾
27'	864	81
27'9"	888	83¼

Table 12A-5

This Table allows one to determine easily the number of 9 in. × 9 in. tiles or the linear feet of 6-ft wide yard goods needed for a given floor area. If the dimension is over a given value, then use the next larger value. The room width is given as a subtitle, and lengths up to double the width are arranged under it.

TABLE 12A-6. Stain Removal

Stain	Linoleum, Linoleum Tile, Cork Tile, Vinyl Sheet Flooring, Cushionflor	Asphalt Tile, Vinyl Asbestos Tile	Rubber Tile, Solid Vinyl Tile
Acids, alkalies, cleansers, detergents, drain cleaners, strong soaps	Wash area with rag dipped in water or liquid detergent floor cleaner. If necessary, rub with 00 fine steel wool dipped in floor cleaner, then rinse, or apply a dilute solution (1:1) of vinegar and let stand for several minutes. Rinse, let dry and wax.		
Alcoholic beverages, catsup, coffee, food dye markings, fruit and fruit juice, ink, iodine, vegetable, mercurochrome, mustard	Wash with cloth dipped in liquid detergent floor cleaner and water, then rinse. If necessary, rub with 00 fine steel wool dipped in floor cleaner, then rinse. If stain still remains, wet with a diluted Chlorox (1:1) solution and let stand for 10–15 min. Rinse well, let dry and wax.		
Rubber heel marks, shoe polish	Rub lightly with cloth or fine steel wool to which a solvent wax has been applied. Wipe with clean cloth before wax dries completely. Buff when dry. If necessary, rub lightly with cloth dipped in alcohol, then rinse. Polish when dry.	Rub with 00 fine steel wool dipped in liquid detergent floor cleaner, then rinse. If this fails, dust with mild household abrasive cleanser, then rub with fine steel wool dipped in floor cleaner. Rinse. Polish when dry.	
Dry-cleaning fluids, lacquer, nail polish, nail polish remover	Mop up freshly spilled liquids by blotting or remove excess with putty knife. Rub with 00 steel wool dipped in liquid detergent floor cleaner, then rinse. If this fails, dust with mild household abrasive cleanser, then rub with 00 steel wool dipped in floor cleaner. Rinse. Polish when dry.		
Asphalt, candle wax, chewing gum, grease, oil, tar	If dry, remove excess with putty knife. Rub lightly with cloth or fine steel wool to which a solvent wax has been applied. Wipe with clean cloth before wax dries completely. Buff when dry. To make scraping gum easier, freeze stubborn gum with dry ice; then scrape. The gum may be softened for easier removal with naptha. Then rub with fine steel wool and floor cleaner.	If dry, remove excess with putty knife. Rub with fine steel wool dipped in floor cleaner, then rinse. If this fails, dust with mild household abrasive cleanser, then rub with fine steel wool dipped in liquid cleanser. Rinse. Polish when dry. To make scraping gum easier, freeze stubborn gum with dry ice, then scrape. Do not use naptha on asphalt or VA tile. The gum may be softened for easier removal with naphtha. Then rub with fine steel wool and floor cleaner.	
Candy	Scrape off with a putty knife. Then rub with fine steel wool and liquid floor cleaner.		
Plaster	Scrape off with a putty knife. Then, clean with fine steel wool and a solution of liquid floor cleaner. Plaster that resists this removal may be softened by soaking with a 50–50 solution of vinegar and water.		
Adhesive, flooring	Sometimes a newly laid tile floor will present this problem. Remove with steel wool and liquid floor cleaner.		
Cigarette burns, rust, mildew, dye, blood, grass	Rub with 00 steel wool dipped in liquid floor cleaner, then rinse. If this fails, dust with mild household abrasive cleanser, then rub with 00 steel wool in liquid cleaner. Rinse. Polish when dry. If rust stain does not respond, use a 10% solution of oxalic acid. Then clean with liquid floor cleaner.		
Paint, solvents, varnish	If freshly spilled, take up immediately with blotting action. Wash with cloth dipped in liquid floor cleaner, then rinse. If dry, remove excess with putty knife. Rub with 00 steel wool dipped in liquid floor cleaner, then rinse. If this fails, dust with mild household abrasive cleanser, then rub with steel wool dipped in liquid cleaner. Rinse. Polish when dry.		
Shellac	Wash with cloth dipped in liquid floor cleaner, then rinse. If necessary, rub lightly with cloth dipped in alcohol then rinse. Polish when dry.		
Urine	Use liquid floor cleaner. If stain is old and does not respond, use 10% oxalic acid followed by liquid floor cleaner.		

Most spills and stains are easily removed with a quick wipe.

If the floor is waxed, chances are the stains will be kept on the surface and will not penetrate through to the flooring.

Most stains respond to scrubbing with detergent, liquid detergent floor cleaner or a light rubbing with fine steel wool dipped in liquid detergent floor cleaner.

More stubborn stains may be handled as indicated in the chart.

However, before some of the stubborn type stains are removed, it is desirable to know the type of floor. Different kinds of floors react differently to various cleaning agents.

Vinyl. Vinyl floors may be any one of the following:

VINYL TILE. Usually identified by clear, translucent or clean opaque color effects. May be solid with design all the way through, or backed with coarser vinyl or other backing material.

SHEET INLAID VINYL. Surface similar to vinyl tile, though in 6-ft widths and with backing material.

VINYL ASBESTOS TILE. A blend of vinyl resins and asbestos. Lower gloss than other types of vinyl floors.

ROTO VINYL. Clear vinyl coating over pattern printed by rotogravure printing process. Usually backed with heavy, flexible felt.

Inlaid Linoleum. Basically made of wood flour, resins, and color pigments. Comes in 6-ft widths and in tile form.

Asphalt Tile. Made of asbestos fibers, fillers, pigments and asphalt or resin binders.

TABLE 12A-7. Maintenance Problems—and How to Resolve Them

Problem	Cause	Solution
Dull appearance	Too little polish	Follow instructions carefully as prescribed on high-grade wax containers
	Improper cleaning and rinsing of floor	Follow instructions carefully as prescribed on liquid detergent cleaner and wax container.
	Wrong polish used	Clean floor completely as prescribed on liquid detergent floor cleaner container and then finish with suitable self-polishing wax or vinyl wax. Only the self-polishing wax needs buffing to increase its gloss.
	Coarse floor	After freshly applied thin coat of wax is dry, buff and apply another coat of wax and buff again. Do not use heavy-duty cleaners. Use liquid detergent floor cleaner.
	Floor not completely dry after washing	Always make certain floor is fully dried after washing; incomplete drying commonly occurs in humid weather.
Yellowed film (build-up of wax)	Too many coats of wax in non-traffic areas	Remove old wax with liquid detergent floor cleaner. Apply thin coat of self-polishing wax or vinyl wax.
	Too frequent application of wax	When spot waxing, apply wax only on bare surface.
	Wrong wax	Remove old wax with liquid floor cleaner. Apply thin coat of self-polishing wax or vinyl wax.
"Tacky" finish	Too much wax	
	Wrong wax	
	Wax applied over improperly cleaned and improperly rinsed floor	Remove old wax with liquid detergent floor cleaner and reapply wax, following instructions carefully.
Black heel marks	Some rubber heels mark any flooring	Rub with fine steel wool dipped in liquid detergent floor cleaner.
	Wrong polish	Clean floor with liquid detergent floor cleaner and apply self-polishing wax or vinyl wax. When dry, only the self-polishing wax needs buffing to increase its gloss.
Uneven glossy and dull appearance	Uneven wax removal	Remove all old wax completely with liquid detergent floor cleaner. Then apply self-polishing wax or vinyl wax evenly as directed. Only the self-polishing wax needs buffing to increase its gloss.
	Uneven surface collects dirt and excess wax due to indentations	Using liquid detergent floor cleaner, remove dirt and wax with steel wool or fine synthetic fiber pad and floor machine. When floor is completely clean, apply thin coat or coats of self-polishing wax or vinyl wax. Buff the self-polishing wax when dry after each application.
Faded, washed out appearance	Heavy-duty cleaners	Use liquid detergent floor cleaner.
	Cleaning too often	Follow recommended floor care program.
	Abrasive pads and cleaners	Use finer-grade pads and liquid detergent floor cleaner.
	Direct sunlight	Scrub with #1 steel wool and liquid detergent floor cleaner (solution: 1 part cleaner, 32 parts water—½ cup/gal). Rinse. Apply self-polishing wax.
Streaking when applying wax; uneven wetting, spreading or leveling of wax	Too much or not enough wax in mop or on applicator	Use proper amount of wax.
	Excessive rubbing with applicator	Apply wax lightly and evenly.
	Improper rinsing	Rinse carefully. When surface is dry, apply wax.
	Wrong polish	Clean with liquid detergent floor cleaner and apply self-polishing wax or vinyl wax.
	Dirty mop or applicator	Use clean mop or applicator.
Traffic paths (yellowing)	Improper maintenance	Scrub area with machine and fine steel wool pads and a strong detergent solution. Apply wax. Damp mop area periodically. Renew wax when worn off. Check for track-in source such as paint, asphalt driveways, oil, concrete, etc.

PART B: Carpeting

LEONARD MOZER*

American Carpet Institute
New York, New York

The development of synthetic fibers by the United States carpet industry is another chapter in the manifold story of how plastic materials have created a revolution in American business.

Before World War II—except for a few experimental fabrics—all of the pile yarns used in American carpets and rugs were produced from natural fibers. Of these fibers, wool was almost completely dominant, though some low-priced rugs were also made of cotton, and one could also find some floor coverings woven of linen. Synthetics were virtually unknown in the carpet industry.

By 1963, synthetic fibers accounted for virtually half of all the pile yarns used by American carpet manufacturers, and the outlook is for continued expansion. The introduction of synthetic fibers has made it possible for the carpet industry to sustain a fantastic growth record in the postwar period. It has enabled the industry to produce hundreds of millions of yards of carpet at moderate prices, and has led to new types of carpets with unique characteristics of performance and styling.

WOOL — THE HISTORIC CARPET FIBER

Wool, the traditional carpet fiber since the birth of civilization, dominated the fiber picture in the carpet industry in the pre-war period. The types of wool used in carpets differ greatly from those used in fine apparel fabrics. They are longer, more coarse, tough, durable, springy and resilient—all factors vital to good carpet performance

*Present address: Wool Carpets of America, New York, N. Y

and wear. The high-bred, domestically-grown sheep produce wools which are soft and fine, and ideally suited for apparel fabrics, but not suitable for carpets. For this reason all of the wools used in American-made carpets are imported from areas of the world where low-bred sheep produce the coarse wools required.

Before and immediately following World War II, these carpet wools continued to be in a readily available supply for such countries as Argentina, China, New Zealand, India, Iraq, Syria and other Middle Eastern nations.

When this supply was cut off at the outbreak of the war, American carpet manufacturers began producing some fabrics made of cellulosic fibers—rayon and acetate—but even this output ended when the carpet industry converted to war production.

When carpet wools again became available to the industry at the end of the war, there was no great stimulation for any volume production of synthetic fibers. Some low-priced carpeting made of rayon was manufactured, but its output was extremely limited—amounting to only 1 per cent in the immediate postwar years of 1948–49.

In the next two years, there was a sudden turn of events. First, Communist domination of China eliminated this nation as an important source of carpet wool to the American industry. Secondly, the outbreak of the Korean War in June, 1950, created panic buying which greatly boosted demand and skyrocketed the cost of carpet wools.

Thus the industry vitally required another raw material on which it could depend for a stable supply and with which it could manufacture carpets for the expanding American market at prices that the average consumer could afford.

The cellulosic fibers met this need at that moment, and manufacturers began to increase the usage of this material. This is indicated by the following consumption figures for the years 1950 and 1951.

	Wool (lb)	*Cellulosic* (lb)
1950	273,800,000	12,537,000
1951	141,000,000	31,600,000

THE GROWTH OF SYNTHETIC FIBERS IN CARPETS

Though the cost of carpet wools eventually subsided to normal levels by 1952, the carpet industry never returned to its all-wool dependence. In the years that followed, intensive research was conducted by the carpet manufacturers in close cooperation with the major chemical companies to develop and produce completely new types of synthetic fibers in volume. The results of these efforts bore fruit during the ensuing decade with the introduction of completely new types of carpet yarns made from fibers of nylon, acrylic, modacrylic and, more recently, polypropylene and polyester fibers.

These new fibers have been engineered specifically for carpets. They are generally heavier, coarser, springier and tougher than their counterparts used for clothing or blankets. In some cases they closely resemble wool in appearance and performance. But in addition, these fibers offer special properties that make them quite distinctive from wool.

The degree of public acceptance of the synthetics can be judged by comparing total yardage output of carpets and fiber consumption in the years 1948 and 1963. In 1948, United States carpet manufacturers produced 90 million square yards of "broadloom" (6 feet or wider) carpeting. This was an all-time record for production of carpets in this country up to that time. In that year carpet wool accounted for 292,500,000 pounds of fibers consumed, while cellulosics—the only synthetic fiber in use then—accounted for just 2,753,000 pounds.

By 1965, sales of carpet had reached an annual volume of approximately 295 million square yards—more than triple the 1948 output. The fiber picture, however, had changed drastically. Consumption of synthetic fibers that year accounted for an estimated 353,000,000 pounds, while wool consumption was at 115,000,000 pounds. Furthermore, the newer synthetic fibers had replaced the cellulosics as the leading manmade material used in broadloom carpet pile yarns. This is indicated by a breakdown of fiber consumption for the years 1961 through 1965 (Table 12B-1).

TABLE 12B-1. Broadloom Pile Fiber Consumption
(millions of pounds)

	1961	1962	1963	1964	Est. 1965
Wool	147	149	160	122	115
Filament nylon	45	70	90	131	155
Staple nylon	23	25	30	45	53
Acrylics and modacrylics	12	22	45	85	120
Rayon and polypro	20	15	11	17	25
Cotton	10	10	5	3	2
Totals	257	291	341	403	370

The different synthetic fibers offer styling and performance characteristics which are comparable in some respects to wool, and unique in others. Some of the fibers' dyeing properties make possible deep, intense colorings. Some also have distinctive textures, with a high luster or sheen. As to performance, some of the fibers have outstanding resistance to abrasive wear when constructed in good quality carpets. Some

TABLE 12B-2. Chart of Hotel-Motel Carpet Fibers

Fiber	Wearability	Resiliency	Soil Resistance	Stain Resistance	Cleanability	Static Generation	Price Range	Special Characteristics
Wool	High in good quality construction	High	High	Medium	High	Medium to high (antistatic agents help)	Medium to high	The most versatile carpet yarn—wool resists abrasion, gives long life, resists crushing, and has a soft hand. It can be used in the heaviest traffic areas.
Cotton	High (if in a dense construction)	Low	Low	Low	Medium (vacuuming is necessary often to raise pile)	Low	Low	Cotton offers bright color and a soft hand. Unless found in a very dense quality construction, it should only be used in light traffic areas.
Acrylic brands	High	High	High	High	High	Medium to high (antistatic agents eliminate static)	Medium to high	The acrylics have many characteristics similar to wool. They are considered excellent long wearing carpet yarns. Colors are bright and intense.

Fiber	Wearability	Resiliency	Soil Resistance	Stain Resistance	Cleanability	Static Generation	Price Range	Special Characteristics
Nylon (there are two types of nylon: staple and continuous filament)	Extra high	Medium to high	Medium to high	High	High	High (anti-static agents help)	Low to medium generally; high-priced nylon is available in special qualities	Nylon is considered by most of the trade as the most durable and longest wearing carpet fiber.
Rayon	Medium to low, depending on density	Medium to low	Low	Low	Medium	Low	Low	Carpet rayon is suitable only for light traffic areas. It is used primarily in scatter rugs in hotel and motel bathrooms.
Polypropylene	Extra high	Medium	High	High	High	Low	Low to Medium	Thermoplastic, melts. Durable outdoors.
Other fibers	Polyester is just coming into use as a carpet fiber and cannot be rated as yet.							
Blends	The advantages of each fiber in a blend are gained provided there is at least 20% of each fiber. Wool/nylon blends of 70/30 or 80/20 are becoming more common. Acrylics are usually blended with either 20 or 30% of modacrylic fiber.							
Flame resistance	Wool, nylon, acrylics in blends, cotton and rayon are self-extinguishing—if the source of flame is removed, the carpet ceases to burn. When nylon meets a flame, it melts. Hard beads form which can easily be snipped off. If this is fairly extensive, the carpet may be re-burled. Black char remains when either wool or acrylic blends meet flame. This can be easily scraped off. The carpet should then be cleansed with a detergent.							

are more resilient than others. Some of the fibers are hydrophobic—resistant to water absorption—and thus permit easier removal of water-soluble stains. Some of the synthetic yarns are more resistant to shedding than others when specially processed.

There are several characteristics that are universal to all of the synthetic fibers. They are all nonallergenic, unaffected by mildewing and not subject to damage by moths or other insects. It should be pointed out, however, that in the mid-1950's chemical treatments were perfected that have made woolen carpets immune to moth or insect damage for the life of the carpet, even after repeated shampooings.

The normal tendency has been to compare each of the synthetic materials to wool since the latter has been the standard carpet pile fiber for so many years. However, this can be misleading. The pile yarns are just one component of a finished carpet. The amount of yarns used, the density or closeness of their construction, the backing foundation which holds the pile yarns, and a number of other factors all play a role in determining the quality, appearance and performance of the finished carpet.

A good carpet can be made from any one of the carpet fibers. On the other hand, a "bad" or poor-performing carpet can be produced from these same materials—including wool. How well these materials are used and the quality of the construction must be considered as well as the fiber itself.

Following is a description of each of the synthetic fibers currently used in the manufacture of carpets in the United States.

Acrylic Fibers

According to the definition of the Federal Trade Commission, acrylic is a manufactured fiber in which the fiber-forming substance is any long-chain synthetic polymer composed of at least 85 per cent by weight of acrylonitrile units. The acrylonitrile is usually combined with small amounts of other chemicals to improve the ability of the fiber to absorb dyes and other properties.

Initially brought out for apparel fabrics in 1950, acrylic yarns were first introduced commercially in carpets in 1957. The extent of their use grew slowly in the years immediately following, but showed a sharp increase from 1961 to 1965.

Characteristics. Of all the synthetic carpet fibers in use today, acrylic bears the greatest resemblance to wool in appearance and other properties. Like wool, it has a soft "hand," providing the warm, luxurious feel and appearance often associated with wool carpets. It has a high resiliency—ability to bounce back after being subject to pressure— and thus is resistant to crushing and matting down.

A pure white fiber in its original state, acrylic takes dyes well, and thus makes possible carpet yarns of pure, rich colors.

Being a hydrophobic fiber, it is resistant to water-soluble stains, permitting them to be easily removed. Carpets of acrylic yarns have excellent soil resistance and can be readily cleaned.

In a good-quality construction, an acrylic yarn has an excellent resistance to abrasive wear, quite similar to that of wool. The fibers have high elasticity and are able to maintain excellent twist retention when spun into yarn.

Acrylic carpets have a medium-to-high tendency to generate static electricity, which becomes apparent on cool, dry days, or when humidity in a room becomes abnormally low. However, this problem can be eliminated by application of antistatic agents to the carpet surface.

Acrylic fibers are frequently blended with modacrylic fibers in carpet yarns, usually in combinations of 80 per cent acrylic and 20 per cent modacrylic by weight. There are also blends of acrylic with wool or acrylic with nylon.

The cost of acrylic carpets is usually in the medium-to-higher price ranges.

Manufacturers of Acrylic Fibers

Trade Name	Manufacturer
"Acrilan"	Chemstrand Company
"Creslan"	American Cyanamid Company
"Orlon"	E. I. du Pont de Nemours & Company
"Zefran"	Dow Chemical Company

Modacrylic Fibers

The Federal Trade Commission Rules define modacrylic as a manufactured fiber in which the fiber-forming substance is any long-chain synthetic polymer composed of less than 85 per cent, but at least 35 per cent, by weight of acrylonitrile units.

Modacrylics are made from resins that are combinations of acrylonitrile and other materials as vinyl chloride, vinylidene chloride or vinylidene dicyanide. First introduced in apparel fabrics in 1949, modacrylic yarns were initially used in carpets in 1957. Though some carpets made of all-modacrylic yarns are produced, most of these materials are used today for blending with acrylic fibers for carpet yarns.

Characteristics. In a number of respects, modacrylics resemble the acrylics, dependent upon the degree of their acrylonitrile content. They have a warm, soft and luxurious hand. They do not have quite the resiliency of acrylic yarns. Their resistance to abrasive wear is good. The fibers are difficult to ignite, and when exposed to flame, are self-extinguishing. They resist acids and alkalies. Modacrylics, like acrylics, can be dyed in a wide range of colors. The modacrylics are heavier than acrylic fibers (greater in specific gravity) being closer to cotton and wool in this respect.

Manufacturers of Modacrylic Fibers

Trade Name	Manufacturer
"Verel"	Eastman Kodak Company
"Dynel"	Union Carbide Chemicals Company

Nylon Fibers

The Federal Trade Commission Rules define nylon as a manufactured fiber in which the fiber-forming substance is any long-chain synthetic polyamide having recurring amide groups as an integral part of the polymer chain. Nylon 66 is made from adipic acid and hexamethylene diamine, while nylon 6 is made from caprolactam.

Though first introduced in hosiery and other apparel fabrics in 1938, nylon was not employed in carpet yarns until after World War II. Initially, carpet nylon fibers were made only in "staple" form. In this form, the finished fiber is chopped into short pieces, which are then spun into yarn as in the "woolen system." In 1958, nylon yarns made of continuous-filament fibers were introduced in carpets. The yarns are also subjected to various texturizing processes.

The use of nylon had a steady but slow growth in carpet manufacture prior to the development of the continuous-filament type. However, its application registered a phenomenal boost when this type of nylon was introduced. Continuous-filament nylon quickly became the second most important carpet fiber, after wool. Consumption leaped to 155,000,000 pounds by 1965. Staple nylon, used either in 100 percent pile content or blended with other fibers, has grown rapidly in the past few years to 53,000,000 pounds in 1965.

Characteristics. Nylon carpet yarns are outstanding in their resistance to abrasive wear. They are tough and highly durable. In staple form, nylon is well-suited to cut-pile or plush textures. However, it has a tendency to "pill"—form little balls of fiber at the tips of looped pile yarns. The continuous-filament type, whether constructed in dense, looped or uncut pile fabrics, does not pill and resists shedding.

Nylon tends to have a harder "hand" than wool or the acrylic fibers. Its texture also is somewhat glossier. Although they can be made in de-lustered forms, most nylon carpets generally appear more shiny or lustrous than the other carpet yarns.

Nylon carpets are hydrophobic, resistant to water absorption. As a result, they tend to generate static electricity under low-humidity conditions. However, as in the acrylics, this problem can be corrected by introducing moisture into the atmosphere or by application of antistatic agents to the carpet.

Nylon carpet yarns have good resiliency, particularly in dense pile constructions. In cost, nylon carpets tend to be priced lower than those made of wool primarily because less yarn is required to provide corresponding wear.

Nylon takes dyes well, and carpets made of this fiber are available in a wide color range. Water-soluble stains are readily removed from nylon carpets. Resistance to soiling is considered almost as good as wool or acrylics, and nylon can be cleaned easily.

Staple nylon is frequently blended with wool, usually in proportions of 70 percent wool and 30 percent nylon, to take advantage of nylon's excellent abrasive resistance. (In carpet yarn blends, the carpet will tend to appear and perform like the fiber that is predominant in the mixture. In the case of blends with nylon, it should be pointed out, the addition of at least 20 percent nylon is necessary for any noticeable gain in the finished carpet's durability.)

Manufacturers of Nylon Fibers

Trade Name	Manufacturer
"Caprolan"	Allied Chemical Corporation
"Cumuloft"	Chemstrand Company
"Enkaloft"	American Enka Corporation
"501"	E. I. du Pont de Nemours & Company
"Nyloft"	Firestone Synthetic Fibers Company
"Tycora"	Textured Yarn Company

Cellulosic Fibers

The two cellulosic fibers used in carpets are rayon and acetate. Rayon is defined by the Federal Trade Commission as a manufactured fiber composed of regenerated cellulose, as well as manufactured fibers composed of regenerated cellulose in which substituents have replaced not more than 15 percent of the hydrogens of the hydroxyl groups. Acetate is defined as a manufactured fiber in which the fiber-forming substance is cellulose acetate.

The type of rayon most prevalently used in carpet fibers is viscose rayon. This is made by converting purified cellulose to xanthate, dissolving the xanthate in dilute caustic soda and then regenerating the cellulose from the product as it emerges from the spinneret.

As noted, some carpets of cellulosic yarns were made before World War II. It reached its peak in consumption in the 1950's. In 1957 about 76,000,000 pounds of these fibers were consumed by the carpet industry. With the introduction of the acrylic and continuous-filament nylon synthetics, however, use of rayon and acetate in broadloom carpet manufacture declined, and by 1963 had dropped to about 7,000,000 and has declined still further since then.

Some of the cellulosics are produced in solution-dyed form; the color is introduced before the fiber is spun and is thus locked into the fiber. This prevents fading.

The cellulosic fibers are low in cost and are still used in quantity in low-priced scatter rugs and, to a lesser degree, in broadloom rugs and carpets designed for light duty. Their abrasion resistance is lower than that of wool, nylon or the acrylics. They have less resiliency than the other fibers, and unless they are employed in thick, dense constructions, the cellulosics will tend to mat or crust more readily.

They have an excellent ability to take dyes and can be produced in a wide range of colors. Their resistance to soil, particularly in a smooth fiber form, is fair to good, but they can be readily cleaned.

Carpets made of cellulosic fibers have a soft hand and luxurious feeling. Their static generation is low. Some rayon carpets are blended with nylon for improved abrasion resistance.

Manufacturers of Cellulosic Fibers

Trade Name	Manufacturer
"Avicolor," "Avicron" and "Super L"	American Viscose Division, FMC Corporation
"Corval," "Fibro" and "Kolorbon"	Courtaulds of North America, Inc.
"Skybloom" and "Skyloft"	American Enka Corporation

Polypropylene Fibers

Polypropylene fibers are classified as "olefins." These are defined by the Federal Trade Commission Rules as manufactured fibers in which the fiber-forming substance is any long-chain synthetic polymer composed of at least 85 per cent by weight of ethylene, propylene or other olefin units.

American carpet manufacturers began using polypropylene yarns in 1962. Growth has been rapid, and these fibers account for most of the estimated 25 million pounds for "rayon and polypropylene" in 1965.

Characteristics. For carpet yarns, polypropylene has been used mostly in continuous-filament form. In appearance, it is quite similar to carpets of continuous-filament nylon, though it is less lustrous. It combines light weight with high strength and good abrasion resistance. Its cost is relatively low, so that it offers carpets of good performance at moderate prices. It has low static generation.

The yarns have medium resiliency. They are unaffected by water and have a good resistance to sunlight. Their use in carpets was initially impeded by their inability to accept normally available dyes, so that their color range has been limited. However, development of new dyeing techniques is rapidly widening the color spectrum of these carpet yarns.

Manufacturers of Polypropylene Fibers

Trade Name	Manufacturer
"Herculon"	Hercules Powder Company
"Polycrest"	U. S. Rubber Company
"Vectra"	Vectra Company Div., Natl. Plastics Corp.
"Marvess"	Alamo Industries

13 PLASTIC PIPE

J. S. SCHAUL JR.

Celanese Plastics Company
Plastics Research and Development Center
Clark, New Jersey

WHY PLASTIC PIPE?

Plumbing is associated, historically and etymologically, with lead pipe and joints, but today this material is one among many. Other metals, with ceramics and composite materials, have dominated piping and fixture manufacture. Opposite lead on the weight scale is the most recent group to enter the field, plastics. This chapter presents information on the use of plastics to convey and control fluids in and around buildings. (Bathroom fixtures of glass-reinforced plastics are included in Chapter 5.)

Few building components have been made of so many diverse materials as has pipe, yet no one material is wholly satisfactory—certainly not for all uses. This testifies to the severe functional requirements imposed on most piping systems. In a building, pipe must do some or all of these:

(1) Convey fluid quantitatively, i.e., without leakage or seepage;

(2) Convey it efficiently, i.e., with minimum loss of pressure and flow;

(3) Convey it inertly, without chemical interaction;

(4) Withstand hydraulic pressures exerted by the fluid;

(5) Have structural strength, inherent or derived from other systems;

(6) Resist or absorb movement imparted by its support or other agencies;

(7) Resist external loads normally occurring;

(8) Keep heat exchange with the environment to a minimum;

(9) Resist fire, heat, cold, shock, corrosion, organisms and other environmental factors;

(10) Retain these characteristics with minimum maintenance for the life of the building.

In addition, it should be

(a) Available in all required diameters, wall thicknesses and lengths;

(b) Joinable to itself, to distribution and collection piping and to appurtenances, including provision for size and direction changes, branching, and controls;

(c) Specifiable from recognized standards and acceptable by constituted regulatory bodies;

(d) Shipped, handled and installed successfully by normal means and personnel.

Finally, unless a pipe has some unique advantage, it must be competitive, with installed cost the point of reference.

Plastic pipe, less than 20 years old in this country and barely 30 years old anywhere, having become established in several other parts of the economy, is knocking on building doors. What are its claims to admission?

Its major claim is simply that it can perform the required functions and save money. In certain respects, i.e., those that follow from its chemical inertness, light but impermeable structure, smooth, hydrophobic surface and attractive joining characteristics, it equals or excels all other pipe. In others, broadly involving mechanical strength, plastic cannot match some competitors; closely examined as pipe, however, it looks unexpectedly good. For example, breakage in handling or service is rare because plastics usually are merely deformed under external loads that crack brittle materials; the extra wall-thickness allowance for corrosion and the extra diameter allowance for rust buildup are not needed; joints, which are the critical points of other systems because they are weakest, most susceptible to corrosion, or least reliably tight, are not limiting factors in the strength of plastic pipe.

Probably hundreds of basic types of plastics have been developed. Dozens are commercial. Only a few have succeeded as pipe; four of these are produced in large volume and important for building use. In alphabetical order, their names and trade symbols are: acrylonitrile-butadiene-styrene (ABS), polyethylene (PE), polyvinyl chloride (PVC) and styrene-rubber (SRP). They are listed, with annual sales[11] as pipe and fittings, in Table 13-1.

TABLE 13-1. Sales Volume of Major Plastic Pipe and Fittings

| | | Millions of pounds | | |
		1962	1963	1964
ABS	Acrylonitrile-butadiene-styrene	10	12	18
PE	Polyethylene	49	59	58[a]
PVC	Polyvinyl chloride	18	30	43
SRP	Styrene-rubber	16	20	25

[a]Poundage decrease reflects higher design stress assignments; footage increased.

As noted in Chapter 2, these four materials contain synthetic organic materials of high molecular weight called polymers, or mixtures thereof; they are thermoplastic and are produced in many varieties for many purposes. Thanks to standardization, however, confusion of trade names does not plague pipe identification; plastic materials for pipes and fittings have been classified, on a performance basis, into relatively few types and grades within each chemical family.

Other kinds of plastic pipe are manufactured: acetal, biaxially oriented polyethylene, butyrate, chlorinated polyether, cross-linked polyethylene, fluorocarbon, nylon, polypropylene, reinforced thermoset, vinylidene, and also plastic lined or covered pipe. Some of these may be passing out of the picture; others are about to enter it; still others may be costly or otherwise not suitable for building use; only polypropylene will be mentioned here again. The four important plastics survive because they are best able to meet the functional requirements, paralleling the selection process in other piping materials.

These plastics have survived first because of cost. They belong to large plastic material groups that are produced at about two billion pounds per year and sell for under 50¢/lb, some less than 25¢. On a volumetric basis, this is cheaper than steel but higher than clay, for example. A second reason is their environmental stability, or resistance to deterioration by air, water, gas, sewage, soil and chemicals, in which they surpass most other plastics. PVC and ABS qualify as engineering materials in other areas. The final reason, of course, is their ability to be formed into tubes by the convenient process of extrusion.

Other reasons are peculiar to the individual pipe. PVC is a strong, rigid structural thermoplastic; PE has modest strength but convenient lightness. ABS and PVC are easily joined to their fittings by solvent cement; PE cannot be joined this way but its flexibility eliminates many joints. PVC is more fire and corrosion resistant, but the other two are tougher at low temperatures. SRP has an advantage over all the others in an important area—price—but it lacks other virtues. A comparison of properties is found in Table 13-2.

The most important uses of these plastic pipes, here and abroad, have been as shown in Table 13-3.

MANUFACTURE AND TESTING OF PLASTIC PIPE AND FITTINGS

The processing of thermoplastics[3] utilizes their properties of softening when heated

TABLE 13-2. ASTM Requirements for Thermoplastic Pipe and Fitting Materials[a,b]

	ABS—D1788-62T			PE—D1248-60T			PVC—D1784-60T		
	TIG1	TIG2	TIIG1	TIG3	TIIIG2	TIIIG3	TIG1	TIG2	TIIG1
Specific gravity (density, g/cc)	1.0–1.2	1.0–1.2	1.0–1.2	0.926–0.940	0.941–0.965	0.941–0.965	—	—	—
Tensile properties									
Tensile strength, psi	4000	4500	7500	1800	2800	3200	7000	7000	5500
Elastic modulus, psi	210,000	210,000	350,000	—	—	—	400,000	400,000	300,000
Ultimate elongation, %	—	—	—	400	75	100	—	—	—
Flexural strength, psi	—	—	—	—	—	—	11,000	11,000	8500
Izod impact strength, ft-lb/in.									
at 73°F	3	6.5	4	—	—	—	0.65	0.65	5.0
at −40°F	—	1.5	—	—	—	—	—	—	—
Rockwell hardness (R scale)	85	85	110	—	—	—	—	—	—
Deflection temperature (264 psi), °F	185	185	214	—	—	—	158	158	151
Brittle temperature, max, °F	—	—	—	−76	−67	−94	—	—	—
Flammability (SE = self-extinguishing)	—	—	—	—	—	—	SE	SE	SE
Chemical resistance	5.0% max weight change after 40-hr immersion in heptane			—	—	—	Max limits on changes in weight and flexural strength after elevated-temperature immersions in sulfuric acid, and in weight after oil immersion		

[a] All properties are minimum values at 73°F unless otherwise stated.
[b] Properties in this Table apply to test results under specified conditions and are not for design purposes. In general, they define and identify the materials on a test performance basis.
[c] TIG1 is Type I Grade 1, etc.

TABLE 13-3. Important Uses of Plastic Pipes

	ABS	PE	PVC
Agriculture	X	XX	
Artificial skating rinks		X	
Chemical process	X		XX
Drain, waste and vent	X		X
Electrochemical			X
Food and beverage	X	X	XX
Gas distribution	X	X	X
Irrigation	X	X	X
Laboratory drainage		X	X
Lawn and turf sprinkling	X	XX	X
Marine	X		X
Metallurgical			X
Mine drainage		X	
Petroleum			X
Pharmaceutical			X
Photographic			X
Pulp and paper	X		XX
Refrigeration and air conditioning			X
Sewer and drain			X
Slab radiant heating		X	
Swimming pools	X	XX	X
Textile	X		XX
Water supply and distribution	X	XX	XX

SRP pipe has been used largely for sewer and drain.

to force flow into the desired shapes and hardening when cooled to set these shapes. Pipe, having a constant cross section and indefinite length, is produced continuously by extrusion. A plastics extruder, usually of highly developed design, is fed pellets or powder prepared by compounding polymer with additives. The material is conveyed through a heated cylinder by means of a rotating screw whose shearing action also melts it, mixes it and forces it through an annular opening in a die. The extrudate from the die is pulled continuously through stations which successively size, cool, and cut it to length or coil it.

Fittings, being discrete bodies of which all dimensions are determined, are formed by high-pressure injection of plastic melt into closed molds. A reciprocating plunger forces material past heated surfaces, through a nozzle and, by way of runners or channels and a gate, into the mold cavity, which includes suitable cores to form the hollow interior. A rotating screw that may also reciprocate is used on some machines to do the plunger's job of plastication, and it sometimes does it better. When the piece has cooled, the mold opens and the piece is pushed out. Injection molding machines, like extruders, are of sophisticated design and operate automatically or semiautomatically.

Where economic or technical reasons prevent molding, other methods are available. Fittings that have axial symmetry—couplings, bushings, etc.—may be machined from extruded rod or tube stock by modified metal-working techniques. In addition, any configuration can be fabricated by welding, cementing and/or screwing together parts which have been cut, machined and/or thermoformed from sheet, rod, pipe and/or other fittings; their reliability in general depends on the joining technique as well as on material quality. Finally, several molded or machined shapes may be assembled to make a valve or other complex item.

The designer and the consumer are interested in the variables of processing as they affect product quality.[13] Accurate and stable dimensions, critical when parts are to be joined, result from skilled attention to many details including die and mold design, pressures, heating and cooling conditions. Optimum realization of a material's potentialities in the finished product, which is expected when specifying it for a construction item, depends on such points as attaining homogeneity, complete fusion, uniform temperatures, and cooling without stress or distortion, as well as proper reunion and welding of divided flows in an extruder or molding machine, absence of polymer degradation by heat or oxygen and, almost obviously, use of high-grade starting material.

Property and quality tests have been performed regularly by responsible plastics processors and laboratories, and they now have been written into product standards;[24] these tests regulate most of the conversion of engineering plastics into pipe and fittings. Devising tests which can be meaningfully correlated with performance and durability has been the activity of many technical people.[4] This was needed because different types of plastic pipe tend to "look alike" and the defects, if any, are not always apparent. Another reason is that behavior is complex and not readily predicted by simple or quick tests; often it depends on the duration of the load or the frequency of load application, as well as on the temperature.

Some familiar properties such as tensile strength or its hydrostatic analogue, burst strength, are of limited value for plastic pipe and fittings; nevertheless, when intelligently interpreted, short-term mechanical and chemical tests can be reliable guides. Accordingly, an entire technology of evaluation has been developed by producers, consumers and technical committees. Some tests serve to identify or characterize materials or products on the basis of how they perform under defined conditions, others are used for control of quality, and a few provide directly usable design information. A test is preferably performed on the pipe or fitting itself but, in many cases, must be done on the raw material.

JOINING PLASTIC PIPE

While thermoplastic pipe can be threaded for joining with screw-type fittings, in practice other systems are usually more suitable. Cut threads lessen toughness of notch-sensitive plastics, some pipe walls are too thin for threads, and in any case threads reduce pressure ratings and take time to make. Instead, joining techniques utilizing special properties of the materials are commonly employed and have important advantages: joints are quickly made with minimum preparatino and equipment, and most kinds are at least as strong and resistant as the pipe itself and are bottle-tight.

Solvent-cemented Joint

Specific organic solvents can soften, swell and partially dissolve ABS, PVC and SRP when applied to the surface; two such treated objects brought into contact coalesce,

TABLE 13-4. Tests Used on Plastic Pipe and on Pipe Materials

Test	Significance
Tensile properties	Relative strength, stiffness and ductility in tension at medium loading rates
Flexural properties	Relative behavior as simple beam at medium loading rates
Izod impact strength	Energy to break notched cantilever specimen under arbitrary shock load conditions
Dropweight impact strength	Energy to break pipe specimen or fitting; more realistic than Izod
Quick burst	Rough measure of relative pressure capacity; a control test
Long-term hydrostatic	Used to establish design stress for material and pressure rating for pipe
Parallel-plate bearing (flattening)	Provides engineering data on ring flexibility and stiffness, indicates quality
Sand bearing	Earth-load capacity of buried rigid conduit; inapplicable to plastic pipe, being removed from standards
Visual examination	Indicates general workmanship but not performance characteristics
Dimensional	To assure proper assembly fits and maintenance of minimum wall thickness for pressure resistance
Density (specific gravity)	For weight and cost calculations; determines PE type
Chemical resistance	Roughly predicts relative life in corrosive environment
Water absorption	Indicates relative take-up but not effect on properties
Dimensional stability	Intended to show effect of heat and load; does not represent use conditions
Reagent immersion	May detect improper extrusion or molding, such as incomplete fusion or residual stress; for quality control
Deflection temperature (heat distortion point)	Rough estimate of maximum service temperature
Flammability	Burning rate or self-extinguishing property under test conditions

Tests listed in Table 13-4 and their requirements for compliance appear in published standards.[2] Their significance is indicated in the Table.

and an integral, monolithic joint results on drying. Solvent cementing of plastic pipe points is based on this behavior, where the surfaces involved are the plain end of a pipe and the socket of a fitting (or the belled-out end of another pipe). The process is also called solvent welding, in analogy to heat welding. Rather than solvent alone, the cement is usually a viscous solution of the pipe plastic, which provides body to fill the annular gap.

In contrast to the sweated copper joint, which it somewhat resembles, the solvent-cemented plastic joint is prepared by applying adhesive to both parts *before* assembling. They will first have been given a moist solvent wipe to remove moisture, dirt, oil and grease. A light, continuous coat is brushed into the socket, and a heavier layer is brushed on the pipe to the engagement length; this requires a natural-bristle paint brush of appropriate size and should take not over 45 seconds. The parts are immediately joined and pushed home, and thrust is maintained while turning one 90° relative to the other to distribute cement. Handling is possible after about 10 minutes; nearly full strength develops in 24 hours.

Points to observe are: cut pipe square and clean; use only materials recommended by pipe supplier; join only clean and dry pipe; do not take more than one minute for the whole operation; wipe excess cement from pipe beyond joint. Keep container covered when not in use; return brush to cement container during use; clean it with solvent when stopping work and shake dry before reusing, or let it dry and clean it with wire brush; do not thin cement unless recommended. Use two men on 4-inch and larger pipe.

Sockets are made to a slight taper; some are designed for as much as 0.040-inch diametral clearance to pipe, i.e., they are oversize, the gap being filled with cement. Others provide interference fit in the bottom section, for initial mechanical grip while cement sets, and take a thinner cement; they may require brief holding to prevent backout after assembling.

While the socket is usually incorporated in a fitting, it may also be integral with the pipe. Such a bell-and-spigot joint, eliminating the fitting, is practical with large-size or thin-wall pipe for long straight runs.

Fusion Joints

PE and a few other pipe plastics do not respond to solvents but do have a well-defined melting temperature; hence, their surfaces may be coalesced by heating above this point, bringing together and cooling. In socket fusion, a tool whose one side enters and fits the socket, and whose other side closely surrounds the pipe end, is heated and thermostatically controlled. An elastic band around the fitting prevents undue expansion. After sufficient heating, as indicated by incipient oozing, the parts are withdrawn from the tool, engaged and turned. Cooling to full strength takes seconds or minutes, depending on size. The heating tool must be cleaned before each use. In butt fusion, a heated plate is similarly used before bringing ends together.

Insert Fittings

The most popular way to join flexible PE pipe is with internal couplings, tees, etc., having several circumferential barbs or serrations to resist pullout. They are metal or molded of various rigid plastics. After lubrication with hot water (no other) and insertion to the shoulder, an all stainless-steel hose-type clamp is tightened around the pipe over the smooth cylindrical shank of the fitting to lock it in and seal the joint. Insert fittings are convenient; they restrict flow, but are widely spaced in most PE piping systems.

Gasket Joint

This more recent application of an older type of mechanical joint to plastic pipe involves an integral bell at a pipe end, a circumferential groove formed in it and a rubber O-ring or other gasket placed in the groove. The spigot end of the adjoining pipe is preferably chamfered to pass the gasket. Thorough application of a soapy lubricant is generally necessary before "making" the joint.

Its main advantage is adaptation to wet outdoor conditions, which handicap cementing or fusing. Some axial and angular displacement can be absorbed by this joint, although the need for this may not be important. Greater care and time are required to prepare it, but it is ready for immediate use. The joint is considered a satisfactory but not ideal substitute for the stronger and probably more reliable integral types.

Screwed Joints

Subject to the limitations mentioned above, plastic pipe may be conventionally threaded. Sharp, clean dies, preferably having 0 to 5° negative rake, are best. Fittings with molded or machined threads are supplied. Only thread tape or shellac-base compound is suitable. Strap wrenches tighten the joint about one-half turn beyond handtight; overtightening should be avoided. Temperature changes, deflections and vibration are enemies of screwed connections, but many installations have been successful, and they are readily taken apart.

PRESSURE PIPE

Thermoplastic pressure pipe today is a highly engineered article, the result of three technical accomplishments: hydrostatic design stresses, standard dimension ratios and approval for potable water. The economic problems of marketing a new structural product that is attractive but not inherently strong or cheap stimulated this outstanding development by American industry.

Hydrostatic Design Stresses (HDS)

Allowable stress in a thermoplastic depends on time under load. To design against structural damage, using the criteria of safety and efficiency, the probability of failure by rupture or by excessive deformation must be known as a function of applied load and the duration of its application at a given temperature. From these relationships, predictions can be made, with due use of statistical safeguards, for direct engineering application to structural design with high confidence.

This knowledge has been gathered for thermoplastic pipe perhaps more thoroughly than for other plastic configurations, certainly more so than for other types of pipe at corresponding points in their existence.

Work begun at Battelle Memorial Institute in the early 1950's and later continued by the industry itself has evolved a rigorous test method[10,28] and resulted in objectively assigning hydrostatic design stress (HDS) ratings to over 50 commercial plastic pipe and fitting materials. The ratings, a series of "preferred numbers" increasing by 25 per cent steps, provided the designer with a 73°F pressure value for any pipe which, if maintained continuously, he can confidently expect not to cause failure for at least 100,000 hours (11.4 years). (Higher temperatures and longer times are under study.)

The designer should note the limitations of the HDS rating. It applies only to static pressure free of surges, shock pressures and other transient effects; these, if present, must be allowed for. Pressure is usually not the only load on a pipe: beam and ring flexure, earth load in a ditch, impact, and thermal expansion and contraction may impose stresses additive to the hydrostatic. The rating is for water at 73°F; other fluids and temperatures may lower it. Finally, while HDS refers to an indefinite period of service, it is an extrapolated value. Plastic pipe has not been around long enough to outlast a building.

Standard Dimensions Ratios (SDR)

As plastic pipe pushed into markets having various pressure requirements, producers made use of a simple physical relationship: the pressure a pipe of given diameter and material can sustain is directly proportional to its wall thickness. If the magnitude of the job justified it, pipe could be custom designed for the pressure involved. Several diameter systems existed as well, so that eventually over 30 sizes of 2-inch pipe became available in one kind of plastic alone. Simplification and standardization were needed.

For this purpose, the industry adopted a new set of numbers, defined as the ratio of mean diameter D_m to wall thickness t. (Mean diameter is the average of outside and inside diameters.) For each size of pipe there is a regularly stepped series of D_m/t ratios; these also are preferred numbers in approximately 25 per cent increments. Iron-pipe-size (IPS) outside diameters and nominal inside diameters were retained.

However, the D_m/t ratios are not used as such (see below). Each must be increased or decreased by one, depending on the kind of pipe involved; the resulting numbers are standard dimension ratios (SDR).

This system not only standardizes dimensions but also pressure rates the pipe. If HDS values increase by 25 per cent increments, and so do the D_m/t ratios from which SDR values are derived, then pressure ratings (PR) will also have such relationships. Thus SDR-PR plastic pipe is rated for the following pressures: 50, 63, 80, 100, 125, 160, 200, 250 and 315 psi, although each PR is not necessarily available in every size of every material (see Table 13-5).

the wall thickness, and rearranging, the equation becomes

$$\frac{D_m}{t} = 2 \times \frac{S}{P}$$

Thus D_m/t, a parameter of pipe dimensions, permits calculation of stress from working pressure or of pressure rating from hydrostatic design stress.

A complication arises in expressing the parameter in terms of measurable dimensions, i.e., outside diameter (OD) or inside diameter (ID) rather than mean diameter. For ABS and PVC pipes, which are joined by external fittings, OD is basic; with PE pipe, using insert fittings, ID is important. To accommodate both, the SDR is defined in two ways:

TABLE 13-5. Pressure Rating of Thermoplastic Pipe as Determined by Standard Dimension Ratio and Hydrostatic Design Stress

D_m/t ratio	8	10	12.5	16	20	25	31.5	40	50	63
SDR: ABS, PVC	—	—	13.5	17	21	26	32.5[a]	41[a]	—	64[a]
SDR: PE	7	9	11.5	15	—	—	—	—	—	—
HDS					*Pressure Ratings*					
500	125	100	80	63	—	—	—	—	—	—
630	160	125	100	80	63	50	—	—	—	—
800	—	—	—	—	—	—	—	—	—	—
1000	—	—	160	125	100	80	63	50	—	—
1250	—	—	200	160	125	100	—	—	—	—
1600	—	—	250	200	160	125	100	80	—	50
2000	—	—	315	250	200	160	125	100	—	63

[a]PVC only.

The Table is constructed from this formula:

$$PR = \frac{2 \times HDS}{D_m/t}$$

Hydrostatic design stresses and pressure ratings are in lb/in.² (psi).

The SDR system is derived as follows. Elementary stress analysis for fluid in a pipe discloses that the component of internal hydrostatic pressure normal to a diametral plane is opposed by tensile stress in the wall across that plane. The equilibrium is

$$P \times D_i = 2 \times S \times t$$

where P is pressure, D_i inside diameter, S stress and t wall thickness. Substituting D_m for D_i, to adjust for stress distribution over

For OD-based pipe, SDR $= D_o/t = (D_m + t)/t = D_m/t + 1 = 2S/P + 1$

For ID-based pipe, SDR $= D_i/t = (D_m - t)/t = D_m/t - 1 = 2S/P - 1$

To illustrate, if a system pressure is 75 psi and the design stress for a certain ABS is 1000 psi,

$$SDR = \frac{2 \times HDS}{P} + 1$$
$$= \frac{2 \times 1000}{75} + 1 = 27.7$$

The designer selects the next lower available SDR, which happens to be 26 and is rated at 80 psi in this material, for all pipe sizes required.

To find the pressure rating of PE 2306 SDR-9 pipe:

$$\text{PR} = \frac{2 \times \text{HDS}}{\text{SDR} + 1} = \frac{2 \times 630}{9 + 1} = 125 \text{ psi}$$

Or, calculating the wall thickness of 2-inch PVC 1120 SDR-26:

$$t = \frac{D_o}{\text{SDR}} = \frac{2.375}{26} = 0.091 \text{ inch}$$

Potable Water Approval (NSF)

The third engineering base of plastic pipe, along with physical dimensions and strength rating, is effect on the medium conveyed. Branching into the sensitive area of public health, commercial plastic pipe as long ago as 1955 was established[30] as nontoxic after exhaustive investigation by the National Sanitation Foundation (NSF) of the University of Michigan's School of Public Health. Continuing self-regulation by the producers, conducted by the Foundation's testing laboratory, assures that pipe bearing the NSF seal of approval for potable water was made from a plastic material established as safe and under conditions acceptable to NSF and that it has been checked by the laboratory for compliance with the relevant Commercial Standard.[25]

While analyzing for toxicity by extraction tests with aggressive water and by animal feeding experiments, NSF also studied[30] the effects of weathering, soil burial and prolonged water submersion on their samples, development of taste and odor in the water, effect on chlorine residuals, and disinfection, as well as susceptibility to rodent attack; favorable conclusions were drawn in each case.

On this firm technical tripod—HDS, SDR, NSF—the manufacturers of thermoplastic pipe have been expanding and revising standards and specifications, soliciting code approvals and seeking new markets.

Nomenclature for pipe materials also underwent codification. Code letters designate chemical family: ABS, PE, PVC. The first two digits give ASTM type and grade: 12XX for Type I Grade 2, for example. The second two are the HDS divided by 100, discarding decimals: XX20 for 2000 psi, XX12 for 1250, XX06 for 630. Thus, PVC 2110 means polyvinyl chloride, ASTM Type II, Grade 1, assigned an HDS of 1000 psi.

Table 13-6 summarizes standardization data on the three groups of thermoplastic pressure pipes.

The relations between HDS, SDR, and PR are presented in Table 13-5. In addition, there is a class T pipe in PVC and ABS, intended for threading, which utilizes a single SDR for each size and is pressure rated at one-half the calculated value to allow for the weakening effect of the threads. While SDR-PR pipe already is standard, IPS sizes will continue to be available for some time in

TABLE 13-6. Thermoplastic Pipe Standardization Data

	ABS	PE	PVC
Commercial standard	CS254–63	CS255–63	CS256–63
ASTM Material Specification	D1788–60T	D1248–60T	D1784–60T
Material designations	1106	2305	1120
	1210	2306	1220
	2112	3206	2110
		3306	4116
Pipe sizes, in.	⅛ to 12	½ to 6	⅛ to 12
SDR numbers[a]	13.5, 17,	7, 9,	13.5, 17, 21,
	21, 26	11.5, 15	26, 32.5, 41,
			64
Class	T[b]	—	T[b]

[a]SDR: standard dimension ratio, approximately but not exactly D/t. (See text.)
[b]For threading.

conventional Schedule 40 (standard) and Schedule 80 (extra heavy) wall thicknesses, as will PE pipe in the various current pressure-rated classes.

Much plastic pressure pipe has been installed to carry potable water for human and animal consumption to rural residences, farm, ranch, recreational and temporary buildings, in the form of main-to-house services, jet and submersible well pump leads, and well-to-house lines; similar installations are for swimming pools and lawn sprinkler systems. PE is the favorite for most of this field because the small sizes used come in coils up to 400 feet long, which can be carried, laid down and connected easily in a short time; it costs less than galvanized iron and is not damaged by freeze-up, although burial below frost line is recommended; and a sharp knife cuts it.

A size larger than 2 inches, pressure above 100 psi or burial below 12 feet calls for consideration of PVC or ABS, which offer better performance at some sacrifice of convenience. For the 10- and 20-foot straight lengths of commerce, a complete variety of numerous fittings is available in both materials. A choice between them for water pipe often is made on price, but there are other factors also. ABS is semiflexible, permitting moderate cold bending, and is nearly as light as PE. Like PE, it is flammable and may be deteriorated by long sun exposure. Type I PVC is 30 to 40 per cent heavier, but more than proportionately stronger. It is brittle in very cold weather, but otherwise weather-proof and unaffected by a wider range of incidental chemicals including petroleum products. Type II PVC is more like ABS except for the flammability of the latter.

In designing these systems,[1] pressure ratings should not be exceeded; surge pressures should be minimized by avoiding quick-closing valves or by keeping flow velocities within 5 ft/sec; hot-water backflow and over-pressures should be prevented by suitable devices; damage by vehicles, tools and equipment must be avoided; and 4 to 24 hours should be allowed before pressure testing for joint cement to set (depending on test pressure and duration). Service connection to a conventional main is accomplished by corporation fittings available through pipe manufacturers, as are the adapters for joining to the distribution pipe terminating just outside the foundation wall. Ditches should be at least 3 feet deep under roadways, with the bottom hand-finished to grade and large stones absent; backfill should be tamped on both sides to a few inches over the pipe. (The American Waterworks Association, however, recommends only experimental installation of plastic water *services* pending adoption of ASTM, ASA or AWWA standards. They also do not recommend installing under a paved surface.)

With these precautions, the benefits to be derived are low first cost and upkeep, reliability and protection of water quality.

The use of thermoplastic pressure pipe for inside-the-house water distribution systems has been delayed by one difficulty: lack of a safe, proven, and economical hot-water pipe. In other countries, notably Japan, this has not stopped widespread installation of PVC pipe for cold-water lines, requiring, however, positive protection against water heater thermostat failure and hot-water backflow. Two kinds of water pipe in one building have not been favorably regarded in the United States, which also has plenty of steel and copper. But accessible cold water plastic pipe is under serious discussion[18] for building code inclusion.

Test installations are several. The NAHB Research Houses at Lansing and Rockville[26] employ polyvinyl dichloride, PVC Type IV, for hot water (Figure 13-1). According to the manufacturer[6] of this material, Schedule 80 pipe and fittings safely handle 125 psi pressure at 185°F. Assuming this rating to be acceptable, although some code authorities test at 200°F, such pipe would not be competitive in most areas. It would, however, offer complete freedom from corrosion, pitting, scaling, clogging and contamination of the water, which have been problems[17] where hot aggressive water flows at high velocities, and good intrinsic insulation against heat loss (which also means less sweating of cold-water pipes). Support spacing must be closer than for metal pipe, and allowance should be made for thermal movement. Otherwise installation is no more difficult than that of copper tubing.

FIG. 13-1. Preassembled plumbing wall for 1960 NAHB Research House, East Lansing, Mich., contains all-vinyl piping for kitchen and bath. (*Courtesy B. F. Goodrich Chemical Co.*)

Polypropylene pipe conveys hot water in the NAHB Knoxville House[31] and both hot and cold water in the ICI (Imperial Chemical Industries) development house at Welwyn, England, being part of a prefabricated bathroom unit in the latter.[19] This newer plastic pipe[15] has not made much commercial progress as yet; in strength, it resembles ABS, but it is lighter than PE and promises fair ability as hot-water piping. ABS Type II has also been mentioned as a potential domestic water pipe. Inside water piping is thus not an area about to be invaded by plastics, whose strength-to-price ratio goes down as temperature goes up. Polymer science or economics may change this in 5 to 10 years.[9]

DRAIN, WASTE AND VENT (DWV) PIPING

Plastic drain, waste and vent systems have started to enter buildings[21] on a self-explanatory basis: lower installed cost. For example, at the Capehart housing project for Key West naval base,[14] shop-fabricated preassemblies carried to the point of installation and connected in by one man helped save $65/home. For a typical residence, one cost estimate showed about $50 saving over copper and $90 over cast iron, chiefly in labor.

Plastic DWV pipes are hydraulically smooth, which aids flow, and are unaffected by household wastes, which assures permanence. They offer bonus properties: low thermal conductivity, which keeps greasy wastes hot, delays solidification in the system, and prevents burns on contact; light weight, which reduces support and structural load problems; immunity to corrosion by acid or sulfate waters and soils and by electrolytic action.

Factors such as poured lead joints, burial under concrete slabs and use of power cleanout equipment are commonplace[1] with plastic DWV (Figure 13-2). It offers no attraction to rodents, termites or roots. Mechanics like working with it.

In accordance with Commercial Standards and proposed ASTM specifications, plastic pipe and fittings for DWV application are required to exhibit specified dimensions and dimensional stability, burst strength, crushing strength and ductility, water and chemical resistance, and marking; raw materials and joint cement must meet requirements, and a joint tightness test must be passed.

Pipe is available in 1¼-, 1½-, 2-, 3- and 4-inch IPS sizes with Schedule 40 wall thicknesses. Standard lengths are 10 and 20 feet; as with all plastic pipe, field cuts are easily made with saw and miter box. All sanitary style fittings are supplied, of full bore, free-draining design and customary pitch and laying length dimensions. Joints are typically solvent cemented: the plain end of a pipe is brush coated with the adhesive and inserted into the similarly coated plain socket of a fitting; on setting, a strong, integral bottle-tight joint results. (At Capehart, only three of the 35,000 joints leaked.)

While PE and PVC have long been in use for chemical drainage in laboratories, hospitals, process plants and the like, the materials now contending for residential DWV acceptance

FIG. 13-2. Pouring a lead joint between plastic DWV and a cast iron fitting. (*Courtesy B. F. Goodrich Chemical Co.*)

are PVC and ABS. As in other material families, each has its advantages, neither is perfect.[8,29] Most of the differences are inconsequential for performance.

Heat Resistance

ABS pipe deflects less than PVC under long exposure to extremely hot water; the material has a higher ASTM deflection temperature. In one test,[29] 3-inch ABS DWV supported on 5-foot centers and filled with boiling water sagged less than an inch during several hours. But this is not a service condition; the upper third of a water heater tank, comprising about 10 gallons of water possibly as hot as 160 to 180°F, even if run out all at once without cooling, passes through

only in a matter of minutes. The more common hot-water temperature of 160°F was no problem at all for PVC in the same test series.

Cold Resistance

PVC pipe may get brittle at low temperatures, creating breakage hazards during handling and installation. ABS is better under such conditions, but the difference is academic except on construction jobs below 40°F.

Thermal Expansion

The wide temperature range of ABS may be offset by its greater expansion, about 0.07 inch per ten feet per 10°F temperature rise, compared to a coefficient of about 0.03 for PVC. Thus, to utilize the superior cold toughness and hot rigidity of ABS, the system must be able to absorb thermal movement.

Mechanical Strength

PVC is stronger in every respect except impact, and more rigid than ABS, even somewhat above room temperature. However, the mechanical demands on a DWV system are not severe and are adequately met by ABS.

Chemical Resistance

PVC is superior, being unaffected even by certain strong reagents that deteriorate ABS, but such chemicals are not found in household wastes. However, the need for long-term inertness may favor PVC. Both materials are more inert than cast iron where any acidic condition exists.

Flammability

ABS, once ignited, burns steadily, about as fast as wood. PVC is self-extinguishing, i.e., combustion stops unless supported by contact with flame, but in a hot fire obnoxious fumes are evolved. In either case, fire fighting is not significantly affected by the relatively small amount of pipe.

Weights

PVC is 30 to 40 per cent heavier than ABS; compared to cast iron, the difference is hardly noticeable.

In the above discussion, PVC means Type I, Grade 1 or 2, as specified by ASTM D1784-60T. Type II PVC matches or exceeds ABS in impact strength, including cold toughness, but its rigidity, heat and chemical resistance fall below Type I. The ABS used is Type I Grade 2 per ASTM D1788-60T. The used for 500 homes each having two baths, a sink and a washer; the total saving was $32,805. The plastic line extended 5 feet beyond the foundation wall and joined clay sewer pipe. Six licensed plumbers did the job, besides installing 500 PVC water services, after a two-day training period.

TABLE 13-7. Piping Cost Comparison For Capehart DWV Job

PVC Actual Cost		CAST IRON Contractor's Estimate	
Pipe, solvent cement	$38,603	Pipe, lead, oakum	$51,510
Fittings	23,535	Fittings	15,160
Total materials	62,138	Total materials	66,670
Labor, 4226 hr at $3.50	14,791	Labor, 12,304 hr at $3.50	43,064
Total	76,929	Total	109,734

choice among these materials will rest on individual considerations, including cost experience.[9]

FIG. 13-3. PVC lines being installed in Hidden Assets Building, part of the House of Good Taste Exhibit, 1964-65 New York World's Fair. (*Courtesy B. F. Goodrich Chemical Co.*)

A report[7] on the Capehart DWV installation gave the data in Table 13-7. In this case, 65,000 feet of pipe and 15,000 fittings were

A published comparison[18] of ABS and competitive materials, based on equivalent DWV layout, shows these typical material and labor costs: cast iron, $205.64; copper, $163.81; ABS, $115.71.

Economically and functionally, plastic DWV seems a natural for the residential building. Standardization is now virtually complete. Drawbacks apparently are confined to those associated with new products: trade and code acceptance, based on proven success. The NAHB homes at Louisville and Rockville, drained in plastic, and such projects as Capehart may provide the proof.

Figure 13-3 shows plastic DWV at the New York World's Fair.

SEWER AND DRAIN PIPE

For building sewers, foundation drains, building storm drains, septic tank discharge lines, etc., plastic sewer and drain pipe up to 6 inches in diameter has been available for several years, in both perforated and "solid" form. Besides the more obvious traits of chemical resistance, ease of handling and joining, and competitive price, one property that has won favor for plastic sewer is freedom from root intrusion, infiltration and exfiltration, due to impermeable walls and bottle-tight joints. Sanitary engineers particularly appreciate this feature in areas plagued by cross-pollution or where sewers are overloaded by groundwater. Another advantage is smooth surface, which enhances flow and resists deposition of solids; and water does not deteriorate it.

While earlier versions of this commodity were not noted for anything very worthwhile except low cost, producers now market tough and durable pipe that, in the long run, may well outperform other kinds. This follows not only the above considerations, but also because high mechanical strength, which plastics generally lack, is not required. Nonpressure plastic pipe, properly installed below ground, depends to a large degree on the soil for structural stability.

Traditional kinds of sewer and drain pipe are thick-walled, heavy and sometimes brittle. They are classed as rigid conduit and support earth load by inherent strength and

FIG. 13-4. No Atlas was needed to transport this plastic plumbing tree to its installation site at Glenview Gardens, Ponce, Puerto Rico (Glenwal Development Corporation, builder). (*Courtesy Celanese Plastics Company*)

stiffness. Structural failure, when it occurs, consists of fracture with negligible deformation. Ground settlement or heaving, and excessive earth load or live loads, can crack such pipe or open its joints; otherwise, of course, it performs well.

Plastic sewer and drain pipe presents such

an apparent contrast as to evoke initial disparagement. Relatively thin walls and low elastic modulus combine to permit a man's weight to put it out of round. The accustomed massiveness is missing; but is it necessary? Flexible conduit theory[27] and fact say no.

The weight of earth above buried pipe bears downward on the upper part of it and the trench bed exerts an equal and opposite reaction on the bottom. Rigid conduit resists the crushing effect by brute strength; plastic pipe cannot. Instead, its vertical diameter shortens. Simultaneously, the sides of the pipe extend horizontally, but this movement encounters resistance from the adjacent soil and is arrested. The deflection that occurs before equilibrium is reached is a function of earth load on the pipe, the soil's modulus of passive resistance and, to a very slight extent, the cross-sectional stiffness of the pipe itself. The principal property requirement for the pipe is ring flexibility—the capacity to deflect transversely through several times the required interval, without distress, repeatedly and permanently. The rest is a function of bedding and backfilling.

A common design value for maximum allowable deflection is 5 per cent. In the usual case, this is readily maintained by emphasizing more carefully the good practices followed with other kinds of pipe. Trench bottoms are brought to grade, free of stones; pipe is laid without blocking and is backfilled with granular material. If the backfill is other than moist sand, it should be tamped on both sides of the pipe; a second tamping of rock-free fill 6 to 12 inches over the pipe may be good insurance. The ditch is then filled as usual. Three feet is minimum earth cover under roadways; greater depths present no special problems.[23]

Thus, the flexibility of plastic pipe underground presents no problem with proper installation and, in fact, contributes to keeping pipe and joints intact in shifting ground. The modern concept of performance without great weight or bulk is applied; flexibility becomes a virtue; shipping, handling and pipe laying are more convenient and economical; breakage is reduced; and a new construction material is advantageously employed without prohibitive thickness.

PVC and SRP dominate this area, with some PE also found. The PVC sewer and drain is available in Type I Grade 1 material, which combines optimum chemical resistance and physical properties; in a high-impact grade; and in a composition also containing other ingredients. SRP is produced to comply with Commercial Standard CS228-61 and, as such, has code approval in a number of localities. These types are joined by solvent cementing, either through integrally formed pipe bells or separate couplings. Where cementing is prevented by wet conditions, O-ring gasket joints are offered by some manufacturers. PE sewer and drain is joined by fusion or flanges.

Regardless of type, ring flexibility should be assured by means of the parallel-plate bearing test, in which pipe is deflected 15 per cent or more and observed for cracks; the test also measures stiffness but not crushing strength, as this depends on soil compaction. Use of the sand bearing test is discouraged as inapplicable. Other tests, of impact strength, chemical resistance and joint tightness, are under development by PPI and ASTM.

Plastic sewer and drain pipe is now sized up to 12 and 16 inches in a special OD series that provides nominal inside diameter for hydraulic calculations and prevents connection with pressure piping. Standard lengths are 10 and 20 feet.

OTHER USES

Slab radiant heating, using PE pipe, has been discussed[22] but not widely installed. PVC rainwater disposal systems are more common abroad, although SRP pipe is offered for downspout runoffs.

An ingenious application is a built-in termite control system[16] in Hawaii. PE pipe sinuates under foundations and floor areas; knife-cut slits discharge chemical as needed. Polyethylene film covering the layout retains vapors and prevents clogging.

Special fittings exploit the corrosion resistance and nonconductive nature of plastics. Molded PVC or nylon clean-out plugs and vacuum breakers are quickly removed because threads do not rust and seize. Water

heater connections, where dissimilar metals may be joined, are isolated by dielectric fittings bushed with nylon.

STANDARDS AND SPECIFICATIONS

ASA—American Standards Association
10 East 40th Street
New York, N. Y. 10016
  B16.27–1962 Plastic Insert Fittings for Flexible Polyethylene Pipe
ASTM—American Society for Testing and Materials
1916 Race Street
Philadelphia 3, Pa.

D1598-63T	Time-to-Failure of Plastic Pipe Under Long-Term Hydrostatic Pressure
D1599-62T	Short-Time Rupture Strength of Plastic Pipe, Tubing, and Fittings
D1939-62T	Quality of Extruded Acrylonitrile-Butadiene-Styrene (ABS) Pipe by Acetic Acid Immersion
D2105-62T	Longitudinal Tensile Properties of Reinforced Thermosetting Plastic Pipe and Tube
D2122-62T	Determining Dimensions of Thermoplastic Pipe
D2143-63T	Cyclic Pressure Strength of Reinforced Thermosetting Plastic Pipe
D2152-63T	Quality of Extruded Poly(Vinyl Chloride) Pipe by Acetone Immersion
D2153-63T	Calculating Stress in Plastic Pipe Under Internal Pressure
D1503-62T	IPS Cellulose Acetate Butyrate Pipe
D1527-58T	Dimensions of Iron Pipe Size (IPS) Extruded Acrylonitrile-Butadiene-Styrene (ABS)
D1528-58T	Dimensions of Solvent Welded (SWP Size) Extruded Acrylonitrile-Butadiene-Styrene (ABS) Plastic Pipe
D1694-59T	Threads for Reinforced Thermosetting Plastic Pipe
D1785-60T	IPS Rigid Poly(Vinyl Chloride) (PVC) Plastic Pipe
D2104-62T	Polyethylene Plastic Pipe
D2235-63T	Solvent Cement for Acrylonitrile-Butadiene-Styrene (ABS) Plastic Pipe and Fittings

USDC—U. S. Department of Commerce
Write to:
Superintendent of Documents
U. S. Government Printing Office
Washington, D. C. 20402

CS197-60	Flexible Polyethylene Plastic Pipe
CS206-57	Solvent Welded (SWP Size) Cellulose-Acetate Butyrate Pipe
CS207-60	Rigid Unplasticized Polyvinyl Chloride Pipe
CS218-59	Rigid ABS Plastic Pipe (IPS Dimensions)
CS228-61	Styrene-Rubber Plastic Drain and Sewer Pipe and Fittings
CS254-63	Acrylonitrile-Butadiene-Styrene (ABS) Plastic Pipe (SDR-PR and Class T)
CS255-63	Polyethylene(PE)Plastic Pipe (SDR-PR)
CS256-63	Polyvinyl Chloride (PVC) Plastic Pipe (SDR-PR and Class T)

CS270-65 Acrylonitrile-Butadiene-Styrene (ABS) Plastic Drain, Waste and Vent Pipe and Fittings
CS272-65 Polyvinyl Chloride (PVC) Plastic Drain, Waste and Vent Pipe and Fittings
GSA (FSS)—Federal Specifications
General Services Administration
Federal Supply Service
Washington, D. C. 20407
L-P-00320 Interim Federal Specification—May 25, 1964. Pipe and Fittings, Plastic (PVC Drain, Waste and Vent)
L-P-00315 Interim Federal Specification—August 16, 1963. Pipe, Plastic (Polyethylene, PE, SDR-PR)
L-P-540 Plastic Tubes and Tubing, Heavy Walled, Polyvinyl Chloride, Rigid
FHA—Architectural Standards Division
Federal Housing Administration
Washington 25, D. C.
WW-P-00380 Pipe, Drain and Sewer, Plastic
Bulletin UM-31b Flexible Polyethylene Plastic Pipe (August 16, 1961)
Bulletin UM-33 ABS Plastic Drainage and Vent Pipe and Drainage Fittings
USDA—U. S. Department of Agriculture
Soil Conservation Service
Washington, D. C. 20250
Engineering Irrigation Pipelines (Low Head Underground Plastic Irrigation Pipelines)
Memorandum
SCS-46 (September 1963)
MILITARY SPECIFICATIONS—Department of Defense
Washington 25, D. C.
MIL-P-19119A(1) Pipe, Plastic, Rigid, Unplasticized, High Impact, Polyvinyl Chloride
MIL-P-22011 Pipe Fittings, Plastic Rigid, Unplasticized, High Impact, Polyvinyl Chloride
MIL-P-22245A (Docks) Pipe and Fittings, Glass Fiber Reinforced Plastic.
MIL-P-22296 Plastic Tubes and Tubing, Polytetrafluoroethylene, (TFE-Fluorocarbon Resin), Heavy Walled
MIL-P-22634(1) Pipe and Pipe Fittings, Polyethylene for Low Pressure Waste and Drainage Systems
MIL-P-26692 Plastic Tubes and Tubing, Polyethylene
MIL-P-14529(1) Pipe, Extruded Thermoplastic
WPOA—Western Plumbing Officials Association
520 Mission Street
P. O. Box 247
South Pasadena, Calif. 91031
WPOA TSC 6-61 Plastic Drain and Vent Pipe—Drainage Fittings for Trailer Coach Drainage and Vent Systems ABS-Type 1 and 1A
WPOA PS17-65 (January 12, 1965) Materials and Property Standards for Acrylonitrile-Butadiene-Styrene (ABS) Plastic Drain, Waste and Vent Pipe and Fittings.
WPOA IS 5-65 Installation Standard for ABS Drain, Waste and Vent Pipe and Fittings (January 12, 1965)

MODEL PLUMBING CODE

Suggestions for Inclusion of Plastic Pipe and Fittings in Governmental, State, Municipal and other Regulatory Body Plumbing Codes. A voluntary model plumbing code of the plastic pipe and fittings industry published by the Plastics Pipe Institute, a division of the Society of the Plastics Industry, Inc., 250 Park Avenue, New York, New York.

OUTLINE OF CONTENTS

1.0 Standards for Plastic Plumbing Materials. Any plastic material which meets one or more of the following organizational standards and is cited therein shall be considered acceptable for plumbing; also the local administrative authority may accept materials on the basis of other tests, or their own tests pending the development of standards by organizations listed below:

1.1 Abbreviations: Refer to the following organizations:

ASA   American Standards Association
          10 East 40th Street, New York 17, New York

ASTM   American Society for Testing Materials
          1916 Race Street, Phila. 3, Pa.

AWWA   American Water Works Association
          2 Park Avenue, New York, New York

CS   Commercial Standards

TS   Comm. Stds. Div., Office of Ind. and Comm., U. S. Dept. of Comm., Wash. 25, D. C.

FS   Federal Supply Service, Standards Div. General Services Adm., Wash. 25, D.C.

NSF   National Sanitation Foundation Testing Laboratories, Inc. School of Public Health, Univ. of Mich. Ann Arbor, Michigan

1.2 Existing Applicable Standards

Plastic Pipe and Fittings (Water Supply)

NSF   National Sanitation Foundation

CS254-63   Acrylonitrile-Butadiene-Styrene(ABS) Plastic Pipe (SDR-PR Class T)

CS255-63   Polyethylene (PE) Plastic Pipe (SDR-PR)

CS256-63   Polyvinyl Chloride (PVC) Plastic Pipe (SDR-PR Class T)

CS197-60   Flexible Polyethylene Plastic Pipe

CS207-60   Rigid Unplasticized Polyvinyl Chloride Plastic Pipe

CS218-59   Rigid ABS Plastic Pipe (IPS) Dimensions

CS220-59   Dim. and Tolerances for Lightweight Rigid ABS Plastic Pipe

CS237-61   Dim. and Tol. Sched. A Type I and Schedule A Type II, Rigid Polyvinyl Chloride Pipe (Lightweight PVC Pipe)

FHA UM-31   Flexible Polyethylene Plastic Pipe

ASTM D1785-60T   IPS Rigid Poly (Vinyl Chloride) (PVC) Plastic Pipe

Plastic Pipe and Fittings (Drain, Waste and Vent)

TS5607   Acrylonitrile-Butadiene-Styrene (ABS) Plastic Drain, Waste and Vent Pipe and Fittings

TS5608   Polyvinyl Chloride (PVC) Plastic Drain, Waste and Vent Pipe and Fittings

FHA UM-33   ABS Plastic Drainage and Vent Pipe and Drainage Fittings

WPOA-TCS-61   Trailer Coach Standard

WW-P-00380   (GSA-FSS) Int. Fed. Spec. Pipe, Drain and Sewer, Plastic

Plastic Pipe and Fittings (Sewer and Drain)

CS228-61   Styrene Rubber Plastic Sewer and Drain Pipe and Fittings

FHA UM-26   Plastic Drain and Sewer Pipe and Fittings

American Society for Testing Materials (ASTM) specifications are as follows:

D1503-57T   Solvent Welded (SWP Size) Cellulose Acetate-Butyrate Pipe

D1527-58T	Iron Pipe Size (IPS) Extruded Acrylonitrile Butadiene-Styrene (ABS) Plastic Pipe, Dimensions of
D1528-58T	Solvent Welded (SWP Size) Extruded, Acrylonitrile-Butadiene-Styrene (ABS) Plastic Pipe, Dimensions of
D1598-58T	Time-To-Failure of Plastic Pipe Under Long-Term Hydrostatic Pressure
D1599-58T	Short-Time Rupture Strength of Thermoplastic Pipe, Tubing, and Fittings
D1785-60T	IPS Rigid Poly (Vinyl Chloride) (PVC) Plastic Pipe

The Federal Specifications and Military Specifications for plastic pipe and fittings include:

L-P-540	— Plastic Tubes and Tubing, Heavy Walled, Polyvinyl Chloride, Rigid, (21 Jan. 59)
Interim Federal	Specification WW-P-00380 (GSA-FSS) Plastic Drain and Sewer Pipe and Fittings
MIL-P-22011	Pipe Fittings, Plastic, Rigid, Unplasticized, High Impact, Polyvinyl Chloride, (29 May 59)
MIL-P-14529	(1) Pipe, Extruded, Thermoplastic, (5 May 58)
MIL-P-19119A	(1) Pipe, Plastic, Rigid, Unplasticized, High Impact, Polyvinyl Chloride, (21 Feb. 58)
MIL-P-26692	Tubes and Tubings, Polyethylene, (12 Mar. 59)
MIL-P-22624	Pipe and Fittings, Polyethylene, For Low Pressure Wast and Drainage Systems (Sept. 9, 1960)

2.0 Plastic Pipe and Fittings for Portable Water Service

2.1 ABS, PVC and PE Pipe and Fittings. Acrylonitrile-Butadiene-Styrene (ABS) pipe and fittings; Polethylene (PE) pipe and fittings; and Polyvinyl chloride (PVC) pipe and fittings which meet Commercial Standards established by the United States Department of Commerce may be used in potable cold water services for such applications as well-to-building; well drop pipe; main-to-building service lines; lawn sprinkler systems and cold water lines inside the building.

2.2 Commercial Standards. Plastic pipe mentioned in Section 2.1 shall comply with the following applicable Commercial Standards: ABS-CS218-59; ABS-CS219-59; ABS-CS220-59; Polyethylene-CS197-60; PVC-CS207-60; PVC-CS237-61 and Federal Housing Administration Use of Materials Bulletin No. UM-31, dated March 1, 1961, or revisions thereto.

2.3 Marking. All plastic pipe and fittings used for potable water systems shall bear the Seal of Approval of the National Sanitation Foundation Testing Laboratory, Inc., School of Public Health, University of Michigan, Ann Arbor, Michigan, or other approved testing laboratories acceptable to public health officials. When the NSF or other certification is used, this is indicated by the symbol "nSf" or other symbols at not more than 2 foot intervals on the pipe and at least one "nSf" or other symbol on each fitting.

2.4 Fittings

2.4.1 Markings. Fittings shall be marked with the manufacturer's name or trademark, material designation and size. In addition to this, fittings used for conveying potable water shall be marked with the seal of approval of a qualifying tested laboratory such as the nSf seal of the National Sanitation Foundation, Inc., or other testing laboratory acceptable to public health officials. Material identification symbols shall be as follows: PVC-Polyvinyl Chloride; PS-Hi Impact Styrene; ABS-Acrylonitrile-Butadiene-Styrene; N-Nylon; PE-Polyethylene; PP-Polypropylene. Markings or symbols may be molded, hot stamped or applied to fittings by any other suitable method such as printing. Where recessed marking is used care must be taken so that marking, in no case, causes cracks or reduces the wall thickness of fittings below the minimum specified. Where the size of fitting does not permit complete marking identification, marking may be omitted in the following sequence: Size, Material Designation, Manufacturers Name or Trademark.

2.4.2 Joints

2.4.2.1 ABS and PVC pipe may be joined by either threaded or solvent weld type fittings. No threaded joint shall be made from Schedule 40 or thinner wall pipe.

2.4.2.2 Polyethylene. Polyethylene pipe may be joined either by fusion welding or by serrated plastic insert type fittings made tight by means of a clamping band and tightening screw, each made of stainless steel.

2.4.3 Polyethylene Fitting Standards. Polyethylene fittings shall conform to the tentative standard of ASA Committee B-16 on plastic insert fittings for Flexible Polyethylene Pipe.

2.4.4 ABS. ABS fittings shall conform to the tentative standard of ASA Committee B-16 on plastic fittings for ABS pipe.

2.4.5 PVC. PVC fittings shall conform to the tentative standard of ASA Committee B-16 on plastic fittings for PVC pipe.

2.5 Polyethylene Installation and Handling Precautions

2.5.1 Storage, Handling & Use of Potable Water Pipe. Some of the common materials used around building construction and warehouses which will contaminate polyethylene are: Gasoline, Lubricating oils, Liquid or Gaseous Fuels, Aromatic Compounds, Paint Solvent, Paint Thinners, Paints, and Acid Solder. Any pipe which has been in contact with such materials is no longer suitable for use as potable water pipe and must be rejected.

2.5.2 Installation. Polyethylene pipe must be cut by a knife or hand saw. The edges of the cut end are smoothed with a knife or rough file.

2.5.3 Expansion and Contraction. Polyethylene has a linear coefficient of expansion 8.3×10^{-5} inch per degree Fahrenheit. For each 10°F change in temperature an allowance for contraction and expansion of 1 inch per 100 feet of pipe shall be allowed. In trench work, this may be accomplished by snaking the pipe in the bottom of the ditch to take up the slack allowed. The snaking should be uniform throughout the length of the ditch.

2.5.4 Lubricants for Polyethylene. Only water should be used to lubricate the pipe and fittings which are to be joined. The use of pipe dope, oil, detergents, or other chemicals is prohibited.

2.5.5 Junction with Other Materials. For attaching plastic lines to metallic systems, it is recommended that an insert adapter be used. This is attached to the plastic pipe in the same manner as other plastic insert fittings. Threaded end only of adapter is coated with a plastic joint compound and tightened into female connections. Do not use joint compound on the plastic pipe itself.

2.5.6 Maximum Depth of PE Pipe Below Grade

Pressure Rating	Depth
75 psi pipe	7.7 feet
100 psi pipe	12.7 feet

2.5.7 Excavations and Backfilling of PE Pipe

2.5.7.1 Excavations. The trench shall be excavated to a smooth bottom, free of projecting rocks or other hard materials, and shall be wide enough to allow a moderate amount of snaking of the pipe in the trench to provide for expansion and contraction with ground and water temperature cycling. The backfill should consist of lump-and-rock free material to a depth of 6 inches over the pipe at which time power equipment can be employed to complete the backfill.

2.5.8 Installation Techniques for Serrated Insert Fittings. Joint compound shall not be employed on serrated insert fitting except where the threaded end of such fitting engage metallic pipes. At such points, a non hardening joint sealer should be employed. The clamps should be slipped over the pipe before the insert fitting is attached and the clamp tightened firmly over the cylindrical part of the fitting between the shoulder and the molded serrations.

2.5.9 Lawn Sprinkling and Irrigation Systems

2.5.9.1 Back-Flow Prevention. Each lawn sprinkling system shall be equipped with one or more properly installed and acceptable back-flow preventers or anti-siphon devices.

2.6 Polyethylene Well Piping

2.6.1 Well Installations. Polyethylene piping may be used for jet and submersible well or other well systems provided the following conditions are followed:

Maximum Settings For Well Installations At 73° Farenheit

For other maximum settings at temperatures other than 73°F consult plastic pipe manufacturers literature.

Pressure Rating of Pipe, PSI	Depth at Pump 40 PSI	50 PSI	Shut-off Pressure 60 PSI
75	77 ft.	55 ft.	
100	132 ft.	110 ft.	88 ft.
125	187 ft.	165 ft.	143 ft.
150	242 ft.	220 ft.	198 ft.

It is recommended that polyethylene plastic pipe be used down to depths as indicated in the table above in 2.6.1 for the approximate cutoff pressure of the system. It is recommended when polyethylene pipe is used in submersible well systems that the pump be supported by a cable. It shall not be used for deep well turbine pump installations.

2.6.2 Bending Radii Permissible

Pipe Size	Minimum Radius	Pipe Size	Minimum Radius
½"	7½"	1¼"	12"
¾"	10"	1½°	16"
1"	10"	2"	20"

3.0 ABS Pipe (Acrylonitrile-Butadiene-Styrene)

3.1 Installation. ABS pipe shall be installed in accordance with the following procedures and in accordance with table above in section 2.6.1 for Maximum Settings For Well Installations. For additional details refer to "Tentative Installation Manual for ABS Pipe and Fittings" published by The Society Of The Plastics Industry, Inc., 250 Park Avenue, New York 17, New York, dated September 1, 1961.

3.1.1 The trenching, laying and backfilling procedures presented in Sections 2.5.7 and 2.5.7.1 shall be followed in the use of ABS pipe installed underground.

4.0 PVC Pipe (Polyvinyl Chloride)

4.1 PVC Installation Procedures. PVC pipe shall be installed in accordance with the following procedures and in accordance with table above in section 2.6.1 for Maximum Settings For Well Installations. For additional details refer to "Tentative Installation Manual For PVC Pipe and Fittings" published by The Society Of The Plastics Industry, Inc., 250 Park Avenue, New York 17, New York, dated May 12, 1961.

5.0 Plastic Sewer and Drain Pipe and Fittings

5.1 Plastic Sewer and Drain Pipe and Fittings are suitable for non-pressure drainage of sewage and drain water where resistance to deterioration from water and chemicals, dimensional stability, resistance to aging, and strong tight joints are required. Sewage is defined as the water carrying human or organic wastes together with such underground, surface, storm, or other water, as may be present.

5.1.1 Building Sewers and Underground Drains in dwellings of four families or less. The building sewer and drain pipe is the lowest part of the piping of a drainage system which conveys its contents to a public sewer, private sewer, individual sewage-disposal system or other points of disposal.

5.1.2 Storm Drainage. The Storm drain is that part of the disposal system used for conveying rain water, surface water, ground water, sub-surface water, condensate, or similar discharge to a building storm sewer or a combined building sewer.

5.1.3 Leaching System for Septic Tank Effluents. This pipe is that part of the system which would receive the liquid discharge from a septic tank for further treatment under the surface of the ground through a system of perforated pipe laid in gravel or crushed stone.

5.1.4 Footing Drains. This pipe composes that portion of the drainage system which is used to surround the outer walls of a building for subsoil drainage. This pipe should be perforated. Drainage should then be conveyed through unperforated pipe to a sump pump, storm sewer, or other point of disposal.

5.1.5 Sanitary Sewer and Storm sewer. A sanitary sewer is a pipe which carries sewage and is intended to exclude storm, surface, and ground water. A storm sewer is a pipe used for conveying rain water, surface water, ground water, subsurface water, condensate, cooling water, or other similar discharge. In some cases a sanitary sewer and storm sewer may be combined although this practice is generally unacceptable.

5.2 Governing Specifications

5.2.1 Commercial Standard CS228-61. Styrene Rubber Plastic Drain and Sewer Pipe and Fittings. This Commercial Standard covers requirements and methods of test for materials, dimensions, workmanship, chemical resistance, crushing strength, water resistance, dimensional stability, and joint tightness of styrene-rubber plastic pipe and fittings. A form of marking to indicate compliance with this standard is also included. Refer to Section 5.6 and 2.4.1.

5.2.2 Interim Federal Specification for Plastic Sewer and Drain Pipe Made of Styrene or Styrene-Rubber. WW-P-00380 (GSA-FFS) dated September 23, 1960 plus Amendment-1. This Federal specification covers plastic pipe and fittings which are resistant to the action of organic matter, alkalies and acids normally existing in soils and in drainage systems. The pipe is intended for use in drains and sewer systems. Refer to Section 5.6 and 2.4.1.

5.3 Pipe Sizes — Plastic sewer and drain pipe to be manufactured in 8 nominal sizes 2-inch through 12-inch.

5.3.1 Building Sewer. Shall be a minimum of 4-inch diameter, but not less than minimum size required for the installation served.

5.3.2 Foundation Drains, Footing Drains, and Building Storm Drains shall be a minimum of 3-inch diameter but not less that the minimum for the installation serveed.

5.3.3 Septic Tank Absorption Fields. Shall be a minimum of 4-inch perforated pipe.

5.4 Pipe Joining — Method of Connection

5.4.1 Plastic to Plastic. Connections for solid pipe shall be made by solvent welding. This does not exclude other types of connection. The socket and the pipe or fitting which fits in the socket shall be free of dirt, grease, or foreign matter. A solvent cement shall be applied, with a natural bristle brush inside the socket and to the pipe for a length equal to the socket depth. The socket and pipe shall immediately be forced together with a slight twisting motion if possible to insure full engagement of pipe end into the socket. Reasonable handling is permissible within one to two minutes after joining.

5.4.1.1 Perforated Drain Pipe. Connections may be left dry if so desired.

5.4.2 Plastic pipe connections to pipe made of other materials shall be sealed by solvent cement, cement mortar, or other methods recommended by the manufacturer, provided the joint tightness test as described in CS228-61 can be met.

5.5 Testing. The building sewer shall be tested by insertion of a test plug at the point of connection with the public sewer. It shall then be filled with water under a head of not less than 10 feet. The water level at the top of the test head of water shall not drop for at least 15 minutes.

5.6 Marking of Pipe. Pipe shall be marked at intervals not greater than 24″ with the manufacturer's name or trade mark, pipe size, and symbol of applicable standard.

5.7 Installation — Trenching and Backfill

5.7.1 Trench Depth for building sewers connecting to sewer mains shall be sufficient to provide a minimum cover depth of 30″ under driveways and streets. No minimum cover depth is prescribed for building storm sewers, subsoil drains, or pipe used in septic tank installations because of out-fall location and elevation.

5.7.2 Trench Width shall be sufficient to provide at least 4″ of clearance on both sides of the pipe.

5.7.3 A Firm Smooth Foundation shall be provided for the pipe. Ditch shall be excavated to a depth to provide at least 2 inches of thoroughly compacted sand or earth free of rocks or debris under the pipe, except where existing soil is adequately clean and sound.

5.7.4 Grade. To be established in accordance with good sound engineering practice for a given flow and size of pipe. Local practice suffices.

5.7.5 Backfill. Pipe shall be firmly bedded and back-filled with selected backfill material free of rocks, boulders, and foreign matter over 1 inch in diameter, to at least 3 inches above the pipe. Backfill is tamped in thin layers not exceeding 4 inches in depth and thoroughly compacted to provide solid support between the sides of the pipe and the sides of the ditch. Remainder of ditch may be mechanically filled if desired and should be compacted by puddling, flooding, flooding, or tamping. Stones larger than 8 inches at their greatest dimension shall not be used in the backfill.

6.0 Plastic Drain, Soil, Waste and Vent Pipe for Interior Drainage Plumbing

6.1 Visibility of Marking. Pipe and fittings shall be so positioned that identifying marking shall be readily visible for inspection.

6.2 Joints in Plastic Drain & Vent Pipes. All pipe cuts shall be square and smooth. All burrs shall be removed. All joining surfaces shall be clean of all foreign matter. No pipe shall be bent. Pipe shall be joined by approved fittings, and when joined shall be in alignment with proper slope or plumb, if vertical.

6.2.1 Socket Joints. Solvent cement shall be lightly applied to the socket and more heavily to the male end of the pipe. The male end shall be inserted to the full depth of the socket. The excess solvent-cement shall be immediately wiped off. Under no circumstances attempt to adjust a socket fitting after the solvent-cement has set. Depending on cement, temperature, and humidity, the time of initial setting ranges from 30 seconds to 2 minutes.

6.2.2 Threaded Joints. Schedule 40 pipe shall not be threaded. If a transition from Schedule 40 to threaded Schedule 80 or 120 pipe, or to metal pipe is necessary, a socket to threaded adapter fitting or a flange shall be used.

6.2.2.1 Tightening. Threaded plastic joints shall be tightened by means of a strap wrench not to exceed one full turn beyond hand tight.

6.2.2.2 Only thread lubricants which have the approval of the manufacturer of the pipe or fittings are to be used.

6.3 Pitch Loading and Sizing. It is recommended that plastic drain and vent piping be sized and sloped in accordance with the tables covering pipe with smooth interiors such as DWV cooper — lead, etc., except that no building sewer shall be less than 4″ ID.

6.3.1 Storm Drains. Underground storm drains shall be a minimum of 3″ ID.

6.4 Plastic Traps. Acceptable plastic traps shall have their down-stream connection made by means of proper adaptor fittings, minimum size 1Wy.

6.5 Joints. Between plastic pipe and other types of pipe with poured, precast, or lead caulked joints, or with threaded or flanged joints, an acceptable adaptor or fitting shall be used.

7.0 Supports for Plastic Pipe. Plastic pipe up to one inch in diameter shall be supported at intervals of 4 feet. Larger sizes shall be supported at intervals of not more than six feet, except in dwellings in which the distance from floor to ceiling does not exceed 8 feet. Supports at each floor will be acceptable for vertical piping. Continuous trough supports may be used for horizontal pipe installation.

7.1 Hangers and Clamps. Only metal or other acceptable hangers shall be used. The inner face of the support shall not scrape or deface the pipe in normal expansion and contraction, or flatten or crimp the pipe.

8.0 General Regulations.

8.1 Definitions: For definition of building sewers, storm sewers, storm drains, main drains, branches, risers, traps, vents, rough plumbing, stacks, fixture supply, water service, backfilling, trench work, etc. refer to such modern plumbing codes as ASA A 40-8 as amended June 1, 1961, The Uniform Code of the Western Plumbing Officials 1961 issue, The Illinois State Plumbing Code, or the Plumbing Code of the City of Detroit, City of Chicago or the New York State Code.

8.2 Cold Water Piping for Building Distribution

8.2.1 Normal Temperatures. Caution must be exercised to make certain that boiling water or water near boiling cannot back into cold water plastic pipe lines.

8.2.2 Heating Supplies. If plastic pipe is used to distribute cold water in the building, the plastic supply branch or branches leading to either a domestic hot water heating unit or to a space heating boiler, shall terminate not less than 3 feet from the supply opening of the heating equipment. In distribution systems including a space heating boiler an expansion tank of 2 gallon capacity or two percent of the volume of the hot water system, whichever may be greater, shall be installed on the hot water system to prevent pressure buildups which would cause the pressure relief valve to discharge pripr to hazard.

8.3 Firestopping, Sleeving, Sealing and other general requirements. See the codes referred to in Section 8.1, as well as the recommended Building Code of the Building Officials Conference of America, or The National Board of Fire Underwriters.

8.4 Septic Tank Piping. The installation of piping to and from septic tanks shall conform to ASA A40.8 as amended June 1, 1961, or The Septic Tank Manual of the U. S. Public Health Service.

REFERENCES

1. ABS Plastic Pipe Manual, Marbon Chemical Division, Borg-Warner Corporation, Washington, West Virginia, 1962. Book I, General Information; Book II, Water Supply and Distribution Systems; Book IV, Residential Drain, Waste and Vent Systems.
2. ASTM Parts 26 and 27, June 1965, Standards, American Society for Testing and Materials, Philadelphia, Pa.
3. Bernhardt, E. C., Editor, "Processing of Thermoplastic Materials," New York, Reinhold Publishing Corp., 1959.
4. Committee D-20 on Plastics, Report for 1962, American Society for Testing and Materials, Philadelphia, 1963.
5. Faust, R. J., (Executive Secretary, American Waterworks Association), letter to Joseph Broslaw (Market Research Director, Plastics Pipe Institute), March 14, 1963.
6. *Geon Hi-Temp Newsletter No. 1*, B. F. Goodrich Chemical Company (1963).
7. *Goodchemco News*, B. F. Goodrich Chemical Company (Autumn 1962).
8. Holtz, R. T. (B. F. Goodrich Chemical Company), private communication.
9. "Keeping Up With Plastics," *Plumbing-Heating-Cooling Business*, **25,** 55–10 (June 1963).
10. Killeen, N. D., and Schaul, J. S., "Method of Determining Hydrostatic Design Stress for PVC Pressure Pipe," *Interpace Technical Journal* (International Pipe & Ceramics Corp., Parsippany, New Jersey), **1,** No. 1, 17 (1964).
11. Market Research Release, Plastics Pipe Institute, Society of the Plastics Industry, January 1964.
12. Model Plumbing Code 163–10; Suggestions for Inclusion of Plastic Pipe and Fittings in Governmental, State, Municipal and Other Regulatory Body Plumbing Codes, Plastics Pipe Institute, Society of the Plastics Industry, New York, 1963.
13. "Modern Plastics Encyclopediá and Engineering Manual," New York, Breskin Publications, 1963.
14. "New Building Products of Geon Vinyls," IV, No. 1, B. F. Goodrich Chemical Company.
15. "New Line on Pipe List," *Chemical Week*, p. 37 (August 24, 1964).
16. "New Permanent System for Termite Control with Plastic Pipe," *Hawaii Plastics Bulletin*, **2,** No. 3 (March 1963) (Honolulu).
17. Obrecht, M. F., and Quill, L. L., *Heating, Piping Air Conditioning*, **32,** 165 (January 1960); 109 (March 1060); 131 (April 1960); 105 (May 1960).
18. "Plastic Pipe: Is It Ready to Go inside the House?" *Plumbing-Heating-Cooling Business* (March 1963).
19. "Plastics in Building," *Brit. Plastics*, **36,** 622 (November 1963).
20. "Plastics Pipe: A New Plateau," *Mod. Plastics* (August and September 1962).
21. "Plastics Piping for the Home," *Plastics World* **21,** 54 (June 1963).
22. Platts, R. E., "Where Polyethylene Pipe Challenges Metal for Slab Radiant Heating," *Can. Builder*, **13,** 55 (1963).
23. Tentative Recommended Practice for Underground Installation of Thermoplastic Sewer Pipe, ASTM D2321-64T. ASTM Standards, Part 26, June 1965, American Society for Testing and Materials.
24. Reinhart, F. W., *SPE J.*, **17,** 159 (1961).
25. 1964 Seal of Approval Listing of Plastic Materials, Pipe, Fittings, and Appurtenances for Potable Water Supplies, National Sanitation Foundation Testing Laboratory, Inc., Ann Arbor, Michigan, March 1964.
26. "Showcase for Plastics in Building," *Mod. Plastics*, **40,** No. 10, 86 (1963).
27. Spangler, M. G., "Soil Engineering," Scranton, Pa., International Textbook Company, 1951.
28. "Tentative Method for Estimating Long Term Hydrostatic Design Stress of Thermoplastic Pipe," Plastics Pipe Institute, Society of the Plastics Industry, New York, 1963.
29. Thompson, E. R. (Marbon Chemical Division, Borg-Warner Corporation), private communication.
30. Tiedemann, W. H., and Milone, N. A., "A Study of Plastic Pipe for Potable Water Supplies," National Sanitation Foundation, Ann Arbor, Michigan, June 1955.
31. *Time*, 89 (October 27, 1958).

14 | UTILITIES

J. A. Baumann and R. C. Hess

Union Carbide Corporation
Plastics Division
Bound Brook, New Jersey

PART A: *Electrical Fixtures**

Plastics as a class are inherently electrical insulating materials, or dielectrics. Since they also possess many other attributes, such as ease of fabrication and a wide choice of physical properties, plastics have come to play an important role in the insulation of electrical equipment. Electrical properties alone are generally not sufficient to determine the suitability of a plastic material for a particular application. Due consideration must be given to mechanical, chemical, thermal, water absorption, aging, and weathering properties and other characteristics as well. Two types of plastics, because of their combination of mechanical, electrical, processing and economic properties, practically monopolize the electrical insulation field in building—*polyvinyl chloride* and its copolymers for wire and cable insulation, and molded *phenolics* for sockets, receptacles, and other wiring devices, and more recently outlet, switch, and conduit boxes and covers.

Wire and Cable Insulation

Time and again vinyl compounds have proved themselves to be reliable, economical and versatile insulating and jacketing materials, rendering outstanding long-term service in a host of general-purpose as well as highly specialized wire and cable constructions. In addition to building wire they are used in such applications as appliance, machine, radio, instrument, and hookup wire; flexible cords; radar communications; telephone equipment; and police and fire alarm systems. The vinyl thermoplastic insulations are fully accepted by the National Electrical Code[4] and accredited by the Underwriters Laboratories and various government specifications; significant tests and specifications have been promulgated by the American Society for Testing and Materials.

The vinyl materials are characterized by high electrical resistivity, good dielectric strength and excellent mechanical toughness over a wide range of operating temperatures. They possess superior resistance to oxygen, ozone, and most corrosive acids, alkalies, and other chemicals. This insulation is lightweight and flame resistant, and its electrical and mechanical properties are relatively unaffected by moisture.

The vinyl compounds are extruded easily onto wire at high rates; they have smooth glossy surfaces, which contribute to ease of stripping, splicing, and pulling through conduits. This extrusion behavior, coupled with their excellent properties and low cost, makes them so highly competitive with older type constructions that the major portion of

*This part by J. A. Baumann

building wire installed today is insulated with PVC compounds.

In 1963 it was estimated that 60,000,000 pounds of PVC and 25,000,000 pounds of styrene butadiene rubber (SBR) were used for building wire alone.[1] The total market for PVC-type insulations was about three times as great; about equal to the insulation market for polyolefins which are generally used in higher-voltage power transmission applications. The reported use of vinyl resins in all types of wire and cable insulation for the years 1959, 1960 and 1962–1965 is shown in Table 14A-1.

TABLE 14A-1. Estimated Use of Vinyl Resins in Wire and Cable Insulation

	million lb
1959[2]	105
1960[2]	90
1962[3]	170
1963[3]	184
1964[15]	220
1965[15]	250

In 1962 the catalog of a major mail-order distributor of consumer goods listed only "thermoplastic" insulated electrical building wire. This included steel armored cable, single wire conductor, and nonmetallic cable. Its best 2-wire grounded cable sold for 5.2¢/ft in 250-foot lengths and was advertised for "use anywhere even outdoors underground."

No. 14 single wire conductor sold for less than 1¢/ft. Outdoor wire for use from pole to house or building to building overhead was neoprene covered. Much wire for this application now uses vulcanizable polyethylene insulation.

The Underwriters Laboratories (UL) have a number of designations for insulated wire, some of the more important of which are listed in Table 14-A2.

The American Society for Testing and Materials in its "standard specifications for non-rigid vinyl chloride polymer and copolymer molding and extrusion compounds" (D-1432) list 22 resin compounds of which six are designated "Type II—electrical insulation general-purpose compounds." Specifications for these compounds are listed in Table 14A-3, which also shows additional properties of four typical vinyl insulation compounds and the Underwriters Laboratories designations for which they are suited. The important ASTM specifications and methods pertaining to these plastic wire and cable insulations are:

D-470-59T Methods of test for rubber and thermoplastic insulated wire and cable

D-734 Standard specifications for insulated wire and cable: vinyl chloride plastic insulating compound

TABLE 14A-2.

UL Designation	Description	Uses
T and TW	General-purpose and moisture-resistant building wire, 60°C	Building wire, raceway conduit, switchboard, machine tool, and control circuit use
THW	Moisture-resistant, heat-resistant building wire, 75°C	Same
NMC and UF	Nonmetallic sheath cable (corrosion resistant) and underground feeder	All thermoplastic construction suitable for direct burial
NM	Nonmetallic sheath cable	
ACT	Armored cable	Thermoplastic insulated armored building cable
SPT 1, 2, 3	Parallel cord, 60°C	Lamp cords
SPT 1, 2, 3	Parallel cord, 75°C	Appliances
SVT (60°C)	Flexible cord—light duty	Vacuum cleaners, mixers, etc.
ST	Flexible cord—heavy duty	Portable tools, motors, portable power supply
SRT	Electric range cables	
TF	Fixture wire	Wire electrical fixtures, solid and stranded
TFF	Flexible fixture wire	Flexible stranding
TA	Switchboard wire	

TABLE 14A-3. Typical Properties of Vinyl Wire and Cable Insulating Compounds for Building Wire

Properties	Test No.	Typical Vinyl Building Wire Compounds:				Specifications for ASTM Grade No. (D-1432):					
		QFD-9031	QFD-9033	QFD-9252	QFD-9530	17	18	19	20	21	22
Maximum cont. operating temperature, °C	UL std	60	80	75	60	60	60	80	90	105	Low temp.
Specific gravity at 25°C	D-792	1.42	1.36	1.37	1.37	max 1.35	1.45	1.45	1.40	1.40	1.40
Dielectric strength, volts/mil at 1/32 in.	D-149	790	740	760	700						
Dissipation factor at 1 kc (dry)	D-150	.092	.079	.091	.095						
Dielectric constant at 1 kc (dry)	D-150	5.51	5.16	5.60	6.00						
Volume resistivity, megohm—cm at 50°C	D-257	8×10^6	3.5×10^6	3.0×10^6	8.0×10^6	1×10^7	5×10^6	3×10^6	2×10^6	1×10^6	5×10^5
Insulation resistance constant(K)	D-470	3600	3600	2150	2000						
Tensile strength, psi	D-412	2500	2500	2650	2400	min 2200	2000	2200	2200	2000	2000
Elongation, %	D-412	290	300	260	315	min 300	250	275	275	275	300
Retention of elongation % (aged 4 hr at 70°C in SAE No. 20 oil)	IMSA[b]	76	85	—	80						
Durometer hardness, shore A	D-676	85	82	84	78						
Brittle temperature, 50% non fail, °C	D-746	-15	-20	-14	-23	max -25	-20	-10	-10	-10	-45
Stiffness in torsion, psi	D-1043										
23°C		2100	2000	3800	1600						
0°C		50,000	20,000	60,000	16,000						
-25°C		225,000	140,000	250,000	130,000						
-50°C		500,000	390,000	510,000	410,000						

		T and TW	T and TW	THW	T and TW					
Retention of elongation, % (Test on No. 14 AWG wire, .031-in. wall)	UL std									
7 days at 100°C		80	90	92	82					
at 113°C		—	85	84	—					
at 121°C		—	—	76	—					
Deformation at 120°C, % (AWG No. 14, .031-in. wall, 500g)	UL std									
Mandrel blend; ½: mandrel		20	24	24	25					
Pass temperature, °C (5 rpm, 5 lb wt)		−58	−47	−40	−55					
Volatility at 105°C					max 3.0	5.0	2.0	1.5	1.0	4.0
Water absorption, %					max .35	.60	.40	.40	.50	.30
Listed for UL designations		T and TW, NM[a], ACT, TF, TFF	T and TW, NMC and UF, UF, NM, SPT 1, 2, 3, 75°C, SVT 60[a], SJT 60[a], ST, TF, TFF,[a] TA	THW	T and TW, NMC and UF, SPT 1, 2, 3 (60°C), SVT (60°C), SJT (60°C), ST, SRT, TF, TFF					

[a]Both insulation and jacketing.
[b]International Municipal Signal Association.

D-1047   Thermoplastic vinyl chloride plastic sheath compound for electrical insulated cords and cables

D-1351   Polyethylene insulated wire and cable

D-1432   Nonrigid vinyl chloride polymer and copolymer molding and extrusion compounds

Boxes, Covers, Sockets and Switches

For over 50 years molded phenolics have been used for electrical applications. They thus qualify as "traditional" building materials. However, new applications are also being developed. Among the latest are phenolic molded nonmetallic outlet and switch boxes and vinyl chloride conduit, boxes and fittings.

The electrical industry is the largest consumer of phenolic molding compounds. General electrical devices such as switch gear, panel boards, wiring devices, and other equipment used in electrical production and servicing constitute about 40 per cent of total production.[7] Phenolic molding materials cost approximately 1¢/in.³; this is less than most metals. The future of phenolics in electrical applications seems secure since there is nothing to match their combination of heat resistance, electrical properties, moldability, and low cost.

The first commercial phenolic molded items were bushings produced for Weston Electrical Instrument Company in 1910 (Figure 14A-1). In 1916 molded weatherproof sockets were being produced that were not unlike those being made and sold today (Figure 14A-2). One of the first applications

Fig. 14A-2. Weatherproof sockets (1916). (*Courtesy Union Carbide Corp.*)

of phenolics for household electrical appliances was to replace molded shellac. This involved two-way sockets molded by National Lead Company for the Hemco Company in 1920. The photograph, Figure 14A-3, could serve to describe two-way sockets available in hardware stores ever since. Successful experience has led to the present widespread use of phenolics and

Fig. 14A-1. First commercial and smallest phenolic molded part-bushings for Weston Electrical Instrument Company. (*Courtesy Union Carbide Corp.*)

Fig. 14A-3. Two way sockets, 1920 to today. (*Courtesy Union Carbide Corp.*)

other thermosetting compounds in lighting fixtures, switches, plugs, outlets, sockets, fuse boxes, wall plates, plug-in circuit breakers, and control panels for hundreds of types of electrical appliances.

One of the more recent developments (1957) is a line of phenolic molded outlet and switch boxes.[8] Use of these has been growing since changes in the National Electrical code in 1962. Typical boxes are shown in Figures 14A-4 through 14A-9. At this writing the

ious phenolic boxes also meet the REA Specifications for Farmstead Wiring and the requirements of the Trailer Standards Asso-

FIG. 14A-5. Switch box. (*Courtesy Union Insulation Co.*)

ciation. The major deterrents to sales of these nonmetallic boxes are breakage and individual codes.

FIG. 14A-4. Phenolic molded switch box. (*Courtesy Union Insulating Co.*)

major markets are on the West Coast, Florida, and the New Jersey area. The major uses are in mobile homes, prefabricated housing, and farmstead wiring. The boxes are all listed by Underwriters Laboratories.[10] Advantages of these boxes include lower cost and greater safety since there are no exposed parts that might become energized and there are no sharp corners to cut into insulated conductors. Also, the use of nonmetallic sheathed cable and insulated boxes eliminates box grounding required under NEC Section 2542, so that much labor and copper wire cost is avoided, and the long-term danger of a disconnected ground wire is eliminated. Var-

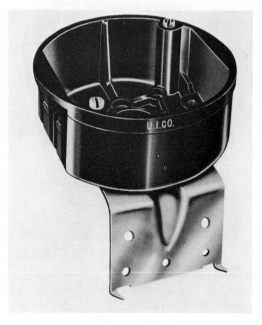

FIG. 14A-6. Four-inch round box. (*Courtesy Union Insulating Co.*)

Conduit and Fittings

The electrical conduit and fittings industry is (outside of the oil and gas industry) one of the largest single end-use areas for pipe. In 1962, conduit and fittings required 366 thou-

FIG. 14A-7. Non metallic conduit box. (*Courtesy Union Insulating Co.*)

sand tons of steel or almost 6 per cent of the total U.S. production of steel pipe. Additional quantities of aluminum brass, and nonmetallic materials, e.g., fiber, clay and

FIG. 14A-8. Weatherproof duplex receptacle cover. (*Courtesy Union Insulating Co.*)

plastic, are also used in the manufacturing of conduit and fittings.

Electrical conduit can generally be divided into two major use areas: above ground (rigid metallic) and below ground (nonmetallic including plastic). However, because of its desirable properties and economics, plastic conduit, especially rigid PVC pipe, is expected to gain more acceptance in both above and below-ground applications.

Electrical conduit and fittings is one of the areas where rapid growth has been forecast for plastic pipe, particularly rigid PVC. By 1972 it is predicted about 50 MM pounds of plastic conduit will be consumed annually in

FIG. 14A-9. Non metallic device box. (*Courtesy Union Insulating Co.*)

the United States (80 per cent rigid PVC). Relatively more use has been made of thermoplastic conduit in Europe than in America; but there as in the United States, the majority of conduit has been steel. In England, a flexible PVC base molding (called a skirting board) is sold which doubles as conduit.[12] PVC conduits are reported to have widespread use in Holland where experience has been quite favorable.[11] The principal advantages quoted are:

(1) Lower installation cost,
(2) Reduction in number of fittings required,
(3) No corrosion.

Recent action of the Underwriters Laboratories and the National Electrical code opens the way for increased use of thermoplastic conduit. A "proposed standard for rigid plastic conduit" was prepared in 1963[13] with the intention of publishing the standard when appropriate requirements have been developed for non-PVC types of rigid plastic conduit which can then be included in the standard. The National Electrical code[14] and the Underwriters Laboratories consider rigid PVC conduit, boxes, and fittings to be special-use products, intended for severe conditions. Presumably it is the authorities' intention, if experience is good under the severe conditions listed in Section 347-2 of the code, to consider expanding the section to include general use applications.

The requirements for conduit as listed by the proposed Underwriters Laboratories standard are summarized below:

(1) Tensile strength, 5000 psi.

(2) Tensile strength undiminished after aging 168 hours at 133°C.

(3) Heat distortion, 70°C or greater at 66 psi, 63°C or greater at 264 psi.

(4) No surface flaking on immersion in acetone.

(5) No chipping or cracking when 30-inch piece of conduit at −20°C is dropped twice from a height of 5 feet onto a concrete floor.

(6) Finished conduit to absorb no more than 0.5 per cent water while submerged 24 hours.

(7) Conduit to withstand the following lateral crushing loads in 6-inch sample.

Conduit Size (in.)	Load (lb)
½, 1¼, 2½, 3½	1000
1½	750
2	700
4	900
6	850

(8) Conduit shall withstand impact of a 20-pound, 2-inch diameter cylinder dropped from the following heights:

Conduit Size (in.)	Height of Drop (ft)
½	2½
¾	4
1	5
1¼	6
1½	7½
2	9½
2½	10½
3	11

TABLE 14A-5. U. S. Electrical Conduit Materials Prices and Economics

Materials	Size (in.)	lb/100 ft	Average Price ($/100 ft) Exposed Conduit		Underground Conduit Installed
			Conduit Only	Installed	
Galvanized steel	½	79	16	71	
	1	150	29	117	
	2	330	61	304	200
	3	690	123	465	
	4	987	190	743	
Aluminum	½	30	16	66	
	1	60	30	110	
	2	129	63	293	
	3	268	128	440	
	4	382	200	715	
Plastics (PVC)	½	9	11	66	
Thin conduit	1	15	17	94	
(160 psi)	2	41	50	295	150–200
	3	90	108	450	
	4	147	170	715	
Plastics (PVC)	½	15	19	75	
Schedule 40 pipe	1	30	37	125	
	2	65	81	325	200
	3	135	165	500	
	4	190	240	775	

TABLE 14A-4. U. S. Manufacturers' Plastic Electrical Conduit and Tubing Shipments

	1958	1962	1967	1972
Million dollars	1	3	11	30
Thousand tons	1	2	9	26
Million feet	2	5	20	60

(9) Flame retardant properties to be such that conduit will not flame longer than 5 seconds following 60-second applications of a standard flame.

(10) If conduit will be wet by a specific reagent, it shall not gain or lose more than 2½ per cent in weight on immersion for 120 days. Crushing strength shall be at least 85 per cent that of similar unaged specimens.

Table 14A-5 illustrates the economic advantage attendant on the use of PVC plastic conduit as compared to galvanized steel. Light weight is an important advantage both in handling and in pipe footage obtained per pound of material. As craftsmen become more familiar with plastic conduit, installation costs may be expected to decrease. Increased code acceptance and economic advantages should make the estimates of Table 14A-4 easily attainable.

REFERENCES

1. *Chem. Eng. News*, p. 38 (October 14, 1963).
2. *Mod. Plastics*, **38,** 97 (January 1961).
3. *Mod. Plastics*, **42,** 164 (October 1964).
4. Underwriters Laboratories, Inc., Chicago, Illinois, "Wires, Thermoplastic—Insulated," UL-83, April 1963.
5. Union Carbide Corporation, Plastics Division, New York, "Kabelitems," No. 124, April 1963.
6. American Society for Testing and Materials, Philadelphia, Pa., "ASTM Standards on Plastics," thirteenth ed., D-1432, November 1962.
7. *Mod. Plastics*, **38,** 108 (January 1961).
8. Union Insulating Company, Parkersburg, W. Va.
10. Underwriters Laboratories Inc., Chicago, Illinois, "Outlet Boxes and Fittings," UL-514, March 1951.
11. Imperial Chemical Industries Ltd., London England, "Plastics in Building," p. 121, 1963.
12. *Brit. Plastics*, **35,** 247 (May 1962).
13. Underwriters Laboratories Inc., Chicago, Illinois, "Proposed Standard for Rigid Plastic Conduit," UL-543, first ed., July 1963.
14. National Electrical Code, Section 347-2.
15. Union Carbide Corp., Plastics Div., Market Research Estimates, April 1965.

PART B: *Heating and Air Conditioning Applications**

RIGID VINYL DUCTS FOR CORROSIVE INDUSTRIAL INSTALLATIONS

The use of rigid polyvinyl chloride plastic (PVC) for process ductwork has become rather common, and many designers and installers have become familiar with details concerning this engineering material. A great many factors must be considered in evaluating the use of a plastic material for industrial process work. The principal use of PVC in industrial ventilation applications is for processes of a corrosive nature. This is the most important design criterion with which the engineer must be concerned.

Generally, the corrosion resistance of PVC is very good. Its structural characteristics are adequate for most situations. Temperature resistance has been somewhat limited. This may soon be improved with developments now in progress.

At least two grades of PVC are available. These are normal-impact (Type I) and high-impact (Type II) materials. Certain modifiers added to the normal-impact base resin formulation provide greater impact resistance, thus producing the high-impact type of PVC. High-impact PVC provides greater resistance to a striking force than does the normal impact material. This, however, is accomplished at the expense of corrosion resistance. Consequently, the normal-impact material is used wherever superior chemical resistance is required, where impact is not a critical factor, or where a structural requirement can be provided by protective reinforcement. High-impact PVC should be specified wherever

*This part by R. C. Hess.

resistance to external damage is the primary consideration and some sacrifice in chemical resistance is permissible.

Reference to the data in Table 6-1 provides a comparison of physical properties between normal- and high-impact PVC. Table 14B-1

provide protection across the entire range of corrosion problems. Accordingly, care must be exercised in the selection of a certain plastic to withstand a specific corrosion environment.

Mechanical Strength. PVC provides a very

TABLE 14B-1. Chemical Resistance of Rigid Polyvinyl Chloride:

Reagent	Concentration	Maximum Temperature (°F)	Reagent	Concentration	Maximum Temperature (°F)
Acetic acid	10	100	Aluminum chloride	All	160
Acetic acid	100	75	Ammonium chloride	All	160
Benzoic acid	All	150	Ammonium nitrate	All	160
Boric acid	All	150	Calcium chloride	All	160
Chromic acid	50	165	Nickel sulfate	All	160
Citric acid	25	165	Potassium dichromate	50	140
Formic acid	100	125	Potassium permanganate	25	125
Hydrobromic acid	All	160	Silver nitrate	All	160
Hydrochloric acid	25	160	Sodium bisulfite	All	160
Hydrochloric acid	100	150	Sodium sulfide	All	160
Hydorfluoric acid	25	125	Stannous chloride	25	125
Hydrofluoric acid	50	70	Zinc chloride	All	160
Lactic acid	25	160			
Nitric acid	25	160	Acetaldehyde	50	70
Nitric acid	50	160	Butyl alcohol	100	160
Nitric acid	100	100	Carbon tetrachloride	100	125
Oxalic acid	All	160	Ethyl alcohol	100	100
Perchloric acid	20	100	Formaldehyde	50	160
Phosphoric acid	All	160	Glycerine	100	160
Sulfuric acid	30	130	Methyl alcohol	100	125
Sulfuric acid	50	160			
Sulfuric acid	80	160	Alums	100	160
Sulfuric acid	100	130	Chlorine gas, dry	10	100
			Hydrogen peroxide	30	160
Ammonium hydroxide	All	160	Ozone	100	100
Calcium hydroxide	All	160	Sea water	100	100
Potassium hydroxide	All	160	Beer	100	125
Sodium hydroxide	All	160	Wine	100	160

lists a number of chemicals at various concentrations and indicates the maximum operating temperature at which rigid polyvinyl chloride can be satisfactorily used in contact with these chemicals. Rigid polyvinyl chloride is not recommended for use with ketones, ethers, esters, aromatic hydrocarbons and chlorinated hydrocarbons.

Advantages

The advantages offered by PVC which have led to its use in process ventilation systems include:

Corrosion Resistance. PVC withstands a great many chemicals as shown in Table 14B-1. No plastic material will necessarily

high degree of structural strength on a weight basis. Hanger supports can be located as is customary for metal systems.

Nonconductor. Galvanic action will not occur, hence electromotive potential is eliminated. Grounding a duct system fabricated from PVC is unnecessary, unless external metal bracing might require such protection.

Low Internal Coefficient of Frictional Flow. PVC ductwork provides an interior surface lower in friction to air flow than is possible with a metal system.

Ease of Installation and Handling. Equivalent strength densities of PVC average 40 per cent less when compared with steel. Plastic duct and fittings can be pre-joined to reduce on-the-job forming. Thus, installation becomes a matter of final assembly of previously joined component parts of a duct system.

Ease of Repair. PVC ductwork lends itself to easy and inexpensive repair using hot-air welding techniques.

Disadvantages

While the aforementioned advantages make PVC a logical choice for many installations, PVC is limited in some respects. These are noted as follows:

Limited Resistance to Temperature. PVC decreases rapidly in mechanical strength over 150°F. Also, corrosive attack increases at higher temperatures with the likely consequence that the PVC will deteriorate more rapidly at these elevated temperatures.

Limited Physical Strength. While this factor was mentioned as an advantage it can also be a disadvantage. While PVC has high strength on a pound-to-pound basis, specified wall thicknesses of plastic duct are generally greater than those of steel. An analysis must thus be made to determine whether or not equivalent strength has been achieved.

Limited Fire Resistance. PVC plastic burns, but it does not support combustion. It is self-extinguishing, and the fire-retardant characteristic is enhanced by the addition of antimony oxide. Thus, this limitation does not preclude the use of PVC in this application.

Fig. 14B-2. Fabricated PVC hoods and ductwork used in the plating industry. (*Courtesy Joseph T. Ryerson & Son. Inc.*)

High Coefficient of Thermal Expansion. PVC expands at 3 to 4 times the rate for steel. Consequently, any design which may be subjected to extreme fluctuations in temperature must provide allowance for expansion and contraction of the component members.

Typical PVC ductwork is shown in Figures 14B-1 and 14B-2.

VARIED EQUIPMENT USAGE

Engineering plastics are now making a serious bid for a share of the air-conditioning equipment market. *Impact styrene* is the big factor in the industry, being used for the basic housing and various other parts. *ABS* (*acrylonitrile-butadiene-styrene*) is being used for grilles, drip pans and escutcheons. *Styrene-acrylontrile* plastic materials are also bidding for this market. A *polycarbonate* has been employed for a molded frame. *Polypropylene* is also gaining acceptance in some of these applications. Its use has been noted in an air-conditioner grille in which polypropylene louvers are set in a styrene frame.

An example of the increasing attention

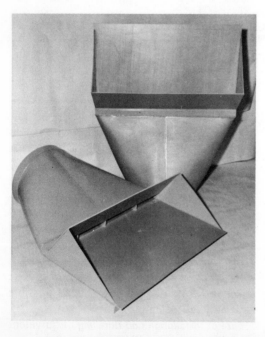

Fig. 14B-1. Fabricated PVC ductwork used in the plating industry. (*Courtesy Joseph T. Ryerson & Son, Inc.*)

being given by equipment designers in industry to plastics as engineering materials is provided by examination of a new range of ventilating units made by Vent-Axia Ltd.[2] Thirty-eight different plastic components comprise the whole assembly. This is a strong indication of the extent to which plastics are now capable of displacing metals in engineering applications. The range of models (window, wall and roof) all use the same basic components, except for variations in shape to suit the particular application. *Melamine* and *phenolic* materials are used for the housings, the former for light-colored models, and the latter for dark-colored ones. *ABS* is used for the impeller, shutter frame and the grille in the window model. Various small components including shutter blades and cam mechanisms utilize *polyacetal* materials because of their delicacy of molding, dimensional stability and low coefficient of friction. Use is made of *high-impact polystyrene* for fascia of the wall model.

REFERENCES

1. Huscher, J. L., "Fabrication and Use of Rigid Polyvinyl Chloride Plastics," *Materials and Methods*, **39**, 119 (1954).
2. "Thirty-eight Plastics Components in Ventilating Unit Range," *Brit. Plastics*, **34**, (September 1961).
3. Brown, R. A., "What You Should Know When Designing Plastic Ventilation Systems," *Heating, Piping Air Conditioning*, **34**, (September 1962);
4. "The Coming Market in Appliances," *Mod. Plastics*, **39**, (July 1962).

15 PLASTICS IN LIGHTING

SVEND W. BRUUN AND JOSEPH R. LORING

Joseph R. Loring & Associates
New York, New York

LIGHTING TODAY — AN ARCHITECTURAL TOOL

The history of the role which lighting, both natural and artificial, has played in the evolution of architectural forms throughout the ages is well known to any serious student of architecture. The development of artificial light sources, however, has been so rapid over the past thirty years that century-old requirements concerning the need for natural light have been reduced to psychological rather than functional necessities.

Complete independence from daylight as a source of interior illumination, however, was not achieved until the introduction of large lighting elements—a direct result of the development of the efficient, low-brightness, fluorescent lamp. Large luminous areas, such as false skylights and indirectly lighted ceilings, were in use before the advent of the fluorescent lamp; however, the inherent presence of heat, both radiant and convected from incandescent sources, necessitated the use of metal or glass as shielding media because of their high heat-resistant qualities.

The development of the fluorescent lamp, with its inherent low brightness, high efficiency, and long lamp life, has given the architect and engineer greater freedom in the integration of architecture and light and has also created a need for large translucent shielding media—a need which was quickly recognized by the plastics industry. Although

plastics of various types were first used primarily to replace glass as a light diffusing and shielding medium, recent developments have permitted applications in areas where glass would be impractical.

The improvement in the efficiency of light sources brought with it the long-needed increase in recommended lighting levels. The practical limit for comfortable interior illumination with incandescent light sources is reached in the vicinity of 50 to 75 foot-candles, while the latest research in the field of illumination has indicated the desirability of levels considerably above 100 foot-candles for performing many daily tasks in offices, schools, hospitals, industrial plants, etc. These higher lighting levels resulted in the increased use of large area lighting elements using fluorescent lamps as the source and plastic as the light-controlling medium.

While the use of plastics is not limited to application in combination with fluorescent lamps, the "perfect marriage" between the two was nevertheless quickly recognized. It would appear that the phenomenal advances in the development of plastics for the lighting industry could be attributed in large part to the rapid improvement of the fluorescent lamp as a light source.

Plastics in lighting, as an adjunct to contemporary architecture, is enjoying an ever-expanding area of use. It is the purpose of this chapter to evaluate the many uses, to

312

suggest new fields of application, and to call for caution in the use of plastics in unsuitable applications.

CURRENT USES OF PLASTICS IN LIGHTING

The use of plastics in lighting may be broken down as follows:

(1) Plastics used as light-controlling devices
  (a) Refractors—lenses, sheets, lamp enclosures
  (b) Reflectors—clear or coated (reflector-louver combination)
  (c) Louvers—clear, translucent or opaque (coated)
(2) Plastics used as light modifiers
  (a) Diffusers—panels, dished forms, luminous ceilings
  (b) Enclosures—globes, panels
  (c) Walls—luminous walls, false windows, panels
  (d) Polarizers—panels
(3) Plastics used as light transmitters
  (a) Sheets (signs)
  (b) Rods
  (c) Electroluminescent forms
  (d) Directional signs
(4) Plastics used as color transmitters
  (a) Special decorative effects
  (b) Signs
(5) Plastics used as selective radiation filters
  (a) Control of ultraviolet, deleterious and fading effects

Since the use of various plastic materials in the lighting industry is of relatively recent origin, new uses are still being found. When the rapidly expanding development of new light sources is considered, it may well be that certain plastic materials which are unsuitable for particular applications today will find acceptance in the future with radically different light sources.

WHY PLASTICS?

To answer the question, "Why plastics?" let us consider the various elements with which the user or designer should be familiar. These "elements" have played a major role in the increased use of plastics for lighting due to the ability of the plastics producers to "tailor-make" the material economically to the requirements of the task by varying the characteristics of those elements. As a result, plastics have been produced which have controllable degrees of heat resistance, hardness, translucency and fire resistance, etc.

To evaluate these characteristics properly, the following advantages and disadvantages must be considered:

Advantages

(1) Weight. In general, plastics as a group are considerably lighter than glass. Lightness, *per se*, is only part of the story, since plastic may be molded or formed to add rigidity far beyond its plain, or unworked state. The lesser weight of the material reduces installation time and simplifies maintenance. Framing members may be made of thinner metal or eliminated entirely.

(2) Workability. Whether of the "thermoplastic" or "thermosetting" types, plastics may be worked in the field by use of simple drills, saws, files, or scissors—an advantage in both customized and regular installation work.

Thermosetting plastics (urea, melamine, most polyesters, and phenolics) cannot be altered as to shape and form once molded, but the large family of thermoplastics (acrylics, polystyrenes, and vinyls) may be relatively easily shaped or reshaped by proper application of heat. The joining of two or more pieces of plastics may be accomplished by the use of adhesives composed of essentially the same basic material. Thus, acrylics may be joined with acrylic liquid cement and phenolics with phenolic resin, etc. The joints thus formed are comparable in strength to a welded joint.

(3) Strength. Rigidity of the thermoplastics compares favorably with most building materials. Their modulus of elasticity is in the range of 150,000 to 500,000 psi. The thermosetting plastics are considerably stronger and, when used in conjunction with reinforced polyesters, approximate structural lumber in stiffness. Where characteristics of flexibility and shatter resistance become important, such as in cases where large surfaces

or panels are being considered, the use of plastics is indicated.

(4) Versatility. Plastics are used today in connection with light and lighting in sizes ranging from fractions of square inches to areas measurable in acres. It should be noted that the trend toward large area lighting, made possible by plastics, has resulted in generally improved luminous environments based upon the following:

(a) The greater the ratio of luminous ceiling panel area to floor area, the greater is the comfort ratio, provided proper brightness control can be achieved.

(b) Formed ceiling (and wall) panels as large as 6 feet in width or diameter are not uncommon while compression or injection molded one-piece panels are available in lengths up to 6 feet. Entire ceilings are often constructed of large, molded, optically designed panels. Architectural considerations frequently dictate the form and extent of luminous surfaces. The availability of shapes, thickness, optical control characteristics, and even color tints, can assure results which match the architectural concept.

(5) Control of Translucency. A major factor in the vast acceptance of plastics in lighting is the availability of these materials in almost unlimited degrees of translucency ranging from the efficient transparency of clear acrylics at 92 per cent to complete opacity. Control of the light passing through the plastic may be attained by forming the material in a prismatic pattern. "Hiding power" of the material is increased by the addition of diffusive materials to the compound.

(6) Adaptability. The term "plastic" represents a compound of many materials, each of which may be modified by additives and manufacturing processes. Therefore, desired specification of characteristics regarding translucency, formability, hardness, light control, color or thermal limitations may generally be obtained.

Disadvantages

(1) Permanence. Plastics, in general, are more susceptible to environmental influences than glass and cannot be considered equal in permanence. However, experience over the past two decades would lead to the conclusion that such permanence is not necessarily required. The art and science of illumination is a vast and rapidly changing field. Rare indeed is the sight of a 25-year old lighting fixture that is still considered proper or adequate. On the other hand, when permanency in translucent media, in the real sense of the word is required, such as in museums, churches and other monumental-type projects, the full knowledge of the "life" of a material should be carefully considered.

(2) Temperature considerations. Plastics, as a group, are affected by temperature fluctuations in both the higher (above 125°F) and the lower ranges of environmental ambient. They should be selected with full realization of these limitations.

Present day light sources, i.e., lamps of all types, are essentially heating elements. This fact may be appreciated when one considers that of all the energy consumed in the operation of the highly efficient fluorescent lamp only 18 per cent of its radiant energy is transmitted as visible light. The remaining 82 per cent is radiated or distributed to lamp sockets and fixture parts (including plastic materials) in the form of heat. In the case of incandescent lamps only 10 per cent of the energy consumed is emitted as visible light. This leaves 90 per cent to be disposed of by convection, radiation (70 per cent) and conduction. The concentrated heat emission of the incandescent lamp imposes more serious demands upon plastics than that of the larger-dimensioned fluorescent lamp. Lamps mounted too close to the plastic material may cause warping, sagging, and discoloration, and proper precautions should be exercised in the design. (For specific data concerning the heat resistance of various plastic materials refer to Tables 15-1, 15-2 or 15-3.)

Ultraviolet, near-ultraviolet (from fluorescent lamps), and infrared radiations may have deleterious effects upon certain plastics. Discoloration and brittleness may result from improper design and application of equipment.

(3) Static Dust Collection. Unless guarded

against by destaticizing measures, dust collecting on lighting equipment will become a problem. Most plastics are excellent electric insulators due to high surface resistivity, thus presenting a surface conducive to static buildup. The use of proper cleaning agents will help minimize the dust problem. Caution should be exercised in the selection of such cleaning materials for the various plastics react differently to the several available cleaners. The manufacturer's instructions should be followed.

(4) Flammability. Some ideas die hard. Since 1868, when the most famous plastic, cellulose acetate (celluloid), was first manufactured in the United States, apprehension has existed toward all plastics as potential fire hazards. Certain building codes still appear overly cautious in this respect. It should be noted that many plastics, including those popular in lighting applications, have relatively high burning rates. Others, including vinyls, acrylics, some styrenes and certain polyester-glass combinations, are self-extinguishing. Therefore, caution should be taken not to expose the plastics to excessive heat or open flame. All plastics, however, are organic in origin and can be destroyed by fire.

(5) Hardness. Surface hardness is limited in most plastics varying, according to composition, between thermoplastics and thermosetting. No plastic has attained the hardness of glass; hence their use must generally be restricted to applications reasonably free from abrasive influences such as are prevalent in certain industrial areas where grit and sand are normally present in the air. Coarse cleaning agents such as scouring powders must also be avoided.

The responsibility for proper selection of a plastic rests upon the designer, or specifier, based upon the knowledge and consideration of the above characteristics, as well as the cost. An awareness of all the characteristics of a material will usually reveal certain drawbacks which are inherently present. The final determination should be made after careful evaluation of both the positive and negative aspects of the material. In order to assist in the comparison of the relative advantages and disadvantages of the many plastics used in lighting applications, the specific characteristics of each group will be listed in Tables 15-1, 15-2 and 15-3.

THE TREND TOWARD IMPROVEMENT AND UNIFORMITY

By 1947, the need for interaction between the plastics and the lighting industries had become obvious; the various manufacturers had not yet standardized their terminology, resulting in a confusion of terms. A joint industry committee was established at that time, and in 1956 a "Plastics for Lighting" committee was formed. This committee, combining the two industries in a single body, seeks to compile standards on plastics when applied to fluorescent lighting for eventual industry adoption. The organizations joined in this clarifying effort are the Society of the Plastics Industry (SPI), the Illuminating Engineering Society (IES) and the National Electrical Manufacturers Association (NEMA).

Two reports have emerged to date as a result of the joint efforts:

(1) "Recommended Light Characteristics of Polystyrene Used in Illumination" and

(2) "Recommended Light Characteristics of Acrylic Used in Illumination."

Both reports establish scope, classification of material composition, test procedures, and requirements of test specimens.

An area of great importance to the lighting industry which is still awaiting uniform testing and evaluation in the plastics industry is the "yellowing" or "color stability" factor.

Some manufacturers report "yellowing" according to hours exposure to fluorescent lamps under operating conditions; others according to approved Fade-O-Meter tests. The latter is an accelerated test which can produce equivalent exposure time in a matter of months instead of years.

Tables 15-1, 15-2, and 15-3 have listed those characteristics of the various plastics which are especially pertinent to the lighting industry.

To further the understanding of the inherent characteristics of each material the following discussion is included:

TABLE 15-1. General Properties of Acrylics in Lighting Applications

	ASTM Test No.	IES-SPI-NEMA Requirements and Classifications				Self-extinguishing	Manufacturers' Data Tabulated				
		A	B	C	D	E	A	B	C	D	E
Optical											
Light transmission, %	D791	91	90	90	90		93	93	93	>92	92
Index of refraction	D542	1.50	1.50	1.50	1.50		1.49	1.49	1.49	1.49	1.49
	D791	1.48	1.48	1.48	1.48						
Stability of yellowing**		500	1000	1000	1000		500+	1000+	1000+	1000+	1000+
Heat distortion temperature, °F***	D648	185	183	162	149		166 / 190	198 / 206	189	136 / 155	185†
Burning rate, in./min.	D635	1.5	1.6	1.5	1.4	SE	.9	.7	2.0	.9	SE
Elongation in 2 in. (minimum), %	D638	2	2	2	1.5		1.2 / 5	1.2 / 5.5	4.0	1.2 / 3.5	3.6
Tensile strength (minimum), psi	D638	8000	8000	8000	8000		10,500	10,500	10,000	9,500	12,500
Impact strength, notch Izod	D256	.3	.2	.2	.2		.4	.4	.3	.3	.3
Generally used in lighting as:											
Flat sheets — plain or configurated							X	X	X	X	X
Cast panels and dishes								X	X	X	
Extrusions							X	X			
Vacuum formed dishes							X				

*50 to 63% in white opal.
**Fade-O-Meter. Yellowing factor not exceeding 3.0.
***At 264 psi fiber stress.
†155° for white.

Acrylics

Inherently crystal clear thermoplastics: This family of methyl-methacrylates is extremely well-suited for lighting applications.

(a) Most acrylics withstand long exposure to light (more than 10 years) as well as to weathering without discoloration depending upon the precise composition.

(b) The index of refraction of commercial acrylics is close to 1.49. This variance from that of glass is sufficient to demand its being taken into account in the design of lenses and refractors for the sake of accuracy. Two lenses of identical design, one acrylic, one glass, will result in two different light patterns from an identical light source.

(c) In sheet form, acrylics can be softened at elevated temperatures and formed (usually vacuum-formed) into practically any desired three-dimensional shape used by the lighting industry. Formed acrylic parts resist heat up

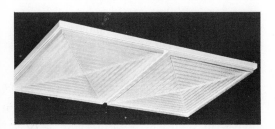

FIG. 15-1. Clear, prismatic acrylic panels 2ft. × 2ft. for use in very shallow fluorescent fixtures. (*Courtesy Holophane Co.*)

to 200°F, although the behavior of different grades will vary somewhat. Parts made of acrylic molding powder (certain lenses and bowls) have lower heat distortion temperatures than those produced from cast sheets (diffusers, "wrap-around" light shields, etc.).

(d) Acrylics, with other thermoplastics, have a relatively high coefficient of expansion, 3.3×10^{-5}. Adequate provisions, therefore, must be made for movement when acrylics are attached to nonplastic materials.

(e) Bonding between acrylic parts, as well as between acrylics and other plastics, is positive when solvent cementing agents such as monomers, aromatic or chlorinated hydrocarbons are used. Many manufacturers utilize this characteristic to good advantage in the joining of extrusions to cast or injection molded pieces. The bonded assemblies are, in general, fully as stable as a one-piece molded unit, and both methods are in common use in the lighting industry.

Classification. The IES-SPI-NEMA Industry committee recommendations * attempt to classify the acrylics according to their light characteristics and to identify and concentrate on "thermoplastic acrylic cast sheet and molding compounds for use in the manufacture of fluorescent luminaires." The recommendations cover four types of acrylic compositions as listed in Table 15-1:

Class A—Heat-resistant cast sheet.
Class B—Heat-resistant molding powder.
Class C—General-purpose molding powder.
Class D—Easy-flowing molding powder.

Properties. Since lighting acrylics are available in a number of compounds and vary according to raw materials (molding powders), the profusion of types, as well as the complexity of manufacturers, as yet non-uniform property specifications, may confuse the average user. The authors have therefore listed those properties of plastics, which most critically affect the suitability of their application in the lighting industry, according to:

(1) Manufacturing methods and compounds (Classes A thru D)
(2) Resistance to heat (heat distortion)
(3) Flammability (burning rate)
(4) Color stability (yellowing)
(5) Impact strength
(6) Embrittlement
(7) Transmission

All the above factors have great influence upon performance, durability, safety, and cost of the plastics.

Resistance to Heat (Heat Distortion). While the ASTM test method (D648) only measures the relative behavior of a plastic under heat and stress, it affords a valuable measure of comparison. Heat is present in every incandescent and fluorescent luminaire; often attaining unexpectedly high temperatures. Tests have shown that the inside temperature

*Published in *Illuminating Engineering*, **50,** 284 (May 1958).

in poorly designed recessed fluorescent units may reach 140°F or higher. (Ideal temperature for optimum lamp performance is 77°F.) Some plastics will experience distortion or will sag at temperatures as low as 130°F. The combination, therefore, of a fixture which runs "hot" and non-heat-resistant plastics should obviously be avoided. Self-extinguishing acrylics with a heat distortion point of less than 140°F are not recommended by plastics manufacturers for use in flat, horizontal panels, but they may be used in "formed" or "dished" shapes. Manufacturers' recommendation of maximum sizes of panels should be closely adhered to. Most acrylics of the non-self-extinguishing type will tolerate temperatures well above the 140°F level; some can reach 205°F and higher before distorting. Conservative design, however, would dictate that continued in-service design temperature should be limited to 20 to 25°F below the distortion temperature.

Flammability (Burning Rate). The development of self-extinguishing acrylics has been accomplished only recently and at the apparent sacrifice of the high heat-resistance characteristics of the material. Self-extinguishing acrylics are the only types approved for large area plastic installations in a number of cities. Among the slow-burning acrylics and plastics are those which, when exposed to open flame, will burn with no detectable fumes. Other types develop considerably sooty and, under some circumstances, toxic fumes.

Burning rate is measured in inches per minute of test specimen of certain size and thickness. The BR/min of the various acrylics range from 0 (self-extinguishing) to 1.2 (slow-burning).

Stability to Yellowing. Among the plastics developed to date, only the acrylics have shown the ability to withstand exposure to artificial and/or natural light for extended periods of time without "yellowing." "Yellowing" is a gradual change in the appearance of the plastics from a clear colorless substance to one with an increasingly deepening yellow-brownish cast. The change may take place in as little as a year for some nonstabilized plastics or may be unnoticeable in some acrylics even after 15 to 25 years of normal service. The "yellowing" is the result of constant impingement on the plastic of the infrared, the near-ultraviolet and the ultraviolet rays produced by the light sources. The latter emissions are produced in various degrees by fluorescent, mercury, and other arc-type vapor lamps.

The degree of "yellowing" has been measured in laboratory tests by means of "accelerated" exposure of test specimens. These test specimens are exposed to a carbon arc aging device (Fade-O-Meter) under laboratory atmospheric conditions standardized at 23°C. A 1000-hour exposure without discernible yellowing (factor of less than 3) is considered satisfactory. Most acrylics pass this time test. The ASTM "Test Method #D791 and paragraph 6(c)" employing type FDA-R Fade-O-Meter, appears to the authors to be the most positive, informative, and impartial laboratory test established to date, and such test results should be made available by all manufacturers on all plastic compounds.

Some manufacturers seem to prefer non-accelerated tests in the form of "Life Tests," exposing test specimens to 100-watt fluorescent lamps at a distance of 2 to 4 inches to lamp bulb wall. This is the method by which the 10-year or longer performance guarantees have been substantiated. No ASTM test method covers this procedure since the time duration involved precludes close laboratory type control which is possible in the shorter, accelerated laboratory test.

Other manufacturers use actual fluorescent fixtures in their tests, exposing test specimens to the radiation of 3 or 4 fluorescent lamps separated from the specimen by a selected distance, 2 to 4 inches. Because of the non-uniformity of such tests, however accurate and impressive, the absence of common denominations with other manufacturers' and with the Industry Committees' standards, the comparative values are lost.

The equation used in determining the perceptible color change is

Yellowing Factor

$$= 100 \frac{(T420 - T'420) - (T680 - T'680)}{T560}$$

where

$T420$ = per cent transmittance of same thickness of unexposed material at 420 $m\mu$

$T560$ = per cent transmittance of same thickness of unexposed material at 560 $m\mu$

$T680$ = per cent transmittance of same thickness of unexposed material at 680 $m\mu$

$T'420$ = per cent transmittance of specimen at 420 $m\mu$

$T'680$ = per cent transmittance of specimen at 680 $m\mu$

$m\mu$ = wavelength in millimicrons.

Tolerable Yellowing: Acrylic specimens tested as above should be considered as objectionably yellow if a yellowing factor of 3 is exceeded.

Experience over the past several years has, however, proved this formula somewhat unreliable insofar as incongruities often occur between the visual and the mathematical results. A new formula has therefore been developed by the ASTM at the request of the IES-SPI-NEMA Committee and subject to its approval. The new formula is based on the tri-stimulus color evaluation system and is as follows

Yellowness Index YI

$$= \frac{100 (1.28\, Xcie - 1.06\, Zcie)}{Ycie}$$

(ASTM Designation D1925 − 63T)

where $Xcie$, $Ycie$ and $Zcie$ = the tristimulus value of the specimen relative to light source C. (Yellowness is defined as deviation in chroma from whiteness or water-whiteness in the dominant wavelength range from 570 to 580 $m\mu$.)

The general industry acceptance of this formula is expected and should eventually result in new uniform test reporting.

Impact Resistance. This is a figure normally available from the plastics manufacturer upon request. Its importance lies in its application in locations where vandalism or very rough handling is a factor, such as outdoors. The impact resistance figures will range, according to composition, from 0.3 to 12.0 foot-pounds. However, the latter compound is not suited for normal lighting applications.

Embrittlement. An awareness of this factor is of extreme importance to the prospective user in view of the fact that certain plastics, outside of the acrylics, become brittle beyond practical use after relatively limited exposure to artificial and natural light or to extreme temperatures. At this moment no authoritative data concerning brittleness are available, nor has any industry norm been established.

Transmission. Finally, plastics may be classified according to their actual value as Lambert or Brightness transmitters and regulators (optical properties.) While last on this discussion of properties, light-transmission is, of course, of greatest importance and the main reason for the use of translucent-transparent plastics in connection with light and lighting. Hence several allusions to this subject have been made through-out the preceding pages (see "Current uses of plastics in Lighting", "Why Plastics" (5), Table 15-1 etc.).

Thermoplastics have outstanding total luminous transmission, clear acrylics reaching 93% (Table 15-1) while styrenes in their initial stage are somewhat lower, 88 to 90% (Table 15-2). Others, such as polyesters and polycarbonates are about in this same range.

Thermosetting plastics, such as ureas and polyesters, being inherently of diffused transmittance, show initial light transmission of 50% (total transmission as for instance when used in fixtures and luminous ceilings is somewhat higher.) Phenolic and urea formaldehydes were successfully applied for many years in luminous bowl-indirect and other incandescent fixtures.

A review of the foregoing properties with regard to their comparative importance for lighting system applications, reveals that heat resistance, flammability, stability to yellowing, and impact strength embody the values which are of the greatest importance to the user.

In view of the complexity of the alternatives, insofar as selection of suitable properties of plastics materials is concerned, the four classifications A, B, C, and D, as agreed by the IES-SPI-NEMA committee, still appear to constitute a reasonable common meeting ground and thus are advocated for industry use. To the four categories should now be added a fifth, "E"—self-extinguishing acrylics, which were introduced subsequent to the original issue of the committee recommendations.

Styrenes

First developed in 1938 and available as clear, translucent or opaque thermoplastics, styrenes or polystyrenes have been widely applied in the lighting industry.

(a) Styrenes are lightweight and are relatively simple to mass-produce in complicated shapes.

(b) Styrenes are available in an unlimited

Fig. 15-2. Twenty-four inch diameter dish of styrene sealed against dust and vapors. Circline fluorescent lamps. (*Courtesy The Dow Chemical Co.*)

range of colors, have good dimensional stability, and are generally slow burning.

(c) Styrenes are less resistive to ultraviolet radiations and heat in general than the acrylics and should not be used for outdoor application, unless in a blend with acrylics.

TABLE 15-2. General Properties of Polystyrenes (Thermoplastics) in Lighting Applications

	ASTM Test	IES-SPI-NEMA Requirements and Classifications			Manufacturers' Data Tabulated			
	No.	A	B	C	Light-stabilized**			Unstabilized
Optical								
					68	88	88	
Light transmission	D791	—	—	—	−90	−90	−90	
Index of refraction	D542	1.585	1.585	1.585				
		1.60	1.6	.16	1.59	1.59	1.59	
Stability to Yellowing*	D791	100	100	500	800	1250	1200	625
Heat distortion temperature,					165		170	
°F	D648	165	176	165	−172	205	195	
					1.0	1.5	1.0	
Burning rate, in./min.	D635	2.	2.	2.	−1.5	1.8	−1.5	
							1.2	
Elongation in 2 in. (minimum), %	D638	1.0	1.0	1.0	1.2	2.	2.9	
Tensile strength (minimum), psi	D638	6.0	7.0	6.0	4.5	— to —	9.5	
					.32	2.	.45	
Impact strength, notch Izod	D256	.25	.25	.25	−.65	2.5	−.5	

*Fade-O-Meter test. Tolerable yellowing factor 15.
**The values in these columns have no direct relation to classifications A, B and C as manufacturers data are individually and not collectively classified.

(d) Polystyrenes are workable in extruded, molded, or vacuum-formed panels and cost less than acrylics.

(e) The index of refraction of styrenes is

FIG. 15-3. Outdoor, opal acrylic fluorescent highway lighting unit. Approximately 4ft. × 6 in. (*Courtesy Rohm & Haas*)

1.58 to 1.60. As this differs considerably from glass and acrylics, it is a factor which must be considered in the design of refractive devices.

Classification. The IES-SPI-NEMA Industry committee has classified the three types of polystyrene compounds as follows:

Class A—Unmodified polystyrene with or without the addition of diffusing pigments and small amounts of lubricants.

Class B—Essentially, Class A material characterized by improved heat-distorting properties.

Class C—Essentially polystyrene with or without the addition of diffusing pigments and incorporating additives to inhibit discoloration resulting from fluorescent light radiation.

Properties. An evaluation of polystyrenes according to Resistance to heat, flammability

and color stability previously described under acrylics would emphasize the following

Resistance to Heat (*Heat Distortion*). The IES-SPI Industry norms set at 165 to 176°F appear to be either met or exceeded according to data from certain manufacturers. However, not all manufacturers have made their data available. In general, heat appears to be a greater factor in the application of polystyrenes than acrylics. This simply means that greater care must be exercised by the lighting fixture designer when using a polystyrene.

Flammability (*Burning Rate*). Available industry data show that manufactured polystyrenes exceed the IES-SPI norms and in general compare with the performance of acrylics. One manufacturer has produced a self-extinguishing, medium-impact styrene sheet which meets the rather stringent requirements of the city of New York for self-extinguishing materials (Group A).

Color Stability (*Yellowing*). Polystyrene can be classified in two groups–light-stabilized and unstabilized. Of the two, the unstabilized should be considered only for intermittent usage as it yellows quickly and is generally unsuitable for lighting applications.

Light stability is achieved either by protecting the polystyrenes from direct exposure

FIG. 15-4. Configurated vinyl panels in beamed ceiling. Fluorescent lamps. (*Courtesy Union Carbide Corp.*)

to air (oxygen) and ultraviolet radiations, or by the addition of sufficient antioxidants and ultraviolet absorbers to the styrene mixture.

Styrenes are also blended with acrylics for still greater light stability.

Most commercially available light-stabilized styrenes today purportedly pass the Class C requirements, although some manufacturers seem reluctant either to submit their materials to the IES-SPI-NEMA tests or to publish their own figures. "Tolerable yellowing" or "yellowing factor" of polystyrenes has, for one reason or another, been set by the Industry committee at 15. This means that specimens are not considered objectionably yellow unless the yellowing factor of 15 is exceeded. It should be noted at this point that the yellowing factor for acrylics is 3.

Here again the importance of an industry-wide test procedure for yellowing is made apparent. Because such a test is not used, and certain manufacturers are reluctant to reveal their figures, no clear over-all picture of this important factor can be made available to designers, buyers, and users of the product.

Application. Styrenes are available in plain and configured sheet form, clear or made opaque by the addition of selected materials which, while regulating or scattering light source brightness, also cut down total light transmission. Solid opaque polystyrene is used extensively in the manufacture of plastic louvers. Patterns of egg-crate types and multicircular forms are available in white or tints.

Because of their excellent workability, polystyrenes are extruded, molded or vacuum-formed into diffusing and prismatic light-controlling panels.

Vinyls

As the third component of the main grouping of plastics, vinyls, especially in sheet form, found early and wide acceptance in the lighting industry through their use in luminous ceilings.

(a) The main features of vinyls are: uniformity in light diffusion, light weight, versatility in design, and low cost.

(b) Vinyls are self-extinguishing.

(c) Vinyls have a low resistance to heat.

(d) Vinyls are less resistive to ultraviolet radiation than either the acrylic or light-stabilized polystyrenes.

(e) Vinyls are workable in extruded, molded or vacuum-formed panels and cost much less than either acrylics or polystyrenes.

Composition. Vinyls are composed of vinyl chloride-acetate copolymer resins formed into sheets at high temperatures.

Vinyl is available in a highly diffusing

TABLE 15-3. General Properties of Vinyls and Styrene-Acrylic Copolymers in Lighting Applications

	Vinyls High Impact	Vinyls Medium Impact	Styrene-Acrylic Copolymers
Optical	White only		
Light transmission, %			91
	50	50	
Index of refraction	—	—	1.533
Stability to yellowing	Not available*	Not available	
Heat distortion temperature, °F	144	140	205
Burning rate, in./min.	S. E.	S. E.	1.7
Elongation in 2 in. (minimum), %	20	20	4 to 5
Tensile strength (minimum), psi	8000	8000	9000
Impact strength, notch Izod	1.0	.50	.4
Generally used in lighting as:			
Louvers	X	X	X
Flat sheets, plain or conf.	X	X	X
Cast panels—dishes			X
Extrusions			X
Vacuum-formed dishes	X	X	
Calendered	X	X	

*Not available in ASTM—Industry Committee norms.
Note: No IES-SPI-NEMA Classification Available.

matte finish which assures direct light transmission values of 50 per cent or more.

Properties. An evaluation of vinyls according to resistance to heat, flammability, and color stability previously described under acrylics would emphasize the following:

Application. Vinyls have had their greatest application in luminous ceilings; particularly those which have sprinklers located within the ceiling cavities. Should a fire occur below

ity tests are available for comparative purposes.

FIG. 15-5. Regressed acrylic dome fixtures, fluorescent. Dome is slightly concave for strength, 36 in. diameter up to 5 ft. square available. (*Courtesy: Rohm & Haas*)

Resistance to Heat (Heat Distortion). Resistance to heat is low as the 140°F softening point would indicate.

Flammability (Burning Rate). Vinyl will not support combustion and will decompose only when continuously exposed to flames.

Color Stability (Yellowing). The color stability of vinyls, under exposure to fluorescent lamps and normal aging, does not come up to the performance of either acrylics or light-stabilized polystyrenes.

Light stability of the standard vinyl sheet can be approximately doubled by conventional hydraulic press over-lamination of ultraviolet absorbing clear vinyl films. A similar technique is also used in the manufacture of hollow louver panels which are overlaid by the ultraviolet absorbing sheet.

No standard IES-SPI-NEMA light stabil-

the vinyl ceiling, the plastic, because of its 140°F softening point, will fall out and thus allow the sprinkler system to function as soon as the room temperature exceeds 165°F. One commercially available vinyl laminate can be obtained with minute perforations; it acts as an acoustical ceiling as well as a luminous ceiling.

Vinyl is available in configurated sheet or corrugated roll forms as well as panels and special louver construction. It is also used as a base material in which minute glass flakes are suspended for polarization of light. Rigid polarized panels are made up of many layers through which light travels and is eventually transmitted in a radially symmetrical distribution reducing direct glare markedly.

From a cost standpoint, the vinyl thin sheet material is lower in cost on a square foot basis than either acrylics or polystyrenes.

Combination Thermoplastics

In recent years copolymer chemistry has produced a new copolymer of methyl methacrylate and styrene. The combination material costs less than pure acrylics and bridges the gap between acrylics and styrenes for certain applications, particularly outdoor usage. This copolymer can be injection molded, extruded, vacuum or pressure formed, and it retains many of the specific characteristics of the parent plastics. The original material is crystal clear and in annealed form is resistant to heat up to 205°F. In Fade-O-Meter tests the combination material passes the 500-hour test for polystyrenes and approaches the 1000-hour test for acrylics showing a yellowing factor of less than 5. (See Table 15-3.)

Thermosetting Plastics in Lighting

Polyesters and urea formaldehyde are thermosetting plastics often used in conjunction with other materials. Thermosets undergo an irreversible chemical transformation when molded. Subsequent heat applied will not change their shape, although extreme heat and open fire will destroy them. All plastics, of course, thermosetting or thermoplastic alike, are organic materials and thus destructible by fire. Polyesters are translucent plastics used in lighting (natural or artificial) almost exclusively in combination with and reinforced by glass fibers. In later years another combination has developed, that of polyester with flaked glass to produce a light-polarizing panel. Fiber-glass panels are mainly applied in the control and modification of daylight, although use has been made of them as room dividers and trans-illuminated walls.

Fiber glass attains a very high impact strength and is subject to slight color changes when exposed to daylight or fluorescent light. No specific data are available.

Polarized panels are used in large area fixtures or luminous ceilings.

Fɪɢ. 15-6. Regressed dome type fluorescent fixture designed to deliver both natural as well as fluorescent light to the interior. (*Courtesy Rohm & Haas*)

Other Applications of Plastics in Lighting

Incandescent, Mercury and Other Nonlinear Light Sources. The major part of the foregoing discussion has been centered around the fluorescent lamp as the light source in plas-

considerations in these examples have been the observance of proper distance relation between lamp and plastic as well as unobstructed heat dissipation.

Polystyrene has been used broadly in the

Fig. 15-7. Five-foot square diffusing opal acrylic panels in combination lighting-air conditioning ceiling. Deep perforated baffles minimize noises in the room. (*Courtesy: Rohm & Haas*)

tics lighting applications. But while the fluorescent lamp with its relatively low energy per square inch emission, as has been evidenced, is easily compatible with most plastics, more serious problems arise when plastics must combine with concentrated light sources such as incandescent and high-pressure metallic vapor lamps, e.g., mercury and color-corrected mercury lamps. Here very high energy and heat concentrations are encountered which limit the design of equipment.

Cylindrical lanterns have been used successfully for years. Twelve-inch diameter cylinders made from high heat-resistant acrylic may employ single lamps up to 500 watts. Opal cylinders of smaller diameter and lamp wattages are extensively used for decorative and semi-decorative purposes. Main design

design of globe-type incandescent fixtures, while, especially prior to the arrival of the fluorescent lamp, urea-formaldehyde was extensively used in open bowl-type semi-indirect commercial luminaires.

Acrylics are popular both in small exterior pole fixtures which may employ incandescent, mercury, or fluorescent lamps, while cone-shaped large-area light fixtures measuring nearly 6 feet in diameter are available for parking field or similar lighting.

Self-luminous panels, a form of light still under intensive development, are becoming available for everyday use. The phenomenon known as "electroluminescence" employs acrylics inside of which the real light source is encapsulated, whose thickness is measured in thousandths of an inch. The entire area of such panels becomes evenly luminous when voltage is applied. In one pioneering installation the panels run the entire length of each step. Other and readily available electroluminescent applications are small

recessed lighting fixture or an expanse of luminous ceiling, a new situation is created in which fire safety is directly involved. Fireproof material is, in effect, replaced with a

FIG. 15-8. Corrugated plastic (acrylic) luminous ceiling. (*Courtesy*: *Rohm & Haas*)

night-light discs plugged into one 120 to 130 volt convenience outlet and luminous switchplates. These luminesce in a darkened interior and indicate the location of the light switch in the dark.

Building Code Considerations and the Changing Codes

Some prevailing misconceptions as to which of the specific characteristics of plastics are of predominant importance regarding "safety" must be briefly touched upon.

In lighting:

(a) Is a "flameproof" translucent plastic desirable?

(b) When is distortion due to heat desirable in a plastic?

(c) Why is low "smoke density" of greater importance in fires than "self-extinguishing" features?

When an area of fire-retarding ceiling material, such as plaster or mineral tile, is removed or omitted in order to give room for a

nonflameproof substance, be it thermosetting ureas, phenolics or glass-reinforced polyesters or thermoplastic acetates, acrylics, polystyrenes, or vinyls, each of which possesses its very own fire-responding characteristics.

The Underwriters Laboratories have approved over-all luminous ceilings placed below a sprinkler system provided a selfextinguishing, low-softening point (140°F) material is used. Such plastics will actually deflect and fall out of their ceiling structure when room temperature has reached 140°F, well in advance of the sprinklers actuating point of 165°F.

However, no flameproof plastic has, so far, been developed. One reason is that plastics are of organic origin and thus will ultimately be consumed in a fire. Therefore, the use of thermosetting plastics as light transmitters in, for instance, recessed lighting fixtures, may be questionable from a fire-hazard standpoint. Such plastic members could actually be set on fire at superheated temperatures and burn while in place. Experience therefore leads to the use of translucent plas-

FIG. 15-9. Official New York World's Fair street lighting luminaires. Opal acrylic panel design. In background may be seen one of several "bubble-roofs" of vinyl, inflated and internally lighted. (*Courtesy: Rohm & Haas*)

tics which are thermoplastic and thus will automatically drop out under the same circumstances.

The question now is not so much whether a plastic has a low or a high burning point, but rather how it burns. Most self-extinguishing plastics, because of their chemistry, will give off excessive quantities of black, sooty smoke. Other plastics, specifically certain acrylics, will cause next to no smoke and scarcely detectable fumes.

A number of fires of public concern within the last several years have shown that "smoke represents the greatest threat to occupants of a building on fire" (*The Fire Protection Handbook*, 12th Ed.). People have perished in many of these fires not from heat but from inhaling the fumes which simultaneously blocked vision completely. Firemen lose

their bearings under such situations, thus rendering fire fighting impossible.

As of this writing, building codes are being

FIG. 15-10. Street lighting globe fixture. Globe made of Butyrate in opal composition. Unusual impact resistance. (*Courtesy: Sterner Lighting Inc.*)

revised to cope more realistically with some of these phenomena. As a result, plastics, notably clear acrylics with very low smoke-producing tendency, are being approved for use in public areas, egresses, etc., where they were formerly either banned or allowed only

TABLE 15-4. Smoke Density of Various Materials Under Standard Conditions.

Material	Smoke Density (%)	Max. Smoke Production Rate(%/min.)
Red oak	2	1
Ponderosa pine	48	44
Acrylic—sample #1	2	4
Acrylic—sample #2	4	5
Acrylic—sample #3, self-extinguishing	97	114
Acrylic—sample #4, self-extinguishing	98	123
Polystyrene	100	296
Polyester, flame-resistant	199	151
Polyester, glass-fiber reinforced	89	124

in very limited extent. Recent publications by the National Fire Protection Association report the following results from closely watched laboratory smoke tests [*Quarterly of the N.F.P.A.*, Table 5 (January, 1964)].

The reader is advised to check with the most recent local building code regarding these matters, which, as noted, are now taking on aspects quite different from earlier concepts.

16

PERMANENT FIXTURES

J. A. BAUMANN

Union Carbide Corporation
Plastics Division
Bound Brook, New Jersey

The plastics applications discussed in this chapter are all technically suitable; but acceptance has been mixed. Plastic laminates, seating and hardware items have been commercially successful. Plastic molded drawers provide superb performance, but usage has been confined largely to the quality-conscious commercial and industrial areas.

HARDWARE

Plastics have been used in building hardware for over 35 years. Back in October, 1929, the *Bakelite Review*[1] carried a description of phenolic door knobs "for the better homes." In 1963, 5,350,000 pounds of plastics valued at $9,807,000 were used for hardware.

Recent guides to building products reveal many additional modern applications and new plastic materials [2-4]:

(1) Plastic tracks, slides, rollers, rails, edgings, bearings, etc., for sliding doors, drapes, windows, blinds and louvers.

(2) Handles, knobs, finger plates, parts of locksets and closers, glazing, thresholds, thermal breaks, trim, latches, rain baffles and fittings of all kinds for doors and windows.

(3) Towel rings, bars, holders, toilet floats, and other bath accessories.

(4) Louvers, ventilation registers, ventilators, and vent tubes for ventilation of stud spaces.

(5) Molded capping for hand rails. Sink hole mounts, sump pumps, numerous tool and appliance housings, liners, knobs and handles.

These items are made from a great variety of plastics of which the most prominent are nylon, acrylics, vinyls, phenolics, polystyrene and polyethylene. *Nylon* is characterized by unusual strength and stiffness, low coefficient of friction, good corrosion resistance, and a price competitive with many metals. It has appeared as latches, rollers, wheels, pulleys, bearings, and similar molded hardware which do not have to be lubricated and which provide ease, smoothness and silence of operation. It has been reported that after 1.2 million cycles—equivalent to at least 80 years of use—certain unlubricated nylon locksets operated even more smoothly than before.[5] Figure 16-1 illustrates a modern plastic lockset and knob. These features have found favor with consumers everywhere. *Polyethylene* has been used largely for its low price, extrudability, and low coefficient of friction to make such items as rain baffles and slide tracks for windows. *Phenolics* are found in molded electrial hardware, finger plates and knobs, where outstanding heat resistance, electrical insulation, rigidity and low cost are of most advantage. The *vinyls* are found both molded and extruded, rigid and flexible as glazing bead, door thresholds, thermal breaks, and interior (jalousie) trim. The *acrylics* are most noted for their brilliant clarity together with other properties which make them popular here and abroad[3] for

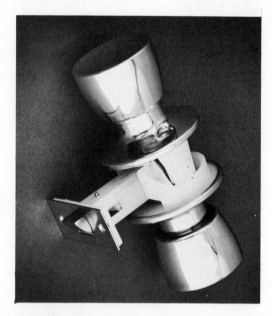

Fig. 16-1. Plastic lockset. (*Courtesy E. I. duPont de Nemours*)

such items as knobs, towel rings, railings, etc. Their attractiveness draws immediate approving attention.

Polystyrene is much used in appliance housings such as the sound shell of a waste disposer, bath accessories, and ventilation louvers and registers, where its low cost, moldability, and colorability give it the edge over other candidates. The sump pump mentioned above is manufactured of asbestos reinforced *polypropylene* with advantages claimed to be:[6] (1) better wear and corrosion resistance, (2) lighter weight, (3) good impact, (4) no welding required, (5) molded-in screw holes, and (6) true dimensional stability for easy, fast assembly.

DECORATIVE LAMINATES

There are three types of laminates important in building. Oldest, best known and most used are the high-pressure decorative laminates based on *phenolic*-impregnated kraft paper with *melamine*-impregnated decorative surface sheets. The others are colored, printed and/or embossed *vinyl* cloth laminates used for wall coverings and upholstery fabrics, and *polyester* films, sometimes reverse printed but often clear, laminated to wood, hardboard and other surfaces as durable prefinishes.

The decorative, high-pressure thermosetting laminates are seen on counter tops everywhere today in homes, restaurants, stores, offices, schools, hospitals, etc. (Figure 16-2). With their fine colors and patterns, durability and ease of cleaning, they have found extensive use as well in desk and table tops, cabinet fronts, convector covers, door and wall surfaces, window stools, and bath and shower enclosures (Figure 16-3). Exterior applications have been reported, among them 5000 square feet of facing panels on three buildings of the Manor Park School, Newcastle-on-Tyne.[9] Decorative effects include a rainbow of colors, many patterns including all the fine wood grains, marbles, textured finishes, checks, linens, and basket weaves.

Four types of high-pressure laminates are recognized:[7,8]

(1) General purpose,
(2) Vertical surface,
(3) Post-forming,
(4) Hardboard core.

The general purpose is, as the name implies, the common choice in the above applications. Vertical surface-type laminate is designed specifically for vertical applications where good appearance, durability, resistance to stains and resistance to heat from ordinary sources are required. Thinner ($\frac{1}{36}$ inch), and hence lower-cost, laminates are used. The post-forming laminates are used where other than flat shapes are desired. A major use of the laminate or hardboard core is one-piece shower and bath enclosures.

To make these laminates, the manufacturer lays up several layers of phenolic-impregnated paper over which are layed a melamine-impregnated, printed, fine paper, and on top of that a melamine-impregnated translucent sheet. Melamine is used in the surface layers because of its light color. The

FIG. 16-2. Decorative laminates in an office. (*Courtesy Union Carbide Corp.*)

layers are pressed for approximately 1 hour at 1500 psi and 300°F between mirror-polished stainless or chrome-plated sheets which give fine glossy surfaces (Figures 16-4 and 16-5). The sheets may then be buffed to

FIG. 16-3. Plastic laminate wall panels. (*Courtesy Union Carbide Corp.*)

FIG. 16-4. Laminating press. (*Courtesy Union Carbide Corp.*)

give variations in luster, and the underside can be sanded for better adhesion. Similar undecorated laminates are made with cotton, or synthetic fabrics, and asbestos for industrial, particularly electrical, applications.

Vinyl laminates are made by a calendering and embossing or laminating process in

Fig. 16-5. Laminates being pressed. (*Courtesy Union Carbide Corp.*)

which the plasticized vinyl is bonded to an inexpensive cloth backing. They have been used in commercial establishments and homes as fine, durable wall coverings. Recognition of their admirable stain resistance, ease of maintenance, and water resistance is generating increasing use in residential construction for kitchen and bath wall coverings. Vinyl laminates are proposed for exterior use on certain wall systems, sidings, doors, and similar uses;[10] they are also employed as protection for plasterboard used as base for tile around baths and showers.

Low-pressure laminates have usually been based on polyester resins. In a recently introduced thermoplastic system, film is applied as a protective stain- and wear-resistant surface for fine wood paneling. Colored and/or printed film is used on

cheaper backing for other panels.[11] Other low-pressure laminates use paper sheets to give more flexible, formable structures suitable for home craftsmen and applicable where radii as small as ¾ inch are required.[12]

History

Laminates were some of the first applications of the phenolic resins developed by Dr. L. H. Baekeland near the turn of the century. Industrial and electrical laminates came first, but by 1929, decorative laminates had entered the building industry as window sills in Pullman coaches and houses, deal plates in the Chase National Bank, tops for desks, tables, and dressers.[13] Wood finishes and grains, marble effects, and colors were available. Resistance to alcohol and to lighted cigars and cigarettes were noted.

Decorative laminates provided a $150,000,000 business in 1963, one that grew at the rate of 14 percent per year from 1961 to 1963. The U.S. Department of Commerce's "Current Industrial Reports, Series M 30D" provide the following data on production and dollar value of high- and low-pressure decorative laminates:[14]

High-pressure Thermosetting Decorative Sheets	1961	1962	1963
Value, dollars	106,643,000	121,474,000	138,164,000
Production, lb	—	75,210,000	89,026,000
Low-pressure Thermosetting Sheets			
Value, dollars	12,152,900	9,322,000	9,890,000
Production, lb	—	3,977,000	5,195,000

The value of shipments of high-pressure laminated sheets was only $90,358,000 in 1958; it leveled off between $116,000,000–$118,000,000 in 1959 to 1961, and then reached $135,546,000 in 1962.[15] The phenolic resin used in these applications amounted to 97,708,000 pounds in 1962 and 105,423,000 pounds in 1963.[16]

While sales in building and construction,

tend to follow the general business trend these high-pressure laminates are finding increasing use within that market. A factor in this expansion of laminate markets has been the extreme price stability of phenolic resins, their price having risen little if any over the past decade while prices of many other products have doubled.

Characteristics

Resistance to wear, heat, and stain are among the most advantageous properties of the high-pressure laminates. Even so, the following precautions will serve to prolong their useful and aesthetic life:

(1) Use pads under hot utensils.

(2) Keep surfaces dry beneath pots.

(3) Use a cutting board.

(4) Wipe up strong solutions.

(5) Do not pound (softer substrate may indent, cracking the laminate).

(6) Wax the surface.

(7) Wash with soap and water.

The surfaces are unaffected by such materials as gasoline, water, alcohol, amyl acetate, acetone, carbon tetrachloride, moth and fly sprays, soaps and detergents, trisodium phosphate ("Oakite"), olive oil, ammonia and citric acid solutions, coffee, mustard, wax crayons, urine, and shoe polish. Other liquids such as tea, beet juice, vinegar, bluing, dyes, washable inks, iodine, mercurochrome, and phenol-solutions ("Lysol") may cause stains which can easily be removed with light abrasive powders. It is recommended that certain other materials not be allowed to remain in contact with decorative-material:[8] bleaches (chlorox, peroxide), strong acids, lye solution, sodium bisulfate ("Sani Flush"), potassium permanganate, berry juices (grape, raspberry, etc.), silver nitrate, gentian violet, and silver proteins (argyrol).

Nema standards[7] specify test methods and performance for decorative laminates as well as the wide range of electrical laminates. These tests include: resistance of surface to wear, boiling water, high temperature, cigarette burns and stains; color fastness; immersion in boiling water; dimensional change; flexural strength; modulus of elasticity and deflection at rupture and appearance.

Installation

The high-pressure laminates are usually applied by fabricators, wood-working shops or contractors on the job. They can be sawed, sheared, routed, and filed. They may be hot veneered at not more than 15 psi and 180°F, or cold veneered with room-temperature cure thermosetting glues or contact adhesives. Balanced construction, using laminate on both sides of a core, is recommended to avoid warping. One side may be less expensive nondecorative sheet. The usual core materials are particle board, plywood, and hardboard. Sheet is available in a wide variety of standard widths and lengths, e.g., 24, 30, 48, and 60 inches wide. Common lengths are 60, 72, 84, 96, 120, and 144 inches. Thicknesses to ¼ inch are available, but generally ⅟₁₆-inch general-purpose grade is used for horizontal and vertical application together with .020-inch backing sheet. Vertical surfaces may be faced with ⅟₃₂-inch sheet, and post-forming sheet is usually .050-inch stock.

SEATING

A well-established and growing application for both thermoplastic and thermosetting materials is seating, particularly high-performance seating, where moldability and colorability of plastics make them especially suitable to modern, colorful, body-cupping designs.

Applications

Plastics have found enthusiastic acceptance for seating where rough usage is commonplace. Perhaps foremost has been the highly satisfactory use in schools and other institutions, not only for classroom furniture but also for stacking chairs for auditoriums, cafeterias, libraries, and general-purpose rooms. Short-range transportation facilities, railroads and subways, have used—and are reordering—plastic seating. In bowling alleys, recently built or modernized, plastic settees are used almost exclusively (Figure 16-6). Recently such seating has been used outdoors in a number of stadiums, music bowls, and coliseums. High-style chairs have been designed in plastic for several years; today one can buy desk chairs, arm chairs,

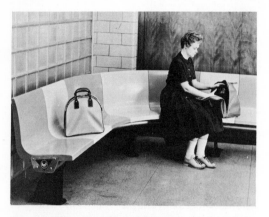

FIG. 16-6. Reinforced-plastic bowling settee. (*Courtesy Cincinnati Milling Machine Co., Cimastra Div.*)

and bar stools of plastics from many local stores and through the mail-order catalogs.

Properties

Favorable over-all economics and superior performance have combined to make plastic

FIG. 16-7. Smooth-surface FRP withstands high impact with no cracking or delamination. (*Courtesy Cincinnati Milling Machine Co., Cimastra Div.*)

seating the choice of architects, school boards, institutional administrators, purchasing agents and owners. The following are important factors in the selection of plastics.

Durability. School service is especially severe. Resistance to cuts, scratches, and scraping feet is imperative. A restless child can flex a seat more than 1000 times in just one class period. Outside seating will be walked on, jumped on, rained on and snowed on as well as sat on (Figure 16-7).

Resistance to Soiling. Ink, dirt and spilled foods do not permanently stain.

Maintenance. Plastic seating cleans easily with detergent and water, and through colors minimize the effect of scratches.

Light Weight. This is vital for stacking chairs which custodians must move, set up, and rearrange frequently.

Comfort. Forming methods make it possible to design shape and texture for maximum comfort. Textured surfaces provide friction and air circulation on materials

FIG. 16-8. Blow-molded polyethylene seating. (*Courtesy American Seating*)

which would otherwise be slippery and sweaty. Slight flexibility of the plastics is easier on the human frame than hard rigid wood seats.

Aesthetic Appeal. Simple, one-piece, clean construction and good material properties permit light, airy, modern appearance. Excellent colorability makes possible a wide range of colors.

Materials and Processes

Both thermosets and the thermoplastics provide the advantages listed above. The thermoplastics most used are high-density polyethylene, polypropylene, ABS, impact styrene, and rigid vinyls. Depending on the design, the estimated market, and the manufacturer's preference, these may be shaped into seating by injection molding, blow molding, or thermoforming (Figures 16-8 and 16-9). Some vinyl-coated steel and aluminum

Fig. 16-9. Blow-molded polyethylene school seating. (*Courtesy American Seating*)

seating may be covered by laminating or by fluidized bed coating processes.

The most important thermoset construction is glass fiber-reinforced polyester (Figure 16-6). In some simple, low-volume cases, hand layup has been used, but the majority of high-quality seating is made by match metal molding of polyester-impregnated glass mat preforms. High-pressure decorative laminates have been used for decades in furniture applications and are still widely used, but this material is best adapted to flat or simply curved surfaces rather than to the compound curved shapes of modern seating.

Plastic foams are used extensively for cushioning. Figure 16-10 shows a sample of

molded vinyl foam. Urethane foams are also used extensively in cushioning and are probably the major factor in this market today.

Markets

Estimated markets for high-performance seating in institutions and schools were reported in 1962 to be:[17]

Institutional Seating Market

Year	Number of chairs
1958	18,419,000
1965	19,882,000
1970	19,780,000

School Classrooms

1958	3,920,000
1965	4,709,000
1970	4,380,000

School: Other (Auditoriums, Cafeterias, Study Halls, Libraries, Offices)

1958	4,612,000
1965	5,627,000
1970	5,130,000

Use of plastic seating in outdoor stadiums has focused attention on the approximately 6½ million seats in 141 stadiums in the

Fig. 16-10. Molded vinyl foam. (*Courtesy Union Carbide Corp.*)

United States with capacities greater than 20,000 (Figure 16-11). Recently just two such installations have required 96,000 plastic seats. In September, 1964 the Los Angeles

FIG. 16-11. Seating at Buffalo Stadium, West Texas State College. (*Courtesy American Desk Manufacturing Co.*)

Coliseum had ordered 46,000 blow-molded high-density polyethylene seats as replacements for wooden benches. The Memphis Municipal Stadium will have injection-molded high-density polyethylene chairs plus many reinforced-plastic benches.[18] The costs of various stadium seats are:[18]

Injection-molded polyethylene	$15–18
Blow-molded polyethylene	$15
Reinforced plastics	$18
Wood	$8–10

Residential seating can be purchased at typical retail prices from $9.95 (desk chairs) to $18.50 (arm chairs).

PLASTIC DRAWERS

The total number of drawers made and sold each year in the United States is enormous, and the trends in economics and availability of wood drawers are such that plastic drawers with their many practical and aesthetic advantages will eventually make major advances in this market.

The principal plastic drawers which have been manufactured are molded phenolic, and injection-molded and thermoformed polystyrene. Considerable work has been done also on molded reinforced polyesters, wood particle board, polypropylene, and molded plywood. Economics and distribution have been the major problems encountered. While plastics have so far not succeeded in making a major penetration into the furniture drawer market, some are available in related form as tote boxes and as clear display boxes. A typical use allied to drawers is tote boxes to store materials in school sewing and home economic classes; retail stores are using clear molded styrene boxes for lingerie, shoes, dry goods and other items.

There are several advantages to plastic drawers:

(1) One-piece construction with no joints to come apart,

(2) Dimensional stability—drawers will not warp and stick with humidity changes,

(3) Smooth surfaces which do not snag hosiery and fine lingerie,

(4) Surfaces which can be cleaned with a damp sponge and which have no sharp corners to collect dirt,

(5) Molded-in colors which provide clean attractive interiors and exteriors,

(6) Excellent uniformity, providing interchangeable drawers with no fitting or planing.

In addition, drawer divider slots can be molded in, provision can be made for the separate attachment of wood fronts, very sturdy light-weight drawers can be made, and costs can be brought within the range of high-quality wood equivalents.

The furniture industry predicts at least four other long-range and continuous trends which signal an eventual switch from wood:

(1) Wood is gradually disappearing at the current rate of use.

(2) Quality of available wood is decreasing.

(3) Cost of wood is increasing.

(4) Labor cost of drawer fabrication is increasing.

History

One of the first plastic drawers was a molded-phenolic item produced in 1954 (Figures 16-12 and 16-13). These were fine drawers ideally suited for certain specialty drawer applications but too costly for the mass furniture market. They were followed about a gle cavity compression mold. Consequently, only three modular sizes were then available. Phenolic drawers are available today, advertised for hotel and motel furniture.

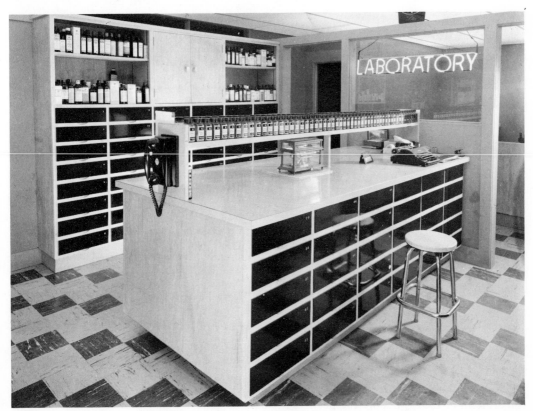

FIG. 16-12. Molded phenolic drawers in laboratory bench with decorative laminate top. (*Courtesy Union Carbide Corp.*)

year later by injection-molded, high-impact polystyrene drawers. In 1956–1957 a vacuum-formed polystyrene drawer was manufactured. These are no longer available. Another high-impact styrene drawer, sold about the same time, was featured by a prominent mail-order retail distributor. Some 200,000 drawers were utilized, but the line was apparently dropped about 1959

While possessed of many advantages, *phenolic* drawers were restricted to dark colors unless painted; the phenolics are inherently brittle; even careful molding at times produced warped drawers, and the drawers could not be trimmed to fit irregular frames. The raw material cost was reported to be twice that of styrene drawers.[19] Tooling in 1957 cost approximately $15,000 per sin-

Injection-molded styrene drawers were somewhat cheaper, but addition of separate fronts added to over all costs. Tooling costs were comparable to the above, but the molding cycle was faster. Problems with these drawers were: size limitations, sound, thin appearance, brittleness and breakage especially in cold weather.

Drawers thermoformed from *sheet styrene* were still lower in price. The tooling cost for aluminum production molds was about ⅛ that of comparable compression and injection molds, and experimental molds for market testing of drawers could be made of epoxy for roughly $500. Drawers were molded of impact styrene sheet, .014 inch thick, using a female mold with plug assist.[19] They are no longer on the market.

Market

The size of this market is difficult to ascertain, but it is probably 75 to 100 million drawers per year, of which kitchen drawers

FIG. 16-13. Plastic drawers for built-in furniture. (*Courtesy Union Carbide Corp.*)

constitute from 10 to 20 per cent. In 1957 kitchen drawers were estimated at 10,000,000; in 1962, 15,000,000. Consumption of plastics for drawers in 1957, possibly the peak year, was estimated to be 1,500,000 pounds.

There is practically no standardization of sizes, each drawer designer setting his own size. This size variation is easily accommodated in wood but not in molded plastic due to mold costs. One manufacturer has hazarded a guess that some 80 per cent of the requirements could be satisfied by 15-inch-deep drawers in roughly 15 widths and 11 heights, a total of 165 different drawers.

At the present time, the major materials for molded drawers are wood particles and polypropylene.

REFERENCES

Hardware

1. *Bakelite Review*, 3 (October 1929).
2. 1963 Building and Remodeling Product Guide, Hudson Publishing Co., Los Altos, California, December, 1962.
3. Imperial Chemical Industries Ltd., Plastics Division, "Plastics in Building," Welwyn Garden City, Hertfordshire, England.
4. *Brit. Plastics*, **34**, 630–8 (December 1961).
5. *Mod. Plastics*, **38**, 110 (January 1961).
6. *Mod. Plastics*, **39**, 98 (March 1962).

Laminates

7. NEMA Standards Publication No. LD1–1964, National Electrical Manufacturers Association, N. Y.
8. *Formica Corporation Bulletin SP 601–63*, Cincinnati, Ohio.
9. Imperial Chemical Industries Ltd., "Plastics in Building," London, 1963.
10. *Building Products*, 39 (January, 1963) (Columbus Coated Fabrics Co., Columbus, Ohio).
11. "What's New in Plastic Laminates," *Building Products* (April 1963).
12. Latham, M. E., "Low Pressure Decorative Laminate," Report presented at 15th Annual Meeting of Reinforced Plastics Division, SPI, Chicago, Ill.
13. *Bakelite Review* (July and October 1929).
14. U. S. Department of Commerce, Current Industrial Reports, Series M 30D (62)—1, January 15, 1964; Series M 30D (63)—1; November, 1964.
15. U. S. Bureau of the Census, Annual Survey of Manufacturers 1962, Value of Shipments of Selected Classes of Products M 62 (45)—2 (revised), Washington, D. C., 1964.
16. *Mod. Plastics*, **42**, 160, 161, 164 (October 1964).

Seating

17. *Mod. Plastics*, **39**, 87–9, 176, 178 (August 1962).
18. *Mod. Plastics*, **42**, 110–113, 189 (September 1964).

Drawers

19. *Mod. Plastics*, **35**, 114–119 (October 1957).

17 ARCHITECTURAL AND MAINTENANCE COATINGS

ANTHONY ERRICO

Paint and Varnish Production (Magazine)
New York, N. Y.

Technological progress has made the word "paint" obsolete. Today's paints are so advanced that they are essentially chemical coatings. The unique properties of modern coatings have vastly expanded their use in many new applications such as protecting against chemical fumes, acids and alkalies; preserving wood, metal, and masonry; providing a clean and sanitary environment; effecting good visibility and safety; promoting cooling, and even resisting the immense heat and abrasion encountered in space flights.

Moreover, there are paints available today that are quick drying, self-cleaning, possess little or no odor, can be washed and scrubbed, produce unusual decorative effects, and even dry in the presence of moisture.

The compounding and manufacturing of paints is no longer an art, but a true science. In the last decade, the paint industry has expended considerable money and effort to upgrade paint quality to the degree that the appearance, durability, and protective properties of present-day paints can truly be described as a chemical achievement.

The coatings industry continues to provide the products needed to decorate and protect a large proportion of all construction today. It is also developing new products to meet the requirements resulting from changes in construction practices.

PAINT PERFORMANCE AND CONSTRUCTION PRACTICES

The performance of paint on the exterior of a house is closely linked with the construction practices used in erecting the dwelling. It is essential that particular attention should be given to the control of condensation from inside the house as well as the control of moisture from the ground and other sources.

Today the average house has less space than those constructed some 35 years ago. Ceilings are lower and basements are often omitted. As a result, the heating plant, laundry equipment, and other utilities must be installed on the first floor. Also, in the interest of achieving economies in labor and materials, many new homes do not provide the overhang at the eaves and gable ends which formerly protected the outside walls.

Each day, several gallons of water vapor are added to the air from such daily activities as bathing and cooking and the extensive use of home appliances (clothes washers, dishwashers, dryers, etc.). Because of the tighter and more compact construction of the modern home, air and moisture become entrapped in the living area of the house.

Condensation is often responsible for damaging exterior paint. Condensed water, in the form of free water or ice, often collects behind the siding of a building. This excess

339

moisture may absorb extractives from the wood and result in stains as it runs out over the surface of the siding. If an excessive amount of moisture reaches the painted sur-

TABLE 17-1. Labor Requirements for Interior and Exterior Building Painting*

Preparation	
Siding (sand and putty)	200 sq ft/man-hr
Trim (sand and putty)	100 lin ft/man-hr
Remove varnish	30 sq ft/man-hr
*Painting***	
Cement block (waterproof)	175 sq ft/man-hr
Corrugated siding	240 sq ft/man-hr
Stucco (oil paint)	150 sq ft/man-hr
Plaster (flat finish)	175 sq ft/man-hr
Plaster (enamel finish)	175 sq ft/man-hr
Wood trim	150 lin ft/man-hr
Doors	150 sq ft/man-hr

*Based on "Labor Factors: Painting" by William G. Clark, Chemical Engineering **66**, No. 25 (Dec. 14, 1959).
**Based on first coat; for additional coats, add 25–30% to productivity.

face, a loss of paint adhesion and formation of blisters can occur under the paint film. Rainwater, entering the wall at siding laps through capillary action, also may increase moisture in the wood beneath the coating of paint.

For these reasons, adequate protection of exterior walls should be provided against moisture arising within the home and from outside sources. There are a number of effective methods for preventing condensation. The booklet, "Improved Paint Performance through Sound Construction Practices,"* describes control measures and construction features which curb moisture vapor and assure proper paint performance.

EXTERIOR HOUSE PAINTS

Drying Oil Base

Exterior house paint is the most important of the products known as trade sales paints, i.e., sales over the counter. Included also in

* This publication was prepared with the combined efforts of the National Lumber Manufacturers Association and the National Paint, Varnish and Lacquer Association. Copies may be obtained by writing to the National Lumber Manufacturers Association, Technical Service Div., 1619 Massachusetts Ave., N. W., Washington, D. C., 20036.

this group are primers, trim and trellis paints, porch floor and deck paints and enamels, and various clear finishes.

Over the past twenty-five years, considerable improvement has been made in the durability of exterior house paints. The early ready-mixed products were prone to staining, dirt collection, cracking, flaking, and failure due to moisture. Modern technology and improved raw materials not only have eliminated the above deficiencies but have produced new properties which enhance the life of the paint itself.

For many years, linseed oil-based paints dominated the exterior wood market. More recently, latex paints have moved into this area with promising results. Indications are that they will become an important factor in this market in the 1970's.

In the formulation of quality exterior oil paints, a refined grade of linseed oil is used, particularly for white products. For tinted and dark-colored paints, raw linseed oil is generally used.

The second most common vehicle component of a house paint is bodied linseed oil. The main advantages of bodied linseed oil are control of consistency, improved flow, and greater durability. Depending on the type and amount of bodied linseed oil used, it is possible to obtain the following improved film properties: water resistance, dirt collection, mildew resistance, better gloss and appearance, and resistance to checking and cracking.

Linseed oil may be replaced by other types of drying or semi-drying oils in house paint formulations; e.g., soybean oil, fish oil, safflower oil and dehydrated castor oil. Economies plus properties desired determine whether a substitution is advantageous.

Soybean oil must be modified chemically to be of value in house paints. Untreated soybean oil results in films which dry too slowly and tend to collect dirt and mildew. Also, untreated soybean oil causes film failure by "cissing," a combination of checking and crawling.

Dehydrated castor oil provides exterior finishes with superior elasticity and a high degree of water resistance.

One very important ingredient of house paints is small amounts of a fortifying resin, usually an alkyd vehicle. The main purpose of the fortifying resin is to improve film properties and reduce cracking and checking, chalking pigment such as rutile titanium dioxide, which is chalk-resistant. However, the use of a pigment leads to a serious problem of dirt collection and mildew formation. This can be alleviated by using anatase titanium

TABLE 17-2. Exterior Coatings*

Type	Production (thousands of gallons)	Value (thousands of dollars)
Oil and alkyd vehicle exterior house paint	50,022	176,460
Enamels other than alkyd	16,132	62,629
Primers	8,686	27,845
Barn and roof paints	4,398	10,178
Bituminous paints	6,297	5,027
Metallic paints	6,657	19,796
Clear varnishes	6,073	15,669
Stain, shingle, and shake	3,174	8,460
Cement paints (water-thinned)	29,380	4,763
Water-thinned, latex emulsions, alkyd emulsions, epoxy emulsions, etc.	4,338	13,186

*Production and Shipments of Paints, Varnishes, Lacquers, and Allied Products by all Manufacturing Establishments (1958).
Source: U. S. Dept. of Commerce, Bureau of Census, Industry Div., Washington, D.C., 20233.

particularly in formations which do not contain zinc oxide.

Pigmentation

The above discussion dealt with the vehicle or binder component of house paints. Of equal importance is the pigment component, which may be of three types: prime pigments, modifying pigments, and extenders.

The prime pigment is usually titanium dioxide, which has high power. The rutile grade is resistant to chalking; the anatase grade gives control of dirt collection and mildew through its chalking behavior.

Modifying pigments—lead, leaded zinc, oxide—improve water resistance, control mildew, improve adhesion, and stop cracking and checking.

Extenders in house paint pigmentation are incorporated primarily to impart improved film properties at lower cost. Among the most widely used extenders are magnesium silicate, calcium sulfate, and calcium carbonate.

Tint Base Pigments. The important problem encountered in tinted or light color house paints is one of retaining the original color. This problem can be solved by using a non-dioxide, which chalks; but in tinted products, the chalking of anatase leads to very poor tint retention. Therefore, in any tinted house paint formulation, a compromise must be reached between the tint-retentive properties of the chalk-resistant rutile and the desirable chalking properties of the anatase which prevents dirt collection and mildew.

Among the most popular tinting pigments are earth colors such as iron oxides, umbers, and siennas. Also used are chrome green, hydrated chromium oxide, phthalocyanine green, chrome yellow, phthalocyanine blue, ultramarine blue, iron blue, and carbon black.

Dark House Paints. Dark colored house paints, as opposed to tinted house paint, are those paints sold in the dark shades of red, green, black, or brown. Dark paints ordinarily do not contain titanium dioxide but rely on modifying pigments such as zinc oxide which inhibits mildew formation and dirt collection. Extender pigments such as magnesium silicate or calcium carbonate are necessary to obtain proper body.

The most popular pigments used are chrome greens, chromium oxides, iron oxides, umbers, siennas, and black pigments.

Alkyd Base

As already mentioned, linseed oil is the major vehicle for house paints. In the interest of obtaining more durable paints, considerable research was directed toward the use of alkyd resins in house paint formulations. As a result, acceptable alkyd house paints were developed which had excellent durability on wood but had poor brushability properties. A few years ago, the brushability problem was solved and alkyd paints are now accepted for exterior applications because of their excellent film properties, especially in moisture resistance. The problem of moisture in the wood, and its effect on paint peeling is one of the most common of paint failures. Today, this problem is more serious than it was thirty years ago because houses built then were not as tightly constructed, and insulation in the walls and attics was hardly used. Fortener[1] makes this interesting observation.

"In more recent years many changes in the living habits of the average American have all contributed to this moisture problem. Our houses are constructed more snugly, with storm windows so that they are more tightly sealed, and with insulation in the walls and attics. All are beneficial moves as far as savings on fuel bills are concerned, but they all drastically affect the house paint problem. More frequent baths, use of showers rather than tubs, more bathrooms per home, more frequent use of the family washer, clothes dryers, and the like, all contribute to the problem of pouring literally tons of water into the interior of the house.

"With the tighter construction of today's homes, much of the water vapor, from the various sources mentioned above, cannot escape, but condenses on the cold exterior walls, settles in the rock wool insulation or the wood siding or in both. When the wood siding becomes wet many house paints tend to lose their adhesion to the wood. In some cases, the warming action of the winter sun on the exterior surface tends to volatilize some of this water causing blisters to pop out on the paint film. At other times, the film will tend to crack along the grain lines of the wood substrate after which the typical moisture curl begins to appear."

According to Fortener, a correctly formulated alkyd house paint has these advantages: easy application, good flow, requires no special primers, good blister resistance, and good stain resistance.

Water-thinned Paints

After many years of extensive research and testing, latex paints for exterior wood were introduced to the consumer in the spring of 1961. Consumer reaction to this new concept in house paints has been most favorable because of the remarkable performance qualities of these paints plus their easy application and cleanup features. Claimed advantages of these water emulsion paints include quick drying; high resistance to fading, yellowing, cracking, blistering and peeling; and increased durability over conventional oil paints.

However, producers of such paints insist that application instructions must be closely followed in order for these latex paints to perform successfully on outside wood. Most instructions recommend careful surface preparation followed by an oleoresinous primer. However, an all-latex system—primer and topcoat—is most desirable. Such systems are currently being evaluated in exposure testing programs.

Latex house paints are by no means perfect. They do have some deficiencies, mainly poor adhesion to badly chalked surfaces, staining over redwood and cedar, and grain cracking along the line of wood. However, their good properties such as tint retention, cleanliness, and high durability overshadow these shortcomings which can be corrected by proper surface preparation and priming.

Water-thinned paint systems include latex emulsions (polyvinyl acetate and acrylic) and the water-based linseed oil products (emulsified and water soluble).

Latex Emulsions. Before going into the various types of latex emulsion used in exterior application, a brief discussion of the basic concepts concerning latex systems is in order.

An emulsion paint is quite different from an oil-solvent paint in constitution and film formation. In the oil-solvent paint, the pigment is wetted by and dispersed in the vehicle, resulting in a continuous matrix in which the pigment particles are uniformly distributed. In a pigment emulsion paint, the pigment and binder particles are independently suspended in water, and complete wetting and dispersion of the pigment in the binder does not develop in the film. Actually, latices form a film by coagulation of discrete particles. The film has been described as a closely-packed mass of spherical particles, each individual particle more or less discrete.

Acrylic Latex. According to Allyn,[2] acrylic latex paints have many advantages when used for exterior wood:

(1) Reduced Blistering. Properly formulated acrylic emulsion paint films have relatively low rates of swelling when immersed in water. Work by F. L. Browne of the Forest Products Laboratory has demonstrated that paint systems with relatively low swelling rates in water have the best chance of resisting blistering when used on wood surfaces. It is necessary, of course, to use a blister-resistant primer in order to get a highly blister-resistant paint system.

(2) Good Resistance to Cracking and Checking. Both paint films and wood, when subjected to changes in temperature or moisture, undergo changes in their dimensions. Changes in dimensions of acrylic paint films come somewhat closer to those of wood than many other types of films particuarly linseed oil films containing zinc oxide. The polymer in acrylic emulsion paints forms tough, flexible films which retain the major portion of their flexibility and elongation on aging. The acrylic paints also have exceptionally good adhesion to previously painted surfaces. This property has been confirmed in a great many commercial applications.

(3) Outstanding Resistance to Weathering and to Degradation by Ultraviolet Light. While there is some reduction in elongation and an increase in tensile strength, the acrylic paints show excellent color retention and retain their whiteness or tinted appearance very well on aging.

(4) Application to Damp Surfaces. Since emulsion paints themselves are thinned with water, it is not necessary to wait for wet wood surfaces to dry out.

(5) Easy Application. There is a characteristic absence of brush drag which is typical of emulsion systems. However, this is also a disadvantage because there is often a tendency to apply too little paint.

(6) Easy Brush Cleanup. Brushes can be washed in water.

(7) Fast Drying Speed. If two coats of acrylic emulsion paint are to be applied, the second coat can be put on 30 minutes to an hour after the first coat. As a result, there is a considerable saving of time as one scaffold setting will take care of both coats. This quick drying also reduces the problem of bug and dirt collection, characteristic of oil drying paints.

Polyvinyl Acetate Latex. Many of the advantages cited for the acrylic type are also available in properly formulated polyvinyl acetate emulsion paints: non-yellowing of white paints, non-blistering, easy application, quick drying, good color retention, and resistance to ultraviolet degradation.

One problem with all latex systems is their lack of penetration on chalky surfaces. These paints have difficulty in wetting and absorbing the layer of loose chalk during application. Consequently, latex systems have trouble in obtaining good adhesion to the film under the chalk surface.

The need for a simple, easy-to-use, all-latex system for repainting overaged and chalking oil surfaces resulted in a technique[3] whereby 10 to 20 per cent of a drying oil (linseed) is stirred into the latex paint before use. However, this technique should not be attempted unless the manufacturer specifically makes this recommendation in his instructions on the label.

Staining is another problem with latex paints, particularly on bare cedar and redwood siding, shingles, and shakes. Staining is caused by the presence of water-soluble stains in the wood. The water-borne paint carries such stains through the surface, creating an unsightly appearance, particularly in white and light-colored paint jobs. One successful approach to this problem has been the application of a special primer, usually alkyd or oil type, specifically formulated to prevent staining after the application of the topcoat. A polyurethane water-thinned primer is now available for such jobs.

Water-thinned Linseed Oil Paint. These materials were introduced in 1961 as an answer to latex systems for the exterior wood market. Two types are available: (a) a water-soluble linseed oil and (b) an emulsified linseed. They are easy to apply and clean up, and are odor-free.

The water-soluble type is one-coat hiding, and has adhesion to chalky surfaces (no special primers needed), ability to resist mildew attack, excellent gloss leveling and flow properties, and good freeze-thaw stability. The *emulsified type* has good adhesion to chalky surfaces, good blister resistance, mildew resistance, and good flow and leveling.

Some of the drawbacks of these paints are longer drying time (overnight) and yellowing, an inherent disadvantage of all linseed oil systems. These paints are not recommended over bare wood, especially staining types such as cedar or redwood, in which case solvent, oil based primers are necessary.

INTERIOR FINISHES

Two types of wall construction are used in architectural practice today—walls having plaster surfaces and those made of various wallboards. Payne[4] points out that porosity, alkalinity, and moisture are two problems associated with finishing the above surfaces. Since porosity of plaster wall may vary considerably over a given area, differences in hiding and color may occur because of variations in absorption of the paint. However, this condition can be corrected by using a good sealer before applying the topcoat.

Sealers may consist of a coat of shellac or a quick drying hydrocarbon varnish or any polyvinyl acetate type paint.

Free lime in plaster is another source of trouble for paints, particularly with oil or resin types which readily saponify. This problem can be alleviated if architects specify the use of Type S lime, which is completely hydrated. It is slightly higher in cost and not as easily workable as Type N lime and, therefore, is not generally accepted by the construction industry.

The moisture problem is caused by painting the wall before the plaster is dry enough. Moisture in the wall not only accelerates the "burning" action of the lime, but also causes the paint to blister resulting in loss of adhesion. It should be pointed out that moisture is not a problem with latex emulsion paints unless the plaster is very "green."

Types of Interior Paints

Oil and Varnish Flats. These are generally low-cost paints and susceptible to lime burning and, therefore, should be used over a sealer.

Calcicoater Flats. These paints were developed originally to adhere to walls which had been painted with calcimine. Today, they are widely used as a one-coat finish on ceilings in low cost construction housing. They have good dry hiding. They are porous and difficult to clean, but this is no problem since

TABLE 17-3. Interior Coatings*

Type	Production (thousands of gallons	Value (thousands of dollars)
Flat wall (alkyd)	27,494	80,471
Gloss and semi-gloss (alkyd)	29,087	102,554
Primers	6,769	20,045
Multicolored finishes	2,312	7,515
Varnishes (natural resin)	2,601	7,260
Varnishes (synthetic)	5,840	17,179
Shellac varnish	3,367	7,862
Stains	1,989	5,499
Latex (acrylic, Water-thinned)	4,677	14,739
Latex (styrene-Butadiene, water-thinned)	32,990	104,448
Latex (vinyl, water-thinned)	12,023	36,063
Resin emulsions, (water-thinned)	1,170	3,668

*Production and Shipments of Paints, Varnishes, Lacquers, and Allied Products by All Manufacturing Establishments (1958).
Source: U.S. Dept. of Commerce, Bureau of Census Industry Div., Washington, D.C., 20233.

ceilings are not apt to require frequent removal of finger marks and other stains.

Odorless Alkyd Flats. These flat wall paints are formulated with heavy bodied alkyds cut in odorless mineral spirits. They are characterized by easy brushing, non-penetration which provides good results with one-coat application, low odor, and fairly good resistance to lime burning.

Copolymer Oil Flats. These paints are based on oils reacted with styrene or vinyltoluene to provide improved properties such as fast drying and better alkali resistance.

Alkyd Gel Flats. These are novel paints having a gel-like consistency which is so firm that the paint does not flow readily from the can when turned on its side. Sagging and settling problems are eliminated in these polyamide-modified alkyds.

Latex Emulsion. Among the most successful latex emulsion paints used for wall interiors are styrene-butadiene, polyvinyl acetate, and acrylic. These water-reducible paints have many advantages, particularly ease of application, good coverage, low odor, fast drying, nonflammable solvents, easy cleanup features, and good washability properties.

Gloss Finishes. These finishes are formulated with oleoresinous or alkyd vehicles. For dark colors, oleoresinous vehicles such as a phenolic type are satisfactory, since after-yellowing of these vehicles will have little or no effect on the dark shade. However, for whites and very light pastel shades, a soybean-modified alkyd type formulation shows very little after-yellowing.

For faster-drying (4 hours) interior enamels, a low oil modified (dehydrated castor oil, linseed, or soybean) alkyd vehicle gives good results.

Multicolor Finishes. A multicolor finish, produced in a single application is a coating having two or more separate colors.

Basically, multicolor finishes are a two phase system consisting of (a) a colored non-aqueous phase and (b) a clear-water phase. One type of multicolor finish is a suspension of nitrocellulose lacquer in water containing a stabilization agent such as methyl cellulose. The lacquer phase is dispersed in the form of droplets which are small enough to stay in suspension but large enough to be clearly visible. As many as three or four different colored lacquers may be dispersed in the same water phase without coalescing, but often only two colors are used. On drying, the color present in largest amount forms a background which is flecked with the other color.

The solvents in the lacquer phase should not be miscible with water. The viscosity of the lacquer phase affects the shape of the particles; high viscosity tends to produce elongated shaped, and low viscosity gives spherical shapes. The size of the particle is large if the agitation is mild, becoming smaller with vigorous agitation.

Multicolor finishes may also be formulated with styrene-butadiene, vinyl toluene-butadiene, or butyrate resins.

In order to obtain the multicolor effect, this finish must be applied by spraying because brushing or roller coating tends to coalesce the individual particles. Generally the spraying is done at a low pressure.

Multicolor finishes find many architectural outlets. One particular use is as a wall finish in public buildings, schools, hotels, motels, offices, etc., because multicolor coatings do not show soiling as do conventional types of flat wall paints. Moreover, these finishes can be easily cleaned, are very durable, and can stand a great deal of abuse. They can be used on both interior and exterior surfaces.

EXTERIOR MASONRY PAINTS

For best appearance and durability, masonry surfaces require painting to provide protection against weathering, particularly rain and frost. Poured concrete, cinder blocks, brick, stucco, asbestos siding, cement roofing tiles, etc., are standard masonry materials used in huge quantities for commercial and residential buildings.

Moisture has a very destructive effect on masonry surfaces. As Allyn[5] points out, most untreated masonry surfaces will absorb considerable quantities of water from rainfall and dew, and this eventually results in several types of deterioration.

Spalling occurs when moisture freezes in the masonry wall. Pressure exerted by the formed ice causes a gradual disintegration of the masonry surface.

Efflorescence is the deposition of crystallized soluble salts on the masonry surface because of moisture penetration. The moisture brings the soluble salts to the surface of the masonry. These salts, chiefly sodium, potassium, calcium, magnesium, and aluminum, usually give a white appearance. In some instances, salt crystallization below the surface may cause cracking and spalling.

Surface Preparation

Without proper surface preparation such paint failures as peeling and blistering may occur soon after painting. On new or unpainted masonry surfaces, it is necessary to remove dust and dirt which may have collected on the surface. Allyn[5] recommends that if a water-thinned paint is to be used, the surface can be washed down with clean water and painted while damp.

Newly poured concrete may have an oil surface from oil or wax type curing compounds. These materials should be removed by sandblasting before painting. For cinder block, special penetrating primers should be used before painting.

No special treatment is required for asbestos cement shingles, providing they are clean and the surface is sound. However, in some cases, newly installed shingles may have a glaze which could cause adhesion difficulties. For best results, asbestos cement shingles should be painted only after some weathering. If they are old, heavily eroded and very porous, washing with water is recommended. According to Allyn,[5] the application of a concrete hardener such as magnesium fluorosilicate solution will provide a suitable base for painting on badly eroded cement asbestos shingles.

Surface preparation is especially important on masonry which has been previously painted. If the old painted surface shows no sign of failure and is devoid of peeling or blistering, with only light chalking, repainting can be started. However, if the surface is showing extensive chalking, flaking, peeling, and blistering, the old coating should be removed by sandblasting. Such a treatment will also provide a surface which will impart good paint adhesion. For heavily chalky surfaces, special conditioners have been found useful in strengthening and binding the chalk to the masonry surface. Efflorescence can be removed by washing with a 5 per cent solution of hydrochloric acid (muriatic acid) followed by a thorough rinsing with clear water. If mildew is present, it may be removed by scrubbing the surface with a solution of bleach and trisodium phosphate.

Types of Paints

There are several types of paints specifically formulated for exterior masonry surfaces. All of these will give good performance and service, providing they are applied according to the manufacturer's recommendations. It is important to remember that one system will perform differently from another, depending on the surface conditions.

Cement Paints. The ingredients which make up cement paints consist of cement, lime and pigment. Allyn[5] recommends that these paints must be used on *bare* masonry or over *previous coats of similar cement paint*, since adhesion to other types of paints is generally poor.

Cement paints give good protection in one or two coats. The surface should be dampened before application, and slick spots in poured concrete should be etched with a strong solution of hydrochloric acid. Cement paints should not be applied before the masonry has been allowed to cure for at least a month, and painting is not recommended in freezing weather.

Solvent Coatings. Oil-based, alkyd, synthetic rubber, chlorinated, rubber, epoxy, and polyester comprise this group of masonry coatings.

Oil based paints have been successfully used on masonry surfaces for many years. Because of the porous nature of masonry surfaces, several coats may be necessary to give adequate-hiding and uniformity. These paints cannot be applied to damp surfaces. Highly alkaline masonry surfaces will have a deleterious effect on oil-based paints, and it is very important that new masonry be well dried before application of such paints.

Neutralization of free alkali can be easily accomplished by washing with a solution of zinc chloride in water and allowing to dry thoroughly before painting.

Alkyd paints give good durability and appearance on masonry surfaces. They are very similar to the oil types but dry faster and give harder films, and also have less penetration. They have a tendency to brush harder than the oil variety.

For the past fifteen years, synthetic and chlorinated rubber paints have been available for masonry. These paints are characterized by excellent penetration and good adhesion to chalky and new surfaces. Moreover, they boast good chemical, alkali, acid, and water resistance.

A more recent development has been epoxy coatings, which possess several outstanding properties that make them particularly adaptable for painting masonry surfaces. Such finishes have exceptional adhesion, flexibility, dimensional stability, abrasion resistance, tensile strength, durability, chemical resistance, and water-proofness.

A dramatic application of epoxy-based paints is in the rapidly growing cinder block construction field. Cinder blocks have long provided a low-cost approach[6] to the construction of commercial and industrial buildings where aesthetic appearance has not been of utmost importance. However, protection of these surfaces from weathering, moisture penetration, abrasion, and chemical attack is still very essential. Most gasoline stations are constructed from cinder blocks and faced with enameled tile.

It is now possible to protect cinder block walls with a one-coat application of an epoxy paint. In such applications, the paint is supplied in two packages, mixed on the job in 2-gallon quantities, and has a working life of 2 to 3 hours. The films dry hard in 18 to 24 hours depending on ambient temperatures. The paint may be applied by brush, spray, or roller coat. Painting is not recommended at temperatures below 50°F unless external heat can be applied.

Some types of epoxy paints show rather fast chalking on outdoor exposure. One answer to this problem is an air-dry epoxy-modified acrylic coating,[7] which is reported to combine the excellent adhesion, hardness and moisture resistance of epoxy resins with the weather resistance and gloss retention properties of acrylic resins. The system consists of (a) a modified epoxy primer coat, (b) a polyamide-epoxy intermediate coat, and (c) a topcoat of epoxy-acrylic.

Polyester coatings are doing an outstanding job in the masonry field, but trained applicators are necessary to insure best performance and appearance. According to Weinman,[8] these coatings work well on rough porous surfaces, completely covering voids, cracks, and mortar joints.

On nonporous masonry such as poured concrete, steel-trowled cement, and unglazed tile, adhesion is a problem. Depending on the nature of the masonry surface, a high or low-viscosity primer may be used. For cinder blocks or rough porous surfaces, a pigmented primer is applied by trowel and squeegee to fill the voids and level the surface of the substrates. The average coverage of the surfaces is 100 to 150 sq ft/gal. depending on the nature of the substrate. The surface requires a 3 to 4 hour curing period prior to applying the finish coats. Two finish coats are necessary and are applied 5 to 7 mils each with an interval of 6 hours between coats. These coatings may be applied by spray gun, roller, or brush. In spraying applications, special equipment and experienced spray operators are required for polyester coatings.

Air-drying urethane enamels have met the stringent requirements as a coating for masonry surfaces. Of particular interest has been the use of urethane enamels for swimming pools, since these coatings offer, in addition to high durability, good chemical-resistant and adhesion properties.

Latex Emulsion Paints. Latex emulsion paints are widely used on exterior masonry surfaces today. On the whole, styrene-butadiene, vinyl, and acrylic emulsion paints give excellent performance. They are easy to apply, dry quickly, may be applied on damp surfaces, and have good resistance to fresh stucco, concrete, and mortar. All three show good moisture vapor permeability, permitting entrapped moisture in the wall to escape slowly without blistering.

Silicone Repellents. The application of silicone water repellents to exterior masonry surface is very effective in reducing damage caused by frost. These clear solutions can be used on concrete, stucco, brick, cinder block, and stone. They are usually applied by low-pressure spraying or by flooding the surface. The solution penetrates into the masonry surface, often as much as ¼ inch, providing a highly water-repellent, non-wetting surface. This treatment produces no change in the surface appearance of masonry; in fact it helps to prevent darkening of the masonry by water and stops efflorescence and spalling.

PAINTING METAL

Estimates are that the annual cost of metal lost due to corrosion plus the cost of preventing corrosion runs some five billion dollars in the United States alone. One of the most effective means of preventing and controlling corrosion is through the use of protective coatings.

In the face of increasing costs, engineers and architects are vitally interested in holding maintenance painting to a minimum. This can be achieved only by carefully applying high-quality, properly designed paints to properly prepared metallic surfaces.

Surface Preparation

For maximum coating protection which will result in low maintenance cost, proper surface preparation is most essential. Several methods are employed; among them are flame cleaning, acid pickling, sandblasting, mechanical cleaning, and phosphatizing.[9]

Flame Cleaning. This method makes use of the high heat of an oxyacetylene flame passed over the steel surface. The temperature difference between the interior and the exterior of the steel helps to set up stresses which loosen the mill scale. The high temperatures also dry the steel surface, dehydrate the rust, and leave the steel slightly warm. These conditions promote faster drying and better wetting by the paint.

Acid Pickling. A hot solution of (5 to 10 per cent hydrochloric or sulfuric acid removes rust and mill scale. The object is then rinsed in hot water and then immersed into a 2 per cent phosphoric acid bath at 185°F for 3 to 4 minutes and allowed to dry and painted while still warm. This treatment gives excellent paint performance.

Sandblasting. Cleaning is accomplished by making use of sand or grit impinged on the surface by a stream of air or water. Water-soluble inhibitive compounds, usually amines, are sometimes included in wet sandblasting to provide temporary protection against corrosion while the metal is drying, prior to painting. Sandblasting surfaces give excellent base for metal priming.

Mechanical Cleaning. Most steel surfaces are cleaned by mechanical tools such as chipping hammers, scrapers, wire brushes, and grinding wheels. It is generally felt that with the exception of the grinding wheel, none of these tools is capable of totally removing all of the rust to provide a surface which is comparable to one achieved with sandblasting.

Phosphatizing. This method uses a metallic phosphate solution in combination with activating agents. Phosphatizing is a common surface treatment before finishing automobiles and appliances, and could be applied to pre-finishing building components.

Requirements

A surface coating controls corrosion primarily by serving as a barrier which prevents contact of the corrosive environment with the underlying surface. However, this is not as simple as it seems, according to Munger.[10] For a protective coating to be effective, it must meet several requirements. If it is to prevent contact by the corrosive environment, it must obviously be resistant to the environment. In other words, if it is to be exposed to a chemical solution or fumes, the coating must be inert to this atmosphere. If the coating is exposed primarily to weathering, it must resist the effect of oxygen, moisture, and sunlight.

A most essential requirement of a coating is that it must be highly adherent to the surface[10] to prevent blistering and other film failures.

Pigments

The pigment component of a metal protective paint has several important functions:

(1) Corrosion inhibitive properties.

(2) Good package stability in the can.

(3) Good film forming properties.

(4) Good chalking resistance and color retention.

(5) Controlled reactivity with the vehicle in the dried paint film.

(6) Low specific gravity.

Common anticorrosive pigments in metal protective coatings are zinc yellow, basic zinc chromate, basic lead chromate, red lead, zinc dust, basic lead silicochromate, and dibasic lead phosphite.

Zinc yellow is used in corrosion-resistant primers, especially for aluminum.

Basic zinc chromate is used in so-called wash primers (vinyl-butyral resin mixed with phosphoric acid) which are applied as a very thin film.

Red lead is the most widely used anticorrosive pigment that inhibits corrosion by producing an alkaline condition, by reacting with fatty acids to produce soaps which are water-repellent, and by having an oxidizing effect.[11]

Zinc dust is used principally in paints for galvanized surfaces and in zinc-rich coatings for protecting iron and steel.

Basic lead silicochromate is a white pigment that has very low solubility in water and produces chromate ions in solution. Because the chromate ions have both oxidizing and passivating actions, this pigment is reported to be quite effective in inhibiting corrosion.

Dibasic lead phosphite is a white pigment to possess very efficient anticorrosive properties.

Types of Metal-protective Paints

There are several types of metal-protective paints. The most widely used are the linseed oil type. Bodied linseed oil has improved drying, water resistance and brushability over raw linseed. One important feature of raw linseed oil rust-inhibitive paints is their ability to penetrate mill scale and crevices between metal surfaces. Also, they have the ability to displace moisture on metal surfaces, particularly when lead pigments are present. On the other hand, linseed oil paints dry slowly, harden, and become brittle on aging. They are sensitive to water and alkali.

Another important group are resinous paints which include phenolic-tung oil varnishes, long to medium oil alkyds, epoxy esters, vinyls, and polyamides. Alkyd paints are used extensively because of their combination of fast drying, excellent adhesion and durability. They are sensitive to moisture but have good flexibility in normal atmospheric exposure. Epoxy esters coatings have comparable properties as alkyds plus good water resistance. Vinyl-type primers have extreme toughness and resistance to water and chemicals.

Combination of epoxy and polyamide resins are used in fast-drying primers which have excellent toughness and adhesion. This type of coating is a two-package system.

Air-drying silicone-alkyd paints have shown considerable promise for protecting steel surfaces. They exhibit excellent adhesion to steel surfaces and various primers, have improved color and gloss retention, and markedly reduce corrosion.

A more recent development is the availability of an acrylic latex water emulsion paint designed for maintenance applications.[12] In addition to good film properties, these paints are reported to possess good corrosion resistance and gloss and tint retention plus easy application and cleanup properties. Other advantages of this latex paint are: no thinner losses, nonflammability, no irritation, very low odor, and rapid drying. Such coatings adhere well to most metallic surfaces and to a variety of other substrates such as "Transite," plywood, and galvanized steel.

Aluminum Paint

The biggest outlet for aluminum paints is in the protection of metal, particularly for iron and steel. Properly formulated aluminum paints provide a tough, protective coat of high durability and resistance to moisture.[13] Because of these properties, aluminum paint is being used extensively to protect the steel work of bridges. The vehicle is usually an alkyd resin.

Film thickness is an important factor in the durability and protective value of aluminum paint on metal. Tests have shown that optimum protection requires three coats, since the resistance to penetration by moisture increases directly with the thickness of the film. Generally, a good primer followed by two coats of aluminum paint does an adequate job.

Since aluminum paint spreads easily and smoothly, a minimum of brush work is necessary to obtain proper coverage. Excessive brushing will coalesce the aluminum particles, ruining the appearance and smoothness of the film. Best results are obtained when the finish strokes are made in the same direction. It is also essential that aluminum paint be kept well stirred to prevent settling.

Aluminum paint has found particular application in the protection of hot metal surfaces. Steel should first be thoroughly cleaned of all scale, rust, and loose paint, preferably by sandblasting. Silicone-aluminum paints are reported to give the best protection on hot surfaces, especially when exposed to weather, as in the case of steel stacks. On oil tanks, aluminum paint not only protects the steel tank from corrosion, but reduces evaporation losses by reflecting radiation.

Galvanized Steel

One of the problems associated with the painting of galvanized steel is the poor adhesion of the coating to the surface. Tests conducted by the *American Iron and Steel Institute* disclosed that zinc dust and cement-in-oil paints provide excellent results. Proprietary latex paints, both vinyl and acrylic, specifically intended for galvanized steel can also be used; one coat can do the job, but two coats are often better. Weathering of the substrate is desirable but not necessary to achieve good adhesion when the correct paint is used. The zinc dust paints are generally a drying oil or alkyd type. If underwater or other wet conditions are involved, a phenolic type is needed.

Portland cement-in-oil paints incorporate the cement as part of the pigment. Their

formulations vary, but the composition usually consists of 60 per cent pigment and 40 per cent vehicle.

Painting Aluminum

Aluminum is being used more extensively in home construction today. It is the easiest of all metals to paint. This is fortunate because exposure to the elements soon dulls the original brightness of aluminum and often creates a mottled appearance. In coastal and industrial atmospheres, aluminum will often pit badly.

Aluminum is generally given a protective coating of oil in the factory to protect it against damage during shipment or erection. Unless the metal has weathered, this must be removed by washing with a phosphoric acid compound.

The first step in painting is to apply an exterior metal primer. Zinc chromate is recommended, particularly where there are corrosive conditions. When the prime coat has dried hard, one or two coats of the finish paint can then be put on with a brush, roller, or spray.

Any quality exterior enamel, e.g., an alkyd, will give good results over properyl primed aluminum. Two coats will give best resistance to moisture and corrosion. Exterior aluminum paint can also be used.

If it is desired to retain the shiny look of the new metal, use a clear, non-yellowing acrylic lacquer or cellulose acetate butyrate lacquer omitting the primer.

When painting aluminum which has been exposed for some time, be sure to brush away any loose dirt or oxide. To get rid of oil or grease, use a detergent solution or a paint thinner. Then prime and finish as with new metal.

Economics

The economics factors involved in painting metal can be expressed empirically by the following equation[14]

$$C = \frac{M + L}{T}$$

where:

C = annual charge for painting upkeep of a structure

T = time interval allowed to lapse between paintings

M = cost of paint and other materials

L = cost of labor for surface preparation, application of paint, loss involved due to interruption of business during painting, scaffold charges, etc.

As Eickhoff[9] points out, any change in operations which increases T (the time interval between paints), with other factors constant, results in a lower value of C. The maintenance supervisor can also vary M and L to achieve a minimum value of C.

SPECIAL COATINGS

For specialized applications where conventional paints were considered inadequate, the availability of new polymers provided the stimulus for the development of unique coatings having improved film properties. The capsule digest below consists of the more important types of special coatings currently being marketed covering their properties and uses. It is interesting to note that some of these were introduced some twenty-five years ago and are still finding service in various applications today.

Epoxies

Epoxy coatings exhibit good adhesion, flexibility, chemical and corrosion resistance, they are used as primers and as finishes for masonry and metal surfaces. Epoxy ester coatings (epoxy resin reacted with a fatty acid) are lower in cost than straight epoxy coatings. They generally have better flexibility, adhesion, toughness and chemical resistance than alkyd coatings, but do not have quite as good color retention. As air-drying finishes, epoxy esters are used for floor varnishes, primers for steelwork in chemical plants, and marine finishes.

Polyurethanes

Polyurethane coatings have a wide range of unique properties which include resistance to chemicals, salt solutions, vegetable and mineral oils, and many solvents. As a result these coatings have many and varied uses on practically all substrates such as metal, wood, rubber, and fabrics.

As a metal finish where maximum chemical resistance is required, application of at least 5-mil thickness is necessary. In ordinary atmospheric exposure, a primer and finish will suffice.

Because of their excellent abrasion and scuff resistance, urethane coatings find a big outlet for finishing wood floors. They are able to retain their initial high gloss for long periods of time, even under heavy wear with a minimum of maintenance such as cleaning and polishing.

There are several types of related urethane coatings which are of interest in the maintenance field. These include two-package and one-package systems. The two-package systems are designed for application where a very high degree of chemical and abrasion resistance is required.

The one-package systems include two types: oil-modified and moisture-cured. Oil-modified urethanes are coatings made by reacting polyisocanate with esters of polyol and unsaturated fatty acids. Such coatings are fast-drying. Moisture-cured urethanes are relatively slow drying, especially in low-humidity areas, but they have good abrasion resistance, chemical resistance, toughness, and flexibility.

Polyesters

One outstanding property of polyester coatings is that of film thickness. Any thickness is possible, since the viscous mixture of polyester and styrene is 100 per cent reactive, with no solvents to evaporate. Thus, high film buildup can be obtained in a minimum number of coats. Hardness, good chemical and abrasion resistance, plus high clarity are some of the other important properties of these coatings. Room-temperature-curing polyester paints shrink considerably, leaving cracks and checks. This condition can be alleviated by using reinforcing glass mat, fiber glass, or chopped glass to provide the necessary strength.[15]

Phenolics

Air-drying phenolic paints are based on phenolic oil varnish. Because of their excel-

TABLE 17-4. Comparative Properties of Twelve Air-Dry Coatings

Coating	Exterior Durability	Salt Spray	Alkali Resistance	Acid Resistance	Water Resistance	Abrasion Resistance	Adhesion	Flexibility	Color Retention	Initial Gloss	Gloss Retention	Drying Time	Coverage (sq ft/gal.)	Cost materials plus labor (¢/sq ft/mil dry)
										Decorative Properties				
Alkyd	E	E	F	F	G	G	E	G	G	E	E	3 hr.	450	1.50
Bituminous	E	E	E	E	E	—	E	E	G	P	—	24 hr.	Low	—
Epoxy (100%)	G	E	E	E	VG	E	E[1]	E	E	VG	F	2 hr.	450	1.75
Epoxy ester	G	E	P	F	G	E	VG	G	E	E	F	2 hr.	450	1.75
Latex emulsion														
Acrylic	G	—	G	F	G	F	F[2]	G	G	—	—	30 min.	450	2.00
Polyvinyl, acetate	G	—	G	F	G	F	F[2]	G	G	—	—	30 min.	450	1.75
Styrene-butadiene	F	—	G	F	G	F	F[2]	G	G	—	—	30 min.	450	1.75
Linseed oil	G	G	F	G	F	F	G	F	P	F	F	24 hr.	450	1.50
Phenolic	E	E	E	E	E	E	G	G	P	VG	F	30 min.	350	1.75
Silicone	E	E	F	F	E	F	G	F	G	E	E	2 hr.	350	6.00
Urethane-oil	E	E	E	E	E	E	E	E	G	E	P	1–2 hr.	—	2.00
Vinyl chloride resins	E	E	E	E	E	E	VG	E	VG	G	F	30 min.	250	2.50
Chlorinated rubber	E	E	VG	E	VG	E	E	G	G	F	F	30 min.	450	1.50
Hypalon	E	E	E	E	E	—	VG	E	E	P	—	30 min.	350	—

Ratings: E-Excellent; VG-Very Good; G-Good; F-Fair; P-Poor
1. Poor over old paint.
2. Poor over chalky surfaces.

lent water resistance, they are used on the interior of water tanks. Such coatings have been known to give good service under water for many years. Chemical resistance of these coatings is fair, but their weather resistance is considered good.

Vinyls

Vinyl coatings are particularly effective in protecting metal. When properly pigmented, vinyl paints have excellent weathering properties. They have good chemical, acid and alkali resistance, and they perform very satisfactorily in fresh and salt water.

Vinyl butyral resins are used to formulate wash primers which provide excellent anti-corrosive properties and good adhesion for subsequent topcoats. The primers dry by solvent evaporation, and remain tough and flexible over a wide range of temperature.

Since ordinary vinyl-solution coatings require multiple coats to obtain adequate film thickness, special vinyl formulations may be hot-sprayed to provide much thicker films having longer life and good weather resistance.

Chlorinated Rubber

Chlorinated rubber coatings can be formulated to give maximum protection against most common chemicals. They have good resistance against most alkalis, oxidizing agents, and oils, and they perform well in salt spray environment and during fresh and salt water immersion. These coatings are used as traffic paints, swimming pool paints and masonry paints, on concrete floors, and as general maintenance paints.

Styrene-butadiene

Lacquer type styrene-butadiene coatings are recommended for general maintenance work such as protecting masonry and wood.

Silicones

The outstanding property of silicone coatings is their high heat resistance. Enamels based on silicone resins can withstand temperatures as high as 750°F. As maintenance coatings, silicones are especially useful on stacks, furnaces, or any surface where heat is extreme. The high heat resistance can be achieved only through baked silicone coatings. Obviously, surfaces which are hot during operation provide the necessary heat to convert the silicone. Silicones also have excellent resistance to oxidation and weathering, plus good color and gloss retention. Another important advantage of silicones is their innate water repellency and moisture resistance.

"Hypalon"

"Hypalon" (chlorosulfonated polyethylene) is an elastomeric material developed in the early 1950's. One of its more important uses is in the formulation of flexible, decorative and protective coatings for fabric, metal, rubber, and masonry surfaces.

Suitably compounded "Hypalon" coatings have these interesting properties: complete resistance to sunlight and weather; resistance to chemicals, especially oxidizing agents; good resistance to abrasion; excellent color stability; low temperature flexibility; excellent resistance at temperatures of 250 to 300°F; good adhesion to rubber fabrics, metal, wood and masonry; and a high degree of flexibility and excellent flex-life. Because "Hypalon" coatings retain their original brillance and hue, they are used for color-coding piping systems, marking safety areas, or brightening up plants and equipment while providing a high degree of protection against corrosion. They can also be used as linings for tanks, ducts, and similar installations.

Coal Tar Epoxies

Epoxy resins can be modified with coal tar to provide coatings having long-time protection underwater. Such coatings can prevent corrosion by sealing water away from the metal. They are resistant to most salts and a few acids except nitric.[14] Coal tar epoxies give good service on undisturbed locations such as underground pipelines.

FIRE-RETARDANT PAINTS

Over 800,000 fires occur in the United States each year causing an estimated loss of over one billion dollars in property damage, the death of 12,000 persons, and injury to 75,000. Home fires account for half the deaths.

While certain states and municipalities have building codes enforcing the use of fire-retardant paints and products in multiple-residence dwellings and public halls, the general feeling about fire retardance has been apathetic. However, as the result of a series of fires in schools, hospitals, and industrial plants, more awareness and emphasis are being placed on using fire-retardant materials in such buildings. Many fire marshals are considering institutional safety codes that may become the basis for statewide building laws affecting the type of paint to be used on public buildings.

It has been theorized that much of the loss —both human and property—is caused by the swift spread of flame through the structure. Several methods are currently being advanced to help reduce the rapid spreading of flame. One of these calls for building materials which are flame-resistant or fire-retardant.

Properly designed paints can effectively reduce the spread of flame. The few minutes thus gained might be enough for complete evacuation of personnel and for fire-fighting equipment to effectively combat the blaze.

There are a number of methods for flame-proofing different materials, utilizing coating, gas, thermal, chemical, or insulation techniques.[15] The insulation method, one of the most effective, involves intumescence—the formation of a heat-insulating mat of spongy tough cells. Many chemicals (intumescent agents) are capable of producing this "puffing" action under the influence of heat. They include ammonium phosphate, borates, vermiculite, casein, starch, benzene sulfonyl hydrazide, isano oil, urea, paraformaldehyde, aminoacetic acid, methylene disalicylic acid, ammonium phosphate, dicyandiamide, etc.

Intumescent fire-retardant paints are available in aqueous or nonaqueous two-package systems or in a single-package solvent system. Since the solvent system is usually prepared with flammable solvents, it cannot be considered fire-retardant until after all the solvent is evaporated from the film.

Latex Type

A stable, single-package interior fire-retardant latex paint based on polyvinyl acetate emulsion[16] was deveolped some three years

TABLE 17-5. Solids Content of Four Representative Architectural Paints

Type	% Solids
Linseed oil paints	90
Latex emulsion paints	50–55
Flat alkyd	55–60
Enamel (interior)	60

ago. Its exceptional stability is attributed to the use of a polyvinyl acetate emulsion that accepts high loadings of intumescent (di- and trivalent salts) and other materials used in fire retardant coatings. Ordinarily, use of these salts causes precipitation or coagulation of latex systems.

On the negative side is the tendency of intumescent paints to weather, wear, and wash poorly.[16] Intumescing agents are usually water-soluble, and such paints tend to lack durability, particularly under damp or humid conditions.

In some applications, particularly on vertical surfaces, and especially in the presence of vibration, a paint film which has become intumesced from the effect of flame does not always adhere well. Also, there is a tendency for the paint film to lose its original degree of fire-retardance through the loss of the intumescing agents as the paint ages and weathers.

Alkyd Type

One approach in formulating effective fire-retardant paints involves the use of a chlorinated alkyd resin[17] as the vehicle component. Paints with a chlorinated alkyd resin base provide, along with fire-retardance, the excellent appearance, weatherability, scrubbability and other desirable properties associated with conventional alkyd-type paints.

A protective enamel based on chlorinated

alkyd was developed by the U.S. Navy for use on such metal surfaces as bulkheads. The unusual fire-retardant qualities of this enamel were readily demonstrated as it passed a Navy test requiring that the paint film on a steel panel would not ignite when heated electrically for 30 seconds to a temperature of 2300°F.

Antimony silico-oxide pigment[18] can be used to advantage in formulating fire-retardant paints. In this particular approach, the flame-retardant activity is based on the reaction of silico-oxide and a chlorine-containing binder under the influence of heat.

Similarly, a formulation using chlorinated paraffin and antimony trioxide exhibits good fire-retardant properties.

Application

Fire-retardant paint is applied like conventional paint. Brush, roller, or spray gun may be used. It is important that the surface be thoroughly prepared prior to painting. Dirt, grease, or oil, and loose paint should be removed. Effective fire protection can be attained with one coat of fire-retardant paint having a coverage of 250 to 300 sq ft/gal.[19] Two heavy coats will provide an extreme degree of fire protection.

A fire-retardant paint is usually applied in three types of locations:

(a) where the possibility of fire is slight, but the potential loss in life and property is great,

(b) in fire-sensitive areas where equipment, materials, or the building structure itself are particularly flammable, although loss of life is unlikely, and

(c) on temporary wooden structures.

The first type of location includes structures where there is a heavy concentration of personnel, e.g., schools, hospitals, apartments, etc. It is in these locations that the greatest quantity of fire-retardant paint is used. Chemical plants, petroleum refineries, storage tanks, warehouses, etc., make up the second category. In the third type, temporary wooden structures such as plywood wall-panelled offices and trade-show exhibits are included because the potential fire loss is substantial.

PREFINISHED BUILDING COMPONENTS

Residential construction is undergoing a major change today with the trend toward in-plant manufacture of complete building components. In the interest of saving on site labor costs, the builder is using precut, preassembled, pretreated, preprimed, and prefinished materials. The impact of this trend has been particularly significant for the lumber industry. Wood siding has decreased in usage.[20] A study undertaken by the California Redwood Association revealed that in 1950, wood siding commanded about 45 per cent of the residential exterior market. By 1960, the figure dropped to about 23 per cent—a strong indication that the lumber industry is fast losing its wood siding market to such materials as masonry, brick veneer, aluminum siding, hardboard siding, and other surfaces which do not necessarily require paint.

The performance of paint on exterior wood has always been a problem to the paint industry. While considerable progress has been made in upgrading the quality of paints for exterior wood, there always exists the possibility of improper use of quality paints by the painter or homeowner. Poor application, particularly thin coats can lead to very early paint failures on wood.

Factory-applied Finishes

The lumber industry reasoned that the high-quality exterior wood coatings with improved durability could be formulated for factory application and that applying these finishes under controlled conditions, coating failures would be minimized.[21] By getting uniform and correct film thickness as well as uniform composition, paint performance could be much improved. Another advantage gained by factory finishing is the opportunity to use products that cannot be applied at the building site because of poor brushing, or slow drying, or both, but which can be applied and cured in the factory.[22] It is known that the coatings industry has topcoats which will give good service for 5 years or better when applied on carefully prepared panels, but which often fail in 1 to 3 years on homes because of inferior substrates. Better primed siding will help the topcoats to give better service. Also, the application of the primer in the factory eliminates the weathering and abuse to which raw wood siding is too often subjected prior to painting.

Preprimed siding is readily available. Completely prefinished wood siding, guaranteed not to require repainting for at least seven years, is now being marketed in limited quantities, by a leading lumber concern. Offered in two sizes and five colors, the siding has a 4-mil-thick finish. Next to the substrate is a blister-resistant alkyd primer; the topcoat is a baked-on acrylic that gives a satin finish. This prefinished siding sells for about two-thirds more than vertically grained material.

The lumber industry is actually seeking a 10-year maintenance-free exterior wood coating and a 5-year clear coating. To attain this goal, Nichols[21] feels that the coating must show improvement in holdout or sealing, in resistance to mildew, and in resistance to staining from water solubles in the wood.

As far as the topcoat is concerned, it must have all of the desirable properties of any house paint—resistance to cracking, excellent tint retention, blister resistance, and mildew resistance. Also, it must cure fast and be nonblocking when the finished lumber is packaged.

Laminating Technique

One approach offered by Nichols[21] which seems rather novel, is a single coat on siding rather than a system of primer plus topcoat. This would involve "laminating" a single coat of liquid film, e.g., polyesters, epoxies, or isocyanates, to wood. Such a technique would be cheaper than any precoat film laminated to wood by adhesives. To implement such a technique on a large scale would necessitate the development of new types of application equipment or processes to get the liquid films onto the wood and cured in a minimum amount of time. Once cured, the films should not be thermoplastic and should not be subjected to further change by oxidation.

Clear Finishes

Improved clear coating is equally important as pigmented coatings. It must be agreed that the natural beauty of wood is something that cannot be duplicated by any other material. If this beauty can be preserved and protected during exterior exposure, the lumber industry believes that much more natural siding will be used in home construction.

Present clear finishes are very unsatisfactory because of poor durability and difficult maintenance.

The answer to durabilities of five years lies in factory applied coatings.[21] However, before a clear coating will perform satisfactorily over wood, stabilization of the wood itself is necessary. Most clear coatings begin to fail at the wood-film interface. It is postulated that ultraviolet light transmitted through the film causes some type of degradation on the surface of the wood which has a deleterious effect on the adhesion of the film.

Research

In connection with a joint research program sponsored by the *National Paint, Varnish and Lacquer Association* and the *National Lumber Manufacturers Association*, the *U.S. Forest Products Laboratory* reported that in a surface stabilization study, efforts have been made to learn how to obtain concentration gradients of stabilizing chemicals in the surface of the wood and to determine the correlation between the amount of chemical present and the degree of stability achieved. Tests indicate that optimum stability can be achieved when the chemical concentration is greatest close to the wood surface and diminishes in concentration as it penetrates into the wood.

The study on photochemical degradation of wood was directed toward determining the chemical compounds formed at the wood surface as a result of the action of ultraviolet light, and the effect these compounds have on wood properties and finishes. Studies have shown that lignin (the cementing substance in wood) is most affected by exposure to light and weather.

At the *Armour Research Foundation*, another project under investigation by the above groups is to find a satisfactory laboratory method for predicting the ultimate durability of paint systems on wood, avoiding the necessity of long term panel and house tests to evaluate paint systems. The Armour study indicated that stress-strain and stress-relaxation measurements and certain measures of surface friction appear promising in forecasting paint performance.

Stress-strain and stress-relaxation measurements were made on paint films that had previously been subjected to varying conditions of exposure, such as temperature and humidity cyclic variations, ultraviolet radiation, ozone and microwave frequencies. Several approaches appear worthy of further investigation, including a study of the surface friction characteristics of film which have been exposed to ultraviolet radiation and further studies of the effect of ozone on the elastic properties of paint films.

Presently, the production of factory-coated lumber for exterior use is considered relatively small, but there has been an increasing trend toward factory priming at various plants in the last two years. Some two dozen major lumber producers are now doing prefinishing or prepriming, and several more are planning to enter this field.

Aluminum Siding

Estimates are that 4 per cent of exterior wall surfaces in new residential frame building were covered with aluminum siding in 1960.[23] This figure is expected to increase to 7 or 8 per cent by 1975.

The big advantage claimed for aluminum siding is that it is maintenance-free and will give service up to 10 years or better. Present finishes used on aluminum siding are vinyls, modified alkyds, and acrylics. Aluminum siding is finding extensive use in the north central region of the United States.

Fluoride Film

A system for finishing exterior building products was developed in late 1962 by E. I. duPont de Nemours & Co., using preformed sheets of fluoride film ("Tedlar") which it is claimed, will withstand weathering much longer than conventional liquid-finished materials.

The building products are laminates of standard structural materials and "Tedlar" PVF film. In the lamination process, this plastic film is bonded to substrates to form decorative surfaces with a predicted maintenance-free life of 15 to 30 years. The life expectancy of the film depends on the intensity of sunlight and the weather at the geographical location. "Tedlar" film is described as extremely tough, flexible, chemically inert, abrasion-resistant, and highly weatherable.

GLOSSARY*

Alligatoring—The appearance of a paint film that is cracked into large segments, resembling the hide of an alligator.

Ambient Temperature—Temperature of the medium surrounding an object.

Antifouling—An antifouling paint is one which contains toxic or poisonous substances to prevent growth of barnacles on the hull of ships or objects submerged in water.

Blistering—Formation of bubbles or blisters on the surface of a paint film after it has dried.

Blocking—Adhesion between touching layers of materials.

Chalking—A type of paint failure characterized by the appearance at the surface of loose pigment resulting in loss of gloss.

Checking—Checking is very similar to alligatoring except that the finish is broken into smaller segments.

Cissing—Another term for the defect known as "crawling."

Coverage—Hiding power of paint expressed in square feet per gallon.

Cracking—A fissured surface condition of a paint film.

Crawling—Defect of a finishing composition in which the adhesion to the surface is too low to prevent the material, while still wet, from pulling together, thereby leaving uncoated areas.

Crazing—Type of film failure usually due to disrupting the continuity of the topcoat resulting in fine wrinkles and minute surface cracks.

Dispersion—In paint technology a "good" dispersion means that a pigment is finely divided and deflocculated in the binder. Where aggregates are present in the disperse phase, the material is considered without exception a "poor" dispersion regardless of the state of flocculation.

Efflorescence—Certain hydrated salts (soda crystals) gradually lose their water of crystallization when exposed to the air, forming a white powder of the dehydrated material on the surface.

Extender—Inert pigment use for dilution of colored pigments.

Fastness—The stability or resistance of pigments to influences such as light, alkali, etc.

Filler—A material usually containing considerable quantities of pigment used for building up or filling the imperfections in the surface to be finished.

Film Thickness—The thickness of any applied coating.

*Based on "Glossary for the Protective Coatings Industry" 3rd Ed., 1954, by L. J. Radi, R-B-H Dispersions, Interchemical Corp., Bound Brook, N.J.

Flocculation—Formation of clusters of particles separable by relatively weak mechanical forces or by a change in the physical forces at the intefacre between the liquid and the solid dispersed particles.

Grinding—Process by which mechanical work is applied to reduce the size of pigment aggregates.

Inhibitor—Any substance which slows or prevents chemical reaction or corrosion.

Livering—The progressive, irreversible increase in consistency of pigment-vehicle combination.

Masstone—The color of pigmented film sufficiently thick to eliminate transmitted light.

Non-volatile—The portion of a paint, lacquer, or varnish which does not evaporate at ordinary temperatures.

Pastel—A tint. A masstone to which white has been added.

Pinholing—A film defect characterized by the presence of tiny holes.

Porosity—Presence of numerous minute voids in the cured material.

Reducer—A thinner to reduce the viscosity or body of a paint, coating, etc.

Saponify—Decomposition of an oil or ester by an alkali.

Thixotropy—Property of a material which undergoes an isothermal gel-sol-gel transformation upon agitation and subsequent rest.

Tint—A masstone color to which white has been added. A pastel color is a tint.

Vehicle—The liquid portion of a finishing material, consisting of the binder and volatile thinners.

Viscosity—The resistance to flow in a liquid.

Wetting—Process by which a liquid comes into contact with a solid to form a solid-liquid interface.

Wrinkling—Formation of small ridges or folds in surface film.

Yellowing—Clear finishes and white paints and enamels sometimes turn yellow upon long standing.

REFERENCES

1. Fortener, R., Official Digest, **33,** No. 12, 1634 (December 1961).
2. Allyn, G., *Paint and Varnish Production,* **50,** No. 11, 81 (October 1960).
3. Lalk, R., *Paint and Varnish Production,* **50,** No. 11, 87 (October 1960).
4. Payne, H. F., Interior Architectural Finishes, Paint, Research and Technology, Bull. No. 86, Vol. X, No. 12, p. 68, Florida Engineering and Industrial Experimental Station, University of Florida, Gainesville, Fla.
5. Allyn, G., Field Applied Coatings, Publication NAS-NRC 653 (1959) pg. 40 Building Research Institute, Washington 25, D.C.
6. Maslow, P., Epoxy-Based Masonry Materials, *Paint and Varnish Production,* **48,** No. 6, 37 (May 1958).
7. Non-Chalking Exterior Epoxy Coating—Developed by Plas-Chem Corp., St Louis 30, Mo.
8. Weinman, J., *Official Digest,* **33,** No. 7, 842 (July 1961).
9. Eickhoff, A., Field Applied Coatings, Publication NAS-NRC 653, p. 53 (1959), Building Research Institute, Washington 25, D.C.
10. Munger, C. G., Paper presented at Washington Paint Technology Group Symposium on Anti-corrosion Coatings, Washington, D.C., April 30–May 1, 1963.
11. Payne, H. F. "Organic Coating Technology," Vol. II: Pigments and Pigmented Coatings," p. 1266, New York, John Wiley & Son, Inc. (1961).
12. Acrylic Latex for Maintenance and Industrial Finishes, *Paint and Varnish Production,* **53,** No. 3, 26 (March 1963).
13. Edwards, *et al,* Aluminum Paint and Powder, New York, Reinhold Publishing Corp., 3rd Ed., p. 71, 1955.
14. Evans, U. R., Metallic Corrosion, Passavity and Protection, London, E. Arnold & Co., 1937.
15. Garlock, N., *et al.* Paper presented at the Building Research Institute on Coatings Maintenance Concepts, Washington, D. C., April 23, 1963.
16. Liberti, F., "Fire Retardant Latex Coatings," *Paint and Varnish Production,* **51,** No. 12, 57 (November 1961).
17. Ewalt, W. M., *et al.,* Chlorinated Alkyds for Fire, Retardant Paints," *Paint and Varnish Production-* **51,** No. 12, 53 (November 1961).
18. Zimmermann, E. K. et al, Flame Retardant Coatings Based on Antimony Silico Oxide Pigment, Paint and Varnish Production, Vol. 51, No. 12, November 1961, p. 79
19. Redlin L., Fire-Retardant Paints—A Profitable Business in Fire Protection, *Spotlights,* June–July 1961. Painting and Decorating Contractors of America, Chicago, Ill.
20. Laughnan, D. F., "What the Lumber Industry Requires of the Paint Manufacturer." Paper presented before Pre-Finished Wood Conference, 75th Meeting of National Paint, Varnish and Lacquer Association, Los Angeles, Calif., November 6, 1962.
21. Nichols, G., "Impact of Factory Coated Wood on the Chemical Coatings Manufacturers." Paper presented before Pre-Finished Wood Conference, 75th Meeting of National Paint, Varnish and Lacquer Association, Los Angeles, Calif., November 6, 1962.
22. Herndon, D. L., "Impact of Factory Coated Wood on the Trade Sales Manufacturer." Paper presented before Pre-Finished Wood Conference, 75th Meeting of the National Paint, Varnish and Lacquer Association, Los Angeles, Calif., November 6, 1962.
23. Bratt, L., "Trends in the Consumption of Exterior-Grade Forest Products by the Building Industry in the United States." Paper presented at the American Chemical Society Div. of Organic Coatings and Plastic Chemistry, Spring Meeting (March 31–April 5, 1963).

18 PLASTICS IN ROOFING

Joseph W. Prane

Skeist Laboratories, Inc.
Newark, New Jersey

From time immemorial, roofs of structures have had to be sealed against the elements. The tarred and pitched roofs of the ancients did a fairly adequate job. The modern built-up and hot-mopped asphalt deck, today's counterpart of the tarred roof, is serving satisfactorily in many residential and industrial roofing applications, but newer, better materials are achieving increasing acceptance.

Three geometric forms of roofs are common, each with its own specific characteristics and challenges:

(1) *Flat roof:* This horizontal surface must withstand the ravages of sunlight, wind, dust, rain, snow and extremes of temperature. Together with its supporting subroofing and drainage system, it must protect the rest of the building from the weight and persistent wetting, penetration and seepage of snow and standing water.

In many institutional buildings, such as schools and hospitals, flat roofs must bear foot traffic and light-wheeled vehicle traffic, since the roof is often used as a recreation area. In many industrial structures, roofs are subjected to corrosive and/or solvent-bearing fumes and other industrial fallout. Also, in large apartment complexes and industrial installations, roofing materials must withstand the vibration and mechanical shock associated with exhaust systems,

air-conditioning systems and cooling towers.

(2) *Pitched roof:* This angled or sloped roof construction is normally associated with residential structures. Some types of institutional structures have been built with pitched roofs, but this is no longer common architectural practice. Modern factories rarely employ this type of roofing; here flat roofs are found to be more functional.

Design of pitched roofs must allow for most of the weather and use elements referred to above. Although standing water is rarely a problem, snow loads are still hazardous, particularly at low pitch angles.

(3) *Free-form roof:* Many structures having hyperbolic, parabolic, ellipsoidal or circular roof contours (or combinations thereof) have already been built; many more are on drawing boards as architects all over the world have been released from the aesthetic restrictions of the more conventional flat or pitched roofs. Much of this freedom is due to the availability of new plastic materials or plastic coating systems employed in conjunction with imaginative and novel roof construction methods using formed plywood and prestressed concrete.

Motels, hospitals and airport buildings with free-form roofs are much in evidence. The daring and imagination of their design have created a distinctive and unusual archi-

359

tecture; however, this construction has also given rise to challenges to conventional roofing methods and joint sealing techniques. Many of the newer methods to be described below have been designed specifically for these new roof systems.

Any discussion of the use of plastic materials in roof construction must begin with a review of the present conventional systems.

The most common system is called the *built-up roofing* system. This type of roofing is applied over a variety of decks including metal, wood, concrete (poured, precast or prestressed), precast gypsum with concrete fill, pre-formed reinforced insulation (mineral

TABLE 18-1. Plastics in Roofing

Name of System	Principal Chemical Type	Used on Roof Type	Number of Coats and/or Plies	Reinforcing Materials	System Thickness (in.)	Weight (lbs/ 100 sq ft)	Typical Cost of Materials (per 100 sq ft) in $
Built-up Roofing	Asphalt or pitch	A, B	5-10	Roofing felt, tarred paper	$7/8$-$1\frac{1}{8}$ (1)	250-275 (1) 550-650 (3)	6.80-7.50 (1)
Membrane Roofing "Last-O-Roof"	Poly iso-butylene	A, B, C	1	Woven glass fabric	0.040	35-40	20-25
Butyl	Butyl rubber	A, B, C	1	None	3/32	58	45
Neoprene and "Hypalon" coated fabric	Neoprene, "Hypalon"	A, B, C	1	Polyamide, polyester fabric	0.020-0.030	15-20	225-300 (5)
"Travelon Weatherdeck"	Neoprene	A	2	Slate tile	0.175	150	175-225 (5)
Roof Coatings "Cocoon"	Polyvinyl chloride— plast.	A, B, C	5-7	Glass fabric	0.025-0.030	15-20	24-26
"Dex-O-Tex Weatherwear"	Neoprene-latex and paste	A, B, C	8	Asbestos fabric	0.370	200-250	65
Neoprene-"Hypalon" (fluid applied)	Neoprene, "Hypalon"	A, B, C	5	Glass fabric	0.020-0.030	10-30	20-25
Polysulfide	Liquid polysulfide polymer	A, B, C	3	Glass fabric	0.020-0.030	18-25	20-25
"EPO-440"	Epoxy-polyamide	A, B, C	1	None	0.030	15-25	N.A.
Plastic Paneling Acrylic	Polymethyl methacrylate	A, B, C	1	None	$3/16$-$3/8$	115-225	N.A.
Vinyl	Rigid PVC —un-plasticized	A, B, C	1	None	0.060	44	50-55
Integral, Laminated Systems "Tedlar" (T/NA-200)	Polyvinyl fluoride	A, B, C	1	Asbestos felt	0.020-0.030	15	23-26

Notes: The figures shown above are only typical. Prices and characteristics are variable, depending on geographical location, auxiliary materials, quality of installation, etc.
(1) Smooth surface — no surface treatment with slag, gravel or granules.
(2) Can be improved by surface treatment with reflective roofing granules.
(3) With surfacing.
(4) Black non-staining — can be painted with white "Hypalon" paint.
(5) Total cost — applied — includes materials, labor, markup, profits.

or synthetic, such as polyurethane). The roofing system consists of primers (where indicated) followed by alternate layers of roofing felt or tarred paper and hot-mopped asphalt or pitch. In buildings with severe water problems, a vapor barrier (asphalt-coated base sheets, polyethylene or aluminum foil) is commonly included in the system. The top surface is usually covered with gravel, chips, slag or colored roofing granules imbedded into the last coat of asphalt or pitch.

Meticulous attention must be paid to adhering and sealing roofing details and openings such as drains, ventilators, skylights, expansion joints, curbs, reglets, conduits, electrical connections, flashing,

TABLE 18-1. Plastics in Roofing (Cont.)

Colors Available	Reflective Properties	Traffic Properties	Flexibility	Resistance To					Major Materials Manufacturer
				Standing Water	Snow and Ice	Weathering	Fire Spread	Chemicals	
Black	P (2)	F	F-P	G	G	G	P	F-P	Barrett Ruberoid
White, aluminum, metallic pastels	G	F-P	G	G	G	G	P	F	Johns Manville
Black (4)	G (4)	G	G	G	G	G	P	G	Enjay
Several	G	F-G	G	G	G	G	G	G	Du Pont
Several	F	G	G	G	G	G	G	G	(Du Pont) Armstrong Cork
Many (30 colors)	G	F	G	G	G	F-G	G	F-P	Cocoon Diversified Corp.
Several (12 deep tones)	G	G	G	G	G	G	G	G	(Du Pont) Crossfield Products
Many	G	G	G	G	G	G	G	G	Du Pont
Many	G	G	G	G	G	G	F	G	Thiokol
Several	G	G	G	G	G	G	G	G	Bradco
Transparent —clear tinted	—	F	G	G	G	G	F	F	Rohm and Haas
Translucent —tinted, opaque— 5 colors	G	F	G	G	G	G	G	F-G	Barrett
White	G	G	G	G	G	G	G	G	Du Pont Ruberoid

Roof Types	Properties
A = Flat	G = Good
B = Pitched	F = Fair
C = Free form	P = Poor
	N. A. = Not available

coving, down-spouts, gutters, and all other projections. Roof edges receive extra treatment to carry protection beyond the vertical walls.

In cases where large roof areas (8000 square feet or more) are installed by trained roofers in accordance with roofing material manufacturers' specifications, bonded guarantees of as long as twenty years are available. Two of the major manufacturers are Barrett Division, Allied Chemical Corporation, New York, N. Y., and the Ruberoid Company, New York, N. Y.

Another common system is based on the use of *shingles* over a suitably waterproofed roof deck. Shingles are most commonly used on pitched roofs. One well-known type of asphalt-asbestos shingle comes in a multilayer construction, comprising an exterior layer of mineral granules, followed by a layer of asphalt and asbestos fibers, a layer of mineral granules and vermiculite, another layer of asphalt and asbestos, a layer of asphalt-saturated felt, and a back coating of asphalt and asbestos with a fine mineral surfacing.

Shingles are mounted over the previously waterproofed deck by nailing in a staggered, overlapping design, starting from the bottom. The shingles described meet a Class "A" fire rating, which signifies a high degree of protection from flame spread.

Other surfacing materials include *wood shingles* (usually impregnated and/or stained) and *clay tile* (flat or barrel). These systems have had long usage in residential structures, but they offer less protection and durability than built-up roofing or asphalt-asbestos shingles.

Modern roofing methods, using plastic materials, may be divided into four categories:

(1) Membrane roofing,
(2) Roof coatings,
(3) Plastic paneling or sections,
(4) Integral, laminated systems.

Membrane Roofing

This type of roofing comprises a reinforced polymeric sheet which is adhered to the roof deck. Four specific systems will be described.

"Last-O-Roof" (Johns-Manville, Manville, N. J.). This system consists of a weathering surface of heavy *polyisobutylene* film supported by a woven glass fabric. These are combined into a one-ply membrane. The weight per 100 square feet is 35 to 40 pounds, and the over-all thickness is 40 mils. The membrane is cemented to the surface with a solvent-type polyisobutylene adhesive, applied by trowel or knife.

The advantages of this system are light weight (compared to built-up systems), flexibility, durability and ease of maintenance. Color and reflective properties can be supplied with copolymer-based coatings in aluminum, white and several metallic pastel colors.

The system is somewhat tricky to apply and seal. Also, it is not as amenable to heavy foot traffic and abuse as built-up systems. Deck surfaces must be scrupulously clean before application. Compatibility with previous asphalt roofs is a problem.

Butyl (Enjay Chemical Co., New York, N. Y.). This system comprises butyl rubber sheets of several thicknesses supplied by Enjay to skilled applicators. The butyl sheets are adhered to the roof deck with waterproof rubber-base cements.

The excellent chemical and weathering properties of butyl rubber, together with good flexibility, are transmitted to this roofing system. Several installations have been made in the Southwest and are performing well to date.

Neoprene and "Hypalon" Coated Fabrics (E. I. du Pont de Nemours, Wilmington, Del.). Neoprene and "Hypalon" (chlorosulfonated polyethylene) coated fabrics (nylon and dacron polyester) are being used as protective covers for applications requiring exceptional weather resistance and waterproofness. These fabrics are finding increasing use in such applications as roofs and side walls for integral portable storage tents, temporary covers for building construction operations, air-supported radomes, etc.

Neoprene Sheet (E. I. du Pont de Nemours, Wilmington, Del.). Neoprene sheet stock has been used as a waterproof membrane in a roofing system for promenade decks which is supplied by the Building Products Division of the Armstrong Cork Company, Lancaster, Pa., under the name of "Travelon

FIG. 18-1. "Travelon" weather deck system showing application of neoprene sheet (*Courtesy Armstrong Cork Co.*).

Weather Deck System." Here a base sheet of neoprene is adhered to a prepared deck and covered with a durable natural slate design tile. Besides making use of the excellent performance properties of neoprene, the system is said to resist mold, scorching and indentation damage, while expanding and contracting with the deck for complete watertightness.

The future may well see such polymers as *hydrocarbon rubber* (such as "Nordel," made by du Pont) and *polycarbonates* (such as "Lexan," made by General Electric and "Merlon," made by Mobay Chemical) used as roofing membranes because of their excellent performance properties.

Roof Coatings

Many types of *thin film* coatings are available based on acrylic and vinyl emulsions, and butyl latexes. These are pigmented with aluminum powder, titanium dioxide and pastel colors and are usually reinforced with asbestos fibers. They perform well as heat-reflective coatings, reducing temperatures within the structures to as much as 15 to 30°F below temperatures which would result internally from the use of black-topped roofs.

Of more pertinence to this discussion are the *heavier films*, 20 mils and greater, of which the following are examples.

"*Cocoon*" (Cocoon Diversified Corp., Camden, N. J.). "Cocoon" is a sprayable vinyl plastic protective coating originally developed by the R. M. Hollingshead Corp. in 1945 for "moth-balling" guns and other vital parts of ships for the Navy. The material is a clear or pigmented plasticized polyvinyl chloride lacquer (25 parts of dioctyl phthalate to 100 parts of PVC) supplied at 24 to 30 per cent solids in conventional lacquer solvents.

"Cocoon" is applied by hot or cold spray to the clean and primed roof deck in several coats to a 5 to 10 mil thickness. Glass cloth reinforcement is set in, followed by additional coats to a total film thickness of 25 to 30 mils (including the glass cloth). It forms a tough, strong, waterproof, jointless membrane over a variety of roofing surfaces. It has good ability to bridge cracks and does not support combustion. It is available in thirty colors, in a gloss or matte finish.

Considerable skill is required to apply the "Cocoon" system properly; therefore, it can be applied only by trained franchised distributor applicators.

Many successful installations have been made, particularly on the West Coast, in New England and in the Southwest. However, several problems have arisen, such as a tendency to bleach and discolor, blister formation and poor adhesion, sensitivity to heat and ultraviolet light, and plasticizer migration. Some controversy exists relative to this last item. There have been reports that building sealants (such as polysulfides) have shown occasional adhesion failure when used in contact with the "Cocoon" membrane. However, the use of the "Cocoon" system is continuing to grow.

"*Dex-O-Tex*" *Weatherwear* (Crossfield Products Corp., Roselle Park, N. J.). This roof covering is applied in a series of trowel operations, starting with a divorcing layer of perforated asbestos felt over the roof deck. The felt is covered with a waterproof membrane which consists of a neoprene latex combined with a dehydrating powder and a mineral aggregate. This is followed by a

FIG. 18-2. "Cocoon" system, Memphis Metropolitan Airport, Memphis, Tenn. (*Courtesy Cocoon Diversified Corp.*)

layer of asbestos fabric embedded in two coats of neoprene paste. The final traffic surface is formed by a neoprene-cement composition, followed by two coats of a penetrating sealer. The complete system weighs about 200–250 pounds per 100 square feet and is approximately $\frac{3}{16}$ to $\frac{1}{4}$ inch thick.

"Dex-O-Tex" is available in a range of colors. It is said to be flexible, waterproof and to have excellent durability and resistance to traffic. Installations have been made successfully in several areas of the United States.

Neoprene-"Hypalon" (E. I. du Pont de Nemours, Wilmington, Del.). This system comprises a combination of fluid-applied elastomers to produce the final finish over a variety of roof decks. Although many variations are possible, the following is a typical method of application:

The system consists of five coats—one prime coat (1 part neoprene plus 2 parts xylol), two coats of neoprene solution, followed by two coats of "Hypalon" solution. (The neoprene solution is approximately 30 per cent solids, at 33 per cent maximum pigment volume concentration, and contains up to 45 parts of heat reactive phenolic resin

per 100 parts neoprene to impart self-priming properties to the coating.) Some applications involve the use of a nonwoven glass mat between neoprene coats to aid in bridging cracks. Application is by brush, roller or spray.

FIG. 18-3. Neoprene-"Hypalon" fluid applied roofing system (*Courtesy du Pont*).

Both neoprene and "Hypalon" have excellent flexibility, abrasion resistance, chemical and fire resistance and weatherability. Neoprene confers sealing and waterproofing qualities; "Hypalon" brings exterior durability and the ability to be made in a wide variety of colors.

This system can be built up to a film thickness of 20 to 25 mils. (Higher film thicknesses have been achieved in fewer coats recently through the use of neoprene emulsions instead of solutions for the first coat.)

Labor costs are high, although they vary with geographical area. The approximate cost to applicators for fluid materials is $20 to $25 per 100 square feet. The du Pont Company distributes the neoprene and "Hypalon" solutions to approved contractors, some of which are: Gates Engineering Co., Gaco-Western, Gibson-Homans Co., Jones-Blair Paint Co., Miracle Adhesives Corp. Over 500 installations have been made all over the country, including the roofs of many of the pavilions at the 1964–1965 World's Fair in New York.

Polysulfide (Thiokol Chemical Corp., Trenton, N. J.). A roll-on elastomeric polysulfide-base coating has been promoted by the Thiokol Chemical Corp. for roof coating applications. This system is based on "paint-grade" polysulfide compositions which are otherwise similar in makeup to conventional two-component polysulfide sealants. "Solids" are in the range of 85 to 95 per cent, of which polysulfide LP (liquid polymer) contents are in the range of 45 to 60 per cent (based on the total nonvolatile content).

The polysulfide system is applied in a manner similar to the neoprene-"Hypalon" system described above. However, because of the higher solids possible with polysulfides, a 20 to 25 mil coating can be built up with as few as three coats (including primer) as compared to five coats for the neoprene-"Hypalon" system. Although the material costs are approximately the same, the savings in labor time are significant. Many colors are available. Performance properties are excellent and typical of polysulfides. Several polysulfide formulators have put in successful installations, particularly in California and the Southwest.

Epoxy-Polyamide (Bradco Plastics Ltd., Houston, Tex.). An epoxy-polyamide base coating has been developed for use on roof decks. The coating, "Epo-440," is said to require no primer and to adhere to both porous and nonporous surfaces. It can be applied by brush, roller or spray in thicknesses up to 30 mils in a single coat without sagging. Other properties claimed for the coating include a pot-life of 12 hours at 80°F, drying time of 6 hours at 80°F, initial cure of 24 hours, complete cure in 7 days; it is non-flammable after curing and does not become brittle at temperatures down to −40°F.

At this time, no information is available concerning installations using this potentially excellent material.

Following their development as polymers for building sealants, it is expected that roof coating systems based on *polyurethane* and *silicone* elastomers will be making their

FIG. 18-4. Clear "Plexiglas" acrylic plastic dome (50 foot diameter. Parsons Ford Agency, Kingston, N. Y. (*Courtesy Rohm & Haas*).

appearance in the near future. In fact, the roof of the General Electric Pavilion at the recent New York World's Fair was coated with a two-part silicone system.

Plastic Paneling or Sections

Plastic panels have been discussed extensively in other chapters; hence their use in roofing will be reviewed here only briefly. Plastic skylights are usually based on *acrylic* polymer systems. Rohm and Haas (Philadelphia, Pa.) in this country and ICI in England have pioneered in the use of clear, translucent and/or colored panels in protective and decorative roofing and skylighting applications.

Many installations have been erected, using flat and curved sections of sheet acrylic in a variety of configurations. When joined and sealed properly to structural members, they afford all the advantages of weatherability and water resistance with the further ability to admit light to the interior and render the surroundings of the building visible. The major problems of acrylic roofing in the past have involved difficulties in sealing, due to the rather large coefficient of thermal expansion of acrylics, and the stability of the plastic under long-term ultraviolet and infrared irradiation. Both problems have been brought under control—the first by proper joint design and the use of modern elastomeric sealants; the second by the incorporation of suitable stabilizers and absorbers. For additional information on acrylics, see Chapter 15.

Vinyl building panels are also being used in roofing and skylighting applications, especially in northern Europe, where heat and ultraviolet light are less of a problem than in some sections of the United States. Properly stabilized PVC panels can also be decorative and weather-resistant, strong and lightweight, flexible and capable of good light transmission. They are less expensive than acrylic paneling and have better fire resistance, as well as better resistance to many chemicals and solvents. One of the several manufacturers of vinyl building panels is the Barrett Division, Allied Chemical Corp., New York, N.Y. (see also Chapter 8).

Reinforced polyester panels are discussed in Chapters 5 and 6, and elsewhere.

Integral, Laminated Systems

In this classification, "Tedlar," a factory-applied film developed by du Pont, is clearly the leading contender. "Tedlar" is *polyvinyl fluoride* film, factory-bonded with special elastomeric adhesives to a variety of building materials such as wood, metals, insulation board and asbestos felt. The film has shown excellent chemical resistance, weatherability, flexibility, water resistance, and toughness maintained after more than twenty years of exterior exposure.

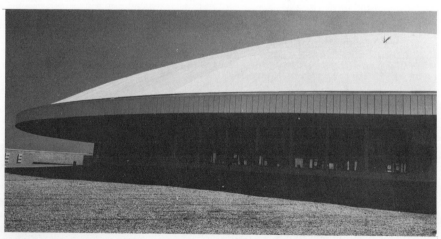

FIG. 18-5. "Tedlar" roof dome. Randhurst shopping center, Mt. Prospect, Ill. "Tedlar" film (du Pont); "T/NA-200" roofing membrane (*Courtesy Ruberoid Co.*).

One of the more rapidly growing applications for this fluorocarbon resin is in roofing. The Ruberoid Co. has developed a built-up roofing material called Ruberoid T/NA 200 Roofing Membrane. In T/NA 200, "Tedlar" film is laminated, using an elastomeric adhesive, to an asbestos felt sheet, impregnated with an elastomeric binder. The elasticity and flexibility of this combination make it suitable for covering roofs of any contour. T/NA 200 comes in white, weighs about 15 pounds per 100 square feet, and has a thickness of approximately 20 to 30 mils.

Many installations using T/NA 200 have been made all over the country. It is anticipated that this type of roof construction will continue to grow because of its adaptability to such a variety of roofing surfaces and shapes.

Systems based on *extrusion-coated polyvinyl chloride* on steel and masonry sheets have appeared and have enjoyed some use. No information is yet available on their performance.

In conclusion, it is evident that new roofing systems based on a variety of plastic forms, sheets and coatings will play a significant part in future building plans. They probably will not replace the conventional built-up roofing systems altogether, partly because of cost. However, their use will be indicated where architect and builder require beauty, color, extreme resistance to weather, water and chemical attack, and complete freedom of roof design.

19 | PLASTICS ABROAD

PART A: Western Europe

ARMAND G. WINFIELD

Plastics Consultant
New York, New York

INTRODUCTION

This section is a short survey of some of the more interesting developments in Western European usage of plastics in building as observed by the author in two visits.

The United States is considered to be the world leader in the use of plastics in building, but where as we are equally concerned with decorative and functional uses of plastics, the European concentrates on the functional. This may be due in part to his frugality, his conservativism or his resistance to change. Yet despite these limitations many interesting and unusual developments are emerging in Europe.

This paper deals with some interesting high lights in the following countries: Belgium,* Denmark, England, France,* Germany,* Italy,* and Switzerland. The European Common Market has had a marked influence on the plastics industry, increasing the interexchange of plastic products. Plastic products heretofore unknown in many European countries are now gaining popularity. Skilled labor is at a premium, and workers move to countries where wages and advancement are best. With higher pay, workers can buy better clothes, more appliances, better homes.

*Common Market members.

Many of the large cartels are providing the means for mass-produced and prefabricated homes. Coincidentally, the use of plastics as building materials is beginning to make inroads.

DENMARK

During the fall of 1961, Denmark held its first International Plastics Fair or "Plastic-Messe" in Copenhagen. It was the largest plastics exhibition ever held in Scandinavia.

The Danish plastics manufacturing industry, it was stated,[1] has become a social factor of great importance during the 16 years after World War II, its annual production value amounting to something between £25 millions and £50 millions.

Many papers were presented dealing with plastics in building. According to M. Rodeyns, Solvay S.A., Belgium, the use of lead stabilizers in rigid PVC water pipes is perfectly compatible with the requirements of public health, provided the concentration of the stabilizers is kept under 1 per cent.[2] According to Henry Duhot of U. S. Rubber, Naugatuck Chemical Division, U.S.A., accelerated tests have proved that ABS plastics possess good weathering characteristics.[3]

The Plastic-Messe contained a number of items for use in building which are worthy of mention:

(A) Glass fiber-reinforced polyesters are used for telephone booths (Figure 19A1), bathtubs, ventilators, walk-in refrigerators, storage tanks and building facades.

FIG. 19A-1. Glass fiber-reinforced telephone booths designed and produced by Abieco A/S, Copenhagen. (*Photo by author*)

(B) Extremely large sintered polyethylene tanks have been made by the Engel Process—upward of 1000 liters—and can be used for water storage, reservoirs, etc.

(C) Sinks and fixtures of molded non-corrosive polyvinyl chloride were shown—many of German origin.

(D) Polyvinyl chloride pipe in a variety of sizes from 1″ to 14″ diameters are available for water mains, sewage and irrigation.

(E) Polyvinyl chloride is available molded and extruded as gutters and drains for household use.

(F) Extruded polyvinyl chloride is available as floor coverings and wall coverings in a wide variety of textures, colors and effects.

(G) Extruded polyvinyl chloride profiles have been made as stair rails, stair runners, window casings, molding and trim.

(H) Polyvinyl chloride has been extruded as corrugated sheet, with and without wire reinforcement, to supplement fiber glass-reinforced polyester sheet (some of the samples were Japanese imports).

(I) Polyvinyl chloride was extruded as "barbed wire." The polyvinyl chloride is extruded over wire strands and barbed edges and have been applied to the polyvinyl chloride edging.

(J) Also on exhibit were two lightweight aggregates using resin-bonded organic fibers and concrete. Known as "Durisol" and "Stramit," they can be used as insulation or nonstructional walls.

(K) Foamed styrene was molded into a series of insulation applications. Well-designed integral fitting pipe covers were of note.

The use of polyvinyl chloride gutters and downpipes in Denmark is increasing. PVC is also being used for window framework, some insulation, and in flooring. Flooring, however, is restricted to schools or limited use in the older homes—in kitchen and bathrooms. The Danes do not feel sure about using polyvinyl chloride tile in hospitals—floors or walls—because the static electricity generated attracts dust, and they believe that there may be retention of disease-carrying bacteria in this dust.

Acrylonitrile-butadiene-styrene copolymer

FIG. 19A-2. Acrylonitrile-butadiene-styrene toilet reservoir; glass fiber-reinforced polyester bath-tub as shown in the Byggecentrum, Copenhagen, Denmark. (*Photo Courtesy of the Biggecentrum, The Danish Building Center, Copenhagen, Denmark*)

has been used as toilet reservoirs since about 1958 (Figure 19A-2) and glass fiber-reinforced polyesters are being used in bathtubs, in test installations as experimental prototypes. Other appropriate plastics are being used for toilet seats, shower curtains and bathroom wall and floor covering.

Glass fiber-reinforced polyester is also being used in roofing, but since this aspect was introduced only a few years ago, it is used mostly for patio covers in new small houses.

Plastic insulation has been used for more than a decade. Foam insulation seems very good in this country where normal temperatures average -5 to $-10°C$ during the winter. Mineral wool is widely used, but styrene foam is expected to become a large competitor.

Plastic ceilings are beginning to achieve acceptance in institutional use such as banks and insurance companies. Melamine counter tops are going into new homes and buildings. There is some use of polyethylene film in association with concrete. Polyethylene film has been used in wall cavity insulation for about eight years.

A remarkably designed extruded vinyl (Figure 19A-3) waterstop is being used as a peripheral insulation. The diamond-shaped center portion serves as a mechanical spring. When the concrete expands, the diamond collapses; when the concrete contracts, the diamond expands pushing the fins tightly

FIG. 19A-3. Extruded vinyl waterstop. (*Courtesy Cementa A/S, Copenhagen, Denmark*)

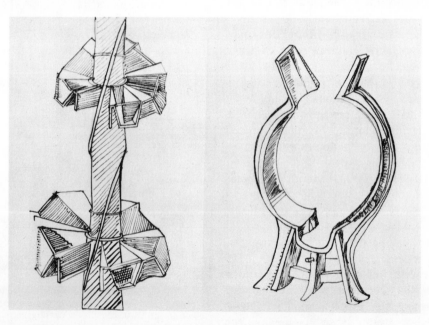

FIG. 19A-4. Injection molded polyvinyl chloride separators used between steel rods in reinforced concrete. (*Courtesy Cementa A/S, Copenhagen, Denmark*)

into position. Molded polyvinyl chloride separators are acceptable between the steel reinforcing rods in precast concrete (Figure 19A-4).

WESTERN GERMANY

At Dynamit-Nobel A/G in Troisdorf (Bez Köln), flame retardant phenolic foams are being produced for the building field, for use in sandwich insulation. Dynamit-Nobel is also using polyvinyl chloride plus styrene foam beads mixed in concrete as "swinging ceilings" 2 to 3 inches thick.

According to Dr. Horst Elsner of the German firm, Europe is generally one to two years behind the United States. The big German plastics applications today in building are in flooring, piping, doors, wall coverings, electrical insulation, and fiber glass-reinforced polyester components.

German standards require water pipes to withstand pressures of 7 atmospheres (102.2 psi). Dynamit-Nobel A/G is now making polyvinyl chloride pipes that have been successfully tested to 70 atmospheres (1020 psi).

covered interior living area, 20 square meters is covered porch and 10 square meters is overhang. The total weight of the "Haus," exclusive of the concrete foundation, is 3.5 tons (3500 kg).

The Haus was built in a "dry" method, except for the concrete slab. No plastics were applied in an uncured state. To break down the 3.5 tons into its components and to show a space-weight relationship, the following analysis is made:

	Volume (m³)	Weight (kg)
Foams: Phenolic		
Rigid polyvinyl chloride	3.5	150
Plastic plates, sheets; surface covering; pipes	1.45	2050
Safety glass	0.18	500
Plastic-covered steel profiles	0.12	750
Miscellaneous		50
Total	5.25	3500

The Haus is 94 per cent plastics by volume. If one discounts the steel profiles (together

Fig. 19A-5. The Troisdorfer Kunststoff-Haus, Grounds of Dynamit-Nobel A/G, Troisdorf, West Germany. (*Courtesy Dynamit-Nobel A/G*)

An experimental bungalow[4] built in 1959 by Dynamit-Nobel A/G utilized only commercially available, semifinished plastic products (Figures 19A-5, 19A-6 and 19A-7). The bungalow has 60 square meters of roof covering—of which 30 square meters is

with their polyvinyl chloride coverings) and the safety glass (with its polyvinyl butyral interlayer), the Haus is 65 per cent plastics by weight.

The Haus, which consists of a living room, bedroom, kitchenette, toilet and covered porch, can be transported by truck. It can be packed into a container 2 × 3 × 1.3 meters (approximately 6½ × 9¾ × 4¼ feet). It can be erected by five persons, each working 14 hours, or in a total of 70 man-hours of labor (Figure 19A-6).

modules (approximately 50 × 95 inches). Structural frames or "carrying" frames were made from polyvinyl chloride covered hollow steel profiles. These were used for windows and doors, as well as walls.

They were pre-cut to length and cemented

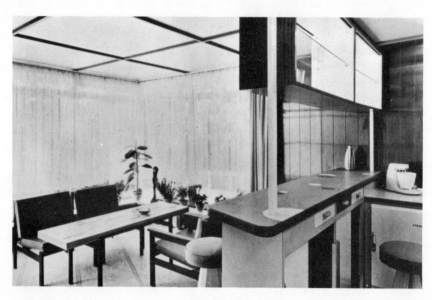

Fig. 19A-6. Interior view of das Troisdorfer Kunststoff-Haus showing furniture, wall partitions, breakfast bar, windows, wall modules, etc. (*Courtesy Dynamit-Nobel A/G*)

Since this bungalow was constructed as an experiment in economics, certain plastics were not used. For example, fiber glass-reinforced polyester profiles were dropped in favor of polyvinyl chloride coated steel, and acrylic was far more expensive than safety glass. Of the plastics chosen, the "Duroplasts" (thermosets) were used for wall covers, roofing, underflooring, and insulation (phenolic foams). "Thermoplasts" (thermoplastics) were used as the floor coverings, electrical insulation, water pipes, elastic insulation (caulking), covers over steel profiles and beams, and for decoration. As previously stated, all plastics were prefabricated or cut to size in advance.

The foundation was made of a concrete slab, protected against moisture with polyethylene sheet. The steel beams were placed on top of the slab based on a construction module of 127 cm (approximately 50 inches), and anchored into the slab.

The walls were standard 127 × 240 cm

together with epoxy cements, then the polyvinyl chloride was welded to provide continuity. Porosity is checked electrically to insure a waterproof protection against rust or corrosion.

The wall slabs are sandwiches of flame-retardant phenolic foams against which melamine laminates are cemented to each face with a neoprene adhesive. The total thickness of this sandwich is 40 mm. and a sandwich of this nature provides the same insulation as a 70 cm brick wall. Most interior panels are 1.3 mm melamine veneers, and the breakfast bar uses a 1.5-mm polyvinyl chloride cover.

The porch door is made of slide louvers of rigid polyvinyl chloride—and resembles the top of a rolltop desk.

The walls are made on movable modules, so that the house can be increased in size. Part of this can be accomplished by extending the walls around the open porch area (Figure 19A-7).

The floors are 16-mm (⅝ inch) thick plates of "Lingnofol," a phenolic-impregnated plywood serving as an underfloor. On this underfloor a foamed "Airex"* polyvinyl

Fig. 19A-7. Das Troisdorfer Kunststoff-Haus showing how to enlarge living area by extending wall modules around open porch area. Compare Fig. 19A-5. (*Courtesy Dynamit-Nobel A/G*)

chloride sheet is placed, and on top of this a prewelded polyvinyl chloride floor covering is laid. The floor meets the walls via a rigid polyvinyl chloride baseboard. The total thickness of the floor is 22 mm (½ inch). It is regarded as an ideal floor because of its insulation, comfort, wear, and maintenance. The vinyl foam gives it a slightly elastic feeling for comfort (like a deep pile rug), and there are no joints in the floor covering since it is prewelded.

The roof supports are made of profiles of rigid polyvinyl chloride covered steel. A fiber glass-reinforced polyester corrugated cover is rolled over these beams. Actually, the roof is like a hollow box. The floor of this box is made of plates of phenolic foam. An air space separates the top from the bottom, and the top layer is the corrugated fiber glass-reinforced polyester.

The caulking is "Prestik."** Sandwich wall panels are caulked to the mullions, slab and roof. Also, all seams where water is a problem, such as in the bath, are "gunked" tight with this caulking.

The house is electrically heated, and all electric wires are covered with polyvinyl chloride. The bathroom utilizes plastics

except for the toilet bowl. The sinks are made from glass fiber-reinforced polyester. Piping is polyvinyl chloride and polyethylene—with cemented joints and hot-welded bends. In the kitchen, the refrigerator is made of thermoformed polyvinyl chloride copolymer. All furniture is covered with veneers of melamine.

The house was well designed, well built, and in excellent condition after two years.

According to Dr. Ing. Karl Mienes, a consulting engineer in Bad Godesberg, German building codes are very strict and differ from state to state—a condition similar to that in the United States. Nevertheless, progress is being made in getting plastics into building. German industrial firms have been doing work with polyvinyl chloride film on aluminum. They have been successful with phenolformaldehyde foam because it can be made flame retardant. Other plastics are being used in flooring and in prefabrication—which Dr. Mienes feels has an important future. Lightweight concretes are being made with epoxies and preblown styrene, and these aggregates can be used to advantage in building.

In furniture, the restrictions are not as critical as in the structural applications and the Germans are using a large assortment of plastics and plastics applications. More and more acrylonitrile butadiene styrene copolymers are being used in furniture where the low static loading permits.

Developments of Badische Anilin- & Soda-Fabrik A/G (BASF) were discussed by Dr. Hans A. Brauns and Dr. Rudolf Gaeth. "Styropor"* is a styrene foam which can be used as sandwich panels in housing or furniture. The density is 20 kg/m³ (8 to 9 pcf). With a wood or synthetic wood veneer (melamine), it makes an attractive laminate. A high-frequency electrical field is used for foaming in place and sealing the skins in place. This method is economical. One cubic meter costs between 100 and 110 Deutsch marks (approximately $.75 per cubic foot or $.06–.07 per board foot), compared to 200 to 250 Deutsch marks for normal chip board. The high-frequency method can foam the

*Trademark, Dynamit-Nobel A/G.
**Trademark, Boston Blacking Co.

*Trademark, BASF

styrene in 3 to 10 seconds; with veneers, in 30 to 40 seconds.

Urea-formaldehydes are being used as adhesives and as foams in large quantities in the building field.

BASF is pushing the use of polyvinyl chloride in homes and institutions, specifically as wall and floor coverings and as pipes. The difficulty, however, is that the German housing authorities restrict most plastics to industrial usage only (Figure 19A-8).

FIG. 19A-8. Polyvinyl chloride used as flooring, stair rails and stair treads. Sales office in the Friedrich Engelhorn House, BASF. (*Courtesy Badische Anilin & Soda-Fabrik*)

Polyethylene films are used in buildings during construction as protective sheaths against weather, but polyisobutylene is used more than polyethylene as insulation film in walls and floors.

BASF is using glass fiber-reinforced polyesters and rigid polyvinyl chloride faces with "Styropor" cores for various building and furniture applications—walls, floors, doors, etc. Foamed styrene squares are also molded, designed, and painted for use as decorative insulative and acoustical ceilings (not unsimilar in appearance and characteristics to the American "Cellulite."*)

Styrene beads are mixed with concrete to produce lightweight aggregates to 0.70 kg/dm³ (approximately 40 pcf).

Resin-coated wood fibers can be overlayed with melamine or urea-formaldehyde skins. These would be used as prefabricated insulat-

ing type walls. Laminations of wood plies using standard urea-formaldehyde adhesives are being used in applications where critical load-bearing structures are involved, e.g., structural laminated arches.

The field of prefabricated houses using plastics is a most promising market.

Rigid polyvinyl chloride corrugated sheets now indicate a better potential in building than corrugated glass fiber-reinforced polyesters.

The application of polyethylene film as an aid in curing concrete is not as successful as anticipated. Straw mats placed on top of uncured concrete are still preferred in road building. It appears that the polyethylene film slows the water evaporation from the concrete slab, and this seems to be more detrimental than helpful.

In Germany, as in most of Europe, very little plastics are used for decorative applications. The Germans are more functional and practical and are more concerned with basic uses than with decoration.

There is also an interesting corrugated sheet for building facades, "Hostalit Z,"* which is primarily a mechanical blend of polyvinyl chloride with chlorinated polyethylene as plasticizer.[6] It is used outdoors for building panels, jalousies, roof gutters, downspouts and ventilators, and indoors for electrical insulation.

Dr. Otto Jordan, of Isar-Chemie GmbH in Munich, pointed out that the per-capita consumption of plastics is higher in Germany than in the United States. In building, the Germans are working toward lightweight concrete aggregates and toward quick-setting cements. In one of the latter, "LaForouche," aluminum oxide combined with polyvinyl acetate is added to the cement mix.

Dr. Jordan has produced modified acrylic dispersions that can be heat-converted at 130 to 140°C. As these are insoluble in perchloroethylene, they open up new possibilities in the rug industry where fibers are "crumpled," impregnated, and attached to linen backings. This produces an inexpensive, dry-cleanable rug or floor covering.

*Trademark, Gilman Brothers Co.

*Trademark, Farbwerke Hoechst A. G.

Trichloroethylene and/or methylene chloride with after-chlorinated polyvinyl chloride makes an excellent adhesive for polyvinyl chloride pipes. This combination does not "show through" when the joint is cut for examination, in contrast to such vinyl solvents as cyclohexanone and tetrahydrofuran, which are slow acting and continue to outgas or "show" for some months after cementing.

Polysulfide-type caulking compounds for sealing and insulating are used rather extensively throughout Germany.

SWITZERLAND

According to Professor Dr. Heinrich Hopff of the Swiss Federal Institute of Technology at Zurich and Dr. Rudolf Gaeth of BASF (Germany), the three main plastics acceptable as building materials in Switzerland are polyvinyl chloride, polyethylene, and polypropylene. A fourth material, nylon, has possibilities.

Polyvinyl chloride pipe is used in the food industry for beverages and in the chemical industry. The Swiss produce about 2000 tons of polyvinyl chloride annually. They import many plastics, especially polyethylene and methyl methacrylate.

Portable polyethylene pipe has been suggested for bringing milk down from the mountain herds. The problem of sterilizing the pipe remains to be solved, possibly by steam.

ITALY

Italy has always been a European leader in plastics applications. As early as 1958-1959, polyvinyl chloride profiles were in use as window frames, stair rails, and garage doors (of slats making a slide roll type).

Plastics played a key role in the recent rewiring of St. Peter's Basilica in Vatican City. The million-dollar project, carried out by Phillips Radio and Television Trust as a gift, was required to safeguard art treasures by eliminating fire hazards, and to lessen maintenance problems. It was necessary to disassemble altars, remove works of art, remove marble floor slabs, and lay in PVC pipe, all without interrupting normal functions.

Polyvinyl chloride served as a protective

FIG. 19A-9. Polyvinyl chloride pipe in Vatican installation showing formed shoulder joint. (*Photo by author, with special permission of Director S.E. Primo Principi, Palazzo San Carlo, Vatican City, Rome, Italy*)

tunnel sheath for polyethylene-covered conduit and cable. The polyvinyl chloride pipes were of two shades of color and were used in at least three diameters ranging from 2¼-inch OD with a wall thickness of ³⁄₁₆ inch to a 7-inch OD with a wall thickness of ⅛ inch. They carried the marking: "Ceramica Possi" —Milano—160A. The pipes were joined with adhesives. Some pipes had formed shoulders (Figure 19A-9) to facilitate easy joints; others had to be beveled to fit during the application (Figure 19A-10).

FIG. 19A-10. Polyvinyl chloride pipe in Vatican installation being laid on gravel bed. Joints are beveled to fit during application. (*Photo by author, with special permission — see Fig. 19A-9*)

The method of installation was to lift the marble wall or floor slabs with as little damage as possible and to lay polyvinyl chloride pipes on a gravel bed. The pipes were placed in concrete before slabs were replaced. Occasionally the marble had to be cut and left as an opening (with false wall-door).

The Basilica's interior is 691 feet in length, and the ceilings vary from 75 feet at the arcades of the central nave to 137 feet at the dome.[7] Since the installation was around the periphery of the Basilica, with at least three various sized pipes being used, and since this periphery interweaves into the various chapels, crypts, vaults, and niches, the floor area alone is quite extensive. In addition, the cables had to circumvent the altar and statuary in order to reach the upper heights of the arcades and domes, canopies, crowns, lanterns and lamps, pillars and medallions. Cables were installed in trunks between the dome walls, and branched out into many pipes and receptacles into the dome's interior.

The installation of the polyvinyl chloride pipe and the polyethylene-covered cables in St. Peter's Basilica should be proof of the safety, practicability, and even economy of such installations for buildings in general.

FRANCE

As noted earlier in this chapter, most Europeans are less concerned with the aesthetic uses of plastics than with the functional and structural. In France, however, the aesthetic uses of plastics took on an exciting aspect. These aspects are most pointedly demonstrated by the work of Jean Pierre Fisholle of Compagnie Européenne du Crystopal.

M. Fisholle has created a unique process for the controlled cracking of translucent thermosetting resins. In color, the products offer unique architectural effects. Called "Crystopal," this material may be translucent or opaque, and can be used for light walls, stairs, doors, door handles, facades, columns, counter tops, table tops, lighting, "stained glass," lamps, and accessories. Cast in masses weighing as much as 200 kg (440

pounds), panels can be made flat or semicircular.

Société Félicie, in Paris (Figure 19A-11), has used a two-toned "Crystopal" in green

FIG. 19A-11. Société Félice showing use of "Crystopal" facades, pillars and door handles. (*Photo by author, Courtesy Crystopal, Ltd., Hazardville, Conn.*)

and deep yellow to accent the smart decor of the shop. The outside panels at the sides of the shop and above the windows (on which the name is mounted) are 1-inch-thick slabs of the material. Using the same color scheme throughout, the columns visible inside the window (and in the interior of this couturiére) are made of split cylinders of "Crystopal" mounted around steel posts. The door handles are also of the same material. The outside panels have successfully withstood the elements for over three years.

The famous glass company, St. Gobain, has used this material for push plates on its glass plate doors and as the illuminated back wall of a bar.

As a light panel, "Crystopal" has been successfully used in a stair well in Fabrique du Television; Ste. Ribet—Des Jardin, Siége Social—Mont Rouge. These panels, mounted like stained glass, are used as lights in the dark stairwell. The color and texture of the plastic produce an iridescent effect.

Deep amber "Crystopal" sheets, approximately 1¼ inches thick, have been suspended and underlighted to form counter tops of a leading hairdresser (Figure 19A-12).

The Agency Immobilière has utilized "Crystopal" in a pale gray "Niche" some 7 feet tall, semicircular in shape, and lighted from behind. A series of curved panels

FIG. 19A-12. "Crystopal" counter tops, Paris hairdresser. (*Courtesy Crystopal, Ltd., Hazardville, Conn.*)

approximately 30 inches wide and 7 feet high, mullion joined together and dramatically lighted, makes a most unusual rotunda, also,

FIG. 19A-13. "Crystopal" Rotunda, Information Immobilière, Paris. (*Photo by author, courtesy Crystopal, Ltd., Hazardville, Conn.*)

in the Information Immobilière, Boulevard du Capucines (Figure 19A-13).

The material has also been used semistructurally. In association with steel supports, "floating" stairs of "Crystopal" have been in daily use for over three years at the Charbonnages de France, Avenue Déclassé (Figure 19A-14). The material looks weak, yet is very strong.

FIG. 19A-14. Plastic "floating" stairs at the Charbonnages de France. (*Courtesy Crystopal, Ltd., Hazardville, Conn.*)

"Crystopal" has been used out-of-doors in Paris as theater doors (Cinema La Rotonde, Boulevard du Mont Parnasse), building facades, and as inside-outside light walls (Café du Rond-Point, Les Champs-Elysées). After three years of outdoor weathering, the panels were holding up surprisingly well.

M. Fisholle has also created a second art medium known as "Luminail." He applies to sheets of translucent fiber glass-reinforced polyester various catalyzed colored resins in patterns which his artists create. Sometimes these are realistic portraits or scenes, sometimes they are abstract. At other times the result resembles stained glass. To achieve a third dimension, he incorporates broken "Crystopal." Murals using this technique have been installed in the children's dining room (Tourist Class) of the new French luxury liner, *France* (Figure 19A-15).

FIG. 19A-15. "Luminail" decorative panel in children's dining room on French luxury liner The France. (*Courtesy The French Line, New York, N. Y.*)

A second group of exciting French applications of plastics for building and interior architecture was seen at "L'Objet," an extensive exhibition of avant-garde painting, sculpture, and architecture at the Palais du Louvre.

FIG. 19A-16. "Fontaine Transparente." Henri-George Adam. (*Photo by Pierre Joly-Vera Cardot, courtesy Palais du Louvre, Pavillon de Marsan, Paris France*)

Among the most interesting uses of plastics was a fountain by Henri-George Adam made of polyester and iron. Called "Fontaine Transparente," it is 2 meters high (approximately 6½ feet) and 1.5 meters (5 feet) in breadth[8] (Figure 19A-16). Fountains of this type can be used indoors or outdoors.

In the field of architecture, several building models using or projecting the use of plastics were most unusual. One by André Bloc, called "Sculpture Habitacle,"[9] was a sculp-

FIG. 19A-17. "Sculpture Habitacle," André Bloc. (*Photo by Pierre Joly-Vera Cardot, courtesy Palais du Louvre, Pavillon de Marsan, Paris, France*)

tural free-form plastic structure. Using simple and complex sculptural forms, Bloc creates an internal labyrinth of pleasing shapes—allowing light to enter in a pattern controlled by apertures in the sculptural form itself (Figure 19A-17). Bloc's model is designed for glass fiber-reinforced polyester. There seems to be an inside sculptural surface and an exterior one with an insulating air space between. The model was $3 \times 2 \times 2$ meters ($9\frac{3}{4} \times 6\frac{1}{2} \times 6\frac{1}{2}$ feet).

The second of the housing structures, in model form, was by a team of Michel Genier, painter; Piotr Kowalski, architect; and Philippe Muel, painter and sculptor.[10] Using glass fiber-reinforced polyesters, they created free forms for building structures mounted on concrete and brick slabs.

Piotr Kowalski also exhibited alone with glass fiber-reinforced polyester shelters designed as "Maquettes Pour Un Musée d'Art Contemporain (en Plein Air); Côte Ligure, Italy"[11]* (Figure 19A-18). These models in-

FIG. 19A-18. "Maquettes Pour Un Musée d'Art Contemporain (en Plein Air), Côte Ligure, Italy," Piotr Kowalski. (*Photo by Annet Held. Courtesy of Palais du Louvre, Pavillon de Marsan, Paris, France*)

dicate what can be accomplished with versatile reinforced polyesters in size, shape, and feel.

BELGIUM

An experimental house (Figure 19A-19) created by Designer Jacques Ladyjensky in Belgium utilizes 65 per cent plastics. Its

FIG. 19A-19. Belgium experimental plastics house designed and built by Jacques Ladyjensky. (*Courtesy Modern Plastics Magazine*)

structural upright supports are made by filling T-shaped polyvinyl chloride extrusions (Figure 19A-20) with reinforced concrete. The polyvinyl chloride covering remains as a

* Translation: Sketches (models) for a Museum of Contemporary Art (in the open air), Côte Ligure, Italy.

surface facing over the structural concrete. The roof and other components are added to this basic unit.

FIG. 19A-20. T-shaped polyvinyl chloride extrusions which are filled with reinforced concrete and which serve as the structural beams. (*Courtesy Modern Plastics Magazine*)

ENGLAND

England's use of plastics in the building field is growing rapidly, accelerated by such giants as Imperial Chemical Industries Limited and the subdivisions of American and German companies. The Plastics Institute has spurred usage through its Building Sub-Committee, which has collected histories of the uses of plastics in building to provide information for architects, quantity surveyors and civil engineers. The institute has also sponsored educational courses on plastics in building.

This survey of English uses of plastics in buildings will encompass three areas: (a) outdoor applications, (b) indoor applications, and (c) accessories.

Outdoor Applications

Among the outdoor uses of interest is a spire of fiber glass-reinforced polyester[13] which has been installed at St. Andrew's Presbyterian Church in Dartford (Figures 19A-21 and 19A-22). It has been constructed

FIG. 19A-22. Engineer checks fiber glass-reinforced polyester base to spire of St. Andrew's Church. (*Photo by Associated Press Studio. Courtesy Bakelite, Ltd., London*)

FIG. 19A-21. Installation of fiber glass-reinforced polyester spire at St. Andrew's Presbyterian Church, Dartford, England. (*Photo by Walter A. Lee. Courtesy Bakelite, Ltd, London*)

with a base or skirt, also of glass fiber-reinforced polyester, which has been joined to the spire proper. The entire unit provided a quick and simple installation to the supporting tower and did not interfere with the other building work in process.

At the Nant-y-Moch Dam near Aberystwyth, England, a sheet of "Darvic"* polyvinyl chloride has been applied to a dam wall, serving as a water level gauge. Polyvinyl chloride was chosen because of its non-corrosive properties.

*Trademark, Imperial Chemical Industries, Ltd.

FIG. 19A-23. Polytetrafluoroethylene expansion bearing plates on deck of bridge at Comber, County Down, Northern Ireland. (*Photo by Stewart Bale. Courtesy Imperial Chemical Industries Ltd.*)

Expansion bearings of polytetrafluoroethylene are on the deck of a bridge in northern Ireland (Figure 19A-23). These plates, made from a prefinished, high-performance bearing material containing "Fluon" P.T.F.E.,* require no lubrication in view of their low coefficient of friction. In building, this material might be used where sections must rotate—revolving stages in theaters, revolving restaurants, etc.

In more conventional applications, the English are making use of lightweight protective panels of .005 polyethylene film mounted skintight over a Canadian western red cedar grid framework in 1-foot squares. These panels are easy to handle; a 4 × 8 foot section weighs about one-half pound. These sashes are used as an economical form of weatherproofing during road and house building, swimming pool construction, over sports arenas, etc. They will withstand wind gusts up to 70 mph and are waterproof and "hard-wearing."

For factory lighting, corrugated "Perspex"* acrylic sheets have been fabricated as the entire roof (Figure 19A-24). This well-tested outdoor weathering material provides an attractive and functional cover. Flat acrylic sheets topped with corrugated sheets form the domes and lanterns at the Brook County Secondary School (Figure 19A-25).

FIG. 19A-25. Dome lights and lantern lights made from flat and corrugated acrylic sheets at the Brook County Secondary School, Loughton, England. (*Courtesy Imperial Chemical Industries Limited*)

Polyvinyl chloride sheets are being used both functionally and decoratively as store and building facades and as gables on residential housing. Some of these panels have

FIG. 19A-24. Factory roof of G. & J. Weir, Cathcart, Scotland constructed of corrugated acrylic sheets. (*Photo by Scottish Studios. Courtesy Imperial Chemical Industries Limited*)

*Trademark, Imperial Chemical Industries, Ltd.

FIG. 19A-26. Polyvinyl chloride extrusions as gutter and downspout on bungalow at Durley, near Bishops Waltham, England. (*Photo by Studio Cole. Courtesy Imperial Chemical Industries Limited*)

been successful in outdoor applications for over 5 years. Polyvinyl chloride is also being used for gutters and downspouts (Figure 19A-26). A window marketed under the name "Woodplast"* consists of a wood frame covered with extruded polyvinyl chloride (Figure 19A-27).

FIG. 19A-27. Window made by extruding polyvinyl chloride over wood framework. (*Photo by Studio Cole. Courtesy Imperial Chemical Industries Limited*)

Indoor Applications

The English are using polyvinyl chloride as indoor wall partitions over wood partitions, particularly in industrial applications, as

FIG. 19A-28. Illuminated ceiling made from "Corvic"* vinyl chloride polymer for the showrooms of Kennings, Redhill, Surrey, England. (*Photo by Bedford Lemere. Courtesy Imperial Chemical Industries Limited*)

*Trademark, Imperial Chemical Industries Limited

floor covering and as electrical insulation. Luminous ceilings of vinyl chloride polymer have been made as diffusers (Figure 19A-28).

"Perspex" acrylic sheet has likewise been

*Trademark, Woodplast Associates, Ltd., Harpendon, England.

used for ceiling lights and produces brilliancy and beauty found in few other plastic materials (Figure 19A-29). Both as ceilings and light walls (Figure 19A-30) this material produces the effect of frozen light.

The use of polyester film as a vapor barrier has been successfully demonstrated with "Asbestolux"* acoustical panels, installed in

FIG. 19A-29. "Perspex"* acrylic sheets, opal color, .040 inch thickness, used as ceiling light diffusers in main reception hall at the B.B.C. Television Centre, London, W.12, England. (*Photo by Studio Cole. Courtesy Imperial Chemical Industries Limited*)

*Trademark, Imperial Chemical Industries Limited

the main swimming area at the new swimming baths at West Bromwich. In these 24 × 24 inch panels, a .002-inch "Melinex"** polyester film backing provides the necessary blockoff to the wet, damp atmosphere.

*Trademark, Cape Building Products Ltd., Uxbridge, Middlesex, England.
**Trademark, Imperial Chemical Industries, Ltd.

Accessories

In the accessory field, the English are making most unusual uses of the acrylics. Whereas, in most of the other countries covered in this survey, the accessory field utilized limited amounts of acrylics and considerably more of glass fiber-reinforced polyesters,

FIG. 19A-30. "Perspex" acrylic light wall serving as screen between offices and showroom of Williams Motor Co., Ltd., Trafford Street, Manchester, England. (*Photo by Stewart Bale. Courtesy Imperial Chemical Industries Limited*)

acrylonitrile-butadiene-styrene materials and polyvinyl chlorides, the English have created a series of functional accessories based on the beauty, abrasion resistance, weathering and water repellency of the acrylic resins. Figures 19A-31, 19A-32 and 19A-33 show a selection of these most interesting applications, which include sinks, drains, tubs, fountains and urinals.

CONCLUSIONS

There are many peripheral areas such as agriculture and road building which utilize plastics. In this category are the Italian method of enclosing multi-acre fields under large plastic film tents,[15] and the German experiments in air-inflated structures. Also of interest is the use of plastics in Vienna's airport (Figure 19A-34), experimental Scandinavian plastic houses, irrigation problems in Finland and Spain, and road building in the "Satellite" countries using Soviet techniques.

Had Antonio Gaudí (1852–1926), the Spanish architect-designer, lived during the

FIG. 19A-31. "Crelene"* acrylic sink and double drainer. (*Photo by Carlton Studio. Courtesy Imperial Chemical Industries Limited*)

*Trademark, Troman Bros. Limited, Warwickshire, England

FIG. 19A-32. "Cleopatra"* acrylic bathtub, transparent. (*Photo by Studio Cole. Courtesy Imperial Chemical Industries Limited*)

*Trademark, P & S Plastics Ltd., Gloucester, England

era of plastics, we would probably be seeing innovations far more advanced and revolutionary than any known today. Practically everything that Gaudí designed is plastic in

Fig. 19A-33. Prototype drinking fountain of "Perspex" acrylic sheet. (*Courtesy Imperial Chemical Industries Limited*)

feeling. From the unadulterated beauty of nature, he transposed the undulating surfaces and flowing forms to create a new and exciting architecture.

Fig. 19A-34. Roof of new Vienna Airport showing use of thermoformed acrylic hemispheres as skylights. Multiplicity of lights serves as design as well as in the functional application of lighting and main area of the terminal below. (*Photo by author*)

Gaudí's school on the grounds of the Famillia Sagrada first uses the zig-zag barrel vaulting,[16] now popular through "the innovation of structural plastic foam form boards."[17] Pier Luigi Nervi's exhibition hall in Turin uses tilted branching supports directly attributable to Gaudí. Nervi's UNESCO Building in Paris exemplifies the Gaudí influence in the Assembly Hall. Le Corbusier's warped forms in his Philips Pavillion at the Brussels Exposition in 1958 are directly attributable to a Gaudí influence; and Felix Candéla, in his church of Santa Maria Milagrosa, in Mexico City, used the tilted columns to support a concrete roof of hyperbolic paraboloidal shells—another Gaudí innovation which can be made more feasible through the use of plastics.

In our world of new and exciting plastic materials, complex curves and obtuse angles are as simple to achieve as the flow of the material itself. If we are to continue to upgrade our plastic materials as well as to uplift our aesthetic standards, we must look to the guiding spirits of the great innovators, past and present, European and American.

Acknowledgment. The author is greatly indebted to the many scientists and technologists who assisted him in the preparation of this material.

REFERENCES

1. "Officielt Messekatalog," Introduction, p. 1, Copenhagen, International Plastic-Messe.
2. *Ibid.*, Section C: Applications, p. 11.
3. *Ibid.*, pp. 12, 13.
4. Von Dipl.-Ing. Reinhold Frenz, "Ein Kunststoff-Haus in Bungalow-Stil," Troisdorf *Kunststoffe*, **50**, (1960).
5. Licenses for this BASF process are available in the United States through the Dow Chemical Company, the Koppers Company or the Monsanto Chemical Company.
6. "New Polymer Blend Upgrades PVC," *Mod. Plastics*, 24-95 (April 1961).
7. Venturini, E., "The Eternal City," pp. 168-186, Rome, Lozzi Publisher, 1961.
8. Catalogue of "Antagonismes 2, L'Objet," p. 1, Musée des Arts Decoratifs, Palais du Louvre, Pavillon de Marsan, Spring 1962.
9. *Ibid.*, p. 12.
10. *Ibid.*, p. 53.
11. *Ibid.*, p. 78.
12. "New Day for Plastics in Architecture: Part 1," *Mod. Plastics*, 88-91 March 1962.
13. Polyester resin by Bakelite Limited; engineering by Brylan Plastics.
14. "Polysash," produced by British Cellophane Ltd, Henrietta House, London, England.
15. Ferrais, Enrico, "Il Film de Polietilene Nell'-

agricoltura," *Materie Plastiche*, **12**, No. XXVII, (December 1961.

16. Dietz, Albert G. H., Contemporary Shell Structures," *Mod. Plastics* 91-94 (March 1962.

17. Tenney, H. W., Jr., "Plastics—A New Dimension in Buildings: Versatile Plastic Foams for Building Insulation," p. 47, published by the Plastics in Building Professional Activity Group of the Society of Plastics Engineers, Inc., Stamford, Connecticut, 1961.

PART B: *The Soviet Union*

ARMAND G. WINFIELD

Plastics Consultant
New York, New York

The writer received an American Specialist Grant* during the summer of 1961 to accompany the U.S.I.A. exhibition, "Plastics—U.S.A." to the Soviet Union, where it was shown for three-week periods in Kiev, Moscow and Tbilisi. Two-thirds of all the questions asked at the exhibitions were concerned with the use of plastics in building. In addition, the writer gave lectures and interviewed architects, designers and builders.

The Soviet government has undertaken staggering programs of building and rebuilding its country, and Soviet construction specialists are keenly aware of the potential that plastics offer. It is extremely important that the Soviets continue to build at a rapid rate and in a better manner than at present, to relieve their critical housing shortage.

At Kiev, the Academy of Building was constructing an institute devoted entirely to building problems which would be the largest in all of the Soviet Union—6 million square meters.** This laboratory will deal with many problems that are foreseen in the use of plastics as building materials.

Additives to concrete are of much interest, to increase the weather, water and moisture resistance not only in housing applications but also in hydroelectric dams. The Soviet specialists informed us that they are using

"furfural."* They are experimenting with silanolates† as additives to concrete in roads so that during the strenuous winter months

FIG. 19B-1. Polymethyl methacrylate capitals for fluorescent lighting, department store, Kiev. Designed by Oleg Konstantinovich Koshevoi, 1952. (*Photo Courtesy of O. K. Koshevoi*)

---

*U. S. Department of State.

**Projected on an American basis, this space would provide for approximately 30,000 chemists. Engineers require more space and would deplete this number by approximately 16 to 20 per cent.

*Specific identity of the furfural material was not offered.

†$RSiX_3 \xrightarrow{MOH} (RSiO_2M)_n$

ice can be easily removed from the surface of the roads with an ice breaker; the silicone layer keeps the ice from sticking fast to the road surface.

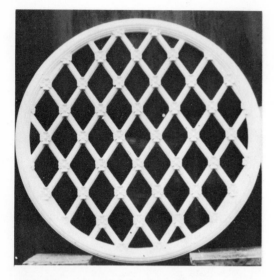

FIG. 19B-2. Grill used in Kiev and Moscow Metros, 1956—Developed by Oleg Konstantinovitch Koshevoi. (*Photo Courtesy of O. K. Koshevoi*)

Soviet builders are progressing rather cautiously with the use of plastics in building applications. They are placing considerable effort in their Institutes and are field testing many plastic materials in a number of buildings in Moscow and Leningrad. A major problem is the lack of craftsmanship among the artisan workers who are responsible for installation.

In the laboratories of the Institute of Building Materials, PVC and other floor tiles were being tested. A tile made of coumarone resin and petroleum by-products has good impact resistance and good wear resistance on the flat, but the edges break easily. A very cheap material—rosin—is added as an anti-slip.

Another series of experimental floor tiles were made of PVC coated with styrene butadiene. Still a third series comprised PVC tiles cemented to wood particle board. In this manner, an entire floor including the particle underflooring could be laid in one operation. Although the indication was that this was an economic saving, in all probability it was also one way of assuring a level floor as well, since evenly laid tile could be applied to the underfloor at the factory.

PVC film is being manufactured in the Soviet Union on a limited basis for wall covering, curtains, and lamp shades. Experimentally, PVC film has been backed with

FIG. 19B-3. Sculptures, 3.5 meters in height, made of acrylic and styrene copolymers, gold leafed. Installed on facade of the Machine Construction Pavilion, Vystvaka Perovodogo Opyta, Kiev. Sculpture by Oleg Konstantinovitch Koshevoi, 1956 (*Photo Courtesy O. K. Keshevoi*)

paper fabric and pressure-sensitive adhesive. The Soviets produce 150,000 square meters of unsupported PVC film per year for building applications, slightly more than 1 per cent of their needs for the projected building program.

Styrene tiles, in limited use, are attached to walls with coumarone adhesives.

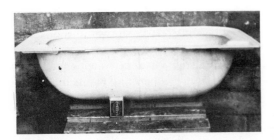

FIG. 19B-4. Experimental sink made of acrylic with reinforced glass fibers by Oleg Konstantinovitch Koshevoi, Kiev, 1955–1956, (*Photo courtesy of O. K. Koshevoi*)

The Soviet building specialists are using particle board composition flooring made with urea-formaldehyde binders and laminated PVC covering. This is preferred to ply-

FIG. 19B-5. Interior walls of Lenin Hills Metro Station, Moscow, light blue melamine. Manufactured in Leningrad. (*Photo by author*)

wood because it is cheaper. The boards are made with German equipment. Although the Soviets have been producing particle boards on a limited scale since the end of World War II, the current particle board industry

was started in 1960 with a production of ½ million m³/yr, to be increased sevenfold by 1965. The boards are made from wood particles, filings, chips, sawdust, etc., mixed with amino resin binders and pressed under heat and pressure. They can be made in one, two or three layers. In a three-layer board, the middle layer would be two-thirds of the entire thickness. The middle layer is made up

FIG. 19B-6. Superstructure made of glass fiber-reinforced polyester on experimental high speed pleasure boat, 48 feet long, being tested on Black Sea area near Odessa. Boat was designed by Sergei Kotchubey and manufactured in Leningrad. (*Photo courtesy Sergei Kotchubey*)

of regular or large particles while the skins are of very fine particles. Boards are produced in standard building modules of 3500 mm in length, 1250 to 1500 mm in width

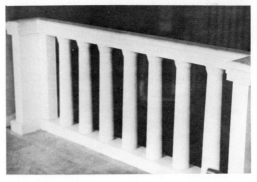

FIG. 19B-7. Balustrade of cast acrylic, made by Oleg Konstantinovitch Koshevoi, Kiev. (*Photo Courtesy O. K. Koshevoi*)

and 8-50 mm thick. For flooring use, smaller sizes are made, which, when covered by a mastic, can have the surface tiles applied.

The density of the board is controlled by the particle size. Boards are classified as

Light	300–500 kg/m³
Medium	500–700 kg/³
Heavy	750–1000 kg/³
Very heavy	Over 1000 kg/³

The most popular board in use today is a medium board of around 600 to 650 kg/m³. Lightweight boards are used for insulation; medium weight for furniture and partitions; heavy and very heavy for flooring. The boards have the following physical-mechanical properties:

Density, kg/m³	Light (to 450)	Medium (450-750)	Heavy (750)	Very Heavy (1100)
Flexural strength, kg/cm²	50	50–250	210	500
Flexural modulus of elasticity kg/cm²			28,000	70,000
Breakage parallel to surface, kg/cm²			21	175
Stability against breakage perpendicular to surface, kg/cm²			19	28
Compressive strength parallel to surface kg/cm²			240	280
Water absorption in 24 hours	to 90%	35%	15%	40%
Coefficient of thermal conductivity, kcal/m hr °C	0.045			

To make the board, particles are obtained either by grinding or by hammer-milling, classified according to particle size, and dried in either cylindrical or ribbon type dryers. Resin binder is then added, preferably urea-formaldehyde, in amounts of 7 to 12 per cent of the weight of the "dry" particles (which still retain 7 to 8 per cent water, however). The binder is half the cost. The boards are preformed cold under pressures of 5 to 20 kg/cm², then transferred to multiplaten presses where they are pressed at 190°C and pressures of 15 to 35 kg/cm². Finally, they are removed and trimmed.

Phenol-formaldehyde foams which are fire resistant are being used in prototype insulation-type wall sandwich sections.

Styrene seems to be a very popular material, both in resins and in foam. The resins are used in film and filament, in electrical insulation, as packages for foods and medicine, and as foams for acoustical barriers, insulation, refrigeration and packaging.

Flame-retardant PVC is increasing in popularity as a building material. Most plastic pipes and ducts are made of PVC because of its anti-corrosive properties. Some polypropylene is used in limited quantities, experimentally, where higher temperatures must be tolerated.

Extruded PVC bannisters, floor and baseboard trims were seen in many of the buildings visited.

PVC films are used as moisture barriers as well as decoratively in shower curtains, wall coverings, etc.

Chlorinated PVC as a water emulsion is finding uses in lacquers and paints for out-of-door surfaces.

Polyester resins, reinforced with fiber glass, are being used as ceilings, skylights and superstructures to boats. They are also incorporated in paints, providing a hard surface and high temperature resistance at low cost.

Polymethyl methacrylate is used extensively for lighting.

It appears that the Soviets can make in their laboratories or pilot plants almost anything in the plastics field that we can produce. However, in mass production they are far behind us.

At the Lenin Hills Metro Station in Moscow, the entrance is through methacrylate doors with cream-colored melamine laminate paneling as an archway. Tan-brown colored melamine laminates are also used on the sides and the tops of the dividing sections of the escalators as well as bright blue panels on the interior walls in the station proper. Acrylics are used as the diffusers over the fluorescent lighting throughout the station.

At the Youth Hotel in Moscow, the floors

in the main lobby were vinyl tile and some vinyls were used as wall coverings. The acoustical ceilings were of experimental plastic and fiber-glass tiles produced in the Building Academy. Most of the lighting fixtures throughout the building used acrylic light-diffusing grills. A motion picture theater in one part of the hotel had a ceiling made of yellow glass fiber-reinforced polyester corrugated panels, and the cocktail lounge had melamine laminate countering.

Fig. 19B-8. "Torshiri" lamp posts, Moscow, 1955 – present. Designed by Oleg Konstantinovitch Koshevoi, Kiev. (*Photo Courtesy O. K. Koshevoi*)

Corridor lights extending the full length of long corridors were encased in methacrylate. Melamine laminates were used for table tops, counter tops and dresser tops in the hotel rooms.

The Soviet specialists were extremely interested in mass-production techniques and better usage of plastics, and would like to purchase American technical know-how. Unlike us, the Soviet planner prefers an integrated plant handling all phases of pro-

duction from the manufacture of the raw material to the finished end product.

At Kiev, a leading Soviet architect-sculptor, Oleg Konstantinovitch Koshevoi, has been working with plastics in building and art since the early 1950's. He and his group were primarily interested in cast acrylics, PVC, polyethylenes, styrene and styrene copolymers. These materials, converted to art forms, were one-sixth the cost of bronze statues and one-ninth the cost of marble ones—a great economic saving. Plastics could also be used in building, in building decoration, and in lighting. Mr. Koshevoi made a balustrade for his house of cast acrylic in sections weighing 2000 kg each. He also cast some 4000 grills of an acrylic-styrene copolymer for Metro Stations in Moscow and Kiev. Other grills are indicated as being of cast acrylic and PVC.

Soviet museums have a multiplicity of plastic sculptures, some imitating bronze, marble, ceramic, bone, various stones, asbestos or wood, others taking advantage of the peculiar characteristics of the various plastic materials—translucency, light transmission, light and color stability.

Mr. Koshevoi, a pioneer in plastics art, saw in these materials ease of handling, unlimited potentials, inexpensive molds and great economic savings. He has developed large pieces done in sections as well as small pieces done as total entities. For outdoor usage, he worked with polymethyl methacrylate (beads), polystyrene (beads), and polyvinyl chloride (powder). He also used various copolymers: vinyl chloride–vinyl acetate (85:15), methyl methacrylate–styrene (90:10), and styrene-acrylonitrile (72:28). Some casting was done from monomer.

Plaster molds were used; they were cored and steam heated to 100 or 120°C for a 3 to 4 hour cycle (240°C for accelerated cures). Metal molds were employed only rarely, because of expense.

In order to cut back on cost of plastic materials, Mr. Koshevoi first built up his armature with plaster or concrete. Over this, he started to build his surface detail with layers of polymer, to which fillers, colors,

FIG. 19B-9. Soviet helicopter using glass fiber-reinforced polyester tail fins and propeller blades, Moscow 1961. (*Photo by author*)

etc., could be added. Hollow castings could also be made.

One of Mr. Koshevoi's formulations for architectural details and sculpture is as follows:

"In vessels of 8 to 10 liters, pour 3 kg of methyl methacrylate in which is dissolved 2 per cent stearic acid and 0.2 per cent benzoyl peroxide and 3 to 4 per cent dibutyl phthalate plus very little color (for white—300 to 400 grams of zinc, however).

"Prepare polymers by taking 2 kg of copolymer made of methyl methacrylate and styrene and 2.2 kg polyvinyl chloride in powder form and 300 grams of "Egelite" resin or styrene-acrylonitrile copolymer.

"The first batch is mixed for 10 to 20 minutes and the second for 1 to 2.

"They are then both mixed together and poured into the mold. Heat is applied (120°C) to aid polymerization.

"Cold-curing materials are achieved by adding bronze powder to the polymer or a liquid activator such as dimethyl aniline or dimethyl-*p*-toluidine to the monomer.

"These materials have good weatherability, can be made flame retardant. They can be assembled by cementing, can be sanded and can be surface finished with polyamide lacquers.

"Cracks can be filled with mixtures of methyl methacrylate and 3 per cent each of dichloroethane and benzoyl peroxide."

In the middle' fifties, Mr. Koshevoi experimented with sinks and tubs made of acrylic reinforced with glass fiber, and eventually produced some 200 of these units. He also produced tables of glass fiber-reinforced polyester.

He has also used methyl methacrylate capitals for fluorescent lighting in Soviet department store columns and polystyrenes

for decorative lamp posts, some up to 2.2 meters in height. Some 9000 of his acrylic lamps, 3.2 meters long, weighing 6.5 kg each are installed in Moscow and Kiev.

In addition to these utilitarian applications of plastics, Mr. Koshevoi and other members of the Kiev group have been making thousands of large monuments and friezes, resin castings, as exterior decorations for buildings. In 1956, the sculptures of the Machine Construction Pavilion at the Permanent Exhibition Grounds in Kiev were cast 3.5 meters high in acrylic and styrene materials. These have been covered with gold leaf and are quite impressive. The fountain behind the main pavilion of Kiev Vystvaka was also his work as was the 10-meter-high statue called "Harvest" made of polyester-reinforced glass fiber, weighing 2800 kg, executed in 1955, which graces the pinnacle of the main agricultural building in the same park.

It is also interesting to note that massive sculptures as well as small ones have been executed using Mr. Koshevoi's techniques over the past 20 years, and most of them seem to be in excellent condition after out-of-door weathering for over a decade. These materials are continually achieving more widespread usage throughout the Soviet Union.

To sum up, the Soviets have a very keen interest in the potential for plastics in building. They are continually experimenting and borrowing outside technology, whenever possible. Until they are able to master mass-production and installation techniques, however, they will remain behind the United States and the Western world. Plastics usage in building will depend very much upon the attitude of the government.

In view of the continued interest of the new generation of young modern architects in the experimental, and accelerated programs to build more and more plastics laboratories, the indications are very favorable for a substantial breakthrough in Soviet usage of plastics in building in the not-too-distant future. We in the Western world should be aware of what these Soviet specialists are accomplishing so that perhaps we may learn something through their efforts as well as through our own.

PART C: Japan

MASANORI KANAI* AND KAORU MAEDA

Sekisui Chemical Co., Ltd.
Central Research Laboratory
Mishimagun-Hirose
Osaka, Japan

In describing plastics as building materials in Japan, it is necessary to touch briefly on the characteristics of Japanese architectural style and the development of plastics as building materials.

Japanese Architectural Style and Mode of Living

In Western countries there is not much difference between styles of living in the business office and at home. In Japan, however, most people at home are still enjoying the old mode of living handed down from generation to generation, although it is gradually changing. Western styles of living and construction already prevail at the office, but at home Japanese people still follow earlier customs. Kawara (earthen tiles) are still the predominant roofing materials. In view of the difference in the manner of living, it is no wonder that the materials used in the furnishing of the interior of the house are also quite different from those used in western countries.

Of late, however, research on prefabricated construction of both small and large buildings has made remarkable progress, and prefabricated houses in which plastics are used are gaining considerable popularity. Plastics are becoming more important as buildings become taller and larger, with the adoption of curtain-wall construction.

Development of Plastics in Japan

Production of plastics in Japan has increased fivefold in the last five years, surpassing the growth rate in other countries.

*Deceased.

Japan ranked third in the production of plastics in 1961, following the United States and West Germany. Table 19C-1 compares the production of individual resins in Japan and the United States. It is noteworthy that PVC accounts for 44 per cent of all resins in Japan as against 15 per cent in the United States. Production of rigid PVC is about the same as that of flexible PVC. The rigid vinyl is formed mainly into pipes, sheets and corrugated sheets, which are used in great quantities as building materials. The high usage is largely attributable to the successful establishment of molding techniques for rigid PVC, which had previously been thought very difficult to mold.

TABLE 19C-1. Percentage Comparison of Resin Production between Japan and the United States

Resin	Japan %	United States %
PVC	44	15
Polyethylene	7	24
Polystyrene	4	17
Phenolics	8	11
Urea resin	23	} 6
Melamine resin	2	
Alkyd resin	3	9
Polyester	3	3
Others	6	15
Total	100	100

Following PVC, the production of urea resin occupies second place, accounting for 23 per cent of resin production in Japan as against 6 per cent in the United States. The greater part of the urea resin is used as adhesives for wood bonding. In Japan, long

FIG. 19C-1 Prefabricated houses in which plastics are used for furnishing of the interior. (*Courtesy the Sekisui House Co., Ltd.*)

and large pieces of lumber of good quality are unavailable; therefore, adhesives are required for the manufacture of laminated board, particle board and chip board. The increase in the production of melamine resin is also remarkable. More than 30 per cent

FIG. 19C-2. A "Sekisui cabin" made entirely of plastics, using glass fiber-reinforced polyester for exterior walls and "styrol sponge" (polystyrene foam) as an adiabatic (i.e., insulating) material.

of it is used as decorative laminated boards and about 25 per cent as paints.

The production of phenolic resin has not shown a very great increase, but it is making steady headway in molding, lamination, adhesives, paints and shell molding. Among new resins are polysulfide and epoxy. These are used for the manufacture of sealing materials and adhesives for concrete, and considerable growth is expected.

Materials for Floors

The popularization of plastic floor materials in recent years has been so remarkable that almost all floor coverings are now made of some sort of plastic. They are being used increasingly for homes as part of the trend toward westernization of the mode of living. In addition, they are now being used in stores, shops, and large buildings, as quality and installation techniques improve, and as new colors and designs are added every year. Approximately 80 per cent of the monthly demand for tiles of about 2 million square meters is met by those made of plastics belonging to the PVC family. Of all types, tiles made of vinyl asbestos are most popular.

Materials for Walls and Ceilings

Wall and ceiling materials made of plastics include PVC rib overlay laminated board, sheets for walls, tiles for walls, etc. The PVC rib overlay laminated board began to be popular eight or nine years ago. It was widely used for a time because of its smooth finish, ease of installation, and availability of long pieces. However, because of shortcomings such as deformation by shrinkage and ease of soiling from static electricity, it has been losing ground lately to other interior furnishing materials.

Two additional overlay laminated boards are in use. A decorative board is made by molding paper impregnated with melamine or polyester resin, applying heat and pressure. The other decorative overlay is made by cementing a PVC sheet onto the surface of a laminated board. These are well liked, and their future as furnishings materials is assured, since they combine the beauty and durability of plastics with the ease of installation and strength of laminated board. As for the core materials, metal sheet, asbestos sheet, hardboard and styrene foam are used in accordance with the characteristics of each.

Wall tiles of polystyrene were introduced about ten years ago, but were not used much because of the difficulty of installation. Sheets and tiles for the wall are not very popular as yet because of the difference in the mode of living. However, the demand for those items, it is predicted, will increase greatly in the future as westernization of the mode of living advances and installation techniques are improved.

As for ceiling materials, there is little worth mentioning. Overlay laminated board is used, as is painted styrene foam, because of its light weight and excellent sound-absorbing and adiabatic thermal insulating properties.

Roofing

Corrugated sheets made of plastics are used mostly as roofing materials for lighting. They are of two kinds—PVC and glass

FIG. 19C-3. Screen using transparent (blue) PVC corrugated sheets.

forced PVC corrugated sheets have been recognized legally as incombustible materials and are used mainly for lighting of large-scale structures such as factories, arcades and large-sized parking lots.

FIG. 19C-4. Transparent PVC sheet for lighting in a carbarn.

Ordinary PVC corrugated sheets are being used for dwelling houses and stores and shops in quantity because they are cheap, easy to handle and yet beautiful. The monthly

FIG. 19C-5. Bicycle barn of PVC corrugated sheet.

fiber-reinforced polyester (FRP). It is a phenomenon peculiar to Japan that wire-reinforced PVC corrugated sheets are widely used. FRP corrugated sheets and wire-rein-

demand for them is estimated at between 1,500,000 and 2,000,000 sheets. They are now widely used as accessories of dwelling houses, not only for roofing, but also for parts of the exterior walls, partitions and screens, as a result of recent standardization of quality and price.

Adiabatic Materials

Adiabatic (i.e., thermal insulating) materials for building formerly consisted chiefly of such natural or synthetic inorganic sub-

FIG. 19C-6. PVC corrugated sheets in arcade over a shopping street.

stances as diatomaceous silica, asbestos, glass wool, plaster board and insulation boards. Recently, as a result of the develop-

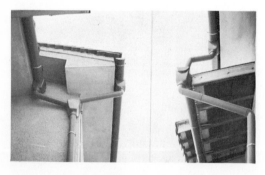

FIG. 19C-7. Gutters made of PVC.

ment of the synthetic high-polymer industry and advances in foaming techniques, foamed plastics such as polystyrene, PVC, urethane,

mercialized. Of these, polystyrene foam, particularly, is widely used for ceilings and floor walls. It is expected that other foamed resins will also expand greatly in the future.

Materials for Facilities

Piping. Plastic pipe includes rigid PVC, polyethylene and polypropylene. Rigid PVC is used chiefly for water supply pipes, drain pipes and electrical conduits. Uses are phenolic and acrylic plastic have been com-

FIG. 19C-8. A bathtub made of FRP (Glass fiber-reinforced polyester).

expanding all the time as new adhesives and joints are developed and installation techniques are improved.

Gutters. In the past, almost all gutters were made of galvanized iron sheet, but of late, gutters of PVC are fast taking their place. Large quantities of gutters and drain pipes are made by extrusion molding, while connectors between the gutter and drain pipe, such as funnels and water collectors, are made in standardized sizes and shapes by injection molding.

Lighting Fixtures. Artificial illumination has turned from the point light source to the line light source, using fluorescent light, and now is turning to the surface light source, using various covers.

Plastic materials for lighting fixtures include acrylic, polystyrene and glass-reinforced polyesters, but the major material is PVC, used in large quantities for illuminated ceilings, lighting fixture covers, and illuminated sign boards.

Miscellaneous

Furniture and Furnishings. PVC components are very much used for sliding doors, doors, partitions, window sashes and panes. Veneers of melamine are utilized so widely as table tops that it is not too much to say that almost all tables are covered with them. Veneers of

Fig. 19C-9. Water warming tank using pipes made of PVC.

melamine or polyester are used in large quantities for chests of drawers, cupboards, sinks and other kitchen fixtures. Chairs and benches made of polyethylene or PVC are also steadily gaining in popularity.

Bathtubs. Bathtubs formerly were almost all made of wood or ceramic tiles. However, tubs made of plastics such as glass fiber-reinforced polyester, PVC, acrylic, or polyethylene, using polystyrene foam as lagging materials, have recently become available commercially. Their future is looked upon as very promising in view of their beautiful and sanitary appearance and good heat insulation.

Water Warming Tanks. Gas water heaters and bathtubs using gas as the fuel have spread considerably in recent years. Along with these, water warming tanks which can warm the water to 60 or 70°C, utilizing solar energy as the heat source, are quite often seen installed on the roofs of residences. They save the time and trouble of heating

water for bathtubs, and make effective use of the natural heat source.

Adhesives and Caulking Materials. Adhesives for building are used for the manufacture of building materials such as PVC-covered steel plates, sandwich panels and wood products and for the installation of tiles, gutters, pipe joints and the like. The progress and the development of adhesives have really been remarkable; they are fast becoming the second nail. The importance which caulking materials, sealing materials and waterproof materials occupy in architecture is becoming increasingly large in view of the advance in architectural techniques, particularly curtain-wall and prefabrication methods. It will not be long before adhesives made of polyester or epoxy, for use with concrete, will be in the limelight, as prefabrication methods improve.

Soil Stabilizers. Japan offers many problems, from the viewpoint of architectural technique, which are not met in western countries, because of the particular terrain of Japan and the formation of her cities. Land is scarce. Large areas of big cities are

Fig. 19C-10. Water warming tanks installed on the roofs of dwelling houses (Close-up and distant views).

situated on the soft ground of moraine layers, large buildings are built close together, traffic is congested, and there are many subterranean structures such as the subway, water pipes, drain pipes and telephone lines. For these reasons, it has now become necessary, in many cases, to improve the soft ground before constructing a large building.

The need for stabilizing the ground was most keenly felt in the past in mines and in civil engineering projects. Cement or water

recently in our country. Advantages include light weight, shortened construction period, and ease of installation. There is an almost unlimited variety of combinations of materials and dimensions.

An experimental Sekisui plastics house makes use of sandwich panels with rigid PVC facings. To obtain the optimum in rigidity and thermal insulation, a triplex construction was employed. The inner panel has a PVC facing backed by noncombustible polysytrene. The exterior wall panel has an

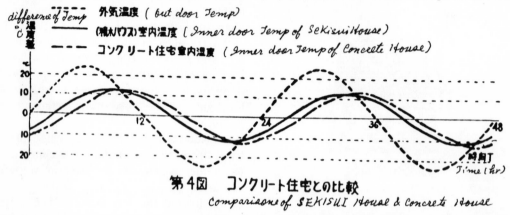

FIG. 19C-11. Time-temperature cycles in Sekisui house *vs* concrete house

glass have mainly been used for this purpose. However, soil stabilizers using acrylamide, urea or phenolic resins have recently been developed, and much is expected of them in the future.

Water Barriers. To prevent water from leaking through the clearance in the joint between two concrete walls, copper plate or galvanized iron plate was used in the past; now PVC sheet is largely replacing these materials.

Building Panels

Research and utilization of sandwich panels for building have made great progress

aluminum honeycomb for rigidity. Between the two is an aluminum honeycomb for stiffness.

Heat insulation was found to be equivalent to that of a concrete structure.

Figure 19C-11 shows the results of an experiment in which the outside temperature was caused to fluctuate sinusoidally, with a 24-hour cycle, and the indoor temperature was measured. Temperature fluctuation inside was half that outside for both the Sekisui house and a concrete house of the same dimensions, with a lag of approximately 8 hours for the Sekisui house compared with 9 hours for the concrete house.

PART D: International Developments in Plastics Structures

Z. S. MAKOWSKI

Battersea College of Technology
London, United Kingdom

Initial interest in plastic structures was aroused mainly by the research sponsored by Monsanto Chemical Co. and especially through their plastics "Monsanto House of the Future," which was a very important contribution. Their structure, built in 1956, consisted of four curved wings cantilevered from a central core. The basic unit was an 8 × 16 foot prefabricated shell made as a laminated sandwich panel with a 4-inch honeycomb core. A glass fiber-reinforced polyester plastic was selected as the structural material; a fire-resistant polyester resin having chemical- and water-resistant characteristics and good resistance to heat distortion was chosen for the laminated parts. Periodic on-site tests of this structure proved that the structural performance of the house was outstanding. No evidence of structural weakness could be detected.

The major controlling factor in the design of the Monsanto house was its stiffness. The house had to be rigid enough to prevent undue deflection of its parts under load. In building construction, the deflection of floors under full load should preferably not exceed $\frac{1}{360}$ of the span.

On a cost basis, such an all-plastic structure in 1956 could not compete with the traditional techniques, even taking into account all the advantages offered by plastics. However, the impact of this experimental structure upon the architectural profession was very significant. As a result of the Monsanto house, various projects on all-plastic houses have been put forward by architects and engineers.

An experimental French all-plastic house was built in 1956 for the Salon des Arts Menagers de Paris, according to the design of Yonel Schein, Yves Magnant and R. A. Coulon. This structure is an excellent example of a prefabricated panelized system. The circular core of the house consists of eight prefabricated segments. The roof is constructed of eight light units overhanging along the perimeter and joined together to a central hollow column collecting the rainwater from the whole roof area. The main feature of the design of this house is its flexibility—one can add one, two, three or four rooms to the central core, according to the needs of the occupants.

The floor units are strong but light plastic sandwich panels. The wall panels are filled with plastic foam giving the required stiffness and thermal insulation. All the interior partitions in the house are also made in light glass-reinforced polyester sections, including the built-in plastic furniture in the bedrooms, kitchen and bathroom. The windows, in clear acrylics, are built into the wall units and form an integral part of the load-carrying elements. The whole house weighed only 1800 pounds and had 6000 cubic feet of useful volume.

The same designers produced, also in 1956, a most interesting plastic cabin, which could be used as a beach hut or a temporary hotel cabin for tourists. This cabin consists of two upper and two lower molds and included a bathroom in a bulged portion to the right of the entrance door.

As a result of another early development

during the Interbau—the industrial exhibition in Berlin in 1957—the Owopor house has been constructed using prefabricated plastic segments. These units consisted of 2-inch-thick "Styropor" foam core having the outer facings in glass-reinforced plastics, the inner ones in plywood. It was a modest but highly interesting project.

In 1958, a German architect, Rudolph Doernach, displayed at the Stuttgart Plastics meters. It has been built of four identical segments constructed in glass-reinforced polyester resin with saturated paper honeycomb core. These prefabricated plastic boxes can be jointed in a variety of ways to form larger houses.

In some of these plastic houses, electric heating elements have been embedded in the plastic floor or wall units, using a special type of graphite-coated glass cloth. In other

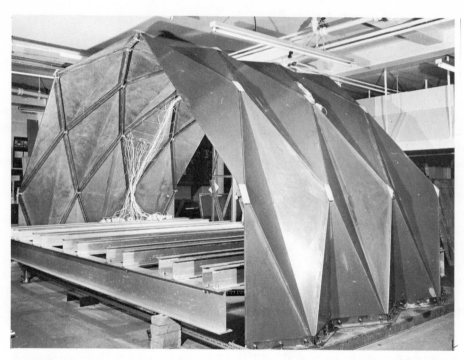

Fig. 19D-1. A prototype of an all-plastics barrel vault built at Battersea College from prefabricated plastics sandwich panels. They consisted of 1/16″ thick glass fiber reinforced polyester laminates facing a ½″ thick rigid polyurethane foam core. The span of this model is 20 ft. Various loading tests proved a remarkable rigidity of this structure.

Exhibition another version of a prefabricated plastic house using doubly curved segments consisting of plastic foam core covered with thin aluminum skin. The structure was supported at four corners only and was meant to be a small weekend country house. Two or more units could be linked to provide increased accommodation.

In the year 1957, during the Milan Exhibition (Triennale di Milano) a considerable amount of attention was drawn to an Italian all-plastic house designed by an architect Cesare Pea. The prototype consisted of a box having basic dimensions 4.80 × 4.80 × 2.70 experimental houses, the wall and floor units are plastic panels ducted for air conditioning.

Recent reports from Russia suggest that several government-sponsored investigations are being carried out on prefabricated plastic houses.

An experimental all-plastic house was displayed in 1962 during the first International Exhibition of Prefabrication, held in Milan. This house, of a hexagonal layout, was made in glass-reinforced polyester, designed by a team of young Italian architects and engineers under Professor Giordano Forti and was based on identical, interchangeable components for wall and roof. Panels consist of two layers of polyester with a sandwich insulation layer.

Various German companies are now experimenting with low-cost prefabricated

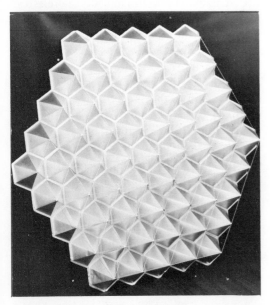

FIG. 19D-2. Models of pyramidal double-layer stressed skin space grids. These structures developed by Professor Makowski consist of FRP or PVC molded pyramidal units. Have been used as roofs or canopies.

plastic houses and bungalows, and the work of Schwabe, Doernach, Schulze and Freuz is receiving an increasing amount of publicity.

Japanese engineers also take great interest in such systems—the "Sekisui" plastic house has met with considerable commercial success and has turned the attention of Japanese architects to the unique potentials of plastics for structural use in building.

In Britian, the Mickleover Transport Ltd. is one of the progressive firms which for some years has been actively engaged in an intensive evaluation of the potential for plastics in structural applications. This firm developed in 1961 special prefabricated plastic relay buildings for the signaling system on British Railway's Eastern Region. The introduction of automatic signaling required the construction of new relay rooms for housing electrical equipment at existing signal boxes. These rooms are often needed at sites where there is no easy access, and they must be capable of enlargement. The plastic buildings can be erected within a few hours, do not need painting and require no maintenance.

The all-plastic buildings developed by Mickleover Transport Ltd. are composed of three basic types of units: a corner unit and side units of two different spans. A unit comprises wall and roof in one shell of double curvature. There is an outer laminate of polyester reinforced with glass fiber about ⅛ inch thick with a smooth face from the mold and a core of ¾-inch thick phenolic foam to give thermal insulation and fire resistance. The inner laminate is of polyester reinforced with glass fiber about ⅛ inch thick, formulated to give a low surface flame spread and faced with a surfacing mat. The units are bolted together with stiffening flanges of solid polyester.

These plastic structures have also been recently used as substations for the South of Scotland Electricity Board. The same firm built, in 1963, a two-story telephone exchange-office block in Birmingham using the same technique of prefabricated plastic sandwich panel units consisting of skins in polyester resin reinforced with glass fiber bonded to a core of phenolic foam.

Full-size tests on prototype units proved the exceptional rigidity of this form of construction. Tests on the phenolic foam used for the core showed also that it has a Class I surface spread of flame rating according to the British Standard No. 476, it does not soften with heat, and it is self-extinguishing.

The interest in such prefabricated plastic structures is increasing. The architectural firm of McNab and Jamieson of London, acting on behalf of John West Design Group Ltd., has prepared very interesting design proposals for prefabricated plastic structures, consisting of multipurpose shell units adaptable to many types of building use. These units are fabricated from glass fiber-reinforced polyester with a phenolic core erected on site with the maximum use of identical components. The junctions of panels are achieved by means of metal unequal-leg channels wrapped around the edge of the panel to reinforce it, with shim spacers which are bolted through.

Radomes

A spectacular use of plastics as main load-carrying structural material is provided by the plastic domes, especially the radomes, built in many countries during the last few

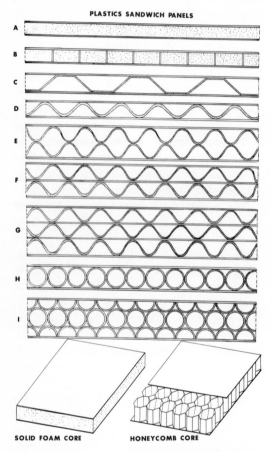

PLASTICS SANDWICH PANELS

SOLID FOAM CORE   HONEYCOMB CORE

FIG. 19D-3. Plastics sandwich panel cross-sections tested at the Structural Plastics Research Unit at Battersea College.

years. In many cases, plastics are the only structural materials which can satisfy all the requirements. The main requirement is that the structure must be transparent to electromagnetic radiation. In addition, because of their translucency, plastics can be used as the structural unit enclosing the space, which can, at the same time, admit light into the interior of the building. The plastic ground

radomes protect delicate radar installations from the weather. They are light and modular in design, resulting in economy in production and erection.

Fundamental research has been carried out in Canada, under the auspices of the R.C.A.F, on the use of plastic foam as the structural material for radomes. It is known that low-density foams are practically transparent to radio waves. The sizes of the units for domes up to 60-foot diameter are about 4 × 3 feet and for larger domes they reach 6 to 7 feet; the thickness of the panels is normally 3 to 4 inches. Most encouraging results have been obtained by using polystyrene and polyurethane foams. The density of polystyrene foam is about 2½ pcf. To get an adequate mechanical strength for domes of larger diameter, higher-density foams are required. Polyurethane gives excellent service in such cases, in a density of 6 pcf.

In order to protect the foam from weathering and accidental damage, the outer surface is covered with a layer of glass cloth cemented to the foam with epoxy resin. The field tests proved that the conventional joints of the polyester-glass cloth laminate radomes, with flanges and bolts, are not as satisfactory as the tongue-and-groove joints used to interconnect the panels of the Canadian plastic domes. The tests on real structures prove that plastic radomes can stand up to a maximum wind velocity of 250 mph. Also they were exposed to temperatures ranging from −60 to +180°F without any deterioration taking place in their mechanical properties.

In the reinforced plastic laminate types of radomes, the fundamental units consist of flanged diamond-shaped panels molded in vacuum bags with glass mat-reinforced polyester resin. In many cases, the membrane is only 0.050 to 0.060 inch thick, and the molded flanges are generally ¼-inch thick. Their heights vary between 3 and 5 inches depending on the diameter of the dome. To reinforce the diamond units, the minor axis of the panels is strengthened by means of a premolded post-bonded reinforcing rib which forms an integral part of the panel. The general tendency nowadays is to avoid making larger units of small composite jointed panels, as this leads to considerable energy losses through scattering reflection and refraction.

A huge plastic dome has been designed, fabricated and built recently by Goodyear

Fig. 19D-4. A basic unit used in plastics stressed-skin double-layer grid structures.

Aircraft Corporation as part of the Ballistic Missile Early Warning system. This dome acts as a protective cover for an 84-foot-high radar antenna and drive; it has a 140-foot equatorial diameter, a height of 116 feet and a base circle of 105 foot diameter. This structure consists of 1646 plastic panels, following a dodecahedron arrangement.

A dodecahedron exploded onto a surface of a sphere can be divided into 12 identical pentagonal faces. Each pentagon is further divided into hexagonal and pentagonal sections with a pentagon at each vertex of the original network.

There are 10 basic panel shapes, all of the same curvature. The panels are of a honeycomb sandwich construction. The basic skin thickness is 0.042 inch, and the honeycomb core consists of kraft paper 6 inches thick. Extensive tests proved that the honeycomb core provides the best structural answer leading to a highly economical solution. It has also been shown that honeycomb core presents a reduced electrical obstruction. "Hetron 92* fire-retardant

*Trademark, Hooker Electrochemical Co.

resin was used in the manufacture of the plastics. Watertight seals were obtained using a strip of caulking compound placed around the outer edges of each panel. The adjacent panels were bolted together during the erection, squeezing the sealing compound between them and forming an efficient water seal.

In May 1962, installation began of radar and electronic equipment at the ballistic missile early warning system station on Fylingdale Moor, in Yorkshire. The station consists of three main buildings, each of which carries on its roof a tracking radar inside a plastic radome 140 feet in diameter.

Three techniques are used in the manufacture of plastic radomes: (a) reinforced plastic laminate, (b) structural foam, and (c) honeycomb sandwich. There are also various types in which the component parts are arranged to form a spherical surface. The geodesic type of division of the surface into triangles or pentagons and hexagons is very popular as it leads to a relatively small number of different units. The simplest type

Fig. 19D-5. A roof structure built in London using plastics hexagonal pyramids interconnected by a three-way aluminum grid.

of geodesic dome is based on a spherical icosahedron, but in practice, for smaller diameters, the segmented orange peel type has proved to be the most economical, mainly on account of the low cost of tooling since very simple molds are required. This type has also been used recently for plastic domes built for various other purposes, not connected with radar operation. Several British firms have already gained a considerable amount of practical experience in the production of such all-plastic domes.

Other Plastic Domes

In Britain a number of plastic radomes of large diameter have been built recently by English Electric Ltd. This firm is also producing commercially a plastic summer house consisting of triangular sections of glass-reinforced resin bolted together. Another British firm taking keen interest in plastic domes is C. F. Taylor (Plastics) Ltd.

Precision Reinforced Mouldings Ltd. uses a fire-retardant grade of polyester resin, reinforced with glass fiber, which passes the stringent fire-retardancy tests of the L.C.C.

In the United States, demountable plastic domes are available in various standard sizes. The larger size structures of 22-foot diameter can be used as industrial shelters, farm domes, etc. At least one American firm is introducing low-cost greenhouses composed of unbreakable translucent glass fiber-reinforced panels, forming hemispherical domes.

After the dramatic use of translucent polyester fiber-glass umbrellas designed for the American Exhibition in Moscow in 1959, another equally exciting design in fiber glass-reinforced plastics has recently been carried out in France, where a market in Fresnes was covered with 18 large-size interconnected plastic umbrellas. Owing to the low-bearing strength of the ground, use of steel or concrete was ruled out, and the construction was possible due to the light weight of the plastic. Certain parts of the umbrellas were translucent, transmitting light to the interior of the building. A similar technique has been used by the same firm, Société des Chantiers Réunis Loire-Normandie, for a market in Ivry, composed of four rows of vaults, covering an area of 1620 square feet. Each vault is made up of four elements resting on a central column, which is also made of plastic. Elements are bolted together, two by two, on the ground, and the half-vaults made in this way are raised by a small crane and placed on the columns. The hollow columns are

bolted to cubes of concrete 50 cm across, which provide the entire foundation for the market. On the curved parts of the umbrellas, bolts are screwed through small rectangular plates-which rise above the raised edge of the vault elements. These plates are placed alternately on either side of the joint, and the raised parts serve as a guide for a thick PVC cover strip clipped on after the elements are

Fig. 19D-6. Glass fiber-reinforced polyester roof units used in Italy for houses and industrial buildings. Developed by architect Mario Scheichenbauer.

bolted. A thicker plastic gel coat has been used for the roof at Ivry to prevent the fiber-glass reinforcement from showing on the surface after a few months.

The same firm recently put on the market a large prefabricated plastic bus shelter. It proved successful, and a number of such shelters have already been erected in France.

In England, some music bandstands of considerable span have been built in polyester glass fiber supplied by Fibreglass Ltd.

In Canada, a garden shelter recently built in Strathcona Park created a considerable amount of interest. It was designed by Green, Blankstein, Russell and Associates, as a dome in reinforced polyesters with overhangs on all four sides, and is supported at four corners only. The over-all diameter of the dome is 54 feet and the height 16 feet. The dome consists of thin-skin sections reinforced with ribs which are integrally molded with each unit. The sections were epoxy bonded and bolted on the site. The material used was a fire-resistant polyester resin reinforced with a laminate of alternate layers of rove cloth and mat. The total weight of this structure is 3000 pounds. It has proved to be remarkably rigid, and shortly after the erection resisted an 80-mph gale without any ill effects.

Another interesting development is a canopied garden in Houston, Texas over the

FIG. 19D-7. Prefabricated plastics house developed in Germany by architect Rudolf Doernach.

Dow Center designed by the architects Caudill, Rowlett and Scott. The garden, between two buildings, is covered by prefabricated polyester glass-fiber units 38 feet long. In order to obtain the required stiffness, each unit is conceived as a space, curved membranal folded truss ¼-inch thick. It weighs only 240 pounds and is translucent with a light penetration of 20 per cent. These units are supported and bolted only at four points at their ends, but they are stitched together to each other with bolts at intervals of 2 feet. Tests proved that the pattern of stiffening contours finally adopted successfully resists the buckling tendency, even under 40 lb/ft² live load over the whole 38-foot span.

Current trends put a special emphasis on membranal structures in which bending is either minimized or eliminated entirely. A typical example is the hyperbolic paraboloid, studied at M.I.T. under the sponsorship of the Monsanto Chemical Company, described in an earlier chapter.

Pyramids

A most interesting concept is the idea of using plastic sheet pyramids for the construction of double-layer stressed-skin grid systems. These systems consist of a large number of prefabricated three-dimensional units, molded from thin sheets, interconnected along the edges and arranged in regular geometrical patterns. They possess several advantages and can be highly economical in use. The stress distribution is of the membrane type, eliminating bending moments. Owing to the modular design, the erection of such systems is exceptionally simple. Also, it has been found that such pyramidal structures possess the remarkable acoustic advantage of acting as sound baffles, reducing the noise level in the interior of the building.

Most of the structures described so far in this article have been built in glass fiber-reinforced plastics. However, for certain types it is feasible to use even unreinforced plastics. It is thought that pyramidal structures of the stressed-skin type represent such a field of application for PVC. Recent tests carried out by the author as a part of the research sponsored by the I.C.I. on the structural use of plastics on plastic pyramids made in PVC have revealed a surprisingly high load-carrying capacity of the units. One hypothesis explaining this is that the compression edges of the sheet units receive additional lateral restraint from the adjacent sheets, thus effectively preventing their tendency to buckle. In England such pyramidal structures have already been built by C. F. Taylor (Plastics) Ltd. as prototypes in polyester glass fiber, but it is evident that it is also possible to construct them even in PVC.

Barrel Vault

Very recently, a most interesting design has been carried out using such prefabricated hexagonal plastic pyramids for a swimming pool at Mill Hill, near London. The units are interconnected forming a cylindrical barrel vault, 48 feet long and 25 feet wide. The light transmission is over 80 per cent. The plastic modules are bolted together along their mating flanges and tied by light aluminum tubes, forming on the surface a three-way grid.

In hot weather the whole barrel can be

wheeled back, and in cool weather even a short spell of sunshine through the translucent roofing material raises the temperature rapidly. This plastic barrel vault is a permanent structure, but if the need arose it could easily be dismantled and re-erected elsewhere.

In Poland one of the recently constructed exhibition pavilions in Poznan is covered with such a pyramidal system consisting of a

FIG. 19D-8. Prefabricated plastics house developed in Germany by architect Rudolf Doernach.

large number of prefabricated glass fiber-reinforced plastic pyramids.

Several plastic barrel vaults have been built in the United States. One type has been constructed in Texas by Structural Plastics, Inc. to cover a factory, and hyperbolic paraboloids 4 × 4 feet of glass fiber-reinforced plastics were used, and were locked together along their edges to form shallow pyramids fixed to very light steel tubular struts forming a space grid framework of a barrel vault shape spanning 78 feet. The joints in this structure were sealed by means of "Thiokol" caulking compound and the resulting structure is remarkably rigid. It withstood winds up to 70 mph without any trouble. Static tests have been carried out to an equivalent of 20 psi live load. Plastic hyperbolic paraboloids used in this barrel vault are mostly opaque white, with translucent yellow and blue sections for light transmission.

Recently, the same firm built a number of very interesting petrol station canopies, using large prefabricated plastic hyperbolic paraboloids, readily assembled on the site. These components, as a rule, weigh less than 1 lb/sq ft; they transmit light, reflect heat and can be easily insulated.

An investigation is being carried out at the Battersea College of Technology on the behavior of a barrel vault consisting of prefabricated plastic shallow pyramids of hexagonal shape, bolted together along the edges and stiffened at the upper layer by a three-way grid of light aluminium tubes. Tests up to destruction will be carried out in the near future under the guidance of the author on a plastic prototype of such a barrel vault covering an area of 24 × 40 feet.

Foam/Concrete

Another progressive concept in thin reinforced concrete (r.c.) shell construction is the use of preformed or shaped polystyrene foam boards to act as a permanent shuttering for concrete. This foam polystyrene plastic is characterized by a lightweight unicellular structure having low thermal conductivity, excellent vapor barrier qualities, durability and permanence. Urethane foam can also be used, and has better heat resistance than polystyrene—up to 250°F without the danger of distortion. Urethanes can be sprayed and foamed directly on roofs to form a monolithic rigid surface requiring only a weatherproof covering. Both polyurethane and polystyrene foams are available in self-extinguishing or fire-retardant formulations.

Air-supported Structures

Air-supported structures are proving popular for a wide variety of uses, ranging from temporary, portable covers to permanent installations. The pressure differential between the inside and outside of such buildings is roughly equivalent to that between the first and seventeenth floor of an office building. This amount of pressure differential affords safety in wind velocities in excess of 70 mph. Many structures of this type have already been erected during recent years in the United States and on the continent, especially in Germany by Kruppsbaubetriebe. They include greenhouses, swimming pools, skating rinks and storage buildings. In Germany, they are frequently used as shelters for construction projects.

Miscellaneous; Space Structures

Irradiated plastics, still in the research stage, will all possess immensely increased fire resistance at low weight.

Plastics seem to have a very promising future in aerospace applications. Goodyear Aircraft Company is working at present on foamed-in-place solar collectors. Several prototypes have already been built on the ground, using plastics mostly from the polyurethane family.

Most interesting experiments have been carried out recently in the United States by the Flight Accessories Laboratory, Directorate of Aeromechanics, Aeronautical Systems Division, on plastic expandable self-rigidizing honeycomb space structures. Various geometric configurations have been tried out, e.g., a sphere and a torus. These structures, once placed in orbit, are expanded by air pressure; the skins either attach themselves to the core material or rigidize as well.

Fig. 19D-9. Two-story plastics house developed by Mickleover Transport Ltd.

The cells of the honeycomb core contain pressurized gas. After its release, the elastomeric material is rigidized by ultraviolet cross-linking or vaporized catalysis. The resulting structure has a high strength-to-weight ratio and can be transported in small, compact packages. It is envisaged that space stations, shelters, solar collectors, etc., will be built using such techniques. Designs have already been prepared for space plastics hangars to protect launch pads.

There is no doubt that once these techniques prove their worth in such applications, they will be gradually applied to more "down-to-earth" practical structures.

Some firms originally specializing in the construction of large reinforced plastic trucks or boats have now turned their attention to the possibilities existing in the building industry.

Several 30-foot-high and 12-foot-diameter plastic bins have been constructed for bulk sugar storage. The bins are made in two halves, each consisting of six identical segments bolted together. Their advantages are considerable—savings in height, lower installation and maintenance cost, elimination of problems of corrosion, and superior cooling and drying qualities.

Conclusions

In spite of several limitations involved in the use of plastics, they offer a tremendous potential for the building industry, especially in the field of prefabricated stressed-skin elements. They are transforming building manufacturing techniques and are beginning to influence building design.

It is the firm belief of the author that plastics will achieve a real "breakthrough" in building during the next decade, but the plastics industry must invest in research and in the education of civil engineers and architects in the properties and uses of plastics. At the moment, plastic as structural material is not even mentioned in the syllabuses of most universities and colleges. There is an urgent need for a long-term research in the structural use of plastics, not on small-scale models, but on full-size prototypes. Only such tests will convince the general public and will lead the way for the development of mass-produced plastic constructional systems.

PART E: Other Developments Outside the United States

IRVING SKEIST

Skeist Laboratories, Inc.
Newark, New Jersey

CANADA

Usage of plastics in countries outside the United States varies with the technical proficiency and the climate. In Canada, both factors are favorable. Technology is essentially the same as in the United States. Because of the northern latitude, deterioration from ultraviolet radiation is greatly reduced. The cold winters give an added impetus to the use of plastic foam insulation, with its especially low thermal conductivity.

"Building With Plastics" was the subject of a conference sponsored by the Society of the Plastics Industry (Canada), Inc. in 1965.[1] Expenditures for building in Canada were 8.65 billion dollars in 1964 and an estimated 9.8 billion dollars in 1965. They are expected to be 15 billion dollars by 1970, half of this amount going to materials. A target of 15 per cent of the value of all construction materials, or more than a billion dollars, is suggested as an attainable goal for plastic materials.

Among the leading plastics applications are vinyl tile, polyethylene pipe, kitchen counter laminates, stair tread and stair nosing, curtain wall gasketing and caulking, silicone water repellent, vinyl wall fabrics, and polyethylene film for translucent enclosures, vapor barriers and blankets for curing concrete slabs. Polyvinyl chloride siding, sash, door frames, eaves troughs and shutters are beginning to appear. Sewer pipe, drain waste and vent pipe and pressure pipe are expected to receive CSA (Canadian Standards Association)[2] certification and code approval. Plastics are taking over for weather stripping and are making progress in urethane foam insulation.

The Canadian Standards Association has developed certification service for plastic pipe, including polyvinyl chloride (PVC), acrylonitrile-butadiene-styrene (ABS) and polyethylene. Applications include drain, waste and vent; cold-water service (pressure pipe); gas service; underground drain and sewer pipe. A list of certified manufacturers of pipe, fittings and solvent cements is available.

The Canadian Government Specifications Board[1b] has complemented the work of the Canadian Standards Association and the U. S. Commercial Standards with standards on:

41-GP-6 Sheets, Thermosetting Plastics, Glass-Fiber Reinforced
41-GP-16 Polyurethane; Rigid, Cellular
41-GP-18 Septic Tanks; Glass-Fiber Reinforced Plastics

They have also worked together with CSA to produce standards for laminated thermosetting decorative sheets, polyethylene for cold water service, and rigid PVC pipe. In addition, they have been working on acrylic sinks and lavatories and on vinyl extrusion for windows.

Electroplated plastic plumbing fixtures are seen as having a good future.[1c] Platable plumbing fixtures include shower heads, escutcheon and base plates for taps, tap handles, faucet aerators and spouts, soap dishes, towel holders, drain pipe traps, etc. Toilet flush valves from unplated ABS are already in use.

The building industry, like the auto industry, is discovering that metal-plated ABS is less expensive than brass or zinc die castings, and at least as serviceable. Plated ABS is 25 to 40 per cent cheaper than metal castings. The strength is that of the plastic rather than that of the plated film. The plating can be as thin as 0.5 to 2 mils, utilizing new techniques of plating on plastics. The weight of ABS is only $\frac{1}{7}$ that of die cast zinc. It is expected that 30 million pounds of ABS will be used in plated plumbing applications in Canada by 1970, replacing more than 200 million pounds of zinc, primarily for shower heads and faucet handles.

of blocks and boards. The materials include rigid vinyl, plastics manufactured from polyester and melamine resins, and polystyrene and polyurethane foams.

Half the materials have a flame spread index of 25 or less, but only 8 per cent have smoke-developed ratings of less than 100. Thus, it is apparent that a reduction in smoke level is necessary to make many plastic materials more acceptable in schools, hospitals, and other institutional buildings.

In the province of Saskatchewan,[1e] the

Fig. 19E-1. FRP panels shade the Queen Elizabeth II Grandstand at Ascot, England. The panels, 40 ft. long, are sufficiently light in weight to permit a cantilever structure without view-obstructing supports. (*Courtesy: "Filon" B.I.P. Reinforced Plastics, Ltd. International Filon Producers' Association*)

The Underwriters Laboratories of Canada has adopted the Steiner 25-foot tunnel test (ASTM E84-61) utilized in the United States for the measurement of flame spread.[1d] More than 200 products have been tested, including flattened corrugated glass fiber-reinforced panels, corrugated translucent sheets, translucent and opaque panels, perforated translucent panels, louver and die-formed translucent panels, laminated plastic sheets (secured to asbestos-cement board or unbonded) and expanded plastics in the form

Department of Agriculture has instituted a program for replacing outdoor privies with indoor facilities, using polyethylene, ABS and PVC pipe. In addition, fiber glass is making strong inroads on precast concrete for the construction of septic tanks, increasing its penetration from 8 per cent in 1963 to 13 per cent in 1964. However, experimentation with screw-type plastic fittings has been abandoned as unsatisfactory.

At McGill University,[1f] architectural students are being taught the advantages and the pitfalls of plastics usage. A laboratory course includes practice in the microscopic examination of materials, the preparation and evaluation of thermosets and thermoplastics, and tension and compression tests on composite materials such as concrete, wood and fiber glass. An interesting facet of the course will be the exploration of the simultaneous use of one plastic part for enclosure, structural strength and light transmission.

The use of rigid vinyl in windows has grown substantially.[1g] While wood retains most of the rural market for sash, rigid vinyl tracks and weather stripping have overcome windows. Many commercial windows use rigid vinyl thermal barriers in the frames. The all-vinyl window is gaining acceptance. It is an excellent thermal barrier, better than wood and far superior to aluminum. It requires no maintenance, is self-extinguishing and has a warm feel. In gray and white, at least, it maintains its appearance indefinitely in Canada.

It is predicted that 75 per cent of the residential and apartment windows built in 1970 will have vinyl sash. More and more wood frames will be clad with vinyl to make them maintenance free. Commercial windows will be made of vinyl sash and frame members reinforced on the inside with wood and metal. Thus, the consumption of rigid vinyl by the window industry is likely to quintuple in the next decade.

In Canada as in the United States, glass fiber-reinforced plastic (FRP) has been used for the waffle pan construction of large-span ceiling slabs of concrete.[1h] The FRP provides a smooth architectural finish. A standard 30 × 30 × 10 inch FRP pan costs only $9.00 and weighs only 10 pounds, as compared with $14.00 and 35 pounds for 12-gauge steel. The lighter weight means lower labor cost as well as shipping and handling costs. The FRP is not easily dented, is more readily removed, does not rust or stain the surface finish. The plastic pans can be reused fifteen or twenty times.

Among the concrete structures built with the help of FRP waffle pans are Place Victoria in Montreal, Malton Aeroquay,

Scarborough College, a circular church in Quebec, the Table Rock House observation platform at Niagara Falls, the St. Clare Shopping Centre, the window arches at Kitchener Laboratory. Permanent FRP structures include the D.O.T. radome at Malton Airport, radomes for the Dew Line, balcony panels for a prestige apartment building in Ottawa, a one-piece self-flashing translucent dome at Loyola College. A monkey house at the Winnipeg City Park Zoo in Toronto, 28 feet in diameter with a 5-foot central opening, was constructed from 22 curved and tapered segments mounted on a wooden framework. At Brentwood Mall in Vancouver, an even larger dome, 36 feet in diameter, was fabricated in sections.

Northwest Design and Fabrication Ltd. in Winnipeg has developed a home based on sandwich panels with RP facings and foam plastic cores. Initial cost is 20 to 25 per cent less than if built of conventional materials, and heating is much cheaper.

UNITED KINGDOM

Consumption of plastics in the United Kingdom has been estimated by ICI officials at 150,000 tons/yr for mid-1965:[5]

Consumption of Principal Organic Polymers in the United Kingdom Construction Industry, Mid-1965

	Rate (thousand tons/yr)
PVC	80
Thermosetting resins	35
Polyethylene[a]	12
Polystyrene	10
Acrylics	5
Polyesters and epoxies	4.5
Polypropylene	1.5
Others	1
Total (approximate)	150

[a] "Polythene" in the United Kingdom.

Building currently utilizes about one-fifth of British plastics production, almost the same as in the United States. But the annual growth of plastics in building applications is about 15 per cent, as compared with 12 per cent for plastics as a whole, and only 4 per cent for the entire construction industry. If the usage of plastics in construction continues to leap forward at the current rate, consumption will be 600,000 tons/yr by 1975.

Great growth is foreseen for PVC in rigid sheets, especially for cladding. A considerable volume of wire-reinforced translucent PVC

Fig. 19E-2. At Tarancon, Spain, translucent FRP roofing panels are tightly fitted to keep out the elements, yet permit illumination of this large warehouse without artificial lighting. Circular vent openings in brick walls at roof level provide natural air cooling. (*Courtesy "Reposa" Resinas Poliesteres, S.A. International Filon Producers' Association*)

PVC is by far the leading material. It dominates the rigid pipe and wire covering field, and is the fastest growing resin for resilient flooring:[5]

Main Building Applications for PVC in the United Kingdom—1965

Application	% of Total Polymer
Rigid pipe	33
Flooring	30
Wire covering	19
Rigid sheet	10
Flexible sheet	5
Flexible extrusions	3

The steady increase in vinyl usage for resilient flooring in the United Kingdom is shown in statistics from the Board of Trade:[5]

Synthetic Floorings Production

	Jan.-June 1964 (1000 sq yd)	Jan.-June 1965 (1000 sq yd)
Paper or paperboard based (other than vinyl)	32,260	31,293
Textile based:		
Linoleum (printed and inlaid)	14,108	11,152
Vinyl	1,232	1,339
Rigid and semi-rigid titles		
"Thermoplastic" (coumarone-indene)	6,522	6,430
Vinyl asbestos, etc.	6,484	6,575
Flexible vinyl floorings		
Printed	8,496	11,845
Inlaid	2,203	2,173
Other types	626	2,959
TOTAL	75,931	73,766

sheeting is being imported into the United Kingdom from Japan.

The thermosets—phenolics and amino resins—go predominantly into bonding and electrical applications:[3-5]

Main Building Applications for Thermosetting Resins in the United Kingdom—1965

Applications	% of Total
Laminates	28
Electrical fittings	25
Particle board	21
Doors	11
Sanitary ware	9
Plywood	6

Polyethylene has a large percentage of the pipe market and is the leading material for film and sheet, for moisture barrier and other applications.

FIG. 19E-3. Beach cabin of sandwich panel faced with corrugated vinyl. (*Courtesy: Fabbrica Prodotti Termoplastici Corea Pasquetti & Co., Italy*)

In the United Kingdom as in the United States, lack of prior performance history is the main impediment to plastics usage.[3-5] Requirements for combustibility and surface spread of flame are given in United Kingdom Building Regulations B.S.4.76: Part 1:1953. The conservatism of builders and buyers is an even greater obstacle in the United Kingdom than in the United States. Nevertheless, the efforts of the Building Committee of the British Plastics Federation are resulting in a gradual breaking down of barriers.

A 1964 conference on plastics in building construction, held at Battersea College of Technology, indicated problems similar to those in the United States.[6] A significant difference is the greater usage of polymethyl methacrylate, even for bathtubs, as the result of vigorous efforts by ICI.

The marketing of *adhesives* for building in the United Kingdom has been described by Dunlop Chemical Products Division.[7] The materials in most demand are adhesives for ceramic tile and for styrene foam. Other significant products are those for the bonding of rubber and plastic floor tiles, acoustic tiles, foam panels and decorative plastic laminates.

Rubber-based adhesives are being used extensively for fixing tiles and other coverings to floors, walls and ceilings.[8]

In a recent publication, "Plastics in Building," Imperial Chemical Industries, Ltd. (ICI) notes the wide range of uses for their PVC, acrylic and other plastic materials in construction. In addition to the usual applications for vinyl, acrylic, polyethylene, polyurethane foam, silicone water repellent, urea-formaldehyde adhesives, etc., they show:

(1) Polyethylene floats and other plumbing fittings for cold water;

(2) Polypropylene plumbing for hot water;

(3) Vinyl copolymer foil as a lining for concrete molds;

(4) Cellular urea formaldehyde, foamed *in situ*, at low cost;

(5) PVC foil for paneling, ceilings, partitions, and covering kitchen furniture;

(6) PTFE (polytetrafluoroethylene) tape for sealing pipe threads.

For the future, they anticipate greater use of geodesic principles in design, and the application of space frames and hyperbolic structures, through materials having higher strength-to-weight ratios.

Reporting to an American audience, McLeod[3] stated that acrylic bathtubs have shown abrasion resistance superior to that of enameled cast iron. ICI has had two years' successful experience with hot-water storage tanks of polypropylene. Polyethylene is replacing galvanized iron for cold-water storage tanks on roofs, but PVC is the dominant plastic material. Factors favoring PVC there are the narrow temperature range and the paucity of ultraviolet exposure.

A conference on sandwich construction was held by the Plastics Institute in late 1963.[9] Cores are in use made from resin-impregnated kraft paper, reinforced plastics, a furan-treated kraft paper, a foam-filled paper honeycomb, non-impregnated papers, resin-impregnated glass cloths and resin-impregnated cotton cloths. Applications include ground radar equipment, building panels, molds and goedesic domes. Much promise is seen in combination of plastics with traditional materials such as metals or wood.

Additional information on the use of plastics in the United Kingdom has appeared in several issues of *British Plastics*.[10-13]

GERMANY

The journal *Kunststoff-Rundschau* has devoted several issues to comprehensive reviews of plastics in building. In September 1962, they reported on a symposium on plastic foams carried out in Aachen in 1961. Among the problems discussed were the physics of thermal insulation (Mahler), the use of phenolic resins in foam (Juenger), polystyrene (Stastny) and PVC (Eichenberger).[14a-f]

The February 1963 issue of *Kunststoff-Rundschau* begins with papers by architects (Schwabe, Engel) on their requirements. Engel points out the desirability of a modular structure such as has been used in Japan for many years. Among the materials discussed are rigid PVC (Fischer), polyurethane foam (Hoppe, Cap), phenolic foam (Laeis), and polysulfide sealants (Goebel). Hanusch indicates the usefulness of glass-reinforced fiber-glass and concrete reinforcement; Winfield reviews the use of resins in architecture in the Soviet Union.[15a-c]

Hostachem's *Hostalit Z* is indicated to be a blend of PVC and chlorinated polyethylene. It is used principally for corrugating sheeting

and panels.[16] A good stabilizer system is necessary for outdoor use, e.g.,[17]

PVC or Hostalit Z	100
Basic Ba-Cd stabilizer	2-3
Organic phosphite	0.5-1
Epoxy compound	1-2
UV absorber	0.2-0.3
(Antioxidant for pigmented lubricant compounds)	0.5 (as required)

Man-sized hexagonal sheets of Hostalit Z were used to cover the huge concrete domed hall built in 1963 by Hoechst in celebration of its 100th anniversary.[18]

Typical applications[15d] shown for corrugated sheets of PVC or Hostalit Z include the cover for a quarry bridge, a roof deck, a ramp, a bicycle shelter, an exposition stand, an apartment house, curtain wall construction, building facades, a chapel hall covered with hexagonal plates, and a window element of cement asbestos faced with plastic.

The flat sheets are approximately 0.4 mm thick (0.016 inch). Unlike polyesters, they have a mat appearance. They are cleaned with styrene cleansers or with fine emery paper without impairing the appearance, as the color goes all the way through.

Glass-fiber polyester is recommended by Thomas[15n] as a material for windows. A typical formulation has the following properties:

Heat conductivity	0.16 kcal/m·h/°C
Specific heat	0.32 cal/°C g
Tensile strength	950 kg/cm²
Elongation	1.5%
Flexural strength	1750 kg/cm²
Impact strength	60 kg cm/cm²
Compressive strength	1950 kg/cm²
Modulus	92,000 kg/cm²

The low heat conductivity is particularly desirable, as is the low flammability. Chemical resistance is excellent, and the windows are easy to clean.

Phenolic resin foams[15h] are much more used in Germany than in the United States. Manufacture is relatively simple. The liquid phenol-formaldehyde is mixed with the propellant, and a small amount of hardener is added to promote cross-linking. After rapid agitation, the fluid mixture is dropped upon a form covered with paper or plastic film and exposed to heat. The resin rises and foams. It fills the wooden form over a period of 2 to 4 hours at a temperature of 50 to 60°C. More recently, a cold foaming resin has been discovered which cures by the exothermic heat of reaction.

The fully cured foam has a specific gravity of 0.03 to 0.10 (i.e., 2 to 6 lb/cu ft). It is approximately 40 per cent open cell. It has a high heat distortion temperature and can

Because of its heat resistance, it is found to be especially useful as a roof covering, withstanding the temperature of 190°C at which bitumen is used as a cement. The bitumen is applied to the concrete roof, followed by perforated roof paper, phenolic foam, then glass mat with a bitumen cement.

(In the United States, phenolic resins have not achieved the popularity of polystyrene and urethane in cellular plastics. In 1958, Dietz[19] characterized them as the

FIG. 19E-4. Twenty-eight randomes, 15 ft in height, have been erected in Canada for meteorological studies, using reinforced low density fire-retardant polyester resin. The material has low wave-interference properties and high physical strength, enabling it to resist shocks of parachute delivery and heavy snow loads. (*Courtesy: "IC-6006" Interchemical Corporation, Clifton, N. J.*)

withstand a temperature of 130°C for a long period of time, or 180°C for a short period. It can also withstand temperatures as low as −200°C without visible change in properties.

The material is self-extinguishing, and is rated "difficultly flammable," according to specification DIN 4102. In this respect, phenolic resin foam is superior to other plastic cellular materials. Its main use is as an insulating material against cold or heat. At a specific gravity of 0.04, it has the same thermal conductivity as ten times its thickness of stone wall. It is easily machined and readily bonded to paper or other substrates.

cheapest but also the most brittle and weak. Furthermore, acid catalysts are said to make them corrosive to metals in the presence of moisture.)

Engel[1c] sees increased interest in prefabricated houses. Traditional Japanese dwellings have long utilized the principle of *modular* construction. The Japanese house is assembled from horizontal and vertical prefabricated panels. Although the house is put together by hand, the building operation is simplified, since the building elements are mostly of the same size, approximately 6 × 3 feet. Using these modules, the Japanese can build homes of any size, can divide the rooms in any way into 3-foot sections, and can easily change the divisions of the room. Inner and outer passageways are readily added. A variety of building elements are available, giving the possibility of individual artistic expression.

Casting resins can be used in three different ways in concrete structures, according to Gotthard:[20]

(1) As a bonding agent in concrete,
(2) As a surface layer on concrete,
(3) As a bond between precast concrete units.

If the resin is substituted for concrete and is used as a suitably graded sand, the result is a high-class mortar. With the addition of gravel, it becomes a concrete with twice the strength of conventional structural concrete.

A layer of plastic applied to concrete provides for protection against impact and forms a thin film across the unavoidable hairline cracks. The rapid setting of cast resins and their high strength and adhesion recommend them for bonding concrete blocks.

An entire issue of *Kunststoff-Rundschau*[21] has been devoted to plastics in agriculture. The use of pipe for irrigation has been discussed by Gaertner[21a] and by Schneider.[21b] Both polyethylene and plasticized PVC film are shown to be used extensively for silage covers, greenhouses and mulches.[21c] A revolutionary development that may disturb the traditionalist is the storage of wine in casks of glass-reinforced polyester.[21d]

The rapid progress of German plastics usage in construction has been revealed by Schwabe:[22]

	Million DM[a]	
	1963	1964
Total	1244	1609
Floor covering	391	525
Panels	164	198
Piping	126	178
Profiles	122	146
Rigid foam	70	135
Corrugated sheets	89	102
Building elements (including skylights, sandwich panels, etc.	45	82
Shutters	44	54

[a]1 DM = $0.25.

SOVIET UNION

In the Soviet Union, as in other countries, acrylic-modified polyester is utilized in the production of translucent reinforced plastic panels.[24] A recommended formulation is:

Polyester resins	100
Styrene	25
Methyl methacrylate	25

The optimum ratio of glass fiber to resin is 2.5:1 to 3:1. Light transmission is 80 to 85 per cent. After outdoor weathering for five years, light transmission is reduced by only 10 per cent.

A Russian publication on fiber-glass building materials is available in English translation.[25] Methods for producing fiber glass-reinforced plastics are described, including: contact molding, employing a single mold, bag molding, vacuum injection molding, low-pressure compression molding, high-pressure compression molding, continuous laminating, and continuous molding of flat and corrugated laminates.

The Russians produced a small portable plastic dwelling to house nomads in the south of the Soviet Union, according to an international review of plastics by Griff.[26]

Lubin[27] describes the Russians as quite enthusiastic about the potential of plastics in construction. They have no restrictive building codes and complete freedom for new ideas. Because of their inexperience with the materials, workmanship is far from American standards. For example, a fiber glass-reinforced bathtub was found to have an inadequate gel coat, resulting in exposed fibers. But research is being carried out at the Plastics Research Institute, the Moscow Architectural-Structural Bureau, and the Moscow-Project Institute in many directions:

(1) Study of materials for flooring and interior lining of buildings;

(2) Study of water-resistant phenolic and related resin-bound wood laminates;

(3) Manufacture of furniture, concrete-casting forms and lighting fixtures;

(4) Sanitary technical equipment for homes (bathrooms and piping);

(5) Plastics for laminated structural appli-

cations including walls, ceilings, partitions and doors;

(6) Other laminated fiber-glass applications;

(7) Window frames from plastics;

(8) Use of furfural binders in construction;

(9) Design of model homes using plastics.

FIG. 19E-5. Rain water system made from vinyl chloride polymer. (*Courtesy: "Corvic" Imperial Chemical Industries, England*)

OTHER EUROPEAN COUNTRIES

Belgium

The U.S. Pavilion at the Brussels World's Fair was enclosed in a curtain wall of clear rigid vinyl 42.5 feet high, extending around the entire 1000-foot circumference. The light weight of the panels permitted the use of a steel lattice for support. The material was supplied by Bakelite, the panels by Laminations, Inc. of Scranton, Pa.[23]

France

The progress of plastics in building was reviewed in the French journal *Techniques and Architecture*.[28] Emphasis was placed on the freedom of design afforded the architect by plastics.

Epoxy resins and polyesters have been used effectively in France for the bonding of concrete.[29] Entire bridges of reinforced concrete have been made in concrete sections bonded together with resin to spread the load. This parallels a similar development in railroad trestles in the United States.

The Netherlands

Bouwcentrum, the Building Research institute at Rotterdam, has been actively investigating the utilization of plastics in conjunction with the Research Institutes of TNO in Delft. A major publication has dealt with reinforced polyesters.[30]

PVC and other plastics have been compared with galvanized for gutters, downspouts, etc.[31] The relative merits of PVC and polyethylene for pipe are presented in another publication.[32]

Specifications and standards organizations in various countries have been listed.[33] Other publications deal with foams,[34] plastic materials for transportation of potable water,[35] and plastic film water barriers.[36] Finally, Wulkan[37] has reviewed experimental developments in the design of buildings with plastics.

Schwabe[38] lists the per capita use of plastics in various countries as follows for 1962:

	kg		kg
West Germany	18.2	Holland	10.4
United States	15.7	France	9.4
Belgium	14.8	Great Britain	8.7
Switzerland	14.5	Italy	8.3

Plastics amount to some 3.2 per cent of total building costs in Germany. It is believed by some specialists at Hüls that the proportion of plastic materials could be raised to 10 per cent of the building costs. A high potential is seen in other countries as well.

THE DEVELOPING COUNTRIES

Lien[39] suggests reasons for the utilization of plastics in the developing countries: light weight, moldability, workability, design flexibility, and durability. Furthermore, many of these countries have naphtha or other raw materials which are not being utilized completely. He proposes an integrated program for making plastic materials from such natural resources, then using the plastics in building.

Aldis[40] points to many uses of plastics in Africa and other parts of the world. In Southern Rhodesia, the inside of the roof of the Kariba Dam Power Station is lined with 1,250,000 sheets of vinyl, 96 feet long, 4 feet wide, and $\frac{1}{16}$ inch thick. In Jamaica, a church has made effective use of acrylic

FIG. 19E-6. A picture gallery for the Earl of Bradford is illuminated by daylight diffusing through acrylic sheet. (*Courtesy "Perspex" Imperial Chemical Industries, Ltd., England*)

sheet in various colors for an entire triangular wall. A radome and a serial tower for television, both on Mt. Barrow in Tasmania, are built from glass fiber-reinforced polyester resin. In some Indian villages, PVC water piping is relieving the women of a chore that formerly required two hours a day. But these are only rudimentary beginnings, and there is a vast potential for plastics in these countries.

Foam plastics have been investigated for housing in underdeveloped areas, in a project conducted at the University of Michigan under the sponsorship of the U.S. Department of State.[41] Further research is needed before foam systems will be feasible for the production of housing in underdeveloped areas.

REFERENCES

1. "Building With Plastics," Society of the Plastics Industry (Canada), Inc., 23rd Annual Conference, Brockville, Ont., May 19–20, 1965.

   (a) Gauthier, R. J., "The Scope of the Construction Industry."
   (b) Hanna, J. E., "CGSB Plastics Standards for Building."
   (c) Davies, T. L., "Plastics in Plumbing Products."
   (d) Pearce, Norman S., "Specifications and Standards of the Underwriters Laboratories of Canada."
   (e) Nemaneshen, W., "Privyless Prairie."
   (f) Bland, J., "Plastics in Architectural Education."
   (g) Tillotson, R. D., "Rigid Vinyl Window Applications—Now and To Come."
   (h) Szasz, Paul, "Reinforced Plastics in Building."

2. CSA Testing Laboratories, Mechanical-Chemical Dept., 178 Rexdale Blvd., Rexdale, Ont., *Plastic Pipe Newsletter*, 3 (Spring, 1965).
3. McLeod, N. D., and deNormann, J., "Properties and Applications of Plastics Experience in the United Kingdom," page A-133 of *Polymers and Plastics in Construction, Preprints* (symposium sponsored by the Division of Petroleum Chemistry, American Chemical Society), 10, A-133 (September 12–17, 1965), Atlantic City, N. J.
4. Anon., *Chem. Eng. News*, 29 (September 27, 1965).
5. Anon., "Plastics in Building, Today and Tomorrow," *Brit. Plastics*, 38, 643 (November 1965).
6. Davies, R. M., Editor, "Plastics in Building Construction," London, Blackie & Son Ltd., 1965.
7. Anon., "New Approach to Marketing Adhesives," *Adhesives Age*, 6, No. 8, 24 (August 1963).
8. Tilley, Simon P. E., *Adhesives Age*, 6, No. 2, 22 (February 1963).
9. Anon., "Sandwich Construction," *Brit. Plastics*, 37, No. 1, 35 (January 1964).
10. Anon., "Plastics in Building," *Brit. Plastics*, 36, No. 11, 622 (November 1963).
11. Anon., "Building Exhibition Report," *Brit. Plastics*, 36, No. 12, 662 (December 1963).
12. Anon., "Sandwich Construction," *Brit. Plastics*, 37, No. 1, 25 (January 1964).

13. Quarmby, Arthur, "An Architect Looks at Plastics in Housing," *Brit. Plastics*, **37**, No. 1, 28 (January 1964).

14. "Kunststoff-Schaumstoffe im Bauwesen," *Kunststoff-Rundschau*, **9**, 429–454 (1962).

(a) Joehren, J., "Einteilung der Kunststoffe," 430.

(b) Mahler, K., "Physikalische Grundlagen der Waerme- und Schallisolierungstechnik sowie der Wasserdampfdiffusion," 430–437.

(c) Juenger, H., "Phenolharzschaum, seine Eigenschaften und Anwendungsmoeglichkeiten," 437–442.

(d) Haumann, H., "Isoschaum im Bauwesen," 442–443.

(e) Stastny, F., "Polystyrol-Schaumstoffe—Eigenschaften, Anwendungsmoeglichkeiten und Verlegung im Bauwesen," 444–448.

(f) Eichenberger, W., "Eigenschaften und bisherige Anwendungen von PVC-Schaumstoffen im Bauwesen," 448–454.

15. *Kunststoff-Rundschau*, **10**, 53–106 (1963).

(a) Anon., 53.

(b) Schwabe, B. A., "Wuensche und Anregungen des Architekten an die Kunststoffindustrie fur eine breitere Anwendung der Kunststoffe in der Vorfertigung," 54.

(c) Engel, H., "Architektonische Gestaltungsgrundsaetze fur Bauelemente aus Kunststoff. Probleme des Bauens mit Kunststoff-Bauelementen," 57.

(d) Fischer, K., "Schlagfestes Hart-PVC im Hochbau," 63.

(e) Hoppe, P., "Hartes Moltopren im Bauwesen," 70.

(f) Cap, P. C., "Die Anwendung des Polyurethan-Hartschaumes im Bauwesen der USA," 79.

(g) Anon., "Das Verschweissen von Hart-PVC-Rohren und Dachrinnen," 82.

(h) Laeis, W., "Phenolharz-Schaumstoff—ein neues Baumaterial," 83.

(i) Schwabe, B. A., "Die Verwendung von Acrylglas im Hochbau," 86.

(j) Anon., "Resartglas im Bauwesen," 88.

(k) Winfield, A. G., "Kunststoffe in der Architektur der Sowjetunion," 89.

(l) Hanusch, H., "Formen aus glasfaserverstaerkten Polyesterharzen bei der Herstellung von Beton-Fertigbauteilen," 95.

(m) Goebel, G., "Anwendung von Thiokol im Hochbau," 99.

(n) Thomas, G., "Das HGS-Glasfiber-Fenster, ein Vollkunststoff-Bauelement," 101.

(o) Anon., "Verzeichnis von Kunststoff-Erzeugnissen fur das Bauwesen," 102.

(p) Anon., "Kalwall-Lichtwaende, ein modernes Fertigbau-Element," 103.

(q) Anon., "Steigender Kunststoff-Verbrauch im Hochbau der USA," 107.

(q) Anon., "Steigender Kunststoff-Verbrauch im Hochbau der USA," 107.

16. Anon., "New Polymer Plant Upgrades PVC," *Mod. Plastics*, (April 1961).

17. Frey, Hans-Helmut, "Licht- und Wetterbeständigkeit von schlagfestem PVC" (Stability to Light, Weatherability of Impact Resistant PVC), *Kunststoffe*, **52**, 667 (1962).

18. Lang, G. H., Hostachem Corporation, Mountainside, N.J., private communication.

19. Dietz, A. G. H., "Rigid Plastics Foams in Building," quoted in *Mod. Plastics*, **36**, No. 4, 91 (December 1958).

20. Gotthard, Franz, quoted by Coppa-Zaccari, "European Plastics Report—West," *Plastics Design Process* **3**, No. 8, 6 (August 1963; from *VDI Zeitschrift* for March 11, 1963).

21. *Kunststoff-Rundschau*, **11**, No. 3 (March 1964)

(a) Gaertner, G., 151.

(b) Schneider, R., 154.

(c) Anon., 161.

(d) Proksch, W., 142.

22. Schwabe, A., "Der Architekt und die Kunststoffe," Kunststoffe im Bau—Die Fassade, Strassenbau Chemie und Technik Verlagsgesellschaft, m.b.H., Heidelberg, 1965.

23. Anon., "Transparent Vinyl Wall," *Mod. Plastics*, 88 (July 1958).

24. Santholzer, Robert, "European Plastics Report—East," *Plastics Design Process* **3**, No. 8, 8 (August 1963); quoting from *Plasticheski je Massy*, **4**, 46–49 (1963).

25. Barbarina, T. M., Sukhof, M. P., and Sheludyakov, N. A., "Fiberglass Building Materials," Publication OTS: 63-31431, U. S. Department of Commerce, Office of Technical Services, Joint Publications Research Service, Washington, D.C., 1963.

26. Griff, Allan L., "Worldwide Plastics," *Mod. Plastics* (August 1963).

27. Lubin, George, "Reinforced Plastics in Russia," *SPE J.* **18**, No. 11, 1360 (November 1962).

28. Palatchi, Paul, Editor, "Les Matières Plastiques dans le Bâtiment," *Techniques & Architecture*, **22**, No. 1 (November 1961).

29. (a) Csillaghy, J., private communication.

(b) Lezy, R., "Une possibilite nouvelle d'emploi des résines synthétiques dans les bétons hydrauliques," *Travaux*, 193 (April 1965).

(c) Meunier, André, "Les problemès de l'étanchéité des joints dans le bâtiment," *Rev. Generale de l'Etaucheitré*, No. 56.

(d) Anon., "Les Colles Pour Béton," *Les Chroniques du Laboratoire*.

30. "Kunststoffen in de Bouw: Overzicht van Toepassingen van Polyester en al dan niet decoratief Plaatmateriaal," Stichting tot rationalisatie van het Bouwen, Rotterdam, 1963.

31. "De Toepassing van Kunststoffen Voor Dakgoten," Bouwcentrum, Rotterdam, 1963.

32. "De Toepassing van Kunststoffen voor Hemel-waterafvoerbuizen," Centrale Directie van de Volkshuisvesting en de Bouwnijverheid, Rotterdam, 1961.

33. "Herzien Rapport over De Stand Van de Normalisatie in Diverse Landen Met Betrekking Tot de Toepassing van Kunststoffen in de Bouw," Rotterdam, 1963.

34. "Kunststofschuimen," Bouwcentrum, Rotterdam, 1962.

35. "Plastic Materialen Voor Binnenleidingen Voor Drinkwater in Woningen," Rotterdam, 1960.

36. "Toepassing van Plastiekfoelies in de Bouwnijverheid," Rotterdam, 1963.

37. Wulkan, E. K. H., "Experimentele Woonhuizen van Kunststof," *Plastica* (July, August, September 1963).

38. Schwabe, A., "Uses of Plastics in Buildings in Continental Europe," talk given at SPI National Plastics Conference, New York, June 1–3, 1964.

39. Lien, Arthur P., "Plastics and Housing in Developing Countries," *Battelle Technical Review*, **14,** No. 3, 6 (March 1965).

40. Aldis, Basil C., "Plastics Progress in the Building Industry in the British Commonwealth," paper given at SPI National Plastics Conference, New York City, June 1–3, 1964.

41. Paraskevopoulos, S. C. A., Borkin, H. J., Darvas, R. M., and Larson, C. T., "The Potential Use of Foam Plastics for Housing in Underdeveloped Areas," U.S. Department of State, Agency for International Development, ORA Research Project 05215, July 1962 to February 1963, conducted at University of Michigan, Ann Arbor, Mich.

20

NAHB RESEARCH HOUSES DEMONSTRATE PLASTICS

JOHN M. KING

*National Association of Home Builders
Research Foundation
Washington, D. C.*

One of the forces behind the expanding volume of plastics production has been the development and marketing of new products for single- and multiple-family dwelling units. Many of these products found an immediate foothold in the market by virtue of their meeting a need that was not wholly satisfied by products of other materials. Other products, merely substitutes of plastics for other materials, did not find wide acceptance. The producers of successful products recognize the necessity of designing to use *efficiently* the least amount of material to perform the function and to provide the lowest in-place cost. The wide variety of plastics and their many desirable properties allow the imaginative designer almost unlimited scope in developing products which will contribute to the building of better value houses.

Since its establishment in 1952, the Research Institute of the National Association of Home Builders has been working with producers of basic materials and end products for the building industry to stimulate the development of new products, equipment and methods of construction. NAHB represents most of the builders who construct single- and multiple-family buildings in this country. Thousands of building product manufacturers and their dealers also partici-

pate in NAHB activities through associate memberships.

The research activities of the Association and its Research Institute are now being carried on by a wholly-owned subsidiary, the NAHB Research Foundation, with a laboratory and staff in Rockville, Maryland. The programs of the Foundation include manufacture consultation, research and development, industrial engineering studies, and sponsored or contract projects for manufacturers. In addition, the Foundation works closely with other organizations in the field of building standards.

A major program of the Institute since 1956 has been the development and construction of research houses. The objectives of this program are: the design and development of better construction systems, materials and equipment; the obtaining of data from the analyses of methods of construction and the performance of products; and the dissemination of information to home builders and the industry in general. The program has also aided manufacturers in obtaining the acceptance of products by the Federal Housing Administration, major building code organizations, and local code authorities.

The five research houses constructed to date were developed by the Research Institute following the principles and objectives set forth by its trustees. The houses were constructed by builder members of the Association on a nonprofit basis and, after builder and public showings, were sold on the open market. A covenant in the deeds of sale provides that representatives of the Institute may instrument and inspect the houses for a period of time. The manufacturers have generally warranted their products used in the houses in the event that they may require replacement.

Plastic products of all types and forms have been used in the research houses (Table 20-1). Most of these are illustrative of the tremendous development work being undertaken by the plastics industry. A number of products resulted from ideas suggested by the Research Institute and were used in the houses for the first time. Others were only recently on the market at the time the houses were designed. In any event, the selection of products was based on their known or potential contribution to improved housing and their advantages in terms of the specific house structure and finishes. Additional information about the products and their uses may be obtained from the NAHB Research Institute in Washington, D. C.

THE HOUSE STRUCTURE

Past experimental work in housing and other building types has produced a number of interesting structural shapes which have been used to form floors, walls, and roofs. Perhaps the most dramatic display of structural plastic components has been in the Monsanto House of the Future now displayed in Disneyland. Interior space was formed by combinations of glass-reinforced polyester laminate curved shells and flat sandwiches cantilevered from a central foundation element. Considerable engineering analysis and testing was carried out to take advantage of the desirable characteristics of plastics and to design around their limitations.

Although the Monsanto house and other experimental structures have been useful in exploring the potential of plastics, it is unlikely that curved roof shapes will find home buyer acceptance in the near future even if they are competitive in cost with traditional construction. This is so because the home buyer is aware that a future return on the sale of his largest single investment depends on how well his house conforms to an accepted pattern of individual and community preferences. For the most part, these are deeply rooted in the past, although there does appear to be a gradual acceptance of contemporary expression in house design. These appearance or design preference factors also affect applications of plastics other than for the house structure.

Another factor that has a significant bearing on the use of plastics in the house structure, even more so than in other building types, is cost. The operative home builder, who builds the vast majority of today's single family homes, operates in a free private enterprise system with competition for the consumer dollar. Furthermore, the ability of the consumer to buy houses is largely related to his income and credit financing. The builder chooses design, materials and construction methods which provide the best possible house at the least possible cost to the home buyer and with a reasonable profit to himself.

As home building continues to depart from its ties to localized craft traditions, efforts are being made by the builders and manufacturers to reduce labor costs through the use of more efficient construction methods. The development of prefabrication or the off-site assembly of components has contributed significantly to this objective during the last two decades. House floor, wall and roof components, primarily of wood frame construction, found their way into over 40 per cent of the single family houses in 1963. Following the lead of the early prefabricators, the builders, lumber yards, specialty fabricators, and even building product manufacturers have found the advantages inherent in the preassembly of parts and pieces into larger house components under controlled shop conditions not adversely affected by weather. Other advantages of shop fabrication include: the ability to use automated power equipment to reduce labor costs; the application of techniques and ma-

TABLE 20-1. Plastics Used in the Research Houses of the NAHB Research Institute

Plastics Applications	Kensington, Md. 1957	Knoxville, Tenn. 1958	South Bend, Ind. 1958	E. Lansing, Mich. 1959	Rockville, Md. 1963
The House Structure					
Floor panels				Polystyrene foam core—asbestos cement faces	
Exterior load-bearing wall panels			Polystyrene foam core—plywood faces	Polystyrene foam core—plywood faces	
Exterior non-load-bearing panels			Polystyrene foam core—plywood faces	Polystyrene foam core—plywood and asbestos cement faces	
Roof panels			Polystyrene foam core—plywood faces	Polystyrene foam core—plywood faces	
Interior partitions			Polystyrene foam core—gypsum board and plywood faces	Polystyrene foam core—gypsum board and plywood faces	
Adhesives	Phenol-resorcinol			Modified casein	Epoxy (wood to steel) Epoxy mortar
Exterior Finishes					
Site applied paints and coatings	Alkyd primer and acrylic top coats "Hypalon" roof coating	Alkyd primer and acrylic top coats	Urethane on walls and carport roof	Alkyd and acrylic "Hypalon" and neoprene	Coal tar enamel (corrosion resistance)
Shop applied paints and coatings	Neoprene undercoat on roof plywood		Urethane primer	Urethane on roof panels	
Film on wall panels				"Hypalon" on wall panels	Polyvinyl fluoride Calendered "Hypalon"
Film on roof panels					"Hypalon"
Flashing	Neoprene Neoprene	Vinylidene chloride	Vinylidene chloride Urethane	Neoprene "Hypalon"	"Hypalon"
Caulking	Urethane		Butyl		
Interior Finishes					
Paints and coatings	Alkyd	Alkyd	Urethane Vinyl	Alkyd Acrylic Melamine	Urethane Acrylic Melamine
Films and sheetings	Polyester Vinyl coated fabric	Polyester	Woven vinylidene chloride filament Supported vinyl sheeting	Vinyl coated fabric Woven vinylidene chloride filament	Vinyl sheeting and film
Flooring	Vinyl sheet Rayon/nylon rugs "Hypalon" tile	Vinyl tile	Vinyl tile Rayon/nylon rugs	Vinyl asbestos tile Vinyl sheet Ceramic tile in GRS rubber	Vinyl asbestos Ceramic tile with epoxy grout

Other Interior Finishes					
Kitchen counter and vanity tops	Melamine laminate	Melamine laminate Gel coated polyester	Melamine laminate Gel coated polyester	Melamine laminate Gel-coated polyester	Melamine laminate Ceramic tile with epoxy grout Gel-coated polyester
Cabinet drawers		High impact polystyrene	High impact polystyrene	High impact polystyrene	Formed ABS sheet
Closet doors					
Bathtub and shower enclosures	Acrylic				
Trim				Vinyl Polyethylene Vinyl handrail cap	Vinyl window and door casing
Windows and Doors	Nylon door handle and lockset			Foam urethane door core Vinyl-coated steel door faces Nylon locksets and knob	Vinyl and aluminum windows Foam polystyrene door core
Heating and Cooling					
Vapor barrier	Polyethylene		Polyethylene	Polyethylene	Polyethylene
Insulation	Foam polystyrene Phenolic foamed in place				Foam polystyrene
Ducts			Vinyl-covered fiber glass	Vinyl-covered sheet steel	
Electrical Distribution and Lighting					
Wiring	Acrylic-fiber-reinforced acrylic sheet		Calendered vinyl sheeting	Rigid vinyl baseboard Nylon-encased wires	Rigid vinyl baseboard
Lighting—ceiling			Nylon-reinforced acrylic	Nylon-reinforced acrylic	Glass-fiber-reinforced acrylic
Plumbing					
Pipe and fittings					
House supply	Polyethylene			Polyethylene	
Cold-water supply	ABS and PVC			PVDC	PVDC
Hot-water supply	Polypropylene			PVDC	PVDC
Waste, drain and vent	PVC			PVC	ABS
Drainage field	Rubber modified polystyrene			PVC	
Gas service					ABS
Plumbing fixtures	Glass-fiber-reinforced polyester vanitory	Glass-fiber-reinforced polyester vanitory	Glass-fiber-reinforced polyester vanitory	Glass-fiber-reinforced polyester vanitory and shower	Glass-fiber-reinforced polyester shower, vanitory and wall sections, and bathtub
Other plumbing items	Nylon water closet valve parts and shower heads Polyethylene water closet valve parts			Nylon ball-cock assemblies, faucet valves, toilet seat hinges and shower heads	

terials that cannot be used on the building site, such as adhesive bonding; better quality control; and the potential of material savings with increased volume of production. Of course, on the site the house structure can be erected in shorter time to provide savings in labor and other costs.

Even in the early stages of experimentation with prefabrication, house panels were fabricated in the form of stressed-skin or sandwich panels using a variety of materials. The development of plastic resin adhesives permitted the employment of efficient bonding techniques. Resins were also used to give greater durability and strength to the paper honeycomb core materials used in many of the earlier sandwich structures.

One of the first introductions of a plastic for a sandwich core came about with the design of panels for exterior walls, interior partitions and roof for several houses constructed in Midland, Michigan in 1952. The wall panels were 3 feet 6 inches × 8 feet with ¼-inch plywood faces and 1⅝-inch thick foam polyester core. Faces were bonded to the core with a resorcinol-type thermosetting adhesive cured with dielectric heat. Other experimental and a few commercial sandwich panels for houses also utilized low-density polystyrene foam in board form. In more recent years, other materials including urethane, phenolic, and vinyl foams have been successfully incorporated into panel constructions.

SOUTH BEND RESEARCH HOUSE

In 1956, the NAHB Research Institute began to work with Koppers Company, Inc., on expandable polystyrene core sandwich panels. Rensselaer Polytechnic Institute obtained test data on many types of panels produced by Koppers' pilot plant. The test data and the experience gained in the fabrication of panels were applied to the analysis of construction systems. It was evident that the use of sandwich panels would influence other elements of the house such as plumbing, electrical, heating, windows, and doors. Also, different materials and methods for finishing walls, ceilings, and roofs could be used to advantage.

The decision of the Institute to work toward the development of a sandwich panel house was based largely on a cost analysis which revealed that foamed-in-place polystyrene core panels were competitive with conventional frame construction. This analysis included not only basic material and labor costs, but also costs related to plant and equipment investment, marketing and distribution.

By the spring of 1958, considerable data had been gathered, and a number of manufacturers were ready to try out prototypes of materials and equipment. To test the panels and related items, the Institute set in motion the design and construction of a research house.

The basic plan objective was a house with three bedrooms, family room, living room, kitchen, one bath, and ample storage (Figure 20-1). The area of the 32 × 36 foot house is 1150 square feet. Analysis of the floor plan in relation to panelization led to the choice of a 4-foot module. This module also related to the dimensions of the fabrication equipment and the available widths of sheet materials for panel faces. The two sizes of exterior wall panels are 2 × 8 feet and 4 × 8 feet; they vary only in the height of the windows placed in the panels. Two 4 × 8 foot panels differ only in the location of the door opening, either at the right or left side of the panels. Panelization of the interior walls required further study in order to obtain flexibility with as few panels as possible. In the final design, 1-, 2- and 4-foot-wide panels were used. All roof panels are 4 feet wide. The car shelter and breezeway were designed to demonstrate additional applications of the foam core panels.

Structural Design

In their investigation of the use of expanded polystyrene foam in structural building components, RPI determined the structural capacity of various panel types and verified by test the validity of proposed design procedures. The objective was a sandwich panel performance equal to or better than conventional frame construction. Formulas and values were derived for constants which correlate theoretical load deflection curves with actual curves (Table 20-2). Tables were prepared to simplify the selection of panel thicknesses with given loading conditions and face materials, and with adequate factors of safety. All of this technical data was put in a form presentable to regulatory agencies.

The structural design of the South Bend research house was influenced by three main factors. First, in view of the panel construction used in testing, plywood was chosen for the faces of all load-bearing panels. Secondly, it was obviously uneconomical to use core thicknesses greater than needed for thermal insulation. The third consideration dealt with wall panel thickness in relation to acceptance by the general public. In other words, a two-inch thick exterior wall panel would perform satisfactorily but from a sales standpoint might be too great a departure from traditional frame wall thickness.

Roof Panels

An initial test series of panels loaded transversely showed that under short-time loads, sections of core and plywood faces performed acceptably. However, if the loads were continued over a period of time, the deflection of the panels continued to increase and an objectionable amount of permanent set remained after the loads were removed. These findings led to the introduction of continuous longitudinal ribs or side rails with a depth equal to the core thickness and their

FIG. 20-1A. NAHB 1958 research house constructed in South Bend, Indiana.

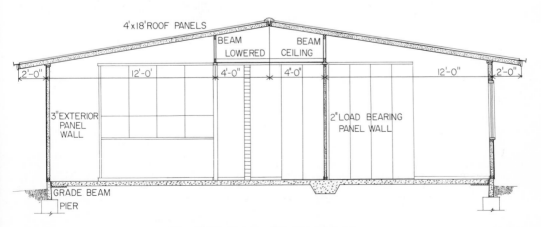

FIG. 20-1B. Cross-section through house.

edges continuously adhesive-bonded to both faces. These rails serve to resist shear stresses imposed by loading and the core serves structurally to stiffen the facing skins and prevent their buckling under stress. Therefore the roof panels perform more like a stressed-skin construction with a structural frame acting as the webs of a series of I-beams and the plywood faces serving as the flanges.

Under certain loading conditions, only a portion of the plywood of a stressed-skin panel may be counted on to resist tension and compression stresses when the panel bends. However, if the plywood is restrained from buckling by a continuous core, the full sectional area of the faces contributes to an increased moment of inertia. Test results verified that the introduction of the wood rails serves the intended purpose, substantially stiffening the panel, and eliminating the deflection increment under sustained loading.

A 3½-inch core thickness for the roof panels is ample for insulation; however, the maximum simple span for a 4-inch panel with ¼-inch plywood faces is 10 feet. By cantilevering the roof panels at two supports, it was possible to obtain a 12-foot clear span between exterior walls and two beams placed 8 feet apart, each 4 feet from the ridge (Figure 20-1B). This gives each 18-foot-long roof panel a 4-foot cantilever from roof peak to beam, a center span of 12 feet from beam to exterior wall and a 2-foot cantilever overhanging the exterior wall. The 4-inch-thick, 4 × 18 foot panels were fabricated with ¾-inch perimeter rail members. These members were held back 1 inch from both edges of the panel for the site insertion of splines. The peak and fascia ends of the panels are formed by 1⅝ inch members. The exterior faces of the panels are ¼-inch B-C Exterior Douglas fir plywood, and the interior faces are ¼-inch Douglas fir plywood with an overlaid plastic-impregnated paper surface on the underside. Scarf-jointed plywood was used to give continuous panel length faces.

Wall Panels

The selection of exterior and interior load-bearing wall panels was based on the results

TABLE 20-2.   Typical Load Deflection Curves.

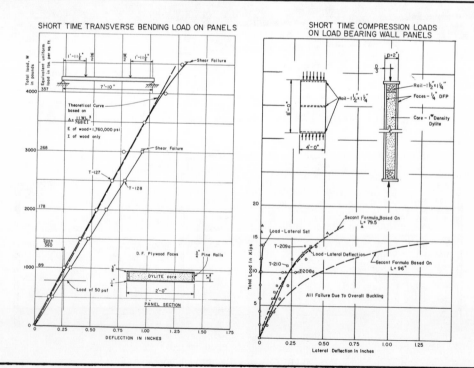

of compression, racking and impact tests as well as the previously mentioned transverse load tests. The polystyrene foam core serves structurally to provide lateral support to the relatively thin and flexible faces, and through its bond to the faces, it insures that the whole assembly acts as a structural unit rather than as individual parts. The top and bottom rails glued to the faces serve the same function as the end connectors in a spaced wood column, and they prevent either face of the panel from slipping with respect to the other. Three-inch thick, 4 × 8 foot panels with ¼-inch plywood faces had, under test, an average load of 13,500 pounds at ¼-inch deflection and an average ultimate load of 23,400 pounds. At 80 per cent of the ultimate load, the faces were still within the elastic limit and the deflection was less than ¾ inch. Under racking loads, the continuous core stabilizes the faces to aid the entire panel to resist deformation.

The exterior wall panels (Figure 20-2) were

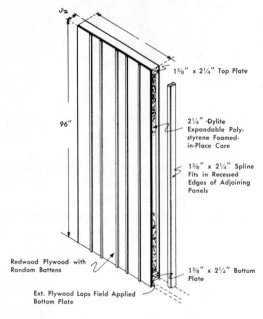

Fig. 20-2. Typical foam core wall panel used in the South Bend research house.

fabricated with an interior face of ¼-inch B-C Douglas fir plywood and an exterior face of an experimental ½-inch redwood surfaced siding panel. At both edges of the panel, the core was recessed about 1 inch to accept the joint splines. These splines were cut short from bearing on the top and bottom panel rails. At the top of the wall, the roof loads are distributed through a field-applied plate that bears on the edges of both panel faces. The bottom edge of the interior face bears on the field-applied sill plate.

Panel Fabrication

All of the panels for the South Bend research house and later the East Lansing house were fabricated with equipment developed by Koppers Co. to utilize "Dylite" expandable polystyrene foamed in place between two panel faces. The faces are pre-coated with an adhesive and assembled with the necessary wood rails. In the restraining press, pre-expanded beads are blown into the panel cavities and steam probes are inserted through predrilled holes in the side rails. When the steam is introduced, the beads expand into a cellular core structure with a 1¼ lb/cu ft density. The adhesive is heat reactivated to bond the faces to the foam core and the wood frame members. This fabrication process permits the use of a wide variety of facings including those with corrugated or other irregular shapes.

Construction

In August of 1958, the builder prepared the site and poured the foundation and concrete slab. On the morning of the house erection, the builder's crew of four carpenters, two laborers, and a foreman were briefed on the sequence and method of erecting the panels. They started with the wall erection at 9:00 a.m. (Figure 20-3) and anchored the last roof panel shortly before 5:00 p.m. The first wall panel was set at a corner of the house with one edge on a perimeter module line. The panels along an end wall were then placed in sequence to the next corner. Since the panels were an exact 4- or 2-foot width and some accumulation of wall length was expected, the last panel in a length of wall was allowed to overlap the module line at the corner. In practice, it was found that this overlap did not amount to more than ½ inch and the difference could be easily taken up in the width of the corner post. Panel faces were nailed to the wood splines at all joints and to the sill plate. The erection of window, door, and solid panels continued around the perimeter of the house to the first corner.

Interior non-load-bearing panels were fabricated with polystyrene core and faces of ¼- or ⅜-inch gypsum board. The panels are 2 inches thick and 1, 2, or 4 feet wide. In the bedroom areas where the walls were required

FIG. 20-3. Erection of South Bend house wall panels.

The interior load-bearing panels were set in place simultaneously with the roof beams. The panels were anchored to the concrete and, in turn, the beams were connected to the panels. All of these panels are 2 inches thick and 8 feet high with faces of ¼-inch B-C Douglas fir plywood or 3⁄16-inch Lauan plywood. The joining system is similar to that used for the exterior walls.

The roof erection sequence started with the placement of the first panels at the center of the house. Four men lifted the 192-pound roof panels over the exterior walls and laid them in place on the beams and walls. Working outward from the center, additional panels were placed toward both ends of the house with wood splines inserted in the recessed edges of the panels and nailed in place. Anchorage of the roof to the beams and exterior walls was accomplished by nailing through the splines with 7-inch ring nails.

to reach the underside of the sloped ceiling, 10-foot-long panels were shipped to the site and then cut at an angle to fit the ceiling slope. The joint system for the non-load-bearing partitions is the same as for the load-bearing panels. Partitions were anchored to the concrete slab by 2 × 6 inch 26-gauge sheet metal strips nailed to the slab and bent up and nailed to the bottom plate of the panels.

Performance of the House

For a year following the completion of the house, close observation was made of the expected movement of the exterior wall and roof panels. The movement was caused by seasonal changes in temperature and humidity varying the moisture content of the plywood faces of the panel. Minor repairs were made to hide cracking of the interior paint on exterior walls where the joints had been filled with a spackling compound. The maximum bowing in the 8-foot vertical dimension of the wall panels was approximately ⅜ inch. The major source of trouble developed at the intersections of interior panels with the outward bowing of exterior panels. These cracks were later covered with trim pieces. An approximately ½-inch variation in roof panel deflection was not noticeable.

Further research will be required to find solutions to dimensional instability of sandwich panels. Consideration should be given to the development of more stable face materials, and to the design of connection systems to control or hide panel movement.

The heating cost of the house during the first winter was slightly more than half the cost of heating houses with similar areas in the neighborhood. The savings can be attributed largely to the excellent insulation provided by the foam core. The 4-inch roof panels have a "U" factor of .065, and the 3-inch panels have a factor of .093. Summer air-conditioning costs are also low.

able than in other houses in which they lived. This "drum" affect has been observed in other structures with sandwich roof panels.

EAST LANSING, MICHIGAN, RESEARCH HOUSE

In 1959, Koppers Company and the Research Institute cooperated in the development and construction of another research house. To demonstrate the versatility of the polystyrene foam core sandwich panels for residential construction, a two-story house was designed with load-bearing interior and exterior wall panels and roof panels. In addition, an unusual first floor system, using foam core asbestos-cement-faced panels laid directly on a sand bed, was tried for the first time. The fabrication techniques involved in producing the panels were similar to those in making the South Bend house panels.

The 28 × 36 foot house contains 2000 square feet of living area with an attached one-car garage (Figure 20-4). All wall panels are 4 feet wide to conform to the modular

FIG. 20-4. East Lansing, Michigan, research house.

The owners of the house have indicated their satisfaction with its functional performance, but commented that sound transmission of noises within the house has attracted their notice. Tests of interior partition panels indicate, however, that they have sound transmission losses approximating those of conventional partitions. The owners also commented that the noise of rain on the roof was definitely more notice-

plan of the house. The roof panels and second-floor wood frame floor span across the three bays of the house and transmit their loads to the two end and two interior bearing walls. Since the house was constructed on an upward-sloping site, the back of the first floor level is about 6 feet below grade and the lower portion of the back wall serves as a retaining wall. The panels span between the sill plate and the second floor (Figure 20-5).

The load is transmitted to the sill and to the second floor which acts as a diaphragm to transmit load to the lateral walls with their racking resistance. To provide waterproofing, the exterior of the panels was factory finished with three coats of "Hypalon"* and field coated with neoprene for a total thickness of about 15 mils.

Laboratory tests, which involved the exposure of one side of panels with various face materials to a high-humidity atmosphere, indicated that aluminum foil bonded to the faces of panels might contribute to lessening or at least retarding their bowing. To further evaluate the laboratory tests, all of the exterior wall and roof panels of the research house have 2.5-mil aluminum foil bonded to both plywood faces with a neoprene adhesive. Foil was also carried around the edges of the panel faces. A clear epoxy prime coat was applied to the foil for bonding of finish and joint materials.

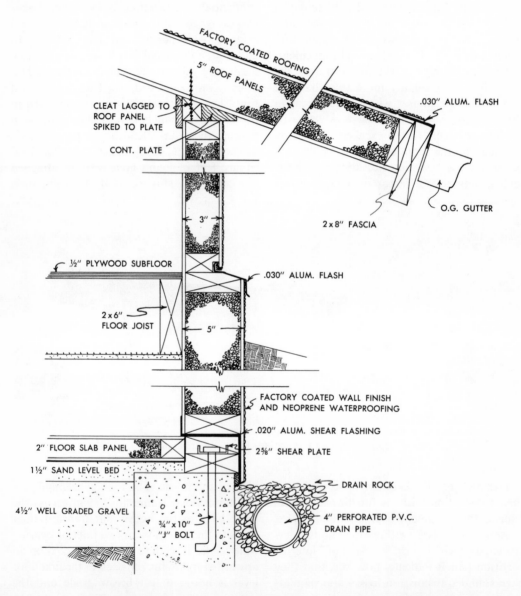

FIG. 20-5. Section through back wall of the East Lansing research house.

*E. I. du Pont de Nemours & Co., Inc.

Floor Panels

Following the installation of the house footings and foundation walls, the slab area was filled with 4 inches of compacted gravel topped by a 2-inch leveled and compacted bed of sand. A continuous 6-mil polyethylene film was placed over the sand. The foam core floor panels are 2 inches thick and 4 feet wide

FIG. 20-6. Placing foam core cement asbestos-faced floor panels of the East Lansing research house.

by 12 feet long (Figure 20-6). Faces of the panels are either ⅛- or ¼-inch asbestos cement board. The panels are laid directly on the polyethylene film and fastened only to each other by means of treated wood splines inserted in the edges of the panels. The entire slab area was covered in approximately 2 hours and 15 minutes during bad weather.

Structural Wall Panels

The 4 × 16 foot rear wall panels have ¼-inch plywood foil-faced skins bonded to the expandable polystyrene core (Figure 20-7). The first floor portion of the panels is 5 inches thick over-all, and the upper portion is 3 inches thick. The inside plywood face is continuous for the 16-foot height. All other wall panels are 3 inches thick with full-height scarfed ¼-inch plywood faces. Three panels with asbestos cement faces, the exterior faces covered with a plant-applied masonry coating, form a two-story accent wall. The two interior bearing walls are similar in construction to the exterior walls except that the foil was omitted. With the exception of the masonry coated panels which were set with a boom crane, all panels were erected by the carpenters on the job. Panels were joined

FIG. 20-7. East Lansing house wall panels are joined together on the floor and tipped into place.

with wood splines in the recessed panel edges and nailing through the faces.

Roof Panels

The 4-foot wide panels for both the house and the garage are 5 inches thick and ⅜-inch thick foil-faced plywood faces (Figure 20-8).

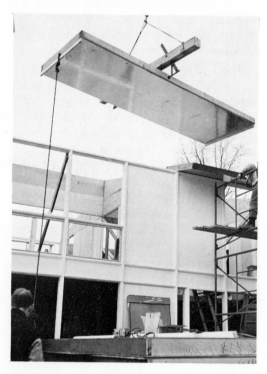

FIG. 20-8. Boom crane simplifies placement of East Lansing house roof panels.

Longitudinal wood rails were placed 24 inches on center in the panels to allow them to span the 12 feet between bearing walls. Splines fasten the panels together. Wood cleats attached to the bottom faces of the roof panels dropped into recesses provided along the top of the bearing walls as the panels were set in place by a hydraulic boom. Construction of the exterior walls, bearing partitions, and roof panels required about one week.

Performance

Even with the use of the aluminum foil to reduce moisture pickup in the plywood faces, panel movement has caused some problems with exterior and interior finishes. Bowing of the wall panels in the 4-foot direction, rather than the vertical direction, appeared to be the cause of the failure of some paint films at joints. From measurements of dimensional and moisture content changes of the panel faces, it did appear that loss and gain of moisture was slowed down. Horizontal movement in the roof panels soon caused failure of the taped joints between the plant finished urethane-coated panels. The roof was finally covered with asphalt shingles to eliminate leaking.

The excellent insulation provided by the foam core of the panels has given comparatively low heating costs during severe winters. The occupants of the homes claim that they have the only warm floor "slab." There has been no indication of any problems resulting from the foam panels on the sand bed. The rear wall with its earth back-fill has not presented any problems.

Regulatory Experience

It was recognized by Koppers Company that their foam core sandwich would require acceptance by building officials and other regulatory agencies. Extensive testing and engineering analyses provided data on structural capabilities, fire safety, durability, and sound transmission. Technical presentations permitted the Company to go far in obtaining the acceptance of the panel systems by the Federal Housing Administration, Building Officials Conference of America, and numerous cities and towns, some with their own archaic codes, but with officials who were willing to accept change.

The East Lansing House, built on land owned by Michigan State University, was not subject to code requirements. In the case of the South Bend research house, the city officials were very cooperative. After examining the technical data, the Building Commissioner helped obtain a waiver of the code from the Board of Public Works and aided in satisfying the South Bend Fire Marshal that the panels with the foam polystyrene core would not present any greater fire hazard than conventional nonrated house construction. An impromptu test at the site demonstrated to the Marshal that a hollow panel may cause a more rapid spread of fire due to the flue action in the open spaces between the framing members and panel faces; whereas a panel with a foam core has, in effect, a continuous fire stop from top to bottom of panel. Even when a local flame burns through a face, the core melts to form a cavity which hinders further combustion due to lack of oxygen. If an entire wall was subjected to intense heat, however, the core would recede and thereby reduce the structural effectiveness of the panels. In this case, the wood splines in the panel joints would provide a certain amount of support. Load tests of 2-inch thick panels with ¼-inch plywood faces indicate that even without the core, the splines and the plywood enable the panels to withstand the design load for a period of time which would either result in the death of the occupants by heat, smoke or toxic gases, or allow them to escape.

The widespread adoption of sandwich panels will depend largely on the technical data accumulated by the fabricator and, equally important, the existence of standards which will provide regulatory agencies with a basis for the evaluation of panels and systems. The uniform adoption of these standards, particularly by the communities in the market area of the fabricator, is essential. Variation in standards will require the fabricator either to design for the most severe requirements or to provide a multiplicity of components to meet the provisions of the different codes. Reasonable standards will enable sandwich panel systems to be designed with strength and rigidity consistent with house performance. Attention must be given also to regulations pertaining to other elements of the house which may be affected by a sandwich panel structure. For example, prefabricators of early enclosed panels found themselves in difficulty until the National Electric Code provided for the "fishing" of wires through the panels after they were erected.

The Future of Sandwich Panels in Housing

Following the construction of the two research houses, Koppers Company continued the development of the polystyrene core. A new plant was established in the Detroit area to provide home builders with complete component house systems, including finishes and special windows and doors required to fit the nonstandard wall thickness. A number of builders constructed houses with the panel system in the Midwest and East. Usually these houses were similar in plan and outward appearance to the builders' standard models.

In 1960, the Research Institute cooperated with Koppers Company in the construction of fourteen low-cost houses in Hampton, Virginia. These houses used modular panels for the exterior walls and interior non-load-bearing partitions. The builders' conventional trusses were used for the roof and ceiling system. Time studies of the house erections, using different methods for assembling the panels, showed a very low site labor content. Even so, the total in-place costs of the panel houses were slightly more than the builder's standard houses built with efficient wood framing methods. The houses were sold with Federal Housing Administration mortgage insurance. To date, their performance has been satisfactory.

Aside from ever present code problems, sandwich panel systems, regardless of the core material, have several problems that will not be overcome without other pioneering efforts and probably a somewhat changed attitude on the part of the home buyer. Sandwich panels have gained many of the economies inherent in shop-fabricated prefinished components and have the potential of reducing material costs with engineered design for strength and rigidity without exorbitant factors of safety. In addition, low-cost core materials, particularly the lower-density plastic foams, can compete successfully with wood frame and provide excellent wall and roof insulation. The key to achieving these economies, however, lies in the ability to use single layer panel faces. In combination with a continuous foam plastic core, these faces may often be thinner than materials required to span between framing. Certainly there is a large variety of materials, textures, colors, and finishes that is suitable for the structural faces of panels. But one pattern that is traditional, the appearance of lap or horizontal siding, is not available. Another one, still in an experimental state for panel faces, is brick. Recent efforts at producing marketable sandwich panel systems for housing have recognized the need for adhering to traditional design.

The sandwich panel and particularly the sandwich with the foam plastic core, will eventually be produced in volume sufficient to obtain high quality with lower costs. This will aid in changing the traditional attitudes of home buyers. Urethane and polystyrene will continue in the forefront of panel production, but other plastics, used by themselves and in combination with paper honeycomb and other materials, will find quick acceptance where they can perform multiple functions of adding to the strength, rigidity, and insulation of house components.

The Contributions of Adhesives

The development of synthetic adhesives has contributed to the growth of shop-fabricated structural components for use in houses. Panel construction, both stressed-skin and sandwich, has been made possible through the development of bonding techniques and adhesives with long-term strength and durability. The NAHB Research Institute has demonstrated applications of structural and semi-structural adhesives in their research houses.

Truss construction, providing a clear interior space within the house, has largely replaced the conventional joist and rafter roof system. Trusses have plywood gusset plates glued to the wood framing members to form rigid joints. Casein glue, the first bonding agent for the gussets, was rapidly replaced by more durable thermosetting resin adhesives. In the first NAHB research house, constructed in Kensington, Maryland, in 1956, a 32-ft span kingpost truss was designed to use ½-inch plywood bonded with a phenol-resorcinol glue. Pressure for bonding during curing of the adhesive was provided by nailing through the gussets into the wood.

The second floor of the East Lansing research house was constructed with shop-built 4 × 12 foot panels with ½-inch plywood nail-glued to the 2 × 6 floor joists. The combination of plywood and lumber in a stressed-skin construction allowed 2 × 6 joists to be used for a 12-foot span in place of the normally required 2 × 8's.

In the 1963 house, built in Rockville, Maryland, there is a separate two-car garage located in front of the house. The garage structural system has plywood bents 4 feet on center with preassembled split block masonry curtain wall panels between the bents.

Two-inch thick concrete blocks were bonded with an epoxy mortar to provide the joint strength required by the 8-foot-high thin panels. For the privacy fence in front of the house, the blocks were spaced to provide openings in a decorative pattern.

Other uses of adhesives in the NAHB research house have included the use of a two-part field mixed epoxy system to adhere prefinished wood flooring planks to steel bar joists; mastic type adhesives to adhere prefinished gypsum wall board to the interior of wood framing; a new epoxy grouting and bonding system developed by the Tile Council of America for preassembly of stock ceramic tile patterns to sheets of plywood; and a variety of other adhesives for the application of counter top material, the installation of various types of flooring materials, and the factory and field application of a variety of plastic film and sheetings.

Considering that an average size one-story house usually requires over 40,000 mechanical fasteners of many different types, the future of adhesives in housing looks particularly promising. Also in favor of the use of adhesives is the trend toward preassembly of components under controlled shop conditions. Improved adhesives systems and longer experience will help convince regulatory agencies of the performance of adhesive bonded structures. Better standards and quality control procedures will also help gain confidence. Eventually the industry may see the site adhesive bonding of house components even during adverse weather conditions.

EXTERIOR FINISHES

Since the early 1950's the accelerated development of plastic paints, coatings, and films has contributed to providing durable and colorful exterior finishes that have reduced the home owner's concern with maintenance. For the most part, plastics have been combined with structural materials such as aluminum, lumber, hardboard, and cement asbestos board, to serve as the exterior wear and weather-resistant surfaces. Baked enamels on aluminum, off to a bad start in the early remodeling market, are now established as a premiun siding finish. The lumber industry turned to plastics to help solve the problems produced when moisture meets paint on the house exterior.

Alkyd paints first started to supplement conventional oil-based paints and were followed by three principal types of water-

FIG. 20-9. The first NAHB research house constructed in Kensington, Maryland.

thinned paints, styrene-butadiene, polyvinyl-acetate, and acrylic. These water-base paints have greater alkali resistance and allow the passage of water vapor to reduce blistering and cracking of the paint films.

One of the new paint systems was used during its developmental stage on the exterior of the Kensington research house in 1957 (Figure 20-9) and a year later on the Knoxville house (Figure 20-10). In both cases the

FIG. 20-10. NAHB research house built in Knoxville, Tennessee, in 1958.

paint was applied to hardboard panel siding and trim. The recommended application called for three coats starting with an alkyd resin primer and finishing with two coats of "Lucite"* acrylic emulsion. The exterior finish of the Kensington house was still in good condition when it was refinished in the summer of 1963.

Several plastic coatings, including epoxies, urethanes and polyesters, have established themselves as extremely durable surfaces with excellent bonding characteristics. These coatings form their films by chemical action rather than oxidation or evaporation as in the case of the paints. A urethane coating was used for the car shelter and breezeway panels of the South Bend house. This two-part system promises excellent weather resistance and color retention. One clear coat of the formulation was plant applied during fabrication of the sandwich panels. After the initial color coat was mixed and brush applied at the site, an additional coat which contained a pure silica sand for texturing finished the surfaces. The coating has performed well and appears to be particularly able to conceal plywood grain raising and checking.

Plastics market researchers have found enthusiastic endorsement of the idea of prefinished materials and components for the building industry. Excellent cooperative work between the plastics producers and building product manufacturers has led to the introduction of a number of coatings, sheetings, and films which are factory applied to various materials. For house construction these products have generally been limited to sheet and lap wall siding. The problem has been primarily one of finding suitable mechanical fastening systems, preferably concealed systems which do not require penetration of the finishes. On the roof, the problem is compounded by a more severe weather exposure and limited means for concealing the joints between panels or sheets of material.

One of the earlier plastic roof coating systems has performed very well since 1957

*E. I. du Pont de Nemours & Co., Inc.

on the roof of the Kensington research house. Sheets of ½-inch plywood (4 feet × 8 feet) were factory coated with two 5-mil thick coats of neoprene. Neoprene granules were imbedded in the second coat to give a textured surface. In the field, the plywood sheets were nailed to the top chords of the trusses and a neoprene caulking was laid down in the chamfered joints between the sheets. Finally a turquoise color coat of "Hypalon"* synthetic rubber was applied with a paint roller. Aside from a slight chalking there has been no failure of the coating.

"Hypalon" was used again for the exterior wall coatings on the East Lansing research house. In the factory, the vertical edges of the exterior wall panels were masked back 1½ inch to provide for the field-applied joint treatment. Next, a prime coat of "Hypalon" was sprayed on the exterior foil face of the panels. A second tack coat was sprayed over the dry primed surface, and sand was spread over this coat for the desired texture. After the excess sand was shaken off the panel, a final binder coat of "Hypalon" was sprayed on.

Following erection of the wall panels and nailing of the splines, a mixture of sand and "Hypalon" was trowled on the joints in an attempt to match the factory finish. This method of finishing the joints did not provide a uniform color and texture and the walls were field coated with a final coat of "Hypalon." The total thickness on the house is approximately 10 mils, with the exception of the retaining wall area which is 15 to 18 mils. It is possible to paint over these coatings for repair or change of color.

The joint problem is best illustrated by the roof finish system of the East Lansing research house. Again, the roof panels were masked back at the edges with 1½-inch wide masking tape. Urethane prime and tack coats were applied to the panel surfaces. Sand for texture and a binder coat provided the final finish of the panels. When the panels were in place and the masking tape was removed to expose the clean foil, a 1-inch wide vinyl tape was bonded to the foil. Finally, a 3-inch wide tape, sand textured to match the panel coating, was applied with an adhesive over the joint. It was felt that this system with the flexible vinyl undertape would withstand movement and dimensional changes of the panel faces. However, some of the tape and adhesive joints were not firmly bonded, or worked loose, and leaks developed. The house roof was covered with asphalt shingles. The garage roof, however, has caused no problems and the urethane coating remains exposed and in good condition.

The 1963 Rockville house (Figure 20-11) degradation, mechanical wear and chemical reagents. The plywood panels were nailed to the wall studs with aluminum nails. "Tedlar"-wrapped wood battens, 1×3 inches, were attached 24 inches on centers, over each stud, with double pointed nails used as concealed fasteners. "Tedlar"-covered 1×4's and 1×3's were also used for corner and frieze boards and exterior door and window casings. "Tedlar"-faced ⅜-inch plywood encloses the eave soffits. The gable end walls

FIG. 20-11. Completely prefinished exterior of the 1963 research house in Rockville, Maryland.

featured components and systems developed to reduce on-site labor times and the effects of adverse weather conditions. Plastic prefinished materials contributed substantially to meeting these objectives. The entire exterior of the research house required no-site applied paints or coatings. Starting with the component foundation system, light gauge steel channel grade beams and their supporting steel H-beams in the ground were coated with an epoxy enamel to resist the corrosive action of the earth in contact with the steel.

The wood frame exterior wall panels were fabricated on the floor and tipped up in place after the application of 4×8 foot sheets of ½-inch A-C Exterior grade Douglas fir plywood with a plant laminated 2-mil polyvinyl fluoride film. The Research Institute previously cooperated with du Pont on field tests of their "Tedlar" film and was convinced of its superior resistance to solar

were covered with a horizontal one-piece cedar sheathing and siding material prefinished with a water repellent and stain.

The Douglas Fir Plywood Association cooperated with du Pont in the development of a folded interlocking Bermuda roof system using ½-inch A-C grade exterior Douglas fir plywood with a 10-mil calendered "Hypalon" film. The tough flexible film is factory laminated with a phenolic paper glueline to 2×10 foot plywood panels. The long edges of the panels are milled on their back sides so that the "Hypalon" can act as a continuous hinge for folded horizontal joints. The roofing is installed starting at the eaves by folding up successive courses of the panels. All nailing is concealed. The butt joints at the rafter chords were sealed with a pressure sensitive adhesive backed "Hypalon" tape. "Hypalon" tape flashings were also used at the chimney housing and vents. Subsequent movement of the plywood sheets have required the re-taping of some of the butt joints.

Several difficult flashing problems have been solved with the use of plastic sheets. "Hypalon" film was used as flashing in three of the research houses. The vent stack of the East Lansing house was flashed with a preformed neoprene unit. "Saraloy," * a vinylidene chloride copolymer sheet material, was used for flashing the plumbing vent stacks and flue housings on the roofs of the Knoxville and South Bend houses. This $\frac{1}{16}$-inch thick flexible material can be shaped and bonded to a wide variety of materials.

In addition to the flashings, several caulking compounds have been used in the research houses. These have included compounds of polysulfide, butyl rubber, urethane, and neoprene. These were used under wall sill plates, at joints between sandwich panels, and for glazing and sealing parts of two aluminum roofs.

Other plastic exterior finishes and accessories that have been considered by the Research Institute include vinyl sheeting laminated to wood, hardboard and metals; polyvinyl fluoride film on aluminum siding; rigid vinyl siding and rain carrying equipment; and glass-reinforced polyester siding.

FINISHING THE INTERIOR

From floors to ceilings, the five research houses have demonstrated many of the new plastic materials and products which have contributed to improving the quality of the house interior. Plastic products have departed from the mere decorative imitation of other materials to assume a prominent role in providing attractive, wear-resistant and cleanable surfaces. Plastics by themselves and in combination with other materials have shown that their unique characteristics can provide better value to the home owner. Many of these products have been used in the NAHB research houses. Other products were tried experimentally and are still in the process of development.

Interior finishes used in the research

*Dow Chemical Co.

houses include alkyd, latex, vinyl and acrylic paints, and urethane coatings. In addition to providing a wide range of colors for interior decoration, several paints were formulated to allow easier and quicker application with spray equipment. Improved coatings, such as the clear urethane used to finish the oak flooring of the Rockville house, enhance the beauty of the natural wood floors of four of the houses.

The prefinishing of wall sheet materials, largely for use as decorative paneling, has increased as a result of new clear and textured plastic finishes suitable for wood, plywood, and hardboard. The Rockville house study walls are cherry plywood faced with a clear acrylic coating. Prefinished wood tiles in the Knoxville and South Bend houses have a resin finish. Several prefabricated interior panels of the Knoxville house are faced with $\frac{1}{8}$-inch hardboard, factory surfaced with clear melamine over a printed simulated wood grain. These panels with a strip insulation board core came in widths of 1, 2, 3 and 4 feet. Even the bathroom walls including the tub surround show the versatility of materials such as the high-pressure malamine laminates. This surface on a $\frac{3}{16}$-inch-thick wood particle-board, in panels 30 inches wide, was applied as a tub wainscoating in the East Lansing house. The panels were applied to the framing with mastic, and a white vinyl caulking material was used at the joints and corners. Generally, these plastic-surfaced panel materials have not obtained wide acceptance for the bath areas, undoubtedly because of the preference for ceramic tile. As discussed later, the development of one-piece shower stalls and plastic tubs with integral wall surround have advantages which weigh heavily in their favor.

A wide variety of plastic films and sheetings, both factory and site applied, attracted favorable comment on the part of the visiting public and home builders. Like many of the coated prefinished materials, these finishes add value with their improved wear resistance and cleanability and attractive textures and colors. In addition, their site application to the surfaces of prefabricated wall components offers a means of concealing the joints between panels. Both the South Bend and the East Lansing research houses used several materials to achieve this end. A plastic fabric developed by the Dow Chemical Company is woven from a vinylidene chloride copolymer filament yarn on multi-shuttle automatic looms. A variety of colors is available, and decorative patterns can be obtained by embossing the woven fabric with heat and pressure. A final coating of an acrylic resin gives the material additional durability and water resistance. A vinyl acetate adhesive was used to apply the material to plywood panel surfaces. One application of the fabric was for the wainscoat around the bathtub. The material is still performing well. For the same purpose, the South Bend house used an embossed and colorful backed vinyl wall covering by Columbus Coated Fabrics Corporation. The East Lansing house used a vinyl covered fabric material by du Pont.

The first research house in Kensington, Maryland, began a series of applications of plastic films which are factory applied to interior surface materials, primarily hardboard and gypsum board. "Mylar,"* a clear polyester film, was laminated to a decorative paper which was factory applied to the gypsum board panels used for the interior of the house. The 1-mil thick "Mylar" film provides a very strong and durable surface that can be readily cleaned. The Rockville house carries its prefinishing to the inside with the use throughout the house of vinyl-faced gypsum board bonded by a rubber resin adhesive to the wood framing to do away with exposed nailing. One construction problem with this material, as well as with other prefinished materials, is the special trimming often required to hide the edges of the panels.

The use of decorative prefinished materials has been generally limited to special wall areas in the house, since the bevelled edge or V-joints between panels, whether or not "concealed" by random or regular grooves, are not yet completely acceptable in place of smooth continuous drywall and plaster surfaces. However, the inherent advantages of

the plastic films or sheeting materials and their decreasing costs will create an increasing demand for their use. Another practical use of the films has been their application to acoustical ceiling tile to provided washable surfaces without diminishing the acoustical characteristics of the tile. The Kensington house kitchen ceiling tile was faced with "Mylar" polyester film. For the Knoxville house, Owens-Corning Fiberglas provided an experimental acoustic and insulating material consisting of $\frac{1}{2} \times 12 \times 32$ inch fiberglass acoustic tile covered with "Mylar" and backed with $5\frac{1}{2}$ inches of "Fiberglas" insulation. The Rockville house also has several types of acoustical insulating ceiling materials by Owens-Corning Fiberglas, all faced with a washable embossed vinyl surface.

Plastic flooring materials used in the research houses have shown improvements in the wear resistance of floor surfaces since the introduction of the asphalt tile. A low-cost all vinyl tile on the floors of the Knoxville and South Bend houses has performed well despite its thinner thickness. The tile has the color pattern through the entire thickness. Other flooring materials used include vinyl asbestos tile, vinyl sheet flooring, and a sheet vinyl backed with an integral layer of foam rubber to give greater resiliency. Plastics for carpeting were on display in several nylon and rayon rugs with an integral foam rubber backing and a colloidal silica application to minimize soiling. An interesting exterior flooring application in the Kensington house made use of a "Hypalon" film applied with mastic to concrete patio blocks.

Other uses of plastics, both decorative and functional, on the interior of the research houses, although too numerous to describe in detail, deserve listing.

(1) High pressure laminate melamine sheets for kitchen counter and vanitory tops.

(2) Wood particle-board with surfaces of phenolic and melamine laminates used for the working surfaces and cabinet doors of a new kitchen cabinet system, and also for built-in storage cabinets.

(3) Cabinet drawers of molded high-impact polystyrene.

*E. I. du Pont de Nemours & Co., Inc.

(4) Closet doors with a decorative molded face of acrylonitrile-butadiene-styrene (ABS).

(5) Sliding bathtub enclosure, sliding kitchen cabinet doors, and decorative panels of methyl methacrylate polymer (acrylic) translucent sheets with embedded decorative patterns.

(6) Sliding tub enclosure with opaque rigid vinyl sheets.

(7) Shower door of polyethylene folding panels.

(8) Stair handrail with a vinyl cap heat-applied over an aluminum "T" section.

(9) Rigid PVC extruded trim with integral color for interior door and window casings.

WINDOWS AND DOORS

In the late 1940's, wood, the traditional material for windows and doors, found itself competing with aluminum and steel. The metals provided lighter, thinner frame and sash sections but had to face up to their own problems, primarily those of insufficient rigidity and corrosion resistance and conduction of low temperatures. Just as wood windows found the advantages of new plastic paints and coatings for finishes, so have the efforts to combine metal and plastic resulted in matching the good characteristics of each material.

The Rockville research house incorporated a new extruded vinyl and aluminum insulating window, manufactured by Caradco, Inc., of Dubuque, Iowa. The basic structural frame of the window is aluminum with an acrylic coating on the exposed portions. The upper light of double layer glass is fixed in rigid PVC sections which are adhered to the glass to combine the strength and stiffness of the two materials. The vinyl sections, with their low thermal conductivity, provide a continuous thermal break to reduce condensation problems. They also require no additional finishing in the field. The one disadvantage of the window is the necessity of obtaining an entire sash with glass and perimeter sections in the event of glass breakage.

For the Rockville house and the previous East Lansing house, translucent glass sandwich panels with a large cell polystyrene core were used for attractive light-admitting insulated units in a gable end and entry panel.

Three of the exterior doors in the East Lansing house were constructed with a foam core of a low-density urethane between faces of 22-gauge steel pans connected at the door edge with a neoprene weather seal to stop conductance through the metal. A similar type door in the Rockville house combines acrylic primed steel sheet faces with an expandable polystyrene foam core. Both of these doors provide excellent insulation and have remained dimensionally stable. Bifold garage door panels in the East Lansing house have $\frac{1}{8}$-in. plywood skins on a polystyrene foam core to give lightweight construction.

Nylon and "Delrin," * an acetal resin, have contributed to excellent working door hardware including injection molded hinge bushings, lockset latch bolts, and pins. The visible as well as the wearing parts of the "Delrin" front door handle and lockset of the Kensington house show the possibilities of new styling with integral color and excellent wear and corrosion resistance. These parts have all performed well since 1957.

HEATING AND COOLING

Forced-air counterflow heating and cooling systems have been used in all the research houses with the exception of the Knoxville house with its electrical resistance heating elements. System development has emphasized methods of air distribution, although several new types of equipment have been demonstrated.

Vinyl-coated, 22-gauge steel provided a unique solution for a portion of the air supply duct in the East Lansing research house. For distribution of air to the second floor, it was necessary to run the main supply duct perpendicular to the floor joists. Normally this sheet metal duct would be enclosed in a space below the ceiling. For the research house the framing was omitted and the duct with its attractive vinyl finish was left exposed. A continuous indirect light

*E. I. du Pont de Nemours & Co., Inc.

trough for strip fluorescent lighting was formed into the lower edge of one side of the duct for a slight additional cost.

Return air distribution in the South Bend research house was handled by lightweight duct sections of glass-fiber insulation encased in a vinyl film. The insulated duct has the added advantage of transmitting less equipment sound and noises from room to room. Ducts sections are easily cut and joined with an adhesive-backed tape.

Plastic films have offered an economical and efficient way of providing for continuous vapor barriers for the walls, floors, and ceilings of houses. Four of the research houses have a 4-mil polyethlene film under the concrete floor slabs, or panels, in the case of the East Lansing house. Six-mil material was used in the crawl space of the Rockville house. Polyethylene film was also used for temporary shelter of building materials on the site and for protection of partially completed construction.

Fig. 20-12. Placing board polystyrene foam over polyethylene vapor barrier for insulation of the crawl space in the Rockville house.

Foam polystyrene in board form has contributed to reducing heat loss through the edges of concrete slabs on grade. In the Kensington house 1-in.-thick foam poly-styrene, "Styrofoam,"* was placed around the entire edge of the slab and 12 in. under the slab. "Styrofoam" was also used under the steel channel grade beam of the Rockville house to reduce heat loss from the crawl space plenum (Figure 20-12).

An unusual insulation problem was solved with a plastic foam in the Kensington house. In this house, the building drain is above the slab and projects through the side wall with a 90° elbow. The drain drops straight down to the building sewer located below the frost line. That portion of the building drain above the frost line and outside the house wall is encased with a 3-in. thickness of an economical foamed-in-place phenolic of about a 2-lb/cu ft density.

ELECTRICAL DISTRIBUTION AND LIGHTING

Wiring

One of the problems inherent in continuous core sandwich panel construction is the lack of space to run wiring for wall outlets and switches. Although wiring can be fished through vertical voids in the panel core, horizontal wiring is next to impossible. In the South Bend house, conventional metal raceways systems were used to contain all convenience outlets and serve as a baseboard along interior and exterior wall panels. Shallow switch boxes were fastened to the plywood panel faces by special sheet metal clamping devices. Vertical runs from the raceway to switches were through voids in the foam polystyrene at panel edges.

The cost of installing a raceway system was reduced in the East Lansing research house by the development of an extruded rigid vinyl section which serves as the baseboard and covers nonmetallic cable stapled to the wall about 2 inches above the floor. The baseboard is $^{13}/_{16}$ inch $\times$ 3 inches and contains two compartments which are divided by double fins to enclose the screws for connection to the walls. The vinyl was stamped out in the house at the desired places to allow a porcelain receptacle outlet to project through the base. The upper larger compartment carries one or more

*Dow Chemical Company.

line voltage cables, and the smaller lower compartment carries telephone wires. This system offers the advantage of easy addition of wiring and outlets at a later date.

Vertical fishing of wires through the foam core panels was made easier by the use of a nonmetallic cable with a plastic covering and over-all smaller size. Two vinyl-covered wires with a bare ground are encased in a semi-clear tough and durable nylon.

A further refinement of the extruded vinyl baseboard raceway was developed for the Rockville house (Figure 20-13). There

FIG. 20-13. Rigid vinyl baseboard raceway sections used in the Rockville house.

are two sections, a continuous vinyl retaining clip which is nailed to the bottom of the wall, and a 3-inch snap-on cover installed after the wiring is in place. A separate compartment is available for running telephone and television wires. Both systems were developed with the cooperation of the B. F. Goodrich Chemical Company. It is expected that the eventual cost to the builder of the baseboard, wiring, and receptacles will be less than 30¢/lineal ft.

Lighting

Translucent plastic sheets have been used for many years for interior diffused lighting under fluorescent tubes. The Research Institute has tried a number of materials and suspension systems with the objective of finding lower cost installations. These materials and systems include: 90-mil sheets of nylon-reinforced clear acrylic plastic suspended in a 1 × 2 inch wood egg crate framing; acrylic fiber reinforced 55-mil

acrylic sheets suspended by a similar wood grid; a 15-mil rigid calendered vinyl chloride-acetate sheeting with a three-dimensional pattern; and glass-fiber-reinforced acrylic panels suspended in a lightweight steel grid. The cost of a translucent ceiling system for the residential market, exclusive of lighting, should be less than 20¢/sq ft to obtain acceptance for use in large areas of the house.

PLUMBING

Pipe and Fittings

The Research Institute since its inception has followed the development of plastic piping systems. Improved materials and the creation of dimensional and quality standards have gradually led to acceptance of plastic pipe and fittings by state and local plumbing officials. The Federal Housing Administration acknowledged the advent of plastic plumbing in housing with the acceptance of polyethylene water supply to the house and acrylonitrile-butadiene-styrene (ABS) building drainage and vent systems. The biggest barrier to be overcome is the reluctance of the trades to accept the new materials and the techniques required to assemble the systems.

Despite the problems, plastic pipe and fittings have such existing or potential advantages that they will eventually replace traditional materials for most applications. From the builder and trade point of view, one of the advantages is the comparative light weight of plastic pipe, as little as $\frac{1}{10}$ that of metals. Yet, the materials are sturdy enough to allow rough handling in the field. Longer lengths of pipe and continuous sections of flexible tubing require fewer joints, and the connections are generally easier and faster to make. This means reduced labor costs which, with competitive material costs, particularly when fitting prices are reduced, will contribute to lower in-place costs. From a performance standpoint, plastic pipe is acid- and alkali-resistant and not subject to galvanic or electrolytic action. Smooth inside surfaces provide improved flow conditions and reduce the collection of deposits.

The Knoxville research house utilized an all-plastic plumbing system (Figure 20-14). Starting with the water service, a continuous one-piece length of flexible polyethylene tubing extends from the street to the house, with a pressure reducer at the curb and shutoff at the house. Within the house, two

(Figure 20-15). Connections to the fixture drains were made with solvent-welded and threaded adapters. The exterior sewer and drain field line from the treatment tank are 4-inch rubber-modified polystyrene, plain and perforated pipe.

Preassembly of plastic plumbing went the

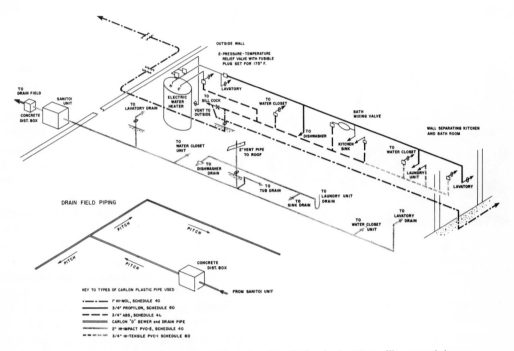

FIG. 20-14. Schematic of plastic plumbing system installation in the Knoxville research house.

types of material were used for cold-water supply, ¾-inch Schedule 40 ABS with solvent-welded connections and ¾-inch Schedule 80 PVC pipe and fittings with both solvent-welded and threaded connections.

One of the first installations of plastic residential hot-water supply lines took advantage of a newly developed high-temperature polypropylene pipe and fittings with threaded connections. A back-flow valve was placed in the cold-water supply to eliminate any chance of hot-water flow into the cold-water system. Two 175° fusable plug pressure-temperature relief valves were provided for the hot-water heater.

The interior drain lines and vent pipe are 2-inch high-impact Schedule 40 PVC with solvent-welded connections. The system was partially prefabricated and placed in the ground before the concrete slab was poured

full course in the East Lansing research house. The two-story house design with kitchen and baths back-to-back and above each other allowed the development of a plumbing core wall which was completely shop assembled. (Figure 20-16). All drain and supply lines were preassembled in a

FIG. 20-15. Plumber solvent–welds sections of plastic drain line for the Knoxville research house.

12 foot wide × 18 foot high frame wall constructed with 2 × 8 studs. The completed wall including pipe weighed approximately

FIG. 20-16. Plumbing wall with completely preassembled plastic piping is set in place for the East Lansing research house.

800 pounds. After the wall was set in place with a boom crane, the sewer was connected to the vertical stack, and the hot- and cold-water lines were connected to the water service and hot-water heater.

The hot- and cold-water pipes and fittings were manufactured from a new material by the B. F. Goodrich Chemical Company. The polyvinyl dichloride (PVDC) plastic has demonstrated an ability to withstand relatively high-temperature and pressure conditions. Schedule 40 pipe was used throughout in ½-, ¾- and 1-inch diameters. All plastic pipe and fitting connections were made by solvent welding, usually in less than one minute per joint. Connections to metal fittings were accomplished with the use of plastic-to-copper adapters. Water for the house is obtained from a well through a 1-inch polyethylene service line. Waste and vent pipe and fittings are polyvinylchloride (PVC) with solvent-welded connections. The drain field for the sewage disposal system is also PVC.

PVDC pipe and injection-molded fittings were also used for the hot- and cold-water

supply systems of the Rockville research house. The vent and drainage system is assembled with fittings and pipe made from ABS by the Marbon Chemical Division of the Borg-Warner Corporation. A single 3-inch stack is used to serve the first and second-floor baths and a 2-inch drain runs from the kitchen. Valves were installed in the vent stacks to allow partial or complete blocking of the vents, and transparent traps were installed at the fixtures to observe possible trap loss. Gas service to the house is ABS pipe, one of the first installations allowed by the local utility.

In addition to the plastic piping installations in the research houses, the Research Institute cooperated with the B. F. Goodrich Chemical Company in the installation of complete plastic plumbing systems in three field test houses in Baltimore. The performance of all of the plastic plumbing systems installed in the research and other houses has been excellent. There has been no indication of failure or degradation of the pipe and fittings. From a construction viewpoint, the drain and vent systems with the larger-diameter pipe have been installed with few problems. On the other hand, the hot- and cold-water systems have presented problems in assembly, largely due to the rigidity of the pipe, in comparison with copper tubing which can be bent to fit site conditions. Eventually, a suitable flexible plastic tubing with simple connections may allow water supply pipes to be fished through the walls similar to electrical wiring.

Plumbing Fixtures

When the Research Institute decided to use molded plastic vanitory units in the Knoxville and South Bend houses in 1958, these fixtures were somewhat of a novelty. The following year one of the East Lansing house bathrooms contained a double bowl vanitory with bowl, top, and back splash molded in one piece. A one-piece molded shower stall attracted attention in the same room. These fixtures were all glass fiber-reinforced polyester resin laminates.

It was the first-floor powder room of the Rockville house with its molded plastic fixtures and walls that really gave a glimpse into the future. The componentized bath was designed by industrial designers Loewy and Snaith for Owens-Corning Fiberglas Corporation (Figure 20-17). The bath con-

FIG. 20-17. Top view of model shows molded plastic components of a bathroom in the Rockville research house.

sists of a one-piece shower stall, presently available; an experimental wall-length single bowl vanitory with provision for conventional wall-hung toilet; vanitory side panels with integral medicine cabinets and decorative doors; and connecting wall panels to completely enclose the room, including one panel with a built-in recess for towels. All of these components were plant fabricated of gel-coated glass-fiber-reinforced polyester. They were bolted together in the house. The second-floor bathroom has a practical and attractive one-piece molded bathtub and wall enclosure of the same materials.

Early glass-fiber-reinforced polyester bathtubs have been performing satisfactorily for over 8 years. The first standards for these units, and another for shower receptors, were formulated in 1958 and established as Commercial Standards. In the meantime, resin producers improved their formulations and fabricators worked out better methods of hand and spray molding. As a result, fixtures produced in 1964 represent a considerable improvement over previous units. A matched metal mold shower stall came on the market in 1963. The same year a plastics industry advisory committee working with the NAHB Research Institute established a revised set of test methods and performance standards which allowed the gel-

coated glass-fiber-reinforced polyester bathtubs to be accepted by the Federal Housing Administration. These materials appear to be firmly entrenched. However, future development will lead to other materials which will provide attractive and durable shower, tub, and vanitory units. These units will be preferred by the home buyer because of their attractive design, warmth to the touch, and ease of cleaning. Completely molded bathroom units or molded components such as in the Rockville house are on the horizon.

Other Plumbing Assemblies

The East Lansing and other research houses have demonstrated other uses of plastics for house plumbing systems. Plastics such as nylon reduce corrosion and provide self-lubrication and, therefore, a longer life. Water closet ball-cock assemblies, valve assemblies of lavatory fittings, shower heads and toilet seat hinges, all fabricated from nylon, have performed excellently over a period of seven years.

CONCLUSION

The NAHB research houses and other demonstration houses developed by associations and manufacturers have led to a better understanding of the production, installation and performance of new plastic products. This knowledge reaches to the builder-contractor and general public and, in the case of the home building market, will help create not only an acceptance of new plastics but a demand for their superior qualities. As is usually the case with new materials, acceptance without substantial experience is not always easily obtained. Sound technical evidence to relate to up-to-date specifications and standards must be relied upon by the designer, user and regulatory agencies. In the design of new products for the residential market, the manufacturer must remain cognizant of the economic situation prevailing in a highly competitive market. To this end, the leading plastic products will be designed for the most efficient use of material to perform the required structural, protective, or decorative functions.

21 EXTENDING THE HORIZON

IRVING SKEIST

Skeist Laboratories, Inc.
Newark, New Jersey

The volume of new construction in the United States is expected to double in thirteen years—from $61 billion in 1962 to $120 billion in 1975. Of this total, one-fourth will be for non-residential building; nearly one-third for utilities, highways and other non-residential non-building; the remaining and largest fraction (also the fastest growing) for residences.[1]

Plastics should make an increasing contribution to this growth. The new materials have achieved their acceptance most rapidly in *industrial* and *commercial* buildings. The architects who design these buildings have appreciated the high functional performance and economy of plastic components. The companies who occupy the buildings want them to reflect a progressive, forward approach. Increased use of air conditioning will result in a swing back from the present excessive employment of glass exteriors, with their poor thermal insulation. Two-thirds of exterior walls for commercial building will be of paneling. This can open a tremendous market for plastics, in view of their low weight—important for high-rise buildings—and the reduced use of on-site labor. (Bricklayers get nearly $7.00 per hour in metropolitan areas.[2]

The typical *home* buyer is more conservative. Although the kitchen may be replete with shiny new gadgetry, the exterior must not be too great a departure from the surrounding architecture. Indeed, some communities even require a degree of conformity in outward structures that tends to stifle radical innovation. Specification-type building codes have also hindered the utilization of new materials, but this obstacle is being overcome gradually through the adoption of performance-type codes. The greatest promise for increased plastics usage in the home lies in the blending of synthetics with older materials, in composites, rather than in wholesale substitution. Another helpful factor is the trend toward factory prebuilt components, with savings in labor costs and improved quality control.

Institutional construction—schools, hospitals and government buildings—generally has added non-flammability requirements. The resin manufacturers are steadily improving the flame spread and smoke development ratings of their plastics, coatings and foam insulation.[3] Briber points to two broad categories of flammability requirements: avoiding danger to human life and preserving the mechanical strength of the structure. In the first requirement, urethane foam compares favorably with the standard material (red oak) in flame spread, fuel contributor factor and toxicity of combustion products. However, it gives a high smoke rating. With regard to structural considerations, urethane foam shows promise when tested in roofing, and in floor and

444

ceiling assemblies. For wall assemblies, it is suggested that the thermoplastic nature of polystyrene foam might actually be an advantage, since on melting, it would leave behind an air space which would insulate against the transmission of heat. In other words, the thermoplastic polystyrene would function as a fuse. Of course, once it had served this purpose, it would have to be replaced.

The major volume plastics used in building have already had more than a decade of successful experience. As far back as 1954, the Building Research Institute held a conference on building, at which speakers discussed fiber glass-reinforced plastic facings and sandwich panels, acrylic glazing, polystyrene foam thermal insulation, polyethylene film vapor seals, resilient vinyl floor coverings, etc.[4] The following year, a group at Massachusetts Institute of Technology published an authoritative brochure on the accomplishments and potentialities for plastics in housing, under the auspices of the Monsanto Chemical Company.[5] Yet, a recent review on building construction notes that designers and builders consider plastics to be "exotic."[6]

Government figures for 1963 and 1964 show generally increasing acceptance of plastics in construction.

TABLE 21-1. Value of Shipments of Miscellaneous Plastics Products and Quantity of Resins Consumed: 1964 and 1963[3]

Product Code	Product	1964			1963		
		Value of Shipments Including Interplant Transfers[1] ($1,000)	Resins Consumed in the Manufacture of Products Shipped: (1000 lb)		Value of Shipments Including Interplant Transfers[1] ($1000)	Resins Consumed in the Manufacture of Products Shipped: (1,000 lb)	
			Thermoplastics	Thermosets		Thermoplastics	Thermosets
30796	Construction plastics products, total	c322,026	255,265	33,644	c280,604	219,823	29,449
3079611	Corrugated and flat panels	b42,835	16,006	24,242	b40,761	13,857	25,264
3079621	Doors and partitions, folding accordion type	c18,740	1,326	—	c19,105	(D)	(2)
	Unsupported plastic floor, wall, and counter covering:						
3079631	Sheet goods	b14,894	16,756	(2)	b11,379	14,472	(2)
3079635	Floor tile	43,632	42,437	—	45,200	44,310	(2)
3079637	Wall tile	a10,263	14,232	—	b9,895	14,320	—
3079651	Plumbing fixtures and parts (excluding pipe and fittings)	b14,773	4,000	3,184	a13,613	4,920	2,356
	Pipe:						
3079653	½ to less than 2 in. inside diameter	35,911	74,305	(2)	32,452	62,776	(2)
3079655	2 in. and over, inside diameter	a21,206	44,505	(D)	16,837	33,271	(D)
3079654	Not specified by size	9,097	18,138	—	b8,379	14,889	—
3079657	Fittings and unions	b24,879	15,127	2,620	b21,394	10,431	1,829
3079698	Other construction plastic products	c84,015	8,175	(D)	c60,694	6,577	(D)
3079600	Construction plastic products, not specified by kind	c1,781	258	—	b895	(D)	—

—Represents zero.   rrevised.
(D) Withheld to avoid disclosing figures for individual companies.
[1]Quantities of resins consumed in manufacture were reported by establishments which accounted for 95 percent of more of the value of shipments of each specified product unless indicated as follows:

(a) From 90 to 94 %.
(b) From 75 to 89 %.
(c) Less than 75 %.

These percentages are not only based upon quantities of resins consumed and not reported, but also include value of shipments of products made from purchased sheets, rods, tubes, foam, other intermediate stock shapes, laminates and parts purchased for assembly.
[2]Less than 100,000 lb.
[3]Source: Current Industrial Reports Series M30D (64)-1, U. S. Department of Commerce, Bureau of the Census.

Codes and the SPI Plastics in Building Construction Council

The building codes, examined in depth in Chapter 3, are at last being updated to permit the use of new materials. New York City has finally adopted a code based on performance, and the various regional codes are gradually being revised to permit the greater utilization of plastics for pipe and other purposes. Much progress has been achieved through the efforts of various federal agencies and associations, especially the Society of the Plastics Industry, which in 1964 set up the SPI Plastics in Building Construction Council. Among the interested groups are the National Board of Fire Underwriters[7], Underwriters' Laboratories, Inc.[8] American Society for Testing and Materials (ASTM),[9] and the Building Research Institute.[10] Underwriters' Laboratories, Inc., Chicago, Illinois, has provided the flame spread, fuel contributed and smoke developed ratings for the plastic products of approximately 100 companies in its Building Materials List for January 1965, The companies and their products are listed in the Appendix.

The U. S. Department of Commerce, acting on the recommendations of organizations such as SPI, publishes voluntary standards, for example, Commercial Standard CS214, "Glass-Fiber Reinforced Polyester Corrugated Structural Plastics Panels." An SPI committee is developing improved standards for gel-coated reinforced plastic bathtubs (CS221) and shower floors (CS222). Shower floors and enclosures have generally been accepted by the FHA (Federal Housing Administration) and most local code authorities. The FHA insures mortgages on some houses containing reinforced plastic bathtubs—single-family houses in a few states, multiple-family dwellings in all areas.[11]

The National Research Council, through its Building Research Advisory Board (BRAB), is sponsoring a study by the National Bureau of Standards which will set up performance characteristics for plumbing fixtures.[12] Professor Walter H. Lewis of the University of Illinois sees a savings of $75 to $100 per home by substituting plastic for other types of pipe in residential drain-waste-vent systems, but much union opposition must be overcome. Early in 1965, the Western Plumbing Officials Association approved the use of thermoplastic pipe and fittings for one-story and two-story residences.[13]

Plastics in the "Conventional" Home

While code restrictions and inertia have inhibited the use of plastics in the home, the more progressive house builders are utilizing the synthetics for many non-structural purposes. For example, National Homes Corporation of Lafayette, Indiana,[14] a leader in prebuilt house construction, made use of the following plastic items in its 1964 homes:

Joint tape for roofs and flashing applications: "Tedlar"* polyvinyl fluoride.

Siding facing: "Videne"** polyester film.

Underslab vapor barrier and conceal flashing: polyethylene film, 6 mils.

Underslab insulation: polystyrene foam, approximately 1 pcf density.

Roof sheathing: Douglas fir plywood ⅜ inch.

Structural window glazing and thermal barrier: rigid vinyl.

Window frames and surrounds: rigid vinyl on wood frame.

Window mullions: extruded and molded vinyl, attached non-structurally for decorative purposes.

Window sills: "Formica"† phenolic-melamine laminate.

Window hardware: upper and lower sash fitted with "Delrin"* polyacetal; rigid vinyl latches to retain sash in desired position.

Magnetic door weather strip: flexible vinyl with hidden extrusion of magnetic oxide in plastic.

Door drip cap: rigid vinyl.

Door sweep: flexible vinyl.

Door: polystyrene foam core between aluminum skins.

Trim for interior: flexible vinyl for hiding joint of butting wall panels.

Facing materials for ceilings and walls: flexible vinyl film, 3 mils thick.

Acoustical ceiling: "Sonocor"‡ — fiber glass faced with rigid embossed vinyl film, 2.5 mils thick. Vapor barrier permeance or transmission rating of

*Registered trademark E. I. du Pont de Nemours & Co., Inc.
**Registered trademark The Goodyear Tire & Rubber Co., Inc.
†Registered trademark American Cyanamid Co.
‡Registered trademark Owens-Corning Fiberglass Corporation.

0.50 perm. The ceiling has a K value of 0.24. The vinyl face film has a flame spread of less than 0.25. Flexible vinyl plastic extruded joint strips cover the joints.

Electrical hardware and wiring: various plastics.

Hardware parts: nylon for gears, sliders, etc., in door knobs and sliding door hardware.

Bathroom sills and vanity: marble dust reconstituted with polyester resin to give marble pattern.

Kitchen countertops: "Formica" laminate.

Kitchen drawers: injection molded plastic mounted on a 20-gauge metal track with removable plastic guides.

Sub-flooring: Douglas fir plywood, ⅝-inch, 5-ply interior grade.

Floor tile: vinyl, vinyl-asbestos and asphalt.

At Midland, Michigan, home of The Dow Chemical Company, a conventional house[15] has made even greater use of plastics, including large-cell styrene–methyl methacrylate copolymer rigid foam glazing panels in gables, front door sidelight, skylights in kitchen and bathroom; foamed styrene roof board; latex-modified stucco; thin-wall brick construction utilizing saran polymer-aggregate mortar and insulated with polystyrene and polyurethane board; epoxy marble vanity; polyethylene foam gasketing for windows; latex-modified mortar walkway and driveway topping; acrylic light rod fixtures; flexible polyurethane foam ceiling; polyethylene rod stock screen retainers and gasketing; polyethylene film moisture barrier; vinyl floor covering; acetal knobs; styrene drawers; silicone floor protector and water repellent; saran flashing.

As already discussed in Chapter 20, sandwich panels with "Dylite"* foamed polystyrene cores, faced with plywood, were utilized successfully in the 1958-1959 research house of the National Association of Home Builders.[16,17] After obtaining an Engineering Bulletin from the Federal Housing Administration, the Koppers Company was able to secure FHA mortgage insurance and building code approval from the four model codes for houses containing these panels. Usage of the panels is promoted through a Koppers affiliate, General Homes, which prebuilds entire homes and ships them to the building site in sections. Within

*Registered trademark Koppers Company, Inc.

300 miles of the plant, they can deliver house packages which are sold in-place at prices no higher than those charged for homes of equivalent size and quality built by conventional methods.[18]

FIG. 21-1. Vinyl siding can be snapped into place. (*Courtesy Monsanto Co.*)

The New York World's Fair

In marked contrast to the rectilinear structures of the tradition-bound home builder were the domes and other compound curvatures of the 1964-1965 New York World's Fair. The Fair served as a proving ground for new design concepts as well as materials.[19]

Fiber glass-reinforced plastic (FRP) panels played a dominant role.[20] The Marina, a permanent installation to accommodate approximately 700 boats, is made up of a modular docking system of FRP pontoons, like building blocks, fitted together to form headers and finger slips, that maintain a constant level above the water. Because of their light weight, the flotation blocks are easy to install or remove.

The AT&T Pavilion, designed by Harrison and Abramovitz, was completely sheathed with 450 white FRP panels—185,000 square feet. The panels, as large as 40 × 12 feet, were constructed by Lunn Laminates, Inc., of Wyandanch, New York. The backs of the panels were sprayed with a ½-inch layer of asbestos for maximum fire safety. A steel-ribbed backing was built into each panel for attaching and handling. The panels were joined with a Dow-Corning silicone sealant.

The U. S. Pavilion, designed by Charles Luckman Associates, was sheathed with striated, textured panels to give a stained-glass effect and a uniform distribution of soft light. The 65,000 square feet of 4 × 10 foot panels, in six different types and designs, were made by Dimensional Plastics of Miami, Florida. The 7-up snack pavilions were made from free-form pods, each 25 feet square, with honeycomb cores between outer surfaces of molded FRP. The West Virginia Pavilion, designed by F. P. Weidersum, had two 38-foot circular domes, each covered with 12 pie-shaped, translucent FRP sandwich panels. The New York State Pavilion, designed by Philip Johnson,[21]

an oval roof. They were built by Kalwall Corp. of Manchester, New Hampshire.

FRP was also utilized in serpentine phone booths designed by Henry Dreyfuss, and in the Sinclair dinosaurs sculptured under the direction of Louis Paul Jonas.

Acrylic was employed to give an airy structure creating a feeling of euphoria[23] in the Schaefer Center designed by Eggers and Higgins (Figure 21-3). Light-gray transparent sheet, one-half inch thick, manufactured by Rohm & Haas Company, was vacuum formed in a bubble pattern by Just Plastics, Inc. of New York City, to provide a "foamy beer" look, as well as extra rigidity.

In the Coca-Cola Pavilion, three-dimensional acrylic grill work provided a sculptured look. The transparent walls of the Chun King Pavilion utilized acrylic sandwich panels. The firm plans to build a nationwide chain of Chinese restaurants, using the same type of construction.

FIG. 21-2. More than 1400 translucent reinforced plastic panels were required to build the roof of the New York State pavilion. (*Courtesy Kalwall Corporation*)

had a huge oval translucent roof of FRP sandwich panels laid up on cable suspension —said to be the largest suspension roof in the world (Figure 21-2).[22] The 57,500 square feet of sandwich panels, with glass-reinforced acrylic-modified polyester skins and an aluminum I-beam core, had to be trapezoidal in shape in order to produce

Moire patterns were produced in "Row-lux" multi-lens sheet made by Rowland Products, Inc., of Kensington, Connecticut. During the extrusion process, the sheet is embossed on both sides with tiny parabolic lenses. There are slightly more lenses per square inch on one side than the other, giving varying patterns of reflection. The material was employed by designer Jo Mielziner for the twinkling votive lights to frame *La Pieta* at the Vatican Pavilion. It also served to provide a moire effect in portions of the Bell, General Electric, Swiss and other exhibits.

COMPOSITES

A common theme in much of the new plastics development is the use of composites. The objective is to get a product that combines the best properties of the individual members. Such a composite can be all

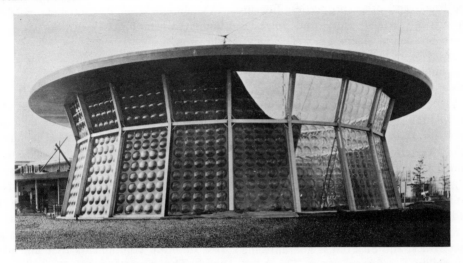

Fig. 21-3. Installation of "Plexiglas" acrylic exterior walls in the 90-ft diameter Schaefer structure. (*Courtesy Rohm & Haas Co.*)

IBM's giant plastic egg was encased in *cellulose acetate butyrate* (CAB). Embossed CAB panels also formed the curtain wall of the Kodak Pavilion. Rigid vinyl clapboard siding and plumbing were employed in the House of Good Taste. The Minnesota Pavilion was constructed of sandwich panels with rigid PVC skins and polystyrene foam cores, from Structural Plastics Corp., Osseo, Minnesota. For the walls of the Formica house, polystyrene foam cores were faced with laminated plastic. General Electric's nuclear fusion demonstration was capped by a transparent *polycarbonate* dome. The roof of the Chun King Inn was covered with sculptured tiles of painted urethane foam, light in weight, and high in thermal insulation. The Brass Rail refreshment stands had inflated roofs of high-strength nylon and white vinyl. The du Pont exhibit and several others were surfaced with polyvinyl fluoride.

Polyester, acrylic and polycarbonate were among the materials employed by Winfield[24] in designing the American Express Company's "Map of the World" mural and other decorative exhibits.

plastic, as in the case of FRP sandwich panels with styrene or urethane foam cores. More often, however, a plastic is mated with a non-plastic.

The various types of laminated plywood and particle board have been described in Chapter 7. According to Bryant,[25,26] the leading overlay for plywood is phenolic-impregnated paper, but smaller amounts of other materials are being used: melamine, polyester, polyvinyl fluoride ("Tedlar"*), vulcanized fiber, aluminum and acrylic. (The polyester film referred to here is a saturated polyester, such as du Pont's "Mylar" or Goodyear's "Videne"; it is chemically quite different from the unsaturated polyester resins used in the manufacture of reinforced plastics.) Other materials which are being promoted actively include PVC, "Hypalon"* (chlorosulfonated polyethylene), and thick fiber overlays. But liquid finishes, especially urea-alkyd and epoxies, are beginning to compete with the film overlays.

*Registered trademark E. I. du Pont de Nemours & Co., Inc.

Many other materials besides plywood—gypsum wallboard (as well as plaster itself), hardboard, wood siding, aluminum siding, steel panels, etc.—are being laminated with plastic facings for improved appearance, texture, washability, weatherability, warmth to the touch and other properties. For interior vertical surfaces, vinyl and polyester film are becoming widely used. The vinyl, in thicknesses up to 10 mils, may be applied by roll laminating, calendering, or adhesive bonding. Advantages of interior film finishes include decorative appearance, light fastness, color, reduced flame spread, less on-site labor costs, resistance to staining, ease of cleaning, scratch resistance, surface hardness and impact resistance.

Polyvinyl fluoride (PVF) was first produced by du Pont in 1942. Long-term testing, started the following year, has indicated that this material has remarkable weathering characteristics, and du Pont is guaranteeing its durability for fifteen years. The 1-mil Tedlar film is laminated with special adhesives to steel, gulvanized steel, aluminum, ABS (acrylonitrile-butadiene-styrene) plastic, resin-impregnated asbestos felt, asbestos-cement board, plywood and lumber. When used with fiber glass-reinforced polyester, it replaces the gel coat, and no adhesive is necessary. It may be either pigmented or transparent, containing ultraviolet screening agents.

At Merritt Island in Florida, a "Tedlar" composite is being used to build the windows for the huge Vehicle Assembly Building (VAB), in which the Apollo Saturn V moon rocket will be put together.[27] The largest structure (in volume) ever built by man, it occupies almost 8 acres and is over 50 stories high. More than two thousand 4 × 12 foot panels of the plastic composite will be needed. Plastic glazing is required instead of glass because of the great shock waves and acoustical pressures, up to 145 decibels.

The weather resistance of fire-retardant fiber glass-reinforced "Hetron"* panels is tripled by lamination with a film of

*Registered trademark Hooker Chemical Corp.

PVF, according to Fiber Glass Plastics, Inc.[28]

Polyvinyl fluoride ("Tedlar") and polyvinyl chloride (Columbus Coated Fabrics Corp.'s "Colovin") have been laminated to aluminum in the manufacture of Alcoa's "Vynalate." The PVC-coated panels are highly resistant to corrosion, stain and abrasion.[29]

Adhesives and Binders

In composites for building, each of the components is a solid at the time of use. If at least one of the materials is a liquid at some time during manufacture, it may also function as an adhesive. This is the case, for example, with the polyester resin in the FRP/ "Tedlar" laminate described above, as well as the sandwich panels with urethane cores, foamed in place, to be discussed below.

Usually, however, it is necessary to bond two or more components that are already solid. The importance of the adhesive in most "Tedlar" laminates has already been noted.

Binders for plywood and particle board have received attention in Chapter 7; resin additives for latex were discussed in Chapter 4; other adhesives, in Chapter 11. The present section reviews advances made in the use of epoxy and polyester liquid resins for structural adhesives and as binders in such applications as terrazzo flooring.

In the last decade, the *epoxy resins* have emerged as outstanding adhesive materials.[30(a),(b)] The resins most often used as binders are amber-colored viscous liquids. In adhesive applications, they are usually cured with amine or polyamide/amine hardeners.

The liquid *polyesters* are viscous blends of unsaturated polyester and styrene monomer, hardened with the aid of organic peroxides and other curing agents. While their greatest use is in fiber glass-reinforced plastics, as discussed in Chapter 5, they are being employed to an increasing extent for other applications.

Both epoxies and polyesters can be cured without pressure, since neither one gives off volatiles during the hardening process. Also, they can be hardened at the ambient temperature of the building site. Unfortunately, these "room-temperature" cures require the use of a two-part or three-part mix, in which the components must be blended in precisely the right proportion to achieve optimum thoroughness of cure, strength and heat resistance. This fussiness, required especially for the epoxies, has delayed their acceptance by the building trades. The epoxies shrink less during cure than the polyesters and adhere better to some surfaces, but they are also more expensive than the polyesters.

Bonding Concrete, Brick and Cinder Block. A blend of liquid epoxy and liquid polysulfide resins, cured with an amine hardener, has been employed for bonding old to new concrete for more than a decade. It was pioneered by the California Public Works Department in 1955.[31]

The railroads have been utilizing epoxies as adhesives to join prestressed beam sections of concrete in bridges.[32] The epoxy spreads the load among the beams. Concrete structures are being repaired by filling the cracks with liquid epoxy.[33]

A blend of epoxy resin and cement is utilized as a mortar for concrete blocks or cinder blocks in a Dow Chemical Company composition. The blocks must have planar surfaces to insure good contact.

"Stained-glass" Windows. At Washington University in St. Louis, the reading room of the Gaylord Music Library is paneled with "faceted slab glass," a variation of the traditional stained-glass window.[34] In the technique developed by Emil Frei Associates for the Benesco Company, pieces of colored glass 1 to 2 inches thick, are laid out horizontally, in the desired design and epoxy resin is poured around them. The epoxy matrix is far tougher, lighter and easier to work with than lead, the material used in medieval churches. Furthermore, the epoxy may be either transparent or opaque, in any desired color.

The windows of the Novitiate Chapel of the Sisters of Mercy in Dallas, Pennsylvania, are made by a patented process developed by Baut Studies involving epoxy resins, aluminum sheets and stained glass. The tough-

ness of the epoxy permits panels to be as large as 72 square feet in area, compared with 18 square feet by older handicrafting techniques.[35]

Epoxy resin has also been utilized in the preparation of three-dimensional murals, bonding pieces of glass, marble or other materials.

Binders for Hard Flooring. Both polyesters and epoxies are finding increased acceptance as binders for tile and terrazzo flooring. At the research center of Tile Council of America, epoxy adhesives and grouting compounds have been developed which show outstanding resistance to water and chemicals. The good sanitary properties of these materials make them desirable for floors, walls and countertops in hotels, restaurants, schools, hospitals, dairies, breweries and other food-processing plants.[36]

Terrazzo flooring, bonded with epoxy resin, can be as thin as ¼-inch instead of the thicknesses approaching 1 inch required when inorganic cements are used. Tishman Reality Company,[37] New York builders of high-rise structures, have employed terrazzo in some apartment foyers. They see two important advantages of the epoxy over the conventional terrazzo: lighter floor load and taller ceilings.

Epoxy/sand blends have had more than ten years successful experience as flooring compositions in factories, warehouses, garages, and other locations requiring excellent wearing qualities under heavy load.[30b]

Coatings of epoxy/aggregate blends have also achieved success in exterior wall and roof construction. A 15-mil film of coating is applied to plywood panels in the factory. The aggregate, crushed marble and quartz, adds color as well as protection. Cost of the applied coating is only 16¢ to 25¢/sq ft, and no painting is necessary. Life expectancy is 20 to 25 years.[38]

An entire small office building was assembled at Gilman, Connecticut, with the aid of a two-part epoxy adhesive (supplied by Pittsburgh Plate Glass Company), in which the components are used in equal proportion. Polystyrene foam was bonded to plywood skin panels in the shop. The panels were joined with wood splines of pine spreading a bead of adhesive from a gun with a ½-inch nozzle. The insulated panels were used for floor, walls and roof. Speed of erection resulted in lowered construction

usage of both materials is growing very rapidly.

To an increasing extent, the plastic foams are being used in sandwich construction or other composites. Monsanto Chemical Com-

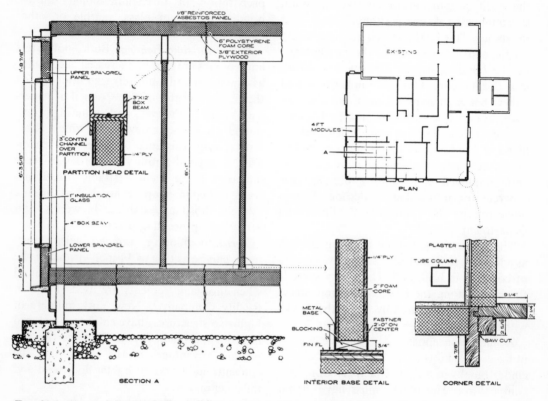

FIG. 21-4. Plan and details of office building constructed from sandwich panels with plywood faces and poly ethylene foam cores, bonded with epoxy adhesive. (*Courtesy Pittsburgh Plate Glass*)

cost.[39] Figure 21-4 shows construction details. The building was designed by Juster & Gugliotta and Richard Sharpe.

Plastic Foams in Composites

As noted in Chapter 9, polystyrene foam has been the leading type of cellular plastic used in construction, with polyurethane in second place. In the future, the situation could be reversed, according to Siren,[40] but

pany's "Loc-Pac" structure is made up of panels with cores of polystyrene laminated to kraft paper. These "Rib-Cores" are adhesive bonded, in turn, to ¼-inch exterior plywood faces, which are covered on both sides with polyvinyl chloride sheets.[41] These composites, in various sizes and thicknesses, are used for floors, exterior and load-bearing wall panels, and roof panels. They are available in a modular system, easily shipped and assembled. They can also be taken apart readily for relocation.

Utilizing the "Miller system," the Dow Chemical Company has constructed a wall with excellent strength and insulation value by adhesive bonding ½-inch of polystyrene foam to a 4-inch-thick brick wall.[42] The bricks are bonded with a mortar which con-

TABLE 21-2. Foams in Construction[40]

| | Million Pounds | | |
	1962	1964	1967-1970
Rigid urethane	3	12	35–137
Polystyrene	26	35	60–120

tains saran latex, adding greatly to tensile strength and impact strength. The brick walls can be preassembled, and a single wall of this construction will give strength at least equivalent to a double wall of brick assembled with conventional mortar.[43] Thermal insulation is excellent; the composite has a *U* factor of only 0.13.

Buildings in Barrels. The U. S. Army Engineers Research and Development Laboratories, Ft. Belvoir, Virginia, have developed an Arctic building of modular design, utilizing stressed skin panels of glass fiber-reinforced polyester and polyurethane foam cores.[44] Each module contains wall, ceiling and floor components. The modules are keyed to each other by means of a tapered tongue-and-groove system, and are sealed with pressure-sensitive tape. A combination of four wall panels, four floor panels and two ceiling panels gives 6 linear feet of building, 16 feet wide. The end walls are fabricated in one piece (Figure 21-5).

FIG. 21-5. Interior of glass fiber-polyurethane plastics building located in the arctic. (*Courtesy U.S. Army Engineer Research and Development Laboratories, Ft. Belvoir, Va.*)

The buildings are designed so that the materials and equipment can be moved with a minimum of shipping space. On location, molds are set up, coated with release agent, and sprayed with polyester resin and chopped glass fiber, then compacted by rolling

with paint rollers. Both outside and inside faces are made in this manner. Then the molds are assembled, leaving a cavity which is filled with polyurethane foam. After the foam has expanded, the composite is separated from the molds and post-cured for 24 hours prior to assembly.

A more recent modification, shown in Figure 21-6, utilizes a module constructed

FIG. 21-6. Module for arctic building. (*Courtesy U.S. Army Engineer Research and Development Laboratories, Ft. Belvoir, Va.*)

of two identical halves, with a single joint at the ridge.

Vinyl/Wood Windows

The use of rigid vinyl as the sole construction material for windows has been noted in Chapter 8. One of the problems of all-vinyl windows is the difference in coefficient of thermal expansion between vinyl and glass. Another is the difficulty of extruding very rigid vinyl in the complex profiles required for window construction. Both problems have now been eliminated by extruding the vinyl over wood (Figure 21-7).[45]

The wood provides the rigidity, while the vinyl protects the wood against moisture which could otherwise cause large dimensional changes. Since there is no paint, there is no blistering problem. The extrusion process was developed in Italy by Luigi

Zanini and is carried out by Crane Plastics, Inc., of Columbus, Ohio, for the Anderson Corporation, Bayport, Minnesota. Both rigid and plasticized vinyl are utilized. The plas-

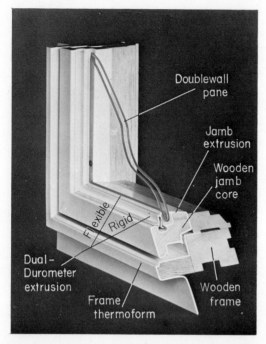

FIG. 21-7. Vinyl is extruded over wood to make superior frame for insulating window. (*Courtesy Modern Plastics and Anderson Corporation*)

ticized vinyl is an effective sealant, excluding water.

Plastics in Radiant Heating Panels

An electric radiant heating system that is rolled on like wallpaper has been developed for The Goodyear Tire & Rubber Co. The "Sun-Glo"* composite is a flexible sandwich made up of two outer layers of thin vinyl and a filling of nylon net interwoven with resistance wiring. Temperature of the system is only 100°F. It is applied to ceilings with mastic. [Figures 21-8(a) and 21-8(b)].[46]

A different type of ceiling-embedded "furnace" is used at the Kingswood Regional High School, Wolfeboro, New Hampshire. The 2 × 4 foot heat sheets, developed by Thermal Circuits, Inc., of Beverly, Massachusetts, each contain steel foil grids

*Registered trademark The Goodyear Tire & Rubber Co.

laminated between a layer of "Mylar"* polyester film and a layer of glass-reinforced epoxy. They generally operate at temperatures up to 200°F.[47] The excellent electrical properties, moisture resistance and heat resistance of the polyester film are essential to its function.

LOOKING AHEAD

Plastics have accomplished much in a short time. The chemists and other technologists who have created them have reason to be proud, but important tasks remain. The architect, the builder and the code official must be provided with more precise information about the properties of these new materials. Levitt[48] is emphatic that direct collaboration with the leaders in home building is necessary before the chemical industry can begin to scratch the potential in this market. Do not imitate or substitute, he says. Instead, emphasize the unique

FIG. 21-8A. Knitted fabric containing a zig-zag resistance wire woven into nylon is the essence of Sun-Glo electric radiant heat panels. (*Courtesy The Goodyear Tire and Rubber Co.; Yale Forman Designs, Inc.*)

*Registered trademark E. I. du Pont de Nemours & Co., Inc.

features that the polymers can contribute. Build interchangeable parts; use standard groups.

FIG. 21-8B. Vinyl-covered radiant heating panels are bonded to ceiling. (*Courtesy The Goodyear Tire & Rubber Co; Yale Forman Designs, Inc.*)

Modular Construction

Plastics will advance along two seemingly divergent paths. On the one hand, the light weight and easy transportability of plastics facilitates their use in prebuilt components, or even entire prebuilt homes. Alternatively, plastics offer the architect the opportunity to liberate himself from the rectangular strait jacket of conventional materials and techniques.

The prebuilt structure with plastic components, shipped in panels and other sections marked for quick assembly, is already a reality, thanks to the leadership of companies such as Koppers, Monsanto and National Homes Corp. In view of the light weight of plastic-based structures, it may be entirely feasible to move completely assembled houses by helicopter, thus overcoming the restrictions imposed by the width of highways.[23]

Just as the ability to mass-produce repetitive structures from plastics is important, so is the capability of reinforced plastics to function as molds for the repetitive casting of concrete, Figures 21-9A and 21-9B.[49-52] In the construction of the Marina City Twin

Towers in Chicago,[51] the RP (reinforced plastic) cores were reused an average of 67 times. The forms were less expensive than forms of conventional materials, stood up well under rough handling, were sufficiently light in weight to be set by hand, and gave an excellent surface finish.

(a)

(b)

FIGS. 21-9A,B. Reinforced polyester form (21-9A) is used for the repetitive casting of massive concrete structures shown in Fig. 21-9B. The polyester is an economical material because the form is reusable. (*Courtesy Archer Daniels Midland Company*)

Plastics processing is well adapted to continuous production and the manufacture of large numbers of identical parts, whether by extrusion, RP processing, thermoforming and other post-forming, calendering, plastisol processing, injection molding, or foam processing.[53]

Makowski[54] has emphasized the variety and strength of structures that can be built up from modular units.

Buckminster Fuller,[55] inventor of the geodesic dome (U. S. Patent 2,682,235), sees ever larger structures being built from repetitive interlocking tetrahedrons. He can even envisage a plastic dome that would cover forty blocks of Manhattan from river to river.

Free Form

To the artist and the designer, a fascinating aspect of plastics in their potential for free-form structures. At the Bath Academy of Art in England, urethane foam and reinforced plastics were combined to make the floating dock shown in Figure 21-10.[56]

FIG. 21-10. Floating bathing place of foam-filled reinforced plastics. (*Courtesy Bath Academy of Art*)

Winfield[57a,b] visualizes five main areas in which plastics have special promise as materials for construction:

Laminated sandwich constructions
Combinations of plastics with senior structural materials
Inflatable plastics and films
Continuous sequence structures
Cell-pod constructions.

Tomorrow's panels will be structural, load-bearing members, containing utilities in the core. Not only radiant heat but electroluminescent lighting will be built in.

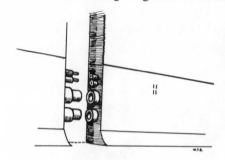

FIG. 21-11. Modular panel design with built-in utilities. (*Courtesy Armand G. Winfield*)

Heating, plumbing and air-conditioning facilities will be buried in the panels with butt attachments from one panel to another (Figure 21-11).

Second-story roadbeds will be built eco-

FIG. 21-12. Mural by Peter Ostuni in laminated plastic in dining room of Sheraton Palace Hotel, San Francisco, depicts the life of Henry VIII.

nomically by first laying down arches of somewhat flexible styrene foam, then spraying with concrete.

Giant filament-winding machinery will make it possible to construct pipes, tubes or profiles on a continuous basis, as large as 30 feet across, suitable for buildings or vehicular tunnels. The winders can be portable, permitting construction on the site with the most advanced techniques.

Blow molding equipment, also gargantuan in size, will enable the production of rooms or pods with doors and window frames as inserts.

These are "blue sky" projections, of course. But of this we can be sure: the ingenuity of the chemist and the architect will lead us to new vistas.

REFERENCES

1. "Forecast by F. W. Dodge Corporation," reprinted from Architectural Record (September, 1963).
2. Schmidlin, Emil A., speaking at SPI World's Fair Conference (June 1964).
3. Briber, Alex A., "Flammability Requirements for Cellular Plastics as Materials of Construction," *J. Cellular Plastics*, **2**, No. 2, 112 (March 1966).
4. Koehler, Charles R., Editor, "Plastics in Building," Publication No. 337 of Building Research Institute, Washington, D. C., 1955.
5. Hamilton, Richard W., *et al.*, "Plastics in Housing," Monsanto Chemical Company, Springfield, Mass., 1955.
6. Rosato, D. V., "Building Construction: What's In It For Plastics?" *Plastics World*, **23**, No. 12, 24 (December 1965).
7. Fowler, E. W., "Building Codes and Fire Safety," *SPE J.*, **18**, 1239 (1962).
8. Davis, E. N., "The Role of Underwriters' Laboratories in the Classification of Plastics for Use in Building Construction," *SPE J.*, **18**, 1240 (1962).
9. Speight, Frank Y., "The Position of ASTM In Setting Standards," *SPE J.*, **18**, 1242 (1962).
10. Building Research Institute, "Information Requirements for Selection of Plastics for Use in Building," Publication No. 833, Washington, D. C., 1960.
11. Young, P. Robert, Fiat Metal Manufacturing Company, Plainview, N. Y., private communication.
12. Rosato, D. V., "Building Construction. What's In It for Plastics?" *Plastics World*, **24**, No. 1, 28 (January 1966).
13. Anon., "Wide Uses of Plastics in Plumbing Are Seen," *The New York Times*, R-1 (September 5, 1965).
14. Warner, Jack R., National Homes Corporation, Lafayette, Ind., private communication.
15. Anon., "A Conventional House—and Plastics are Everywhere!" *Mod. Plastics*, **40**, No. 4, 94 (December 1962).
16. Sarchet, B. R., "New Developments in Construction with Plastics," American Management Association Seminar, "Plastics in the Building Industry," October 1963.
17. Skeist, Irving, "Plastics in the U. S. Building Industry," *Brit. Plastics*, **37**, No. 4, 190 (April 1964).
18. Sarchet, B. R., Koppers Company, Inc., Pittsburgh, Pa., private communication.
19. Ketchum, Morris, Jr., "The Future of Plastics in Building Construction," SPI World's Fair Conference (June 1964).
20. Owens-Corning Fiberglas Corp., New York, N. Y., private communication.
21. Huxtable, Ada Louise, "He Adds Elegance to Modern Architecture," *The New York Times Magazine*, 18 (May 24, 1964).
22. Anon., "New York World's Fair: Testing Ground for Plastics," *Mod. Plastics* (February, March, April, May and June issues, 1964).
23. Keane, Gustave R., "Plastics and the Architect," American Chemical Society, Symposium on Polymers and Plastics in Construction, Atlantic City, N. J., September, 1965.
24. Winfield, Armand G., "Four Unique Plastics Projects at the New York World's Fair," *SPE Tech. Papers*, 21st Annual Technical Conference, Paper XIX-3 (March 1965).
25. Bryant, Ben S., "Film Finishes for Plywood: International Consultation on Plywood and Other Wood-Based Panel Products," sponsored by FOA (Food and Agricultural Organization of the United Nations), Rome, Italy (April 1963).
26. Anon., "Film and Liquid Finishes for Plywood," *Mod. Plastics*, **43**, No. 6, 203 (February 1966).
27. Woodward, Richard J., "Doorway to the Moon," *Du Pont Magazine*, 16 (March-April 1965).
28. German, W. T., Fiber Glass Plastics, Inc., Miami, Fla., private communication.
29. Maher, Robert J., Aluminum Company of America, Pittsburgh, Pa., private communication.
30. (a) Skeist, Irving, "Modern Structural Adhesives for Use in the Building Industry," *Adhesives Age*, **7**, No. 4, 21 (April 1964).
    (b) Skeist, Irving, "Epoxy Resins," New York, Reinhold Publishing Corp., 1958.
31. Kerr, Andre B., "Epoxies in the Building Industry," Paper 1D, Society of the Plastics Industry, Inc., National Plastics Conference, Chicago, Ill. (November 1963).
32. Ruble, E. J., American Association of Railroads, Research Center, Chicago, Ill., private communication.
33. Whitesides, G. W., George W. Whitesides Company, Inc., Louisville, Ky., private communication; see also *J. Am. Concrete Inst.* (1962).

34. Anon., Bakelite Review, Union Carbide Plastics Company, New York, N. Y., p. 1 (April 1963).
35. Anon., "Epoxies Used in New Stain Glass Window Method," *SPE J.*, **20,** No. 12, 1329 (December 1964).
36. Fitzgerald, J. V., Tile Council of America, Inc., Research Center, Princeton, N. J., private communication.
37. Newman, John Tishman Research, New York, N. Y., private communication.
38. Anon., "Epoxy Aggregates Protect, Beautify Exteriors," *Mod. Plastics*, **42,** No. 7, 116 (March 1965).
39. Anon., "Glued Building Construction," *Mater. & Methods*, 168 (July 1962).
40. Siren, Raymond L, Mobay Chemical Company, Pittsburgh, Pa., private communication.
41. Plumb, D. S., and Shand, Lloyd D., Monsanto Chemical Company, St. Louis, Mo., private communications.
42. Anon., "Field and Lab Tests Indicate Experimental Mortar will greatly Increase Load-Bearing Ability of Brick," *Contractor News* (November-December 1962).
43. Lear, John, "Bricks Without Straw Bosses," *Saturday Review*, 45 (February 1, 1964).
44. Swenson, S. B., "Building in Barrels, Part 2," SPI Reinforced Plastics Conference, Chicago, Ill., February 1964.
45. Anon., "Is This the Final Word in Vinyl Windows?" *Mod. Plastics*, **43,** No. 3, 102 (November 1965).
46. Forman, Yale, Yale Forman Designs, Inc., New York N. Y., private communication.
47. Anon., "The School That Ignores Tradition," *Du Pont Magazine*, 25 (September-October 1965).
48. Levitt, W. J., Jr., Levitt & Sons, Inc., Levittown, N. Y., "Mass Production on the Site," New York, The Chemical Market Research Association, May 1960.
49. Pelton, E. R., "The Use of Reinforced Plastics in Concrete Forms," Paper 12-C, The Society of the Plastics Industry, Inc., Reinforced Plastics Conference, Chicago, Ill., 1962.
50. Dietz, Albert G. H., and Bongiorno, Anthony J., "Reinforced Plastic/Concrete Structures," *Architectural & Engineering News*, **4,** No. 7, 10 (July 1962).
51. Anon., "R-P Forms," *Reinforced Plastics*, **1,** No. 5, 14 (November-December 1962).
52. Kreier, George, Jr., George Kreier, Jr., Inc., Philadelphia, Pa., private communication.
53. Anon., "Processing Plastics for Building," *Plastics Technol.*, **12,** No. 1, 31 (January 1966).
54. Makowski, Z. S., "Space Structures in Plastics," *Plastics* (February-March 1963).
55. Anon., "The Dymaxian American," *Time*, **83,** No. 2, 46 (January 10, 1964).
56. Ellis, Clifford, Bath Academy of Art, Corsham, Wiltshire, England, private communication.
57. (a) Winfield, Armand G., "Plastics in Building. . . A 'Blue Sky' Excursion into the Near Future", Society of Plastic Engineers, Inc., Paper XIX-4, 21st Annual Conference, Boston, Mass. (March, 1965).
(b) Winfield, Armand G., "Excursion into a Plastic Future," AIA Journal, page 62 (February, 1966).

APPENDIX

Underwriters' Laboratories, Inc., Chicago, Ill.

Companies supplying plastic products, from "Building Materials List, January, 1965" (consult the publication for flame spread, fuel contributed and smoke developed ratings):

Abco Plastic & Supply Co., Div. of Bro-Dart Industries, Newark, N. J. *Corrugated translucent sheets.*

Alsynite Div. of Reichhold Chemicals, Inc., San Diego Calif. *Flat and corrugated glass fiber-reinforced panels.*

American Louver Co., Chicago, Ill. 60630. *Plastic louvers, open grid type.*

Barclite Corp. of America, Bronx, N. Y. *Flat and corrugated glass fiber-reinforced panels.*

Barrett Division, Allied Chemical Corp., New York, N. Y. *Translucent and opaque panels.*

Benjamin Products, Thomas Industries, Inc., Sparta, Tenn. 38583. *Louver and die-formed translucent panels.*

Butler Mfg. Co., Kansas City, Mo. *Flat and corrugated glass-fiber reinforced panels.*

Ceil-Lite Co., New York, N. Y. *Corrugated or formed translucent sheets.*

Celotex Corp., Chicago, Ill. 60603. *Flat and formed translucent plastic panels.*

Cepco, Inc., San Francisco, Calif. 94117. *Translucent panels.*

Cirvac Plastics, Erie, Pa. *Perforated translucent panels.*

Clopay Corp., Cincinnati, Ohio. *Translucent panels.*

Columbia Electric & Mfg. Co., Spokane, Wash. *Corrugated translucent plastic sheets supported by metal channel member suspended from the structure overhead, forming a suspended ceiling.*

Consoweld Corp., Wisconsin Rapids, Wis. *Laminated plastic sheets.*

Contrex Co., Chelsea, Mass. *Formed and corrugated translucent plastic laminated sheets.*

Curtis-Electro Lighting, Inc., Chicago, Ill. 60608. *Translucent panels.*

Custom Ceilings, Inc., Detroit, Mich. 48211. *Corrugated or formed translucent sheets.*

Diffusa-Lite Co., Conshohocken, Pa. *Flat, corrugated, and formed translucent plastic panels.*

Difus-A-Lite Products, Addison, Tex. *Flat and formed translucent plastic panels.*

The Dow Chemical Co., Midland, Mich. 48641. *Extruded and expanded plastic in the form of blocks and boards.*

Dyplast of Florida, Kraco, Inc., Miami, Fla. *Expanded plastic in the form of blocks and boards.*

Dyplast of Illinois, Inc., Chicago, Ill. 60632. *Expanded plastic in the form of blocks.*

Filon Corp., Hawthorne, Calif. *Flat, corrugated, and special shapes of glass fiber-reinforced panels.*

Formica Corp., Cincinnati, Ohio. *Laminated plastic sheets.*

General Electric Co., Coshocton, Ohio. *Laminated plastic sheets.*

Guth Co., Edwin F., St Louis, Mo. *Plastic louvers, open grid type.*

Hansson, Inc., Elof, New York, N. Y. *Formed and corrugated translucent plastic laminated sheets.*

Iso Industries, Los Angeles, Calif. 90012. *Translucent panels.*

Johns-Manville Corp., New York, N. Y. 10016. *Flat and corrugated glass-fiber-reinforced panels. Expanded plastic in the form of blocks and boards.*

K-Lux Products Div. of K-S-H Plastics, Inc., St. Louis Mo. *Expanded plastic in the form of boards and panels.*
Corrugated or formed translucent sheets.

Kaykor Products Corp., Yardville, N. J. *Translucent and opaque panels.*

Kemlite Corp., Joliet, Ill. *Flat and corrugated glass fiber-reinforced panels.*

Koller-Craft Plastic Products, Inc., Fenton, Mo. *Plastic louvers, open grid type.*

Koppers Co., Inc., Plastics Div., Monaca, Pa. *Expanded plastic in the form of blocks and boards.*

Lasco Industries, Montebello, Calif., Los Angeles, Calif. 90054. *Flat and corrugated shapes of glass fiber-reinforced panels.*

Leigh Products, Inc., Cooperville, Mich. *Flat and formed translucent plastic panels.*

Lightonics, Oakland, Calif. *Formed translucent panels.*

Lin Mfg. Co., The, Clinton Okla. *Expanded plastic in the form of boards and panels.*

Lit Ceilings, Los Angeles, Calif. *Formed translucent plastic panels.*

Lumi-Lucent Ceilings Co., Cleveland, Ohio. *Corrugated or formed translucent sheets.*

Luminous Ceilings, Inc., Chicago, Ill. 60613. *Corrugated translucent sheets or formed panels.*

Macklanburg-Duncan Co., Oklahoma City, Okla. *Expanded plastic in the form of boards.*

Monsanto Co., St. Louis Mo. 63166. *Translucent panels.*

National Gypsum Co., Buffalo, N. Y. *Expanded plastic in the form of blocks or boards. Flat and formed translucent plastic panels.*

Navaco Co., Div. of Howe Sound Co., Dallas, Tex. *Translucent and opaque panels.*

Panelyte Div., St. Regis Paper Co., Kalamazoo, Mich. *Laminated plastic sheets.*

Piolite Plastics Corp., Div. of Pioneer Plastics Corp.,

Salem, Mass. *Corrugated or formed translucent sheets.*

Pittsburgh Reflector Co., Irwin, Pa. *Corrugated or formed translucent sheets.*

Plasteel Products Corp., Washington, Pa. *Flat and corrugated glass fiber-reinforced panels.*

Plastic Specialties, Inc., Los Angeles, Calif. 90011. *Translucent panels.*

Polrized Panel Corp., Beverly Hills, Calif. *Translucent panels.*

Polyplastic United Inc., Union, N. J. *Formed and flat plastic panels.*

Resolite Corp., Zelienople, Pa. *Flat, corrugated and special shapes of glass fiber-reinforced panels.*

Robertson Co., H. H., Pittsburgh, Pa. *Flat, corrugated, or special shapes glass-fiber reinforced panels.*

Sears, Roebuck & Co., Chicago, Ill. 60607. *Flat and formed translucent plastic panels.*

Sinko Mfg. & Tool Co., Chicago, Ill. 60631. *Plastic louvers, open grid type.*

Solux Corp., Woodside, L. I., N. Y. *Corrugated or formed translucent sheets.*

Structoglas, Inc., Cleveland, Ohio. *Flat and corrugated glass fiber-reinforced panels.*

Sylvania Electric Products, Inc., Wheeling, W. Va. *Corrugated or formed translucent sheets.*

Thermotank, Inc., Detroit, Mich. *Corrugated translucent sheets.*

Thermotank, Inc., Luminated Ceiling Div., Detroit, Mich. *Corrugated or formed translucent sheets.*

United Cork Cos., Chicago, Ill. 60613. *Expanded plastic in the form of blocks and boards.*

United Lighting & Ceiling Co., Oakland, Calif. 94601. *Formed translucent plastic panels.*

United States Mineral Products Co., Stanhope, N. J. 07874. *Expanded plastic in the form of blocks and boards.*

United States Plywood Corp., New York, N. Y. 10017. *Laminated plastic sheets. Flat and corrugated glass fiber-reinforced panels.*

Westinghouse Electric Corp., Micarta Div., Hampton, S. C. *Laminated plastic sheets.*

Wilson Lighting, J. A., Div. of Wilson Research Corp., Erie, Pa. *Open grid type louvers.*

Wood Conversion Co., St. Paul, Minn. *Translucent panels.*

Additional Companies Listed in Supplements:

Steelite Buildings, Inc., Pittsburgh, Pa. *Flat and corrugated glass fiber-reinforced panels.*

Boise Cascade Corp., Auburn, Wash. *Expanded plastic in the form of blocks and boards.*

INDEX

The first pages of major sources of information are indicated by italics and appear first.